REVIEW

OF

RESEARCH

CONTRIBUTORS

JOBETH ALLEN

ARTHUR N. APPLEBEE

CARL BEREITER

MARCIA FARR

MICHAEL F. GRAVES

LARRY V. HEDGES

CHARLES TAYLOR KERCHNER

JUDITH A. LANGER

JANA M. MASON

ANNEMARIE S. PALINCSAR

SCOTT PARIS

MARLENE SCARDAMALIA

NANCY L. STEIN

DAVID STERN

RICHARD L. VENEZKY

KAREN K. WIXSON

IN EDUCATION

13   1986

ERNST Z. ROTHKOPF

EDITOR
TEACHERS COLLEGE
COLUMBIA UNIVERSITY

PUBLISHED BY THE
AMERICAN EDUCATIONAL RESEARCH ASSOCIATION
1230 Seventeenth Street, NW
Washington, DC 20036

Copyright © 1986
American Educational Research Association
All rights reserved
Library of Congress
Catalog Card No.—72-89719
Printed in the United States of America
ISBN 0-935302-06-9
ISSN 0091-732-X

Contents

Foreword vii

I. READING ACQUISITION AND INSTRUCTION

1. A Review of Emergent Literacy with Implications for Research and Practice in Reading 3

   Authors: *Jana M. Mason and JoBeth Allen*
   Consulting Editors: *Marie Clay and Linnea Ehri*

2. Vocabulary Learning and Instruction 49

   Author: *Michael F. Graves*
   Consulting Editor: *Joseph Jenkins*

3. Instructional Approaches to Reading Comprehension 91

   Authors: *Scott G. Paris, Karen K. Wixson, and Annemarie S. Palincsar*
   Consulting Editors: *Ann Brown, John Guthrie, and Peter Winograd*

4. Steps Toward a Modern History of American Reading Instruction 129

   Author: *Richard L. Venezky*
   Consulting Editor: *Jennifer Monaghan*

II. WRITING

5. Reading and Writing Instruction: Toward a Theory of Teaching and Learning 171

   Authors: *Judith A. Langer and Arthur N. Applebee*
   Consulting Editor: *David Olson*

6. Language, Culture, and Writing: Sociolinguistic Foundations of Research on Writing 195

   Author: *Marcia Farr*
   Consulting Editor: *Shirley Brice Heath*

7. Knowledge and Process in the Acquisition of Writing Skills   225

   Author: *Nancy L. Stein*
   Consulting Editor: *John Bransford*

8. Levels of Inquiry into the Nature of Expertise in Writing   259

   Authors: *Carl Bereiter and Marlene Scardamalia*
   Consulting Editor: *John R. Hayes*

III. COMPOSITION OF THE TEACHING FORCE

9. Compensation for Teachers   285

   Author: *David Stern*
   Consulting Editor: *Richard Murnane*

10. Union-Made Teaching: The Effects of Labor Relations on
    Teaching Work   317

    Author: *Charles Taylor Kerchner*
    Consulting Editor: *Susan Johnson*

IV. META-ANALYSIS

11. Issues in Meta-Analysis   353

    Author: *Larry V. Hedges*
    Consulting Editor: *Richard Light*

Index   399

Foreword

Volume 13 of *Review of Research in Education* includes reviews of research advances and of evaluated advances in practice in four areas: early reading instruction, the development of writing skills, the teaching force, and meta-analysis of educational experimentation. The authors are forward-looking thinkers and active contributors to the fields on which they report. We owe a great debt to them for taking time out of their busy lives to report on advances in their areas. Special thanks are also due to the Editorial Board, whose wisdom and energetic pursuit of their broad contacts in the educational research community shaped this volume, and to the consulting editors, who generously applied their expert judgment in honing the style and content of individual chapters. I am particularly indebted to my wife, Carol Rothkopf, whose long and varied experience as editor and author proved invaluable in preparing the contributions for publication. Her attention to detail and her devotion to scholarly accuracy greatly strengthened this volume.

Finally I wish to acknowledge my debt to Gloria Burch and Barbara Biesenbach for patient and conscientious editorial assistance.

Ernst Z. Rothkopf
Editor

CORRECTION
to Volume 11

Please note a correction to *Review of Research in Education*, Volume 11 (1984):

In Chapter 1, "Psychosocial Development and Human Variance," by Stella Chess and Susan G. Gordon, on page 23, in line four of the Overview section, the sentence that begins "Prelingual deafness . . ." should read "Postlingual deafness . . . ."

I.
READING ACQUISITION AND INSTRUCTION

Chapter 1

A Review of Emergent Literacy with Implications for Research and Practice in Reading

JANA M. MASON
University of Illinois
and
JoBETH ALLEN
Kansas State University

Current interest in what young children know and how they learn was anticipated many years ago by John and Evelyn Dewey (1915/1962) when they wrote:

Rousseau was almost the first to see that learning is a matter of necessity; it is a part of the process of self-preservation and of growth. If we want, then, to find out how education takes place most successfully, let us go to the experiences of children where learning is a necessity, and not to the practices of the schools where it is largely an adornment, a superfluity and even an unwelcome imposition. (p. 2)

Increasingly, reading researchers are adopting Dewey's perspective, looking at literacy learning before young children receive formal reading and writing instruction. This area of study, which is becoming known as "emergent literacy," replaces the terms "reading readiness" and "early reading and writing." According to Teale and Sulzby (1986), the phrase "emergent literacy" was coined by Clay (1966). "Emergent" denotes the process of becoming, and "literacy" denotes the interrelatedness of writing and reading in young children's development. The study of emergent literacy represents "a new perspective which stresses that legitimate, conceptual, developmental literacy learning is occurring during the first years of a child's life" (Teale & Sulzby, 1986, p. 28).

Portions of this manuscript were presented at a conference on the process of reading acquisition, University of Texas at Austin, March 20–22, 1986. The work upon which this publication is based was performed pursuant to Contract No. 400–81–0030 of the National Institute of Education.

Prior to the 1970s, research on beginning reading focused on first-grade instruction. Most young children were not thought able to read or understand what it means to read or write until they were taught in first grade. For example, research on reading awareness by Denny and Weintraub (1966), Downing (1969), John and Ellis (1976), G. Mason (1967), and Reid (1966) suggested that young children could not describe how they were learning to read. Durkin (1966) tested over 9,500 entering first-grade children on their ability to read a set of sight words and found only 229 who could read at least 18 of the words. These atypical children were termed "children who read early." In Gibson and Levin's (1976) report of Read's (1971) work showing that young children invent their own phonetically regular spelling systems, the subjects were characterized as "not run-of-the-mill children" (p. 253).

Research in the 1980s has focused on precursors of literacy and influences of the home on later reading and writing. This has occurred, in part, because broader definitions of reading have been construed, a larger number of tasks have been given to children, longitudinal studies have been conducted, and approaches have been developed that secure the maximum understanding of what the child knows. This research has made it apparent that preschool children make recognizable story reading attempts before they can read lists of words (Sulzby, 1985), and their scribbles and invented spellings of words anticipate conventional writing (Temple, Nathan, & Burris, 1982). Moreover, interviews with kindergarten children provide reliable descriptions of how they are learning to read (Stewart, 1986).

In this chapter, we review emergent literacy research and attempt to mesh it with more traditional studies on reading acquisition. The first section regarding the social and linguistic contexts for literacy acquisition shows that communication patterns and practices, parent-child interactions, and parent-child literacy activities are critical supports for the acquisition of reading and writing concepts. The second section on oral and written distinctions explains that literacy is not a simple extension of oral language because written language contains concepts that are new and often difficult to learn. The third section reviews the acquisition of early reading and writing skills. The chapter concludes with examples of instructional studies that adopt an emergent literacy perspective.

Throughout this chapter, more descriptive than experimental research is reviewed. One reason is that emergent literacy represents a new perspective. Establishing this perspective involves the development of new constructs and linkages among causative factors, a step that is usually initiated with descriptive research techniques. In addition, a larger number of variables that affect later reading and writing success are being studied. These include oral language, story-listening comprehension, and error patterns in early attempts to write and read. Beginning reading research, by contrast, has been more narrowly directed to letter and word recognition. Finally, emergent literacy research is attempting to trace community and home influences on reading and writing. This involves analyses of social class and cultural attitudes as well as of language patterns. Appropriate experimental research will undoubtedly emanate from the descriptive studies.

THE SOCIAL CONTEXT FOR LITERACY

We cannot consider the literacy of a child or an adult without also considering the context and perspective or purpose in their community. Guthrie and Kirsch (1984) state, "The environment, the social expectations, and the reading activities that others may expect are crucial in determining whether a person is literate" (p. 353). Differing social expectations, for example, have kept the definition of literacy in flux (Clifford, 1984; Resnick & Resnick, 1977; Scribner, 1984). In 1951, the UNESCO definition of literacy was the reading and writing of a short personal statement. In 1962, the definition was modified to include the various skills of reading, writing, and math necessary for a person to function effectively in group and community settings, and the actual *use* of literacy skills for personal and national development.

Purposes for becoming literate vary both within and across countries, and these purposes affect literacy practices and achievement. Downing (1973) pointed out that in Israel, Jewish children must learn to read Hebrew early in order to read the Bible, even though they do not speak Hebrew. In Japan, reading instruction emphasizes moral development through story selection (Sakamoto & Makita, 1973). Cultural values and socialization are stressed in India's primers. In the United States, although identifiable cultural attitudes are not readily apparent today (Blom & Wiberg, 1973), school reading books have in the past emphasized religious, moral or patriotic values (N. Smith, 1965).

Literacy acquisition is further complicated because the value of literacy is not the same for all members of a society. While it is accepted as a matter of individual difference that some people value literacy for themselves more highly than do others, the darker side of the issue is that some educational policymakers systematically discourage certain groups from learning to read and write. In Nepal, as in much of India, lower caste children, especially girls, are not encouraged towards literacy (Junge & Shrestha, 1984). Minority cultures in the United States, as well as other countries, have often received inadequate reading and writing instruction. There is some historical evidence that literacy is intentionally restricted by the literate few in power, if they feel threatened by illiterate factions (Downing, 1973; Goody, 1968). Goody, for example, noted that it took each Chinese "wise man" about 20 years to master the 50,000 characters necessary to be considered fully literate, and that it was this upper echelon who fought any changes in the ideographic system. Now with a national goal of widespread literacy in the People's Republic of China, a simplified writing system is introduced to beginning readers and writers (Jiang & Li, 1985).

In developing countries such as Iran, Chile, and Hindi-speaking India, where education has barely had an impact, most homes do not or cannot support literacy (Thorndike, 1976). Feitelson (1985) warns that in societies that have accepted large numbers of families from underdeveloped countries, such as Israel, the literate traditions valued by the main culture may be missing among immigrants, due to different traditions or situational factors such as poverty. Her fear is that studies of well-educated parents in mainstream cultures whose young children easily make the transition to literacy do not inform teachers about how to work with children from less literate families.

McCullough (1973) illustrated the strength of parental attitudes toward literacy learning with an anecdote. "Before my brother was born, my mother ate gristle and read a complete set of Shakespeare, hoping to make her baby physically strong and a person of taste and competence in reading" (p. 119). McCullough went on to contrast parental attitudes in Scotland and England with those in India where she was involved with an early literacy program. It was common practice for British parents to help their children prepare the next day's reading lesson, but there was a 40% dropout rate in Indian first grades because many parents needed children to work at home or in the fields.

Clay (1971) investigated home influences on several aspects of oral English development, reading, auditory memory, and visual perception in 5- and 6-year-old children with four different language backgrounds. Two groups were Polynesian, two were Pakeha (the Maori word for New Zealand whites). One Polynesian group was the Maoris, with a rural heritage and little command of Maori, a dying language. The other Polynesian group was the Samoans, with 75% speaking fluent Samoan and all having a history of parental educational support. The Pakehas ranged from very proficient to average in oral English. All were being taught in whole language classrooms.

Clay found that although the Maori children exhibited superior oral language development in English to the Samoan children at age 5 and 6, at age 7 the two groups were about equal and the Samoan children had made significantly better progress in reading. In fact, their progress was equal to that of the average Pakeha group. Clay proposed that a critical difference was the parental attitude of Samoans favoring education and their influence as models for reading (at church) and writing letters home (to Samoa). These parents augmented the vital role of "literate other."

In a study directly examining the effect of parental involvement on reading achievement, Sakamoto (1976) found that the earlier Japanese parents begin reading to their children, the more fluently the children read by 5 years of age, a year before formal reading instruction begins. Japanese parents often read to infants; by the time children are 1 year old, 36% of parents have begun reading. Most parents buy books and subscribe to magazines aimed especially at the 4- to 6-year-old audience. Parents do not report "teaching" reading, but they think it important to read aloud, to give children their own books and letter/word/picture blocks, and to answer their children's questions. In Japan, which has exceedingly high rates of literacy, parental encouragement and help with homework is apparently a common practice not only for learning to read, but for learning the difficult writing system.

Thorndike (1976) examined reading comprehension in 15 countries and found two family factors that predict reading achievement, socioeconomic level and availability of print in the home. In comparing literacy development in England, Scotland, and Wales, Goodacre (1973) found that home support, especially the amount of time fathers spent reading with their children, is a significant factor in the higher reading achievement of Scottish children. A meta-analysis of almost 200 studies (K. White, 1982) indicates that family characteristics, such as academic guidance, attitude toward education and aspirations of parent for child, conversations in the home, reading materials and cultural activities, contribute more directly to early reading achievement and account for considerably more variance than socioeconomic status.

These studies reveal that literacy experiences are intertwined with societal expectations. Thus, using correlational studies to study the impact of social context on literacy learning is extremely difficult because the home variables that make a difference are not easily manipulated. In the conduct of training studies, it may be useless to supply reading materials or instructional procedures to parents if the parents do not believe in the value, for themselves and their children, of becoming literate. However, there are researchers who have taken account of what families and communities believe about literacy and the uses they have for it before attempting to design an instructional approach. Similar research is needed to examine the role of the schools in providing literacy experiences and instruction for children who have not had these experiences at home. This is especially important in communities where literacy is viewed as pointless or even detrimental to social acceptance.

LINGUISTIC CONTEXT FOR LITERACY

It is generally assumed that literacy is associated with a distinctive mode of thought and language (Olson, 1977, 1984; Yaden & Templeton, 1986). Literate adults know that language has structure, and that it is comprised of meanings that must to some extent be created or inferred by the listener and reader. Moreover, literate adults use metalinguistic terms, words that reference language, in their talk to children. These include metalinguistic nouns such as *word, sentence, letter;* metalinguistic verbs such as *say, ask, assert, request;* and metacognitive verbs such as *believe, desire, intend, mean, think, know, pretend, wonder, decide, realize, remember, doubt.*

An ability to reference language is thought to be learned to varying degrees depending on the extent of language instruction provided by parents. Based on research reported by Torrance and Olson (1985), Olson (1984) argues that learning to read is affected directly by the extent of the deliberate language instruction provided by parents. That is, as children learn a set of concepts about language, the explicit terms for expressing these concepts, they apply these ways of thinking about language structure and meaning to written language.

Wells (1981, 1985) proposes three major phases of linguistic development. His third phase is similar to Olson's notion that language becomes an analytic tool. First, Wells believes, children discover that patterns of sound take on meaning and purpose and that language represents or stands for objects and events. The second phase is consolidation of language and then diversification. Children listen to and use language conventions to interpret the required social contexts. Third, children learn to detach language from the immediate context. They become conscious of their own mental states, are able to reflect on their own experiences, separate thought from action, and separate language from its context. Wells concludes, as does Olson, that with the acquisition of literacy comes the "ability to abstract linguistic expressions from the particular content and contexts to which they initially referred . . .[so] with the acquisition of literacy comes a more detached and reflective attitude to experience and this, in turn, promotes higher levels of cognitive functioning" (Wells, 1981, p. 243). The importance of reflection is echoed by Ferreiro and Teberosky (1982), who note that "it is not enough to have a language; it is also necessary to reflect on the language and thus become aware of some of its fundamental properties" (p. 284).

How do children become reflective language users? Halliday (1975) speculates that children have an ability as problem solvers, coupled with a need to gain control over their own environments, which leads them to language awareness. Vygotsky (1962) explains the process in terms of language functioning. He proposes that children first learn words and their meanings for social contact and communication purposes. Around age 4, they begin to construct speech for themselves (egocentric speech), and their expressions are turned inward as they try to grasp and remedy situations. In this way speech is "taking on a directing, planning function and raising the child's acts to the level of purposeful behavior" (p. 17). This inner speech serves the reflective or metacognitive purposes of planning, monitoring, and evaluating.

A contrasting view is presented by Olson (1984), who argues that literate parents do not merely allow language to unfold but set about deliberately to teach it. He cites as examples of instruction how parents play word-naming games with their children and shift to more complex language as their children are able to talk.

The ways children learn about language and books are deeply embedded in the family communication patterns (Heath, 1982, 1983; Ninio & Bruner,

1978; Schieffelin & Cochran-Smith, 1984; Snow, 1983; Teale, 1986). Because a community's ways of using printed materials are not separable from the ways the children learn to talk, both being acquired through social interaction, it is not possible to separate oral traditions from literacy. They are intermingled. Observations by Teale in 22 homes revealed literacy-related domains that include: daily living routines, entertainment, school-related, work, religion, interpersonal communication, and storybook time. Ninio and Bruner and Snow focus narrowly on storytime reading, which is a common literacy event in mainstream (middle-class) communities. Here, a structured interaction occurs between adult and child with a dialog that involves questions, comments about the connections between the text and the child's experience, and labeling of pictures and printed words. Heath reports that family literacy events for preschoolers are bedtime stories, reading cereal boxes, stop signs, television ads, and interpreting instructions for commercial games and toys. There are socially established rules for verbalizing what children know from and about the written material.

Among children in a working-class white community, by contrast, there are not extensive parent-child literacy events. Parents make less use of literacy sources and are more likely to direct the child about what to do than to explain how to do something. They expect the child to learn by watching rather than through verbal interaction. Books and other print materials may be listened to but not used for creation of stories.

Similarly, according to Heath, children in working class black families are less likely to learn through parent-guided small steps. Talk that is addressed to them is seldom simplified, and children's reading materials are often not available. In learning to talk, black children from these families are asked to accomplish a more difficult task, that of understanding larger sections of speech. As a result, they often capture intonation patterns before words. They are less often asked for such explanations as "What is that called?" than for analogical questions that call for nonspecific comparisons of items, events, or people—for example, "What's that like?" or "How come you did that?" (examples from Heath, 1982). The questions they hear are dissimilar from questions that teachers ask, so that answering lower-order questions at school is more difficult for them. Moreover, while parents accept children's stories and talk about children's experiences, they are not likely to tutor or relate them to books or other literate events.

In all likelihood, language awareness occurs through self-directed efforts, as Vygotsky and Halliday propose, as well as through deliberate instruction, as Olson suggests, and as part of the cultural milieu, as Heath points out. Case studies by Bissex (1980) and Soderbergh (1977), for example, show that linguistic and written language constructs develop concurrently. Although there are untutored components to language development, there are also aspects taught by parents, such as metalinguistic terms, that may be important for later reading and writing. Tracing this connection has begun in longitudinal studies, and needs to be followed up experimentally. For example, comparisons could be made between preschool programs that focus on metalinguistic constructs with those that do not, evaluating both short- and long-term changes, first of language and listening comprehension, and then of reading. In ways such as these, the presumed links between metalinguistic knowledge and later reading success might be better understood.

ORAL AND WRITTEN LANGUAGE DISTINCTIONS

In reviewing oral language acquisition and its implications for written language learning, Wardhaugh (1976) points out that neither oral nor written forms of learning are simply matters of repetition, imitation, or expansion of words heard or read, but rather that learning centers around meanings. An illustration in the case of written language can be found in Bissex's (1980) son's first written communication, *RUDF*. Paul had never seen this combination of letters in print before. But when he was unable to gain his mother's attention through speech, he communicated his need and frustration in writing with the succinct message, "aRe yoU DeaF?"

Speech and print are both vehicles of meaning, being at times playful, involving experimental endeavors, and requiring context for disambiguation. Both involve complex interactions of sounds, grammatical structure, and meaning-carrying connections to context, intention, and audience. Learning to talk, write, and read also involves invention of the language and a search for language patterns. A beginning talker may overgeneralize by adding "ed" to every verb to form the past tense; the beginning writer may put a silent *e* on many words; the beginning reader may, after reading *help* several times in one passage, misread "helper" for *helicopter* (Allen, 1984) or regularize the vowels in the word *plaid,* saying "played" (Mason, 1976). Finally, oral and written language learners use a kind of shorthand or telegraphic speech (e.g., "Daddy bye-bye" for "Daddy has gone bye-bye") and writing (e.g., captions and labels on pictures).

Nevertheless, since talking and reading are different processes and produce different outcomes (Akinnaso, 1982), it cannot be assumed that written language is acquired merely by applying knowledge about oral language constructs. Chafe (1985) suggests that two basic differences distinguish the linguistic properties of oral and written language. They are based on the fact that writing but not speaking is a slow and deliberate process and that it is usually a lonely activity, while speech can be casual and takes place in a social environment. Using Perena's (1984) framework of *physical, situational, functional, form,* and *structural* differences, we summarize these differences and then consider their implications for written language instruction in the classroom.

Physical Differences

The most obvious difference between written and spoken language is that print is processed by eye and speech by ear (Kavanagh & Mattingly, 1972). Perena (1984) identifies several less obvious physical differences. Sounds are temporarily arranged in time whereas writing is permanently arranged in space. Readers can vary their speed but listeners cannot. The same language sample, such as a paragraph from a speech, may take 6 minutes to write but as little as 1 minute to read aloud and half a minute to read silently.

Because of differences in parental support for literacy, children come to school with varying concepts about these physical differences. Ferreiro and Teberosky (1982) found that children varied in their ability to conceive of reading as voiceless, and to distinguish between oral conversation and a news item or fairy tale when an experimenter held and "read" from a newspaper or storybook. This failure of some children to pick up on physical clues to the nature of reading, or to resolve the conflict between the physical cues and the aural ones, suggests that teachers cannot assume that physical differences will be obvious to all children. Rather, as Jagger and Smith-Burke (1985) suggest, teachers may need to assess children's level of understanding about this and other print concepts in order to clarify and expand the childrens' understanding.

Situational Differences

Oral language most often occurs in a face-to-face context. Readers and writers are usually isolated from each other. Whereas the audience for speech is almost always clearly identified by the speaker, except when a speaker is overheard, the audience for writing may be either intended or unintended. Writers cannot be confident that their readers have sufficient prior knowledge, but speakers either know or can actively assess the prior knowledge of their listeners.

Oral conversation is more dynamic than reader/writer encounters (Adams, Anderson, & Durkin, 1980), although Tierney and LaZansky (1980) point out that dynamic interaction is essential for good writing and meaningful reading. However, the context of most oral language provides immediate and fairly obvious facilitation. The listener "reads" the speaker's gestures and facial expressions for added understanding, and the speaker "reads" the listener's face and reciprocal comments for feedback on clarity, tone, and impact. Language pointers, words like "this," "here," and "her," are often clarified through gesture during speech but could be vague in print (Halliday & Hasan, 1976). If speech referents are unclear, the listener has the option of asking for more information under the implicit turn-taking rules of conversation. The reader must make backward or forward searches of the text and may still end up imploring an unavailable author for a clearer framework.

In classrooms where reading and writing are daily, process-oriented communication events (Calkins, 1983, 1986; Cochran-Smith, 1984; Graves & Stuart, 1985), students do not appear to view writing as a lonely and isolated endeavor. When learning to read and write develop concurrently in an environment that Lindfors (1985) describes as continuous and dynamic, meaning focused, interactive, and creative, the contexts for oral and written language may be very similar.

Functional Differences

People who have command of both oral and written language make choices about which mode is more appropriate for a particular function. People generally use oral language for face-to-face communication and written language when they wish to communicate with others over time or distance. Unique functions of written language include recording and storing information accurately, accumulating and interpreting previous knowledge as in science and history, and labeling streets, products, and buildings. Writing may be a means for expanding one's own thinking. Reading can prompt comparisons and analysis.

There are also functional differences in children's use of language. According to Halliday (1977) children's oral language functions are: instrumental (to get something), regulatory (to control), interactional (to establish social relationships), personal (to express individuality), imaginative (to express fantasy), heuristic (to explore and learn), and informative (to communicate information). Tough (1977) found that most children can use oral language to maintain group status, to direct other people, and to talk about present events. However, some children had difficulties using written language to verbalize past experiences, make associations involving predicting or analyzing, collaborate verbally, or project from concrete experiences to new perspectives. Through extensive observation and categorization of the writing in her first-grade classrooms, Milz (1985) identified six functions of children's written language that are comparable to Halliday's oral functions. Children *establish ownership* by labeling, they *build relationships* through notes and interactive journal entries, they *remind* themselves and others through notes to do things, they *request* information or assistance, they *record* information, and they *create* and fantasize through stories.

F. Smith (1984) argues that literate others, usually parents, lead children to an appreciation and understanding of the multiple functions of written language. However, if children have not had extensive interaction with literate others before they come to school, the teacher must become that person, pointing out varying functions for both oral and written communication, and relating children's reading and writing experiences to their functions.

Form Differences

The 48 sounds used in English speech are represented by 300 distinct letters or letter combinations in English orthography (Jenkinson, 1973). In print, each letter is a distinct visual form, and each word is distinct due to the convention of putting spaces between words. Other format characteristics in print include indentation, punctuation, and capitalization. In contrast, in speech there are no boundaries between phonemes, and even word boundaries may be obscured, as Ehri (1984) demonstrates in contrasting the written "Give me a piece of candy" with the spoken "Gimme a pieca candy."

Written language is more restricted in form than speech. Prosodic features such as pitch, timbre, quality, and loudness, and paralinguistic features such as intonation, stress, and rhythm are only minimally represented by word selection, word order, and punctuation in written language (Perena, 1984). In order to recover the cohesion present in oral language, writers turn to more complex structures such as "passives, variety of tense forms, genitive structures, postpositional noun modifiers, nominalizations, verbalizations, variety of adjectival phrases, variety of subordinate phrases, phrases in apposition, logical and subordinate connectives" and other complex elements, all of which are more frequent in print than in speech (Jenkinson, 1973, p. 159).

An analysis of children's oral reading suggests that connecting the oral form to the written cannot be taken for granted. Clay (1982) found significant rate and accuracy differences between better and poorer readers on measures of juncture, pitch, and stress. For example, better readers read seven words before pausing while poor readers paused after nearly every word. Better readers also ended twice as many sentences with falling pitch, and read four times as many words per stress. Research is needed to determine whether children's reading would benefit if they were taught to capture prosodic features as they read, and if so, how.

Structural Differences

Perena (1984) discusses both syntactic structure and discourse structure. In referring to syntactic structure, she notes that writers, lacking intonation, often place important elements at ends of sentences. While speakers tend to be highly redundant, writers strive to be concise. Speech is also more informal than writing, as evidenced by the greater frequency of incomplete sentences, slang expressions, and meaningless vocalizations that function as place holders allowing time for thought. Some elements of informal speech are consciously emulated in text, for example, dialect, contractions, and elliptical phrases, but these elements occur mainly in narrative texts.

Spoken and written language forms are also structured differently at a discourse level. Speakers present smaller amounts of information at a time, so they can monitor listener response, but may switch topics without notice. Writers rarely have a chance to interact with readers, so they present larger chunks of information and try to signal organization and topic shifts.

The transfer of discourse comprehension skills from listening to reading should be easiest for texts such as narratives because these contain structures commonly found in both speech and writing. However, because narratives are decontextualized stories, they have complex characteristics, vary in arrangement of discourse order (e.g., flashback or flashforward) and in the development of authors' and characters' point-of-view (Brewer, 1985). Even more difficult are expository texts because children typically lack the necessary content, as well as structural knowledge for comprehension (Bock & Brewer, 1985).

Children come to school with widely differing exposure to grammatical and discourse structures. Some may have rich and varied print experiences, some may have heard only oral stories, and some may not have had much exposure to either written or oral texts. Repeated reading activities such as reading books over and over (Holdaway, 1979), reading a wide variety of discourse types including fantasy, information, and poetic texts (Watson, 1985), and reading patterned texts where children can internalize some written structures (Bridge, 1986; McCormick & Mason, 1984) are presumed to help children understand varying text structures.

Implications for Literacy Acquisition

Given that there are physical, situational, functional, formal, and structural differences between oral and written language, what impact do these differences have on the way children learn to read and write? Although the communicative function of language might make the acquisition of written language a natural process (Goodman & Goodman, 1979), research suggests that its acquisition can be fraught with problems.

Dyson's (1984) observations reveal that children coming to school with meager literacy experiences have much to learn about print and are easily confused if they cannot map words onto their oral language or cannot recognize or distinguish letters. A kindergarten child was observed while he was attempting to carry out free writing and copying assignments in his classroom. Dyson found that the child ingeniously applied his little understanding of how written language functions symbolically. In attempting to write, for example, he used the appearance of letters to stand for the resembled word (O for the word *deer*). He called on letter names to represent whole words (R for the word *are*), and he focused on content words and ignored functors. Although he misnamed letters and words, mixed letters with numerals, and ignored or misinterpreted spaces between words, when he was able to write freely, he was able to connect print with his knowledge.

Ferreiro and Teberosky (1982) found that children who entered school without understanding the link between their oral language experiences and formal instruction did not advance at the same rate in learning to read and write as those who did make the connection. They suggest that instruction be designed to build on what children have already learned about print to help them link their experiences with speech to their reading and writing experiences.

Several studies have shown that when text is made more like speech, beginning readers can process it more readily. Tatham (1970) drew from Strickland's (1962) findings on frequent oral language patterns in designing materials for her study. She found that second graders comprehended test sentences written with frequent oral language patterns significantly better than sentences with infrequent oral language patterns. Using a technique of elicited imitation, Amsterdam (1985) had first-grade children repeat, and later recall, "primerese" and "natural language" versions of fables. She found significantly more meaningful consolidation, as well as more complete recalls and fewer unnecessary repetitions, with the natural language versions of the texts.

Allen (1985) found that primary-grade children performed better on inferential comprehension tasks when the texts were closely linked to their oral language. Seventy children varying in reading ability read three kinds of stories: their own dictated stories, peer-written stories, and textbook stories. Even the least able readers inferred well when reading their own texts, and they inferred somewhat better on peer stories than on textbook stories.

Some success has also been obtained by designing beginning texts to lessen the differences between speech and print. Chesterfield (1978) designed "environmentally specific" materials in an attempt to close the "cultural and language gulfs" separating rural Brazilian children from their classroom texts and urban teachers. He changed the pictures and words in initial reading materials to reflect rural life but left the basic structure and situations intact. Subjects were 98 first-grade students who ranged from 6 to 11 years of age (some had been held back in first grade). Four classrooms had experimental texts, and four had the regular texts. Following one year of instruction, subjects using experimental materials scored significantly higher on a reading posttest, and they used more words on a posttest writing sample in which they wrote about their best friend. They were equivalent to the others in the number of different words used and in grammaticality of sentence structure. Chesterfield notes that the gains are especially significant given that the reading test was on regular, not environmentally specific, materials.

Because research in the area of oral and written language comparisons has been most extensive at the level of description, it is not certain which differences between oral and written language cause problems for children in learning to read and write. Put another way, connections that can made automatically or resolved without direct adult assistance need to be differentiated from those which require instruction or opportunity for practice. It is also unclear why some children have more trouble with these transfers than others and what manipulations of beginning reading materials such as Chesterfield's environmentally specific texts might be helpful for at-risk populations. We suggest that in areas where children experience difficulties in transferring from speech to print, research is needed to determine what the sources of the difficulty are and how they might be helped.

ACQUISITION OF READING AND WRITING CONCEPTS

Current research with adults and older children in cognitive psychology, as well as linguistics, has influenced research on emergent literacy. Studies of adult problem solving (Newell & Simon, 1972; Siegler, 1978), higher level cognitive structures to organize comprehension and memory processes (Anderson, Reynolds, Schallert, & Goetz, 1977), and strategies for thinking (Flavell, 1979) suggest that adults usually have effective strategies for learning and remembering print. Children use less effective strategic techniques (Gelman & Baillargeon, 1983). Problem solving also involves flexible and appropriate use of strategies, and an ability to connect, extend and generalize what is being learned from the specific context in which it is learned to the wider contexts in which it is applicable (Brown, Bransford, Ferrara, & Campione, 1982). A question to be discussed subsequently is how a problem-solving approach might be adapted for reading and writing instruction.

Two processes are thought to be involved in literacy acquisition: the translation of written elements into speech and meaning-guided thinking (Perfetti, Beck, & Hughes, 1985), or decoding and comprehension (Gough & Tunmer, 1986). These processes are thought to develop interactively (Stanovich, 1980). Literacy acquisition is analogous to Vygotsky's (1962) notion that language is comprised of two components, word sounds and meanings. Vygotsky proposes that word sounds are learned beginning with small units (single words), while word meanings are learned beginning with the whole context in which the words appear. Similarly, we propose that reading is comprised of two components, word recognition and text meaning, and that word recognition proceeds from the smaller unit to the larger one, while text meaning proceeds from the larger unit to the smaller. Word recognition is probably acquired through differentiation and recognition of letters, letter sounds, and individual words. Later this is broadened to include an understanding of the regularity of letter patterns and how to map print onto speech. Print meaning is probably acquired first within larger contexts through hearing stories, interpreting and relating stories to personal experiences, and recognizing signs and labels in context. Later this is narrowed to critical analyses of texts and their characteristics. This two-component notion of literacy learning is discussed in relation to strategy thinking in the next two sections regarding the development of early reading and writing concepts. Further discussion of the two components is presented under the headings *Phonological and letter-sound principles* and *Acquisition of story-guided concepts*.

Early Reading Development

Beginning reading in the United States has traditionally focused on decoding, that is, on an ability to recognize and use phonemes in identifying words. Chall (1979), for example, states, "The essential aspect of Stage 1 is learning the arbitrary set of letters and associating these with the corresponding parts of spoken words. In this stage, children and adults internalize cognitive knowledge about reading such as what the letters are for, how to know that *bun* is not *bug,* and how to know when they have made a mistake" (p. 39). Similarly, Gough (1972) says, "The Reader converts characters into systematic phonemes; the child must learn to do so. The Reader knows the rules that relate one set of abstract entities to another; the child does not. The Reader is a decoder; the child must become one" (p. 526).

Some researchers who have studied emergent literacy accept decoding skill as part of learning to read, but disagree with those who adopt decoding skill as the only measure of whether or not a child can read. They also assert that components of reading skill begin to emerge long before a child can decode words. They argue that the term "beginning reader" should be applied to children who would be classified by Chall (1979) as Stage 0 nonreaders, not just to children who have moved into the decoding stage.

Mason (1980) examined the emergence of reading-related capabilities in 4-year-old children who were not able to decode words at the outset of the study. When asked to read words without context cues, their responses were entirely unrelated to the graphic structure of the words. Several months later, however, many tried to read words by applying an initial letter-sound strategy, that is, by using the name-sound of the first consonant of a word as the principal cue. For example, one child read *may* as "*mister,*" and another said it was "*mom.*" When they tried to spell, these children applied the same strategy of focusing on the initial sound of the word. They would whisper the word to themselves to hear the initial sound and usually choose a letter that represents the correct phonemic representation (e.g., *B* for *ball* or *K* for *cat*). Mason's results reveal that there is a complex developmental history preceding the emergence of decoding skill.

A similar course of development in spelling is described by Ehri (1985) and Morris (1981). Ehri summarizes as follows:

Once prereaders have learned letter names, they can use this information to invent semiphonetic spellings of words. They distinguish 1 or 2 sounds, usually the first or last, and represent these with letters. . . . When children learn more about letter-sound relations and about phonemic segmentation and decoding, their spellings become more complete phonetically and the letters they choose are more conventional. For example, "giraffe" might be spelled GERAF. As children learn more about spelling patterns in English words, their commitment to the principle of one letter for every sound is relaxed, and they adopt morphemic as well as phonetic patterns to spell. (pp. 6–7)

A partial mapping of children's reading development in New Zealand is proposed by Clay (1967, 1979) based on a year's weekly observations of what children say and do in reading from the time they enter school at age 5. She found reading to involve the integration of four sources of information: language, concepts about print, visual motor skills, and sound sequences in words. At first, children believe that print can be turned into speech simply by their own language inventions. Next, they begin to make up texts using written language structures and then try to tie their construction to the picture. Finally they begin to pay attention to print, using visual cues from letters.

Earlier phases of development in Argentinian children's acquisition of reading concepts are also identified by Ferreiro and Teberosky (1982). At first, print and pictures are not differentiated and a child will point to the picture when asked where there is something to read. Next, although print and picture are differentiated, the child will look at the picture and respond with picture information regardless of the graphic characters. Then the child will gradually consider graphic information.

A common finding in this research is that before children learn to decode words in and out of context, they become able to use some letter-sound information to recognize, remember, and spell words. This is possible even if they are not taught the letter sounds, because the names of the alphabet letters provide clues to the phonemic representations in words. For example, children may hear /j/ in the letter name "jay" and the word "jail" and connect the phoneme with the letter (Ehri, 1983; Ehri & Wilce, in press).

Children's movement into reading is not marked by a clear boundary between readers and nonreaders. Very young children may know where there is something to read but be unable to read it. Somewhat older children may be able to read words in context but not in isolation. Still older children may be able to read isolated words by storing partial letter-sound associations in memory, but they may not be able to read isolated words by decoding the letters into sounds. Which are we to consider readers and which are nonreaders? The term "beginning reader" has the same problem because there is no clear beginning point. Children begin acquiring knowledge about reading long before they begin formal reading instruction and long before they can exhibit any reading production skill. Reading acquisition is better conceptualized as a developmental continuum rather than the all-or-none phenomenon suggested by Chall's (1979) stages.

Early Writing Development

Literacy events almost always involve both reading and writing, either directly, as when young writers attempt to read and revise their written creations (Sulzby, 1986a), or indirectly, as when children's writing reflects elements of the texts they are learning to read (Eckhoff, 1984). They often develop concurrently (Bissex, 1980; Schickedanz & Sullivan, 1984; Taylor, 1983; Teale,

1986). Moreover, concepts about writing, graphic displays, and discourse development have usually been investigated in conjunction with emergent reading concepts and behaviors. As a result, most of the research described next on emergent writing has been pulled from studies that include investigations of reading.

Emergent writing studies have documented the strategies children employ while attempting to write. A major question has been whether children progress through hierarchical levels, or contrariwise, show no stable pattern of development. The data seem to point to a middle ground, characterized by general but not exclusive shifts in development. For example, children scribble-write less as they learn conventional letter forms, but they do not abandon scribbling altogether (Allen, 1986).

Clay's (1975) research suggests that young writers use the following four strategies with increasing sophistication. Children establish a *recurring principle* when they grasp that certain patterns are used repeatedly in English. For example, a child might fill a page with similar lines of scribbles, or linear mode writing. By applying a *generative principle*, they can create unique messages with a limited set of letters or words repeated in different combinations. For example, a limited repertoire of letters or words may lead to a construction of other words by using only the letters in child's name or to patterned sentences such as, "I love Mom. I love Dad," and so on. In grasping a *sign principle*, children make the crucial link between the concrete object and the abstract word. This is evident in labeled drawings. Clay's fourth *inventory principle* describes children's listing of words that they know, so that when asked to write something, unrelated words may be produced.

Ferreiro and Teberosky (1982) propose a developmental hierarchy of five levels of writing, which is based on a year-long study of 30 working-class first-grade children and a cross-age study of over seventy 4- to 6-year-old children from mainstream and working-class families in Argentina. The children were asked to distinguish between drawing and writing, to write their own names and names of family members, to write familiar primer words and unfamiliar words, and to write a sentence.

The first level of writing involves the reproduction of writing features. For example, children may draw broken or connected lines to represent writing. At this level, children mix drawing and writing, but they can distinguish them. They believe that words must have a minimum number of letters, usually three, and that letter arrangements must always show variability. For example "AAA" has a sufficient number of letters to be a word, but there is no variability, so children at the first level would probably reject it as something to read. At the second level, letter forms become more conventional, and children become aware of the importance of letter order. At the third level, children develop the syllabic hypothesis, in which they record one letter per syllable. However, for one- and two-syllable words, this hypothesis contradicts the earlier formed minimum number hypothesis. The fourth level is the alphabetic hypothesis in which they resolve the conflict between the syllabic and mininum number of characters hypothesis by rejecting both and using one letter for each sound they are able to hear. The final level is alphabetic writing in which children approximate the conventional writing system and are more directly influenced by what they read. Their incorrect spellings at this level include common spelling patterns rather than just phonemic representations.

Temple, Nathan, and Burris (1982) identify five levels of spelling strategies that evolve over a 2-year period, beginning typically at age 4 when children begin trying to print letters. Their levels correspond closely to those described in the emergent reading section. Temple and associates illustrate these developmental changes with the spellings for "dragon" from several children: The first level is prephonemic, that is, a letter string such as MPRMRMH. Next is an early phonemic level, some letter-sound correspondence such as J. Children then move to letter-name spelling which has a close phonemic match, such as GAGIN. Transitional spelling mixes correct and invented spelling, as in DRAGUN. The final level is correct spelling.

These developmental changes are thought to be linked to children's background experiences and knowledge of writing strategies, as well as to their purpose for writing, rather than to their age. For example, Crenshaw's (1985) observations of kindergarten children's writing reveal a range from the use of random nonstandard forms to sound/symbol matching and conventional spellings. The hierarchical levels defined by Ferreiro and Teberosky did not "fit" the varied writing produced by these children throughout the year. Similarly, Goodman (1985) analyzed writing samples from five groups of children, aged 3 to 6, 78 altogether, including bilingual Chapter 1 children, inner-city and rural children, and children from the Papagos Indian reservation. She found children using a variety of strategies and forms based on their experiences with writing.

Sulzby (1986b), who studied the story writing samples of 24 kindergarten children, identifies six categories of writing. These are drawing, scribbling, letter-like forms, well-learned units, invented spellings, and conventional spellings. She concludes that children build a repertoire of techniques to write that they can make use of selectively and that they show stability across time in drawing on these varied strategies. For example, a child might "inventory" known words in a conventionally spelled list but use cursive-like scribbles, letter strings, and invented spellings in writing a story.

Graves (1983) proposes that writing begins with spelling and moves through motor aesthetics, conventions, topic selection, adequate information, and revision. However, in his 2-year study of children's writing, he observed that these categories often overlapped, and many children did not fit this ordering. Graves suggests six possible reasons for the absence of an invariant sequence: (1) handwriting and spelling remain central issues for some writers forever but become secondary in others by age 7; (2) children focus on what teachers emphasize; (3) if teachers do not respond to the child's focus, progress may be impeded; (4) all children have concerns in all areas, even though the primary focus may be on one or two; (5) proficient writers also continue to have concerns at all levels; and (6) growth in one category may conflict with growth in other categories.

Integrated writing/reading research is needed to determine how reading and writing are intertwined in the learning process and how they might be assessed. We need to learn more about how reading activities might provide young writers with a repertoire of strategies that become more effective with experience and how writing activities might foster reading. Teachers need to know how reading and writing concepts might be taught together. For example, they should know how phonetic analysis, which is necessary for both reading and writing, might be taught concurrently and how they could help children make the connection between their invented spellings and letter sounds in reading. The role of teachers is also debated but is not resolved. Should teachers simply play the role of responders to what children are trying to write, arranging peer-directed conferences, and celebrate their writing attempts? Or, should they question and challenge children's intents, model good writing, and direct a use of new writing strategies? More research is needed in order to answer questions such as these and to obtain successful writing programs in kindergarten and first grade.

PHONOLOGICAL AND LETTER-SOUND PRINCIPLES

There is strong support for the notion that when children come to understand that words contain distinguishable phonemes and that letters symbolize these phonemes in words, they shift toward more effective word-recognition strategies. This was evident in an instructional study with entering first graders (MacKinnon, 1959). Groups that learned phonologically regular materials were observed to omit and substitute words without realizing their errors at the outset of instruction. However, by the fourth week they were making graphic confusions and helping one another figure out many of the words using both letter-sound and context information. Changes in reading strategy errors were also identified by Biemiller (1970) and Weber (1970). In reading words in stories or in isolation, beginning readers were observed to shift during the school year from a focus on picture or whole word clues to graphic cues and letter-sound relations to a use that included text context.

Lundberg (1984) found that an awareness of words and phonemes was highly correlated ($r > .70$) with later reading achievement. Furthermore, of 46 children with low linguistic awareness scores and low reading scores in first grade, only 6 became average or above-average readers by sixth grade.

A strong relationship between phonemic awareness and reading achievement was also found by Juel, Griffith, and Gough (1985). Phonemic awareness was measured with subtests involving segmentation, blending, and deletion and substitution of the first and last phonemes (taken from a test developed by Roper-Schneider, 1984). Phonemic awareness contributed 49% of the variance in a multiple regression analysis of end-of-first-grade word recognition scores, after accounting for vocabulary (6% of the variance) and listening comprehension (13% of the variance). At the end of second grade it contributed less (30%). Zero order correlations between phonemic awareness and word recognition were high, .83 in first grade and .71 in second grade.

We suggest that the significant correlations between phonological awareness and word recognition are explained principally by children's knowledge about effective strategies for recognizing words. In one study, for example, Mason (1977) gave 40 children a set of 12 words to learn, some of which were in upper case, some in lower case, and some in mixed case. After they practiced identifying the words for four trials, another set of words was substituted in which the letter case was completely or partially changed (e.g., truck was now printed as TRUCK, BIKE became bike, tree became Tree, and Rat became rat). Children who could no longer identify the words were found to use nonphonetic strategies on the reading and spelling tasks. By contrast, children who could read the words after the case shift were found to use letter-sound clues on the other tasks.

A similar influence of strategy on reading was found by Peterman and Mason (1984), who tested 60 kindergarten children's word-reading strategies. Children were given pictures in which printed labels under the picture either closely matched the picture (e.g., a picture of a beach ball was labeled *ball*), or labeled only part of the picture (e.g., under a picture of a car was the label *wheel*). Children were asked to show the examiner where there was something to read, to tell what it said, and to explain how they knew it said that. It was hypothesized that children who do not rely on letter-to-sound relationships to identify words would misguess the unpredictable labels.

All but one child knew that the information to be read was in the print. However, 34% relied completely on the picture information. This was evident because they correctly labeled the predictable pictures (e.g., saying "ball" for the word *ball*) and misidentified every unpredictable label by substituting a predictable label for it (e.g., saying "car" for the word *wheel*). Another 34% made many mistakes, both on predictable and unpredictable labels, but their errors indicated an attempt to rely on the letter information (e.g., saying "white" for *wheel*). These children, by thinking of a word that began with the initial letter of the printed word, were beginning to use a strategy that focused on letter-sound information. An attempt to integrate print and picture was made by 28% of the children. They correctly identified predictable labels and figured out or made good guesses for other words (e.g., saying "wagon" for *wheel* with the pictured car). The remaining 2% of the children were decoders and made essentially no errors on the task. Correlations between children's strategy level on this task and their total scores on a letter and word recognition test were .57 (Mason & McCormick, 1979). Moreover, when the children were retested four months later at the beginning of first grade, it was found that half had advanced to a higher leveled strategy.

Training studies also reveal the advantages of superior knowledge of letter-sound principles for reading and spelling. Ehri and Wilce (in press) studied kindergarten children who knew letter names and were beginning to link initial consonants in words to initial word sounds. They sought to determine whether teaching beginners to use all the letter sounds in three- or four-letter words would enable them to read and spell differently from children who lacked this knowledge. One group of subjects was taught to decipher 12 sets of similarly spelled pseudowords in a way that forced them to pay attention to variations in all letter positions. The other group rehearsed isolated letter-sound relations. Comparisons of the two groups' ability to read real words and to recall their spellings revealed substantial differences favoring the group that had been taught to decipher. In this study, although all of the children had above-average IQs, 6 of the 15 subjects in the deciphering group failed to learn to decode, indicating that this skill is not easily taught. However, the fact that some subjects could be trained and that the training improved their word reading and spelling performance provides evidence for the contribution of an understanding of letter-sound mapping principles.

Bradley and Bryant (1983) obtained moderate correlations between preschool children's ability to detect phonemic similarities and differences in words and their reading and spelling ability measured 4 years later, *rs* = .44 to .57. They provided 40 lessons to three subsamples from the larger group of 4-year-olds. One group was trained to think about how the names of pictured objects shared phonemes. A second group was trained to use pictures and letters to relate print to sound. A third group was trained to categorize names of objects by meaning. The remaining subjects received no training. On reading and spelling tasks administered 3 years later, children in Groups 1 and 2 had significantly higher scores than children in the other trained and untrained groups. Children who received print-sound training (Group 2) outperformed children who received only sound training (Group 1). Bradley and Bryant conclude from their findings "that the awareness of rhyme and alliteration which children acquire before they go to school, possibly as a result of their experiences at home, has a powerful influence on their eventual success in learning to read and to spell" (1983, p. 421).

In a study aimed at measuring word learning under two instructional conditions, Surber and Mason (1977) taught 40 children to recite a letter-sound rule (the long vowel, silent *e* rule) and to read one set of 13 words that appeared in the context of a story that was read to them. One set of words matched the rule (e.g., *cage, later*) while the other set violated it (e.g., *was, large*). Each group recited their set of words from word cards and helped the examiner read the story containing the words. Although both groups learned to recite the long vowel, silent *e* rule and to read their set of words equally well, only the children who had read the story containing words that obeyed the letter-pattern rule were able to read the transfer words (new long *a,* silent *e* patterned words).

Another study was designed to explore the influences of both instruction and reading text. Juel and Roper-Schneider (1985) gave 93 nonreaders 30 minutes of daily, scripted synthetic phonics instruction in addition to their daily basal instruction. Half the children were in a textbook that was characterized as having a variable vocabulary and emphasizing high-frequency words. Half were in a textbook characterized as having a more controlled vocabulary of phonetically regular words. These differences were particularly evident at the preprimer level.

The authors found that while the two groups did not differ in their phonemic ability for items that had been taught, the group using the more controlled vocabulary textbook generalized beyond the taught patterns significantly better than the group using the textbook with a variable vocabulary. Each group adopted decoding strategies consistent with their texts. The group using the controlled vocabulary textbook developed a word-family strategy and could read more words than the other group who relied more on visual strategies. Nonetheless, the groups performed equally well on reading comprehension tests given at the end of first grade. It remains to be determined whether such differences might have an effect on later reading.

Evans and Carr (1985) compared 10 classrooms implementing the British Infant School Model with 10 that featured the use of commercial basal lessons and accompanying reading textbooks and workbooks. Time-sampling techniques in which children in every classroom were observed for four half-days determined that independent activities dominated the Infant Model classrooms while teacher-led activities dominated the basal classrooms. Significantly greater time was spent in the basal classrooms on word analysis, printing, silent reading, and looking at printed display materials. Model classrooms spent more time orally reading the stories they had dictated. Analysis of children's performance revealed differences favoring the basal classrooms on reading and math achievement. No differences were found on measures of basic ability (e.g., verbal fluency, classification, social role-taking).

Differences favoring the basal group are explained by Evans and Carr in terms of lack of effective instruction to build print-specific skills. Word analysis, silent reading, activities focusing on comprehension, the use of context to make predictions, and printing activities were positively correlated with reading. Among the classrooms observed, these activities more often occurred in the basal than Infant Model classrooms, although the authors comment that the Infant Model classrooms could have included those activities.

They conclude that reading instruction varies along two dimensions, one being the extent to which reading is taught as a rule-governed translation task, and the other being the extent to which reading activities are systematically engineered, supervised with corrective feedback, and practiced. Both dimensions are important in reading acquisition.

Perfetti, Beck, and Hughes (1985) studied the relationship between (1) first graders' ability to synthesize and delete phonemes from words and (2) later reading. They found that phonemic knowledge and learning to read develop in mutual support. That is, phonemic awareness seems to lead to more successful reading, and reading activity to a greater understanding of phonemic knowledge. They concluded that it is probably not useful to describe the relationship in simple prerequisite terms. Reading itself "enables the child to analyze words and to manipulate their speech segments. It is not necessary to assume that . . .[the child] performs such manipulations on the orthography. Rather learning some orthographic principles through reading enables the discovery of parallel phonemic principles" (pp. 45–46).

A substantial amount of research exists on this topic, and there are encouraging signs that instructional studies lead to improved outcomes in reading. Still, a number of important, unanswered questions remain—such as how to employ information about children's word-and letter-recognition strategies to improve instruction. In some studies, phonics instruction appears as the significant factor in later reading success; in others, merely the presence of regular patterned words is effective; and in still others, the opportunity to read and reread or figure out the text is what matters. Each seems to foster the development of reading strategies, but whether each is as effective at particular points of development is not known. Clearly, it is important for children to learn about letter-sound relationships, but not if the instruction sacrifices reading comprehension opportunities or independent reading activity.

ACQUISITION OF STORY-GUIDED CONCEPTS

How might reading stories to children benefit their literacy development? It is postulated that a critical aspect is the interaction between adults and children in what Vygotsky (1962) describes as the zone of proximal development, or the area between what learners know and what they come to know with assistance. Parents, teachers, and more capable children operate within this zone by scaffolding conversations (Cazden, 1979). They build one comment or question on the previous one and guide the learner to move from a situation where the task is carried out with others' help to one in which the child operates independently (Brown, 1985). In addition to scaffolding, literate others support learning by holding children accountable for their share of the communication interchange and by guiding them back to the question or subject under discussion. Parents establish routines that contribute to literacy, such as the bedtime reading and talking about shared events (Butler, 1979; Crago,

1975; Heath, 1982, 1986; Hiebert, 1986; Snow, 1983; Sulzby & Teale, 1984; White, 1954). Teachers establish equivalent school routines of story listening or "rugtime reading" and show-and-tell time (Bridge, 1986; Cochran-Smith, 1984; Holdaway, 1986; Mason, McCormick, & Bhavnagri, 1986).

Story Reading at Home

Studying language acquisition of 6- to 10-year olds, Chomsky (1972) found a strong relationship between children's exposure to written stories and their rate of linguistic development. Kindergarten children who had been exposed to many books, particularly those that were linguistically complex, understood more complex language. To exemplify the relationship, Chomsky describes two kindergarteners of the same age and IQ. The child with a low linguistic comprehension score had not heard a single story during the previous week, according to parents' report. She was typically read to less than ½ hour per week and was familiar with very few complex stories. In contrast, a child with a high linguistic score had been read 17,500 words that week, was usually read to more than 2 hours a week, and frequently heard complex stories. Chomsky concludes that there is a distinct language advantage for children if they are read to frequently and hear a variety of rich and complex stories.

In more recent research with reading rather than language as the measure of accomplishment, Wells (1985) found that of all the tests he administered to children on entry at school, the one that had the highest correlation with overall reading attainment 2 years later was knowledge of literacy ($r = .79$, $p < .001$). Knowledge of literacy was defined by a cluster of highly correlated parent-questionnaire variables that tapped parents' support for literacy before their children entered school. These included the number of books owned by the child, the child's interest in literacy, and his or her involvement in activities associated with literacy. The test and questionnaire variables were also significantly associated with the family's social class status.

Close observation of parent-child book-reading sessions indicate their importance in language and reading growth. Ninio and Bruner (1978) analyzed mothers' dialogues that accompanied picture-book reading to young children. They found that mothers direct their children's attention to particular features in a book, ask questions, provide labels, and give feedback by repeating or extending the children's remarks. Harkness and Miller (1982) found that mother-child interactions change over time. Although questions or comments to initiate book-reading interactions are continued, mothers gradually increase the length of time between each interchange by reading longer text sections. Children become able to listen to stories for longer stretches of time. Snow and Ninio (1986), who analyzed videotaped sessions of parents reading to their children, found that children learn many basic concepts about books through joint picture book reading sessions. Parents help children realize that books are for reading, not for manipulating, that the book is in control and the reader is led, that pictures in books are representations of things and events, that pictures can be named, and that events may be fictional and occur outside real time.

Joint picture-book reading was studied by DeLoache and DeMendoza (1986) with 30 pairs of mothers and 12-to-18-month-old infants. They report significant increases over age in requests by the mother for the child to say or do something, in her use of elaboration feedback, particularly to connect the story information with the child's experiences, and in her use of questions instead of labels or comments. Over the age span, children become more able to respond to mothers' questions, to use verbal (compared with nonverbal) terms, and to initiate verbal interactions.

Pellegrini, Brody, and Sigel (1985) compared parent-child book-reading interactions over age (4 and 5 years) and communication status (normal or speech disability). Analyses of 120 parents who each read two stories to their child revealed an effect for communicative status but not age. Parents of speech-handicapped children made fewer story-responding demands, paraphrased greater portions of the text, and gave more turns. The authors conclude that parents adjust their interaction styles to their child's level of communicative competence.

Sulzby (1985) studied the emergent reading attempts of 24 children at the beginning and end of kindergarten, as well as the reading attempts of 2-, 3-, and 4-year-old children. A comparison of the kindergarten data with those obtained from younger children revealed a developmental progression across age levels. Using familiar and unfamiliar stories, children were asked to read or pretend-read the text. At first, stories were not formed. When they were formed, children used an oral language-like structure before they used a written language-like structure. Then, the printed information was watched, and as reading strategies were formed, independent reading began to occur. Sulzby concludes that children progress from a treatment of a book as discrete pieces to a whole unit and use first their own speech and then that of the author to weave a story across the pages. An important implication is that story-reading constructs are formed prior to an ability to read or even attend to print.

The effects of an interactive approach is seen in a study comparing early readers with nonearly readers who were matched for age, intelligence test scores, and social class. Thomas (1985), extending the work of Snow (1983), found that early readers more often talked about literacy with family members and that their interactions contained more instances of semantic contingency (keeping a topic going), scaffolding, and accountability (requiring the completion of a language interaction). The quality and quantity of interaction, not just the presence of reading materials and a storytime routine, was found to shape early reading development.

The studies reported here suggest how children benefit from story reading. Conducted primarily with middle-class families, they indicate that adults act as scaffolds for children during story-reading. As children become more competent, adults adjust their demands and require more complex information. Parents provide just enough support during story reading to enable their children to succeed, but no more. Children learn how to identify story information, relate it to their own experiences, and form stories with written language structures.

Research with working-class families suggests that their children seldom receive these experiences. Feitelson and Goldstein (1986) conducted a study in Israel comparing middle- with working-class families. They found that middle-class homes had an average of 54 children's books whereas working class homes had an average of only 5 books. Middle-class parents read to their children, beginning at age 1, reading up to a half-hour each day. In contrast, 60% of working-class parents did not read to their children. Those that did, read infrequently, and often did not begin until their child was 5 years old.

Social class differences have also been found in this country. Teale (1986) observed 3-year-old children from working-class families. Although many occasions of literacy expression by the parents in the child's presence were observed, these did not necessarily involve children's participation and there were few occasions of parent-child story reading. Similarly, Anderson and Stokes (1984), who studied working-class families, found that story reading encompasses less than 2% of all literacy activities. Both of these studies show that literacy events such as reading the mail or looking at the TV guide do occur, but the troubling finding is that story reading was infrequent. Other literacy events are not likely to yield the same benefits for the child as story reading.

Story telling, as well as story reading, is a less frequent occurrence in working-class homes. Heath (1986) followed three children when they were between the ages of 2 and 4. One child was from a mainstream, white, middle-class family, one was from a white working-class family, and one was from a black working-class family. She observed four types of parent-child interactions surrounding the telling of events and narratives: recounting, in which the child responds to adult requests or questions; accounting, in which the child constructs a personal account of events that the child experienced; event casting, in which the child produces a running narrative of an ongoing event; and story telling, in which the child tells imaginary stories by elaborating on real or imagined events. The surprising finding was that these interactions were seldom observed in the working-class families. Heath observed fewer than 60 such interactions in working-class families but over 1,500 interactions in the mainstream family setting. Heath found that these social class differences were carried into school, affecting children's later ability to talk about or to write stories.

Parents who foster story reading and story talk with their children are thought to ease the task of story reading comprehension (Cochran-Smith, 1983). While no direct evidence is yet available, the lack of parent-supported story activities in the preschool years is likely to be one source accounting for the difficulty that working-class children exhibit in later grades in reading comprehension. However, verifying this connection is extremely difficult. Mainstream parents not only involve their children in more joint picture book reading and story telling than do working-class parents, but also engage them in more language communication activities (Hess, Holloway, Price, & Dickson, 1982; Sigel, 1982). They own more children's books, model literacy more often, take their children to the library and on other outings more often, and discuss educational television programs with them more often (McCormick & Mason, 1984).

Another problem is that data-gathering techniques are inadequate, according to Cochran-Smith (1983). Diary studies of book reading by parents to their infants and young children typically omit explanations of how the data were collected, what the settings for reading were, or how the story-reading process should be analyzed. They are conducted with one or a very few children, making generalization to other children difficult. Cochran-Smith reports that many experimental studies of story reading are also flawed. They have been conducted in unnatural, laboratory contexts; they measure a limited set of factors; and they often contain overly literal measures of listening and reading comprehension.

Available evidence suggests that a rich context for language learning and for understanding written stories is engendered with storybook reading. There are, however, enormous variations in the frequency of story activity at home. Mainstream families typically provide many more occasions of story talk, as well as story listening and reading, than working-class families, and mainstream children are known to become more successful readers than those from the working class. Although additional research is needed to identify factors on the causal chain, a reasonable conjecture is that story reading at home makes an important, if not necessary, contribution to later reading achievement.

Story Reading in School

There is stronger evidence for the importance of story reading in school-based studies. Feitelson, Kita, and Goldstein (1986) had teachers in low socioeconomic status (SES) kindergartens in Israel read to the children three times a week for four months. Matched control classrooms engaged in group games. Posttests indicated that children who were read to better understood stories, were more attentive to picture clues, were better able to infer causal relationships, and could tell more connected stories. In a second study, teachers of first-grade children either read to their students for the last 20 minutes of each weekday or continued their standard reading and writing instruction.

At the end of six months, several posttests were administered. These included oral reading of an unfamiliar expository passage, answering comprehension questions after silently reading five short texts, and telling a story from a sequence of four pictures. They found that children who were read to in school produced significantly fewer word reading errors, had higher comprehension scores, and used more complex language in story telling.

Observations of kindergarten in the United States indicate that teachers seldom use familiar print to introduce children to reading (Aukerman, 1984; Bridge, 1986), although children as young as 3 years of age can identify environmental print words (Harste, Burke & Woodward, 1982; Harste; Woodward, & Burke 1984). Furthermore, according to Bridge, children learn more sight words if they use predictable patterned language books to teach sight words instead of commercial basal text materials.

In a set of four studies, McCormick and Mason (1984, 1986) found that helping children read easy stories after listening to an adult read them can have long-lasting effects. The first study determined that an effective story-reading method is to focus children's attention on the text meaning rather than words or letter-sound relations, to model story reading, and to read the text several times, gradually relinquishing control of the reading task to the children.

A second study with a Head Start classroom documented how repeated readings help children acquire the metacognitive skills of planning, monitoring, and evaluation of stories.

A third study measured the effects of book reading by comparing two groups of kindergarten children. One group received eight books in the mail that they were encouraged to read at home with their parents' help. A control group of classmates matched in IQ did not receive the books. At the end of the kindergarten year, tests of children's story-reading ability, their spelling ability, and their ability to read words out of context revealed superior performance among children receiving the books and benefits that were maintained into first grade.

In the fourth study, school as well as home treatments were provided for experimental and control subjects. The school treatments were 10 lessons of books for the experimental group to read and 10 lessons of story listening with picture materials for the control group. Experimental subjects were sent home three packets of books during the Head Start year and six more during kindergarten. Control subjects received the same number of mailings of materials, but the materials were pictures during the Head Start phase of the study and visual perception work sheets in kindergarten. Significant differences found at the end of the Head Start year and again a year later in kindergarten indicated that experimental children outperformed controls not only on story reading and word reading but also on letter-sound knowledge. Parents and teachers also rated these children as having more knowledge about reading.

Why should story listening and repeated reading experiences affect children's letter-sound knowledge? One possibility is that adults enfold informal phonics and word-reading lessons within story-reading activity. Another is that the activity itself leads children to attend to and ask questions about words and letters.

To answer this question, four kindergarten teachers were videotaped as they read aloud a literature story. Children were individually questioned about their recall of the story and were asked to read four pages from the story. Analyses of story recall and probe questions showed substantial differences among children's story recall as a function both of early reading ability and of the teacher's approach to story reading. The most effective approach was that used by a teacher who read the story through once and then went through it again, helping children see the connections among the key ideas (Dunning & Mason, 1984).

Children also differed in their ability to read the exact words on the four pages. Those who performed better were children whose teacher occasionally asked them to identify words during the story reading and who pointed out how certain words could be identified from the picture or by thinking of the story meaning (Peterman, Mason, & Dunning, 1985). Although this work is correlational and compares the natural variations among only four teachers, it offers support for the first explanation, which is that adults can affect children's word recognition through a focus on the print during story reading.

The second explanation, that reading and rereading causes children to ask questions about print, is also supported in a case study (Lartz & Mason, in preparation). Here, a story was read once and repeatedly discussed for nine sessions with a kindergarten child. The adult limited her responses to answering questions raised by the child. After asking about the pictures and characters, the child eventually began to ask questions about the print and how to read the words. It may be significant that questions about the print did not occur until the story ideas had been thoroughly explored.

It is hypothesized that story-reading activities acquaint children with complex information about written language forms and structures, as well as strategies for reading. This can take place within the larger, more meaningful context because parents or teachers provide support by filling in and modeling the task even though children are able to carry out only a small portion of it. As children become more competent, the adults make more demands and encourage children to take on greater portions of the task. In this way, the story-reading task need not be broken into instructional segments but left as a whole, enabling a focus on meaning and providing the opportunity to develop metacognitive and strategic approaches to reading.

Research needs to address some of the ways that explain how story-reading activities (whether they involve listening, story discussion, story rereading and reciting, or skillful reading) help children understand how to read stories meaningfully. The interplay between story reading and word recognition with possible effects on phonemic awareness and later reading is important. How these might be better integrated in kindergarten and first-grade instruction is an important question. Repeated reading activities, the use of familiar words and texts, word analyses during oral-story reading, and story writing are possible approaches.

IMPLICATIONS OF EMERGENT LITERACY RESEARCH FOR CLASSROOM PRACTICES

Descriptive and experimental studies of individual children, small groups of children, classroom environments, and various home and school settings have begun to clarify the picture of how young children become literate. The overriding evidence is that many, if not most, literacy concepts are acquired through shared adult-child participation in reading and writing activities. Literacy activities, which may be formally or informally provided, involve language interaction with children about literacy events, as well as the use of meaningful tasks and materials. That is, the studies reviewed here point to the importance for literacy development in schools of language-rich social interactions and the use of meaningful tasks.

Language Interactions

Language interactions between adults and children, as well as among children, are proposed to be vital to literacy development. When focused on reading stories to children, these interactions are very similar at home and school for middle-class preschool children (Cochran-Smith, 1984). The interplay serves the dual function of entertaining children and helping them acquire information. Parents are shown to use a scaffolding procedure that allows children gradually to shift from listening and talking about a story to reading or pretend-reading a story. Less information is available about how teachers structure story reading. However, story-reading time can be an "interactive negotiation" of the text in a social, conversational mode. Viable approaches to story reading that have been documented by researchers include reading and rereading of favorite stories, the use of caption or picture books, and reading of one's own written stories.

Literate adults foster the use of language to talk about and analyze language. Specific metalinguistic terms are used to refer to language. The process is thought to help in the analysis of reading and writing concepts and tasks because elements of speech such as letters, syllables, function words, and new vocabulary are discussed. Analytic tasks among preschool children include alphabet-naming games, rhyming and alliteration activities, word-spelling games, and the "What's that?" and "Why" questions that all children ask. These are presumed to help children figure out how to break speech into words and words into phonemes and distinguish words meaningfully.

Typical home language activities of early readers and writers can be extended to schools in part by fostering peer interactions. For example, classroom activities can be arranged to encourage peer discussion of stories, establish opportunities for child authors to discuss their published stories with classmates, and advise others about written ideas (Graves, 1983; Hansen, 1986). Children can learn from each other through sharing insights, asking questions that might not occur to the already-literate teacher, and foster a genuine community of readers and writers. Teachers might also engage young readers and writers in language-rich activities such as word games, storytelling, riddles, and rhymes (Mattingly, 1984), arrange for them to use metalinguistic terminology (Johns, 1984), and intersperse activities such as dictating stories, storytelling, and language play (Holdaway, 1979).

Teachers can organize reading lessons around peer interactions. For example, children in Hawaiian classrooms make substantial gains in understanding texts when they engage in the kind of talk-story social interactions that are similar to their social interactions at home (Au & Mason, 1981). Similarly, first-grade children's reading was influenced after only 10 lessons, if it was structured to encourage peer teaching where children help each other with unknown words instead of working individually with the teacher (MacKinnon, 1959).

Application of successful home-learning strategies to school settings needs extensive research. Although language transfer from home to school seems to be feasible and to have an effect on reading and writing progress, a single model for all children is probably not appropriate. Parent-child interactions and literacy experiences vary with culture, social class, and parents' education. While an effective model for mainstream children has been moderately well specified, the best language-to-literacy instruction for nonmainstream children will require more research before sound guidelines for teachers can be laid out. Some other lingering questions include why siblings in the same home environment often differ in their reactions to parent and teacher literacy efforts, whether an initiation by the child instead of an adult is needed to advance literacy skill, or what activities that are prominent and effective in mainstream homes and schools might be used successfully elsewhere.

Meaningful Literacy Events

Drawing again from observations of mainstream parent-child literacy events, it appears that children usually carry out and benefit from meaningful literacy tasks. For example, children are known to write to communicate, make notes for themselves, label their possessions, and so on. They read to identify words, show off their reading skill to others, enjoy a story, or follow directions. Parents negotiate reading and writing events with children, so that favorite stories, familiar language, and enjoyable literacy activities are featured.

To foster meaningful literacy events in school, Goodman and Goodman

(1983) recommend activities that build on children's interest in environmental print and that encourage reading and writing for communication. They suggest reading signs and labeled products, writing out conversations, and setting up classroom mailboxes for note passing.

Extensive use of books in school is another way to insure a focus on meaningful reading and thoughtful analysis of texts (Doake, 1985; Holdaway, 1979). Holdaway developed an activity that he termed the Shared-Book Experience in which children engage in a variety of talking, writing, reading, and listening activities with favorite books that are read over and over. Bussis, Chittenden, Amarel, and Klausner (1985) recommend using many types of texts in the classroom so that children can gain control of the reading process through wide and varied reading. They also recommend that children be helped to acquire knowledge, a role that includes teaching rules, helping with unknown words, discussing pertinent background information, and supporting attempts to negotiate print successfully.

Book-sharing activities may also lead to meaningful classroom literacy experiences. Hansen (1986) found that literacy was advanced when teachers encouraged children to share favorite books by reading, picture-reading, or retelling the contents, and also to share their own writing with classmates. Morrow and Weinstein (1985) found that a voluntary reading program in kindergarten classroom significantly increased children's use of books in school. Fielding, Wilson, and Anderson (1985) obtained a similar result with fourth graders. These literacy events might be important because children have the opportunity to read materials they find interesting.

A NEW WAVE OF INSTRUCTIONAL RESEARCH

In this last section, we present examples of research that exemplify how teachers might scaffold literacy lessons and use language-rich and print-meaningful contexts to foster the development of effective strategies for reading and writing. While these studies are expressly limited to the particular children who were studied, there are encouraging signs that generalizable instructional techniques have been uncovered.

In an exemplary line of research linking emergent literacy to instruction, Clay (1979, 1982, 1985) developed a reading recovery program for a special population of children. These children were the lowest performers in reading and writing in their schools after one year of instruction. Beginning with careful observation of good teachers teaching, Clay generated three guidelines for accelerating the progress of at-risk readers. The child should have many opportunities for teacher-child interaction in instruction; tasks should foster language use, be drawn from texts that the child can read, and involve practice of tasks where improvement is needed; and the child should be helped to develop flexible approaches to reading.

The program presented teachers with ways to integrate the reading and writing instruction and had them make extensive use of books and encourage independent reading. There were daily individual tutoring sessions of 30–40 minutes each.

A typical tutoring session included the following (Clay, 1985, p. 56):

- Rereading of two or more familiar books
- Rereading yesterday's new book and taking a running record
- Letter identification (plastic letters on a magnetic board)
- Writing a story (including hearing sounds in words)
- Cut-up story to be rearranged
- New book introduced
- New book attempted

Teaching procedures were based on constant evaluation of each child's needs and abilities. Thus, children who had not interacted extensively with print were taught directionality and locating responses. However, these activities were unnecessary for most children.

Clay studied 122 children from five diverse schools who were in the recovery program and compared them to their classmates (a total of 291 children). Teachers kept running records of the second reading of every new book introduced, recorded reading miscues and summaries of the strategies children used as they read, kept detailed lesson records of children's responses to tasks, and constructed graphs showing the progress of the children through levels of increasing text difficulty. Pretests and posttests included measures of reading vocabulary, concepts about print, letter identification, writing vocabulary, and dictation ability. Of the 122 children who began the program, 80 returned to regular classroom instruction after an average of 13.5 weeks of instruction because their performance had reached that of their average-achieving classroom peers, and their teachers judged them to be capable of sustaining progress without special tutoring. Of the remaining 42 children, only 7 did not seem to profit from the program. Four were non-English speaking, and 3 had physical or mental limitations. Statistical comparisons showed that "pupils who received individual tuition made gains which equalled or exceeded the gains made by their classmates who showed initially the higher achievement" (Clay, 1979, p. 85).

A 3-year follow-up study of 68 of the children (34 European, 24 Maori, and 10 Pacific Island) was most encouraging, given the general trend for children to stop progressing after remediation is terminated (Aman & Singh, 1983). Clay (1985) found that the European and Pacific Island children's average test scores were within the normal range in both reading and spelling even 3 years after discontinuing their programs. The Maori children also were at grade level in spelling, but were not making satisfactory progress in reading. This discrepancy led Clay to recommend more time in the program and more conservative discontinuation criteria for the Maori children.

The success of this New Zealand program prompted Huck and Pinnell (1985) to replicate the project in six inner-city schools in Ohio. They compared 70 at-risk children with their classroom peers and tested comparable children in control classrooms that had no Reading Recovery Program. They administered Clay's reading measures and added the reading components of the Stanford Achievement Test. The program was carried out for one year, during which about two-thirds of the children were successfully discontinued and returned to their regular classroom, matching the New Zealand results.

Not only did the Reading Recovery Program children surpass the control group of at-risk children, but they also made significantly higher gains than their classroom peers who had not needed remediation. Statistical analyses showed significantly higher gains for letter identification, concepts about print, reading level, word reading, reading comprehension, word-study skills and SAT reading. Huck and Pinnell are now extending the program to other Ohio schools, and are following the children who were in the original program.

Our last example of innovative instructional research focuses on the social context for learning. In this case, a target community itself was studied in order to design an effective reading instructional program. The Kamehameha Early Education Project (KEEP) in Hawaii has conducted over 15 years of interdisciplinary research with the goal of improving native Hawaiian children's educational achievement (Tharp et al., 1984). The research draws on Vygotskian theory in which learning cannot be explained by looking only at the learner, but must include the context in which the learner has developed.

Research by linguists and anthropologists was designed to explain the socialization of Hawaiian children in their homes and among their peers outside of school. Comparisons were made of home and school culture, of the roles played by parents and teachers, and of the kinds of interactions children engaged in at home and in school. Linguistic analyses of children's production and comprehension of Hawaiian and standard English, its acquisition, and relationships to reading and cognition were also carried out.

A kindergarten through third-grade reading and language arts program was created and has since been continuously modified. Children were tested and compared each year in order to determine whether their performance had improved to the level of nonnative children in Hawaii. When the reading achievement goal of average performance was reached, the program was exported into the public schools. By 1984, 2,000 elementary school students had been in the programs and had shown substantial improvements, with average standardized reading test scores at the 50th percentile for all subjects when collapsed across site and grade.

Instructional procedures involve assisting students in their reading performance through the zone of proximal development. The following correlaries were offered as instructional recommendations:

Assistance should be offered by the teacher in those interactional patterns most likely to be accepted by the child.

To the extent that peers can assist performance, learning will occur through that assistance, and peer-assisted learning should be promoted.

Careful assessment is necessary in order to delineate two points relative to the zone of proximal development: the 'developmental' level of individual competence and the 'instructional' level of assisted competence. (pp. 116–117)

The instructional principles and procedures that foster reading are the following: (1) Work and social contexts of the classroom are made compatible with those of the home and community. (2) Comprehension of the text, rather than mechanics of reading, is the reading instruction goal. (3) Children are helped to increase their facility with standard English and general linguistic/cognitive skills. (4) Instruction is individualized and student progress monitored continuously. (5) Teachers are trained and their performance in the classroom monitored.

The authors warn that the educational community should not focus on the particular instructional approach that has resulted from their research but rather on the process used to do the research. This is because the program was developed in terms of and for local Hawaiian children. Until work with other groups has been carried out, recommendations should be restricted to the method of research, not to the method of instruction. Regarding method of research, the authors recommend that a base of research about children in their own culture and school be created; second, that an effective program in a laboratory school be developed; and finally, that the program be expanded into public schools.

CONCLUSION

The contributions of emergent literacy research to instruction have both clarified and complicated the task of understanding the processes of learning to read and write. It has been proposed that while learning to talk, read, and write are inextricably bound and mutually facilitative processes, they can be expressed through the use of unique, as well as overlapping, strategies. Social and linguistic contexts for learning play profound roles in the course of literacy development. Literacy concepts revolve around two components, phonological awareness and story understanding, which are acquired through informal as well as adult-directed home and school activities.

The research that is needed to verify these proposals is extremely complex and must extend beyond the classroom lesson. We see the need for studies of formal and informal interactions of learners with peers and adults in order to understand the roles played by each participant. Observations of home and community settings are needed to determine how varying linguistic and cultural contexts affect reading and writing development. Interviews and observations of children as they attempt to read and write may determine the strategies that children have available for learning, the background knowledge they can use, and the ways that reading and writing can be intertwined in school instruction. Connections between early home literacy influences and school instructional effects are needed, probably through evaluation of causal models using data that stretch over several years during the time children are learning to read and write. Literacy acquisition in home and school can then be studied to measure reading progress in ways that integrate word recognition and sentence comprehension with the contexts for learning and to measure writing progress beyond spelling and letter formation.

Our review of emergent literacy across cultures, languages, and cognitive disciplines reveals many common findings. Literacy goals, both personal and public, do affect learning. Parents who play crucial roles in assisting literacy have children who come to school prepared for reading instruction. Phonological awareness, knowledge of print-speech relations, and story-reading experiences all contribute to later reading success. There are compelling examples from the United States and New Zealand of effective literacy programs based on a sound understanding of literacy acquisition. There remains a need to study other successful literacy programs and to evaluate the literacy needs of less successful groups of readers, thereby acquiring deeper insights about what instructional procedures can be generalized. As Tharp and associates (1984) conclude, "Applied developmental research forces the collection of locally valid knowledge. This base of knowledge can then serve as the valid data for an eventual higher-order analysis. The paradox returns: Applied developmental research, through its localism, may provoke a valid universalism" (p. 134). By separately studying and then pooling knowledge about divergent readers and writers, a universal understanding of literacy development in young children may someday be achieved.

REFERENCES

Adams, M.J., Anderson, R.C., & Durkin, D. (1980). Beginning reading: Theory and practice. In C. McCullough (Ed.), *Persistent problems in reading instruction.* Newark, DE: International Reading Association.

Akinnaso, F. (1982). On the differences between spoken and written language. *Language and Speech, 25,* 97–125.

Allen, J. (1984). The bottom-up deficit myth: Analysis of a language experience reader. *Journal of Language Experience, 6,* 19–25.

Allen, J. (1985). Inferential comprehensions: The effects of text source, decoding ability, and mode. *Reading Research Quarterly, 20*(5), 603–615.

Allen, J. (1986). *Literacy development in kindergarten: Writing and reading.* Paper presented at the International Reading Association, Philadelphia.

Aman, M.G., & Singh, N.M. (1983). Specific reading disorders: Concepts of etiology reconsidered. In K.D. Gadow & I. Bader (Eds.), *Advances in learning and behavioural disabilities* (Vol. 2). Greenwich, CT: JAI Press.

Amsterdam, L. (1985). *Elicited imitation: A comparison of the effects of text features.* Paper presented at the annual National Reading Conference, San Diego, CA.

Anderson, A., & Stokes, S. (1984). Social and institutional influences on the development and practice of literacy. In H. Goelman, A. Oberg, & F. Smith (Eds.), *Awakening to literacy.* Portsmouth, NH: Heinemann.

Anderson, R.C., Reynolds, J., Schallert, D., & Goetz, E. (1977). Frameworks for comprehending discourse. *American Educational Research Journal, XIV,* 367–381.

Au, K.P., & Mason, J. (1981). Social organization factors in learning to read: The balance of rights hypothesis. *Reading Research Quarterly, 17,* 115–152.

Au, K.P., Tharp, R.G., Crowell, D.C., Jordan, C., Speidel, G.E., & Calkins, R. (1985). The role of research and development in a successful reading program. In J. Osborn, P. Wilson, & R. Anderson (Eds.), *Reading education: Foundations for a literate America.* Lexington, MA: D.C. Heath.

Aukerman, R. (1984). *Approaches to beginning reading* (2nd ed.). New York: Wiley.

Biemiller, A.J. (1970). The development of the use of graphic and contextual information as children learn to read. *Reading Research Quarterly, 6,* 75–96.

Bissex, G.L. (1980). *Gnys at wrk: A child learns to write and read.* Cambridge, MA: Harvard University Press.

Blom, G., & Wiberg, L. (1973). Attitude contents in reading primers. In J. Downing (Ed.), *Comparative reading.* New York: Macmillan.

Bock, J.K., & Brewer, W. (1985). *Discourse structure and mental models* (Tech. Rep. No. 343). Champaign: University of Illinois, Center for the Study of Reading.

Bradley, L., & Bryant, P. (1983). Categorizing sounds and learning to read—a causal connection. *Nature, 301,* 419–421.

Brewer, W. (1985). The story schema: Universal and culture-specific properties. In N. Torrance, D. Olson, & A. Hildyard (Eds.), *Literacy, language, and learning.* Cambridge, England: Cambridge University Press.

Bridge, C. (1986). Predictable books for beginning readers and writers. In M. Sampson (Ed.), *The pursuit of literacy: Early reading and writing.* Dubuque, IA: Kendall/Hunt.

Brown, A. (1985). *Teaching students to think as they read: Implications for curriculum reform* (Reading Ed. Rep. No. 58). Champaign: University of Illinois, Center for the Study of Reading.

Brown, A., Bransford, J., Ferrara, R., & Campione, J. (1982). *Learning, remembering, and understanding* (Tech. Rep. No. 244). Champaign: University of Illinois, Center for the Study of Reading.

Bruner, J. (1984). Language, mind and reading. In H. Goelman, A. Oberg, & F. Smith (Eds.), *Awakening to literacy.* Portsmouth, NH: Heinemann.

Bussis, A., Chittenden, C., Amarel, M., & Klausner, E. (1985). *Inquiry into meaning: An investigation of learning to read.* Hillsdale, NJ: Erlbaum.

Butler, D. (1979). *Cushla and her books.* London: Hodder & Stoughton.

Calkins, L. (1983). *Lessons from a child.* Portsmouth, NH: Heinemann.

Calkins, L. (1986). *The art of teaching writing.* Portsmouth, NH: Heinemann.

Cazden, C. (1979). Peekaboo as an instructional model: Discourse development at home and at school. *Papers and reports on child language development* (No. 17). Stanford, CA: Stanford University, Department of Linguistics.

Chafe, W. (1985). Linguistic differences produced by differences between speaking and writing. In N. Torrance, D. Olson, & A. Hildyard (Eds.), *Literacy, language, and learning*. Cambridge, England: Cambridge University Press.

Chall, J.S. (1979). The great debate: Ten years later, with a modest proposal for reading stages. In B. Resnick & P.A. Weaver (Eds.), *Theory and practice of early reading* (Vol. 1). Hillsdale, NJ: Erlbaum.

Chesterfield, R. (1978). Effect of environmentally specific materials on reading in Brazilian rural primary schools. *The Reading Teacher, 32*(3), 312–315.

Chomsky, C. (1972). Stages in language development and reading exposure. *Harvard Education Review, 42*, 1–33.

Clay, M. (1966). *Emergent reading behavior.* Unpublished doctoral dissertation, University of Auckland Library.

Clay, M. (1967). The reading behavior of five-year-old children: A research report. *New Zealand Journal of Educational Studies, 2*, 11–31.

Clay, M. (1971). Research on language and reading in Pakeha and Polynesian groups. In D.K. Brachen & E. Malmquist (Eds.), *Improving reading ability around the world*. Newark, DE: International Reading Association.

Clay, M. (1975). *What did I write?* Portsmouth, NH: Heinemann.

Clay, M. (1979). *Reading: The patterning of complex behavior.* Portsmouth, NH: Heinemann.

Clay, M. (1982). *Observing young readers.* Portsmouth, NH: Heinemann.

Clay, M. (1985). *Early detection of reading difficulties* (3rd ed.). Portsmouth, NH: Heinemann.

Clifford, G. (1984). Buch und lessen: Historical perspectives on literacy and schooling. *Review of Educational Research, 54*(4), 472–500.

Cochran-Smith, M. (1983). Reading stories to children: A review critique. In B. Hutson (Ed.), *Advances in reading/language research: A research annual* (Vol. 2). Greenwich, CT: JAI Press.

Cochran-Smith, M. (1984). *The making of a reader.* Norwood, NJ: Ablex.

Crago, M. (1975). One child and her books: A case study 11–24 months. *Children's Libraries Newsletter, 11*, 3–8, 41–47.

Crenshaw, S. (1985). *Kindergarten writing: A semiotic focus.* Unpublished doctoral dissertation, University of Missouri, Columbia.

DeLoache, J., & DeMendoza, O. (1986). *Joint picturebook reading of children.* Champaign: University of Illinois.

Denny, T., & Weintraub, S. (1966). First-graders' responses to three questions about reading. *Elementary School Journal, 66*, 441–445.

Dewey, J., & Dewey, E. (1915/1962). *Schools of tomorrow.* New York: Dutton.

Doake, D. (1985). Reading-like behavior: Its role in learning to read. In M. Jagger & T. Smith-Burke (Eds.), *Observing the language learner* (pp. 82–98). Newark, DE: International Reading Association.

Downing, J. (1969). How children think about reading. *The Reading Teacher, 23*, 217–230.

Downing, J. (Ed.) (1973). *Comparative reading: Cross-national studies of behavior and processes in reading and writing.* New York: Macmillan.

Dunning, D., & Mason, J. (1984). An investigation of kindergarten children's expressions of story characters' intentions. Paper presented at the annual National Reading Conference, St. Petersburg, FL.

Durkin, D. (1966). *Children who read early.* New York: Teachers College Press.

Dyson, A.H. (1984). Emerging literacy in school contexts: Toward defining the gap between school curriculum and child mind. *Written Communication, 1*, 5–53.

Eckhoff, B. (1984). How reading affects children's writing. In J. Jensen (Ed.), *Composing and comprehending*. Urbana, IL: National Council of Teachers of English, 105–114.

Ehri, L. (1983). Beginning reading: Summaries and critique. In L. Gentile, M. Kamil, & J. Blanchard (Eds.), *Reading research revisited*. Columbus, OH: Merrill.

Ehri, L. (1984). How orthography alters spoken language competencies in children learning to read and spell. In J. Downing & R. Valtin (Eds.), *Language awareness and learning to read*, New York: Springer.

Ehri, L. (1985). *Learning to read and spell*. Invited address presented at the annual meeting of the American Educational Research Association, Chicago.

Ehri, L. (in press). Sources of difficulty in learning to spell and read. In W. Wolraich & D. Routh (Eds.), *Advances in developmental and behavioral pediatrics*. Greenwich, CT: JAI Press.

Ehri, L., & Roberts, K.T. (1979). Do beginners learn to read function words better in context or in isolation? *Child Development, 50,* 675–685.

Ehri, L., & Wilce, L. (in press). Movement into reading: Is the first stage of printed word learning visual or phonetic? *Reading Research Quarterly, 20,* 163–179.

Evans, M., & Carr, T. (1985). Cognitive abilities, conditions of learning, and the early development of reading skill. *Reading Research Quarterly, 20*(3), 327–350.

Feitelson, D. (1985). *Becoming literate in societies in transition*. Paper presented at the International Conference on the Future of Literacy in a Changing World, University of Pennsylvania, Philadelphia.

Feitelson, D., & Goldstein, Z. (1986). Patterns of book ownership and reading to young children in Israeli school-oriented and non-school-oriented families. *Reading Teacher, 39,* 924–930.

Feitelson, D., Kita, B., & Goldstein, Z. (1986). *Effects of reading series-stories to first graders on their comprehension and use of language*. Haifa, Israel: University of Haifa, School of Education.

Ferreiro, E., & Teberosky, A. (1982). *Literacy before schooling*. Portsmouth, NH: Heinemann.

Fielding, L., Wilson, P., Anderson, R. (1986). A new focus on free reading: The role of trade books in reading instruction. In T. Raphael (Ed.), *Contexts of school-based literacy*. New York: Random House.

Flavell, J. (1979). Cognitive monitoring. In W.P. Dickson (Ed.), *Children's communication skills*. New York: Academic Press.

Gambrell, L. (1986). Reading in the primary grades: How often, how long? In M. Sampson (Ed.), *The pursuit of literacy: Early reading and writing*. Dubuque, IA: Kendall/Hunt.

Gelman, R., & Baillargeon, R. (1983). A review of some Piagetian concepts. In P. Mussen (Ed.), *Handbook of child psychology*, Vol. III. New York: Wiley.

Gibson, E.J., & Levin, H. (1976). *The psychology of reading*. Cambridge, MA: MIT Press.

Goodacre, E. (1973). Great Britain. In J. Downing (Ed.), *Comparative reading: Cross-national studies of behavior and processes in reading and writing*. New York: Macmillan.

Goodman, K.S., & Goodman, Y.M. (1979). Learning to read is natural. In L.B. Resnick & P. Weaver (Eds.), *Theory and practice of early reading*. Hillsdale, NJ: Erlbaum.

Goodman, K.S., & Goodman, Y.M. (1980). Learning about psycholinguistic processes by analyzing oral reading. In C. McCullough (Ed.), *Persistent problems in reading instruction*. Newark, DE: International Reading Association.

Goodman, K.S., & Goodman, Y.M. (1983). Reading and writing relationships: Pragmatic functions. *Language Arts, 60*(5), 590–599.

Goodman, Y. (1985). Children coming to know literacy. In W. Teale & E. Sulzby (Eds.), *Emergent literacy: Writing and reading*. Norwood, NJ: Ablex.

Goody, J. (Ed.) (1968). *Literacy in traditional societies*. London: Cambridge University Press.

Gough, P. (1972). One second of reading. In J. Kavanagh & I. Mattingly (Eds.), *Language by ear and by eye*. Cambridge, MA: MIT Press.

Gough, P., & Tunmer, W. (1986). Decoding, reading, and reading disability. *RASE, 7*, 6–10.

Graves, D. (1983). *Writing: Children and teachers at work*. Portsmouth, NH: Heinemann.

Graves, D., & Stuart, V. (1985). *Write from the start: Tapping your child's natural writing ability*, New York: Dutton.

Green, J.L., & Harker, J.O. (1982). Reading to children: A communicative process. In J. Langer & M.T. Smith-Burke (Eds.), *Reader meets author*. Newark, DE: International Reading Association.

Guthrie, J., & Kirsch, I. (1984). The emergent perspective on literacy. *Phi Delta Kappan, 65*, 351–355.

Halliday, M. (1975). *Learning how to mean*. London: Edward Arnold.

Halliday, M.A.K. (1977). *Explorations in the functions of language*. New York: Elsevier North-Holland.

Halliday, M.A.K., & Hasan, R. (1976). *Cohesion in English*. London: Longman.

Hansen, J. (1986). *Literate environments: Professors, teacher, and children*. Proceedings of the National Reading and Language Arts Educators' Conference. Kansas City, MO.

Harkness, F., & Miller, L. (1982). *A description of the interaction among mother, child, and books in a bedtime reading situation*. Paper presented at the seventh annual Boston Conference on Language Development.

Harste, J.C., Burke, C.L., & Woodward, V.A. (1982). Children's language and world: Initial encounters with print. In J. Langer & M. Smith-Burke (Eds.), *Bridging the gap: Reader meets author*. Newark, DE: International Reading Association.

Harste, J.C., Woodward, V.A., & Burke, C.L. (1984). *Language stories and literacy lessons*. Porstmouth, NH: Heinemann.

Heath, S.B. (1982). What no bedtime story means: Narrative skills at home and school. *Language in Society, 11*(1), 49–76.

Heath, S.B. (1983). *Ways with words: Language, life and work in communities and classrooms*. New York: Cambridge University Press.

Heath, S.B. (1986). Separating "things of the imagination from life: Learning to read and write." In W. Teale & Sulzby (Eds.), *Emergent literacy: Writing and reading*. Norwood, NJ: Ablex.

Hess, R., Holloway, S., Price, G., & Dickson, W. (1982). Family environments and the acquisition of reading skills. In L. Laosa & I. Sigel (Eds.), *Families as learning environments for children*. New York: Plenum Press.

Hiebert, E. (1986). Using environmental print in beginning reading instruction. In M. Sampson (Ed.), *The pursuit of literacy: Early reading and writing*. Dubuque, IA: Kendall/Hunt.

Holdaway, D. (1979). *The foundations of literacy*. New York: Ashton Scholastic.

Holdaway, D. (1986). The structure of natural learning as a basis for literacy instruction. In M. Sampson (Ed.), *The pursuit of literacy: Early reading and writing.* Dubuque, IA: Kendall/Hunt.

Huck, C., & Pinnell, G.S. (1985). *Reading recovery in Ohio: An early intervention effort to reduce reading failure.* Unpublished report of the first year.

Jagger, A., & Smith-Burke, T. (Eds.), (1985). *Observing the language learner.* Newark, DE: International Reading Association.

Jenkinson, M.D. (1973). Meanings in reading. In R. Karlin (Ed.), *Reading for all.* Newark, DE: International Reading Association.

Jiang, S., & Li, B. (1985). A glimpse at reading instruction in China. *Reading Teacher, 38,* 762–766.

Johns, J. (1984). Students' perceptions of reading: Insights from research and pedagogical implications. In J. Downing & R. Valtin (Eds.), *Language awareness and learning to read.* New York: Springer.

Johns, J. & Ellis, D. (1976). Reading: Children tell it like it is. *Reading World, 16,* 115–128.

Juel, C., Griffith, P., & Gough, P. (1985). *The acquisition of literacy: A longitudinal study of children in first and second grade.* University of Texas at Austin, Center for Cognitive Science.

Juel, C., & Roper-Schneider, D. (1985). The influence of basal readers on first grade reading. *Reading Research Quarterly, 20,* 134–152.

Junge, B., & Shrestha, S. (1984). Another barrier broken: Teaching village girls to read in Nepal. *Reading Teacher, 37,* 846–852.

Kavanagh, J., & Mattingly, I. (1972). *Language by ear and by eye.* Cambridge, MA: MIT Press.

Lartz, M., & Mason, J. (in preparation). *Jamie: One child's journey from oral to written language.* Champaign: University of Illinois, Center for the Study of Reading.

Lindfors, J. (1985). Understanding the development of language situations. In A. Jagger & T. Smith-Burke (Eds.), *Observing the language learner* (pp. 41–56). Newark, DE: International Reading Association.

Lundberg, I. (1984, August). Learning to read. *School Research Newsletter,* National Board of Education, Sweden.

MacKinnon, A. (1959). *How do children learn to read?* Vancouver, Canada: Copp Clark.

Mason, G. (1967). Preschoolers' concepts of reading. *The Reading Teacher, 21,* 130–132.

Mason, J. (1976). Overgeneralization in learning to read. *Journal of Reading Behavior, 8,* 173–182.

Mason, J. (1977). *Reading readiness: A definition and skills hierarchy* (Tech. Rep. No. 59). Champaign: University of Illinois, Center for the Study of Reading.

Mason, J. (1980). When *do* children begin to read? *Reading Research Quarterly, 15,* 203–227.

Mason, J. (1985). Cognitive monitoring and early reading: A proposed model. In D. Forrest, G. MacKinnon, & T. Waller (Eds.), *Meta-cognition, cognition, and human performance.* New York: Academic Press.

Mason, J., & McCormick, C. (1979). *Testing the development of reading and linguistic awareness* (Tech. Rep. No. 26). Champaign: University of Illinois, Center for the Study of Reading.

Mason, J., McCormick, C., & Bhavnagri, N. (1986). How are you going to help me learn? Lesson negotiations between a teacher and preschool children. In D. Yaden

& S. Templeton (Eds.), *Metalinguistic awareness and beginning literacy: Conceptualizing what it means to read and write*. Portsmouth, NH: Heinemann.

Mattingly, I. (1984). Reading, linguistic awareness, and language acquisition. In J. Downing & R. Valtin (Eds.), *Language awareness and learning to read*. New York: Springer.

McCormick, C., & Mason, J. (1984). *Intervention procedures for increasing preschool children's interest in and knowledge about reading* (Tech. Rep. No. 312). Champaign: University of Illinois, Center for the Study of Reading. (ERIC Document Reproduction Service No. ED 244 222)

McCormick, C. & Mason, J. (1986). *Use of little books at home: A minimal intervention strategy for fostering early reading*. Paper presented at the annual meeting of the American Educational Research Association, San Francisco.

McCullough, C. (1973). Promoting reading ability at all levels. In R. Karlin (Ed.), *Reading for all*. Newark, DE: International Reading Association.

Milz, V. (1985). First graders uses for writing. In A. Jagger & M. Smith-Burke (Eds.), *Observing the language learner*. Newark, DE: International Reading Association.

Morris, D. (1981). Concept of word. A developmental phenomenon in the beginning reading and writing process. *Language Arts, 58*, 659–668.

Morrow, L., & Weinstein, C. (1985). *The impact of a recreational reading program on children's voluntary use of literature*. Paper presented at annual National Reading Conference, San Diego, CA.

Newell, A., & Simon, H. (1972). *Human problem solving*. Englewood Cliffs, NJ: Prentice-Hall.

Ninio, A., & Bruner, J. (1978). The achievement and antecedents of labelling. *Journal of Child Language, 5*, 5–15.

Olson, D. (1977). From utterance to text: The bias of language in speech and writing. *Harvard Educational Review, 47*, 257–281.

Olson, D. (1984). "See! Jumping!" Some oral language antecedents of literacy. In H. Goelman, A. Oberg, & F. Smith (Eds.), *Awakening to literacy*. Portsmouth, NH: Heinemann.

Paley, V. (1981). *Wally's stories*. Cambridge, MA: Harvard University Press.

Parker, R. (1983). Language development and learning to write: Theory and research findings. In R. Parker & F. Davis (Eds.), *Developing literacy: Young children's use of language* (pp. 38–54). Newark, DE: International Reading Association.

Pellegrini, A., Brody, G., & Sigel, I. (1985). Parents' book-reading habits with their children. *Journal of Educational Psychology, 77*, 332–340.

Perena, K. (1984). *Children's writing and reading: Analyzing classroom language*. Oxford, England: Blackwell.

Perfetti, C., Beck, I., & Hughes, C. (1985). Reading acquisition and beyond: Decoding includes cognition. *American Journal of Education, 93*, 40–60.

Peterman, C., & Mason, J. (1984). *Kindergarten children's perceptions of the form of print in labelled pictures and stories*. Paper presented at the annual National Reading Conference, St. Petersburg, FL.

Peterman, C., Mason, J., & Dunning, D. (1985). *The storybook reading event: How a teacher's presentation affects kindergarten children's subsequent attempts to read*. Paper presented at the annual National Reading Conference, San Diego, CA.

Read, C. (1971). Pre-school children's knowledge of English phonology. *Harvard Educational Review, 41*, 1–34.

Reid, J. (1966). Learning to think about reading. *Educational Research, 9*, 56–62.

Resnick, D., & Resnick, L. (1977). The nature of literacy: An historical exploration. *Harvard Educational Review, 47*, 370–385.

Roper-Schneider, H.D.W. (1984). *Spelling, word recognition, and phonemic awareness among first grade children.* Unpublished doctoral dissertation, University of Texas, Austin.

Sakamoto, T. (1976). Writing systems in Japan. In J. Merritt (Ed.), *New horizons in reading.* Newark, DE: International Reading Association.

Sakamoto, T., & Makita, K. (1973). Japan. In J. Downing (Ed.), *Comparative reading* (pp. 440–465). New York: Macmillan.

Schickedanz, J., & Sullivan, M. (1984). Mom, what does U-F-F spell? *Language Arts, 61*, 7–17.

Schieffelin, B., & Cochran-Smith, M. (1984). Learning to read culturally: Literacy before schooling. In H. Goelman, A. Oberg, & F. Smith (Eds.), *Awakening to literacy.* Portsmouth, NH: Heinemann.

Scribner, S. (1984). Literacy in three metaphors. *American Journal of Education, 93*, 6–21.

Sigel, I. (1982). The relationship between parental distancing strategies and the child's cognitive behavior. In L. Laosa & I. Sigel (Eds.), *Families as learning environments for children.* New York: Plenum.

Siegler, R. (1978). The origins of scientific reasoning. In R. Siegler (Ed.), *Children's thinking: What develops?* New York: Wiley.

Smith, F. (1984). Reading like a writer. In J. Jensen (Ed.), *Composing and comprehending.* Urbana, IL: National Conference on Research in English. (ERIC Clearinghouse on Reading and Communication Skills, Document No. 08024)

Smith, N.B. (1965). *American reading instruction.* Newark, DE: International Reading Association.

Snow, C. (1983). Literacy and language: Relationships during the preschool years. *Harvard Educational Review, 53*, 165–189.

Snow, C., & Ninio, A. (1986). The contribution of reading books with children to their linguistic and cognitive development. In W. Teale & E. Sulzby (Eds.), *Emergent literacy: Writing and reading.* Norwood, NJ: Ablex.

Soderbergh, R. (1977). *Reading in early childhood: A linguistic study of a preschool child's gradual acquisition of reading ability.* Washington, DC: Georgetown University Press.

Stanovich, K. (1980). Toward an interactive-compensatory model of individual differences in the development of reading fluency. *Reading Research Quarterly, 16*, 32–71.

Stewart, J. (1986). *A study of kindergarten children's awareness of how they are learning to read: Home and school perspectives.* Unpublished doctoral dissertation, University of Illinois, Champaign.

Strickland, R.G. (1962). The language of elementary school children: Its relationship to the language of reading textbooks and the quality of reading by selected children. *Bulletin of the School of Education, Indiana University, 38*(4), 1–131.

Sulzby, E. (1985). Children's emergent reading of favorite storybooks: A developmental study. *Reading Research Quarterly, 20*, 458–481.

Sulzby, E. (1986a). Children's elicitation and use of metalinguistic knowledge about *word* during literacy interactions. In D. Yaden & S. Templeton (Eds.), *Metalinguistic awareness and beginning literacy: Conceptualizing what it means to read and write.* Portsmouth, NH: Heinemann.

Sulzby, E. (1986b). Writing and reading: Signs of oral and written language organization in the young child. In W. Teale & E. Sulzby (Eds.), *Emergent literacy: Writing and reading*. Norwood, NJ: Ablex

Sulzby, E., & Teale, W.H. (1984). *Young children's storybook reading: Hispanic and Anglo families and children* (Report to The Spencer Foundation). Evanston, IL: Northwestern University.

Surber, J. & Mason, J. (1977). Effects of rule consistent examples in learning letter-sound correspondences. *Journal of Reading Behavior, 9*(3), 1–11.

Tatham, S. (1970). Reading comprehension of materials written with select oral language patterns: A study at grades two and four. *Reading Research Quarterly, 5*(3), 402–424.

Taylor, D. (1983). *Family literacy: Young children learning to read and write*. Portsmouth, NH: Heinemann.

Teale, W. (1986). In W. Teale & E. Sulzby (Eds.), *Emergent literacy: Writing and reading*. Norwood, NJ: Ablex.

Teale, W. (1986). Home background and young children's literacy development. In W. Teale & E. Sulzby (Eds.), *Emergent literacy: Writing and reading*. Norwood, NJ: Ablex.

Temple, C., Nathan, R., & Burris, N. (1982). *The beginnings of writing*. Boston: Allyn & Bacon.

Tharp, R., Jordan, C., Speidel, G., Au, K., Klein, T., Calkins, R., Sloat, K., & Gallimore, R. (1984). Product and process in applied developmental research: Education and the children of a minority. In M. Lamb, A. Brown, & R. Rogoff (Eds.), *Advances in developmental psychology* (Vol. III). Hillsdale, NJ: Erlbaum.

Thomas, K. (1985). Early reading as a social interaction process. *Language Arts, 62*(5), 469–475.

Thorndike, R. (1976). Reading comprehension in 15 countries. In J. Merritt (Ed.), *New horizons in reading* (pp. 500–507). Newark, DE: International Reading Association.

Tierney, R. & LaZansky, J. (1980). The rights and responsibilities of readers and writers: A contractual agreement. *Language Arts, 57,* 606–613.

Torrance, N., & Olson, D. (1985). Oral and literate competencies in the early school years. In N. Torrance, D. Olson, & A. Hildyard (Eds.), *Literacy, language, and learning*. Cambridge, England: Cambridge University Press.

Tough, J. (1977). *Talking and learning: A guide to fostering communication skills in nursery and infant schools*. Portsmouth, NH: Heinemann.

Vygotsky, L.S. (1962). *Thought and language*. Cambridge, MA: MIT Press.

Wardhaugh, R. (1976). Theories of language acquisition in relation to beginning reading instruction. In H. Singer & R.B. Ruddell (Eds.), *Theoretical models and processes of reading* (2nd ed., pp. 42–66). Newark, DE: International Reading Association.

Watson, D. (1985). Watching and listening to children read. In A. Jagger & M.T. Smith-Burke (Eds.), *Observing the language learner*. Newark, DE: International Reading Association, 115–128.

Weber, R.M. (1970). A linguistic analysis of first grade reading errors. *Reading Research Quarterly, 6,* 427–451.

Wells, G. (1981). *Learning through interaction: The study of language development*. New York: Cambridge University Press.

Wells, G. (1985). Preschool literacy-related activities and success in school. In D. Olson, N. Torrance, & A. Hildyard (Eds.), *Literacy, language, and learning: The nature and consequences of reading and writing*. New York: Cambridge University Press.

White, D.N. (1954). *Books before five*. Wellington, New Zealand: Council for Educational Research.

White, K. (1982). The relation between socioeconomic status and academic achievement. *Psychological Bulletin, 91,* 461–481.

Yaden, D., & Templeton, S. (1986). *Metalinguistic awareness and beginning literacy: Conceptualizing what it means to read and write*. Portsmouth, NH: Heinemann.

Chapter 2

Vocabulary Learning and Instruction

MICHAEL F. GRAVES
University of Minnesota

OVERVIEW

The orientation of this review is intensely practical. It is an attempt to describe what we know and what we need to learn in order to build vocabulary programs that are based on reasonably accurate empirical estimates of what students already know, what they need to learn, and what they can be taught. The scope of the review is, of course, limited. It deals largely with reading vocabulary, with studies of school-age children, and with published studies. It does not deal with the early history of vocabulary research, word recognition (a topic reviewed recently by Gough, 1984, and Johnson and Baumann, 1984), with readability (a topic reviewed recently by Klare, 1984), or with word lists and word frequency (topics that have not been reviewed recently, but which were excluded because of space limitations).

Two themes will emerge as the chapter progresses. One is that although we have a good deal of information relevant to vocabulary instruction, there are a number of very basic questions to which we have almost no answers. The other is that there are a number of questions for which relatively definitive answers are possible and that speculative answers to these questions are not sufficient.

The first section of this chapter deals with vocabulary size, depth of word knowledge, and assessing word knowledge. The second deals with the effects of vocabulary on reading comprehension and other verbal phenomena, the third with methods of teaching individual words, the fourth with generative vocabulary instruction, and the fifth with the vocabulary instruction currently

I would like to thank Joseph Jenkins of the University of Washington, the editorial consultant for this chapter, for his many helpful comments. I would also like to thank Wayne Slater of the University of Maryland, Maureen Prenn of the University of Minnesota, and my wife, Bonnie Graves, for their useful comments.

taking place in schools. Summaries and suggestions for further research are presented wherever they seem most appropriate, sometimes within the sections and sometimes at the end of them. Finally, the last two sections present a brief summary and two suggestions for making research more productive. Three recent reviews that deal with some of the topics considered here are Mezynski's (1983) analysis of the effects of vocabulary instruction on reading comprehension, Calfee and Drum's (1986) section on vocabulary instruction in their chapter reviewing research on teaching reading, and Stahl and Fairbanks' (1986) meta-analysis on the effects of vocabulary instruction.

VOCABULARY SIZE, DEPTH OF WORD KNOWLEDGE, AND ASSESSING WORD KNOWLEDGE

These three topics are closely linked since interpreting the research on vocabulary size and depth of word knowledge requires consideration of how word knowledge can be assessed.

Vocabulary Size

As Nagy and Anderson (1984) point out, "determining the absolute size of individuals' vocabularies is of more than purely theoretical interest" (p. 304). If the number of words students must learn is fairly small, a program of direct instruction in individual words might teach a substantial proportion of the words needed. On the other hand, if the number of words to be learned is very large, then a program designed to teach individual words could teach only a small fraction of those needed. Nagy and Anderson are not alone in considering vocabulary size an important issue. Dale, Razik, and Petty's *Bibliography of Vocabulary Studies* (1973) includes 35 studies of vocabulary size published between 1891 and 1960, and several studies have been done during the present period of renewed interest in vocabulary.

Studies Conducted Prior to 1960

The studies conducted prior to 1960 are of limited value. As Lorge and Chall (1963), among others, have noted, the estimates of vocabulary size of the various studies are vastly discrepant, differing in many instances by an order of magnitude. Consider several of the examples given by Lorge and Chall. At the first-grade level, M. E. Smith (1926) estimated 2,562 words, Dolch (1936) 2,703, M. K. Smith (1941) 24,000, and Shibles (1959) 26,000. At the university undergraduate level, Kirkpatrick (1891, 1907) estimated 19,000 words, Doran (1907) 157,000, and Hartman (1941, 1946) over 200,000. As Lorge and Chall explain, such factors as the size of the dictionary from which words were sampled, the definition of what constitutes a word, the method of testing, and the sampling procedures used can have huge effects on the estimates of size; and these studies differed from each other on a number of these dimensions.

After carefully analyzing the Seashore and Eckerson (1940) test, which served as the instrument for several of the studies producing the larger estimates, Lorge and Chall conclude that the test has an unrepresentative sample of more frequent words, probably making the larger estimates incorrect, and they go on to suggest that the smaller estimates are likely to be more accurate. Although this position is accepted by Clifford (1978), my assessment is that the studies completed prior to 1960 contain too many shortcomings to be relied upon. Moreover, data from more recent studies indicate that the vocabularies of primary-grade children are at least somewhat larger than the lower estimates produced during this period.

Contemporary Studies

Four contemporary studies will be considered. They are Dupuy (1974), Nagy and Anderson (1982, 1984), Graves, Brunetti, and Slater (1982), and Graves and Slater (in preparation).

Dupuy's study is a carefully conceived, well-documented, and clearly described attempt to create what Dupuy calls the Basic Word Vocabulary Test, a test intended to be used to determine the number of "basic words" known by 3rd- through 12th-grade students. Using this test, Dupuy estimated the size of the average 3rd grader's vocabulary at about 2,000 words, that of the average 7th grader at about 4,800 words, and that of the average 12th grader at about 7,800 words.

As Nagy and Anderson (1982, 1984) have pointed out, Dupuy's study had some major flaws that resulted in its drastically underestimating the number of words known. Two of these flaws are particularly important. First, in arriving at the set of basic words from which to select a sample of words to test, Dupuy required that each of the basic words appear in three specific dictionaries, in addition to the one from which he was sampling. This reduced the sample by about half and excluded a number of words that most would judge to be part of a fairly basic vocabulary. Second, as another part of the selection process, Dupuy eliminated virtually all derived forms from the count, regardless of the semantic distance between the forms or the likelihood that knowing the basic forms might allow someone to determine the meanings of the other forms. The result was a basic word list of only 12,300 words, limiting the largest possible vocabulary that could be estimated by the test to 12,300 words. This is simply not a number that corresponds to the number of words in English.

Nagy and Anderson's (1982, 1984) study can perhaps be best understood if it is seen at least partly as a response to Dupuy's estimate that the vocabularies of school-age children are relatively small and to Becker's (1977) use of Dupuy's estimate in proposing a vocabulary program to systematically teach a basic vocabulary of about 7,000 words to disadvantaged students in grades 3 through 12. Such a program, Nagy and Anderson argued, is not worthwhile if the number of words students need to learn is closer to 70,000 than to 7,000.

Nagy and Anderson's study, like Dupuy's, was carefully conceived, fully documented, and clearly described. It was also very ambitious. Nagy and Anderson set out to estimate the number of different words and different word families (sets consisting of a root word and its compounds and derivatives) appearing in materials used by children in grades 3 through 9.

As part of this study, the authors created some very useful metrics for judging the degree of semantic relatedness of words and developed estimates of the number of different word families occurring in books and other material used by children in grades 3 through 9, a corpus they refer to as printed school English. These estimates differed depending on the exact definition of word family used. However, using the definition that they believed best reflected students' ability to generalize from one form of a word to another, Nagy and Anderson estimated that printed school English contains approximately 88,000 different word families.

This appears to be a very accurate estimate. However, it must be remembered that the figure of 88,000 is the number of word families occurring in the sum total of books and other materials used by 3rd through 9th graders. It is not the number of different word families that any one 3rd through 9th grader will ever deal with (unless, of course, he or she reads all the materials available for these grade levels), and it certainly is not the number of words known by any one student.

Using data and techniques developed in the Nagy and Anderson study, Nagy and Herman (in press) recalibrated the findings of several previous studies of vocabulary size and arrived at extrapolated figures that suggest that average students in grades 3 through 12 learn about 3,000 new words each year. This may well be the case. In fact, this estimate of growth is close to that which Graves and Slater (in preparation) found in a group of academically successful students who were recently tested. However, two things need to be stressed: (1) Nagy and Herman's estimate rested on a good deal of extrapolation, and (2) their estimate was for average students and not for students who were well below average.

The last two studies to be discussed here are considerably less ambitious that those of Dupuy or of Nagy and Anderson. They are attempts to measure students' knowledge of specific bodies of words. In the earlier study, Graves and his associates (1982) tested first- through third-grade middle-class and disadvantaged students on their ability to read the 5,044 most frequent words in the Carroll, Davies, and Richman *American Heritage Word Frequency Book* (1971). The study was conducted near the end of the school year so that students had almost completed their respective grades. It employed a multiple-choice test in which the distractors were clearly wrong, and students were required to read the words being tested. Thus, the test required reading, set a fairly low criterion for word knowledge, and had a definite upper limit in that it could show no more than 5,044 words as being known.

Results indicated that first graders knew an average of about 2,200 words and third graders an average of about 4,000 words. Results also showed marked differences between middle-class and disadvantaged students. For example, the disadvantaged first graders knew about 1,800 of the 5,044 words tested, and the middle-class first graders knew about 2,700 of them. Although the criterion for knowing a word was not a difficult one, these are extremely conservative estimates because of the small corpus of words from which the test was constructed. Obviously, students who knew a large proportion of the 5,044 words tested know a number of words beyond these 5,044.

In a follow-up study, Graves and Slater (in preparation) presented a similar test to first- through fourth-grade children in a rural school enrolling disadvantaged students almost exclusively, an inner-city school also enrolling disadvantaged students almost exclusively, and a surburban school enrolling middle-class students almost exclusively. The test and testing were similar to that employed in the previous study, except that words were sampled from the most frequent 19,050 words in Carroll et al. (1971).

Results indicated that by the end of the year, first graders knew an average of about 4,000 words and fourth graders an average of about 13,000 words. As in the previous study, the test showed marked differences between groups, with the scores of the disadvantaged rural students being the lowest and those of the middle-class suburban students the highest. For example, the disadvantaged rural first graders knew about 2,900 of the words tested, and the middle-class first graders knew about 5,800 of them. Again, the criterion for knowing a word was not very stringent; however, these are still conservative estimates because the corpus of words from which the test was constructed was relatively small. Obviously, students who knew a large proportion of the 19,050 words tested knew a number of words not among the 19,050 that were tested.

Given these data, the huge number of words that Nagy and Anderson showed as occurring in texts, and Nagy and Herman's recalibrations of previous estimates, it appears that students' vocabularies are a good deal larger than Dupuy's estimates and considerably larger than the estimates given in some of the earlier vocabulary studies. Also, the vocabularies of students from different backgrounds vary markedly.

Depth of Word Knowledge

As investigators have repeatedly pointed out (Anderson & Freebody, 1983; Binet & Simon, 1916; Cronbach, 1942; Curtis, in press; Farr, 1969; Feifel & Lorge, 1950; Russell & Saadeh, 1962), understanding vocabulary development requires information on the quality of the information students possess about words, as well as information on the number of words they know. Unfortunately, there has been little research on depth of word knowledge in school-age children.

Several studies (Feifel & Lorge, 1950; Kruglov, 1953; Russell & Saadeh, 1962; Terman, 1916) have shown that children's spontaneous definitions, or those they identify as preferred, progress from being largely concrete or functional to being increasingly abstract. Such findings reveal something about the development of the meaning system and about intellectual development more generally, but they do not say much about the development of the meanings of individual words or suggest specific ways of characterizing the richness of the word knowledge children of various ages have developed.

The work of such developmental psychologists and linguists as Clark (1973), Carey (1978), and Anglin (1970, 1977) provides some insight into the growth in word meaning, although the preponderance of this work concerns preschool children and not all of the work has stood the test of time. Clark's initial theory, the semantic feature hypothesis, was that when children first begin to use words, they may not know the words' full adult meanings but only some of the features of their meanings and will consequently overgeneralize their use. Thus, children may at first learn only the feature "four-legged" for dog, and will overgeneralize the word's meaning, using *dog* to refer to all four-legged animals until they acquire additional features. In this view, the development of meaning proceeds in an orderly fashion, becoming increasingly fuller and more precise.

Carey's (1978) early hypothesis, which she termed the missing feature plus haphazard example theory, differed from Clark's in that Carey saw immature lexical entries as including privilege of occurrence rules, in addition to having missing features. This resulted in children's both overextending and underextending meaning. Thus, to use Carey's example, children might first learn *deep* and *shallow* as applying to swimming pools and could correctly use the words when applying them to unfamiliar swimming pools. But children may not see the similarity between the way in which a swimming pool is deep and the way in which bowls, holes, and puddles are deep, or they may not know that *deep* can be applied when there is no contrast between two parts of a single object (i.e., it need not be paired with shallow, as with a pool), or that it need not concern something filled with a liquid.

Anglin's (1977) position differs from both Clark's and Carey's. His studies reveal that children both overgeneralize and undergeneralize word meanings, with differences between children's meanings and those of adults differing depending on the individual child, the concept being named, and the nature and extent of the child's encounters with instances and noninstances of the concept.

Unfortunately, Anglin's less informative position appears to be the more correct one. Both Carey (1982) and Clark (1983) have repudiated their original theories. Carey has offered no substitute theory. Clark has posited a new theory, but it does not appear to have implications for characterizing depth of word knowledge. At the same time, Clark (1983) has identified one additional relationship that can exist between children's and adults' word meanings that may be of some use in characterizing levels of word knowledge. She has called the relationship "overlapping" and has given as an example a situation in which *dog* might refer to large dogs but not to small ones, but might also refer to other four-legged animals about the same size as a dog.

Another developmentalist construct that may be important in considering depth of word knowledge is Carey's (1978) distinction between "fast mapping" and "extended mapping." According to this view, young children are frequently capable of fast mapping, learning a very gross meaning of a word on a single exposure to the word, but then require an extended period of time, perhaps years, to complete extended mapping, full learning of the word. If the same is true of adults, it may be that the seemingly large vocabularies revealed by studies of vocabulary size contain a large percentage of poorly known words. This possibility is further supported by Dolch and Leads's (1953) survey of adults' knowledge of some fairly common words, which revealed quite poor understanding.

As mentioned at the beginning of this section, there has been little research on depth of word knowledge in school-age children. However, several educators have outlined some dimensions that might be considered in characterizing vocabulary depth.

In one such outline, Cronbach (1942) suggested five dimensions: (1) generalization—defining the word, (2) application—selecting situations to which the word is appropriately applied, (3) breadth—recalling different meanings of the word, (4) precision—recognizing exactly in what situations the word does and does not apply, and (5) availability—using the word in discourse.

Russell (1954) suggested that tests of vocabulary depth should assess (1) precision of knowledge, as in discriminating between *valley* and *canyon*, (2) breadth, taken to mean both the number of different words and the number of different meanings of individual words, and (3) the ability to use words in speaking, reading, and writing.

Taken together, the constructs considered in this section suggest a number of dimensions along which depth of word knowledge might be characterized. However, it is not at all clear which of the dimensions are more important or would lead to more informative characterizations.

Assessing Word Knowledge

The vast majority of tests used to assess word knowledge have used a multiple-choice format. Obviously, researchers and test developers see value in this format, and it is widely agreed that multiple-choice tests can distinguish between those who have no knowledge of a word and those who have some knowledge. However, it is also widely agreed that correctly answering typical multiple-choice items does not require precise knowledge of word meanings and thus provides little or no information on how well students actually know the words they get correct (Cronbach, 1943; Curtis, in press; Dolch & Leads, 1953). Anderson and Freebody (1981, 1983) have recently criticized multiple-choice tests because performance on particular items depends on the nature of the distractors, as well as knowledge of the words being tested. Anderson and Freebody (1981, 1983) also criticize multiple-choice tests because they require test-taking skills. They further argue that a yes/no test in which students simply check words as known or unknown has advantages over a multiple-choice test, and they have briefly presented some data supporting their position. However, the yes/no test has received a good deal of criticism (e.g., Cronbach, 1942; Drum, 1983; Drum & Konopak, in press; Sims, 1929). Although Anderson and Freebody have developed procedures that negate some of this criticism, they have yet to perfect a procedure that provides information on how well students know the words they check as known. Thus, in my opinion, the multiple-choice test still appears to be the most appropriate procedure for group testing used to assess word knowledge.

One solution to the problem of assessing degrees of knowledge, proposed by Cronbach (1943), involved use of what Cronbach termed the "multiple true-false form" in which students were given a class name and asked to check which of half a dozen or so potential members of the class were in fact members of the class. Cronbach reported some success in using the method to characterize students' knowledge of algebra terms, but he admitted that there was little formal experimentation with the method and that the sorts of words with which it could be used were limited. Unfortunately, neither Cronbach nor other researchers appear to have further investigated the procedure.

More recently, Nagy, Herman, and Anderson (1985a) have constructed a multiple-choice test that minimizes the unpredictable and confounding effect of distractors and provides information about depth of knowledge. In developing this test, Nagy and associates employed criteria for choosing distractors that produced items deliberately measuring different levels of word knowledge. In the test, each target word was tested with three items, each of which required a different degree of knowledge for a correct response. The easiest items had distractors representing different concepts and differing in part of speech from the target word. The most difficult items had distractors representing similar concepts and were of the same part of speech as the target word. The items of intermediate difficulty had distractors representing different concepts but of the same part of speech as the target words. Results of this study, which employed both the multiple-choice test and individual interviews to assess level of word knowledge, showed that the levels of knowledge shown by this sort of multiple-choice item correlated well with levels of difficulty determined in the interviews.

Individual interviews are, of course, another procedure that can be used to assess depth of word knowledge. However, aside from the language development work dealing with preschool children and with a limited number of specific word types such as spatial adjectives and kinship terms (e.g., Bartlett, 1976; Haviland & Clark, 1974), interviews are rarely used to probe vocabulary knowledge. Only two studies employing interviews will be discussed here.

In the earlier study, Graves (1980) presented primary grade students with three subtasks, each of which assessed a different aspect of word knowledge. Prior to each task, children were asked to pronounce the target word and, if they could not, it was pronounced for them. For the first task, a multiple-meaning task, children were asked to give one meaning of the word and, if they gave one appropriate meaning, they were asked to give another. For the second task, a meanings-in-context task, children were shown the target word in a sentence, asked to read the sentence (it was read to any children who could not read it), and asked what the word meant in the sentence. Then they were given a sentence that used the same word with a different meaning and asked to give the meaning of the word in that sentence. For the third task, a precision-of-meaning task, children were given two words with similar meanings and asked to explain the difference between the meanings. Thus, this approach yields three separate scores and investigates some of the dimensions suggested by Cronbach (1942).

In the interview portion of the study previously mentioned, Nagy, Herman, and Anderson (1985a) used a three-step procedure that yielded a single index of quality of word knowledge. In the first step, students were shown a word and asked to pronounce it. Mispronunciations were not corrected. In the second step, students were asked to tell what the word meant or to use it in a sentence. If a clear answer was given, the interviewer went on to the next word. If an unclear or incomplete answer was given, the interviewer asked one of three preset questions, the specific question asked depending on students' previous response. For example, one prompt was, "That's one meaning. Do you know another meaning for this word?" Responses were scored on a four-point scale running from no knowledge of the word to totally correct knowledge of the word, and a mean reliability of .7 was obtained. Thus, the procedure provides a reasonably reliable method of scaling the quality of students' knowledge of word meanings.

Summary

It is clear that there are a huge number of distinct words in the materials read by school-age children. It is also clear that even in the primary grades the average student can read an impressive number of words and that middle-class students can read considerably more words than disadvantaged students. However, it is quite possible that students' knowledge of many of the words they know is very limited, and there are no data on how vocabulary size varies with ability. Although a number of dimensions of word knowledge have been considered, little has been done to characterize depth of word knowledge in school-age children. Recently, however, a multiple-choice test format and interview procedures that reliably differentiate levels of word knowledge and an interview procedure that characterizes several aspects of word knowledge have been developed.

In my judgment, in order to plan principled programs of vocabulary development, large-scale descriptive studies are needed that clearly differentiate three or four levels of word knowledge and then provide data on the number of words known by students of various ages, socioeconomic classes, and abilities at each of those levels of depth. Attempts to characterize various aspects of word knowledge should continue as well.

EFFECTS OF VOCABULARY ON READING COMPREHENSION AND OTHER VERBAL PHENOMENA

This section considers the effects of the vocabulary used in written texts on comprehension of those texts; the effects of the vocabulary used in oral and written texts on judgments of the texts and their authors; and the effects of vocabulary instruction on reading comprehension and on writing.

Effects of Vocabulary Used in Texts on Comprehension of the Texts

Vocabulary has repeatedly been shown to be the most powerful component of readability formulas (Coleman, 1971; Klare 1974–1975, 1984) and a major component of reading comprehension (Davis, 1944, 1968; Thurstone, 1946). Given these findings, one would expect that simplifying the vocabulary of texts would markedly influence readers' comprehension of the texts. However, simplifying vocabulary has produced mixed results.

In an early study, Nolte (1938) tested 1,100 6th-grade students on three versions of three passages taken from a standardized reading comprehension test. The three versions consisted of the original passages, passages altered so that they included only words among the 2,500 most frequent words on Thorndike's (1932) list, and passages altered so that they included only words from Ogden's (1934) list of basic words. A multiple-choice comprehension test revealed no differences in overall comprehension of the three versions. However, pictorial tests and interviews revealed that there were points at which vocabulary caused comprehension problems and points at which substitution of easier words aided pupils with particular parts of the passages, and that substituting easier words sometimes increased the difficulty of other parts of the passages.

In a more recent pair of experiments, Marks, Doctorow, and Wittrock

(1974) and Wittrock, Marks, and Doctorow (1975) tested sixth-grade students on two versions of five stories taken from commercial reading materials intended for sixth graders. The two versions were constructed by substituting low-frequency words for high-frequency ones and substituting high-frequency words for low-frequency ones so that the versions differed in the frequency of 15% of the words. Comprehension was assessed with multiple-choice tests. Results of the Marks et al. study showed that students given the high-frequency versions scored 67% while students given the low-frequency versions scored 42%. The researchers concluded that vocabulary markedly influences reading comprehension and suggested that "significant increases in reading comprehension can be produced by giving careful attention to the semantic variable of word frequency" (Marks et al., 1974, p. 262). The results of the Wittrock et al. study showed a similarly strong effect of word frequency.

Two attempts to replicate the findings of Marks and her colleagues have failed. In the first study, Tanner (1976) modified the same materials Marks and her colleagues used and, as in the Marks study, obtained two versions of the passages that differed in the frequency of 15% of the words. However, results of multiple-choice tests failed to show reliable effects of word frequency. In the second study, Ryder and Hughes (1985) tested fifth graders on a basal reader passage in which 25% of the substance words had been replaced by more frequent words using frequency ratings based on family frequencies. Results of a multiple-choice test revealed no reliable differences between the two versions.

Finally, in a series of studies with sixth graders, Freebody and Anderson (1983a, 1983b) obtained results showing weak but reliable effects of frequency. Each of the studies included three measures of comprehension—free recall, summary recall, and sentence recognition. In one experiment, it was found that one substance word in three had to be substituted before reliable effects on comprehension were found. In another, it was found that difficult vocabulary placed in important text elements reliably reduced comprehension, while difficult vocabulary placed in unimportant text elements actually improved comprehension. In another, it was found that vocabulary difficulty produced a reliable effect itself but did not interact with text cohesion. And, in still another study, it was found that vocabulary difficulty had a reliable, although small, effect but did not interact with text familiarity. In summing up these four experiments, Anderson and Freebody (1983) calculated that averaged across the four experiments and the three dependent measures the mean effect size for vocabulary difficulty was 2.1, and they concluded that vocabulary difficulty is definitely related to text comprehension.

Together, the results of these studies suggest that vocabulary difficulty can affect passage comprehension, that the effect it has is seldom a large one, and that a number of words have to be changed to produce the effect. However, all of the studies simplified vocabulary solely or largely on the basis of word frequency and all of them dealt with elementary students reading nontechnical texts. Two topics that seem worth investigation are (1) the effect on comprehension of vocabulary difficulty determined by some less mechanical metric, and (2) the effects of simplifying the technical vocabulary of difficult technical texts for older students.

Effects of the Vocabulary Used in Texts on Judgments of the Texts and Their Authors

Although vocabulary difficulty appears to have a fairly moderate and somewhat inconsistent effect on comprehension, the words used in texts have consistently been shown to affect readers' and listeners' judgments of the texts and their authors. Writing that employs more mature vocabulary has repeatedly been judged as superior to that with less mature vocabulary (Grobe, 1981; Neilsen & Piche, 1981; Stewart & Leaman, 1983). In addition, the lexical diversity of a speaker's vocabulary (the percentage of different words used as indicated in a type-token ratio) is directly related to the listeners' judgments of the speaker's competence, the speaker's socioeconomic status, and the effectiveness of the message (Bradac, Bowers, & Courtright, 1982; Bradac, Courtright, Schmidt, & Davies, 1976; Bradac, Davies, Courtright, Desmond, & Murdock, 1977).

Clearly, vocabulary plays a powerful role in audience reactions to both spoken and written discourse.

Effects of Vocabulary Instruction on Reading Comprehension

There have been two recent reviews of the effects of vocabulary instruction on reading comprehension. In the earlier one, Mezynski (1983) considered eight studies that have been frequently cited in the literature and concluded that while many of the studies did not show an effect of vocabulary instruction on comprehension, those that employed instruction which had certain characteristics did. In the more recent review, a meta-analysis of 14 studies that employed a comprehension measure specific to the words taught, Stahl and Fairbanks (1986) found a mean effect size of .97 and concluded that "vocabulary instruction does have a significant effect on the comprehension of passages containing the taught words" (p. 24). My review of this research revealed a total of 14 studies that have some bearing on the question. Six of these (Jackson & Dizney, 1963; Lieberman, 1967; Margosein, Pascarella, & Pflaum, 1982; Pany & Jenkins, 1978; Pany, Jenkins, & Schreck, 1982; Tuinman & Brady, 1974) failed to increase comprehension by teaching vocabulary. Obviously, not all attempts to improve comprehension by teaching vocabulary are successful.

Moreover, when one critically examines the eight studies that did appear to increase comprehension by preteaching vocabulary, the results of five of them appear questionable. The reasons differ and describing them in detail is beyond the scope of this paper. Briefly, however, the problems are as follows:

Two of the studies (Anders, Bos, & Filip, 1984; Kameenui, Carnine, & Freschi, 1982) used comprehension measures that focused so directly on the vocabulary taught that they were in essence vocabulary measures. Another (Draeper & Moellar, 1971) described a lengthy program in a few pages, making it difficult to know just what was taught and leaving open the possibility that the gains found may have been due to any number of factors. Still another, Barrett and Graves (1981), also employed a lengthy treatment, and although a detailed description of the treatment is available (Barrett, 1979), my interpretation of the results is that they are as likely attributable to the extended use of good instruction as to vocabulary instruction per se. Finally, a study by Stahl (1983) had mixed results in that vocabulary instruction produced comprehension gains in only two of three groups that differed only in the order in which they received the instructional treatments.

This leaves a series of three studies (Beck, Perfetti, & McKeown, 1982; McKeown, Beck, Omanson, & Perfetti, 1983; McKeown, Beck, Omanson, & Pople, 1985) that present convincing evidence that teaching vocabulary can increase comprehension of texts containing the words taught. The studies are convincing for several reasons. First, they replicated the effect three times. Second, they provided the sort of rich, multifaceted, and prolonged instruction that research, theory, and common sense suggest ought to influence comprehension. Third, they employed several dependent measures. And fourth, the reports on the studies are reasonably detailed, and additional information on the instruction and the motivation behind it are available (Beck, McCaslin, & McKeown, 1980; Beck, McKeown, McCaslin, & Burkes, 1979).

Analysis of Beck and McKeown and their colleagues' studies, along with their own summary of their work (Beck, McKeown, & Omanson, in press), Mezynski's (1983) assessment of it, and Nagy's (1985) comments on it, lead to several conclusions.

First, vocabulary instruction can markedly increase comprehension of texts that contain the words taught. Possibly the most dramatic illustration of this appeared in the McKeown et al. (1983) article, in which recall of the group receiving the most extensive instruction was nearly twice that of the uninstructed group, and in which prototypical recalls that graphically illustrated the effects of the instruction were presented.

Second, designing, delivering, and assessing vocabulary instruction that increases comprehension is not easy. More studies have failed, or at least failed to present a convincing case, than have succeeded.

Third, in order to affect comprehension, vocabulary instruction probably needs to be fairly lengthy and to include frequent encounters with the words. Beck and McKeown have provided up to 20 minutes of instruction per word, and children have had up to 24 encounters with each word. Additionally, McKeown et al. (1985) found that while 12 encounters produced reliably higher recall scores, 4 encounters did not.

Fourth, instruction in which words are grouped in semantic categories and taught in relationship to each other and to related concepts is likely to be particularly fruitful. In each of their studies, Beck and McKeown have taught vocabulary in sets of ten or so semantically related words.

Fifth, instruction should probably be multifaceted and require active processing on the part of students. Beck and McKeown's instruction consisted of a variety of increasingly challenging activities, including matching words with definitions, associating new words with a variety of contexts, creating contexts for words, comparing and contrasting words to discover relationships, and using the words outside of class.

Finally, instruction should probably include speeded training designed to build automaticity in word recognition and lexical access. Each of Beck and McKeown's studies included such training.

Providing vocabulary instruction that includes all of these facets of effective instruction is certainly possible. What remains to be determined is where such instruction fits into the curriculum and how much time should be devoted to it. Moreover, the possibility deserves study that other sorts of instruction—particularly instruction that extends over several school years but is less intensive than that of Beck and McKeown—can affect students' reading comprehension.

Effects of Vocabulary Instruction on Writing

The attention that has recently been given to the relationship between reading and writing (see Stotsky, 1983) might lead one to expect to find a number of investigations of the effect of vocabulary instruction on writing. However, my search revealed only two such studies. In one study, Wolfe (1975) taught vocabulary to college students without attempting to induce the students to use the words in their writing and then examined the words appearing in their writing. Results indicated that, as compared to students in a control group, students who received the vocabulary instruction did not include more of the taught words in their writing or use generally more complex vocabulary in their writing. In the other study, Duin and Graves (in press) used instructional procedures similar to those of Beck and McKeown to teach intermediate-grade students a small set of words specifically selected to be useful to them in writing on a particular topic. Students were directly encouraged to use these words and given practice in using them. Results indicated that narratives produced by the students receiving the instruction did employ the taught words and were rated as superior to those of students not taught the words.

Based on only two studies, generalizations are obviously unwarranted. However, it does seem likely that vocabulary instruction can improve some aspects of students' writing and that instruction intended to increase students' use of the words taught should directly encourage them to use the words. It also seems that studying the effects of intensive instruction, such as Beck and McKeown's, on both writing and speaking might be particularly fruitful, as the time spent on such instruction could be partially justified by students' productive use of the instructed words.

METHODS OF TEACHING SPECIFIC WORDS

This section considers the effectiveness, outcomes, and costs of various methods of teaching specific words. Most of the studies that have investigated the effect of vocabulary instruction on comprehension also investigated students' learning of the words taught and, as others (e.g., Beck et al., in press; Mezynski, 1983) have pointed out, most of these attempts at teaching specific words have succeeded. A number of studies have also compared the effectiveness of specific methods of vocabulary instruction (e.g., Gipe, 1979; Johnson, Toms-Bronowski, & Pittelman, 1982; Pany & Jenkins, 1978), and a large number of studies have investigated one specific method, the keyword method (see Pressley, Levin, & Delaney, 1983; Pressley, Levin, & McDaniel, in press). These studies have also shown that most methods successfully teach the instructed words. Stahl and Fairbanks' (1986) meta-analysis revealed an effect size of over 2 when instruction on specific words is compared to no instruction.

Not surprisingly, when specific methods are compared, different methods appear to be differentially effective (e.g., Gipe, 1979, 1981; Johnson et al., 1982; Levin et al., 1984; Pany & Jenkins, 1978; Pressley et al., 1983). And, it is undoubtedly the case that some methods are superior to others. However, effects achieved in one study do not always replicate. For example, Gipe (1979) initially showed what she termed a context method to be superior to several other methods, but she failed to obtain this effect in a subsequent study (Gipe, 1981). Moreover, procedures that are shown to be superior when compared to one method may later be shown to be inferior to some other method. For example, Johnson et al. (1982) found the procedure termed semantic mapping to be more effective than that termed semantic feature analysis, while Levin et al. (1984) found the keyword method to be more effective than either of these approaches.[1]

It is possible, of course, to identify some methods that appear to be generally superior to others. The keyword method, for example, has repeatedly been shown to be superior to a number of other methods for certain sorts of learning (Pressley et al., 1983; Pressley et al., in press). Yet, as will be argued below, no one method is superior in all circumstances.

It is possible to identify some of the general characteristics of effective methods. This is the approach taken by the author in identifying the characteristics of vocabulary instruction likely to affect passage comprehension. It was also the approach taken by Stahl and Fairbanks in their meta-analysis.

In this analysis, Stahl and Fairbanks classified methods as to (1) whether they employed a definitional emphasis, a contextual emphasis, or a mixture of the two; (2) the depth of processing they required; (3) whether they provided one or two exposures of the same type, more than two exposures of the same type, or more than two exposures of varied types; (4) whether instruction was largely individual or done at least partly in groups; and (5) the amount of time given to the instruction. The authors obtained effect sizes for the various levels of each of these factors using three sorts of dependent measures. Although they compared the effect sizes using statistical tests, they cautioned that few of their tests showed reliable differences and that most of their findings therefore described trends.

Results of the emphasis factor showed that a mixed approach produced superior results on all measures. Results of the depth of processing factor showed that depth of processing had no effect on the word measures but that deeper processing did produce superior results on the comprehension measure. Results of the number and types of responses factor indicated that multiple exposures of the same type and multiple exposures of different types both produced superior performance to one or two exposures of the same type, but that the two sorts of multiple exposures did not produce differential results. Results of the group versus individual work factor indicated group and individual work produced similar effects. Finally, the amount of time spent showed both positive and negative correlations with effect size.

Given the huge differences in the quality of the research and the instruction in vocabulary studies, it is not certain how much credence ought to be placed in the results of the meta-analysis. My own reaction to them is as follows: Consistent with Stahl and Fairbanks' results, it is probably the case that methods employing both definitional and contextual activities are generally superior to methods employing either alone, that depth of processing affects comprehension more than it does word learning, and that more exposures produce superior results to fewer exposures. However, contrary to Stahl and Fairbanks' results, it seems likely that exposures of different types will produce superior performance on comprehension measures, and it is difficult to believe that spending more time will not produce superior results. Finally, whether group or individual approaches are superior will often depend on such factors as the students and methods involved, although teaching effectiveness research (see Rosenshine & Stevens, 1984) suggests that group approaches should frequently be superior.

This type of analysis does produce some useful, although very general, information about the characteristics of effective instruction. At the same time, such an analysis misses an important aspect of vocabulary instruction. As has been demonstrated (McKeown et al., 1985), and as Stahl and Fairbanks themselves show, the relative effectiveness of particular aspects of instruction varies depending on just how one measures learning. As I have pointed out elsewhere (Graves & Prenn, 1986), different methods will be more or less appropriate and effective depending on the particular word-learning task students face. Various methods have both their costs (the amount of teachers' out-of-class time they require, the amount of teachers' in-class time they require, the amount of students' time they require) and their benefits (the permanence of the learning, the depth of meaning acquired, the extent to which they promote automatic word recognition and rapid lexical access, and the extent to which they promote generative learning and positive attitudes toward words and word study).

In previous papers (Graves, 1984, 1985, in press; Graves & Duin, 1985), I have identified six word-learning tasks. Three of these will be described and some of the methods that are appropriate with each of them and some of the costs and benefits of each method will be considered. (Note that the three word-learning tasks *not* described here are learning to read known words, learning new meanings for known words, and clarifying and enriching the meanings of known words.)

Learning New Labels

One word-learning task is that of learning new labels for known concepts. The word, *indigenous,* for example, is unknown to the majority of senior high school students (Dale & O'Rourke, 1981), but most high school students would understand "native born." One frequently used method of teaching new labels is to ask students to look up the words in a dictionary and write out their definitions (Petty, Herold, & Stoll, 1968). This certainly is not a very powerful form of instruction; however, Parker (1984) has shown that many junior high school students can learn words by looking them up in the dictionary. Moreover, the method does provide practice in a useful skill, using the dictionary. Of course, students do not fully learn a word's meaning simply by looking it up in the dictionary, but they are likely to learn enough about it to learn more from subsequent encounters with it. Finally, although the cost in both teachers' out-of-class time and teachers' in-class time is very low, the cost in students' time is fairly high, and the method, in my opinion, is unlikely to foster positive attitudes toward words or word study.

A second procedure for teaching labels is the keyword method, which, as already noted, has been tested extensively by Levin and Pressley and their colleagues (see Pressley et al., 1982; Pressley et al., in press). Using the word *carlin,* meaning "old witch," as an example, Levin and Pressley describe the procedure as follows: First, students learn a keyword. A keyword is a familiar imageable word that resembles some salient part of the word to be learned. The word *car* serves as a good keyword for *carlin.* Next, students form a visual image or develop a short episode in which the meaning of the keyword and the meaning of the new word interact. For example, students might think of an old witch driving a car to create an image in which the meanings of *car* and *carlin* interact. When students are asked the meaning of *carlin*, the word *carlin* will remind them of the word *car*, and the word *car* will, in turn, remind them of the image of an old witch driving a car and hence of the meaning of *carlin*.

The keyword method is more costly than the dictionary method because finding a keyword and developing an association is frequently a time-consuming task. However, the method has by far the largest amount of data supporting its efficacy, and there is little doubt that it works well. It establishes a powerful association between the already known meaning and the label for that meaning, the word being taught. At the same time, it does nothing to enrich or refine students' understanding of the new word. Although students could use the keyword method as a generative tool to remember new words, it seems unlikely that many students would choose to use it on their own. Finally, the method appears to be the sort of thing that students would initially find intriguing, but it also seems to be the sort of instruction that could easily be overused.

Learning New Concepts

A second word-learning task is that of learning words that represent new and difficult concepts. For example, fully learning such words as *fulcrum*, *mores*, and *temerity* is likely to require the majority of students to develop new concepts. Procedures for teaching new and difficult concepts are more costly in terms of both student and teacher time than are those for teaching available concepts, but the benefits are, of course, also greater. At the same time, each of these procedures, like each of those for teaching available concepts, has both costs and benefits.

Consider two procedures: The first, which will be called *concept teaching*, was developed by Frayer, Fredrick, and Klausmeier (1969). The procedure can be broken down into five steps: (1) defining the new concept by giving its essential attributes; (2) distinguishing between relevant and irrelevant properties of instances of the concept; (3) giving examples of the concept; (4) giving nonexamples of the concept; and (5) relating the concept being taught to superordinate, subordinate, and coordinate concepts.

This procedure is obviously very costly as it takes a good deal of teachers' out-of-class time to develop such instruction—perhaps 30 minutes for a single concept. It also takes a good deal of both teachers' and students' in-class time, perhaps 10–15 minutes for a concept that is not too difficult. However, the procedure provides a very thorough and effective introduction to new concepts (see Peters, 1974), and it is unreasonable to expect new concepts to be acquired in a very brief period of time. Moreover, although concept teaching is not necessarily a generative procedure, if students internalized the approach, it could certainly aid them in dealing with new concepts. Finally, the procedure is intellectually challenging and seems likely to create some interest in words.

Another procedure for teaching new concepts is the one termed semantic mapping (Johnson & Pearson, 1984; Johnson et al., 1982). With this method, the teacher puts a word representing a central concept on the chalkboard, asks students to work in groups listing as many words related to the central concept as they can, writes students' words on the chalkboard grouped in broad categories, has students name the categories and perhaps suggest additional ones, and discusses with students the central concept, the other words, the categories, and their interrelationships.

This method does not require a great deal of out-of-class preparation, but it does require a good deal of in-class time, possibly 30 minutes per central concept, and the majority of this in-class time is whole-class discussion involving the teacher. Thus, the method is very costly in terms of both teachers' and students' in-class time, but less costly than concept teaching in terms of teachers' out-of-class time. The method has been shown to be effective (Johnson et al., 1982), and it appears to be very beneficial in that students learn a good deal about the interrelationships of the concepts associated with the words, possibly more than they learn in concept teaching. However, it may be that the specific meanings of the words taught are not as fully learned as they are in concept teaching. Still, students appear to enjoy the procedure, and it should spur their interest in words and the relationships among words. Finally, while the procedure probably is not generative in the sense that students will directly use it in learning new words, it is likely to be helpful to them to learn that words are related to each other in a variety of ways, and it may help them to develop increasingly sophisticated lexicons.

Moving Words into Students' Productive Vocabularies

A third word-learning task, that of moving words from students' receptive vocabularies to their productive ones, has received almost no attention. However, it seems likely that getting students actively to use words they learn requires that they both learn words thoroughly and are motivated to use them. Beck and McKeown's studies and a study modeled on their work have attempted to do this.

In each of their three studies (Beck et al., 1982; McKeown et al., 1983; McKeown et al., 1985), Beck and McKeown have included Word Wizard, an activity that encourages students to search for and use the instructed words outside of class and gives them points for doing so. Beck and McKeown reported that "children virtually swamped their teachers with instances of seeing, hearing, or using the words as they worked toward gaining points" (1983, p. 625), and that children sometimes even caused minor disruptions by buzzing with excitement when they heard one of the Word Wizard words spoken.

In the Duin and Graves (in press) study, motivational activities similar to Word Wizard were coupled with instruction and practice in using a set of 10 words. The results indicated that students used an average of 6 of the 10 words in writing a narrative that encouraged the use of these words. Students were excited about the instruction; in fact, they asked for more of it.

The results of these attempts to get students actively to use the words they learn suggest that they can have both cognitive and affective benefits. However, such instruction is very costly in terms of teachers' and students' time.

Summary

Studies of various methods for teaching specific words reveal a number of validated procedures for teaching vocabulary and several characteristics of effective instruction. What is needed in determining the educational implications of those studies and in planning future investigations of methods of teaching specific words is more attention to the types of word-learning tasks each method best serves, the costs of each approach, and the benefits of each of them. What is also needed is consideration of where the various sorts of instruction fit into the curriculum.

GENERATIVE VOCABULARY INSTRUCTION

This section deals with instruction in context clues and instruction in morphological analysis.[2]

Instruction in Context Clues

The research on instruction in context clues has been organized by considering three questions: Can students acquire word meanings from context? What types of clues are available for learning from context and what factors affect the success of such learning? And can children be better taught to use context clues to learn the meanings of novel words? Each of these will be considered in turn, with summaries and suggestions for further research at the end of each section.

Can students acquire word meanings from context?

Studies that attempt to answer this question can be arranged on a continuum ranging from those that investigate learning in very artificial situations to those that investigate learning in nearly natural situations. (Note that the use of the term "artificial situations" is not intended to denigrate the studies.)

At the artificial end of the continuum are studies by Werner and Kaplan (1952), van Daalen-Kapteijns and Elshout-Mohr (1981), McKeown (1985), Shefelbine (1983), and Jenkins and Wysocki (1985). Werner and Kaplan's study is representative of the first three of these, and Shefelbine's is representative of the last two. Werner and Kaplan asked 9- to 13-year-old children to determine the meaning of a pseudoword from a series of six sentences, each of which provided further information about the word's meaning. Although the task was a difficult one and children of different ages showed differential ability to determine meaning, children at all ages learned some meanings from context. The findings of van Daalen-Kapteijns and Elshout-Mohr and of McKeown were similar in this regard. In a quite different study, Shefelbine alerted sixth-grade students to the possibility of using context clues, gave them a brief example of how to do so, and then read short passages from a basal reader to them, prompting them to use the context to figure out the meaning of a difficult word in the passage. Results indicated that students did learn from context under these conditions. Jenkins and Wysocki's results also indicated that children can learn word meanings from context when prompted to do so, and they further showed that merely prompting children to learn meanings does promote learning.

Several studies have employed somewhat more natural learning situations. Carroll and Drum (1983) first asked 11th- and 12th-grade students to define 40 words and then had them read natural passages containing one occurrence of 20 of the words and again define all of them. Results indicated that students produced superior definitions for the words encountered in context.

Jenkins, Stein, and Wysocki (1984) used artificial passages containing richer clues than would be found in natural passages and presented fifth graders with 0, 2, 6, and 10 occurrences of target words without alerting students to the fact that the study concerned vocabulary. Three measures of vocabulary learning were used. Results indicated that 6 presentations of the words were necessary to yield reliable gains on two of the vocabulary measures used and that 10 repetitions were necessary to yield reliable gains on all three measures used.

As part of the study previously mentioned, Jenkins and Wysocki (1985) used similar passages and presented sixth graders with 0, 1, or 5 occurrences of the words, again without alerting students to the fact that the study dealt with word learning. Five measures of vocabulary learning were used. Results indicated that 5 exposures were needed to yield reliable gains in word knowledge and that 5 exposures resulted in gains on all five measures.

In two recent studies Nagy, Herman, and Anderson (1985a, 1985b) used multiple regression analyses to assess learning from context in a very natural situation. In the first study (Nagy et al., 1985a) eighth-grade average and above-average students were asked to read two natural passages that contained one or two occurrences of difficult words without alerting students to the fact that the study concerned vocabulary. Results indicated that students did acquire meaning from context and that the probability of students learning a word well enough to answer a multiple-choice question on its meaning from a single exposure was about .15. In the second study, Nagy et al. (1985b) addressed three limitations of the first one. They provided a longer time interval between the reading and taking the test (6 days as opposed to 15 minutes). They employed a greater range of grade and ability levels (grades 3, 5, and 7 as opposed to grade 8; and ability levels ranging from the 11th percentile to the 99th percentile as opposed to only average and high-ability levels). And they used more passages (four passages at each grade level as opposed to a total of two passages). Results showed that the probability of students learning a word well enough to answer a multiple-choice question on its meaning from a single occurrence of the word was about .05. Even with this low probability of learning a word from a single occurrence, Nagy and his colleagues argued that the volume of reading students do results in their learning a sizable number of words. However, in a further analysis of data from the study, Nagy, Anderson, and Herman (1985) found that context by itself did not assist students in learning conceptually difficult words that required them to learn a network of new concepts and that some of the passages used in the study produced no word learning.

In addition to showing that students do learn word meanings from natural context in a normal reading situation, Nagy and his colleagues have extrapolated from their results to estimate the number of words that students learn from reading. Based on their 1985a study, they estimated that the typical middle-grade child annually learns between 1,500 and 8,250 words from reading outside of school. However, based on their 1985b study, Fielding, Wilson, and Anderson's (in press) study of the amount of reading fifth graders do outside of school, and several estimates of the amount of reading students do in school, Nagy and his colleagues (1985b) estimated that the average child annually learns between 800 and 1,200 words from both in-school and out-of-school reading. It is important to note that in addition to being hugely discrepant, both estimates are based on a great deal of extrapolation.

The studies reviewed in this section clearly demonstrate that students can learn word meanings from context. Moreover, they can learn words from natural context under normal reading conditions. However, much firmer information is needed on how many words are learned from context. Information also is needed on the extent to which learning from context can produce deep and precise meanings for words. What would seem to be particularly useful in estimating the place of learning from context in the total of children's word learning are longitudinal studies that measured students' learning from context over an extended period such as a year and that considered the depth and precision of the meanings learned.

What types of clues are available for learning from context and what other factors affect the success of such learning?

Over the past 40 years, authorities have presented a variety of classifications of the types of context clues that occur in texts. Some are largely or solely the results of intuition (e.g., Artley, 1942; Deighton, 1959; Mc-Cullough, 1943), while others have resulted from empirical attempts to ascertain what sorts of clues readers actually use (Ames, 1966-1967; Quealy, 1969).

More recently, Sternberg and his colleagues (Sternberg, in press, 1985; Sternberg & Powell, 1983; Sternberg, Powell, & Kaye, 1983) have described and begun to test a theory that is more comprehensive than previous attempts and seems likely to become the most widely accepted description of clue types and general explanation of learning from context. The theory has three components. One is a set of eight context clue types. These include clues related to (1) the duration or frequency of the unknown word, (2) the location or possible locations of the unknown word, (3) the value of the unknown word or the effects it has, (4) the properties of the unknown word, (5) the function of the unknown word, (6) the causes of or enabling conditions for the unknown word, (7) the class membership of the unknown word, and (8) definitions of and contrasts to the unknown word. A second component is a set of seven mediating variables. These include (1) the number of occurrences of the unknown word, (2) the variability of the contexts in which the unknown word occurs, (3) the importance of the unknown word to understanding the surrounding material, (4) the helpfulness of the surrounding context in revealing the meaning of the unknown word, (5) the density of unknown words, (6) the concreteness of the unknown word and the surrounding context, and (7) the usefulness of previous knowledge in making use of the context clues available. And, the third component is a set of three knowledge acquisition processes. These include selective encoding (identifying the relevant information), selective combination (combining the encoded information to form a plausible definition), and selective comparison (relating the new information to prior knowledge).

Sternberg has tested parts of the theory in two experiments (both summarized in Sternberg, 1985). He concluded from one experiment that consideration of the clues and moderating variables in a passage yielded good predictions of the definitions given by readers encountering difficult words proximate to them. He concluded from the other experiment that the order of aid given by the clues was in the order one would predict and that the types were differentially effective.

Most other recent work on context clues concerns moderating variables, some of which are those that Sternberg has identified and some of which are not. The results of some of these studies are predictable. For example, both Jenkins and his colleagues' studies (Jenkins et al., 1984; Jenkins & Wysocki, 1985) and those of Finn (1977–1978) and Hoffman (1980) have shown that the number of times a word appears in a text increases the likelihood that it will be learned. Similarly, Drum and her colleagues (Carroll & Drum, 1982; Madison, Carroll, & Drum, 1982) have shown that the proximity of a clue to an unknown word increases the possibility that it will be learned, and Shefelbine (1983) found that words representing familiar concepts were more likely to be learned than those representing unfamiliar concepts. Finally, in a regression analysis that investigated a number of factors, Nagy, Anderson, and Herman (1985) showed that the proportion of conceptually difficult words in a passage and the average length of the difficult words were the strongest factors affecting learning from context, and that the strength of contextual support, readability, and sentence length also affected learning from context. They also found that nouns were better learned than other parts of speech and that simple narratives facilitated learning from context much more than did difficult expositions.

One additional mediating factor that has been considered is students' ability. The typical and expected finding has been that more able students learn more from context than their less able peers (Elvian, 1938; Herman, 1984; Jenkins et al., 1984; McKeown, 1985; Quealy, 1969; Rankin & Overholser, 1969). The notion that learning from context is a basic measure of intellectual ability is also central to Sternberg's theory. Recently, however, Nagy, Herman, and Anderson (1985b) failed to find an interaction between ability and learning from context, and they have used this null result to argue that students of various ability levels are almost equally adept at learning from context and that less able readers should be able to learn the majority of the words they need to learn from encountering them while reading.

Aside from identifying some of the mediating variables that affect learning from context, the work considered in this section raises more questions than it answers. Because of the attention that Sternberg's system is receiving, further investigation of that system seems a definite priority. It also would be helpful if investigations of phenomena closely related to Sternberg's system—investigations of clue types or mediating factors—were directly related to Sternberg's system wherever possible. Finally, the possibility that difficult exposition may not provide much learning from context and the question of the effect of ability on learning from context definitely deserve further study.

Can children be taught to better use context clues to learn the meanings of novel words?

Several studies have investigated the efficacy of teaching students to use context to unlock the meanings of novel words, but this research has produced mixed results. Hafner (1965) reported a one-month experiment with fifth-grade students that produced no reliable difference between the experimental and control groups. Carnine, Kameenui, and Coyle (1984) used both a rule plus practice and a practice only treatment, both of which were very brief, and found that either treatment facilitated students' ability to use context in a contrived passage. Patberg, Graves, and Stibbe (1984) replicated the Carnine et al. study using instruction that employed more active teaching and made greater use of teacher explanations. They found reliable differences favoring the context group over a practice group and a control group on only one of two dependent measures. However, in a follow-up study Patberg and Stibbe (1985) found no effects of instruction in using context clues.

Sternberg has completed two training studies, both of which are briefly described in a general report of his work (1985). In one study, he trained inner-city high school students in six sessions using a variety of procedures suggested by his theory and found a very weak effect of training. In the other, he trained noncollege adults in a single 45-minute session and was able to show that training that emphasized the process of using context, training that taught specific clue types, and training that taught mediating variables each produced reliably greater ability to use context than did either practice alone or no training. Unfortunately, Sternberg did not describe his texts in sufficient detail to determine whether he was testing natural or contrived context, and he did not describe his training in any detail.

In summary, teaching students to use context is difficult. In fact, there is no report that presents a thorough and convincing case that students can be taught to better use context to unlock the meanings of novel words encountered during normal reading. The question of the efficacy of teaching context clues is at about the same state as was the question of the effect of vocabulary instruction on reading comprehension when Beck and McKeown began their investigations of that topic. There is a need for long-term, fully described studies that include at least one dependent measure that uses natural texts read under approximately normal reading conditions.

Instruction in Morphological Analysis

The research on instruction in morphological analysis is organized by considering four questions: What elements are worth teaching? What elements do students of various ages and ability levels know? Are students able to use these elements to unlock the meanings of novel words? And what have been the results of instruction in morphological analysis? Each of these will be considered in turn, with summaries and suggested directions for further research at the end of each section.

What elements are worth teaching?

An empirical answer to the question of what elements are worth teaching would require a thorough analysis and tabulation of the prefixes, roots, and suffixes appearing in a large, representative body of words, an analysis somewhat like that undertaken by Nagy and Anderson (1982, 1984) to estimate the number of words in printed school English. Although nothing as definitive as that analysis exists, several analyses have been done.

In one of the earliest analyses of this kind, Thorndike (1941) analyzed the occurrences of 90 English suffixes in an unspecified corpus of about 50,000 nontechnical words. In another study, Stauffer (1942) tallied the prefixes occurring in the Thorndike (1932) list of 20,000 words and found that 24% of these words had prefixes and that 15 prefixes accounted for 82% of the words. In still another study, Osborn (1954) analyzed the occurrences of Latin and Greek roots in Rinsland's (1945) 15,000-word list and found that 30% of the words contained Latin roots and a very small percentage of them Greek roots, and that 82 Latin roots and 6 Greek roots occurred 10 or more times. And, in a most recent study, White, Speidel, and Power (1985) investigated the occurrences of prefixes and combining forms in the Carroll et al. (1971) 86,000-word list, and identified 16 prefixes and 2 combining forms that occurred two or more times.

A more ambitious attempt to identify the building blocks of English words is that of Becker and his associates (Anderson-Inman, Dixon, & Becker, 1981; Becker, Dixon, & Anderson-Inman, 1980). As part of an attempt to develop a long-term, systematic program of vocabulary instruction, Becker and his colleagues analyzed 26,000 words from the Thorndike and Lorge (1944) list, together with some words from the Carroll et al. (1971) and Harris and Jacobson lists (1972), into what they call morphographs: "[A] group of letters can be considered a morphograph if it contributes meaning to a word or group of words (either historically or currently) and if its structural representation will combine with the other morphographs of a word to form the correct spelling of that word" (Anderson-Inman et al., 1981, p. 4).

The results of this analysis are two volumes, one in which each morphograph is listed alphabetically followed by those words incorporating it (Anderson-Inman et al., 1981) and the other which lists words alphabetically and shows their morphographic breakdown (Becker et al., 1980). Although these lists could be of some use in designing instructional programs, their use is limited by the fact that morphographs include a number of different sorts of elements, and these various elements are not distinguished. For example, morphographs include both prefixes (bound morphemes attached to English roots) and etymological initial units (bound morphemes attached to non-English roots, which may or may not carry their original meaning). Thus, the list includes some elements that are definitely worth teaching and others that almost certainly are not.

Considered together, these studies suggest a number of elements that might be taught. However, the data do not clearly indicate which of the elements are most worth teaching or in what order they should be taught. What is needed is descriptive information on the occurrence of word parts in a representative corpus of words, probably the Carroll et al. (1971) list.

What elements do students of various ages and ability levels know?

There are almost no data addressing this question. In fact, only two studies have been discovered. In one of them, Nicol (1980) investigated fourth-through sixth-grade middle-class students' knowledge of 16 common prefixes and found that correct responses ranged from 88% for *mis-* (wrong) to 20%

for *in-* (not). Unfortunately, specific percentages for the other prefixes were not given.

In the other study, White et al. (1985) tested lower- and middle-class third- and fourth-grade Hawaiian children on the 16 common prefixes and 2 combining forms mentioned above and found that correct responses ranged from 80% for *non-* and *re-* to 20% for *anti-* and *en-*. The survey also revealed that about two-thirds of the elements were known by fewer than 50% of the students.

Clearly, more descriptive data about students' knowledge of word parts are needed.

Are students able to use these elements to unlock the meanings of novel words?

Several recent studies have investigated students' skill at using morphological generalizations. Kaye and Sternberg (1983) found that both secondary school students (grades 8, 9, and 10) and college undergraduates demonstrated some awareness of whether or not they knew a set of Latin roots and prefixes, but that only the college undergraduates appeared to decompose words into their component parts when determining the meanings of unknown words made up of roots and prefixes. It should be noted, however, that all but two of the roots tested were non-English words; thus the study did not investigate the much easier task of decomposing words made up of a prefix and an English word.

Wysocki and Jenkins (1985) tested fourth through eighth graders and found that morphological generalization between suffixed and base forms appeared in modest amounts when a strict criterion for knowing the related words was used but in considerably greater amounts when a weaker criterion was used. They further found that sixth and eighth graders displayed more morphological knowledge than fourth graders. Although Wysocki and Jenkins put more credence in the strict criterion and stressed that their study showed only weak morphological generalization, the weak criterion still required knowledge of the basic word meanings, and it seems plausible to interpret success on that task as evidence of morphological knowledge. It should also be noted that in the majority of cases there were spelling changes between the original word and the transfer word. Thus, as was the case with Kaye and Sternberg's task, Wysocki and Jenkins's task represented a fairly difficult test of morphological knowledge.

In a follow-up study, Wysocki (1986) found that morphological generalization between suffixed and base forms occurred in about twice as many fourth and sixth graders as it had in the previous study. Wysocki attributed this difference to the transformations necessary to arrive at the meaning of the transfer words tested, which were less difficult in the follow-up study than they had been in the original one. The study also indicated that sixth graders displayed more morphological knowledge than fourth graders on some measures used.

Finally, White and associates (1985) found that third- and fourth-grade students correctly separated the root and its suffix in a multiple-choice task 80% of the time when there was no spelling change and 51% when there was a spelling change. Although this task was considerably easier than that presented in some of the other investigations, success on it does require some knowledge of morphology.

In general, then, it appears that while neither elementary nor high school students have sophisticated skills of morphological analysis, students do possess some skill at this task. Again, there is a need for more descriptive data.

What are the results of instruction in morphological analysis?

Several studies have addressed this question. In an early study, which was very cursorily described and which employed no control group, Thompson (1958) reported that college students who were taught 20 prefixes and 14 roots as part of an efficient reading course improved their scores on the elements taught from pretest to posttest by 34%, improved their scores at identifying the elements in words by 22%, and improved their ability to recognize words containing the prefixes by 20%.

In a more recent study, Graves and Hammond (1980) taught seventh graders nine prefixes over a 3-day period and tested the students the day after the training was completed and again 3 weeks later. Results on both the immediate and delayed tests indicated reliable differences between the group taught the prefixes and a control group on a test of the prefixes taught and on a transfer test requiring students to use their knowledge of the prefixes taught to unlock the meanings of novel words containing the prefixes.

In a related study, Nicol, Graves, and Slater (1984) taught fourth, fifth, and sixth graders nine prefixes over a 3-day period and again tested students the day after training and 3 weeks later. As in the previous study, results on both the immediate test and a test given 3 weeks later indicated reliable differences between the group taught the prefixes and a control group on a test of the prefixes taught and a transfer test. The results further indicated that reliable gains were made by children of high, middle, and low ability.

Wysocki (1986) found that six instructional sessions designed to teach students to recognize and define morphologically related base and suffixed words improved low-ability students' performance on one measure of morphological generalization but did not improve high-ability students' performance. Wysocki attributed this differential performance to the fact that low-ability students had more to learn than their high-ability counterparts. She also suggested some deficiencies in the training program that may have lessened its effects on both high- and low-ability students. It should also be noted that the sorts of generalization that the instruction was designed to teach, generalizations from base forms to suffixed forms and vice versa using transfer words that frequently included spelling changes, are quite difficult ones and that the criterion tests were also quite demanding.

Finally, in a general report on their vocabulary research, Pressley and associates (in press) very briefly mentioned a study indicating that both elementary and college students who were taught root words were later better able to remember the names and definitions for novel words containing the roots than students not taught them.

Although each of the studies considered here taught relatively few elements over a relatively brief period of time, it seems clear that at least some sorts of word parts can be taught and that students can use these elements in unlocking the meanings of novel words and in remembering newly learned words. However, precise information on what sorts of elements can be taught to students at various grade and ability levels is lacking.

VOCABULARY INSTRUCTION IN SCHOOLS

There is very little research examining the vocabulary instruction that is currently taking place in schools. Only three studies relevant to the topic were found, and in fact no studies dealt with precisely this issue. Two of the studies examined the vocabulary instruction in selected basal readers, and the third incidentally recorded vocabulary instruction in an observational study of comprehension instruction.

One analysis of basal readers (Beck et al., 1979) examined the vocabulary instruction presented in the third- through sixth-grade books of two series, including prereading activities, during-reading activities, and postreading activities. With regard to prereading activities, one series included none of them, and the other included some words to be taught in sentences specifically designed to reveal their meaning but did not suggest teaching activities. With regard to during-reading activities, both series relied on the students to obtain meanings from natural contexts, contexts that often were not revealing of the words' meanings, and on the students to look up words in the glossary. And, with regard to postreading instruction, one series presented a set of words not previously taught, while the other provided one review of the originally taught words.

In summarizing this work, Beck and colleagues (1980) considered the best and the worst instruction that might occur:

[At best] a new vocabulary word is presented in a sentence that elucidates the meaning of the new word; the word is encountered in the text selection and the student looks it up in the glossary if s/he does not remember its meaning; the word appears a third time in an independently completed, after reading activity. . . .

At worst, a new word appears solely in a selection and the student skips over it because s/he either does not recognize it as an unknown word or does not want to be bothered with the disruption of the glossary. (pp. 7–8)

In the second analysis of basal readers, Jenkins and Dixon (1983) reported an investigation of instruction in several fourth-grade level texts. These authors also compared the best and worst instruction found:

[In the best series the] developers identify several words for each unit . . . , and provide pre- and post-tests for a subset of these words. Instructional recommendations contained in the Teacher's Manual generally involve dictionary work in writing a definition on the board, along with a vocabulary workbook page, which is another version of the pretest. The Teacher's Manual cautions that some words may already be familiar to students . . . , so the teacher need only present selected vocabulary—those words which students would not be able to read (and understand) independently. Thus, the tests, teaching activities, and worksheets are all considered optional. (pp. 245–246)

[In the worst series, they found] no lists of vocabulary identified for emphasis, no lessons specified for teacher-led instruction nor any exercises expressly designed to teach word meanings. (p. 245)

Jenkins and Dixon concluded that, even at best, students would only learn about 300 words a year from the basal program, a fraction of the total number of words students learn each year.

In assessing both their own findings and those of Beck and associates, Jenkins and Dixon suggested that the developers of basal materials

seem not to rely much on direct teaching to produce growth in vocabulary knowledge. Rather, they appear to believe either that vocabulary learning is an unimportant aspect of schooling, or that it occurs chiefly through incidental learning . . . and thus needs only modest attention from teachers and from instructional programs. (1983, p. 247)

In the observational study of comprehension instruction in schools, Durkin (1979–1980), who observed 4,469 minutes of instruction in 4th-grade classrooms, found that only 19 minutes were devoted to vocabulary instruction, with an additional 4 minutes devoted to review. Although Durkin's coding system resulted in some vocabulary instruction being classified as a part of preparation for reading, only about 5% of the total time observed was devoted to all types of preparation for reading. Thus, the total time given to vocabulary instruction certainly was not great.

Admittedly, this is a very small set of studies on which to base generalizations about the amount and quality of vocabulary instruction in schools. Moreover, each of the studies deals with intermediate grade texts or students. Yet, the studies receive added strength from the fact that the findings of all of them are very similar, namely that the vocabulary instruction students receive in schools is quite meager. This finding is consistent with the assessments of a variety of authorities who have observed that the vocabulary instruction in schools lacks purpose, breadth, and depth (Becker, 1977; Calfee & Drum, 1978, 1986; Deighton, 1959; O'Rourke, 1974).

SUMMARY

This section presents a summary of what we know and what we need to learn in order to develop programs of vocabulary instruction based on empirical evidence that informs both the content and the sequence of instruction. Since summaries and suggestions for further research have been presented throughout the review, the section is brief.

The materials students read contain a very large number of words, and the average primary-grade student already has a large reading vocabulary. However, more needs to be learned about the year-by-year growth in students' vocabularies, about the depth of students' word knowledge, and about the vocabularies of less able and less advantaged students.

The vocabulary used in texts has some effect on the comprehensibility of the texts, and vocabulary strongly influences audience reactions to texts and their authors. Particularly rich vocabulary instruction can affect reading comprehension and writing performance. Determining where such rich instruction fits into the curriculum and investigating long-term programs that could affect reading comprehension and writing performance are matters of particular importance.

A variety of methods are effective in teaching individual words. However, different methods make very different demands on teachers' and students' time and produce different results. What needs to be further considered is just what various methods accomplish and where they fit into the curriculum.

Students can learn word meanings from context, and various factors that affect learning from context have been identified. More information is needed on how much word learning is attributable to learning from context, how fully words are learned from context, what factors affect learning from context, and how students can be taught to use context better to unlock word meanings.

Students can use at least some types of morphological elements to find word meanings. Furthermore, instruction can improve their ability at some sorts of morphological analysis. However, just which types of elements and which specific elements students of various ages and ability levels know, which should be taught, and in what order they should be taught have yet to be determined.

Finally, from the sparse data that are available, it appears that relatively little vocabulary instruction takes place in schools; however, any definitive statement on this topic must await further study.

CONCLUSIONS

This review will be concluded by considering two factors that have prevented vocabulary research from having as much effect on instruction as it might. One factor is the lack of long-term attention to vocabulary by most researchers. The most notable exception to this rule was E. L. Thorndike, whose vocabulary research spanned 30 years. The most notable current exceptions are Anderson and Nagy and their associates and Beck and McKeown and their associates, whose vocabulary research now spans nearly 10 years. Additionally, there are another half-dozen individuals and groups of researchers who have consistently pursued research on vocabulary for about the same time period. Such sustained work is essential to producing the sort of data needed to markedly influence instruction.

The other factor is the lack of a coherent, fully articulated, long-term plan for vocabulary instruction. Such a plan should include consideration of what students need to learn, what should be taught, and how it could be taught at various points in the curriculum. Although several sketches for such a plan have recently been presented (Beck et al., in press; Calfee & Drum, 1986; Graves, in press), no comprehensive plan has been described in detail. Once developed, such a plan needs to be widely circulated and thoroughly considered. At the present time, many researchers appear to assume that the particular instructional method they are employing, the particular goal their instruction is intended to achieve, or the particular background factor they are investigating is singularly important. Similarly, many teachers and adoption committees have preconceived notions of what students need, and many publishers have definite and usually quite traditional ideas about what will sell. There needs to be more consensus on the goals of vocabulary instruction and general recognition that various sorts of instruction are needed to achieve these goals.

NOTES

[1] Semantic mapping is a procedure in which a word is placed on the board and related words are solicited from students. Semantic feature analysis is a procedure in which a set of words with similar meanings is listed and features which illustrate the similarities and differences in the meanings are considered. The keyword method is a procedure in which a new word is related to an imageable known word and image or episode involving the known word. Semantic mapping and the keyword method are described in more detail later in this section of the chapter.

[2] Another factor that undoubtedly has a generative effect in fostering word learning, but has not been researched and would be difficult to research, is the teacher's enthusiasm and love for words, his or her skill in using words adroitly, and his or her power to instill in students an interest in words and an appreciation of the precision and power that come from speaking and writing clearly.

REFERENCES

Ames, W.S. (1966–1967). The development of a classification scheme of contextual aids. *Reading Research Quarterly, 2,* 57–62.

Anders, P., Boss, C., & Filip, D. (1984). The effect of semantic feature analysis on the reading comprehension of learning-disabled students. In J.A. Niles & L.A. Harris (Eds.), *Changing perspectives on research in reading/language processing and instruction.* Rochester, NY: National Reading Conference.

Anderson, R.C., & Freebody, P. (1981). Vocabulary knowledge. In J.T. Guthrie (Ed.), *Comprehension and teaching: Research reviews* (pp. 77–117). Newark, DE: International Reading Association.

Anderson, R.C., & Freebody, P. (1983). Reading comprehension and the assessment and acquisition of word knowledge. In B. Hutton (Ed.), *Advances in reading/language research, a research annual.* Greenwich, CT: JAI Press.

Anderson-Inman, L., Dixon, R., & Becker, W.C. (1981). *Morphographs: An alphabetical list with examples.* Eugene: University of Oregon Follow Through Project.

Anglin, J.M. (1970). *The growth of word meaning.* Cambridge, MA: MIT Press.

Anglin, J.M. (1977). *Word, object, and conceptual development.* New York: Norton.

Artley, A.S. (1942). Teaching word meaning through context. *Elementary English Review, 20,* 68–74.

Barrett, M.T. (1979). *A junior high school remedial reading program to teach science and social studies vocabulary.* Unpublished master's thesis, University of Minnesota, Minneapolis.

Barrett, M.T., & Graves, M.F. (1981). A vocabulary program for junior high school remedial readers. *Journal of Reading, 25,* 146–150.

Bartlett, E.J. (1976). Sizing things up: The acquisition of meaning of dimensional adjectives. *Journal of Child Language, 3,* 205–219.

Beck, I.L., McCaslin, E.S., & McKeown, M.G. (1980). *The rationale and design of a program to teach vocabulary to fourth-grade students.* Pittsburgh: University of Pittsburgh, Learning Research and Development Center.

Beck, I.L., McKeown, M.G., McCaslin, E.S., & Burkes, A.M. (1979). *Instructional dimensions that may affect reading comprehension: Examples from two commercial reading programs* (LRDC Publication No. 1979–20). Pittsburgh: University of Pittsburgh, Learning Research and Development Center.

Beck, I.L., McKeown, M.G., & Omanson, R.C. (in press). The effects and uses of diverse vocabulary instructional techniques. In M.G. McKeown & M.E. Curtis (Eds.), *The nature of vocabulary acquisition.* Hillsdale, NJ: Erlbaum.

Beck, I.L., Perfetti, C.A., & McKeown, M.G. (1982). The effects of long-term vocabulary instruction on lexical access and reading comprehension. *Journal of Educational Psychology, 74,* 506–521.

Becker, W.C. (1977). Teaching reading and language to the disadvantaged—What we have learned from field research. *Harvard Educational Review, 47,* 518–543.

Becker, W.C., Dixon, R., & Anderson-Inman, L. (1980, April) *Morphographic and root word analysis of 26,000 high frequency words* (Tech. Rep. 1980–1). Eugene: University of Oregon Follow Through Project, College of Education.

Binet, A., & Simon, T. (1916). *The development of intelligence in children.* Vineland, NJ: Publications of the Training School.

Bradac, J.J., Bowers, J.W., & Courtright, J.A. (1982). Lexical variations in intensity, immediacy, and diversity: An axiomatic theory and causal model. In R.N. St. Clair & H. Giles (Eds.), *The social and psychological contexts of language.* Hillsdale, NJ: Erlbaum.

Bradac, J.J., Courtright, J.A., Schmidt, G., & Davies, R.A. (1976). The effects of perceived status and linguistic diversity upon judgments of speaker attributes and message effectiveness. *Journal of Psychology, 93,* 213–220.

Bradac, J.J., Davies, R.A., Courtright, J.A., Desmond, R.J., & Murdock, J.I.

(1977). Richness of vocabulary: An attributional analysis. *Psychological Reports, 41*, 1131–1134.

Calfee, R.C., & Drum, P.A. (1978). Learning to read: Theory, research, and practice. *Curriculum Inquiry, 8*, 183–249.

Calfee, R.C., & Drum, P.A. (1986). Research on teaching reading. In M.C. Wittrock (Ed.), *Handbook of research on teaching* (3rd ed., pp. 804–849). New York: Macmillan.

Carey, S. (1978). Child as word learner. In M. Halle, J. Bresnan, & G. Miller (Eds.), *Linguistic theory and psychological reality* (pp. 264–293). Cambridge, MA: MIT Press.

Carey, S. (1982). Semantic development: The state of the art. In E. Warner & L.R. Gleitman (Eds.), *Language acquisition: The state of the art* (pp. 347–389). Cambridge, England: Cambridge University Press.

Carnine, D., Kameenui, E.J., & Coyle, G. (1984). Utilization of contextual information in determining the meaning of unfamiliar words in context. *Reading Research Quarterly, 19*, 188–202.

Carroll, B., & Drum, P.A. (1982). Effects of context in facilitating unknown word comprehension. In J.A. Niles & L.A. Harris (Eds.), *New inquiries in reading* (pp. 89–93). Rochester, NY: National Reading Conference.

Carroll, B., & Drum, P.A. (1983) Definitional gains for explicit and implicit context clues. In J.A. Niles & L.A. Harris (Eds.), *Searches for meaning in reading/language processing and instruction* (pp. 158–162). Rochester, NY: National Reading Conference.

Carroll, J.B., Davies, P., & Richman, B. (1971). *Word frequency book*. New York: American Heritage.

Clark, E.V. (1973). What's in a word? On the child's acquisition of semantics in his first language. In T.E. Moore (Ed.), *Cognitive development and the acquisition of language* (pp. 65–110). New York: Academic Press.

Clark, E.V. (1983). Meanings and concepts. In P.H. Mussen (Ed.), *Handbook of child psychology* (4th ed., Vol. 3, pp. 787–840). New York: Wiley.

Clifford, G.J. (1978). Words for schools: The applications in education of the vocabulary researchers of Edward L. Thorndike. In P. Suppes (Ed.), *Impact of research on education: Some case studies* (pp. 107–198). Washington, DC: National Academy of Education.

Coleman, E.B. (1971). Developing a technology of written instruction: Some determiners of the complexity of prose. In E.Z. Rothkopf & P.E. Johnson (Eds.), *Verbal learning research and the technology of written instruction* (pp. 155–204). New York: Teachers College Press, Columbia University.

Cronbach, L.J. (1942). An analysis of techniques for systematic vocabulary testing. *Journal of Educational Research, 36*, 206–217.

Cronbach, L.J. (1943). Measuring knowledge of precise word meaning. *Journal of Educational Research, 36*, 528–534.

Curtis, M.E. (in press). Vocabulary testing and instruction. In M.G. McKeown & M.E. Curtis (Eds.), *The nature of vocabulary acquisition*. Hillsdale, NJ: Erlbaum.

Dale, E., & O'Rourke, J. (1981). *The living word vocabulary*. Chicago: World Book—Childcraft International.

Dale, E., Razik, T., & Petty, W. (1973). *Bibliography of vocabulary studies*. Columbus: Ohio State University

Davis, F.B. (1944). Fundamental factors in reading comprehension. *Psychometrika, 9*, 185–197.

Davis, F.B. (1968). Research in comprehension in reading. *Reading Research Quarterly, 3*, 499–545.

Deighton, L.C. (1959). *Vocabulary development in the classroom.* New York: Teachers College Press, Columbia University.

Dolch, E.W. (1936). How much word knowledge do children bring to grade 1? *Elementary English Review, 13*, 177–183.

Dolch, E.W., & Leads, D. (1953). Vocabulary tests and depth of meaning. *Journal of Educational Research, 47*, 181–189.

Doran, E.W. (1907). A study of vocabularies. *Pedagogical Seminar, 14*, 177–183.

Draeper, A.G., & Moeller, G.H. (1971). We think with words (therefore, to improve thinking, teach vocabulary). *Phi Delta Kappan, 52*, 482–484.

Drum, P.A. (1983). Vocabulary knowledge. In J.A. Niles & L.A. Harris (Eds.), *Searches for meaning in reading/language processing and instruction* (pp. 163–171). Rochester, NY: National Reading Conference.

Drum, P.A., & Konopak, B.C. (in press). Learning word meanings from written context. In M.G. McKeown & M.E. Curtis (Eds.), *The nature of vocabulary acquisition.* Hillsdale, NJ: Erlbaum.

Duin, A.H., & Graves, M.F. (in press). Effects of vocabulary instruction used as a prewriting technique. *Journal of Research and Development in Education.*

Dupuy, H.P. (1974). *The rationale, development and standardization of a basic word vocabulary test* (DHEW Publication No. HRA 74–1334). Washington, DC: U.S. Government Printing Office.

Durkin, D. (1979–1980). What classroom observations reveal about reading comprehension instruction. *Reading Research Quarterly, 14*, 481–533.

Elvian, J. (1938). Word perception and word meaning in student reading in the intermediate grades. *Education, 59*, 51–56.

Farr, R. (1969). *Reading: What can be measured?* Newark, DE: International Reading Association.

Feifel, H., & Lorge, I. (1950). Qualitative differences in the vocabulary responses of children. *Journal of Educational Psychology, 41*, 1–18.

Fielding, L.G., Wilson, P.T., & Anderson, R.C. (in press). A new focus on free reading: The role of trade books in reading instruction. In T. Raphael & R. Reynolds (Eds.), *Contexts of literacy.* New York: Longman.

Finn, P.J. (1977–1978). Word frequency, information theory, and cloze performance: A transfer theory of processing in reading. *Reading Research Quarterly, 13*, 508–537.

Frayer, D.A., Fredrick, W.C., & Klausmeier, H.J. (1969). *A schema for testing the level of concept mastery* (Working Paper No. 16). Madison: Wisconsin Research and Development Center for Cognitive Learning.

Freebody, P., & Anderson, R.C. (1983a). Effects of vocabulary difficulty, text cohesion, and schema availability on reading comprehension. *Reading Research Quarterly, 18*, 277–305.

Freebody, P., & Anderson, R.C. (1983b). Effects on text comprehension of differing proportions and locations of difficult vocabulary. *Journal of Reading Behavior, 15*, 19–40.

Gipe, J.P. (1979). Investigating techniques for teaching word meanings. *Reading Research Quarterly, 14*, 624–644.

Gipe, J.P. (1981, April). *Investigation of techniques for teaching new words.* Paper presented at the meeting of the American Educational Research Association, Los Angeles.

Gough, P.B. (1984). Word recognition. In P.D. Pearson (Ed.), *Handbook of reading research* (pp. 225–254). New York: Longman.

Graves, M.F. (1980, April). *A quantitative and qualitative study of students' reading vocabularies.* Paper presented at the meeting of the American Educational Research Association, Boston.

Graves, M.F. (1984). Selecting vocabulary to teach in the intermediate and secondary grades. In J. Flood (Ed.), *Promoting reading comprehension* (pp. 245–260). Newark, DE: International Reading Association.

Graves, M.F. (1985). *A word is a word.* New York: Scholastic.

Graves, M.F. (in press). The roles of instruction in fostering vocabulary development. In M.G. McKeown & M.E. Curtis (Eds.). *The nature of vocabulary acquisition.* Hillsdale, NJ: Erlbaum.

Graves, M.F., Brunetti, G.J., & Slater, W.H. (1982). The reading vocabularies of primary grade children of varying geographic and social backgrounds. In J.A. Harris & L.A. Harris (Eds.), *New inquiries in reading research and instruction* (pp. 99–104). Rochester, NY: National Reading Conference.

Graves, M.F., & Duin, A.L. (1985). Building students' expressive vocabularies. *Educational Perspectives, 23* (1), 4–10.

Graves, M.F., & Hammond, H.K. (1980). A validated procedure for teaching prefixes and its effect on students' ability to assign meaning to novel words. In M.L. Kamil & A.V. Moe (Eds.), *Perspectives on reading research and instruction.* Washington, DC: National Reading Conference.

Graves, M.F., & Prenn, M.C. (1986). Costs and benefits of various methods of teaching vocabulary. *Journal of Reading, 29,* 596–602.

Graves, M.F., & Slater, W.H. (in preparation). *The development of reading vocabularies in rural disadvantaged students, inner-city disadvantaged students, and middle-class suburban students.*

Grobe, C. (1981). Syntactic maturity, mechanics, and vocabulary as predictors of quality ratings. *Research in the Teaching of English, 15,* 75–85.

Hafner, L.E. (1965). A one-month experiment in teaching context aids in fifth grade. *Journal of Educational Research, 58,* 471–474.

Harris, A.J., & Jacobson, M.D. (1972). *Basic elementary reading vocabularies.* New York: Macmillan.

Hartman, G.W. (1941). A critique on the common method of estimating vocabulary size, together with some data on the absolute word knowledge of educated adults. *Journal of Educational Psychology, 32,* 351–358.

Hartman, G.W. (1946). Further evidence on the unexpectedly large size of recognition vocabularies among college students. *Journal of Educational Psychology, 37,* 436–439.

Haviland, S.E., & Clark, E.V. (1974). This man's father is my father's son. *Journal of Child Language, 1,* 23–47.

Herman, P.A. (1984, December). *Incidental learning of word meanings from expository texts.* Paper presented at the meeting of the National Reading Conference, St. Petersburg Beach, FL.

Hoffman, J.V. (1980). Studying contextual build-up during reading through cumulative cloze. *Journal of Reading Behavior, 12,* 337–341.

Jackson, J.R., & Dizney, H. (1963). Intensive vocabulary training. *Journal of Developmental Reading, 6,* 221–229.

Jenkins, J.R., & Dixon, R. (1983). Vocabulary learning. *Contemporary Educational Psychology, 8,* 237–260.

Jenkins, J.R., Stein, M., & Wysocki, K. (1984). Learning vocabulary through reading. *American Educational Research Journal, 21,* 767–787.

Jenkins, J.R., & Wysocki, K. (1985). *Deriving word meanings from context.* Unpublished manuscript.

Johnson, D.D., & Baumann, J.F. (1984). Word identification. In P.D. Pearson (Ed.), *Handbook of reading research* (pp. 583–608). New York: Longman.

Johnson, D.D., & Pearson, P.D. (1984). *Teaching reading vocabulary* (2nd ed.). New York: Holt, Rinehart & Winston.

Johnson, D.D., Toms-Bronowski, S., & Pittelman, S.D. (1982). *An investigation of the effectiveness of semantic mapping and semantic feature analysis with intermediate grade level children* (Program Report No. 82–3). Madison: Wisconsin Center for Education Research.

Kameenui, E.J., Carnine, D.W., & Freschi, R. (1982). Effects of text construction and instructional procedures for teaching word meanings on comprehension and recall. *Reading Research Quarterly, 17,* 367–388.

Kaye, D.B., & Sternberg, R.J. (1983). *The development of lexical decomposition ability.* Unpublished manuscript.

Kirkpatrick, E.A. (1891). The number of words in an ordinary vocabulary. *Science, 18,* 107–108.

Kirkpatrick, E.A. (1907). Vocabulary test. *Popular Science Monthly, 70,* 157–164.

Klare, G.R. (1974–1975). Assessing readability. *Reading Research Quarterly, 10,* 62–102.

Klare, G.R. (1984). Readability. In P.D. Pearson (Ed.), *Handbook of reading research* (pp. 681–744). New York: Longman.

Kruglov, L.P. (1953). Qualitative differences in the vocabulary choices of children as revealed in a multiple-choice test. *Journal of Educational Psychology, 44,* 229–243.

Levin, J.R., Johnson, D.D., Pittelman, S.D., Levin, K.M., Shriberg, L.K., Toms-Bronowski, S., & Hayes, B.L. (1984). A comparison of semantic- and mnemonic-based vocabulary-learning strategies. *Reading Psychology, 5,* 1–16.

Lieberman, J.E. (1967). *The effects of direct instruction in vocabulary concepts on reading achievement.* (ERIC Document Reproduction Service No. ED-010-985)

Lorge, I., & Chall, J. (1963). Estimating the size of vocabularies of children and adults: An analysis of methodological issues. *Journal of Experimental Education, 32,* 147–157.

Madison, J., Carroll, B., & Drum, P.A. (1982). The effect of directionality and proximity of context clues on the comprehension of words. In J.A. Niles & L.A. Harris (Eds.), *New inquiries in reading research and instruction* (pp. 105–109). Rochester, NY: National Reading Conference.

Margosein, C.M., Pascarella, E.T., & Pflaum, S.W. (1982, March). *The effects of instruction using semantic mapping on vocabulary and comprehension.* Paper presented at the meeting of the American Educational Research Association, New York.

Marks, C.B., Doctorow, M.J., & Wittrock, M.C. (1974). Word frequency and reading comprehension. *Journal of Educational Research, 67,* 259–262.

McCullough, C. (1943). Learning to use context clues. *Elementary English Review, 20,* 140–143.

McKeown, M.G. (1985). The acquisition of word meaning from context by children of high and low ability. *Reading Research Quarterly, 20,* 482–496.

McKeown, M.G., Beck, I.L., Omanson, R.C., & Perfetti, C.A. (1983). The effects of long-term vocabulary instruction on reading comprehension: A replication. *Journal of Reading Behavior, 15,* 3–18.

McKeown, M.G., Beck, I.L., Omanson, R.C., & Pople, M.T. (1985). Some effects of the nature and frequency of vocabulary instruction on the knowledge and use of words. *Reading Research Quarterly, 20,* 522–535.

Mezynski, K. (1983). Issues concerning the acquisition of knowledge: Effects of vocabulary training on reading comprehension. *Review of Educational Research, 53,* 253–279.

Nagy, W.E. (1985, November). *Vocabulary instruction: Implications of the new research.* Paper presented at the meeting of the National Council of Teachers of English, Philadelphia.

Nagy, W.E., & Anderson, R.C. (1982). *The number of words in printed school English* (Tech. Rep. No. 253). Urbana, IL: University of Illinois, Center for the Study of Reading.

Nagy, W.E., & Anderson, R.C. (1984). How many words are there in printed school English? *Reading Research Quarterly, 19,* 304–330.

Nagy, W.E., Anderson, R.C., & Herman, P.A. (1985). *The influence of some word and text properties on learning from context.* Unpublished manuscript, University of Illinois at Urbana-Champaign, Center for the Study of Reading.

Nagy, W.E., & Herman, P.A. (in press). Depth and breadth of vocabulary knowledge: Implications for acquisition and instruction. In M.G. McKeown & M.E. Curtis (Eds.), *The nature of vocabulary acquisition.* Hillsdale, NJ: Erlbaum.

Nagy, W.E., Herman, P.A., & Anderson, R.C. (1985a). Learning words from context. *Reading Research Quarterly, 20,* 233–253.

Nagy, W.E., Herman, P.A., & Anderson, R.C. (1985b). Learning word meanings from context: How broadly generalizable? Unpublished manuscript, University of Illinois, Center for the Study of Reading.

Neilsen, L., & Piche, G.L. (1981). The influence of headed nominal complexity and lexical choice on teachers' evaluation of writing. *Research in the Teaching of English, 15,* 65–73.

Nicol, J.E. (1980). *Effect of prefix instruction on students' vocabulary size.* Unpublished master's thesis, University of Minnesota.

Nicol, J.E., Graves, M.F., & Slater, W.H. (1984). *Building vocabulary through prefix instruction.* Unpublished manuscript, University of Minnesota.

Nolte, K.F. (1938). Simplification of vocabulary and comprehension in reading. *Elementary English Review, 14,* 119–124, 146.

Ogden, C.K. (1934). *The system of basic English.* New York: Harcourt Brace.

O'Rourke, J.P. (1974). *Toward a science of vocabulary development.* The Hague: Mouton.

Osborn, W.J. (1954). Teaching spelling by teaching syllables and root words. *Elementary School Journal, 55,* 32–41.

Pany, D., & Jenkins, J.R. (1978). Learning word meanings: A comparison of instructional procedures. *Learning Disability Quarterly, 1,* 21–32.

Pany, D., Jenkins, J.R., & Schreck, J. (1982). Vocabulary instruction: Effects on word knowledge and reading comprehension. *Learning Disability Quarterly, 5,* 202–215.

Parker, S.L. (1984). *A comparison of four types of initial vocabulary instruction.* Unpublished master's thesis, University of Minnesota, Minneapolis.

Patberg, J.A., Graves, M.F., & Stibbe, M.A. (1984). Effects of active teaching and practice in facilitating students' use of context clues. In J.A. Niles & L.A. Harris (Eds.), *Changing perspectives on reading/language processing and instruction.* Rochester, NY: National Reading Conference.

Patberg, J.A., & Stibbe, M.A. (1985, December). *The effects of contextual analysis instruction on vocabulary learning*. Paper presented at the meeting of the National Reading Conference, San Diego, CA.

Peters, C. (1974). *A comparison between the Frayer model of concept attainment and the textbook approach to concept attainment*. Madison: Wisconsin Research and Development Center for Cognitive Learning.

Petty, W.T., Herold, C.P., & Stoll, E. (1968). *The state of knowledge about the teaching of vocabulary*. Champaign, IL: National Council of Teachers of English.

Pressley, M., Levin, J.R., & Delaney, H.D. (1983). The mnemonic keyword method. *Review of Educational Research, 52,* 61–91.

Pressley, M., Levin, J.R., & McDaniel, M.A. (in press). Remembering versus inferring what a word means: Mnemonic and contextual approaches. In M.G. McKeown & M.E. Curtis (Eds.), *The nature of vocabulary acquisition*. Hillsdale, NJ: Erlbaum.

Quealy, R.J. (1969). Senior high school students' use of context aids in reading. *Reading Research Quarterly, 4,* 512–532.

Rankin, E.F., & Overholser, B.M. (1969). Reaction of intermediate grade children to contextual clues. *Journal of Reading Behavior, 1,* 50–73.

Rinsland, H.D. (1945). *A basic vocabulary of elementary school children*. New York: Macmillan.

Russell, D.H. (1954). The dimensions of children's meaning vocabulary in grades four through twelve. *University of California Publications in Education, 11,* 315–414.

Russell, D.H., & Saadeh, I.Q. (1962). Qualitative levels in children's vocabularies. *Journal of Educational Psychology, 53,* 170–174.

Ryder, R.J., & Hughes, M. (1985). The effect on test comprehension of word frequency. *Journal of Educational Research, 78,* 286–291.

Seashore, R.H., & Eckerson, L.D. (1940) The measurement of individual differences in general English vocabularies. *Journal of Educational Psychology, 31,* 14–38.

Shefelbine, J.L. (1983, April). *Learning word meanings from context*. Paper presented at the annual meeting of the American Educational Research Association, Montreal.

Shibles, B.H. (1959). How many words does the first grade child know? *Elementary English, 31,* 42–47.

Sims, V.M. (1929). The reliability and validity of four types of vocabulary tests. *Journal of Educational Research, 20,* 91–96.

Slobin, D.I. (1966). Grammatical transformations and sentence comprehension in childhood and adulthood. *Journal of Verbal Learning and Verbal Behavior, 5,* 219–227.

Smith, M.E. (1926). An investigation of the development of the sentence and the extent of vocabulary in young children. *University of Iowa Studies in Child Welfare, 3,* 92.

Smith, M.K. (1941). Measurement of the size of general English vocabulary through the elementary grades and high school. *General Psychological Monographs, 24,* 311–345.

Stahl, S.A. (1983). Differential word knowledge and reading comprehension. *Journal of Reading Behavior, 15* (4), 33–50.

Stahl, S.A., & Fairbanks, M.M. (1986). The effects of vocabulary instruction: A model-based meta-analysis. *Review of Educational Research, 56,* 72–110.

Stauffer, R.G. (1942). A study of prefixes in the Thorndike list to establish a list of prefixes that should be taught in elementary school. *Journal of Educational Research, 35,* 453–458.

Sternberg, R.J. (1985). *The psychology of verbal comprehension*. Unpublished manuscript.

Sternberg, R.J. (in press). Most vocabulary is learned from context. In M.G. McKeown & M.E. Curtis (Eds.), *The nature of vocabulary acquisition*. Hillsdale, NJ: Erlbaum.

Sternberg, R., & Powell, J.S. (1983). Comprehending verbal comprehension. *American Psychologist, 38,* 878–893.

Sternberg, R.J., Powell, J.S., & Kaye, D.B. (1983). Teaching vocabulary building skills: A contextual approach. In A.C. Wilkinson (Ed.), *Classroom computers and cognitive science*. New York: Academic Press.

Stewart, M.F., & Leaman, H.L. (1983). Teachers' writing assessments across the high school curriculum. *Research in the Teaching of English, 17,* 113–114.

Stotsky, S.L. (1983). Research on reading-writing relationships: A synthesis and suggested directions. *Language Arts, 60,* 627–642.

Tanner, L. R. (1976). *Some constraints on the word frequency effect in written discourse*. Minneapolis: University of Minnesota. (ERIC Document Reproduction Service No. ED-140-357)

Terman, L.M. (1916). *The measurement of intelligence*. New York: Houghton Mifflin.

Thompson, E. (1958). The "master word" approach to vocabulary training. *Journal of Developmental Reading, 2,* 62–66,

Thorndike, E.L. (1932). *A teacher's word book of the twenty thousand words found most frequently and widely in general reading for children and young adults*. New York: Bureau of Publications, Teachers College, Columbia University.

Thorndike, E.L. (1941). *The teaching of English suffixes*. New York: Columbia University, Teachers College, Bureau of Publications.

Thorndike, E.L., & Lorge, I. (1944). *The teacher's word book of 30,000 words*. New York: Teachers College Press.

Thurstone, L.L. (1946). A note on a reanalysis of Davis' reading tests. *Psychometrika, 11,* 185–188.

Tuinman, J.J., & Brady, M.E. (1974). How does vocabulary account for variance on reading comprehension tests. In P. Nacke (Ed.), *Twenty-third National Reading Conference Yearbook* (pp. 176–184). Clemson, SC: The National Reading Conference.

van Daalen-Kaptejins, M.M., & Elshout-Mohr, M. (1981). The acquisition of word meaning as a cognitive learning process. *Journal of Verbal Learning and Verbal Behavior, 20,* 386–389.

Werner, H., & Kaplan, E. (1952). The acquisition of word meanings: A developmental study. *Monographs of the Society for Research in Child Development, 15*.

White, T.G., Speidel, G. E., & Power, M. A. (1985). *Morphological analysis: A useful strategy for elementary students?* Unpublished manuscript.

Wittrock, M.C., Marks, C., & Doctorow, M. (1975). Reading as a generative process. *Journal of Educational Psychology, 67,* 484–489.

Wolfe, R.F. (1975). *An examination of the effects of teaching a reading vocabulary upon writing vocabulary in student compositions*. Unpublished doctoral dissertation, University of Maryland, College Park.

Wysocki, K. (1986). *Training students to derive word meanings through morphological generalization*. Unpublished doctoral dissertation, University of Washington.

Wysocki, K., & Jenkins, J.R. (1985). *Deriving word meanings through morphological generalization*. Manuscript submitted for publication.

ADDITIONAL READINGS

This paper was shortened somewhat because of space limitations. The readings below originally served as references in those parts of the paper that have been omitted.

Beck, I.L. (1985, November). *Response to William Nagy's "Vocabulary instruction: Implications of the new research."* Paper presented at the meeting of the National Council of Teachers of English, Philadelphia.

Beck, I.L., & McKeown, M.G. (1983). Learning words well—A program to enhance vocabulary and comprehension. *The Reading Teacher, 36,* 622–625.

Beck, I.L., McKeown, M.G., & Omanson, R.C. (1984, April). *The fertility of some types of vocabulary instruction.* Paper presented at the meeting of the American Educational Research Association, New Orleans.

Carroll, J.B. (1956). Introduction. In J.B. Carroll (Ed.), *Language, thought, and reality* (pp. 1–34). Cambridge, MA: The MIT Press.

Chomsky, N. (1957). *Syntactic structures.* The Hague: Mouton

Clark, H.H., & Clark, E.V. (1978). *Psychology of language.* New York: Harcourt Brace Jovanovich.

Clifford, G.J. (1973). A history of the impact of research on teaching. In R.M.W. Travers (Ed.), *Second handbook of research on teaching* (pp. 1–46). Chicago: Rand McNally.

Jensen, A.R. (1980). *Bias in mental testing.* New York: Free Press.

McKeown, M.G., & Curtis, M.E. (Eds.). (in press). *The nature of vocabulary acquisition.* Hillsdale, NJ: Erlbaum.

Miller, G.A. (1962). Some psychological studies of grammar. *American Psychologist, 17,* 748–762.

Miner, J.B. (1957). *Intelligence in the U.S.* New York: Springer.

Nagy, W.E., & Herman, P.A. (1984, April). *The futility of most types of vocabulary instruction.* Paper presented at the meeting of the American Educational Research Association, New Orleans.

Neisser, U. (1967). *Cognitive psychology.* New York: Appleton-Century-Crofts.

Pearson, P.D. (Ed.). (1984). *Handbook of reading research.* New York: Longman.

Rosenshine, B., & Stevens, R. (1984). Classroom instruction in reading. In P.D. Pearson (Ed.), *Handbook of reading research* (pp. 745–798). New York: Longman.

Sapir, E. (1921). *Language.* New York: Harcourt, Brace & World.

Stotsky, S.L. (1978). Teaching prefixes in the elementary school. *The Elementary School Journal, 78,* 278–283.

Terman, L.M. (1918). Vocabulary test as a measure of intelligence. *Journal of Educational Psychology, 9,* 452–466.

Thorndike, E.L. (1921). *The teacher's word book.* New York: Teachers College.

Whorf, B.L. (1956/1940). Science and linguistics. In J.B. Carroll (Ed.), *Language, thought, and reality* (pp. 207–219). Cambridge, MA: The MIT Press.

Chapter 3

Instructional Approaches to Reading Comprehension

SCOTT G. PARIS
KAREN K. WIXSON
University of Michigan

ANNEMARIE S. PALINCSAR
Michigan State University

Learning to read is a foundation for literacy and a gateway to education. Because it is an important objective for elementary education, the methods and materials used to teach students to read are continuously reevaluated. It is important to recognize that many people with diverse agendas and criteria for evaluation examine reading instruction. Sometimes they reach different conclusions and argue for divergent types of reform. Teachers want pragmatic methods of instruction, researchers want particular skills taught, parents want evidence of high achievement, and publishers want to make a profit. Many voices compete for attention wherever decisions about reading instruction are made.

Why are American educators so concerned with evaluating and reforming reading instruction? Several forces are at work. First, Americans are dissatisfied with their children's academic achievement. National reports (e.g., the National Commission's *Nation at Risk,* 1983), surveys (e.g., National Assessment of Educational Progress, 1981), and international comparisons (e.g., Stevenson, Stigler, Lucker, Lee, Hsu, & Kitamura, 1982) have revealed that many American schoolchildren have not learned to read very well. Second, studies of teachers and current reading materials have revealed that essential skills of reading are often not taught to students (Anderson, Osborn, & Tierney, 1984). Third, research during the past 20 years in reading, cognitive psychology, linguistics, and child development has provided tremen-

The authors express their appreciation to Peter Winograd, John Guthrie, and Ann Brown for their helpful comments on drafts of this paper.

dous insights about children's acquisition of skilled reading. Reading educators want to incorporate these new ideas and techniques in classroom practices. Together, these three concerns have helped to initiate new approaches to teaching reading comprehension.

In this chapter, we consider the progressive reconceptualizations of comprehension instruction in America during the past 80 years. We identify three broad views that have had significant influence on the ways in which reading is defined, taught, and measured. These conceptualizations focus successively on component skills of reading, instructional activities that foster learning, and strategies that promote independent, flexible reading. They do not form neat categories according to past history, practice, or research because they are relatively new approaches. We chose these views as representative examples of fundamental shifts in research and practice.

Although many educators are skeptical about the steady stream of "new" approaches to reading instruction that emerge, our review suggests that recent research is not simply the rediscovery of old ideas. The first section of the chapter traces the history of "skills approaches" to reading because they have influenced the way comprehension has been instructed for 60 years (Venezky, 1984, 1986). In particular, skills are taught in a variety of self-instruction and direct instruction curricula. In the second part of the chapter, we examine research on cognitive activities and language experiences that promote comprehension. Next, we summarize recent research on cognitive and metacognitive strategies involved in comprehension instruction that may offer alternatives to traditional guided reading activities and workbooks. We then note four questions that must be addressed in future research on comprehension instruction: (1) How do materials influence learning and instruction? (2) How should reading proficiency be evaluated? (3) How does motivation influence students who are learning to read? and (4) How does the social context of instruction influence students' learning?

READING SKILLS

The most prevalent method of reading instruction today involves the use of basal reading materials. More than 90% of American classrooms use basal series that are designed to provide instruction on discrete skills for decoding, vocabulary, and comprehension. Most basal reading series include a scope and sequence chart that identifies fundamental comprehension skills such as identifying the main idea, identifying temporal/causal sequences, reading for details, and drawing conclusions. These skills are often arranged in a hierarchy of simple to more complicated skills that extend from single words to sentences to whole texts. The basal readers are designed in such a manner that students move through the skills in successive order. Oftentimes, these skills are the main targets of instruction and assessment. As Pearson (1986) and others have asked, "Where did these skills originate and why have they become the predominant mode of comprehension instruction today?"

The 1925 Agenda

Perhaps increased immigration to America and the events of World War I led to renewed emphasis on education and reading. That may be one reason why the National Society for the Study of Education (NSSE) devoted its *Twenty-fourth Yearbook* (Whipple, 1925) entirely to the subject of reading. The Yearbook Committee, chaired by William S. Gray, argued that the essential objectives of reading instruction needed to be enlarged from previous practice. Three objectives were identified. The first was to provide rich and varied experience through reading. The Yearbook Committee indicated that "wide experience . . . contributes to the development of power to interpret effectively what is read" (p. 10). The second objective was to develop permanent interests and strong motives for reading, and the third objective was to develop desirable attitudes, economical habits, and effective skills.

The Yearbook Committee noted that a complete classification of attitudes, habits, and skills had never been made, but that a sufficient number had been distinguished by research on learning to serve as a guide to teachers. Included among the "habits of intelligent interpretation" listed in the 1925 *Yearbook* were the following: concentrating attention on the content, associating meanings with symbols, anticipating the sequence of ideas, associating ideas together accurately, recalling related experiences, recognizing the important elements of meaning, deriving meanings from context and from pictures. They also noted skills used when reading for particular purposes such as analyzing or selecting meanings (e.g., to select important points and supporting details), associating and organizing meanings (e.g., to grasp the author's organization), evaluating meanings (e.g., to interpret critically), and retaining meanings. One need only examine lists of skills in contemporary instructional programs to understand the impact that the habits presented in the 1925 *Yearbook* have had on reading instruction.

According to Smith's definitive review entitled *American Reading Instruction* (1965), the set of objectives described in the 1925 *Yearbook* was undoubtedly more powerful than any other single influence in shaping reading instruction. "Nearly every course of study and basal textbook in reading published after the *Twenty-fourth Yearbook* was issued, set up these same objectives as the ones which its method and materials were designed to achieve" (p. 203). Smith noted, however, that ideas about the teaching of reading were divided in the decade following the 1925 *Yearbook*. One group believed that children should be given practice on sequential skills carefully planned by an adult. The other group was convinced that learning was best when children were permitted to carry out their own purposes, meeting and solving attendant problems within the context of their own experiences. This approach was known as the related-activities orientation. Those who believed in planned skill development continued to use basal readers. Those who supported the activity theory discarded basal readers and used materials prepared by children themselves, along with a wide variety of other materials that children chose to read as a result of their own interests (Smith, 1965).

Modifying Instruction to Teach Skills, Habits, and Attitudes

Over a decade later, NSSE devoted its *Thirty-sixth Yearbook* to *The Teaching of Reading* (Whipple, 1937). The Yearbook Committee, again headed by Gray, recognized the larger role of reading in society and recommended more emphasis on habits, attitudes, and skills for reading to learn. At the same time that the conceptualization of reading was expanding, a preference for the "systematic approach" to instruction was emerging. Citing research conducted by Gates and his colleagues in 1926, Gray stated, "The advantage of carefully planned procedures in attaining specific types of progress in reading has been demonstrated. For example, investigators have found that a systematic method of teaching beginning reading is more effective in promoting the development of basic reading habits than incidental or opportunistic methods" (1937, p. 15). The move toward more systematic reading instruction was enhanced further when the Yearbook Committee recommended "the use of specific periods for carefully planned guidance in reading throughout the elementary-school, secondary-school, and college periods" (Gray, 1937, p. 19).

In a further effort to improve reading instruction, NSSE published *Reading in the Elementary School* as its *Forty-eighth Yearbook* (Henry, 1949). The subcommittee responsible for the preparation of this yearbook, headed by Arthur I. Gates, continued to expand the conceptualization of reading to other types of cognition and to refine the skills approach to reading instruction.

Reading is not a simple mechanical skill; nor is it a narrow scholastic tool. Properly cultivated, it is essentially a thoughtful process. However, to say that reading is a "thought-getting" process is to give it too restricted a description. It should be developed as a complex organization of patterns of higher mental processes. It can and should embrace all types of thinking, evaluating, judging, imagining, reasoning, and problem-solving. (Gates, 1949, p. 3)

The 1949 *Yearbook* was the first with a chapter devoted solely to the "Development of comprehension and interpretation." The author of this chapter, Durrell, indicated that a balance between the related-activity and reading-skills approaches was desirable. However, he favored the skills approach as the best method for addressing the needs of reading education at that time. He cautioned that "the complexities of the reading processes . . . are such that the slow learner especially will find difficulty in the incidental mastery of many of these skills" (p. 198). Further, he concluded that, "thirty years ago when elementary schools eliminated 70 per cent of the pupils before the end of the eighth grade, careful grading of reading skills was not required. . . . Now that the objective is to teach all pupils, great effort is being made to improve systematic sequences by which constant growth is assured" (p. 204). This supports the view of Resnick and Resnick (1977) that the goal of high levels of literacy for the entire population is a relatively recent development, and one for which adequate instructional procedures are still being developed.

Durrell (1949) indicated that research had not yet shown the "perfect" program for the systematic development of reading comprehension and that the order of difficulty or gradation of steps within skills was not well established. He did, however, propose that the essential skills in comprehension be broken down in the following manner: "skills related to simple comprehension; skills associated with oral and written recall; skills related to higher mental processes in reading; [and] comprehension in speeded reading skills" (Durrell, 1949, p. 200). He also described

the general characteristics of a skills program in reading comprehension as follows:
1. Selection of essential skills to be observed and taught.
2. Analysis of difficulties in these skills.
3. Intensive teaching of those skills through graded exercises in suitable material.
4. A motivation program which shows the child the importance of those skills and enables him to see his progress in them. (Durrell, 1949, p. 200)

Smith (1965) observed that during the period between 1935 and 1950 there was a general "tightening up" of informal procedures for teaching reading and an increased emphasis on systematic reading instruction. She indicated that skills began to receive special attention shortly after the publication of the *Thirty-sixth Yearbook* and that it was during this period that authors of reading programs began providing carefully organized skill charts to indicate the many different skills to be developed. She also noted that "in the last years of this period there was a sharp decrease and finally an omission of articles having to do with reading taught only in connection with projects, units of work and the activity program. Furthermore an examination of all 1948–49 courses of study in reading which were available to the writer advocated systematic instruction with the use of basal readers" (N.B. Smith, 1965, p. 270).

A chapter in NSSE's *Sixty-seventh Yearbook* (Robinson, 1968) entitled "What is reading?: Some current concepts," by Clymer, stressed the need to differentiate clearly among the processes required to read, the skills and abilities used in reading, and the procedures used to teach reading. He also indicated that attention to reading skills was most likely to produce "fruitful" results, and presented skill taxonomies that had been developed by Barrett and Gray-Robinson. Clymer's synthesis of various definitions and models indicated that the following "four relatively separate but major outcomes or goals of the reading programs can be listed:" (1) decoding, (2) grasping the author's meaning (literal interpretation); (3) testing and recombining the author's message with the understanding and background of the reader; and (4) application of ideas and values to decisions and actions, and extension of authors' ideas to new settings (Clymer, 1968, p. 28).

An emphasis on detailed skill taxonomies provided a more specialized curriculum for reading, which created a need for new instructional methods and materials. The principles of behavioral psychology provided a framework for instructional design and led to two general methods, self-instruction and direct instruction, which are reviewed in the next two sections.

Self-Instruction

Programmed instruction dates from 1926 when Pressey first introduced a teaching machine, but the idea did not gain acceptance until Skinner popularized it in 1954. By the 1960s, programmed instruction was an idea that had attracted the attention of many reading educators (see reviews of Austin & Morrison, 1963; Della-Piana & Endo, 1973; Robinson, 1968; Smith, 1965). The methods of programmed instruction are derived from the application of S-R principles to learning and instruction. The hallmark of this approach is individualized self-instruction with immediate feedback to the learner (Lumsdaine, 1960), using materials that break the subject matter into small, discrete, sequential steps (Huus, 1968, Smith, 1965).

A number of specific self-instructional programs were developed during the 1960s including Individualized Prescribed Instruction (IPI), Personalized System of Instruction (PSI), Program for Learning in Accordance with Needs (PLAN), and Individually Guided Education (IGE). These programs are the forerunners of skills-management systems that are in use today either as comprehensive reading programs or as accompaniments to basal reading series. An example of one of the better known objective-based programs of reading instruction is the Wisconsin Design for Reading Skill Development (Otto & Chester, 1976). This program was designed to correspond with the principles of IGE developed by Klausmeier and his colleagues at the Research and Development Center for Cognitive Learning at the University of Wisconsin.

IGE provides a framework for organizing instruction that emphasizes the following components: (1) identify essential skills; (2) state objectives; (3) examine individual skill development; (4) identify and carry out appropriate teaching/learning activities; and (5) evaluate the results. The Wisconsin Design for Reading Skill Development (Design) is "completely in tune with instructional programming and other components of IGE" (Otto & Chester, 1976, p. 20). The components of the Design include: skills and objectives, assessment materials, instructional resources, and management techniques and materials.

The structure of the Design is provided by the outline of reading skills, which is a scope and sequence description of what the developers feel are essential reading skills for the elementary school. The skills are grouped into six main areas: word attack skills, study skills, comprehension skills, self-directed reading skills, interpretive reading skills, and creative reading skills. For each skill in the word attack, study skills, and comprehension areas, there is a behavioral objective that prescribes the behavior necessary to demonstrate mastery of the skill. There are also criterion-referenced tests for pretesting and posttesting each behavioral objective.

The instructional component of the Design consists of individual files containing materials, amassed largely by the teacher, that are appropriate for teaching/learning the criterion behavior prescribed by each objective. The management system consists primarily of guidelines for helping teachers plan their instruction, group the students, organize their schedules, and keep records. Pupil Profile Cards are provided for keeping current records of each pupil's skill development in each skill area.

Advocates of skills-management systems believe that sequentially organized objectives and continuous monitoring of students' skill development enable teachers to focus their instructional efforts on the specific needs of individuals (Otto, Wolf, & Eldridge, 1984). Critics are concerned that the approach is too mechanistic and that fractionating the reading process promotes negative attitudes toward reading (Johnson & Pearson, 1978; Winograd & Greenlee, 1986). One report, by Kamm (1978), examined the results of a 5-year study of the effects of implementing the Design in grades K through 6 in 80 elementary schools. In this study, the reading vocabulary and reading comprehension subtests of a standardized, norm-referenced achievement test (Comprehensive Test of Basic Skills) were administered to fourth- and sixth-grade students at the beginning of the program in 1971–1972 and again in 1976–1977. The results indicated that both the percentage of students scoring above the norm and the median percentile had improved. Kamm (1978) concluded that a skill-centered approach is a practical and viable, if not superior, approach to teaching children how to read. However, the lack of any type of alternative method or control group makes it difficult to determine the superiority of this approach.

Direct Instruction

The term "direct instruction" emerged from the Direct Instruction System of Teaching and Remediation (DISTAR) developed by Becker and Engelmann for disadvantaged students (see Becker & Gersten, 1982) and from numerous studies of teacher effects (Anderson, Evertson, & Brophy, 1979; Berliner & Rosenshine, 1977; Rosenshine, 1979). Direct instruction was originally conceptualized as a set of behavioral principles for instruction. Rosenshine is generally credited with popularizing this orientation. Following an extensive review of the research literature on teacher effects, Rosenshine (1979) identified the variables associated with student academic success as "direct instruction:"

[D]irect instruction refers to high levels of student engagement within academically focused, teacher-directed classrooms using sequenced, structured materials. . . . Direct instruction refers to teaching activities focused on academic matters where goals are clear to students; time allocated for instruction is sufficient and continuous; content coverage is extensive; student performance is monitored; questions are at a low cognitive level and produce many correct responses; and feedback to students is immediate and academically oriented. (p. 38)

Direct instruction interventions often include sequenced steps leading to the targeted skill; instruction of each step with the use of scripts to explain and model them; opportunities for a high rate of student participation with designated error correction procedures; and the gradual fading of teacher support in the monitored practice of the skills. The direct instruction advocated by Rosenshine and Stevens (1984) has three classic characteristics: (1) demonstration, (2) guided practice with feedback, and (3) independent practice with feedback.

A fundamental tenet of direct instruction is to make the skill overt and observable by demonstrating, explaining, and modeling it. In this phase of an instructional episode, teachers characteristically show the students what they are to do and explain the particular skill to them. One important stimulus to the influence of direct instruction on the teaching of reading comprehension was Durkin's (1978–1979) landmark study of classroom instruction. She observed the frequency of teachers' verbal instruction, demonstrations, and modeling about reading comprehension and found that less than 1% of teachers' time was devoted to explicit comprehension instruction. The response to the surprisingly low incidence of direct explanations by teachers was the widespread application of principles of direct instruction to the component skills that were embedded in traditional curricula.

Direct instruction interventions have been used to teach a broad range of comprehension skills. For example, in a study by Adams, Carnine, and Gersten (1982), students were taught six steps to extract and remember information from a content area text: (1) preview the passage by reading all the headings and subheadings; (2) recite the subheadings; (3) ask yourself questions about what might be important to learn; (4) read to find the important details; (5) reread the subheadings and recite important details; and (6) rehearse. Researchers found that instruction on these steps produced significantly higher comprehension test scores compared to students who received only corrective feedback for their answers.

Patching, Kameenui, Carnine, Gersten, and Colvin (1983) used direct instruction to teach fifth-grade students rules to detect false generalization, false causality, and invalid testimonial in critical reading. Baumann (1984) taught fifth-graders the identification of explicit and implicit main ideas and supporting detail information embedded in paragraphs and passages. Working with third-grade students, Baumann (1986) provided direct instruction on a series of anaphoric relations including noun substitutes, verb substitutes, and clause substitutes. Strategy use and answers to comprehension questions were facilitated by direct instruction. Approaches that emphasize direct instruction underscore the importance of feedback and correction following independent practice. Carnine, Kameenui, and Coyle (1984) taught students to use context clues to identify new vocabulary words and found that extended practice and feedback enhanced comprehension. A fundamental strength of direct instruction is the potential to teach complex skills in relatively short periods of time.

Evaluation of Skills Approaches

This brief historical review suggests that the 1925 NSSE *Yearbook* has influenced the instructional agenda in reading for many years (cf., Mason, 1985). With each ensuing decade, skills became more specified and valued, instruction became more systematic and dependent upon basal materials, and learning to read became a process of skill mastery beginning with "lower order" literal comprehension and proceeding to "higher order" thinking. By the mid-1960s, skills-based programs had come to define the goals of reading and reading instruction. As the curriculum narrowed and became more focused on learning to read instead of reading to learn, teachers became managers of basal readers, workbooks, small groups, and directed reading activities. Doyle (1983) has characterized the classroom as a workplace, and indeed the emphasis on reading skills encouraged teachers to become managers of materials, records, and skills, and students to become piece-work laborers.

There are both positive and negative features of skills approaches. Teachers view them as easy to use because they provide highly scripted formats for the content and presentation of instruction. But the ease of use may discourage innovative instructional methods. Skills approaches emphasize accountability by teachers and students for mastery of each skill, but critics argue that they promote excessive testing of decontextualized skills. Skills are presented sequentially, yet there is no adequate model of development or learning that underlies mastery. The listing of skills in scope and sequence charts may promote misconceptions by teachers and students that there is a finite list of skills that can be practiced, mastered, and assessed independent of the context of reading. Although skills approaches include many important cognitive components of reading, there is little emphasis on how students regulate and control their reading of different kinds of texts.

ACTIVITIES THAT AID COMPREHENSION

In contrast to the emphasis on planned sequences of skill instruction, several approaches focus on activities that promote comprehension. These activities range from study techniques, to story writing, to cognitive elaborations during reading. Many different labels have been attached to these approaches, and it may be slightly unfair to group them together. However, we would like to call attention to two approaches to instruction that emphasize the activities in which learners engage rather than the skills that they practice. We discuss briefly the language experience approach as a type of a related-activities orientation to reading, then discuss in detail research on instructional aids for learning.

Language Activities

Interest in language activity approaches grew out of the findings of psycholinguistic research during the 1960s regarding the syntactic, semantic, and phonological levels of language that influence reading. For example, Ruddell (1966) demonstrated that children comprehend text that contains high-frequency syntactic structures more easily than text containing low-frequency structures. Subsequently, Bormuth, Carr, Manning, and Pearson (1970) identified a hierarchy of syntactic relations that influence reading. These and other studies led to a view, popularized by Goodman (1967), that reading is a "psycholinguistic guessing game."

This psycholinguistic view of reading has resulted in several language-based approaches to reading instruction, including the instructional use of the cloze technique (Kennedy & Weener, 1973) and sentence manipulation activities (Weaver, 1979). Perhaps the best-known example of the language activity orientation is the language experience approach. This approach provides students with a variety of experiences such as choral reading, dictated stories, and discussion about predictable sentences in text as means of bridging their existing knowledge of oral language to the acquisition of reading. These activities are not presented in a scripted format or regimented curriculum, but are considered instructional opportunities for children to extend their knowledge about oral language to their knowledge about text.

The common theme in these methods is children's use of oral language as a guide for comprehending text. More recently, there has been an emphasis on the sociolinguistic aspects of communication and how the knowledge of the reader-author relationship influences reading (Harste, 1985). One manifestation of the emphasis on sociolinguistics, communication, and language experience has been greater attention to the connections between reading and writing in the curriculum. For example, journal writing, editing, peer conferences, and publication have all been used to encourage students to express their thoughts in writing. One of the strengths of these activities is that students become more aware of authorship and the characteristics of text that influence their reading and writing. One of the weaknesses of the language activities approach is that it is difficult to characterize or to study in traditional research. Partly as a consequence, there has been relatively little empirical research on the effectiveness of psycholinguistic, sociolinguistic, and language activity approaches to teaching reading comprehension, yet they remain popular with teachers in practice.

Cognitive Activities

A second general category of related activities that mediate comprehension includes cognitive prompts for elaborating text. According to this view, learning is mediated by cognitive activities induced by various instructional aids such as directions, questions, organizers, and supplementary material/activities that are provided to readers. Some of these cognitive prompts can be embedded in text, some are adjunctive aids, and some are directions for deeper processing. In general, the mediational views do not emphasize awareness of self-controlled use of the prompts, only the successful execution of the activities that promote comprehension and learning. We discuss the powerful effects of instructional aids derived from the research of Ausubel, Rothkopf, and Wittrock in the 1960s. A more complete review can be found in McConkie's "Learning from Text" (1977).

Advance Organizers

Ausubel's (1963, 1968) theory of meaningful verbal learning emphasizes the importance of prior knowledge, or the existing cognitive structure, in learning. According to this view, material can only be "learned in relation to a previously learned background of relevant concepts, principles, and information which make possible the emergence of new meanings and enhance their retention" (1968, p. 128). Therefore, Ausubel advocates the deliberate manipulation of the learner's cognitive structures through the use of "advance organizers" as a means of facilitating meaningful learning and retention. Ausubel defines advance organizers as "introductory materials at a high level of generality and inclusiveness presented in advance of the learning material" (1968, p. 131). According to Ausubel, "the principal function of the organizer is to bridge the gap between what the learner already knows and what he needs to know before he can successfully learn the task at hand" (1968, p. 147). The organizer provides "ideational scaffolding" for the assimilation and retention of the ideas that follow in the learning passage.

Numerous studies conducted on advance organizers have produced equivocal findings (see reviews by Hartley & Davies, 1976; Luiten, Ames, & Ackerson, 1980). An educational psychology textbook sums it up this way: "Perhaps the safest conclusion that can be reached is that advance organizers may enhance relevant learning if they are formulated with care and clarity; if students are aware of them, know how to use them, and employ them; if they are provided in limited number; and if they are inserted with discretion so that they do not break the continuity of the material" (Vander Zanden, 1980, p. 201).

Research on advance organizers was supplanted by research on "context effects" and cognitive schemata (Anderson & Pearson, 1984; Rumelhart, 1981). Studies demonstrated, for example, that titles, pictures, and cues about a reading selection influenced the kinds of information to which readers attended and the organization of their recall. Moreover, comprehension is greatly influenced by the prior knowledge that readers have about the topics. In a way, both external prompts and internal knowledge serve as advance organizers for comprehension. Research on instructional aids that promote comprehension has remained popular. For example, research by Graves and his colleagues indicates that story previews and structural organizers foster comprehension by students of differing ages and abilities (Graves & Cooke, 1980; Graves, Cooke, & LaBerge, 1983; Slater, Graves, & Piche, 1985). Although current research on schema-driven comprehension processes may be quite different than early work on advance organizers, it is important to recognize the historical connection.

Prompts for Comprehension

Rothkopf's (1965) work on programmed instruction led him to the conclusion that instructional conditions alter the way readers process text and consequently what they learn. He called these cognitive processes "mathemagenic activities," which means activities that give rise to learning. This led naturally to investigations of the effects of different instructional aids on readers' comprehension of text. Although Rothkopf's primary emphasis has been on understanding cognitive processes, he also believes that "the concept of mathemagenic activities suggests a general strategy for approaching the scientific management of instruction" (1970, p. 334). Specifically, he emphasizes identification of instructional aids that promote cognitive activities in students that enable them to achieve instructional goals with available materials.

The instructional aid that has been studied most frequently is adjunct questions (see reviews by Anderson & Biddle, 1975; Andre, 1979; Rickards, 1979). According to Rothkopf (1982), adjunct questions have at least two demonstrable effects on learning from text. First, there is a direct effect that strengthens recall specifically related to the subject of the question. Second, questions may modify mathemagenic activities, and thereby influence the learning of a broad range of information contained in text. The usefulness of adjunctive questions depends on the appropriateness of the mental activities that they elicit. Because questions that accompany text are important instructional aids, they have continued to be investigated (Friedman & Rickards, 1981; Memory, 1983; Reynolds, Standiford, & Anderson, 1979; Wixson, 1983, 1984).

Generative Learning

Ausubel recognized the importance of prior knowledge in comprehension and learning, and Rothkopf recognized the active role of readers in their own learning. Wittrock (1974) proposed a generative model of learning in which "learning is a function of the abstract and distinctive, concrete associations which the learner generates between his prior experience, as it is stored in long-term memory, and the stimuli" (1974, p. 89). Wittrock has observed that "effective instruction does not teach, in the usual sense of the word. Instead, it facilitates the learners' ability to construct meaning from experience" (1978, p. 15). Instruction involves the stimulation of relations between text and mental schemata by inducing readers' elaborations of the information. The learner is responsible for attending to the instruction and for active construction of new ideas. The teacher is responsible for designing and conducting the activities and interactions that facilitate the active construction of mental elaborations.

Research on Wittrock's model has shown that generative activities foster comprehension and fact retention (Doctorow, Wittrock, & Marks, 1978; Marks, Doctorow, & Wittrock, 1974; Wittrock, Marks, & Doctorow, 1975). Linden and Wittrock (1981) demonstrated that fifth-grade students increase their reading comprehension of text when they generate text-relevant images, illustrations, analogies, metaphors, or summary sentences as they read. Instruction to use these cognitive mediators was provided by classroom teachers, and included a procedure for recording the number and quality of students' responses during instruction. These records insured that the teachers actually induced the generative activities among students. This study showed that those students who engaged in the generative activities while reading comprehended better. Generative learning activities have been incorporated in the lesson frameworks used to teach basal stories. Beck, Omanson, and McKeown (1982) have shown that a variety of lesson activities can prompt more elaborative processing of text.

Evaluation of Activities That Aid Comprehension

New agendas for comprehension instruction were established in part by research demonstrations of the importance of advance organizers, adjunctive questions, and other instructional aids that promote students' thinking while reading. Although this research identified many activities that promote comprehension, there are a number of limitations that need to be mentioned. First, the list of cognitive and language activities that influence comprehension is rarely guided by conceptual analyses of text or developmental theories of the learner. A second problem is that most of these activities have been designed to facilitate learning of the content rather than learning the activities as self-controlled tactics that students can use. This may be one reason for the limited generalization found in instructional research on these activities (Brown, Bransford, Ferrara, & Campione, 1983). A third problem is that research on cognitive activities does not provide prescriptions for instruction. We are not told how to present or arrange text so that these activities are meaningful and internalized by students rather than followed blindly. Indeed, Brown, Campione, and Day (1981) have characterized these kinds of training studies as "blind training" because learners are not informed about the usefulness of the particular activities that they were instructed to use while reading. These limitations led researchers to focus on more detailed explanations about comprehension strategies so that students become more aware of the actions that foster understanding.

STRATEGIES FOR COMPREHENSION

Neither the skills nor the activities approach emphasizes understanding of the means readers use to achieve comprehension. Because skills and activities are embedded in worksheets, language experiences, and instructional activities such as question answering, students may not recognize the need to use and generalize these tactics when reading. Several lines of instruction have been devised to make readers more aware of their own strategies and to develop greater self-control while reading. For example, direct instruction, while originally devised in line with behavioral principles, has been expanded to include many cognitive and metacognitive strategies for monitoring meaning. Recent instructional studies have merged aspects of direct instruction, direct explanation, metacognition, and strategy training, so that students can become informed explicitly about the procedures that they use to interact with text.

The term "metacognition" was coined in the 1970s to refer to learners' increased cognitive awareness and self-regulation that often accompany skilled performance (Brown, 1978; Flavell, 1978). The construct is important for reading because it calls attention to students' understanding of reading purposes, tasks, and strategies. For example, research has shown that beginning readers often do not understand many conventions of print (Johns, 1980) or strategies that aid comprehension (Myers & Paris, 1978). Beginning and poor readers often do not monitor their understanding and adjust their reading accordingly (Baker & Brown, 1984). This lack of awareness and executive cognitive skills for self-management offers a plausible explanation for why less skilled readers do not use comprehension strategies spontaneously (Golinkoff, 1975–1976; Paris & Lindauer, 1982). The implication for instruction is to teach better awareness and self-regulation.

In addition to the previously described "blind training" procedures, Brown, Campione, and Day (1983) identified two approaches to strategy training. The first is labeled "informed training" because students are "both induced to use a strategy and also given some information concerning the significance of that activity" (p. 15). For example, students may be given practice and informed about the utility of a particular strategy. The second type of instruction is "self-control training" where students are explicitly instructed how to monitor and self-regulate their use of a strategy. We can see a general correspondence between these types of training and paradigms for comprehension instruction. Self-instruction and activities approaches are essentially blind-training procedures, and direct instruction approaches reflect informed training. Recent procedures for teaching students metacognitive aspects of reading reflect informed, self-control training (Brown & Palincsar, 1982).

Informed Strategy Instruction

Informed strategy training emerged in part from research on the development of memory strategies. Traditional "blind training" failed to establish enduring strategies that children transferred to other tasks (Brown, Bransford, Ferrara, & Campione, 1983). As a consequence, researchers developed instructional techniques that were more persuasive. For example, Paris, Newman, and McVey (1982) showed that first-graders who were informed about the usefulness of memory strategies maintained the strategies without prompting more often than children simply directed to use the strategies. Informed training also led to increased recall and increased metacognition about the strategies. Thus, children's understanding about the benefits of strategic learning can provide a personal rationale for action that motivates continued use of the effective strategies.

Two lines of research support informed strategy instruction for reading comprehension. One line shows that students can gain a richer appreciation of strategies when they are provided with explanations about the uses and benefits of particular strategies. A second body of research reveals that effective teachers explain metacognitive aspects of strategies directly to students. In subsequent sections, it will become evident that these lines of research have contributed to several approaches to comprehension instruction.

Hansen (1981) examined the effects of three different instructional interventions on students' ability to answer inferential comprehension questions. In the first condition, students received a traditional "diet" of literal (80%) and inferential (20%) questions along with "ordinary" story introductions. The second treatment was a "practice-only" treatment in which students received only inferential questions following their stories along with the "ordinary" story introductions. The third treatment included "strategy training" in which students received the traditional assortment of questions; however, prior to reading, they were asked to use their own experiences to predict and evaluate story characters' problems and actions. This final treatment represented an attempt to help students become aware of the "known to new" principle, and to allow them to apply this principle to their reading. The results of this study indicated that both the practice only and the strategy training group demonstrated improved performance on four different measures of comprehension including a standardized achievement test. In a subsequent study, Hansen and Pearson (1983) combined the practice only and strategy training interventions into a single treatment and trained classroom teachers to administer the treatments. The results of this study indicated that the informed strategy training was most effective for poor readers.

In another example of informed strategy training, Raphael and her colleagues conducted a series of studies to inform students about the information sources that are available for seeking correct answers to different kinds of questions. Raphael and Pearson (1985) designed an instructional sequence based on (1) modeling, (2) guided practice, (3) independent practice, and (4) direct feedback. Students were taught to identify different types of questions based on the source of information required for a correct answer. The results indicated that trained students were better than students in the untrained control group at discriminating questions of different types, evaluating their own question-answering behavior, and giving high-quality responses. Subsequent investigations by Raphael and McKinney (1983) and Raphael and Wonnacott (1985) have also shown the benefits of informed strategy training as a method of promoting comprehension.

The other line of research that has contributed to the emergence of informed strategy instruction is research on teachers' explanations. Duffy and his associates (in press) have identified four important characteristics of teachers' explanations. First, explanations provide information to students that is useful for particular tasks. Second, effective classroom teachers cultivate high levels of metacognitive awareness among their students. Third, with regard to reading strategies, good teachers explain what they are, how they operate, and when and why they are effective—categories of metacognition referred to as declarative, procedural, and conditional knowledge (Paris, Lipson, & Wixson, 1983). This information is presented conceptually and within a meaningful framework for students. Fourth, effective explainers are sensitive to their students' level of understanding. Duffy and his colleagues observed that information should be provided gradually and organized sequentially to help students restructure their understanding.

The value of informed instruction and direct explanation is that students learn about the explicit characteristics of the comprehension strategies that they are supposed to use. The underlying assumptions are that many children do not induce comprehension strategies themselves, and that direct explication can facilitate their learning and make instructional episodes more meaningful (Brown, Armbruster, & Baker, 1984; Winograd & Hare, in press). Because students' thinking is guided by the quality of teachers' information, well-structured and informative explanations help students to engage reading tasks in a productive manner.

Self-Control Training

Self-control training procedures instruct students explicitly how to monitor and evaluate their performance. Short and Ryan (1984) designed an instructional intervention to promote comprehension by poor readers. They provided students with self-control training regarding story schemata so that students would ask themselves five questions as they read: (1) Who is the main character? (2) Where and when did the story take place? (3) What did the main character do? (4) How did the story end? and (5) How did the main character feel? Instruction was not designed to provide knowledge about the questions, just the strong encouragement to ask these questions while reading. This plan was compared to an attribution condition in which students recited to themselves positive statements such as "Enjoy the story," "Try hard," and "Give yourself a pat on the back." Skilled and less-skilled fourth-grade readers were assigned to one of these groups or to a group that received both kinds of metacognitive training. Short and Ryan (1984) found that strategy training on story grammar questions enhanced comprehension significantly and that self-encouraging statements had no impact on comprehension. Although less-skilled readers maintained the strategy of asking wh- questions, there was no evidence of increased awareness about reading or generalization of the strategy. This study confirms two limitations of self-control training; first, instruction does not increase students' understanding about the strategy, only the frequency of use; and second, students do not generalize the strategy beyond the context of training.

Interventions that combine informed strategy and self-control training procedures appear more likely to result in transfer of training to appropriate settings. This type of intervention is exemplified by the work of Day (1980; Brown & Day, 1983). Day trained groups of junior college students of average and poor reading and writing ability to use basic rules of summarization that were derived from the work of Kintsch and van Dijk (1978): delete trivia and redundancy, identify superordinates of examplars of a concept, and select or invent topic sentences. There were four conditions to which the students were assigned. In the *self-management* condition, students received only the most general guidelines that summaries are completed by including main idea information and exercising economy with words. In the *rules* condition, students were taught the definition of a summary and the rules for completing a summary outlined above. Students in a *rules + self-management* condition received the same instruction as those in groups one and two but were not provided information on how to integrate these rules. Finally, a fourth group received the rule and self-management instruction and also received explicit directions regarding when to use each of the rules and how to evaluate the effectiveness of implementing the rules. The researchers measured performance on written summaries according to the use of the summarization rules. The data indicated that the *rules + self-management* training was necessary at least for those students who had no identified learning problems in order to implement successfully the summarization rules. For students with learning problems the most explicit of the conditions was necessary to enhance their summarization skills.

Day's (1980) study signaled the need to employ informed self-control training procedures in the instruction of sophisticated cognitive skills (such as the invention of topic sentences), particularly when working with students who have a history of academic difficulty. The essential findings of Day's study were replicated by Kurtz and Borkowski (1985) in their investigation with middle-school students. Using comparable treatment groups, they taught the same summarization skills. The control students wrote summaries on the experimental material. The *strategy* group received instruction in the use of superordinates, the identification of main idea information, and the invention of topic sentences. Students in an *executive* condition received the summarization instruction along with instruction on the value of self-monitoring while reading, the importance of selecting and evaluating strategies to enhance comprehension, and the need to work slowly. The results indicated that students in the two instructional conditions performed better than students in the control group, with students in the executive condition performing better than students in the strategy group.

A Metacognitive Curriculum

The blend of direct instruction, informed training, and metacognitive self-management is exemplified in an experimental curriculum for reading comprehension called Informed Strategies for Learning, or ISL (Paris, Cross, & Lipson, 1984). ISL was designed to teach children directly about what strategies are, how they operate, when they should be applied, and why they foster comprehension. The purpose was to promote children's metacognition about reading strategies which, in turn, would promote their strategic reading and comprehension. But in order to provide a metacognitive curriculum, it was necessary to design instructional methods and materials that would make cognitive strategies tangible and meaningful for 8- to 10-year-olds.

Two of the key features of ISL were the use of metaphors to teach strategies and the use of group discussions. For example, students and teachers discussed how they could be "reading detectives" and how they should "plan their reading trips." These analogies were easily understood by children, and they could elaborate metaphorical relations such as "clues to meaning" or "road signs for reading." The metaphors provided concrete examples of cognitive strategies that could be used before, during, and after reading. In addition, the metaphors stimulated group discussions about thinking; they provided shared insights into children's understanding of reading and thinking for both teachers and peers. It is also important to recognize that the metaphors provided children with a convenient jargon with which to talk about reading strategies and thinking.

The instructional techniques resemble cognitive coaching (Paris, 1986) and include: (1) informing students about particular strategies; (2) using metaphors and visual displays to illustrate concrete analogs of reading strategies; (3) discussing strategies explicitly among the entire class; (4) practicing the strategies immediately and receiving feedback; and (5) using reading selections from various content areas (science and social studies) to promote generalization of strategy use across the curriculum. The strategies addressed three generic comprehension processes: constructing text meaning (e.g., through elaboration, activating relevant background knowledge, and summarizing), monitoring comprehension (e.g., through rereading and self-questioning), and identifying meaning (e.g., inferences and main ideas). The strategies were arranged sequentially and organized in whole-group lesson plans.

In the first study, two third- and two fifth-grade classrooms were taught ISL lessons twice each week for 4 months. Compared to children in control classrooms, children who received metacognitive instruction about reading increased their awareness about comprehension strategies significantly (Paris & Jacobs, 1984). They also exhibited significant advantages on cloze and error detection tasks that required strategic reading, but there were no differences on standardized reading comprehension tests (Paris, Cross, & Lipson, 1984). In a subsequent study, 50 regular classroom teachers taught 20 ISL modules (three half-hour lessons in each module) to nearly 800 third- and 800 fifth-grade students. Again, there were significant improvements in reading awareness and the use of strategies among students in experimental classrooms (Paris et al., 1984; Paris & Oka, 1986). These studies show that principles of cognitive strategies and self-regulation fostered by metacognition can be translated directly into practical classroom instruction that helps students to read better.

Scaffolded Instruction

Considerable attention has been focused recently on the role of scaffolding in cognitive strategy instruction. Scaffolding has been described as instructional assistance that enables someone to solve a problem, carry out a task, or achieve a goal that the person could not accomplish alone (Wood, Bruner, & Ross, 1976). The metaphor of a scaffold calls attention to a support system that is both temporary and adjustable. Central to the notion of scaffolded instruction is Vygotsky's zone of proximal development, "the distance between the actual developmental level as determined by independent problem solving and the level of potential development as determined through problem solving under adult guidance, in collaboration with more capable peers" (Vygotsky, 1978, p. 86). From this point of view, the instructional problem is to choose the best way in which teachers can assist students to move from one level of competence to the next so that, in time, students will be able to apply problem-solving strategies independently and judiciously.

Prescriptions for scaffolded instruction have attended to every facet of instruction from the wise selection of learning tasks to carefully organized practice (Brown & Palincsar, in press). But the hallmark of scaffolded instruction is the interplay between teachers and students in the joint completion of a task. An intervention that reflects the essence of scaffolded instruction is the procedure developed by Palincsar and Brown (1984) to teach poor comprehenders how to enhance and monitor their understanding of text. The procedure, called "reciprocal teaching," is best represented as a dialog between teachers and students as they take turns assuming the role of the teacher. The purpose of the dialog is to arrive at an understanding of the text being read. The dialog is facilitated by the use of four strategies: (1) predicting, or activating relevant background knowledge for the purpose of hypothesizing what the author will discuss; (2) question generating, or identifying key content, framing that information in a question, and self-testing for understanding and recall; (3) clarifying, or noting when there has been a failure to comprehend, identifying the source of the breakdown, and taking the appropriate steps to restore meaning; and (4) summarizing, integrating information across sentences, paragraphs, and pages of text. The person who is assuming the role of teacher for a segment of text gives predictions about what might occur next and, following the reading of the text, generates a question to which the others in the group respond, notes or solicits points to be clarified, and summarizes that portion of text. Other members participating in the discussion comment and elaborate upon the teacher's contributions.

Five years of research have been conducted to evaluate reciprocal teaching, investigate its implementation across a variety of school contexts, extend its use as a form of listening comprehension instruction with nonreaders, and analyze its instructional components. In each series of studies, numerous measures have been used to assess changes in the quality of the dialog, students' responses to criterion-referenced measures of comprehension, scores on standardized achievement measures, performance on training tasks, and maintenance of gains, as well as generalization of improvement to content-area classrooms. Although the size of the instructional effect has been influenced by the number and heterogeneity of students in the groups in which the instruction has occurred, reciprocal teaching has been a robust intervention that promotes significant changes in comprehension and comprehension-monitoring of students (Brown & Palincsar, in press; Palincsar & Brown, 1984, in press).

A component analysis of reciprocal teaching was designed to vary the opportunity for scaffolded instruction (Brown & Palincsar, in press). Four instructional conditions were compared: (1) a traditional reciprocal teaching intervention; (2) a condition in which students received traditional instruction for four days and then proceeded to practice by writing their summaries, questions, clarifications, and predictions while receiving minimal feedback from the teacher; (3) a demonstration condition in which the teacher demonstrated the use of each strategy in the context of reading but provided minimal feedback and instruction; and (4) a condition in which the students were given worksheet activities regarding the four strategies. These worksheets were constructed using a shaping procedure to introduce and instruct the four strategies.

The instruction, conducted with junior high students in developmental reading classes, was implemented by the same teacher/researcher for a period of 12 days in groups of four students each, with a total of three replications for each instructional condition. The results, determined by transfer measures of strategy use as well as criterion-referenced measures of comprehension, indicated that the most effective intervention was the traditional reciprocal teaching intervention. Students in this group showed significant gains over students in the reciprocal teaching/independent writing group and the worksheet instruction group. Making no gains and, in fact, plummeting in performance, were those students who received only the demonstration. This investigation suggests that the scaffolded nature of reciprocal teaching is important for learning the strategies and using instructional time effectively.

Evaluation of Strategies for Comprehension

There is some dissension about the importance of teaching students about comprehension strategies as they learn to read. Tierney and Cunningham (1984) use a gardening metaphor to argue that students should not be taught to use gardening tools but rather that the growth of vegetables is the primary objective. In other words, good comprehension is more important than understanding how to use mental tools. Singer (1985) uses a different metaphor in discussing an explicit metacognitive instructional model. He says, "I wonder if attainment of metacognitive objectives is necessary and whether such attainment might actually interfere with reading acquisition. Analogous to learning to drive a car, we are interested in teaching students how to drive, not how and why the car works. In short, we have to determine whether metacognitive explicitness facilitates, interferes, or is irrelevant to reading acquisition and performance" (p. 411). In contrast, many researchers (e.g., Brown, 1980) argue that students' awareness about language, cognitive strategies, and the processes of reading are crucial to learning to read more effectively (see Downing & Valtin, 1984; Forrest-Pressley, MacKinnon, & Waller, 1985).

A variety of instructional approaches emphasize the value of teaching students about comprehension strategies directly. Although there are differences among these approaches in names and emphases, they share many features of metacognitive explanations. The positive features of strategy instruction include:

- Explicit demonstration, modeling, and explanation about comprehension strategies,
- Informing students directly of the cognitive and motivational characteristics of strategic reading,

- Teaching students to internalize strategies and to transfer them to appropriate tasks,
- Providing teachers with materials and methods to promote comprehension strategies that are frequently missing in basal reading series, and
- Teaching students to use strategies selectively for self-controlled learning rather than acquiring isolated reading tactics.

But critics point out several shortcomings:

- Strategies and metacognition can be taught in regimented ways with worksheets, and then they begin to look like skill hierarchies rather than strategic reading,
- Metacognition, or awareness, may not account for much of the variance in children's reading and should not overshadow reading performance goals,
- Metacognition varies in importance across age and reading skill, and the prescriptions for instruction will vary accordingly, and
- Instruction on metacognition and strategies requires a knowledgeable teacher and oftentimes innovative instructional formats that may tax teachers' time, resources, and creativity.

In retrospect, the emphasis on cognitive strategies for reading and learning has been a driving force in educational research for the past 15 years. Part of the appeal has been the translation of reading skills into explicit strategies that students can be taught directly. Strategies for locating main ideas, making inferences, answering questions, summarizing, paraphrasing, and monitoring comprehension enhance children's reading and can be presented in a variety of instructional formats. Indeed, the rapid proliferation of techniques for teaching reading strategies has led to eclectic methods that often combine features of informed, self-control, metacognitive, and scaffolded instruction. Proficient use of cognitive strategies is certainly not the only aim of reading instruction, and we should be cautious not to repeat the errors of narrow skills approaches. But the new emphases on strategies that promote comprehension have stimulated the creation of new teaching techniques that are noteworthy alternatives to traditional instruction.

DYNAMICS OF COMPREHENSION INSTRUCTION

Progressive reconceptualizations of reading have expanded our knowledge about comprehension instruction. These new ideas have been translated into a variety of materials and methods. Adjunctive reading programs, as well as basal reading materials, are beginning to incorporate ideas about reading schemata, direct explanations of skills, and flexible reading strategies. We describe some of the ways that research can influence classroom practices in the future by addressing four fundamental instructional issues for reading comprehension: (1) How do materials influence learning and instruction? (2) How should reading proficiency be evaluated? (3) How does motivation influence students who are learning to read? and (4) How does the social context of instruction affect students' learning?

Commercial Materials for Instruction

Since 1925, American schoolteachers have relied increasingly on published materials and basal reading series for their instructional programs. Indeed, many authors argue that the basal readers and accompanying workbooks define reading instruction in most classrooms today. Shannon (1983) demonstrated that teachers believe that commercial reading materials are organized to teach reading and therefore they view instruction as a process of administering the materials. The overreliance on published materials has many dangers. First, instruction is based on materials that may remove responsibility from the teacher for explicating the social and cognitive aspects of reading to their students. Durkin (1978–1979) observed that teachers do not supplement basal materials with explicit instruction about comprehension skills and strategies. She further examined basal reading materials in teachers' manuals (Durkin, 1984) and found that the information about comprehension was not included in those materials, and thus teachers remained uninformed. The consequence is that teachers do not provide much information about comprehension skills that students are expected to master. A second consequence of the reliance on basals is that teachers often assume that workbook exercises are beneficial to students. However, the amount of time spent on skill sheets and workbook activities has been found to be unrelated to achievement gains in reading in at least one study (Leinhardt, Zigmond, & Cooley, 1981).

Critical evaluations of commercial reading programs reveal other features that hamper students' reading comprehension. Bruce (1984) compared stories in basal readers with those in trade books and determined that the basal reader stories were more difficult and less interesting because their plots offered less intrigue, the characters were less well-defined, and the goals and motives were unclear. Pictures used in basal readers and the prior knowledge assumed on the part of the students may also be problematic in basal readers. Finally, there is a body of literature (cf., Davison & Kantor, 1982) that describes problems engendered by the use of readability guidelines such as the use of simpler but less informative vocabulary and the use of shorter but less explicit sentences. The conclusion of these studies is that commercial materials must be improved in order to facilitate students' reading and teachers' instruction.

Recent research by textbook publishers, writers, and reading educators has begun to articulate specific ways to improve the quality of commercial materials (Osborn, Wilson, & Anderson, 1985). For example, Brennan, Bridge, and Winograd (1986) observed that second-grade students who read basal stories rewritten to conform with the organizational rules of story grammar recalled significantly more of the explicit information in correct sequence and with fewer errors. Text coherence, as well as text structure, can influence comprehension. Beck, McKeown, Omanson, and Pople (1984) improved the coherence of basal stories by making connections within the text more apparent, by filling potential knowledge gaps, and by organizing text events. Although these revisions increased the difficulty of the texts as defined by readability formulas, the changes enhanced comprehension and memory for third graders. Similarly, Baumann (1986) found that fifth-graders' ability to generate main ideas was enhanced by rewriting selections from science textbooks so that the main ideas were stated explicitly and cued by italics and headings.

Assessing Comprehension

Reading tests are administered to millions of students every year in order to make decisions regarding curriculum, policy, student placement, program evaluation, and diagnosis of individual student performance. But according to Farr and Carey (1986), reading tests have not changed significantly in the past 50 years. Progress in classroom instruction of comprehension depends upon the design and use of comprehension measures that accurately reflect current knowledge about reading. Furthermore, tests must be used appropriately for the particular pruposes for which they are designed.

The widespread use of standardized reading tests rests on assumptions about the normal distribution of component skills and the usefulness of psychometric instruments for identifying students who do not "have" the skills (Messick, 1984). In some studies, we have found that reading comprehension scores on a popular norm-referenced test (the Gates-MacGinitie test) correlate above $r = .70$ with measures of cognitive abilities (Paris, Cross, & Lipson, 1984; Paris & Oka, 1986). It is evident that many reading tests measure a variety of intellectual skills, only some of which are taught as part of a reading curriculum.

Johnston (1984) and others have challenged the assumptions underlying traditional reading tests by noting that these tests do not consider students' knowledge about the topics, they do not permit the use of many elaborate strategies because of the time constraints and question format, and they place a high premium on vocabulary, rapid decoding, and memory. Langer (1985) recently investigated children's responses to standardized multiple-choice questions using a procedure that measured how readers envision the text as they read and how these envisionments change while reading. She states, "If one views reading as a process during which meaning develops and grows as readers progress through a passage, then comprehension assessment needs to be rooted in the growing understanding of what the entire passage is about" (Langer, 1985, p. 587). Prominent among the efforts to develop theory-based assessments of comprehension is the work on the statewide reading tests in Michigan. The tests that are being developed for this project include longer texts that are representative of the various types of materials students read in school at different grade levels. In addition, the test items measure factors that are known to influence comprehension including readers' prior knowledge. metacognitive knowledge, and their attitudes and self-perceptions (Wixson & Peters, in press).

An important area for research is the development of alternative approaches to assessment that are consistent with the different purposes for which reading measures are used. Recent reviews of current practices in reading assessment underscore the importance of the match between the types of assessment that are used and the educational decisions that are to be made (Cross & Paris, in press; Farr & Carey, 1986; Guthrie & Lissitz, 1985). Guthrie and Lissitz (1985) identify three different types of educational decisions for which reading assessment is used: classification of students, program accountability, and instructional process. They indicate that tests that are best suited for one type of decision making in reading may not be well suited for other purposes. For example, the use of norm-referenced achievement tests to evaluate a teacher's effectiveness is misguided because the tests do not measure what teachers say and do in their classrooms. The presumption that a teacher's effectiveness can be determined by these test scores is unfounded, especially given the strong relation between students' scores on standardized achievement tests, IQ scores, and background characteristics.

There is a pressing need for research that examines alternative approaches to the assessment of comprehension that are better suited to the goal of instructional decision making. Guthrie and Lissitz (1985) argue that teachers' decision making is done "on line" as part of dynamic instruction and therefore is likely to be improved with informal, individualized, and curriculum-referenced measures. These measures provide detailed descriptions of how students read and evaluations of instruction that promotes effective learning. Wixson and Lipson (1986) discuss how a variety of informal techniques such as interviews, informal reading inventories, verbal reports, and diagnostic teaching can help teachers make instructional decisions. It is clear that measures of strategic, resourceful, self-managed reading for different purposes across a variety of text genres need to be developed as companions to new instructional approaches.

Farr and Carey (1986) provide a useful summary of the status of comprehension assessment in the form of recommendations for future research in this area. Specifically, they indicate a need for the following: an increased emphasis on analyses of existing instruments; research that analyzes written materials; a comprehensive survey of test use and misuse; assessment strategies to measure emerging models of reading comprehension; a better understanding of the potential and limitations of criterion-referenced measures; an understanding of the full potential of informal assessment; a greater appreciation of reading as a form of communication; and consideration of emerging technologies.

Unmotivated Readers

Many children who experience difficulty learning to read are characterized as unmotivated. But they do not lack energy or incentives in general; they often have specific thoughts and feelings that prevent them from expending persistent and effective effort while reading. Johnston and Winograd (1985) refer to this problem as "passive failure," which is a profile reflecting cognitive, motivational, and affective deficits. Students suffering from passive failure are unaware of their own abilities and strategies; they often attribute failure to their perceived inabilities, while they attribute success to luck or other people; they have low expectations for successful reading, low self-esteem, apathy, and depressed affect. Johnston and Winograd (1985) say that the "key factor underlying the characteristics of passive failure seems to be the perception that responses and outcomes are independent" (p. 283). This notion is partly self-protective because students do not blame themselves for poor performance, but neither do they take credit or responsibility for successful achievements.

According to Covington (1983), students face a double-edged sword when they try to balance attributions to effort and ability. To try hard and fail confirms one's limitations, whereas half-hearted effort allows students to claim that they could have achieved more if they had tried harder. Students who often experience failure may therefore expend less and less effort, which can lead to cycles of failure typical of "learned helpless" behavior (Dweck & Bempechat, 1983.) For children who have difficulty learning to read, negative attributions about the task, teacher, or one's own abilities can have devastating consequences.

One study that exemplifies the impact of motivation on learning was conducted by Butkowsky and Willows (1980). They compared good and poor fourth-grade readers on a learning task in which difficulty and frustration were manipulated. They found that the poor readers had low expectations for success and persisted in the face of failure less strongly than good readers. Apparently, the poor readers had developed an attitude of "learned helplessness" in which minimal effort was expended and minimal success was expected. In contrast, good readers tried harder and longer to solve a new task and maintained their positive self-regard and high expectations in the face of failure. These motivational differences are important for continued efforts to learn to read.

Paris and Oka (1986) analyzed individual differences among students in the ISL project. Information about students' achievement in reading, cognitive abilities, and a variety of self-perception measures provided profiles of individual differences. For example, children were identified who read better than would be expected on the basis of their cognitive ability scores and lower than expected given their aptitude scores. These groups were labeled, respectively, overachievers and underachievers. These groups differed significantly in their reading achievement scores as measured by Gates-MacGinitie tests, but their profiles of test scores were similar in terms of awareness about reading and use of strategies. Yet the groups differed widely on motivational measures. Overachievers had much more positive attitudes toward reading than underachievers. They also had more optimistic views of their own cognitive abilities and more intrinsic motivation. In general, they regarded reading as a positive event, themselves as capable readers, and the source of learning to read as internal motivation. Children with the same cognitive abilities, but significantly worse reading skills, were more pessimistic about themselves, viewed reading as less enjoyable, and regarded learning to read as extrinsically controlled.

Negative attitudes about reading and one's own abilities can lead to active avoidance of reading as well as passive helplessness. These debilitating beliefs about low ability and the futility of trying hard are partly due to students and partly due to teachers. Self-deprecation, negative attitudes, and anxiety have origins in developmental, cognitive, and personality variables. But passive failure is also promoted by giving difficult assignments to poor readers; attributing learning problems to students rather than teachers (Rohrkemper & Brophy, 1983); criticizing less successful students excessively and praising them infrequently (Babad, Inbar, & Rosenthal, 1982); and, generally, by treating successful students more favorably than other students (see reviews by Allington, 1983; Hiebert, 1983; Weinstein, 1986).

It is important for reading educators to recognize how self-regard and motivation are influenced by instructional practices. Johnston and Winograd (1985) suggest that passive failure can be prevented if educators modify instruction to fit individual students; if, for example, they provide easier tasks, reduce evaluations, promote awareness of response-outcome relations, teach students to attribute success and failure to the use of particular reading strategies, and focus students' attention on the processes of reading rather than the normative (comparative) outcomes. Finally, they suggest that students' attributions, attitudes, and affect about reading can and should be assessed by teachers so that research and instruction can be focused on children's learning to read rather than on processes about the teaching of reading.

Social Contexts of Instruction

The contexts of literacy include multiple layers of interactions from teacher-pupil dialogs, to classroom dynamics, to school and community characteristics, to cultural ideologies for education (Paris & Wixson, 1986). Each layer provides a host of factors that influence reading instruction in classrooms. For example, some countries, like Japan, have a uniform national curriculum, whereas other countries consider schooling and literacy largely as vehicles for the religious education of youth. Social values and customs establish agendas for reading and proscribe instructional methods. One example of the influence of culture on instruction is the Kamehameha Early Education Program (KEEP), a K–3 reading curriculum designed for native-born Hawaiian children. It is continually being revised to incorporate new methods and materials, but the underlying objective is to improve the language arts curriculum by making it congruent with children's cultural backgrounds and social customs. For example, "talk story" is an Hawaiian custom that has been used as an instructional method in which many children talk at the same time to create a story or to revise each others' understanding. KEEP was initially piloted in laboratory schools and then extended to public schools in rural, economically depressed areas. Evaluation suggests that KEEP students perform significantly better than control students on standardized achievement tests (Au et al., 1985).

Most research on social contexts of instruction has analyzed classroom interactions and how readers of different abilities are affected by various instructional arrangements. Numerous studies have shown that good readers spend more engaged time on reading tasks and are less distracted than poor readers (e.g., Berliner, 1981). But these differences, which are correlated with achievement differences, may reflect teachers' behavior as much as learners' characteristics. For example, Collins (1982) studied conversations among teachers and pupils in reading groups and observed striking differences in the instructional interactions depending on the background and skills of the students. He found that children with working class, minority backgrounds, as well as poor readers, received far less comprehension instruction (beyond vocabulary words) than other students in the class *even* when they read identical texts.

Rosenbaum (1980) notes that student groups created according to ability level are entities that have social properties and implications. The social properties of ability groups are derived, at least in part, from the fact that: "1) students are grouped with those defined to be similar to themselves and segregated from those who are defined to be different; and 2) group placement is based on socially valued criteria, so that group membership immediately ranks one in a status hierarchy, formally identifying some individuals as better than others" (Rosenbaum, 1980, p. 363). Therefore, high- and low-ability groups established for reading instruction form unique instructional-social contexts that influence the learning outcomes of the individuals within those groups.

Recent reviews of ability grouping for reading instruction suggest that instructional and social reading experiences differ for students in high- and low-ability reading groups and that these differences influence student learning (Allington, 1983; Hiebert, 1983). Several of the instructional differences found between high- and low-ability reading groups have a direct bearing on the teaching and learning of comprehension skills. For example, there is evidence that students in low-ability groups receive less comprehension and more decoding instruction than students in high-ability groups. Gambrell, Wilson, and Gantt (1981) found that contextual reading accounted for 57% of the instructional time in high-ability groups, but only 22% of the time allocated for the low-ability groups. Conversely, instruction in isolated words, letters, and sounds accounted for 17% of the instructional time in low-ability groups, but only 7% of the time in high-ability groups.

Allington (1983) describes a series of studies he conducted using the number of words read as a measure of instructional differences between low- and high-ability reading groups. The results of these studies indicate that students in high-ability groups read two or three times as many words per day as students in low-ability groups. In addition, students in high-ability groups read silently much more than they read orally, while students in low-ability groups read orally much more frequently than silently. Allington (1983) suggests that the differential use of oral and silent reading with high- and low-ability groups is likely to promote different criteria for determining the adequacy of students' reading performance. Specifically, good readers are likely to be judged on the basis of their responses to postreading questions, while poor readers are likely to be judged on the accuracy of their oral reproduction of the text.

Evidence that teacher interruption behavior during oral reading differs between low-and high-ability groups also has implications for the teaching and learning of comprehension skills. Allington (1980) reported that teachers interrupt proportionally more often following errors in low-ability than high-ability groups. Furthermore, he suggests that more frequent interruptions are likely to encourage poor readers' reliance on someone else as an external monitor and, over time, inhibit the development of self-monitoring.

Weinstein (1986) says that grouping practices communicate information to students about their relative ability that eventually influences their learning. For example, she traced children's reading performance from the beginning to the middle of first grade and found that group membership accounted for a significant amount of variation (25%) in achievement scores even when original reading readiness was partialled out (Weinstein, 1976). The performance of children in the low-ability group had declined significantly relative to their counterparts in the high-ability group after only a few months. Brattesani, Weinstein, & Marshall (1984) found that in classrooms where cues about ability were more readily apparent, fourth- through sixth-grade students' own expectations for their future performance in reading were closely aligned with their teachers' expectations for them.

Weinstein (1986) suggests that ability grouping masks the individual differences between students within a group and magnifies the differences between groups. Grouping provides students with messages about their potential for success in reading. Children are aware of these messages and internalize them. For example, in summarizing studies on the effects of ability grouping on self-concept, Rosenbaum (1980) concluded that in most cases average and low-ability students give lower self-evaluations if they are in ability groups than if they are not. It is clear from this brief review that ability groups have social properties that have consequences for both motivation and achievement.

CONCLUSION

In this review we have identified several prominent types of instruction used during the past 60 years to promote students' reading comprehension. The central emphasis on cognitive skills has slowly been modified by new approaches that emphasize cognitive strategies, metacognition, and the social-motivational consequences of instruction. Research on reading has played a significant role in creating new techniques and materials for teaching comprehension. During the next 20 years, we expect reading to be progressively reconceptualized to emphasize the interactive nature of reading and the strategic connections between reading and reasoning. Greater attention will also be paid to the social dynamics of reading instruction and the motivational consequences of successful and unsuccessful reading. We believe that the skills-management systems will continue to capture teachers' attention and to dominate the commercial marketplace. But new materials, new methods, and new assessments of reading comprehension are certain to be created by the year 2000. Along with these changes, we expect that reading instruction will place greater emphasis on enabling students to become strategic readers and empowering teachers to become effective decision makers in their own classrooms.

REFERENCES

Adams, A., Carnine, D., & Gersten, R. (1982). Instructional strategies for studying content area texts in the intermediate grades. *Reading Research Quarterly, 18,* 27–55.

Allington, R.L. (1980). Teacher interruption behaviors during primary grade oral reading. *Journal of Educational Psychology, 72,* 371–377.

Allington, R.L. (1983). The reading instruction provided readers of differing reading abilities. *Elementary School Journal, 83,* 548–558.

Anderson, R.C., & Biddle, W.B. (1975). On asking people questions about what they are reading. In G.H. Bower (Ed.), *The psychology of learning and motivation* (Vol. 9). New York: Academic Press.

Anderson, L.M., Evertson, C.M., & Brophy, J. (1979). An experimental study of effective reading in first-grade reading groups. *Elementary School Journal, 79,* 193–233.

Anderson, R.C., Osborn, J., & Tierney, R.J. (1984). *Learning to read in American schools: Basal readers and content texts.* Hillsdale, NJ: Erlbaum.

Anderson, R.C., & Pearson, P.D. (1984). A schema-theoretic view of basic processes in reading comprehension. In P.D. Pearson, R. Barr, M. Kamil, & P. Mosenthal (Eds.), *Handbook of reading research.* New York: Longman.

Andre, T. (1979). Does answering higher level questions while reading facilitate productive learning. *Review of Educational Research, 49,* 280–318.

Au, K.H., Tharp, R.G., Crowell, D.C., Jordan, C., Speidel, G.E., & Calkins, R. (1985). The role of research in the development of a successful reading program. In J. Osborn, P. Wilson, & R. Anderson (Eds.), *Reading education: Foundations for a literate America*. Lexington, MA: Heath/Lexington Books.

Austin, M.C., & Morrison, C. (1963). *The first R*. New York: Macmillan.

Ausubel, D.P. (1963). *The psychology of meaningful verbal learning*. New York: Grune & Stratton.

Ausubel, D.P. (1968). *Educational psychology*. New York: Holt, Rinehart & Winston.

Babad, E., Inbar, J., & Rosenthal, R. (1982). Pygmalion, Galatea, and the Golem: Investigations of biased and unbiased teachers. *Journal of Educational Psychology, 74*, 459–474.

Baker, L., & Brown, A.L. (1984). Metacognitive skills and reading. In P.D. Pearson, M. Kamil, R. Barr, & P. Mosenthal (Eds.), *Handbook of reading research*. New York: Longman.

Baumann, J.F. (1984). The effectiveness of a direct instruction paradigm for teaching main idea comprehension. *Reading Research Quarterly, 20*, 93–115.

Baumann, J.F. (1986). Teaching third-grade students to comprehend anaphoric relationships: The application of a direct instruction model. *Reading Research Quarterly, 21*, 70–90.

Beck, I.L., McKeown, M.G., Omanson, R.C., & Pople, M.T. (1984). Improving the comprehensibility of stories: The effects of revisions that improve coherence. *Reading Research Quarterly, 19*, 263-277.

Beck, I.L., Omanson, R.C., & McKeown, M.G. (1982). An instructional redesign of reading lessons: Effects on comprehension. *Reading Research Quarterly, 17*, 462–481.

Becker, W.C., & Gersten, R. (1982). A follow-up of Follow Through: The later effects of the direct instruction model on children in fifth and sixth grades. *American Educational Research Journal, 19*, 75–92.

Berliner, D.C. (1981). Academic learning time and reading achievement. In J.T. Guthrie (Ed.), *Comprehension and teaching: Research reviews*. Newark, DE: International Reading Association.

Berliner, D.C., & Rosenshine, B. (1977). The acquisition of knowledge in the classroom. In R.C. Anderson, R.J. Spiro, & W.E. Montague (Eds.), *Schooling and the acquisition of knowledge*. Hillsdale, NJ: Erlbaum.

Bormuth, J., Carr, J., Manning, J., & Pearson, P.D. (1970). Children's comprehension of between- and within-sentence syntactic structures. *Journal of Educational Psychology, 61*, 349–357.

Brattesani, K.A., Weinstein, R.S., & Marshall, H.H. (1984). Student perceptions of differential teacher treatment as moderators of teacher expectation effects. *Journal of Experimental Psychology, 76*, 236–247.

Brennan, A.D., Bridge, C.A., & Winograd, P.N. (1986). The effects of structural variation on children's recall of basal reader stories. *Reading Research Quarterly, 21*, 91–104.

Brown, A.L. (1978). Knowing when, where, and how to remember: A problem of metacognition. In R. Glaser (Ed.), *Advances in instructional psychology* (Vol. 1). Hillsdale, NJ: Erlbaum.

Brown, A.L. (1980). Metacognitive development and reading. In R.J. Spiro, B.C. Bruce, & W. Brewer (Eds.), *Theoretical issues in reading comprehension*. Hillsdale, NJ: Erlbaum.

Brown, A.L., Armbruster, B.B., & Baker, L. (1984). The role of metacognition in reading and studying. In J. Orasanu (Ed.), *A decade of reading research: Implications for practice*. Hillsdale, NJ: Erlbaum.

Brown, A.L., Bransford, J.D., Ferrara, R.A., & Campione, J.C. (1983). Learning, remembering, and understanding. In J.H. Flavell & E.M. Markman (Eds.), *Handbook of child psychology: Cognitive development* (Vol. III). New York: Wiley.

Brown, A.L., Campione, J.C., & Day, J.D. (1981). Learning to learn: On training students to learn from texts. *Educational Researcher, 10,* 14–21.

Brown, A.L., & Day, J.D. (1983). Macrorules for summarizing texts: The development of expertise. *Journal of Verbal Learning and Verbal Behavior, 22,* 1–14.

Brown, A.L., & Palincsar, A.S. (1982). Inducing strategic learning from texts by means of informed, self-control training. *Topics in Learning and Learning Disabilities, 2,* 1–16.

Brown, A.L., & Palincsar, A.S. (in press). Reciprocal teaching of comprehension strategies: A natural history of one program for enhancing learning. In J. Borkowski & J.D. Day (Eds.), *Intelligence and cognition in special children: Comparative studies of giftedness, mental retardation, and learning disabilities*. Norwood, NJ: Ablex.

Bruce, B. (1984). A new point of view on children's stories. In R.C. Anderson, J. Osborn, & R.J. Tierney (Eds.), *Learning to read in American schools*. Hillsdale, NJ: Erlbaum.

Butkowsky, I.S., & Willows, D.M. (1980). Cognitive-motivational characteristics of children varying in reading ability: Evidence of learned helplessness in poor readers. *Journal of Educational Psychology, 72,* 408–422.

Carnine, D., Kameenui, E.J., & Coyle, G. (1984). Utilization of contextual information in determining the meaning of unfamiliar words. *Reading Research Quarterly, 19,* 188–204.

Clay, M. (1979). *The early detection of reading difficulties: A diagnostic survey with recovery procedures* (2nd ed.). Exeter, NH: Heinemann.

Clymer, T. (1968). What is "reading"? Some current concepts. In H.M. Robinson (Ed.), *Innovation and change in reading instruction: The sixty-seventh yearbook of the National Society of the Study of Education*. Chicago: University of Chicago Press.

Collins, J. (1982). Discourse style, classroom interaction and differential treatment. *Journal of Reading Behavior, 14,* 429–437.

Covington, M.V. (1983). Motivated cognitions. In S.G. Paris, G.M. Olson, & H.W. Stevenson (Eds.), *Learning & motivation in the classroom*. Hillsdale, NJ: Erlbaum.

Cross, D.R., & Paris, S.G. (in press). Assessment of reading comprehension: The fit between test properties and test purposes. *Educational Psychologist*.

Davison, A., & Kantor, R.N. (1982). On the failure of readability formulas to define readable tests: A case study from adaptions. *Reading Research Quarterly, 17,* 187–209.

Day, J.D. (1980). *Training summarization skills: A comparison of teaching methods*. Unpublished doctoral dissertation, University of Illinois, Urbana.

Della-Piana, G.M., & Endo, G.T. (1973). Reading research. In R.M. Travers (Ed.), *Second handbook of research on teaching*. Chicago: Rand McNally.

Doctorow, M., Wittrock, M.C., & Marks, C. (1978). Generative processes in reading comprehension. *Journal of Educational Psychology, 70,* 109–118.

Downing, J., & Valtin, R. (1984). *Language awareness and learning to read*. New York: Springer.

Doyle, W. (1983). Academic work. *Review of Educational Research, 53,* 159–199

Duffy, G., Roehler, L., Meloth, M., Vavrus, L., Book, C., Putnam, J., & Wessel-man, R. (in press). The relationship between explicit verbal explanation during reading skill instruction and student awareness and achievement: A study in reading teacher effects. *Reading Research Quarterly.*

Durkin, D. (1978–1979). What classroom observations reveal about reading comprehension instruction. *Reading Research Quarterly, 14,* 481–533.

Durkin, D. (1984). Is there a match between what elementary teachers do and what basal reader manuals recommend? *The Reading Teacher, 37,* 734–745.

Durrell, D.D. (1949). Development of comprehension and interpretation. In N.B. Henry (Ed.), *Reading in the elementary school: The forty-eighth yearbook of the National Society for the Study of Education.* Chicago: University of Chicago Press.

Dweck, C., & Bempechat, J. (1983). Children's theories of intelligence: Consequences for learning. In S. Paris, G. Olson, & H. Stevenson (Eds.), *Learning and motivation in the classroom.* Hillsdale, NJ: Erlbaum.

Farr, R., & Carey, R.F. (1986). *Reading: What can be measured?* (2nd ed.). Newark, DE: International Reading Association.

Flavell, J.H. (1978). Metacognitive development. In J.M. Scandura & C.J. Brainerd (Eds.), *Structural/process theories of complex human behavior.* The Netherlands: Sijthoff & Noordoff.

Forrest-Pressley, D.L., MacKinnon, E., & Waller, T.G. (1985). *Metacognition, cognition, and human performance.* New York: Academic Press.

Friedman, F., & Rickards, J.P. (1981). Effect of level, review and sequence of inserted questions on text processing. *Journal of Educational Psychology, 73,* 427–436.

Gambrell, L.B., Wilson, R.M., & Gantt, W.N. (1981). Classroom observations of task-attending behaviors of good and poor readers. *Journal of Educational Research, 74,* 400–404.

Gates, A.I. (1949). Character and purposes of the yearbook. In N.B. Henry (Ed.), *Reading in the elementary school: The forty-eighth yearbook of the National Society for the Study of Education.* Chicago: University of Chicago Press.

Golinkoff, R. (1975–1976). A comparison of reading comprehension processes in good and poor comprehenders. *Reading Research Quarterly, 11,* 623–659.

Goodman, K.S. (1967). Reading: A psycholinguistic guessing game. *Journal of the Reading Specialist, 6,* 126–135.

Graves, M.F., & Cooke, C.L. (1980). Effects of previewing difficult short stories for high school students. *Research on Reading in Secondary School, 6,* 8–13.

Graves, M.F., Cooke, C.L., & Laberge, M.J. (1983). Effects of previewing difficult short stories on low ability junior high school students' comprehension, recall, and attitudes. *Reading Research Quarterly, 18,* 262–276.

Gray, W.S. (1937). A decade of progress. In G.M. Whipple (Ed.), *The teaching of reading: A second report; The thirty-sixth yearbook of the National Society for the Study of Education.* Bloomington, IL: Public School Publishing.

Guthrie, J.T., & Lissitz, R.W. (1985). A framework for assessment-based decision making in reading education. *Educational Measurement: Issues and Practice, 4,* 26–31.

Hansen, J. (1981). The effects of inference training and practice on young children's comprehension. *Reading Research Quarterly, 16,* 391–417.

Hansen, J., & Pearson, P.D. (1983). An instructional study: Improving the inferential comprehension of fourth grade good and poor readers. *Journal of Educational Psychology, 75,* 821–829.

Harste, J.C. (1985). Portrait of a new paradigm: Reading comprehension research.

In A. Crismore (Ed.), *Landscapes: A state-of-the-art assessment of reading comprehension research 1974–1984*. Bloomington: Indiana University Press.

Hartley, J., & Davies, I.K. (1976). Preinstructional strategies: The role of pretests, behavioral objectives, overviews and advance organizers. *Review of Educational Research, 46*, 239–265.

Henry, N.B. (Ed.). (1949). *Reading in the elementary school: The forty-eighth yearbook of the National Society for the Study of Education*. Chicago: University of Chicago Press.

Henry, N.B. (Ed.). (1961). *Development in and through reading: The sixtieth yearbook of the National Society for the Study of Education*. Chicago: University of Chicago Press.

Hiebert, E.F. (1983). An examination of ability grouping for reading instruction. *Reading Research Quarterly, 18*, 231–255.

Huus, H. (1968). Innovations in reading instruction: At later levels. In H.M. Robinson (Ed.), *Innovation and change in reading instruction: The sixty-seventh yearbook of the National Society of the Study of Education*. Chicago: University of Chicago Press.

Johns, J.L. (1980). First graders' concepts about print. *Reading Research Quarterly, 15*, 539–549.

Johnson, D.D., & Pearson, P.D. (1978). Skills management systems. A critique. *The Reading Teacher, 28*, 757–764.

Johnston, P. (1984). Assessment in reading: The emperor has no clothes. In P.D. Pearson, R. Barr, M. Kamil, & P. Mosenthal (Eds.), *Handbook of reading research*. New York: Longman.

Johnston, P.H., & Winograd, P.N. (1985). Passive failure in reading. *Journal of Reading Behavior, 17*, 279–301.

Kamm, K. (1978). A five-year study of the effects of a skill-centered approach to the teaching of reading. *Journal of Educational Research, 72*, 104–112.

Kennedy, D., & Weener, P. (1973). Visual and auditory training with the cloze procedure to improve reading and listening comprehension. *Reading Research Quarterly, 8*, 524–541.

Kintsch, W., & van Dijk, T.A. (1978). Toward a model of text comprehension and production. *Psychological Review, 85*, 363–394.

Kurtz, B.E., & Borkowski, J.G. (1985, March). *Metacognition and the development of strategic skills in impulsive and reflective children*. Paper presented at the meeting of the Society for Research on Child Development, Toronto.

Langer, J.A. (1985). Levels of questioning: An alternative view. *Reading Research Quarterly, 20*, 586–602.

Leinhardt, G., Zigmond, N., & Cooley, W. (1981). Reading instruction and its effects. *American Educational Research Journal, 18*, 343–361.

Linden, M., & Wittrock, M.C. (1981). The teaching of reading comprehension according to the model of generative learning. *Reading Research Quarterly, 17*, 44–57.

Luiten, J., Ames, W., & Ackerson, G. (1980). A meta-analysis of the effects of advance organizers on learning and retention. *American Educational Research Journal, 17*, 211–218.

Lumsdaine, A.A. (Ed.). (1960). Teaching machines: An introductory review. *Teaching machines and programmed learning*. Washington, DC: National Education Association.

Marks, C.B., Doctorow, M.J., & Wittrock, M.C. (1974). Word frequency and reading comprehension. *Journal of Educational Research, 67*, 259–262.

Mason, J., & the Staff of the Center for the Study of Reading. A schema-theoretic view of the reading process as a basis for comprehension instruction. In G.G. Duffy, L. R. Roehler, & J. Mason (Eds.), *Comprehension instruction* (pp. 26–38). New York: Longman.

McConkie, G.W. (1977). Learning from text. In L.S. Shulman (Ed.), *Review of Research in Education* (Vol. 5). Washington, DC: American Educational Research Association.

Memory, D.M. (1983). Main idea prequestions as adjunct aids with good and low-average middle grade readers. *Journal of Reading Behavior, 15,* 37–48.

Messick, S. (1984). The psychology of educational measurement. *Journal of Educational Measurement, 21,* 215–237.

Myers, M., & Paris, S.G. (1978). Children's metacognitive knowledge about reading. *Journal of Educational Psychology, 70,* 680–690.

National Assessment of Educational Progress (1981). *Three national assessments of reading: Changes in performance, 1970–1980.* (Report No. 11–R–01). Denver, CO: Educational Commission of the States.

National Commission on Excellence in Education. (1983). *A nation at risk: The imperative for educational reform.* Washington, DC: U.S. Government Printing Office.

Osborn, J., Wilson, P.T., & Anderson, R.C. (1985). *Reading education: Foundations for a literate America.* Lexington, MA: Heath/Lexington Books.

Otto, W., & Chester, R.D. (1976). *Objective-based reading.* Reading, MA: Addison-Wesley.

Otto, W., Wolf, A., & Eldrige, R.G. (1984). Managing instruction. In P.D. Pearson, R. Barr, M. Kamil, & P. Mosenthal (Eds.), *Handbook of reading research.* New York: Longman.

Palincsar, A.S. (in press). Role of dialogue in scaffolded instruction. *Educational Psychologist.*

Palincsar, A.S., & Brown, A.L. (1984). Reciprocal teaching of comprehension fostering and monitoring activities. *Cognition and Instruction, 1,* 117–175.

Palincsar, A.S., & Brown, A.L. (in press). Advances in the cognitive instruction of handicapped students. In M.C. Wang, H.J. Walberg, & M. Reynolds (Eds.), *The handbook of special education: Research and practice.* New York: Pergamon Press.

Paris, S.G. (1986). Teaching children to guide their reading and learning. In T. Raphael (Ed.), *The contexts of school-based literacy.* New York: Random House.

Paris, S.G., Cross, D.R., Jacobs, J.E., Oka, E.R., & DeBritto, A.M. (1984). Improving children's metacognition and reading comprehension with classroom instruction. Symposium presented at the annual meeting of the American Educational Research Association, New Orleans.

Paris, S.G., Cross, D.R., & Lipson, M.Y. (1984). Informed strategies for learning: A program to improve children's reading awareness and comprehension. *Journal of Educational Psychology, 76,* 1239–1252.

Paris, S.G., & Jacobs, J.E. (1984). The benefits of informed instruction for children's reading awareness and comprehension skills. *Child Development, 55,* 2083–2093.

Paris, S.G., & Lindauer, B.K. (1982). The development of cognitive skills during childhood. In B. Wolman (Ed.), *Handbook of developmental psychology.* Englewood Cliffs, NJ: Prentice-Hall.

Paris, S.G., Lipson, M., & Wixson, K. (1983). Becoming a strategic reader. *Contemporary Educational Psychology, 8,* 293–316.

Paris, S.G., Newman, R.S., & McVey, K.A. (1982). Learning the functional significance of mnemonic actions: A microgenetic study of strategy acquisition. *Journal of Experimental Child Psychology, 34,* 490–509.

Paris, S.G., & Oka, E.R. (1986). Children's reading strategies, metacognition, and motivation. *Developmental Review, 6,* 25–56.

Paris, S.G., & Wixson, K.K. (1986). Access to literacy. In D. Bloome (Ed.), *Literacy, language, and schooling.* Norwood, NJ: Ablex.

Patching, W., Kameenui, E., Carnine, D., Gersten, R., & Colvin, G. (1983). Direct instruction in critical reading skills. *Reading Research Quarterly, 18,* 406–418.

Pearson, P.D. (1986). The comprehension revolution: A twenty-year perspective on changes in process and practice. In T.E. Raphael (Ed.), *Contexts of school-based literacy.* New York: Random House.

Pressey, S.L. (1926). A simple apparatus which gives tests and scores—and teaches. *School and Society, 23,* 373–376.

Raphael, T.E., & McKinney, J. (1983). An examination of fifth and eighth grade students' question answering behavior: An instructional study in metacognition. *Journal of Reading Behavior, 15,* 67–86.

Raphael, T.E., & Pearson, P.D. (1985). Increasing students' awareness of sources of information for answering questions. *American Educational Research Journal, 22,* 217–236.

Raphael, T.E., & Wonnacott, C.A. (1985). Heightening fourth-grade students' sensitivity to sources of information for answering comprehension questions. *Reading Research Quarterly, 20,* 282–296.

Resnick, D.P., & Resnick, L.B. (1977). The nature of literacy: An historical exploration. *Harvard Educational Review, 47,* 370–385.

Reynolds, R.E., Standiford, S.N., & Anderson, R.C. (1979). Distribution of reading time when questions are asked about a restricted category of text information. *Journal of Education Psychology, 71,* 183–190.

Rickards, J.P. (1979). Adjunct postquestions in text: A critical review of methods and processes. *Review of Educational Research, 49,* 181–196.

Robinson, H.M. (Ed.) (1968). *Innovation and change in reading instruction: The sixty-seventh yearbook of the National Society of the Study of Education.* Chicago: University of Chicago Press.

Roehler, L.R., & Duffy, G.G. (1984). Direct explanation of comprehension processes. In G. Duffy, L. Roehler, & J. Mason (Eds.), *Comprehension instruction: Perspectives and suggestions.* New York: Longman.

Rohrkemper, M.M., & Brophy, J.E. (1983). Teachers' thinking about students. In J.M. Levine & M.C. Wang (Eds.), *Teacher and student perceptions: Implications for learning.* Hillsdale, NJ: Erlbaum.

Rosenbaum, J.E. (1980). Social implications of educational grouping. In D.C. Berliner (Ed.), *Review of Research in Education, 8.* Washington, DC: American Educational Research Association.

Rosenshine, B. (1979). Content, time and direct instruction. In P. Peterson & H. Walberg (Eds.), *Research on teaching: Concepts, findings, and implications.* Berkeley, CA: McCutchan.

Rosenshine, B., & Stevens, R. (1984). Classroom instruction in reading. In P.D. Pearson, R. Barr, M. Kamil, & P. Mosenthal (Eds.), *Handbook of reading research.* New York: Longman.

Rothkopf, E.Z. (1965). Some theoretical and experimental approaches to problems in written instruction. In J.D. Krumboltz (Ed.), *Learning and the educational process.* Chicago: Rand McNally.

Rothkopf, E.Z. (1970). The concept of mathemagenic activities. *Review of Educational Research, 40,* 325–336.

Rothkopf, E.Z. (1982). Adjunct aids and the control of mathemagenic activities during purposeful reading. In W. Otto & S. White (Eds.), *Reading expository material.* New York: Academic Press.

Ruddell, R.B. (1966). Reading instruction in first grade with varying emphasis on the regularity of grapheme-phoneme correspondence and the relation of language structure to meaning. *The Reading Teacher, 19,* 653–660.

Rumelhart, D.E. (1981). Schemata: The building blocks of cognition. In J. Guthrie (Ed.), *Comprehension and teaching: Research reviews.* Newark, DE: International Research Association.

Ryan, E.B. (1981). Identifying and remediating failures in reading comprehension: Toward an instructional approach for poor comprehenders. In T.G. Waller & G.E. MacKinnon (Eds.), *Advances in reading research.* New York: Academic Press.

Shannon, P. (1983). The use of commercial reading materials in American elementary schools. *Reading Research Quarterly, 19,* 68–85.

Short, E.J., & Ryan, E.B. (1984). Metacognitive differences between skilled and less skilled readers: Remediating deficits through story grammar and attribution training. *Journal of Educational Psychology, 76,* 225–235.

Singer, H. (1985). Models of reading have direct implications for instruction: The affirmative position. In J. Niles & R. Lalik (Eds.), *Issues in literacy: A research perspective.* Rochester, NY: National Reading Conference.

Slater, W.H., Graves, M.F., & Piche, G.L. (1985). Effects of structural organizers on ninth-grade students' comprehension and recall of four patterns of expository test. *Reading Research Quarterly, 20,* 189–202.

Skinner, B.F. (1954). The science of learning and the art of teaching. *Harvard Educational Review, 24,* 86–97.

Smith, N.B. (1965). *American reading instruction.* Newark, DE: International Reading Association.

Stevenson, H.W., Stigler, J.W., Lucker, G.W., Lee, S.Y., Hsu, C.C., & Kitamura, S. (1982). Reading disabilities: The case of Chinese, Japanese, and English. *Child Development, 53,* 1164–1181.

Tierney, R.J., & Cunningham, J.W. (1984). Research on teaching reading comprehension. In P.D. Pearson, R. Barr, M. Kamil, & P. Mosenthal (Eds.), *Handbook of reading research.* New York: Longman.

Vander Zanden, J.W. (1980). *Educational psychology: In theory and practice.* New York: Random House.

Venezky, R.L. (1984). The history of reading research. In P.D. Pearson, R. Barr, M. Kamil, & P. Mosenthal (Eds.), *Handbook of reading research.* New York: Longman.

Venezky, R.L. (1986). Steps toward a comprehensive history of American reading instruction. In E.Z. Rothkopf (Ed.), *Review of research in education* (Vol. 13). Washington, D.C.: American Educational Research Association.

Vygotsky, L. (1978). *Mind in society* (M. Cole, V. John-Steiner, S. Scribner, & E. Souberman, Trans.). Cambridge, MA: Harvard University Press.

Weaver, P.A. (1979). Improving reading comprehension: Effects of sentence organization instruction. *Reading Research Quarterly, 15,* 129–146.

Weinstein, R.S. (1976). Reading group membership in first grade: Teacher behaviors and pupil experience over time. *Journal of Educational Psychology, 68,* 103–116.

Weinstein, R.S. (1986). Teaching reading: Children's awareness of teacher expectations. In T.E. Raphael (Ed.), *Contexts of school-based literacy.* New York: Random House.

Whipple, G.M. (Ed.) (1925). *Report of the National Committee on Reading: The twenty-fourth yearbook of the National Society for the Study of Education.* Bloomington, IL: Public School Publishing.

Whipple, G.M. (Ed.) (1937). *The teaching of reading: A second report; The thirty-sixth yearbook of the National Society for the Study of Education.* Bloomington, IL: Public School Publishing.

Winograd, P., & Greenlee, M. (1986). Children need a balanced reading program. *Educational Leadership, 43,* 16–21.

Winograd, P.N., & Hare, V.C. (in press). Direct instruction of reading comprehension strategies: The role of teacher explanations. In E. Goetz, P. Alexander, & C. Weinstein (Eds.), *Learning and study strategies: Issues in assessment, instruction, and evaluation.* New York: Academic Press.

Wittrock, M.C. (1974). Learning as a generative process. *Educational Psychologist, 11,* 87–95.

Wittrock, M.C. (1978). The cognitive movement in instruction. *Educational Psychologist, 13,* 15–29.

Wittrock, M.C., Marks, C.B., & Doctorow, M.J. (1975). Reading as a generative process. *Journal of Educational Psychology, 67,* 17–21.

Wixson, K.K. (1983). Postreading question-answer interactions and children's learning from text. *Journal of Educational Psychology, 30,* 413–423.

Wixson, K.K. (1984). Level of importance of postquestions and children's learning from text. *American Educational Research Journal, 21,* 419–433.

Wixson, K.K., & Lipson, M.Y. (1986). Reading (dis)ability: An interactionist perspective. In T. Raphael (Ed.), *The contexts of school-based literacy.* New York: Random House.

Wixson, K.K., & Peters, C.W. (in press). A theory-based approach to comprehension assessment. *Educational Psychologist.*

Wood, D.J., Bruner, J.S., & Ross, G. (1976). The role of tutoring in problem solving. *Journal of Child Psychology and Psychiatry, 17,* 89–100.

Chapter 4

Steps Toward a Modern History of American Reading Instruction

RICHARD L. VENEZKY
University of Delaware

BACKGROUND

The Status Quo

The history of American reading instruction is an important but generally neglected area of curriculum history. According to annual surveys of reading publications published by the International Reading Association, the number of papers and books on this topic has averaged fewer than a half-dozen a year over the last decade (see also Pugh, 1984), and no major attempt at a full history has appeared for over 20 years. Of the fuller treatments attempted in this century, Reeder (1900) and Lamport (1937), though valuable as information sources, are out of date and generally inaccessible, while N. Smith (1965) and Mathews (1966) are inadequate by modern curriculum history standards, as will be discussed below (*passim*). For reading instruction in England, which influenced American instruction particularly during the Colonial period, only the years from the earliest records until 1612 have been covered in an integrated work (Davies, 1974), although work is in progress on the last several centuries.

This dearth of recent research should not be interpreted as an indicator of exhaustive coverage or consensus on all of the major issues involved. For the most part, the major works focus on public school instruction for the majority population, drawing more on educators' opinions than on classroom evidence. Almost nothing is mentioned in these works on the teaching of reading

I am especially appreciative of the suggestions made by E. Jennifer Monaghan on several versions of this chapter, and of the comments by Robert Hampel on a draft of the present version. Both have helped make this paper more accurate and readable, but neither bears any responsibility for the imperfections that remain.

throughout the 19th century and early 20th century in the evening schools and church schools, and on the Indian reservations and in the slave quarters, even though a sizable portion of the American population took its first steps towards literacy in these settings (Cremin, 1980; Seybolt, 1925; Webber, 1978). In some cases, such as the Cherokee syllabary, limited and probably incorrect information about reading instruction and literacy has been transformed into a mythology that persists to the present day. There is no doubt that the invention and rapid utilization of the Cherokee syllabary were exceptional events in the history of literacy. But the claims made by Mathews (1966, pp. 8–9) and others for the short time needed to acquire literacy with the syllabary have no empirical support. Similarly, critical information is either lacking or inaccessible for a large number of important topics, such as the sales and distributions of most reading texts or the backgrounds of many of the textbook authors such as Edwin Leigh, Charles Sanders, and Lewis B. Monroe.

Equally important, major differences of opinion exist on a number of topics central to this history. Among these are the causes and timing of the shift in instructional emphasis from oral to silent reading; the primary influences on reader content; the effectiveness of public school reading instruction, particularly in the 19th century; and the extent to which comprehension was taught prior to the modern era. Many of these differences reflect scholarly issues that either have not been examined thoroughly, or have been viewed from differing perspectives. As a group they provide a motivation for this chapter, which will attempt to develop a foundation for an integrated history of American reading instruction through an analysis of the major findings and central controversies of this field.

The plan here is to focus on five areas of importance to the history of reading instruction: theoretical frameworks, control of reader content, reading curriculum, instructional technology, and instructional outcomes. In each area, emphasis will be given to important studies, conflicts of methodology or outcomes, and needed research. In part, this chapter will demonstrate how much remains to be done to bring the history of reading instruction into the mainstream of modern curriculum history. But it will also show what parts of the foundation for this task are already in place. The status quo is not a dry and barren landscape, but a patchwork of small oases and occasional flower beds, located in disparate fields and constructed from a variety of perspectives.

Source Materials

The source materials for a history of reading instruction suffer all the inadequacies generally described for educational histories, including unbalanced distribution over regions and time, inadequate school records, inaccurate, ambiguous, and biased reports (Elsbree, 1939, pp. 4–6), and then a few more. In this latter group of problems are, in particular, those attendant to the reading textbooks, upon which so much emphasis has been given in studies of reading instruction. For most of the 17th through the 19th centuries, reading materials were printed on inexpensive paper and had fragile covers and cheap bindings. This, coupled with what Kiefer (1948, p. 4) calls "the traditional vandalism of most children towards books," has led to a low survival rate of early reading materials. Few hornbooks have survived in America, although thousands were probably used in the 17th and early 18th centuries, and no *New England Primer* printed in this country before 1727 is extant, even though this was the most popular reading text of its time and was published in America from at least 1690 (Ford, 1899, pp. 38ff). For the major texts of the 19th century, complete series, including major revisions, are seldom held by any single institution. Aside from the *New England Primer* (Heartman, 1934), Webster's spelling books and readers (Skeel, 1958) and McGuffey's readers (Minnich, 1936), no publication histories are available for American reading series up to the present era.

School texts present special identification problems since revisions were sometimes made and new editions issued with little outward notice of change. Selections and instructional notes present in one edition may not appear in the next. For example, McGuffey's *Third Eclectic Reader* was originally published in 1837. A year later it was revised and recopyrighted under legal pressure from the publishers of Worcester's Readers, for plagiarism. It was revised further in 1843, and 1848, and then radically overhauled in 1853, 1857, and 1879. Slight but unimportant changes were made in 1901 and 1920 when new copyrights were issued (Minnich, 1936, pp. 39–40). Between the original 1837 edition and the 1879 edition the entire world view of the McGuffey Readers changed (Westerhoff, 1978; see below, Control of Reader Content). Similarly, between the first and second editions of Cobb's *Juvenile Readers* a major change in instruction occurred, with the revised editions showing a concern not present in the original for understanding by the child. For the Monroe Readers, the difference between the original series (1872–1874) and the revised series (1883–1885) is reflected not only in changes in selections and instructional methodology, but by a change in authorship. Lewis B. Monroe, who wrote the original series, died in 1879; the revised series was written by his widow, who probably also wrote parts of the first edition. Changing concepts of instruction and changing cultural views can often be dated by a comparison of the various editions of the same reader. But at the same time, when sufficient attention is not paid to editions and copyrights, incorrect conclusions can be drawn on the instruction or world view of a particular author, or on the dating of a change.

There is even less information available about sales records of readers, although many publisher sales books probably lie in the cluttered obscurity of state and local historical societies, university archives, and other institutions.

Several publishers have donated their archives, or parts of them, to libraries (e.g., The American Book Company); others continue to maintain archives of their own (e.g., Ginn & Co.), but no catalogues are available for distribution from any of these collections. Major collections of reading texts are housed in such places as the American Antiquarian Society, the Library of Congress, Trinity College in Hartford (Barnard Textbook Collection), Columbia University (Plimpton Collection), Hofstra University (Nila Banton Smith Historical Collection in Reading), and the McGuffey Museum of Miami University, Oxford, Ohio. For studies of the more popular texts, an adequate literature exists: e.g., Tuer (1896) on the hornbook; Ford (1899) on *The New England Primer;* Monaghan (1983) on Webster's blue-back speller; and Minnich (1936) on the McGuffey readers. In addition, R. Smith (1977) has tabulated all of the spellers published in America up to 1800 and Weeks (1900) lists all of the textbooks published in the Confederacy. General treatments of textbooks, including readers and spellers, can be found in Nietz (1961) and Carpenter (1963).

A CONFLICT OF PERSPECTIVES

Differing frameworks for historical studies are expected for a field as rich as reading instruction with its central position in primary level schooling and its ties, directly or indirectly, to literacy. It is no surprise then to find the wide range of perspectives that have been taken on this topic, particularly during the past 50 years. One reason for this diversity is that many of the writers on the history of reading instruction were trained in fields outside of history—lexicography, education, linguistics, and English, among others. Another reason is that the major works in the field have been produced during a period in which the writing of educational history has changed dramatically. Three perspectives on the history of reading instruction will be illustrated here: (1) *the evangelical perspective,* (2) *the all-for-the-best perspective,* and (3) *the childhood perspective.* A fourth framework, *the propaganda perspective,* is represented by the work in the next section on content analysis.

Evangelism

A number of summaries of the history of reading instruction have been written to promote one or another approach to instruction, the most scholarly of which is Mathews (1966). Mathews is unabashedly in favor of synthetic phonics approaches and views most of the history of reading instruction in terms of a mortal conflict between whole word and phonics advocates. In choosing this framework, Mathews neglects for the most part any instructional issues beyond the introduction of reading (e.g., vocabulary control, role of elocution). His work is rich in information, but suffers from its narrow focus, both in terms of issues ignored and in overemphasis of matters that have had only marginal influence on classroom instruction (e.g., International Teaching Alphabet experiments).

Mathews attributes to Colonel Francis Parker, the first director of the School of Education at the University of Chicago, the credit (i.e., blame) for the triumph of the word method in the United States, with Horace Mann providing intellectual support. There are, however, differences of opinion about Mann's influence. Diack (1965, p. 18) is probably representative of the majority in claiming that Mann had little influence on the teaching of reading outside the Boston area. Mann's objections to the introductory instructional methods of his time were not with phonics approaches per se, but with the ABC or alphabetic method, in which the names of the letters rather than the sounds were used and drill on long lists of nonsense syllables was a tortuous prelude to encounters with real words. In his *Seventh Annual Report to the Board of Education of Massachusetts*, Mann (1842, reproduced in N. Smith, 1965, pp. 77ff.) presented in glowing terms a reading lesson observed in a Prussian school that was a model for phonics approaches. But Mann's emphasis in this report, and in a later article in the *Common School Journal* (1844), was more on meaningful, active learning, based on familiar objects and activities, than it was on introductory approaches to reading. Mann favored whole words for initiating reading instruction, but he also advocated phonics (Balmuth, 1982, pp. 189ff). Modern caviling over initial teaching methods have unfortunately reduced Mann's general reforms to simple advocacy of a whole-word method.

Mathews's focus on introductory methods is understandable, since he wrote at a time when the battle lines in reading instruction were sharply drawn. A year later Chall's book *Learning to Read: The Great Debate* (1967) drew even more attention to introductory methods, in particular to the need to reevaluate the merits of the look-say methods that were then dominant. But a full understanding of reading instruction needs to cover considerably more than just the first few months of reading instruction when the so-called reading methods—look-say, phonics, and the like can be differentiated.

All-for-the-Best

A second perspective often used in historical accounts of reading instruction derives from the Cubberley (1934) *best-of-all-possible worlds* view, which is based on the assumption that intelligent men and women have always labored objectively and unselfishly for the improvement of public education, and that whatever occurred was always in the best interests of students and parents. Thus, the fact that all of the slave states except Kentucky had laws that forbade anyone to teach reading to a slave (Webber, 1978, p. 29), or that Native Americans were once forbidden to read or speak their native languages in reservation schools (Adams, 1946, pp. 50–51) is quietly ignored in N. Smith (1965), whose history is built on this *all-for-the-best* perspective. Smith focuses mostly on primary level reading instruction, but provides sufficient notes on methods and materials at higher levels to give an overview of the entire span of American reading instruction. Her primary interest is in presenting a story of the "ever-increasing attempts to apply science to education" (p. 1), and claims in a concluding section that the supreme achievement of education in this century is the "gift of scientific investigation" (p. 425). Clifford (1973) provides a sobering contrast to this view of direct changes in reading instruction due to research. (See also Instructional Technology, below, on the causes of the shift from oral to silent reading).

In N. Smith (1965), the history of reading instruction is described through the designation of periods, each marked by one or two dominant instructional influences. Thus, the earliest stage (1607–1776) is dominated by theology; the second (1776–1840) by moralism and nationalism; the third (1840–1880) by intelligent citizenship; the fourth (1880–1910) by cultural development; and the fifth (1910–1965) by scientific investigation. As an organizing device, the stages—at least up to the 20th century—provide a simple index to the main trends of reader content. Robinson (1930) provides a similar set of stages, but based solely on reader content. However, there is little support for Smith's boundaries in other studies of educational history. For example, the year 1783 seems to be a more satisfactory date than 1776 for the end of the colonial period (Cremin, 1970), especially since 1783 was the date of publication of Webster's blue-back speller, which was the most popular American reading text for almost 50 years. Then, Cremin (1961, pp. 358ff) places the beginning of the Progressive Movement in education at 1892, the year in which Joseph Mayer Rice's school surveys were published in the *Forum* magazine. For the beginning of the scientific movement in education 1892 appears to be a far more satisfactory date than 1910, when Thorndike's handwriting scale was published. But more importantly, far more was at work in reading instruction during the last two centuries than is reflected in the factors that Smith attributes to each of her last four periods. The works of Garfinkle (1954), Mosier (1947), and Mathews (1966) provide contrasts to these all-for-the-best views, as will be discussed later.

Childhood

While no single work on the history of reading instruction has been built on this perspective, notes about it have emerged from more general studies within this framework, particularly in Wishy (1968) and Kiefer (1948). Of these two, Kiefer's book is most relevant to reading instruction because it traces the changing status of children from 1700 to 1835 as reflected in juvenile literature, including reading texts. The shift in childhood concepts from the early colonial view of *ignorant and recalcitrant men and women* to the mid-19th century view of *undeveloped beings* is reflected both in school books and in other juvenile literature of the period. The stern religious dogma of the early *New England Primer* and the original Webster spelling book is replaced in Cobb's revised *Juvenile Readers* (1842) by examples of right living, occasionally with a humorous twist. The childhood perspective is important as one of several factors not only in reader content, but also in instructional methods. The emphasis on rote memorization of adult concepts that characterized colonial education, particularly at the lower levels, could no longer be fully justified when the child began to be viewed as undeveloped, but willing and able to learn, if led properly.

It is still debated how quickly teaching methods changed in the 19th century to accommodate the nurture view of childhood. Finkelstein (1974–1975, p. 81), for example, concludes that school teaching throughout the 19th century was characterized by rule-mindedness and suppression of subjectivity. Her evidence, however, is drawn primarily from the recollections of teachers, parents, and students. In contrast, Fuller (1982), while acknowledging the prevalence of rote memorization, cites activities that were more intellectually demanding in the district school, such as debating. By the middle of the 19th century many higher level readers stressed interrogative teaching and included passage-related questions that went far beyond literal interpretation. The issue is not only the difference between what occurred in classrooms and what teachers, students, and visitors recollected, but also the cognitive consequences of different schooling activities. Modern psychology gives no cause for favoring present day worksheet exercises on thinking skills over 1860s parsing exercises, if increase in procedural knowledge is the goal.

A second indication of changing attitudes toward childhood in the 19th century is found in the progression of children's literature from religious and moral lessons to what Tebbel (1973, vol. I, p. 195) labels "fantasy and fun and entertainment." Kiefer stresses the vast children's literature that was available and widely distributed from at least the last decade of the 18th century. The rhetoric of reformers (e.g., Eliot, 1898; Judd, 1936) has created the impression that a bookless society existed almost to the beginning of the 20th century, and that children rarely read anything beyond their school texts. Studies by Gilmore (1982) on portions of Vermont and New Hampshire in the period 1760–1830 indicate that books were almost universally found in estates, even among the poorest rural families. Much more work is needed, nevertheless, on the extent of printed material that was available to children in different regions and at different periods in America's history, drawing on estate records, book sales, magazine and newspaper subscription lists, advertisements, and library usage data.

CONTROL OF READER CONTENT

To the outside observer, whether parent, school board member, or ordinary citizen, the method of instruction is not always apparent in a school reader. Often, like a cooking recipe, the ingredients and processes are stated, but the form of the final product can be known only from experience. This is particularly true with 19th-century readers where instructional guidance was laconic at best. But reader content is another matter. The characters and their entanglements in narrative selections, as well as the subject matter of expository pieces, are all accessible and obvious, as are the moral, political, and social views of the compilers, at least to those willing to track them through a text. It should be no surprise then, that this is the aspect of reading instruction on which the largest number of analytical studies have been done.

Central Tendency

The *central tendency* in the study of reader content has been summarized succinctly by Elson in her study of 19th-century textbooks.

The schoolbooks delineated for [an American child] an idealized image both of himself and of the history that had produced the admired American type. They were a compendium of ideas popularly approved at the time, and they offer an excellent index of concepts considered "proper" for the nineteenth century American. (Elson, 1964, p. vii)

This view implies that we could predict the main thrust of reader content at any point during the 19th century from those ideas that had popular approval then. Notice that the emphasis here is not upon accuracy or verisimilitude in any sense, but rather upon idealized images and folk mythologies, that is, upon those beliefs that had popular approval, including those about where as a nation we came from and what we were. The view of history and society that 19th-century textbooks presented was one in which the path of American history revealed God's scheme for moral government, where the heroes of American history were "exemplars of industriousness, honesty, and intelligence," and where hard work and clean thoughts were rewarded by both spiritual and material gains (Cremin, 1980, p. 73).

Viewed against the period in American reading instruction from its beginnings until the early 19th century, the central tendency theory finds support in the heavy religious content of 17th- and early 18th-century New England reading materials (e.g., hornbooks, *New England Primer,* Bible), and in the admixture of religious, moral, and nationalistic selections that were evidenced after the Revolution. Theology was life's guide for the earliest settlers; it regulated not only their daily lives, but also their views of how the young child advanced to adulthood. Original sin and predestination were the justification for continual inculcation of the catechism, with corporal punishment for deviations from expected behavior. The ideas the Puritans accepted and the society they expected to build were, in the earliest days, well represented by the *New England Primer.* As church government gave way to civil government, and old country patterns of family and society changed, morality and good character gained equal footing with religion in the reading texts. With the American Revolution, nationalism was added.

Influence of Reader Content

Although 19th-century readers and spellers provided the bulk of Elson's (1964) data, she also examines texts in geography, history, and arithmetic.

Her basic assumption is that these schoolbooks provide insights into the ideas held by the common people in the 19th century by demonstrating the political, economic, social, cultural, and moral concepts to which they were exposed. While Elson leaves open the question of the extent to which an individual might be influenced by schoolbook concepts, she does point out that schoolbooks in the 19th century were probably more influential than those in the 20th century, due to the lack of competition from the media, and often, from other reading material (Elson, 1964, p. vii).

Cremin (1980) is more certain on this point, claiming that during the national period (1783–1876) textbooks "played a significant role in articulating and shaping the attitudes, values, tastes, and sensibilities of the American people" (p. 70). Although we have no thorough study of this issue, the bulk of the evidence points to a maintenance role for textbooks, which often lagged by years behind the changes occurring in society itself. Schools usually reflected changing practices and beliefs about children and their care and training, rather than initiating these changes. Clifford (1973) borrows the concept of cultural diffusion to explain how new ideas enter school practice. In an analysis of the impact of educational research on school curriculum in the 20th century, she found that changes rarely originated from within the schools and that the impact of those that originated from outside the schools was rarely direct. Instead, ideas entered the general public first, and then diffused into the schools, primarily through teachers who themselves were members of the masses rather than of an elite.

In addition, during much of the 19th century, textbooks were purchased by families and passed from child to child until lost, destroyed, or no longer needed. Since instruction was often based on whichever texts were brought from home, a reader or speller could continue to exert an influence far beyond the time when the ideas and methods it embodied had gone out of vogue. Finally, as many recent studies have shown (e.g., Miles, 1981) public schools, like most other public institutions, tend to be conservative. They act to provide continuity across generations rather than as agencies for change.

Revisionist Views

Elson's (1964) analysis of reader content covers concepts of nature, God and man, nationalism and its attendant concerns, and individualism. She also probes the prevailing textbook views on economic, social, and political concepts and values, and attempts to demonstrate how reader content varied with changing social views. Both Garfinkle (1954) and Mosier (1947) present a less charitable view of the motivation for the content for 19th-century school readers. Mosier (1947) writes exclusively of the McGuffey Readers, focusing mainly on the period from their introduction in the 1830s until the last major revision in 1879. Garfinkle (1954) concentrates on textbooks spanning the period from the first publication of Webster's spelling book (1783) until the

1860s. Both conclude that after 1840 the economic ideas in readers reflected the conservative interests of merchants and industrialists rather than those of the common man. Garfinkle (1954) builds on Curti's (1935) suggestion that the promoters of the common school movement needed the support of the business class, which looked with some alarm on the expanding labor movement and the concomitant spread of radical ideas about property, voting rights, and the like (Curti, 1959, pp. 227ff., 583). Along with religion, education was seen as a force that could instill respect for the established order in the poorer classes; that is, it could promote social control.

In the early 19th-century texts, especially in Webster's spelling books and Lindley Murray's *English Reader* (1799), the gospel of success was conspicuously missing, according to Garfinkle (1954). Murray's *English Reader* extolled "the spirit of true religion . . . [that] teaches men to fit themselves for another world by neglecting the concerns of [worldly success]" (Murray, 1799, pp. 24–27). The poor, according to Murray's *English Reader,* were as well off as the rich; one's talents and goals were assigned from above; and the best one could do in this life was to ". . . serve God, promote virtue, and be useful in this world." Similarly, Webster could find little merit in the Jeffersonian concepts of popular democracy with its concern for widespread suffrage. "I am persuaded," he wrote in a letter to Dr. Joseph Priestley, ". . . that no truth is more certain than that a republican government can be rendered durable in no other way than by excluding from elections men who have so little property, education, or principle, that they are liable to yield their own opinions to the guidance of unprincipled leaders" (quoted in Warfel, 1936, p. 267). In Webster's *American Spelling Book* (the name given from 1787 until 1829 to his 1783 spelling book), the child was taught both to eschew worldly possessions and to treasure labor as man's most important duty. Through labor, men would be kept from vice.

By 1840, however, work-for-reward was firmly entrenched in school readers. Using primarily the textbooks reported to be in use in New York State schools, Garfinkle (1954) found a strong emphasis on property rights and material rewards for labor. Mosier (1947) makes a similar argument for the McGuffey Readers, but he views the guiding philosophy behind the compilers of these texts as in the Hamiltonian tradition, as espoused by Alexander Hamilton, John Marshall, and Daniel Webster. Mixed with these politics are a strong Calvinist religious streak and a middle-class Protestant morality. "God made the poor man as well as the rich man" is a consistent theme, as is the need for religion and education to help reconcile republican institutions with "universal suffrage and the terrors of undisciplined democracy" (Mosier, 1947, p. 156). Nowhere do these readers show any faith in popular government nor any interest in strong individualism. While the beauty and solitude of the West is often compared to the overcrowded urban ugliness of the East, western folk heroes like Mike Fink and Davey Crockett are conspicuously absent.

Revisionism Appraised

As plausible as the arguments of both Garfinkle (1954) and Mosier (1947) might be, they need to be examined against a wider data base than either presents. Garfinkle based his views of early 19th-century American readers on only three texts, the 1826 and 1841 editions of Webster's spelling book and Murray's *English Reader.* Webster's speller was originally issued in 1783, but underwent major revisions in 1804 and 1829 (Monaghan, 1983, pp. 51ff.). Therefore, arguments about early 19th-century values cannot be readily derived from the two Webster texts Garfinkle cited. And, while Webster's speller and Murray's reader were the most widely used texts for teaching reading in the late 18th and early 19th century, they faced increasing competition after the 1820s, particularly from Cobb's spellers and readers, and Pierpont's readers. In New York State, for example, the number of towns reporting the use of Webster's spelling book increased from 302 to 418 (38 %) in the period 1827–1834, while those reporting use of Cobb's spelling book, which was first published in 1821, increased from 59 to 234 (300 %) (*Report of the Superintendent*, 1834). In 1830 Webster complained to the publisher of his spelling book about the loss of sales due to the competition from texts by Emerson, Cobb, Sears, and others (Monaghan, 1983, p. 152). Lindley Murray, although born in the United States, moved to England in 1794 and remained there until his death in 1826 (Belok, 1973). His reading texts were all written in England and contained nothing that could be mistaken for American nationalism. His work, therefore, has limited value as evidence for the attitudes of American textbook writers.

What Garfinkle (1954) interprets as the special interest of conservative businessmen and industrialists might also be attributed to the prevailing Protestant ethic, which found no fault in the doctrine of materialism. "The all pervading religious emphasis in schoolbooks . . . sanctions virtues likely to lead to materialism rather than other-worldliness" (Elson, 1964, p. 252). What Henretta (1973, pp. 102ff.) calls "the new entrepreneurial personality" had its roots in the child-rearing practices and social values of the Protestant sects that settled New England. Supporting the cultural dynamic that transformed the early Puritan society well before the middle of the 18th century were personal responsibility for one's own actions and an unremitting stress on industry, activity, and spirit. What failed to mirror the true interests of the American character was not the materialism-based readers of the McGuffey era, but the conservative, heaven-oriented readers of the generation before (cf. Kaestle, 1983, pp. 67–68).

Industry and thrift are persistent themes in readers throughout the 19th century, and the rewards of one's labors become more and more materialistic as the century progresses. With a focus on character that reaches almost to obsession, many 19th-century textbooks work to death what Commager (1962) called "the essential virtues": industry, sobriety, thrift, propriety, modesty, punctuality, and conformity.

These were the essential virtues, and those who practiced them were sure of success. Success, too, for all the patina of morality that was brushed over it, was clearly material. It was a job, a farm, money in hand or in the bank. Failure was, just as clearly, the consequence of laziness or self-indulgence, and deserved, therefore, little sympathy (Commager, 1962, p. viii).

Wishy (1968) points out that reformers and conservatives in the 19th century agreed that strong character and morality should be the central focus of education. They differed primarily about the role of religious training and the methods of instruction. Commager (1962, p. v) and Westerhoff (1978, p. 24) stress the basic conservatism of the McGuffey Readers, not just in politics and religion, but in pedagogy as well. The reforms inspired by Pestalozzi's teachings in Europe, like the writings of Horace Mann, Henry Barnard, and the other midcentury educational reformers in the United States, are not strongly represented in these readers. McGuffey was certainly not an educational reformer in the style of Keagy, Neef, or Mann, but how he compared to other authors of the same period (e.g., Pierpont, Cobb, Emerson, Worcester, Angell, Goodrich) remains to be worked out. Lindberg (1976, p. xx) is of the opinion that the McGuffey Readers were not markedly different from other readers for the time, and that their success came from shrewd marketing practices rather than noteworthy content or pedagogy. McGuffey flirted with the whole-word approach in his first primer, but changed back to the more conservative ABC method in the first revision. But he did introduce some improvements in instruction, particularly in limiting the number of new words introduced on each page (N. Smith, 1965, p. 107) and in repetition of new vocabulary.

Minnich (1936) credits McGuffey with eliminating spelling as a preliminary step to learning to read. It is true that McGuffey removed the extensive list of one-, two-, three-, and four-syllable words that characterized the interlude between Webster's introduction of the alphabet and his first sentences. Nevertheless, the instructions to the teacher in the *Eclectic Primer* of 1867 (p. 11) are "let the child spell each word in the line, then read the line." Later editions of the primer claimed that the series could be used with the phonic, word or alphabetic [ABC] methods, or any combination of these methods.

Mosier's (1947) views are partially supported in Commager (1962) and Lindberg (1976), but his work suffers from a failure to consider separately the major editions of the McGuffey readers. Few selections survived the entire course of changes that took place from 1836 until 1879 (Nietz, 1964).

For example, Mosier's depiction of the strong sectional bias of the readers, particularly toward the West, is based on two paeans to the glory of western settlers, western geography, and western literature in the first edition of the *Fourth Reader,* both written by Dr. Daniel Drake, a friend of the McGuffeys. But Mosier fails to point out that the most Westernly, chauvinistic of these selections was deleted from the 1844 edition of the *Fourth Reader* and the other was dropped in 1857, neither to reappear. While Mosier claims that "this early sectionalism passes by quiet and easy stages into the broader patriotism and nationalism of the whole series" (1947, p. 36), McGuffey and his publishers apparently strove for a louder and more abrupt change of face. The 1844 revision of the *Fourth Reader* claims in its introduction that "NO SECTIONAL matter, reflecting upon the local institutions, customs, or habits of any portion of the United States, is to be found among [these] contents" (quoted in Lindberg, 1976, p. xxi).

Westerhoff (1978, pp. 74–103) points out that the original editions of the first four McGuffey Readers, which were the only ones written by William Holmes McGuffey, reflected an early 19th-century Presbyterian Calvinism, permeated throughout with salvation, righteousness, and piety. These views were radically altered by the various publishers of the succeeding editions, so that by 1879 the series represented American middle-class attitudes, values, and beliefs, with their underpinning of civil religion. According to Nietz (1964, pp. 122–123), about 30% of the content of the 1844 *Fourth Reader* was religious, while only 3% of the 1901 edition of this text was. Mosier's references to the various readers are rarely to the first four readers (8% according to Westerhoff, 1978, p. 26), and few of these are to the editions published before 1850. By this analysis, the views of William Holmes McGuffey were not those of the second half of the 19th century, but of an earlier time. His publishers were left with the task of catching up to prevailing social attitudes in subsequent editions.

Other Deviations and Limitations

A close inspection of the McGuffey Readers illustrates some of the limitations of the central tendency theory of reader content. These readers, like all others, were commercial ventures, targeted towards a specific audience. "This series of School Books was undertaken . . . for the purpose of furnishing the South and the West with a complete, *uniform,* and *improved* set of School Books," reads the first page of an 1840 edition of the third reader. A few years later, when a national market was sensed, the blatant sectional bias was pulled out and a new national orientation declared. But the South remained important for the McGuffey Readers, and was undoubtedly the reason for an almost total exclusion of readings on the Civil War, save for a single impartial piece. Even in the 1879 edition, the name of Abraham Lincoln, already immortalized in myth and song in American literature, was missing.

Similar deviations from ideas popularly approved at the time are found in the omission of Mark Twain, Walt Whitman, the California gold rush, the Oregon Trail, and, as mentioned already, such backwoods heroes as Mike Fink and Davey Crockett (Commager, 1962, p. xi).

The entrepreneurial element in reader content has not been examined closely, yet is commonly assumed to be present, particularly in the 20th century (Anderson, Hiebert, Scott, & Wilkinson, 1985; Clifford, 1983). Few modern publishers of reading series have included topics in reading selections that might displease the large adoption states, regardless of how popular these subjects might be elsewhere. By contrast, the degree to which Webster altered his content to compete with Cobb and others was probably small, given the limited amount of reading material in the revised Webster spelling book of 1829. But marketing considerations in the selection of reader content increased as single spellers and readers graduated to series of readers, as the school-age population multiplied, and as transportation to national markets became more efficient.

A second limitation on the central tendency notion occurred in the second quarter of the 19th century when primers and first readers began to stress nature themes and simple accounts of everyday observable objects and events. The progression in introductory material from the *New England Primer* and the Webster spelling book of 1783 to McGuffey's revised *Pictorial Eclectic Primer* (1867) provides a case study for the spread of Pestalozzianism. The *New England Primer* is almost totally devoid of secular matter, taking every opportunity to preach the gospel of true faith. Webster mixes moralism and religion but admits an occasional secular paragraph on a didactic topic. In contrast, McGuffey's revised *Pictorial Eclectic Primer* makes almost no mention of moralism and religion. A fly runs, a top hums, a boy hops, a cat gets out of a box, a bird is killed, and a little girl gets a new doll. Of 89 lessons in the text, at most 3 have any obvious religious or moralistic teaching. William Holmes McGuffey had no role in the 1867 revision of the primer (Westerhoff, 1978, p. 17). By the time that this revision was finished, Pestalozzian schooling principles were known throughout the United States. The object lesson had already begun to appear in textbooks and was described in various speeches before the American Institute of Instruction and in articles in the *American Annals of Education*. McGuffey began his moralizing in the original *First Reader,* but by the 1870s even the second and third readers contained mostly nature and childhood stories.

Good Literature Arrives

Yet another deviation from what the central tendency theory would predict began to appear towards the end of the 19th century as college presidents and professors of educational administration began to join the educational reform movement. These administrative progressives, as Tyack (1974, pp. 126ff.)

calls them, attempted to apply the corporate model to school organization, with a stress on strong centralized control. Urban schooling was to be made socially efficient, with schooling differentiated according to the student's position in society. Associated peripherally with this movement was the desire to impose *good literature* on the language arts curriculum. Charles W. Eliot, president of Harvard University, was probably the best known advocate of high literature for reading at the end of the 19th century, but he was not alone in this. Through the National Educational Association and the American Institute of Instruction, reform of the elementary curriculum was pressed, with reading reform a favorite interest. Eliot (1891, cited in N. Smith, 1965, p. 120) called the existing readers "ineffable trash," insisting that all reading instruction be based on great literature.

N. Smith (1965) traces the origins of this cultural emphasis in reading instruction to the 1880s, with acceleration of the movement in the 1890s under the influence of Herbartianism. Herbart, like most other educators of the nineteenth century, saw the elementary school as a central agent in the development of character, but instead of using the Bible or explicit moral tales for achieving this end, Herbart encouraged the use of literary and historical stories. The new education of the 1880s and 1890s strongly stressed the needs and interests of the individual child as the age-graded school was being institutionalized throughout the United States. From Froebel's influence on the spreading kindergarten movement, from the child study movement initiated by G. Stanley Hall, and from the Herbartians, the need to appeal to the child's imagination became the watchword of textbook compilers.

Several trends coincided at the end of the 19th century to make literature a logical basis for school readers. First, silent reading was beginning to be emphasized in place of oral reading, particularly after the elementary grades (see below). The slow demise of school elocution, beginning after the Civil War, reduced the need for short, stage-oriented reading selections. Whereas McGuffey's *Fifth Reader* of 1853 (also called the *Rhetorical Guide*) contained 235 selections from prose and poetry, Cyr's *Fifth Reader* of 1890 had fewer than half this number in roughly the same number of pages. The difference in pages per selection is perhaps more revealing: about 1¾ pages for McGuffey versus almost 4 for Cyr. This trend continued into the 20th century as silent reading became more established. A popular reader from 1918, for example, the *Beacon Fifth Reader* by James F. Fassett, had 9¾ pages per selection for shorter pieces, plus a single, 50-page selection.

Second, children's literature was rapidly becoming an important segment of the publishing trade, particularly after about 1860 (Tebbel, 1973). Juvenile publishing houses like Little, Brown and Houghton Mifflin emerged, particularly in Boston. Rather than preaching the gospel of hard work, thrift, and patience, children's books of this period incorporated adventure stories and other genres that appealed to the child's imagination. Even several national best sellers were children's or young adult's stories, including Joel Chandler Harris's *Uncle Remus* (1881) and Mark Twain's *Huckleberry Finn* (1884). For the most part, the new children's literature had an indirect influence on readers, coming first into supplementary reading materials that began to be used in the last two decades of the 19th century, and only after the turn of the century into the readers themselves.

Finally, and perhaps most importantly, both schooling and society in the United States had matured to the point where culture had become an important concern. With the West settled, movement and opportunity were vertical rather than horizontal—rising up the social and industrial ladder rather than running westward to claim another patch of untamed countryside. A flood of immigrants, many from poor, rural areas of Europe, resulted in further pressures on the schools to homogenize and Americanize. The result was a reader content based on good literature, what one reading textbook called the "famous stories that are the rightful heritage of every English speaking child" (Fassett, 1918, p. iii). This is not exactly what Charles W. Eliot had in mind when he called for the substitution of real literature for readers, but it was as close as reading programs were to come, even up to the present.

The total domination of literary selections in the upper level readers, which came by the first decade of the 20th century, reduced the ability of the reader to convey "a compendium of ideas popularly approved at the time" (Elson, 1964, p. vii). This literary emphasis continued up to the present day, when real life and fantasy account for the majority of the reading selections (Willows, Borwick, & Hayvren, 1981). Changes have occurred in the past 50 years, particularly in the portrayal of minorities and women, but the literary emphasis remains. Current reader content appears to be influenced less by popularly approved ideas than by the constraints of a long list of taboos, created in response to state adoption requirements and the pressures of special interest groups.

In summary, the content of school readers from the middle of the 17th century until the last decade of the 19th century was, with some deviations, regulated by society's idealized image of itself, including its expected future and its ennobling past. This image was, however, primarily of a white, Protestant nation, in which men were strong and noble, and women supportive and caring. In early colonial times, society built its self-image around theological concepts, particularly salvation. With commercial expansion and the elevation of civil religion in the second half of the 19th century, mankind began to celebrate itself, and it presented its children with visions of tangible and immediate rewards for proper behavior. With the shift to silent reading for comprehension, and with the change in child psychology to a nurturing view, society's adult images were sublimated to those of the child. Beginning reading built on fantasy and adventure, while more advanced reading explored good literature. With the introduction in the 20th century of a culturally diverse literature, a clear image of adult American society and of the child's role in it was no longer available. Whether one exists that would be recognized by a majority of Americans remains to be determined.

EVOLUTION OF THE MODERN READING CURRICULUM

Content-Area Reading

In the last several decades, basal readers have generally divided their skill interests across four strands or tracks: (1) decoding, (2) vocabulary, (3) comprehension, and (4) a potpourri that often is labeled *life and study skills,* but might also include literary appreciation and a variety of minor interests and annoyances, arising from special adoption requirements or fads (e.g., survival skills, creativity). The core of this fourth group, study skills and content-area reading, is the most recent historically, entering the reading program as a stated interest in the 1920s, perhaps due to the realization that reading instruction as practiced in the American school curriculum was primarily instruction in reading narrative fiction, and that additional skills were required for expository texts, reference materials, and the like (Venezky, 1982). Whether this bias towards fiction is a universal trait of school reading programs or is unique to particular countries is a worthy topic for cross-national studies.

Content-area reading received brief attention in the mid-19th century through readers that contained science or social studies readings exclusively, but these failed to gain wide acceptance. The emphasis on silent reading that arose after World War I in the United States led to content-area reading, by which was meant reading of science, math, social studies, and other nonliterary materials. Analyses of reading difficulties in content-area materials and suggestions for teaching content-area reading skills were generated by a number of groups, including a special committee established by the National Society for the Study of Education in 1924 (N.S.S.E., 1925). Although this report remains today as an enlightened examination of the topic, there is little evidence that these suggestions ever received more than casual recognition in reading programs.

Moore, Readence, and Rickelman (1983) trace the rise of content-area reading instruction to the influence of humanists, developmentalists, and scientific determinists. According to their analysis, the humanists (e.g., Horace Mann, John Dewey, Colonel Francis Parker) promoted independent thinking, the developmentalists (e.g., G. Stanley Hall), age-stage progression, and the scientific determinists (e.g., E.L. Thorndike, William S. Gray), an empirical base for planning content-area and study skill instruction. But these influences need to be examined (as the authors themselves suggest) against actual instructional practice, as opposed to prominent opinion and research findings.

N. Smith (1965, pp. 282ff.), for example, claims that the first reading texts to emphasize content-area reading skills were the fourth- to sixth-grade books of her own series, published in the middle 1940s. (A second program published in the late 1940s, *The Betts Basic Readers,* had reading selections at the fourth-grade level with settings in foreign countries.) For most reading programs, however, content-area reading is still based upon narrative materials, but with social studies or science themes. The instructional techniques advocated by the 1924 N.S.S.E. Committee are rarely incorporated. At issue here is interpretation of the phrase *content-area reading.* If it means simply the inclusion of expository selections in the readers without provision of instruction on how to cope with the unique features of this genre (e.g., high information content, charts and graphs, noncontinuous text), then content-area reading has been present since at least Webster's original spelling book. If, however, it means specific instruction in content-area reading, as represented, for example, by Kane, Byrne, and Hater (1974), then true content-area reading instruction is probably a practice of recent vintage.

Oral Expression

Besides the first three tracks mentioned above (decoding, vocabulary, and comprehension), which have been represented in the American reading curriculum since the early colonial period, a fourth track, oral expression, once held a prominent position in the reading curriculum, but survives only in the wings and aisles of present-day instruction, stripped of any systematic procedures or rules, and only occasionally admitted to stage center. N. Smith (1965) briefly mentions the importance of elocution in the advanced readers of the 19th century, but gives no attention to the debate that was waged through most of that century between naturalistic and mechanistic speaking styles; or to the influence of James Rush's (1833) text, *The Philosophy of the Human Voice,* on orthography and pronunciation in school readers; or to the role of instructors in elocution and oratory in the design of readers (e.g., Lewis B. Monroe, Mark Bailey, Epes Sargent). Elocutionary excellence was one of the major objectives for advanced reading instruction from the earliest records until almost the end of the 19th century. Prior to the Revolutionary War training in elocution was oriented mainly towards the ministry and law; after the Revolution, according to Robb (1968), elocutionary training was oriented as much towards political roles and education as it was towards the ministry. Harvard introduced elocution instruction in 1756 for nationalistic reasons and in 1806 appointed John Quincy Adams to the first Boylston Chair of Rhetoric and Oratory. Other colleges followed soon after in establishing chairs for elocution and in introducing elocution and oratory courses.

The most fully developed component of instruction in American reading textbooks throughout the 19th century was the component on elocution. At the beginning of the 19th century this included rules and instructions for pronunciation and for proper delivery such as those found in Lindley Murray's *Introduction to the English Reader* (1805/1818). By the middle of the 19th century, more fully developed sections on elocution began to appear. In McGuffey's *Fifth Reader, or Rhetorical Guide,* for example, the first 47 pages are taken up with the principles of elocution, including articulation, inflections, accent in emphasis, instructions for reading verse, cultivation and management of the voice, gesture, and suggestions to teachers.

Elocution fell out of favor in American life in the period immediately following the Civil War, and by the end of the 19th century it was no longer found in the popular reading textbooks. By the end of the first decade of the 20th century, it was practically unknown as a component of American reading instruction (Hyatt, 1943). Gray (1937a, p. 31) pointed out the neglect of oral reading skills in the upper elementary grades, but had little success in restoring any emphasis on this lost art.

Comprehension

One of the main areas of uncertainty in the history of American reading instruction centers on comprehension, and in particular, when comprehension instruction first entered the reading curriculum. Resnick and Resnick (1977, p. 383) and Moore, Readence, and Rickelman (1983, p. 423) claim that independent reading for meaning is a phenomenon of the early 20th century that was prompted by the standardized testing movement. Similarly, the writings of educational reformers like Horace Mann and Henry Barnard could lead to the view that reading for meaning during the 19th century was as rarely seen in classrooms as griffins and unicorns.

An equally defensible view is that gaining meaning from print has always been a goal of reading instruction, but that this goal was disguised by the emphasis on oral expression that pervaded American reading instruction until almost the end of the 19th century. The Massachusetts School Law of 1642, for example, was concerned with "children's ability to read and understand the principles of religion and the capital laws of the country" (quoted in Calhoun, 1969, p. 22). Silent reading for meaning was emphasized in a number of speeches given before the American Institute of Instruction in the first half of the 19th century (e.g., Palmer, 1837). James Pyle Wickersham, the first superintendent of education in Pennsylvania, considered reading as a mental operation to be one of the three main divisions of reading, the other two being reading as a vocal art and delivery (Wickersham, 1867). N. Smith (1965) dates the introduction of comprehension from the 1840s, prompted by whole word introductory methods.

By the end of the 19th century gaining meaning from print was more frequently mentioned as an aim of reading by educators and reading instructors. By the end of the 1920s, the aim of reading instruction was defined as training pupils "to translate the printed words into ideas, thoughts, motives, and actions which make for knowledge and efficiency . . ." (Ayers & McKinnie, 1927, quoted in Gray & Zirbes, 1927–1928, p. 39).

The failure by educational historians (e.g., Finkelstein, 1974–1975) to find reading for meaning in the curriculum prior to the early 1900s also results from the emphasis on primary level instruction in the extant histories, and from a lack of an accepted definition of comprehension instruction. Using amount of time spent on direct instruction in passage meaning as her definition, Durkin (1978–1979) found almost no teaching of comprehension in modern reading classrooms, in spite of a clear emphasis on the topic in current instructional materials. In contrast to Durkin's findings, a survey of 795 schools in larger U.S. cities and towns in the early 1960s found that the percentage of respondents reporting a *considerable* (vs. *moderate, little,* or *none*) amount of time devoted to developing comprehension skills varied from 77.0 (grades 1 and 2) to 81.4 (grades 3 and 4) (Austin & Morrison, 1963, p. 37). It is unlikely that actual or intended emphasis on comprehension declined between the early 1960s and the late 1970s. Although we have no comparable logs of instructional emphasis from the 19th century, anecdotal evidence (e.g., May, 1861, p. 413) gives some support to the claim that comprehension was taught then, although probably not through direct instruction.

Most analyses of instruction have drawn conclusions about comprehension either from the presence of a strong oral/rote emphasis, or the lack of suggested comprehension activities. Both have been accepted as evidence against the teaching of comprehension. But other data relevant to this issue are available, particularly in the textbooks themselves. Careful analyses of vocabulary teaching and of lesson structures, particularly those involving composition, might force a revision of commonly held views on this topic.

INSTRUCTIONAL TECHNOLOGY—THE BATTLE OVER METHODS

Defining Reading Instruction

Methods for teaching reading, as revealed in textbooks, teacher diaries, instruction manuals and other educational literature, play a major role in treatments of American reading instruction (e.g., Davies, 1974; Mathews, 1966; N. Smith, 1965). *Methods* in these accounts generally means the approach to the introduction of reading instruction—that is, such entities as the ABC method, the whole word method, the phonics method, and the sentence method. But the term *method* is also used occasionally to refer to components of these or of other instructional procedures such as organizing word lists by initial sounds, or to the types of reading that were emphasized at different periods throughout the history of American reading instruction.

Both the narrowness and the ambiguity of the conventional use of the term *method* have been barriers to the study of reading instruction and to comparisons with instruction in other disciplines. Debates about reading instruction have always focused heavily on introductory techniques, but even in colonial times school practices extended well beyond the rudiments and incorporated procedures not defined within this domain of labels.

More importantly, the more general development of the philosophy of instruction, from which reading instruction derives, cannot be defined easily through this terminology. For example, educational writings in the two decades prior to the Civil War argued the merits of four basic instructional methods: catechetical, explanatory, synthetical, and analytical (Elsbree, 1939). Each was reflected in contemporary reading practices, but the relationship between these four methods and the so-called reading methods could not be determined from the labels alone. But ambiguity exists even within these reading labels themselves. What has been called the *word method* is in fact at least two, if not more, methods of introducing reading. Samuel Worcester (1826), who was one of the first textbook authors to suggest a break from the ABC approach, advocated teaching words as whole units as a *prelude* to analyzing them and naming their letters. Wells (1860) differed from Worcester in advocating teaching letter sounds after words were introduced. Names of letters might also be introduced, but Wells emphasized mainly the teaching of sounds after whole words were learned. Finally, there is the word or look-say approach that passes directly from whole words to meaning, dispensing altogether with analysis. Michael (1984) cites a text from 1862 that advocated this approach. As Lamport (1937) points out, *word methods* are usually *combination methods,* drawing together whole word and analytical approaches. Mathews (1966, p. 63) suggests the labels "words-to-reading" and "words-to-letters" to distinguish the two major types of word methods.

Gray (1937b, pp. 76–77) presents a five-stage model that is especially useful for viewing the entire span of reading instruction. In this model, reading instruction for kindergarten through senior high school is divided into five phases or stages, each identified with a different developmental goal. These include: (1) readiness, (2) initial teacher guidance, (3) becoming an independent reader, (4) increasing speed and efficiency, and (5) refinement of interests, habits, and tastes. Only in part of stage 2 are the so-called methods relevant. Unfortunately, many of the procedures used in the last two centuries in the later stages (e.g., the interrogative method, elocutionary training) have received little attention in historical accounts. A complete history, nevertheless, needs to attend to methods and materials used in all of these stages.

The Shift from Oral to Silent Reading

Overview

From its origins until almost the end of the 19th century, reading instruction in the American classroom was built around oral activities. By 1925, however, silent reading was strongly emphasized, even to the point where silent reading was sometimes taught from the onset of instruction (Brooks, 1985, p. 88). On the surface, the shift from emphasis on oral reading to an emphasis on silent reading appears to be a simple phenomenon. In the 1870s most reading instruction emphasized oral reading at the lower levels and elocution at the higher levels. By the 1920s reading instruction, even at the beginning levels contained a prominent element of silent reading. At the higher levels, silent reading dominated. However, as simple as this situation may look, two problems remain unresolved: when and why this change occurred. For example, N. Smith (1965, pp. 158ff.) acknowledges a role for the increased emphasis on comprehension that occurred towards the end of the 19th century, but attributes most of the influence for the switch from oral to silent reading to research, especially that done at the University of Chicago in the period 1915–1921, and places the major part of this shift roughly in the period around 1920.

Lamport (1937, pp. 92ff.), on the other hand, attributes most of the influence for this change to the Herbartian movements in the last two decades of the 19th century. Through the efforts of Colonel Francis Parker and others of like mind, the sentence and story methods were strongly advocated for early reading instruction, with a stress on initial silent reading. According to Lamport, a trend towards silent reading had begun by 1900. Kellogg's (1900) survey of reading instruction in ten large cities lends support to Lamport's claim, particularly for primary level reading. But Calhoun (1973) places the major part of the shift even earlier. "Beginning about 1880, the long concern for meaningfulness and oral reading was being transmuted in American normal schools and school systems into a prescription that individual, silent reading for meaningful content should be the main goal of teaching" (p. 82). Part of the influence that Calhoun sees for this switch were the impersonal communication techniques of national commerce. High oral expression was left to the remaining stump orators; meaningfulness now was the criterion of successful reading, and it was not tied exclusively to oral reading.

Hyatt (1943, pp. 30ff.) falls between N. Smith (1965) and Lamport (1937) in that she places the change in emphasis from oral to silent reading in the period 1915–1924, but attributes the change to multiple influences, including the Herbartians, Colonel Francis W. Parker, scientific investigations, standardized tests, and the sentence and story methods. The majority of her evidence is obtained from speeches and writings of educators, pedagogy manuals, and prefaces to reading programs.

The Role of Research

The argument by N. Smith (1965) and, to a lesser degree, Hyatt (1943) that research on the differences between oral and silent reading was the main (or even contributing) factor in this evolution should be questioned on several grounds. First, the research that Smith cites was done in the period from 1913 to about 1921, which is after many reading programs appear to have incorporated silent reading as a primary emphasis, at least at the higher levels. (In contrast, Gray [1925, p. 5] cites several studies done before 1911 which he feels were important for changes that occurred in the 1920s, including studies that showed a clear distinction between oral and silent reading.) Second, the research Smith cites (e.g., Pintner [1913], Mead [1915], Oberholtzer [1915], Judd [1918]) was published primarily in psychological journals or in research-oriented university organs (e.g., *Supplementary Education Monographs*), to which few teachers had access. Clifford (1973) claims from her study of the influence of research on the school curriculum that research results have rarely changed educational practice directly; when they have, generally several decades passed before any influence could be discerned. Educational science in this century has served more to legitimate already accepted practices than it has to initiate new ones.

Missing from the discussions of oral and silent reading is any attempt to distinguish instructional practices in smaller, rural schools from those in larger, urban schools; or practices in educationally progressive areas (e.g., the Northeast) from those in more conservative areas (e.g., the South). Rates of change across these types of schools undoubtedly differed, and may in part account for the differences found in dating the oral to silent shift. But a more significant discontinuity in the research literature is the lack of specification of the instructional context for oral and silent reading. A reading lesson in the 1880s was no more an unremitting chorus of obs and ibs, falling inflections, and orotund enunciations than was a 1920s lesson a demonstration of sustained silence. A variety of instructional activities, some oral and some silent, characterized instruction in both periods. To understand the significance of the oral-to-silent shift, and its relationship to changes in other instructional methods, more refined analyses are needed of the totality of instructional methods across the various grades and time periods.

READING'S REPORT CARD—THE OUTCOMES OF INSTRUCTION

Trends in Current Research

A substantial body of literature on the development of literacy has appeared in the last two decades, particularly in England, France, and Sweden, with work on literacy in North America receiving increased attention (e.g., Graff, 1979; Lockridge, 1974; Soltow & Stevens, 1981; see Kaestle, 1985, for a review). Among the issues attended to in recent years have been the value of different indicators for rates of literacy (e.g., signatures, newspaper circulation), and the relationship of both amount of schooling and instructional quality to literacy acquisition. The first of these issues is discussed in general histories of education (e.g., Cremin, 1970, pp. 546ff.) and more recent specific studies on literacy (e.g., Auwers, 1980; Graff, 1979) and is not of direct interest here. But the second issue, concerning the effectiveness of different amounts and methods of reading instruction, has received little attention from educational historians.

As sketched above, serious debate over methods of teaching reading began at the end of the 1820s in the United States, and has continued to the present day. Implicit in the forensics that have ensued is the assumption that method, by which is generally meant the approach used for at most the first four to six months of introductory instruction, is the main determinant of subsequent reading ability. Admittedly, this debate has occasionally turned to other facets of instruction, such as the roles of rote memorization and oral performance, but nevertheless the focus of reading reform over the past century has been on introductory methods. Current research appears to give only marginal support to this methods/outcome assumption, although a few recent studies show an initial advantage for students taught by phonics approaches, particularly in word identification skills where such an advantage would be expected (Pflaum, Walberg, Karegianes, & Rasher, 1980; Williams, 1985). Differential outcomes as marked by error types have also been attributed to methods in studies by Barr (1974–1975), but more recently attention has shifted to analysis of the importance of academic engaged time and content covered (Rosenshine & Stevens, 1984; Stallings & Kaskowitz, 1974), ability grouping (Barr & Dreeben, 1984), and school effectiveness (see Purkey & Smith, 1983, for a review). While method is a contributing factor in some of these studies, it rarely accounts for any major share of the variability observed in ability outcomes. On balance, the modern research implicates such instructional factors as content covered, time spent relative to what is needed, appropriate diagnosis, and flexible methods as the primary characteristics of effective reading instruction.

The Search for Outcome Measures

The central problem in relating reading instruction to learning outcomes is that few reliable measures of achievement existed prior to the widespread use of standardized reading tests (i.e., before about 1918). Although written examinations were begun by the New York State Regents in 1864, these covered arithmetic, spelling, geography, and grammar, but not reading. Calhoun (1973, pp. 79ff.), in particular, cautions against face value acceptance of school reports and other educational observations of the 19th century. The viewpoint of the observer was an obvious factor in the nature and enthusiasm of what was reported. Those with reform in mind were hardly unbiased observers of the methods they wanted to change. Beginning in the 1840s, according to Calhoun (1973, p. 85), a common educational interpretation can be detected in the school reports, particularly in New York State where specific criticisms of current reading instruction were distributed in 1842 as part of an official statement of instruction in schoolkeeping by the superintendent of common schools. On the other hand, foreign observers were, perhaps out of politeness, overly positive, and generally unable to sample the full range of American schools. This is what might have led J.G. Fitch, an English educator, to claim in 1890 that American schools stressed silent reading, with comprehension tested by subsequent questions (Calhoun, 1973, p. 82), an observation that is not supported by other data from that period.

Data that are perhaps of a slightly more reliable origin were offered by Rice (1893), in reporting on municipal reading programs that he assessed in his journeys in 1892 throughout the East and Midwest. Rice tested third graders in each city he visited, using a third-level reader from which the students were not studying. Students were asked to read aloud from the textbook without preparation. In the schools of Indianapolis, Minneapolis, and two other locations, students in general could read intelligently, at sight, from the text, while in St. Paul there was more variability, but still generally good results. Although Rice gives no criteria for judging oral reading, the information he provides is more objective than most other evaluations from this period. Unfortunately, comparable data are not found until silent reading tests were developed almost 25 years later.

In criticizing particular methods, many observers ignored the possibility that what the canonical method prescribes and what teachers and students did with it might differ. Observations of the ABC method, for example, leave us with little explanation for how literacy could have resulted during the 1,000 years (more or less) that this approach dominated initial reading instruction, yet thousands if not millions began the journey to literacy with this method. Contemporary cognitive psychology offers no explanation if what was reported by 19th-century reformers (e.g., Mann, 1844, pp. 119ff.) was all that was involved. But teacher variability in directing lessons was undoubtedly large and students might have extracted meaningful assistance even when it was not intended. Wickersham (1867, p. 181) offers this interpretation for reading in the mid-19th century, speaking particularly of the alphabetic (ABC) method.

Views on Effectiveness

Introduction

Studies of 19th-century reading instruction have generally emphasized the contemporary criticisms of what were assumed to be ineffective methods and incompetent student performance. Graff (1979, pp. 287ff.), for example, cites reports from England in the middle of the 19th century claiming that fewer than one-third of the students at even the best schools reached expected standards, and reports from Canada, giving similar results. From an examination of such reports and other data on reading instruction, Graff concludes that failure to achieve good reading skills was common at the primary level.

In contrast, Gilmore (1982, p. 165), who studied school records and supporting data on literacy for counties in Vermont and New Hampshire in the period 1760 to 1830, speculates that a child after one term of summer school and one term with good attendance of district winter school would have attained sufficient reading ability to read an almanac, local newspaper, and basic school materials.

Even by modern standards Gilmore's estimates appear excessively optimistic. The abilities Gilmore describes are not obtained by the average child today until well into the third or fourth year of reading instruction, and the total amount of schooling per year today, considering length of term, hours per day, and average daily attendance, is significantly more than it was for a combined summer and winter term in the first quarter of the 19th century (Cubberley, 1934, p. 429). Furthermore, quality of schooling varied dramatically across school districts, and children started school at all imaginable ages (Kaestle & Vinovskis, 1978).

A considerably more conservative estimate is made by Soltow and Stevens (1981, pp. 114–115), who estimate that in the 1860s a child who regularly attended both summer and winter school from the age of 5 through the age of 11 would have been exposed to about 1,100 hours of formal reading instruction. This amount of instruction, they assume, would have been sufficient to guarantee literacy (defined as reading, but not writing). Children with irregular attendance would have had considerable difficulty in becoming literate, especially if strong parental assistance were not provided. Soltow and Steven's figures are based on an assumption of two hours per day for formal reading instruction for ages 5–8 and one hour for ages 9–11 and are derived from selected Ohio school districts together with the schools in Rochester, New York.

Soltow and Stevens (1981) is the best documented attempt so far to relate reading instruction directly to literacy and therefore also reveals many of the difficulties in this particular task. The criticisms that can be made of this study do not invalidate the work so much as they expose problems in the measurement of instructional outcomes, especially for periods prior to the entry of standardized testing. These issues are the concern of the remainder of this section.

Proxies for Achievement

The first point of interest is the assumption that hours of formal instruction is a reliable predictor of achievement. Time-on-task for reading instruction does correlate positively in some studies with achievement gain, but only when instruction is appropriate and error rates are low (Rosenshine & Stevens, 1984). Harris and Serwer's (1966) study of different instructional methods for reading showed that time spent on certain types of reading tasks (e.g.,

vocabulary drill) correlated positively and significantly with reading achievement while time on other reading tasks (e.g., choral reading) did not. Borg
(1980) presents similar results from a series of studies, but also shows the
influence of error rate on achievement gains. (For a general review of the
time-on-task literature, see Karweit, 1983.) Thus, number of hours in formal
reading instruction needs to be considered in relation to type of instruction.
For the latter, no attempt has been made to translate teacher accounts, student
remembrances, and other anecdotal sources on instruction from earlier times
to the types of instructional events that could be used to estimate effectiveness
(i.e., introduction, practice, review, assessment, etc.).

Amount of Reading

Related to the effectiveness issue is the concern over amount of actual reading that is done during formal instruction. Eliot reported a study he had done
in 1890 in which two high school graduates had read all of the school texts
required for grades 1–6 and had needed only 46 hours to accomplish this,
reading aloud at a normal rate. Eliot (1898, p. 185) presented these data as
proof that children did too little reading in school. Judd (1936, p. 575), who
should have known better, cited Eliot's work as a basis for the claim that
schoolchildren in Judd's day read ten times what children read in Eliot's time.
N. Smith (1965, pp. 119ff.) reports Eliot's claims uncritically, as does Clifford (1978, p. 161). That Eliot was striving more for hyperbole than objectivity is apparent from the methodology he used. High school graduates read
from three to six times as fast as first and second graders (Taylor, 1937);
furthermore, the school textbooks were not the only materials read in class
(supplementary reading was well established by 1890). But more importantly,
most of the textbooks were not meant to be read straight through like novels.
Lessons then, as today, were to be read carefully and reread, questions answered, papers written, and problems worked. A four-paragraph selection in
a geography text might be followed by six or eight questions, requiring 10
minutes or more for working, rather than just 2 minutes for reading.

Beyond these inaccuracies, however, lurks the question of interpretation.
What does 46 hours of reading mean at a time when the average school term
was about 135 days and only 3.5% of the population graduated high school?
A recent study of allocated class time (Dishaw, 1977) shows only about 7–8
minutes per day of silent reading in the average primary grade today and
about 15 minutes in the middle grades. In reviewing these data, The Report
of the Commission on Reading (Anderson, Hiebert, Scott, & Wilkinson,
1985) termed the numbers *small,* but gave no indication of how reasonable
expectations might be constructed. At issue is what percentage of the school
day *should* be spent in reading, as opposed to listening, speaking, writing,
problem solving, and so on. This is an instructional issue for which we have

no simple answers, either from observation or theory. It is difficult, therefore, to evaluate Eliot's data (or the more recent data), other than to say that it begs the question of what is instructional.

Distribution of Abilities

Although the average child *might* have become literate after 1,000 or so hours of formal reading instruction, there is no reason to believe that the distribution of abilities across 11-year-olds in Ohio and Rochester in the 1860s would not have fit a bell-shaped normal curve with a standard deviation as large as is found today for rural and urban schooling, meaning that many children who met all the requirements laid out by Soltow and Stevens (1981) for acquiring literacy would still not have reached this level. This is especially true for those eras prior to an emphasis on individual differences. Motivation, parental assistance, intelligence, emotional stability, and other factors enter into the schooling equation in as yet undetermined ways. Perhaps the most important question to ask is what level of reading ability was required to allow the student to continue developing in literacy competencies beyond formal schooling. Then we can ask, for different distributions of entry level abilities, what types and amounts of schooling were needed to achieve this goal.

The Nature of Literacy

As Kirsch and Guthrie (1977–1978) discuss, literacy is not a dichotomous variable, but a continuous, multidimensional one. For example, would an 11-year-old in the 1860s with 4 or 5 years of schooling have been able to comprehend a will or a telegraphy manual, or understand Lincoln's concept of democracy from the 10 sentences he uttered at Gettysburg on November 19, 1863? The skills required to comprehend *The Scarlet Letter* are different from those needed to cope with *Instructions for Using the Singer Sewing Machine No. 27* (Form 7160, February 12, 1897, reissue). Plot, character, and setting are critical to the former, while diagrams, tables, and step-by-step directions are critical to the latter. Mastery of one set of skills does not guarantee mastery of the other, although they share a common set of foundation skills.

Literacy must also be examined as a relative rather than as an absolute ability. Adequate reading ability in 1860 for different roles in society was not the same as for today. Amounts and types of reading required for farming, baking, school teaching, homemaking, and probably every other definable occupation have changed continually over America's history, as have reading vocabulary and preferred sentence structures. Adults certainly read better today on an absolute scale than the Minutemen did, but until we know what advantages and limitations accompanied different literacy competencies in 1776, we cannot judge the significance of this advantage. Studies like Heath's (1980) on the uses of literacy in work and everyday life are needed retrospectively to assess the reading demands and reading habits of earlier times.

Quality of the District Schools

The question of the effectiveness of district schools, particularly in the 19th century, is an issue that goes beyond reading instruction, but is nevertheless important to the instruction-literacy issue. Cremin (1980) and Greene (1965), among others, are particularly negative about the instructional capabilities of the district schools. Cremin (1980) judges the one-room district school for the first half of the 19th century as relatively inefficient, yet ascribes to it a variety of instructional activities that went far beyond the present-day assumption of rote memorization and meaningless drill. In contrast, Fuller (1982) and Soltow and Stephens (1981) present much more charitable views, attributing to this institution a central role in raising educational standards.

By modern standards, the criticisms of the district schools appear valid, but they often fail to consider the context in which schooling took place throughout the 19th century and the different ways in which schooling can affect achievement. Some critics also accept too readily the reports of school reformers as unbiased observations of contemporary conditions. To a predominately rural, poor population, building a new democracy in an unexplored but bountiful land, and confronted with opportunities for self-advancement undreamed of by their European ancestors, neither the physical discomforts of the one-room schoolhouse nor its instructional inefficiencies were insufferable. From the extensive summaries of reports offered by Barnard (1849) on the dilapidated nature of schoolhouses throughout the seven New England states plus Michigan, it could be concluded that these conditions were not significantly different in kind from those occasionally found in the workplace or in many rural homes of the time. John Muir and Abraham Lincoln, for example, both reported home conditions as uncomfortable as those reported for the worst schoolhouses.

It is also well established that primary teachers were often untrained in pedagogical methods and far from experts in the content of what they instructed (e.g., Elsbree, 1939), but current research does not support a strong relationship between either of these factors and student achievement. In direct contrast to this view of the importance of teacher expertise and experience, Stephens (1967) hypothesizes that the primary role of the effective teacher is to orient the student towards what should be learned so that relevant out-of-school experiences will be more effectively utilized for school-directed learning. In this model, the instructor need be only a day or two ahead of the students in comprehension of subject-matter content. If this assumption is valid, the most important characteristic to assess in district school teachers is neither pedagogical training nor subject-area knowledge, at least not for most of the 19th century, but orientation towards learning, as reflected, perhaps, in their attitudes about students' ability to learn. On this particular characteristic we have extremely little information.

Finally, we need to consider the various paths along which different types of literacy might be obtained, including those in which formal schooling does not play a dominant role. The assumption that modern standards of 4 to 5 years of formal schooling are necessary (but not sufficient) conditions for attaining literacy leaves us with the problem of explaining how literacy increased through periods of the 19th century when only a small percentage of the population received this much schooling.

One explanation is that children typically started school at a later age in the middle 19th century than they do now, and that prior to entering school they received training at home in reading, thus making school instruction more efficient than it is now. Calhoun (1973, appendix) analyzed the 1850 census data on literacy and schooling for selected towns in Dutchess County, New York, and among other results showed that the highest percentage of school attendance by age was in the range 8–10 years of age. (Most estimates of the schooling required for literacy assume an entering age to grade 1 of about 6. Kaestle and Vinovskis (1978) report both a steady decline in the number of children below the age of 5 who entered public school after the 1830s in Massachusetts, and encouragements from several school committees and the secretary of the state Board of Education for raising the age limit for entry to 6 or 7.

Another explanation is that the literacy support system in the 19th century, coupled with a pervading drive for self-improvement, led to an unusually high amount of out-of-school learning. Sunday schools, evening schools, on-the-job training, and parental and peer tutoring may have carried a much greater load then than now. While we tend to deride the high readability levels of the 19th century readers (e.g., Nietz, 1961), they may have provided an important goal for continued learning during a period when school attendance was limited to a few years at most. Memorization of excerpts from important speeches and major literary works, even if not understood fully at the time, may have provided both a data base and a set of expectations for later attainment when schooling was short, but motivation for success high. Silly little tales about dogs and cats are a luxury that can be afforded only when schooling can be extended for many years. A child turned out onto the farm or into the sweatshop in the 1840s with only the exposure to print afforded by the first readers of contemporary programs would have had a more limited base for attaining full literacy than one exposed rigorously to the first two Mc-Guffey Readers. While this argument does not justify the adoption of older textbooks for modern use, it does question the procedures through which instructional methods are evaluated, particularly when schooling and societal factors are ignored.

The changes in difficulty levels, content, and methodology of reading instruction over the last 125 years might indicate a much more profound development in the role of the school in American society than they do of change in reading instruction per se. The schools' transition from a locale where exposure was gained to qualities and attitudes, to an institution that was responsible for ensuring acquisition of these abilities, was a radical one, requiring new methods, materials, and organizations. The transformation of schooling that begins with the common school movement was more than a modernization of schooling within a changing American society. It was a radical alteration of the role of the public school vis-a-vis the family and community. Reading instruction was forced to change accordingly.

Conclusions

The linkage between reading instruction and reading achievement is elusive at best. Even for recent times, we must struggle to determine what component of reading achievement is attributable to the school's efforts and what part derives from out-of-school experiences. For earlier periods, we have limited knowledge about instructional approach, amount of time spent in reading, and amount and type of home reinforcement and assistance. In addition we have no objective records of how well students read. Therefore only a wispy thread can be strung from instruction to reading ability in historical studies.

EPILOGUE

Guidelines for a Curriculum History

A history of reading instruction properly fits into curriculum history, a field that now sports its own professional association and a growing literature on methodology and findings. Recently, Kliebard and Franklin (1983) have suggested two guidelines for curriculum history that are especially relevant here. First is the need to attend to the complexities and ambiguities that shape a curriculum over time, rather than subscribing to a single-factor explanation. This is especially critical for reading instruction because of the highly visible position that reading has had both in the curriculum and in society in general. If schools have been as vulnerable to outside pressure as organizational theorists suggest (Miles, 1981; Sieber, 1968), then reading instruction has had a double vulnerability. No other component of the curriculum has been subjected throughout its history to such intense controversy over both its basic methods and its content. N. Smith's (1965) historical stages and Mosier's (1947) and Garfinkle's (1954) hypotheses, for example, are contributions to a growing data base on the history of reading instruction. At the same time, however, they are testimonies to the limitations of single-factor theories. Reading instruction has been influenced by a wide range of social, cultural, educational, and economic factors, and an adequate history needs to account for the interplay among these.

Second, according to Kliebard and Franklin (1983), a history of a curriculum needs to be built upon the evidence for what actually occurred in the homes, churches, schools, and other locales of instruction over time, rather than upon the committee reports, state and local curriculum guidelines, and speeches and proposals of educational leaders. These latter resources may provide barometers for the direction of curriculum change, but they do not always reliably reflect what instructors were actually doing. Uncovering instructional practice is as much an exercise in archaeology as it is exegesis. We attempt to recreate the activities that comprised an instructional process from the fragments and potsherds of old textbooks, copybooks, teacher diaries, artist sketches, and the like. In part, this is building dynamic museum exhibits, perhaps to be realized on film or video disc but, in part, it is also an intellectual exercise that has as its goal a contribution to the social history of the United States.

A Multifaceted Approach

An adequate history of reading instruction needs to be realized through a multifaceted approach, working from description to integration to evaluation. The descriptive or archaeological level should attempt to define how reading was taught throughout the entire history of American education, including the materials and methods used, the settings and times involved, and the backgrounds and abilities of the people who did the instructing and those who were taught. While descriptive in nature, this level needs to assume, either overtly or covertly, a theory of reading instruction to guide the categories it adopts and the objects and ideas on which it focuses. If, for example, reading is viewed primarily as pronouncing from print, then the issue of when and how comprehension was taught in the 19th century is of little concern. However, if reading is defined as gaining meaning from print, this issue is significant, at least for raising the question of how the colonial child learned to read for meaning.

At a deeper level of understanding, a theory of instruction such as that offered by Bruner (1966) forces attention to variables such as motivation, sequencing of skills, and knowledge representation—variables that are mostly ignored in the present treatments of reading instruction. If these are, as Bruner claims, critical for defining instruction, then a diachronic account should be as sensitive to them as a synchronic account. Gray's (1937b) five-stage model for reading development may provide a development framework within which Bruner's theory can guide attention to specific components of instruction.

The second level of a curriculum history should be concerned with the relationship of a particular curriculum to its educational and cultural setting. For reading, this requires an investigation of the factors that led to changes in the methods and materials of reading instruction. Reading was rarely taught in a vacuum; instead it has been integrally tied to changing educational and cultural conditions. Elementary readers did not switch from religious to moral themes and then to materialism because reading teachers found these latter themes to be more conducive to the acquisition of literacy. Nor did methods of reading instruction change from rote memorization to self-interpretation because of factors unique to reading. In both cases, cultural and general educational influences can be shown to be critical determinants of change, the former deriving primarily from a change in Protestant religious dogma and the latter from changing concepts of child development.

The third, or evaluation level, should be concerned with the outcomes of instruction in a particular curricular area, with special emphasis on the growth within the American population of competency in the skills taught. For reading, two issues are of primary importance. First, how well could a child read after specified amounts of schooling, and second, what role did school-based reading instruction play in the rise of literacy in American society? For the latter issue, it is naive to assume a simple cause-and-effect relationship between formal reading instruction and general literacy, especially with the relationships that have been found between student background variables (e.g., parents' education) and school achievement (Sewell, Hauser, & Featherman, 1976). Other factors, such as the roles which the home, church, and workplace have played in literacy training throughout America's history, must be considered. In addition, the drive for self-improvement, among other motivating factors, has often amplified the positive effects of schooling and muted the negative effects. The effects of amount and quality of schooling on skill acquisition are difficult to assess for contemporary instruction; for earlier periods, the task is immense.

REFERENCES

Adams, E.C. (1946). American Indian education, government schools and economic progress. (Reprint, New York: Arno Press, 1972).

Anderson, R.C., Hiebert, E.H., Scott, J.A., & Wilkinson, I.A.G. (1985). *Becoming a nation of readers: The report of the Commission on Reading.* Washington, DC: The National Institute of Education.

Austin, M.C., & Morrison, C. (1963). *The first R: The Harvard report on reading in elementary schools.* New York: Macmillan.

Auwers, L. (1980). Reading the marks of the past: Exploring female literacy in colonial Windsor, Connecticut. *Historical Methods, 13,* 204–214.

Balmuth, M. (1982). *The roots of phonics.* New York: McGraw-Hill.

Barnard, H. (1849). *School architecture; or contributions to the improvement of school-houses in the United States* (3rd ed.). New York: A.S. Barnes.

Barnard, H. (Ed.). (1861). *Memoirs of teachers, educators, and promoters and benefactors of education, literature, and science. Part I. Teachers and Educators* (2nd ed.). New York: F.C. Brownell. (Reprint, New York: Arno Press & The New York Times, 1969).

Barr, R. (1975). The effect of instruction on pupil reading strategies. *Reading Research Quarterly, 10,* 555–582.

Barr, R., & Dreeben, R. (1983). *How schools work.* Chicago: University of Chicago Press.

Barton, A.H., & Wilder, D.E. (1964). Research and practice in the teaching of reading: Progress report. In M.B. Miles (Ed.), *Innovation in education.* New York: Teachers College Press.

Baskerville, B. (1979). *The people's voice.* Lexington: University Press of Kentucky.

Belok, M.V. (1973). *Forming the American minds: Early school-books and their compilers (1783–1837).* Moti Katra, Agra-U.P. (India): Satish Book Enterprise.

Biemiller, A. (1970). The development of the use of graphic and contextual information as children learn to read. *Reading Research Quarterly, 6,* 75–96.

Borg, W. (1980). Time and school learning. In C. Denham & A. Lieberman (Eds.), *Time to learn.* Washington, DC: National Institute of Education.

Bormuth, J.R. (1975). Reading literacy: Its definition and assessment. In J.B. Carroll & J.S. Chall, (Eds.), *Toward a literate society: The report of the committee on reading of the National Academy of Education.* New York: McGraw-Hill.

Brooks, G. (1985). The teaching of silent reading to beginners. In G. Brooks & A.K. Pugh (Eds.), *Studies in the history of reading.* Reading, England: Centre for the Teaching of Reading, University of Reading School of Education.

Brooks, G., & Pugh, A.K. (Eds.). (1984). *Studies in the history of reading.* Reading, England: Centre for the Teaching of Reading, University of Reading School of Education.

Bruner, J. (1966). *Towards a theory of instruction.* Cambridge, MA: Harvard University Press.

Calhoun, D. (Ed.). (1969). *The educating of Americans: A documentary history.* Boston: Houghton Mifflin.

Calhoun, D., (1973). *The intelligence of a people.* Princeton, NJ: Princeton University Press.

Carpenter, C. (1963). *History of American schoolbooks.* Philadelphia: University of Pennsylvania Press.

Chall, J.S. (1967). *Learning to read: The great debate.* New York: McGraw-Hill.

Clifford, G.J. (1973). A history of the impact of research on teaching. In R.M.W. Travers (Ed.), *Second handbook of research on teaching.* Chicago: Rand McNally.

Clifford, G.J. (1984). Buch und lesen: Historical perspective on literacy and schooling. *Review of Educational Research, 54,* 472–500.

Clifford, G.J. (1978). Words for schools: The applications in education of the vocabulary researches of Edward L. Thorndike. In P. Suppes (Ed.), *Impact of research on education: Some case studies.* Washington, DC: National Academy of Education.

Commager, H.S. (1962). Foreword to *McGuffey's Fifth Eclectic Reader, 1879 Edition.* New York: New American Library, 1962.

Commager, H.S. (1950). *The American mind.* New Haven, CT: Yale University Press.

Cremin, L.A. (1961). *The transformation of the school.* New York: Vintage Books.

Cremin, L. (1970). *American education: The colonial experience, 1607–1783.* New York: Harper & Row.

Cremin, L. (1977). *Traditions of American education.* New York: Basic Books.

Cremin, L. (1980). *American education: The national experience, 1783–1876.* New York: Harper Colophon Books.

Cubberley, E.P. (1934). *Public education in America.* Boston: Houghton Mifflin.

Curti, M. (1959). *The social ideas of American educators.* Paterson, Littlefield, NJ: Adams. (First published, 1935.)

Davies, W.J.F. (1974). *Teaching reading in early England.* New York: Harper & Row.

Diack, H. (1965). *The teaching of reading in spite of the alphabet.* New York: Philosophical Library.

Dishaw, M. (1977). Descriptions of allocated time to content areas for the A-B period. *Beginning teacher evaluation study* (Technical Note IV-11a). San Francisco: Far West Regional Laboratory for Educational Research and Development.

Durkin, D. (1978–1979). What classroom observations reveal about reading comprehension instruction. *Reading Research Quarterly, 14,* 481–533.

Dykstra, R. (1969). Summary of the second-grade phase of the Cooperative Research Program in Primary Reading Instruction. *Reading Research Quarterly, 4,* 49–70.

Eliot, C.W. (1898). *Educational reform.* New York: Century.

Elsbree, W.S. (1939). *The American teacher.* New York: American Book.

Elson, R.M. (1964). *Guardians of tradition.* Lincoln: University of Nebraska Press.

Fassett, J.H. (1918). *The Beacon readers.* Boston: Ginn.

Finkelstein, B.J. (1974–1975). The moral dimensions of pedagogy. *American Studies, 15,* 79–91.

Ford, P.L. (1899). *The New England Primer.* New York: Dodd, Mead.

Fuller, W.E. (1982). *The old country school.* Chicago: University of Chicago Press.

Garfinkle, N. (1954). Conservatism in American textbooks, 1800–1860. *New York History, 35,* 49–63.

Gilmore, W. (1982). Elementary literacy on the eve of the industrial revolution: Trends in rural New England, 1760–1830. *Proceedings of the American Antiquarian Society, 92,* Part 1, 87–178.

Graff, H.J. (1979). *The literacy myth.* New York: Academic Press.

Gray, W.S. (1925). Summary of investigations relating to reading. *Supplementary Educational Monographs,* No. 28. Chicago: University of Chicago Press.

Gray, W.S. (1937a). The nature and types of reading. *Thirty-sixth yearbook of the National Society for the Study of Education,* Part I. Bloomington, IL: Public School Publishing.

Gray, W.S. (1937b). The nature and organization of basic instruction in reading. *Thirty-sixth yearbook of the National Society for the Study of Education,* Part I. Bloomington, IL: Public School Publishing.

Gray, W.S., & Leary, B.E. (1935). *What makes a book readable?* Chicago: University of Chicago Press.

Gray, W.S., & Zirbes, L. (1927–1928). Primary reading. In *The Classroom Teacher,* Vol. II. Chicago: The Classroom Teacher.

Greene, M. (1965). *The public school and the private vision.* New York: Random House.

Harris, A.J., & Serwer, B.L. (1966). The CRAFT project: Instructional time in reading research. *Reading Research Quarterly, 2,* 27–56.

Heartman, C.F. (1934). *The New England primer printed in America prior to 1830: A bibliographical checklist* (3rd ed.). New York: R.R. Bowker.

Heartman, C.F. (1935). *American primers, Indian primers, royal primers, and thirty-seven other types of non-New England primers issued prior to 1830.* Highland Park, NJ: H.B. Weiss.

Heath, S.B. (1980). The functions and uses of literacy. *Journal of Communication, 30,* 123–133.

Henretta, J.A. (1973). *The evolution of American society, 1700–1815: An interdisciplinary analysis.* Lexington, MA: D.C. Heath.

Hyatt, A.V. (1943). *The place of oral reading in the school program. Its history from*

1880–1941. Contributions to education, No. 872. New York: Bureau of Publications, Teachers College, Columbia University.

Johnson, C. (1904). *Old-time schools and school-books*. New York: Macmillan (Reprint, New York: Dover, 1963).

Judd, C.J. (1918). Reading: Its nature and development. *Supplementary Educational Monographs*, No. 10. Chicago: University of Chicago Press.

Judd, C.H. (1936). The significance for textbook-making of the newer concepts in education. *Elementary School Journal, 36*, 575–582.

Kaestle, C.F. (1983). *Pillars of the republic*. New York: Hill & Wang.

Kaestle, C.F. (1985). The history of literacy and the history of readers. In E.W. Gordon (Ed.), *Review of research in education* (Vol. 12, pp. 11–53). Washington, D.C.: American Educational Research Association.

Kaestle, C.F., & Vinovskis, M.A. (1978). From apron strings to ABCs: Parents, children and schooling in nineteenth-century Massachusetts. *American Journal of Sociology Supplement, 84*, 539–580.

Kane, R.B., Byrne, M.A., & Hater, M.A. (1974). *Helping children read mathematics*. New York: American Book.

Karweit, N.L. (1983). *Time on task: A research review*. Report No. 332, Center for Social Organization of Schools. Baltimore, MD: Johns Hopkins University.

Kellogg, E.D. (Ed.). (1900). *Teaching reading in ten cities*. Boston: Educational Publishing.

Kiefer, M. (1948). *American children through their books, 1700–1835*. Philadelphia: University of Pennsylvania Press.

Kirsch, I., & Guthrie, J.T. (1977–1978). The concept and measurement of functional literacy. *Reading Research Quarterly, 13*, 485–507.

Kliebard, H.M., & Franklin, B.M. (1983). The course of the course of study: History of curriculum. In J.H. Best (Ed.), *Historical inquiry in education: A research agenda*. Washington, DC: American Educational Research Association.

Lamport, H.B. (1937). *A history of the teaching of beginning reading*. Chicago: Privately printed.

Lindberg, S.W. (1976). *The annotated McGuffey*. New York: Van Nostrand Reinhold.

Livengood, W.W. (1953). *Our textbooks, yesterday and today*. New York: Textbook Clinic, American Institute of Graphic Arts.

Lockridge, K.A. (1974). *Literacy in colonial New England: An enquiry into the social context of literacy in the early modern west*. New York: Norton.

Mann, H. (1839). Reading and reading books. *American Annals of Education, 9*, 289–299.

Mann, H. (1844). Method of teaching young children on their first entering school. *Common School Journal, 6*, 116–125.

Mathews, M.M. (1966). *Teaching to read, historically considered*. Chicago: University of Chicago Press.

May, S.J. (1861). Cyrus Prince. In Henry Barnard (Ed.), *Memoirs of teachers and educators*. New York: Brownell.

Mead, C.D. (1915). Silent versus oral reading with one hundred sixth-grade children. *Journal of Educational Psychology, 6*, 345–348.

Michael, I. (1984). Early evidence for whole word methods. In G. Brooks & A.K. Pugh (Eds.), *Studies in the history of reading*. Reading, England: Centre for the Teaching of Reading, University of Reading School of Education.

Miles, M.B. (1981). Mapping the common properties of schools. In R. Lehming & M. Kane (Eds.), *Improving schools: Using what we know*. Beverly Hills, CA: Sage.

Minnich, H.C. (1936). *William Holmes McGuffey and his readers*. New York: American Book.

Monaghan, E.J. (1983). *A common heritage: Noah Webster's blue-back speller*. Hamden, CT: Archon Books.

Moore, D.W., Readence, J.E., & Rickelman, R.L. (1983). An historical exploration of content area reading instruction. *Reading Research Quarterly, 18,* 419–438.

Mosier, R.D. (1947). *Making the American mind: Social and moral ideas in the McGuffey Readers*. New York: King's Crown Press.

Mott, F.L. (1947). *Golden multitudes: The story of best sellers in the United States*. New York: Macmillan.

Murray, L. (1799). *The English reader*. New York: Isaac Collins.

Murray, L. (1818; copyrighted 1805). *Introduction to the English reader*. New York: Lockwood.

National Society for the Study of Education (1925). Report of the national committee on reading. *Twenty-fourth Yearbook of the National Society for the Study of Education*. Bloomington, IL: Public School Publishing.

Nietz, J. (1961). *Old textbooks*. Pittsburgh, PA: University of Pittsburgh Press.

Nietz, J. (1964). Why the longevity of the McGuffey readers? *History of Education Quarterly, 4,* 119–125.

Noble, G. (1971). Joseph Mayer Rice: Critic of the public schools and pioneer in modern educational measurements. (Doctoral dissertation, State University of New York at Buffalo, 1970). *Dissertation Abstracts International, 31,* 4323A–4945A.

Oberholtzer, E.E. (1915). Testing the efficiency in reading in the grades. *Elementary School Journal, 15,* 313–322.

Oliver, R.T. (1965). *History of public speaking in America*. Boston: Allyn & Bacon.

Palmer, T.H. (1838). On the evils of the present system of primary education. *American Institute of Instruction, 8,* 211–239.

Pintner, R. (1913). Inner speech during silent reading. *Psychological Review, 20,* 129–153.

Pflaum, S.W., Walberg, H.J., Karegianes, M.L., & Rasher, S.P. (1980). Reading instruction: A quantitative analysis. *Educational Researcher, 9,* 12–18.

Pugh, A.K. (1984). The relevance of the study of the history of reading. In G. Brooks & A.K. Pugh (Eds.), *Studies in the history of reading*. Reading, England: Centre for the Teaching of Reading, University of Reading School of Education.

Purkey, S.C., & Smith, M.S. (1983). Effective schools: A review. *The Elementary School Journal, 83,* 427–452.

Report of the Superintendent of Common Schools for the State of New York, made to the Legislature, January 8, 1834. (1834). Albany, NY: Croswell, Van Beuthuysen and Burt.

Reeder, R.R. (1900) The historical development of school readers and of method in teaching reading. *Columbia University Contributions to Philosophy, Psychology and Education, 8,* No. 2.

Resnick, D.P., & Resnick, L.B. (1977). The nature of literacy: An historical exploration. *Harvard Educational Review, 47,* 370–385.

Rice, J.M. (1893). *The public school system of the United States*. New York: Century.

Robb, M.M. (1968). *Oral interpretation of literature in American colleges and universities* (rev. ed.). New York: Johnson Reprint Corporation.

Robinson, R.R. (1930). Two centuries of change in the content of school readers. George Peabody College for Teachers Contributions to Education, No. 59. Nashville, TN: George Peabody College for Teachers.

Rosenshine, B., & Stevens, R. (1984). Classroom instruction in reading. In P.D. Pearson, R. Barr, M.L. Kamil, & P. Mosenthal (Eds.), *Handbook of reading research*. New York: Longman.

Rush, J. (1833). *The philosophy of the human voice*. Philadelphia: J.B. Lippincott, Grambo.

Sewell, W.H., Hauser, R.M., & Featherman, D.L. (Eds.). (1976). *Schooling and achievement in American society*. New York: Academic Press.

Seybolt, R.F. (1925). *The private school*. Source Studies in American Colonial Education, Bulletin No. 28. Urbana: University of Illinois, Bureau of Educational Research.

Sieber, S.D. (1968). Organizational influences on innovative roles. In T.L. Eidell & J.M. Kitchel (Eds.), *Knowledge production and utilization in educational administration*. Eugene: University of Oregon, Center for Advanced Study of Educational Administration.

Skeel, E.E.F. (1958). *A bibliography of the writings of Noah Webster*. Edwin H. Carpenter, Jr. (Ed.). (Reprint, New York: New York Public Library & Arno Press, 1971).

Smith, N.B. (1965). *American reading instruction*. Newark, DE: International Reading Association.

Smith, R.N. (1977). A bibliography of books on language and languages printed in the United States through the year 1800. *Historiographia Linguistica, 4,* 207–243.

Soltow, L., & Stevens, E. (1981). *The rise of literacy and the common school in the United States: A socio-economic analysis to 1870*. Chicago: University of Chicago Press.

Stallings, J.A., & Kaskowitz, D. (1974). *Follow-through classroom observation evaluation, 1972–73*. Menlo Park, CA: Stanford Research Institute.

Stephens, J.M. (1967). *The process of schooling*. New York: Holt, Rinehart, & Winston.

Taylor, E.A. (1937). *Controlled reading*. Chicago: University of Chicago Press.

Tebbel, J. (1973). *A history of book publishing in the United States* (4 vols.) New York: R.R. Bowker.

Travers, R.M.W. (1983). *How research has changed American schools: A history from 1840 to the present*. Kalamazoo, MI: Mythos Press.

Tuer, A.W. (1896). *History of the horn-book*. (2 vols.). London: Leadenhall Press. (Reprint, New York: Arno Press, 1979).

Tyack, D.B. (1974). *The one best system*. Cambridge, MA: Harvard University Press.

Venezky, R.L. (1982). The origins of the present-day chasm between adult literacy needs and school literacy instruction. *Visible Language, 16,* 113–127.

Venezky, R.L. (1984). The history of reading research. In P.D. Pearson, R. Barr, M.L. Kamil, & P. Mosenthal (Eds.), *Handbook of reading research*. New York: Longman.

Warfel, H.R. (1936). *Noah Webster: Schoolmaster to America*. New York: Macmillan.

Webber, T. (1978). *Deep like the rivers: Education in the slave quarter community, 1831–1865*. New York: Norton.

Weeks, S.B. (1900). Confederate text-books (1861–1865): A preliminary bibliography. *Report of the Commissioner of Education for 1898–1899*. Washington, DC: Government Printing Office, pp. 1139–1155.

Wells, W.H. (1860). Report to the Chicago Board of Education. *American Journal of Education, 8,* 530–540.

Westerhoff, J.H., III (1978). *McGuffey and his readers*. Nashville, TN: Abingdon.

Wheat, H.G. (1923). *The teaching of reading*. New York: Ginn.

Wickersham, J.P. (1867). *Methods of instruction*. Philadelphia: J.B. Lippincott.

Williams, J.P. (1985). The case for explicit decoding instruction. In J.W. Osborn, P.T. Wilson, & R.C. Anderson (Eds.), *Reading education: Foundations for a literate America*. Lexington, MA: Lexington Books.

Willows, D.M., Borwick, D., & Hayvren, M. (1981). The content of school readers. In T.G. Waller and G.E. MacKinnon (Eds.), *Reading research: Advances in theory and practice* (Vol. 2). New York: Academic Press.

Wishy, B. (1968). *The child and the republic: The dawn of modern American nurture*. Philadelphia: University of Pennsylvania Press.

Worcester, S. (1826). *A primer of the English language*. Boston: Hilliard, Gray, Little, & Wilkins.

II.
WRITING

Chapter 5

Reading and Writing Instruction: Toward a Theory of Teaching and Learning

JUDITH A. LANGER and ARTHUR N. APPLEBEE
Stanford University

INTRODUCTION: TOWARD A THEORY OF TEACHING AND LEARNING

Reading and writing development are individual processes which reflect the evolving skills of the individual language learner. Instruction, on the other hand, is a social process, rooted in the interaction between teacher and student. Through the intersection of development and instruction, individual learners gain the power to use language to understand their world and to act within it. Reflecting the split between individual and social, most research in the field of reading and writing has concerned itself either with charting the course of individual development, or with delineating the characteristics of effective instruction. Although both traditions have been valuable, we will argue here that they should be integrated through a more general theory that systematically relates individual development to the social processes that surround it. From such a theory, we will emerge with more effective principles for instruction, as well as with a better explanation for the patterns of development that have been described in previous studies. In doing so, we will also clarify our understanding of the deeply related but functionally different activities of reading, writing, and speaking.

The need for a more encompassing theory is evident whether we start independently with either development or instruction. If we start with development, it is quite clear that the skills that individuals learn are constrained (or fostered) by the particular cultural and educational contexts within which the individuals grow up (Au, 1980; Heath, 1983; McDermott, 1977; Scribner

The authors gratefully acknowledge David Olson's helpful comments on an earlier draft of this paper.

& Cole, 1981; Tannen, 1984). What people are expected to read or write as well as how they are expected to approach these tasks has differed across historical periods within a culture and from one culture to another (Graff, 1981; Ong, 1982; Resnick, 1983; Resnick & Resnick, 1977). Some of these differences may be trivial, reflecting simple variations in culturally most acceptable or prestigious forms; others may be more significant, reflecting or perhaps even fostering different modes of thinking and reasoning (cf. Applebee, 1984; Langer, in press; Olson, 1977, in press). In either case, however, the outcomes of individual processes of development are clearly shaped by the social contexts in which they are embedded, and can only be fully understood in relation to those social contexts.

The literature on instruction in reading and writing, on the other hand, has focused on transmission of information from teacher to pupil, with little attention to the nature of individual development. Lacking a broader conceptualization of the nature of instruction and development, the field has been characterized by a relatively unsystematic exploration of microscopic variations of teaching method. Because these studies have not been framed within a theory of teaching and learning, they have not led to powerful generalizations about effective teaching (Langer, 1984). Further, because reading and writing have been treated as separate "contents" to be taught, there has been little systematic exploration of the extent to which reading and writing instruction may be part of a common enterprise of literacy learning. This enterprise builds upon but moves beyond earlier processes of language learning, and is at the heart of learning to function within the specialized contents of the various academic subject areas.

Rather than providing an exhaustive review of previous research on development or instruction in reading or writing, the present chapter will focus on research that contributes to a general theory of learning and instruction in reading and writing. (In keeping with the general topic of this section, our examples will draw somewhat more heavily from writing than from reading, but the argument is a more general one.) The theory that we will present grows out of a view of language learning that has been heavily influenced by the work of both Vygotsky and Bruner.

Vygotsky (1962, 1978) focuses on language as a social and communicative activity. He argues that higher level skills are the result of the child's learning of social/functional relationships; in becoming literate, children learn the structures and processes inherent in socially meaningful literacy activities. In this way, processes that are initially mediated socially become resources available to the individual language user. Interactive events are thus at the heart of learning to read and write; they involve the child as an active learner in settings where an adult provides a systematic structure, and sometimes direct guidance, that governs the child's participation in initial reading or writing activities. In the course of successive experiences, children develop their own self-regulatory abilities. Thus, approaches that are initially socially mediated are eventually internalized, and become part of the repertoire of the individual.

Bruner similarly views the adult/child tutorial relationship as critical to language learning (Wood, Bruner, & Ross, 1976). He uses the term "scaffolding" to describe the tutorial assistance provided by the adult who "knows how" to control those elements that are beyond the child's capabilities. Bruner views language as providing the basis for concept formation, as a tool for cognitive growth (Bruner, Olver, & Greenfield, 1966). Further, he sees writing as a powerful tool essential for thinking (1973), and schooling as promoting the growth of reasoning abilities through training in the mastery of the written language. Bruner believes written language is particularly important in encouraging cognitive growth because it is abstract—the referent is not as frequently present as it is during many forms of oral discourse. The language of school is particularly important in developing abstract literacy skills, requiring students to go beyond the information given and to deal with possibilities and abstractions.

Both Vygotsky and Bruner see language learning as growing out of a communicative relationship where the adult helps the child to understand as well as to complete new tasks. They also see literacy as encouraging the kinds of thinking and reasoning that can support higher levels of cognitive development.

Our general approach to the study of reading and writing is to treat them as an extension and reformulation of earlier language-learning processes, and to embed our analyses in more general frameworks of language learning. While acknowledging the profound effects that literacy may have on cultural as well as individual development, we will argue that there are basic processes of learning and instruction that hold for both written and oral language learning—and, we suspect, for the learning of many other complex skills as well. (On the special demands of written in contrast to oral language, see especially Heath, 1982; Olson, 1977, in press; Tannen, 1982.) It is also true that literacy activities are never content-free; at the root of instructional interaction are the student's goals of learning or explicating some content, or of learning to do something new or to do it differently. These goals affect the nature of the text being written or construed and, in turn, help to shape the nature of the instructional interaction, the skills to be engaged, and the content to be understood. Thus one does not simply learn to read and write: one learns to read and write about particular things in particular ways. This is a process that begins with the cereal boxes and stop signs familiar to the preschool child, and continues in the basal readers of the elementary school, as well as in the specialized content domains of academic discourse that children encounter throughout their schooling.

This chapter will be limited to research that contributes directly to our emerging theory of instruction. We will begin by looking at the role of interaction between adult and child, as revealed in some studies of early language learning. These studies suggest some general principles underlying successful instructional dialogue. (Although these early examples generally focus on oral rather than written language, we believe the roles played by the adult and child are also useful in understanding the roles played in uses of reading and writing.) We will then turn to processes of teaching and learning in more formal instructional settings, including our own studies of classroom instruction. In the final section of the chapter some examples of current research on teaching methods will be examined and reinterpreted in light of the theoretical stance we are taking.

TEACHING AND LEARNING IN ADULT-CHILD INTERACTIONS

Let us begin with the work of Luria (1929/1977–1978) who, with Vygotsky, views language as requisite for thought, and language learning as the result of a social interaction in which the learner has a task to accomplish and the adult serves as facilitator. Both Vygotsky and Luria maintain that the contribution of the social environment is a critical feature of every learning activity because it is through the social interchange that language is mediated and learning takes place.

In keeping with this view, Luria sees writing as developing from the child's ability to use cues in the social environment as functional signs—as a way to express or serve meaning. He showed that children's earliest writing was imitative of adult behaviors, and that as the children's understanding of the adult behavior changed, their engagement in the activities also changed. For the youngest children he observed, their scribbles were socially and culturally acquired behaviors; they did what they saw. They did not use their scribbles as an aid to memory or recall. From this imitative beginning, the children's scribbles evolved into idiosyncratic sign systems, preserving relative length or segmentation of utterances, but not preserving content. In social situations with the people around them, they learned the external conventions of writing—even before they assimilated its meaningful functions. Only later did the children begin to understand the use of writing as a mechanism to encode particular meanings. When this occurred, however, the skills and abilities that they had learned during the earlier, more external, social phases were useful in helping them learn to use writing in more individual and functionally complex ways. (See Ferreiro, 1984, 1985, for an analysis of the cognitive problems being dealt with in these early stages of children's writing.)

In addition to acknowledging the impact of the social environment, Russian studies of the psychology of language learning emphasize the power of the communicative interaction in learning. Vygotsky (1962) puts such confidence in the strength of this interaction that he states, "What children can do with the assistance of others might in some sense be even more indicative of their mental development than what they can do alone" (p. 85).

The notion of interaction, or dialogue, that functions as a kind of "scaffold" to support early language learning has been developed in the work of Bruner and his colleagues (Bruner, 1978; Ninio & Bruner, 1978; Ratner & Bruner, 1978; Wood, Bruner, & Ross, 1976). They use the term "scaffold" to characterize the role of the adult in adult-child dyads, in situations where the dialogue between adult and child serves both as an immediate end in itself, and as the context within which the child gradually learns more sophisticated language functions. Commenting on this concept, Bruner (1978) suggests that the adult caretaker reduces the degrees of freedom with which the child has to cope, concentrates the child's attention into a manageable domain, highlights critical features of the task, and provides models of the expected dialogue from which the child can extract selectively what is needed to fill the appropriate role in discourse. He goes on to describe the caretaker as one who also helps the child extend new language skills to broader contexts of use, and serves as a guardian of newly confirmed communicative hypotheses, preventing the child from sliding back toward earlier forms once more sophisticated ones have been achieved.

To provide a better sense of the phenomenon Bruner is describing, we can turn to the data from particular studies. Ninio and Bruner (1978) investigated the development of labeling skills, in the context of early picture-book reading. Their data consisted of 30-minute videotapes of free play involving one child, Richard, and his mother, every 2 to 3 weeks between the ages of 8 months and 1½ years. Twelve of these sessions included spontaneous book-reading episodes, in which mother and child jointly looked at a picture book, and the major activity was one of attaching verbal labels to the pictured objects. (This activity is also an interesting example of the intermingling of oral language learning in the development of early literacy-related skills.)

Ninio and Bruner's concern in their analyses was with the mechanisms through which this very young child learned how to label. In analyzing their data, they commented that the "most striking characteristic of labelling activity is that it takes place in a structured interactional sequence that has the texture of dialogue" (pp. 5–6), with patterned turn-taking in a rule-governed sequence. This pattern had four elements that occurred in a fixed sequence:

1. Attentional vocative (Look)
2. Query (What's that?)
3. Label (It's an X)
4. Feedback utterance (Yes)   (Order optionally third)

This pattern, with such attendant features as the average number of turns per episode and average length of a turn, remained essentially constant across the period studied, in spite of the extremely rapid growth that Richard was experiencing in other aspects of his language use.

Within this fixed frame, however, there was a clear developmental pattern in Richard's labeling skills. During the period studied, he moved from non-vocal gestures (pointing, smiling) to nonlexical vocalization, and finally to lexical vocalization, using adult-like words as labels for the pictured objects. Ninio and Bruner note a number of characteristics of the mother-child interactions:

1. The picture-book reading ritual builds on already developed skills in dialogue (in the sense of the child's ability to participate in mutually contingent exchanges).

2. No major modification of the mother's customary use of language is required to carry out the book reading; she is acting in a "linguistically conventional manner" (p. 8).

3. Part of this conventional linguistic behavior is the expectation of response, and the imputation of meaning to the responses that occur. The child is seen by the mother as having the intention to carry out the function that she is trying to teach him.

4. The situation as a whole is highly structured, with strict ordering rules and a limited number of critical elements.

5. The situation allows the child to gradually take over one or more of the elements in the labeling routine. The child first learns to respond to a labeling request, and eventually to initiate a labeling sequence.

Ninio and Bruner make two other observations that are relevant to our concerns with instruction. One concerns the role of imitation in the learning of labels. Analyzing the contingent probability of the child uttering a recognizable label, they found it to be much greater if the mother provided the correct conversational setting for labeling (by asking *What* questions or allowing the child to initiate the dialogue), than if the mother offered the label for imitation. Providing the child with a model to imitate actually depressed the probability that he would utter the word immediately.

The second point concerns the mother's tendency to impute meaning to the child's attempts at labeling. Ninio and Bruner comment that this attribution of meaning is "anything but indiscriminate or self-delusory" (p. 10), being based on a constantly updated, detailed inventory of the child's experience. The mother's responses to the child were filled with explanations that made the sources of her expectations clear:

You haven't seen one of those; it's a goose. You don't really know what those are, do you, they are mittens; wrong time of year for those. It's a dog; I know you know that one. (p. 10)

In a parallel paper, Ratner and Bruner (1978) explore the development of language in two other highly structured contexts. In one case, they trace Richard's activity as he learns to play peekaboo between the ages of 5 months and 2 years. In the other, they study a second child, Jonathan, as he learns to play a game involving the appearance and disappearance of a toy clown. In both cases, Ratner and Bruner found that the structure of the game served to (1) limit and render highly familiar the semantic domain within which utterances would be used; (2) provide a highly predictable task structure with clear and reversible role relationships; and (3) allow the child, as mastery developed, to take over the adult's role in the game.

These studies by Bruner and his colleagues provide rich descriptive accounts of individual children learning rules of language and interaction in the process of participating in language episodes with adults whose knowledge of these rules is much more sophisticated and complex than their own. Similar processes have been described in studies involving larger samples of children. Wood, Bruner, and Ross (1976), in a study involving thirty 3-, 4-, and 5-year-olds, examined the tutorial process in which the children were taught how to build a three-dimensional structure. They looked at the changing interaction between tutor and child, and compared these across the three age groups. Their results indicate that it was not so much the amount, but the kind of help that was needed that marked the differences between the younger and older children. The 3-year-olds needed to be "lured" to the task, and shown the activity by demonstration; the 4-year-olds responded more frequently to verbal interaction and prodding; while the 5-year-olds used the tutor to check their own constructions.

Wood, Bruner, and Ross use this work to indicate some of the properties of an interactive instructional exchange in which the requirements of the help are generated by the situational demands:

1. Recruitment—The tutor must enlist the child's interest.

2. Reduction in degrees of freedom—The tutor must reduce the size of the task to the level where the learner can recognize a fit with the task requirements.

3. Direction maintenance—The tutor must keep the child in pursuit of the task goal.

4. Marking critical features—The tutor must accentuate certain features of the task that the learner can use to compare what was actually produced with the desired "correct" production.

5. Frustration control—The tutor must help reduce stress—to make the tutorial situation less stressful than if the adult had not been present.

6. Demonstration—The tutor must demonstrate an "idealization" of the task by means of completing the task or explicating a solution with the expectation that the learner will "imitate" it in a more appropriate form.

This research was based on the view that tutorial interactions are a critical feature of child learning, and these interactions often involve scaffolding that enables children to do what they cannot otherwise do. Scaffolding consists of providing help with elements that are beyond the children's capabilities, while encouraging them to complete those elements that are within their range of competence. This not only helps the children to accomplish the task at hand, but also shows them new strategies that will eventually allow similar tasks to be completed without the help.

Similar processes are evident in studies by Wertsch (Wertsch, 1979; Wertsch, McNamee, McLare, & Budwig, 1980), who sets his work within the general theoretical framework developed by Vygotsky (1962, 1978), concentrating in particular on the role of social interaction in the development of higher psychological processes. The processes Wertsch details are similar to those studied by Bruner and his colleagues: they concern the ways in which children learn to control their own behavior by first participating in situations where that behavior is controlled by adults who understand the rules.

Wertsch and his colleagues (1980) studied the interaction between 18 mother-child pairs in a problem-solving situation. The children ranged in age from 2:7 to 4:7. The task they faced was to assemble a truck puzzle to match a model. The cargo for the truck consisted of identically sized but differently colored pieces, so that the task could be completed successfully only if the model were used for reference. The focus of their analysis was on the extent to which the use of the model was self- or other-regulated; that is, whether the children looked at the model on their own initiative, or only in response to some form of prompting from the mother.

As expected, there was a move from other-regulation to self-regulation in this task, across the age range studied. Of more interest, however, are Wertsch's (1979) analyses of four stages in the children's movement toward self-regulation.

Level 1. At the first level, the child does not share the adult's perception of the task situation, and thus is unable to respond to the adult's directives in the way that the adult intends. One 2½-year-old, for example, simply did not realize that the puzzle represented a truck, and that the truck had windows. When his mother mentioned a "window" section, the child's attention wandered to a window in the room; the same child also decided that the wheels of the truck were cookies, and proceeded to eat them.

In order to regulate the child's activity at this level, it was necessary for the adult to redefine the task in terms of the child's frame of reference—in particular, through the use of deictics such as THIS and THAT, and by nonverbal pointing. This would allow the child to function on the basis of a definition of the situation that consisted of 'this thing' and 'that thing' rather than of a truck with windows, wheels, and a headlight.

Level 2. At the second level, the child interprets the utterances in terms of the task, but fails to understand their full implications. At this stage, the child may, for example, fail to understand the relationship between the model and the task, and will thus be unable to utilize the information in the model without explicit guidance on how to do so. ("I'm looking where you told me, but I still don't see what it has to do with this.")

Level 3. At this level, the child begins to take on a significant share of responsibility for the task. The general rules of the situation are understood, and the child can respond successfully to vague hints and suggestions. Child and adult models of the situation now seem congruent, and the adult role is primarily one of providing reassurance and help when the child gets stuck.

Level 4. Problem solving shifts to self-regulation, and no assistance is needed from the adult.

Examining children's speech in the transition into the fourth stage, Wertsch found striking parallels to the patterns of interaction in earlier stages—except that the child was now playing both roles in the dialogue, talking herself through the task.

In a synthesis paper based on his own work, Wertsch (1977) speculates how metacognition (monitoring, integrating, and coordinating various aspects of a task) is developed through adult-child interactions at home and is then carried over into the orchestration and accomplishment of school tasks. His interpretations, focusing on the early social interaction between child and adult, are an outgrowth of Vygotsky's analysis of higher psychological functions as being first learned on a social (interpsychological) plane, and later moving to the individual (intrapsychological) plane of functioning. In the case of metacognitive development, Wertsch suggests that both mothers and teachers help children solve problems by directing them toward the next step, keeping the goal before them, and helping them plan ways to reach that goal. As part of the instructional interaction, adults provide information about metacognitive procedures. They (1) inform the child about the nature of the goal; (2) make the child aware of the facts relevant to the task; (3) arrange the environment in a way that helps the child deal with each step of the task separately; and (4) remind the child where she or he is in that task.

Wertsch's work, like Bruner's, can be interpreted as a description of the child's gradual internalization of the scaffolding provided by an adult in a rule-governed context. Wertsch (1979) summarizes:

It becomes apparent that what the child has mastered as a result of functioning in other-regulation communicative contexts at the various levels is all the procedures in a language-game. That is, she/he has not simply mastered the ability to carry out one side of the communicative interaction by responding to the directives of others. She/he has taken over the rules and responsibilities of both participants in the language-game. These responsibilities were formerly divided between the adult and child, but they have now been taken over completely by the child. The definitions of situation and the patterns of activity which formerly allowed the child to participate in the problem-solving effort on the interpsychological plane now allow him/her to carry out the task on the intrapsychological plane (p. 18).

Wertsch and Stone (1985) argue that the process of understanding socially defined activities pivots around the child's learning to deal with the signs that are used in social interaction. This mechanism of learning to deal with and control culturally meaningful signs is at the core of the process of internalization.

Rogoff and Gardner (1984) also address the question of the ways in which responsibility for task completion is transferred from adult to child. They describe a situation where a mother was asked to help her 6-year-old son learn to organize pictures of household objects into colored boxes. After the items were sorted, they reviewed where the items had been placed. The mother said, "Just look at it again and see if we can see any similarities that'll help you remember." Then she pointed to a box and helped her son get started, and waited for his response. Her attempts to involve the child were apparent from her pauses, and he filled in the "blanks" more and more as the task progressed. The mother provided a structure to facilitate his recall, but did this to help her son take on the major reconstruction role himself. He understood this aim, and by the end of the task, he took on the burden of the task himself.

Studies such as these highlight both *what* is being learned and *how* it is being learned, in early contexts of language learning. *What* the child is learning includes

1. A definition of the situation; that is, an understanding of the purpose of the activity. Unless the participants construe the activity in somewhat similar ways, learning is unlikely to take place (cf. Wertsch's Level 1);
2. An understanding of the structure and implications of the situation; that is, an understanding of the constituent parts and the ways in which they relate to one another. (In reading and writing, this will include the specialized structures of content domains.)
3. Specific routines for regulating one's behavior in this context.

The *how* includes participation in a dialogue that has a number of characteristics:

1. A clear structure with well-defined roles for the participants.
2. Reversibility—that is, the novice can eventually take over the functions of the more expert participant.
3. An assumption of meaningful intent on the part of all participants.
4. Primary attention to the accomplishment of the task, rather than on the teaching of task-relevant skills, though the purpose of specific steps in relation to the goal may be highlighted by the adult's commentary.

TEACHING AND LEARNING IN INSTRUCTIONAL INTERACTIONS

From one perspective, the studies of early language learning cited here are also studies of instruction; the role of the adult in these interactions is that of teacher or tutor, the role of the child is that of student. The patterns of these interactions bear some resemblance to patterns of classroom instruction, though they also differ from the discourse of most classrooms in a number of important ways, to which we will return later. We have only recently begun to understand the nature of these interactions, and more recently still to begin to use them as a framework for examining instruction. Cazden (1979), in an important paper, summarizes recent research on discourse learning, and proposes Bruner's studies of peekaboo as a starting point for a new instructional model. In our own papers, we have been developing the concept of instructional scaffolding as an important component of effective instruction in reading and writing, functioning much as the adult in the mother-infant pairs: simplifying the situation, clarifying the structure, helping the student accomplish tasks that would otherwise be too difficult, and providing the framework and rules of procedure that the student will gradually learn, so that the instructional support will no longer be necessary (Applebee & Langer, 1983; Langer, 1984; Langer & Applebee, 1984, 1986). In this section we will review this work and that of other researchers who have been looking at instruction from related theoretical vantage points (e.g., Bereiter and Scardamalia; Cole and Griffin; and Palincsar and Brown).

Theory-Based Studies

Palincsar and Brown (1984) developed a reading-comprehension training study based on the notion that intrapsychological (individual) skills could be best developed by interpsychological (teacher-student) activities. Palincsar and Brown wished to develop an instructional environment where the students could participate at any level they could, where they could witness the success of their activities, where they would be involved in actual reading experiences, and where the goal of the activity would be obvious to the students. They also wished to use propleptic teaching (Rogoff & Garner, 1984; Wertsch & Stone, 1979). In propleptic teaching, the student carries out simpler aspects of the task while observing and learning more complex forms from the adult, who serves as a model.

Palincsar and Brown designed an intervention study that emulated the kinds of naturally occurring guided learning interactions described by Bruner and Wertsch, where the adult could model more expert comprehension behaviors while guiding the child to perform with increasing levels of competence. They developed a reciprocal teaching activity, where the adult guides the student to interact with the text in gradually more complex ways as the student takes over the teaching role.

Palincsar and Brown worked with seventh-grade poor comprehenders, and used reciprocal teaching procedures focusing on summarizing, questioning, clarifying, and predicting to improve reading comprehension. The students were divided into four groups, two of which received regular instruction: one group engaged in reciprocal teaching, one group was taught to locate information in the ways generally taught in remedial reading classes, one group took the experimental group's regular assessment tests but did not receive treatment, and one group completed only the criterion tests. Thirteen expository passages were selected for training, and 45 shorter passages were selected for assessment purposes. Ten comprehension questions were developed for each of the assessment passages.

The reciprocal teaching students worked in groups of two with an adult. Each day a passage was introduced, then the students and teacher took turns generating summaries and questions, clarifying more complex sections of the text, and making predictions about what would happen next. Students, as well as the teacher, took turns playing the teacher's role—the students were guided to behave more like the teacher. Throughout the activity, the teacher was available to offer assistance when it was needed. The second experimental group received training to help them answer the types of questions generally asked in remedial reading texts and workbooks. This teaching procedure involved demonstration and practice.

Results indicated that the reciprocal teaching activity led to significant improvement in the quality of the summaries given and questions asked, in performance on criterion tests of comprehension, in generalization to classroom activities, in maintenance of learning, and in standardized test scores.

Cole and Griffin (1984), in developing a remedial study for minority children, wanted to change the children's notion of the process of reading from a focus on letters, sounds, and words to a focus on meanings. To do this, they created an instructional setting where they involved the students in socially mediated, meaningful reading experiences. They planned interpersonal reading "dramas" with the expectation that the social activities would move the students from the interpsychological toward the intrapsychological plane.

An activity they called "Question Asking Reading" was based on Palincsar and Brown's reciprocal teaching procedure (see Raphael and Pearson [1985] for a related questioning activity). The first part of the activity focused on a discussion of the goal of the activity—why they were reading in the first place. This was followed by introduction of the first paragraph of the text (it was difficult for most of the students to read), and handing out of cards with commands to follow after reading the paragraph silently. The cards said: (1) Ask about the words that are hard to say. (You do not have to admit that they are hard for you to read.); (2) Ask about words whose meanings are hard to figure out; (3) Pick the answerers; (4) Ask about the main idea; (5) Ask about what is going to happen next. The children developed their questions, and a scribe wrote down the group's consensus about a good question. This question was added to a list of questions the children were asked to answer at the end of the reading. A researcher and one or more undergraduates were always present as coparticipants to supply assistance as it was necessary. Discussion focused on difficult words, best ways of getting at the main idea, and good questions.

The test consisted of three paragraphs, one of which the children had not already read. Questions were a combination of those the children had constructed themselves and others added by the research team. After the test, the children scored their papers and criticized the various questions (as they had done before). In all cases, the adults worked along with the students to share knowledge, and to create a situation where the children could work on their own to the point where help was necessary.

Cole and Griffin report three levels of change:

1. Children who could not understand (or those who misunderstood) the passage at the beginning of the activity could understand it at the end, and were able to formulate and answer interesting questions.

2. As the training progressed, the children began to anticipate the demands of each of the card commands.

3. Over time, the children approached the reading activities with greater emphasis on meaning.

Cole and Griffin suggest that remediation occurs in the socially cooperative type of environment they set. The children learn to treat print as a symbolically meaningful activity, rather than as a set of arbitrary signs. This is because the children's involvement in learning is coordinated by the adults' definition of reading, and the reorganization of the social environment permits new learning to take place.

Beginning from a different tradition, Bereiter and Scardamalia (1981) have developed the notion of procedural facilitation, an approach in which adults guide students' learning to write and think. They see younger and older students as constructing different problem representations, with younger children perceiving more complex problems in simpler ways. Procedural facilitation is used to reduce the executive demands of a task in ways that help students use the knowledge they already have. However, unlike the instructional procedures discussed above, the adult does not enter into the task as an overt collaborator. Instead, the learner "does it all," but under conditions where the adult has already reduced the task demands.

Bereiter and Scardamalia (1981) describe several instructional studies using procedural facilitation. In one study, Scardamalia asked children to produce all possible combinations of a set of combinatorial stimuli such as shapes, colors, and patterns. She gave them a procedure for dealing with the task, and had them begin by combining only two sets, and working up to more. Her study showed that children as young as eight could develop appropriate strategies themselves. In another study, Anderson, Bereiter, and Smart had children write a list of words they thought they might use in their papers, to facilitate access to topical knowledge. Without adult intervention, the activity resulted in the children's writing longer and better elaborated papers. Bereiter, Scardamalia, Anderson, and Smart facilitated students' switching back and forth between sentence composing and deciding what kind of sentence to produce. The students were asked to choose from among a list of discourse elements before composing each sentence. This approach helped them use a larger number of discourse elements, with greater variety than they otherwise would have used.

Based on these and related studies, Bereiter and Scardamalia conclude that procedural facilitation is helpful either when the overall task demands are high, or when children's ability to understand the task demands exceeds their ability to meet those demands. It enables students to tackle somewhat more complex tasks than they normally could. These conditions occur in writing when children have difficulty orchestrating and applying all they already know, and also have difficulty carrying out the behaviors required to reach their task goals.

Bereiter and Scardamalia suggest several principles to guide procedural facilitation:

1. Use procedures that emulate mature monitoring processes, but in a simpler way through easier routines or surrogate tasks.
2. Reduce the attention students need to coordinate their monitoring routines by setting up patterned routines.
3. Provide finite sets of choices.
4. Structure activities to bypass rather than support immature behaviors.
5. Foster metacognition by making cognitive operations more overt.
6. Provide labels to make tacit knowledge more accessible.
7. Use procedures that can be scaled down or upward in complexity.

Although emanating from somewhat different theoretical traditions, from our perspective Cole and Griffin's structured activities, Palincsar and Brown's reciprocal teaching, and Bereiter and Scardamalia's procedural facilitation share many features with the studies of child language learning that we have already described: assistance is provided during the task, at places where it is needed rather than in isolation from task goals; the aids that are offered are procedures of general utility that can be drawn upon in a variety of other contexts; the procedures model the procedures of more mature language users, highlighting options that are available; and the procedures in general simplify and clarify the structure of tasks that would otherwise be too difficult. They differ in the degree to which understanding of the goals, the means, and the options reside in the learner, as opposed to the teacher.

Components of Effective Instruction

Our own studies of literacy instruction have focused on the nature of effective instructional interaction amidst all of the complexities of ongoing instruction in natural classroom settings. In one series of studies (Langer & Applebee, 1984, 1986), we focused on classrooms where teachers placed particular value on the quality of the child's contribution to the classroom dialogue, and where the emphasis was on higher-order rather than basic skills. Spending anywhere from 4 months to 2 years in individual classrooms, we developed detailed case studies of "model" teachers using such approaches, as well as of experienced teachers beginning to implement such approaches for the first time. Because reading and writing are never content free (and therefore should always be taught in the service of some domain-related or task-related goal), we worked with social studies, science, and literature teachers, helping them use writing activities as a way to foster thinking and learning about the course content. As frequent observers in the classrooms, we were able to compare students' and teachers' goals and understandings, as well as the kinds of knowledge needed for task completion and the nature of the help given.

One of the principal results from these studies has been the conclusion that such an emphasis on writing as a way of learning may be impossible to implement when models of instruction tend to stress the role of the teacher as the evaluator of student learning and emphasize the importance of "coverage" of content rather than mutual exploration of interpretations (Langer, 1984). This has led us to explore "instructional scaffolding" as an alternative model of instruction that is grounded, on the one hand, in the problems that we have observed in our studies of instruction and, on the other hand, in our understanding of the studies of early child language learning, discussed earlier. In its present form, the model falls short of a complete theory of instruction, functioning instead as a metaphor that captures the most important dimensions of change that are needed for effective literacy instruction. In our earlier papers (Applebee & Langer, 1983; Langer, 1984; Langer & Applebee, 1984, 1986), we have proposed five components of effective instructional scaffolding: Ownership, Appropriateness, Structure, Collaboration, and Transfer of Control. We will summarize each of these briefly, highlighting the ways in which they relate to the studies of child language acquisition, as well as the ways in which they seem to fall short in current practice.

1. *Ownership*. Effective instruction gives students the room to have something of their own to say in their writing or in the interpretations they draw in their reading. They must see the point of the task, beyond simple obedience

to the teacher's demands. It is this sense of purposefulness that integrates the various parts of the task into a coherent whole and provides a sense of direction. It is similar to the focusing of attention and interest in Bruner's studies. The focus must be on what is being accomplished through writing or reading, if the student is to learn procedures to carry out those purposes.

In practice, this focusing is often neglected. Studying typical patterns of literacy instruction in American secondary schools, we have found that the majority of school tasks require recitation of previous learning, in which the student has little room to claim ownership for what was being written or read (Applebee, 1981; Langer, 1984; Langer & Applebee, 1984, 1986). In process-oriented writing instruction, the process supports are often seen by the students as separate activities, unrelated to the broader writing goals that the process activities were meant to support. In reading, little room is left for students to interpret texts in ways that are different from that expected by the teacher.

2. *Appropriateness.* Effective instruction builds on literacy and thinking skills the students already have, and helps them to accomplish tasks that they could not otherwise complete on their own. As Vygotsky (1962) puts it, effective instruction is aimed not at the ripe, but at the ripening functions. (More specifically, Vygotsky argues that instruction should be addressed at the zone of proximal development, defined essentially as tasks that a learner can complete with appropriate help, but would be unable to complete unaided.) In each of the studies we examined earlier, the mother-infant dyads drew on language resources the child already had (however simple these might be), stretching them to new and more complex contexts. When the stretch was too far, as for children at the first level in Wertsch's puzzle-solving task, the dialogue fell apart and progress resumed only when the adult redefined the task in terms closer to the child's understanding of the situation.

Again, studies of literacy instruction suggest that this principle is more often violated than observed. When students are asked to undertake new tasks, the tasks too often are not set in the context of skills the students already have. This manifests itself in two ways: (1) as the assumption that all that is necessary is to give students a topic to write about or a passage to read that is at their "level," and they will somehow know how to do it; and (2) as the assumption that every element of a new task must be taught from scratch, as though the students had no resources upon which to draw.

3. *Structure.* Effective instructional tasks make the structure of the activity clear, and guide the student through the activity in a way that provides effective strategies for use in other contexts. Put another way, such tasks produce a natural sequence of thought and language, providing effective routines for the students to internalize.

Structure of this sort is one of the most consistent features in the studies of early language acquisition—the child learns to do new language tasks by being led through them in the context of a supportive dialogue. This insures that skill learning includes a sense of the appropriate contexts for use. New procedures and routines are embedded in the contexts they serve, rather than being presented as isolated components that may or may not be seen as relevant. (Embedded in this way, the use of new procedures and routines may be highlighted by the adult's commentary, but this is very different from teaching the procedures and routines as skills out of context.)

In practice, literacy instruction is usually organized around skills to be learned rather than purposes to be accomplished. Current models of curriculum stress hierarchies of skills, often in elaborate scope and sequence charts, and current teaching and testing emphasize the component skills rather than the whole. Although recent attention to process models of instruction seems to be moving toward teaching that is responsive to "natural" stages in the reading or writing task, very few process approaches have made their way into classrooms. The emphasis, in both reading and writing, remains on isolated skills or isolated content. Most students write little, and when they do write, the writing usually involves a first-and-final draft of a page or less, produced in one class period in response to an assignment that specifies an appropriate length, topic, due date—and little more.

4. *Collaboration*. Effective instructional interactions build upon and recast student efforts without rejecting what the students have accomplished on their own. This is similar to adult-child interactions, in which the adult assumes that the child has something that he or she wants to say or do, and works with the child to carry this through to completion. The adult's repertoire of devices includes telling, modeling, extending, rephrasing, questioning, praising, and correcting. These devices are employed in the service of the task (book reading, peekaboo, puzzle building), rather than to judge the child's performance.

Teachers' roles in literacy instruction, however, are rarely collaborative. Much more frequently, the role is one of evaluation, usually tied to previous learning rather than to learning-in-progress. Collaboration is often thought of as cheating rather than of help, and teachers' responses take the form of grades instead of suggestions of ways to solve a reading or writing problem. Our studies show the role of teacher-as-evaluator as permeating almost all classroom exchanges involving reading and writing.

5. *Internalization*. As students gain competence in new tasks, control of the interaction is gradually transferred from the teacher to the students. External scaffolding for the activity is gradually withdrawn as the new patterns and skills become part of the students' own repertoires. As Cazden (1979) and Griffin and Cole (1984) have pointed out, we are dealing with a peculiar

kind of scaffold, one that self-destructs as the child internalizes its features, allowing the child to complete similar tasks without further help. Thus Richard, in Bruner's studies, eventually took over the labeling sequence in picture-book reading, just as the older children in Wertsch's analyses embedded the parents' directives in their speech to themselves.

In their instructional practices, teachers too often forget to let the scaffolding self-destruct. Rather than allowing students to take over control of the task, teachers perseverate with their favorite teaching practices. In one part of our study of writing instruction, we analyzed popular textbooks in seven subject areas and found that there were few differences in the writing activities suggested between 9th and 11th grades, and no differences in the kinds of activities suggested over the course of a year in individual texts (Applebee, Langer et al., 1984). There was no transfer of control from teacher (or textbook) to student in response to the learning that was presumably taking place.

While we have not elaborated here on the content of the instructional interaction, in any given case the nature of the scaffolding will be shaped by the particular learnings that are needed in order to accomplish the larger goal. In most cases, this will involve both particular content knowledge necessary to carry out the task, and particular reading or writing strategies or approaches necessary to carry it through. And it will be toward the accomplishment of the overall goal that the instructional interaction will be initiated: one or more different kinds of knowledge will be taught in the service of achieving a particular goal. These teachings will have meaning only as they enable the student to move toward accomplishing the goal. In this way, the student can learn (1) new knowledge and (2) new strategies, as well as (3) an understanding of how these are coordinated in the completion of particular tasks. For this to occur, the student must have a clear understanding both of the task itself and of the strategies that are being used to complete it.

REINTERPRETING STUDIES OF TEACHING METHODS

Process-oriented research has come into its own in the past decade, but the bulk of that research has been concerned with cognitive aspects of reading and writing, rather than with the study of instruction, of ways in which those processes can be taught and learned. In the 5-year period 1981–1985, for example, 72% of the articles in *Research in the Teaching of English* dealt with reading or writing, but only 10% discussed alternative methods of instruction. Although the teaching literature has been full of instructional suggestions, the research base for those suggestions is meager at best.

If we consider the instructional studies in terms of the five components of effective scaffolding suggested earlier, virtually all of the recent studies have been concerned with one or another aspect of structure—that is, with the sequence of activities that are provided to support students while engaged in a reading or writing task. Although none of the instructional studies were designed to test the scaffolding model directly, their results are generally consistent with the prediction that tasks that lead students through "a natural sequence of thought and language" are more likely to be effective in the development of new skills.

Some examples follow, selected to illustrate how recent research can be reinterpreted in light of the argument we are developing, rather than to provide a comprehensive review of research on reading or writing instruction.

Hillocks (1979, 1982), in a pair of studies, has examined the effectiveness of a series of observational activities as a prelude to writing, in contrast to more traditional approaches to writing instruction. Essentially, his observational condition leads students through a structured process of observation, recording, and reporting, accompanied in the second study with revision and teacher-response conditions. The sequence of activities in his experimental groups matches our criteria for effective scaffolding rather well: the task has a clear structure with activities that are designed to help students accomplish tasks that they could not successfully complete on their own. The students have room to develop some ownership for what they are doing, since the tasks focus on their own observations rather than a recitation of information previously organized by the teacher. In general, the experimental groups in Hillocks's studies outperformed the controls on posttreatment tasks that required specificity and organizational skills paralleling those in the treatment tasks. Hillocks's studies are limited to one type of writing, but come the closest to offering a test of a well-constructed sequence of instructional scaffolding in the teaching of writing.

Other studies have examined smaller segments of the total writing activity. Glynn, Britton, Muth, and Dogan (1982) compared the effects on persuasive writing of different demands while writing a preliminary draft. In general, their results suggest that, for a complex task like persuasive writing, freeing the students during their early drafts to think about the arguments, rather than about the form of their presentation, simplifies the task for them and leads to a more effective generation of arguments. This approach may also represent a more natural sequence of thought and language than that enforced by the control conditions, which insisted (as teachers so often do) on mechanical correctness and completeness even in the preliminary drafts.

Beach (1979) compared the effects of teacher response, no response, and self-guided response on between-draft revision of expository writing. Teacher-guided revisions were more extensive, and also led to better final drafts, a result that would be predictable if we assume that it is difficult to obtain enough distance from one's own writing to assess where revisions are most needed. Karegianes, Pascarella, and Pflaum (1980), in a small study of low-achieving 10th-grade students, found, on the other hand, that peer editing led to better performance on posttreatment essays than did teacher editing. (Peer editors used the same editing/rating sheets as were used by the teacher.)

Both groups of students improved, which is consistent with Beach's results. However, in this study, the greater improvement attributed to the peer-response condition could have had a number of sources. For example, the process of reading other students' papers may have heightened students' understanding of the process of revision; sharing with a wider audience of peers may have increased the writers' sense of ownership for their work; and the peer-editing group may have been perceived as more collaborative and less evaluative than the teacher editing. Quite likely a combination of those factors was at work.

One of the largest bodies of recent work in writing instruction has examined the effects of sentence combining on writing proficiency. Sentence-combining programs violate two of our principles of effective scaffolding: they are essentially skill practice out of context, and they provide little opportunity for the student to develop ownership of the task.

It is clear that sentence-combining practice leads students to produce more complex sentences. It is much less clear, however, that students write better as a result of such programs. Smith and Combs (1980) found that simply cuing students that sentence complexity will be a factor in assessing their writing leads to comparable increases in complexity. Equivalent gains were obtained from overt cues that stated the criteria and from covert cues that were conveyed, for example, by putting the students through a brief sentence-combining exercise. Although younger students may not be able to vary the syntactic complexity of their writing as easily as did the college students whom Smith and Combs were studying, it is quite possible that the effects of sentence combining on writing quality have as much to do with clarifying students' sense of the task as with their more general writing abilities.

Beck, along with her colleagues at the Learning Research and Development Center, has conducted a series of studies focusing on reading instruction, using basal-reader passages. In one of the most recent studies, McKeown, Beck, Omanson, and Pople (1985) examined successful vocabulary instruction to fourth graders by comparing three types of instruction: traditional instruction using teacher-directed simple associations, rich instruction that engaged the students in exploring various aspects of word meanings for themselves, and extended/rich instruction that included the rich instructional activities but also encouraged the children to become aware of and use their new words in out-of-school contexts. The words selected for inclusion corresponded to those introduced in basal readers during the intermediate grades. Dependent measures were vocabulary knowledge, semantic decision (interpretation of words in context), and story comprehension (recall of stories created around high-encounter and low-encounter words).

The rich and extended/rich instructional environments seem to capture critical aspects of instructional scaffolding in that both conditions permit the students to develop a sense of ownership for the task by encouraging discussion about the students' own meanings. Both also provide a supportive structure in the form of vocabulary-building routines for the students to follow and internalize.

In general, the three groups performed equally well in vocabulary knowledge, but the children in the rich and extended/rich conditions excelled in high-encounter story recall. They also performed their tasks more quickly. The richness of instruction, the authors conclude, provided the students with an opportunity to integrate words and elaborate them in diverse contexts. The extended/rich condition provided them with the opportunity spontaneously to establish even more semantic connections outside of class. We would elaborate these interpretations by conjecturing that the students in these instructional conditions had the opportunity to first use their new vocabulary in social settings that permitted them to move from the meanings they set for themselves toward the more refined definitions they were learning. Further, they had an opportunity to practice their growing understanding of the new vocabulary in social settings where tutorial support was provided to help them understand and use their new learning on their own.

Duffy and Roehler, at the Institute for Research on Teaching, have undertaken a series of studies that look at the effects of instructional explicitness on student achievement. In one recent study (Duffy, Roehler, & Rackliffe, in press), they examined the influence of six teachers' instructional talk during reading lessons. They found that while all the teachers with whom they worked were verbally explicit, some made qualitatively different statements about what was to be learned and how to go about learning, and it was their students who demonstrated a better understanding of the lessons' contents. These teachers were responsive to "where the students were" in their attempts to learn and provided various forms of assistance to help the students understand and complete new tasks.

Analyses of postlesson interviews with students demonstrated that explicitness is a relative term, and the way it is actualized in the classroom makes a great difference in student learning. Duffy, Roehler and Rackliffe conclude that for effective instruction, teachers need not only to be clear about the topic of the lesson, but also to understand the processes good readers go through, and then to offer explicit help based on this understanding.

The behaviors of the successful teachers in this study closely parallel our scaffolding criteria of structure and collaboration. Not only did the teachers understand the natural sequence of language and thought engendered by the activity, but they also served as watchful guides and tutors. They helped students to gain increasing understanding of the nature of the reading activity, and increasing control in carrying it through on their own.

We have cited only a few studies in this section. This is not because of space constraints but because of the dearth of studies that directly focus on literacy instruction: on the roles of teacher and student in the joint enterprise of learning to read and write. However, from these few studies, each quite different in approach and focus, we have been able to demonstrate that the more successful instructional approaches incorporated at least some aspects of the theoretical notions underlying instructional scaffolding.

CONCLUSION

Where does that leave us? We can reorganize and make sense of what we know about reading and writing instruction in terms of the more general principles of language learning processes. That, we think, is ultimately the most productive view, both in defining the research questions we ask in the next generation of reading and writing research, and in helping us to formulate our response to the inevitable questions about what research can tell us about what to do in the classroom tomorrow. Our concern with reading and writing processes has taught us a great deal about the role of the individual; the concept of instructional scaffolding provides a way to bring the role of the teacher, and of instruction, back into our research paradigms—and into our theories of learning to read and write.

REFERENCES

Applebee, A.N. (1981). *Writing in the secondary school: English and the content areas*. Urbana, IL: National Council of Teachers of English.

Applebee, A. (1984). Writing and reasoning. *Review of Educational Research, 54* (4), 577–586.

Applebee, A.N., & Langer, J.A. (1983). Instructional scaffolding: Reading and writing as natural language activities. *Language Arts, 60* (2), 168–175.

Applebee, A.N., Langer, J.A., Butler-Nalin, K., Durst, R., Marshall, J., & Newell, G. (1984). *Contexts for learning to write*. Norwood, NJ: Ablex.

Applebee, A., Langer, J., & Mullis, I. (1985). *The reading report card*. Report of the National Assessment of Educational Progress. Princeton, NJ: Educational Testing Service.

Au, K. (1980). Participation structures in a reading lesson with Hawaiian children: Analysis of a culturally appropriate instruction event. *Anthropology in Education Quarterly, 11* (2), 91–115.

Beach, R. (1979). The effects of between-draft teacher evaluation versus student self-evaluation on high school students' revising of rough drafts. *Research in the Teaching of English, 13*, (2), 111–119.

Bereiter, C., & Scardamalia, M. (1981). From conversation to composition: The role of instruction in a developmental process. In R. Glaser (Ed.), *Advances in instructional psychology* (Vol. 2). Hillsdale, NJ: Erlbaum.

Bruner, J.S. (1973). *The relevance of education* (2nd ed.). New York: Norton.

Bruner, J. (1978). The role of dialogue in language acquisition. In A. Sinclair, R.J. Jarvelle, & W.J.M. Levelt (Eds.), *The child's conception of language*. New York: Springer.

Bruner, J.S., Olver, R.R., & Greenfield, P.M. (1966). *Studies in cognitive growth: A collaboration at the Center for Cognitive Studies*. New York: Wiley.

Cazden, C. (1979). Peekaboo as an instructional model: Discourse development at home and at school. *Papers and Reports on Child Language Development, 17,* 1–19.

Cole, M., & Griffin, P. (1984). Socio-historical approach to remediation. Unpublished paper from the Laboratory of Comparative Human Cognition, University of California at San Diego.

Duffy, G., Roehler, L., & Rackliffe, G. (in press). Qualitative differences in teachers' instructional talk as they influence student awareness of lesson content. *Elementary School Journal.*

Ferreiro, E. (1984). The underlying logic of literacy development. In H. Goelman, A. Oberg, & F. Smith, (Eds.) *Awakening to literacy.* Exeter, NH: Heinemann.

Ferreiro, E. (1985). Literacy development: A psychogenetic perspective. In D.R. Olson, N. Torrance, & A. Hildyard (Eds.), *Literacy, language, and learning: The nature and consequences of reading and writing.* New York: Cambridge University Press.

Glynn, S.M., Britton, B.K., Muth, D., & Dogan, N. (1982). Writing and revising persuasive documents: Cognitive demands. *Journal of Educational Psychology, 74* (4), 557–567.

Graff, H. (Ed.). (1981). *Literacy development in the west.* New York: Cambridge University Press.

Griffin, P., & Cole, M. (1984). Current activity for the future: The zo-ped. In B. Rogoff & J. Wertsch (Eds.), *Children's learning in the zone of proximal development* (New Directions for Child Development, No. 23). San Francisco: Jossey-Bass.

Heath, S.B. (1982). Protean shapes in literacy events: Ever shifting oral and literate traditions. In D. Tannen (Ed.), *Spoken and written language.* Norwood, NJ: Ablex.

Heath, S.B. (1983). *Ways with words.* New York: Cambridge University Press.

Hillocks, G., Jr. (1979). The effects of observational activities on student writing. *Research in the Teaching of English, 13* (1), 23–35.

Hillocks, G., Jr. (1982). The interaction of instruction, teacher comment, and revision in teaching the composing process. *Research in the Teaching of English, 16,* (3), 261–278.

Karegianes, M.L., Pascarella, E.T., & Pflaum, S.W. (1980). The effects of peer editing on the writing proficiency of low-achieving tenth grade students. *Journal of Educational Research, 73* (2), 203–207.

Langer, J.A. (1984). Literacy instruction in American schools: Problems and perspectives. *American Journal of Education, 93* (1), 107–132.

Langer, J.A. (in press). A sociocognitive perspective on literacy. In J. Langer (Ed.), *Language, literacy and culture: Issues of society and schooling.* Norwood, NJ: Ablex.

Langer, J.A., & Applebee, A.N. (1984). Language, learning, and interaction: A framework for improving the teaching of writing. In A. Applebee (Ed.), *Contexts for learning to write: Studies of secondary school instruction.* Norwood, NJ: Ablex.

Langer, J.A., & Applebee, A.N. (1986). *Writing and learning in the secondary school curriculum.* (Final rep. to the National Institute of Education, Grant Number NIE-G-82-0027).

Luria, A.R. (1929/1977–1978). The development of writing in the child. *Soviet Psychology, 16,* 65–114. Translated from *Problems of Marxist Education, 1,* 143–176. (Moscow: Academy of Communist Education).

McDermott, R.P. (1977). Social relations as contexts for learning in school. *Harvard Educational Review, 47* (2), 198–213.

McKeown, M., Beck, I., Omanson, R., & Pople, M. (1985). Some effects of the nature and frequency of vocabulary instruction on the knowledge and use of words. *Reading Research Quarterly, 20* (5), 522–535.

Ninio, A., & Bruner, J. (1978). The achievement and antecedents of labelling. *Journal of Child Language, 5,* 1–15.

Olson, D.R. (1977). From utterance to text: The bias of language in speech and writing. *Harvard Education Review, 47* (3), 257–281.

Olson, D.R. (in press). On the cognitive consequences of literacy. *Canadian Psychology.*

Ong, W. (1982). *Orality and literacy: The technologizing of the word.* London: Methuen.

Palincsar, A.S., & Brown, A.L. (1984). Reciprocal teaching of comprehension-fostering and monitoring activities. *Cognition and Instruction, 1* (2), 117–175.

Raphael, T., & Pearson, P.D. (1985). Increasing students' awareness of sources of information for answering questions. *American Educational Research Journal, 22* (2), 217–236.

Ratner, N., & Bruner, J. (1978). Games, social exchange and the acquisition of language. *Journal of Child Language, 5,* 391–401.

Resnick, D.P. (Ed.) (1983). *Literacy in social perspective.* Washington, DC: Library of Congress.

Resnick, D.P., & Resnick, L.R. (1977). The nature of literacy: An historical exploration. *Harvard Educational Review, 47* (3), 370–385.

Rogoff, B., & Gardner, W. (1984). Adult guidance of cognitive development. In B. Rogoff & J. Lave (Eds.), *Everyday cognition.* Cambridge, MA: Harvard University Press.

Scribner, S. & Cole, M. (1981). *The psychology of literacy.* Cambridge, MA: Harvard University Press.

Smith, W.L., & Combs, W.E. (1980). The effects of overt and covert cues on written syntax. *Research in the Teaching of English, 14* (1), 19–38.

Snow, C.E., & Ferguson, C.A. (Eds.). (1977). *Talking to children: Language input and acquisition.* Cambridge: Cambridge University Press.

Tannen, D. (1982). The oral/literate continuum in discourse. In D. Tannen (Ed.), *Spoken and written language.* Norwood, NJ: Ablex.

Tannen, D. (1984). *Conversational style: Analyzing talk among friends.* Norwood, NJ: Ablex.

Vygotsky, L.S. (1962). *Thought and language.* Cambridge, MA: MIT Press.

Vygotsky, L.S. (1978). *Mind in society.* Cambridge, MA: Harvard University Press.

Wertsch, J.V. (1977). Metacognition and adult-child interaction. Paper presented at the Annual Conference on Learning Disabilities, Evanston, IL. (ERIC Document Reproduction Service No. ED 180-610)

Wertsch, J.V. (1979). From social interaction to higher psychological processes. A clarification and application of Vygotsky's theory. *Human Development, 22,* 1–22.

Wertsch, J.V., McNamee, G.W., McLare, J.B., & Budwig, N.A. (1980). The adult-child dyad as a problem-solving system. *Child Development, 51,* 1215–1221.

Wertsch, J.V., & Stone, C.A. (1985). The concept of internalization in Vygotsky's account of the genesis of higher mental functions. In J.V. Wertsch (Ed.), *Culture, communication, and cognition.* New York: Cambridge University Press.

Wood, D., Bruner, J.S., & Ross, G. (1976). The role of tutoring and problem solving. *Journal of Child Psychology and Psychiatry, 17,* 89–100.

Chapter 6

Language, Culture, and Writing: Sociolinguistic Foundations of Research on Writing

MARCIA FARR
University of Illinois at Chicago

Why is learning to write often so difficult, whereas learning to speak one's native language is not? Why do students from ethnic minority communities generally have even more difficulty in this process than middle-class, "mainstream" students? To begin answering these questions, it is necessary to explore what is known about (1) the language of nonmainstream cultural groups in contrast to the language of the mainstream middle class, and (2) the nature of writing, and the learning of writing, as one kind of language in context.

This chapter will review what we know about writing, and the learning of writing, from the standpoint of language variation, that is, how language differs among users in its structure and in its use. Language variation, of course, can be viewed in both individual and group terms; here the focus will be on the latter, especially as it is reflected in ethnic and cultural identity. Because writing is seen here as one mode, or channel, in which to use language, and because relatively little research on cultural variation in language has focused on writing directly (most of it has focused on spoken language), some of the work to be reviewed deals with cultural variation in oral language.

Research on cultural variation in language is important for research on writing for two reasons: first, because it provides a foundation upon which future work on cultural aspects of writing can be built. Second, knowledge about variation in language, both oral and written, has significant implications for the teaching and learning of writing. While it is clear that there are problems in the teaching and learning of writing in classrooms across the country (Applebee 1981, 1984), it is also clear that these problems are more serious

The author gratefully acknowledges the editorial stewardship provided this review by Shirley Brice Heath, as well as the helpful critical comments of Robert Gundlach and Lawrence Frase on earlier drafts.

among ethnic, minority populations (National Assessment of Educational Progress, 1981). Research that can illuminate the nature of some of these problems is then of crucial importance to any efforts to improve the teaching and learning of writing in this country.

The work reviewed in this chapter will be explored for insights about differences between mainstream standard English writing and various nonmainstream varieties of American English, in terms of both language form and language function. In addition, the work will be assessed for its relevance to the learning of writing. Also included throughout this discussion will be work that has focused directly on cultural variation in writing and in the learning of writing.

After presenting the theoretical framework within which writing can be viewed as one mode of language (and within which variation in both oral and written language has been and can be studied), the role of context in defining writing will be addressed. This will be followed by a discussion of oral and written language patterns and uses among the mainstream middle class, and then a review of research on cultural and linguistic differences among nonmainstream groups. After that, two sections of the review will clarify the terms *dialect* and *bidialectalism,* and also will consider the linguistic effects of learning written standard English on nonstandard dialect speakers. Finally, several studies of effective writing instruction to both mainstream and nonmainstream students will be assessed for the principles underlying their success.

WRITING AS LANGUAGE

Writing can be seen as one way in which to use one's tacit knowledge about language, or one's communicative competence (Hymes, 1971). Within this theoretical framework, learning to write can be seen as adding to one's oral communicative competence and as changing one's tacit competence in language. Researchers have only recently explored written, as opposed to oral, communicative competence within this theoretical framework, and much of this work has focused on reading (see Bloome & Green, 1984, for a synthesis of the work on reading; also Goelman, Oberg, & Smith, 1984; Teale & Sulzby, 1986). Other work has explored the similarities and differences between spoken and written language.

Many investigations of the relationships between spoken and written language were stimulated by Goody and Watt (1963), who suggested that the development of writing has both cultural and cognitive consequences. They argued, on the basis of the historical development of Western civilization, that literacy changes both societies and individuals—that is, that becoming literate affects how people use language and how they think. Initially, researchers explored literacy in opposition to "orality," and defined typical characteristics of each of the two modes of language. For example, Olson (1977) claimed that for written language, meaning resides primarily in the text itself, whereas for oral language, much meaning is communicated in the context in which the language is used. In this sense, written language is more autonomous, or decontextualized, than spoken language.

Olson's work, and other work along these lines, seems to have been based on a characterization of oral language as casual conversation and of written language as the (Western) school essay, not on the full range of *kinds* of oral and written language that more recent research has documented. For example, researchers such as Scribner and Cole (1981), Scollon and Scollon (1981), Tannen (1982, 1984), Heath (1983), and Street (1984) have shown that all language use, whether oral or written, is embedded in a social context that affects both its form and its function. Furthermore, these and other researchers have illustrated how language use in a literate society draws on aspects of orality and literacy in subtle and overlapping ways. In other words, speaking and writing are alternate ways of using one's language capacities, and very often both modes are used within a single speech or literacy event.

Research on children's early writing development also has illuminated the relationships among all the language processes, speaking, listening, reading, and writing (Farr, 1985b). In particular, research on emergent literacy among preschoolers has shown that children employ all their oral and written language capacities to perform reading and writing tasks before they are reading and writing in adult, conventional ways (Harste, Woodward, & Burke, 1984; Sulzby, 1985). Other research has shown the parallels between oral language acquisition and learning to write, especially the role of play in both (Gundlach, McLane, Stott, & McNamee, 1985), and the role of individual variation in the development of both (Dyson, 1985). Furthermore, Greene (1985) shows parallels in the language functions typical of both oral language and writing. Finally, Sowers (1985) shows how the "scaffolding" provided by middle-class mothers in our culture during oral language acquisition parallels the scaffolding provided by teachers in the learning of writing. Scaffolding in this sense is the provision of a temporary, supportive framework by adults to assist a child in doing what he or she cannot yet do alone (Cazden, 1982).

WRITING AS DEFINED IN CONTEXT

Although much research on writing has focused primarily on the act of composing by an individual writer (Farr, 1985a), context increasingly is being viewed as essential to understanding writing (Langer 1985; Schumacher, 1986; Stein, this volume). Context, however, can mean many things, from setting, to situation, to "shared and ratified definitions of situations *and* . . . the social actions persons take on the basis of these definitions" (McDermott, 1976). Thus writing, or oral language, does not so much occur *in* contexts as it does partially constitute them. Moreover, speakers in part *create* the context by the ways in which they use language, including what

Gumperz (1982a) has termed "contextualization cues"—features of intonation, proxemics, and other paralinguistic aspects of behavior. After all, as Erickson (1984a) pointed out, the English word *context* is derived from the Latin *contextare,* meaning "to weave together." Thus, as social processes among people vary, so do contexts, and so does oral or written language, which is part of the texture of those contexts.

Variation in oral language has been documented by several decades of sociolinguistic research, that is, linguistic research which assumes that the social context is essential to an understanding of language. Some of this research has studied ethnic and social class variation in language structure, primarily in phonology and syntax, although some studies have emphasized discourse (i.e., where the unit of analysis includes more than a sentence) and semantics. This work has explored a variety of American English dialects, including Black English Vernacular (Fasold, 1972; Kochman, 1972; Labov, 1972a; Wolfram, 1969); Puerto Rican English (Wolfram, 1974; Zentella, 1981); Appalachian English (Wolfram & Christian, 1976); varieties of American Indian English (Wolfram, Christian, Potter, & Leap, 1979); and others (Amastae & Elias-Olivares, 1982; Ferguson & Heath, 1981; Labov, 1980). The primary finding of all such work is that nonstandard varieties of English, or of any language, are as complex and as regularly patterned as are standard varieties. These patterns, then, do not represent a linguistic or cognitive *deficit* on the part of the speakers, but, rather, represent linguistic *differences* from other dialects of English. These studies also have provided a considerable amount of information about the specific linguistic features in different varieties of American English.

In addition to sociolinguistic studies of language form, other studies have focused on language function, or use. Many of these studies are building toward an ethnography of communication, as suggested by Hymes (1962). They have taken place both within classrooms (Cazden, John, & Hymes, 1972; Cherry-Wilkinson, 1982; Gilmore & Glatthorn, 1982; Green & Wallat, 1981) and within home and community contexts (Bauman & Sherzer, 1974; Gumperz, 1982a, 1982b; Heath, 1983; Kochman, 1981). This work has found that ways of using language can vary sharply from one cultural group to another and that such differences can cause communication to break down between speakers from different groups. Schools, of course, are one significant place in our society where speakers from different cultures meet; once there, however, everyone is expected to interact according to the linguistic patterns of the "school culture" (Green, 1983).

Studies of variation in writing, unlike those of variation in oral language, are less numerous. Work has focused on defining the parameters of the area (Farr Whiteman, 1981b) or on particular contexts: writing in business settings (Odell & Goswami, 1981), and in homes and other nonschool community settings (Heath, 1983; Scribner & Cole, 1981). Two of these studies had a cross-cultural focus: Scribner and Cole studied writing and reading among the Vai in Liberia, and Heath studied writing, reading, and oral language in the Piedmont area of the southern United States. Heath's ethnography included two rural, working-class communities, one white and one black, as well as mainstream black and white families referred to as "townspeople."

Work on variation in writing has shown that writing is not a single entity that occurs in different contexts, but that it is a social practice that varies according to the particular use to which it is put in each context. Similarly, the cognitive demands of writing (and the cognitive effects of being able to write) vary according to particular uses. For example, the Scribner and Cole study found that among the Vai, the Arabic and English literates demonstrated superior performance (over nonliterates) on certain cognitive tasks. However, the specific cognitive tasks in which each group of literates showed superior performance were closely related to the specific ways in which each group used writing or reading (e.g., the practice of letter writing in the Vai script seemed to increase "audience awareness" as a cognitive skill).

"STANDARD" LANGUAGE AND WRITING AMONG THE MAINSTREAM MIDDLE CLASS

Although references frequently are made to "Standard English" as though it were a single dialect used by a particular group of speakers, there is considerable variation across this society in what is considered "standard." In addition to regional differences that are not socially stigmatized (e.g., southern or northeastern pronunciations of English), there are grammatical features that would not be considered "standard" by most teachers of writing in the speech of educated, upper-middle-class people in our society (e.g., Greene, 1980). Also, as Taylor (1983) has pointed out, there is a linguistically describable Standard Black English, which utilizes standard grammar with elements of black verbal style. In sum, there are different kinds of oral standard English in our society that are appropriate in particular situations of language use. Mainstream speakers use these oral varieties along with more formal varieties, or registers, of oral and written English. (Register variation generally refers to variation in language which is conditioned by use, as opposed to dialect variation, which is conditioned by the geographical or social place of the user [Ferguson, 1985]).

If there is not a single oral standard English, is there a unified written standard? The teaching of writing, and much research on writing, seems to be based on an implicit model of "good" writing that approximates a standard. Even with its variations (e.g., stylistic preferences for various kinds of writing), this "standard" seems to be linguistically describable (Chafe, 1982) and largely appropriate in various contexts across time and space. Moreover, the Chomskian grammar of an "ideal speaker-hearer of English" can be said to be a grammar of written standard English, if it is anything, presumably because of what has been called "the written language bias of linguistics" (Linell, 1982). However, even without a fully specified definition of standard English, a primary characteristic of this written standard would have to be a lack of those socially stigmatized features (e.g., multiple negation) associated with nonstandard dialects.

When we teach writing, then, we are teaching, in part, avoidance of nonstandard dialect features. We are also teaching other new ways of using language that are characteristic of the written standard. Academic writing, in fact, calls upon ways of using language that are quite culturally specific. For example, certain kinds of writing may involve specific patterns of reasoning, presentation of argument, and organizational structure. Since such aspects of thinking and of expressing thinking in language can vary greatly from culture to culture, students from nonmainstream groups often are faced with a conflict of cultures when they are learning to produce what we, according to our own cultural beliefs, consider "good academic prose." Such a cultural conflict can be particularly confusing to both students and teachers because these aspects of one's culture are a part of the tacit knowledge that members of a particular cultural group unconsciously share simply by virtue of being members.

All ways of using oral and written language are embedded in cultural beliefs and conventions (Heath, 1983; Street, 1984). This is as true for mainstream as for nonmainstream language use. Consequently, the concept of "good writing" that underlies writing instruction in school is embedded in the cultural beliefs and conventions by which "schooled" people live. As members of what Street (1984) terms "the academic subculture of western society," schooled people immerse themselves in certain kinds of oral and written language, and they value objectivity and explicitness in such language, particularly in writing. Because school in our society is part of mainstream culture, the language use in school, particularly in the case of the written standard, closely resembles the language use of mainstream culture. For example, Heath (1983) shows how members of this mainstream culture in the community she studied used both "expository talk" and expository prose on the job (in this study, as mill executives and teachers) and at home as parents.

NONMAINSTREAM USES OF LANGUAGE AND WRITING

Most students who begin school using language in nonmainstream ways leave school without acquiring written standard English. This is so despite the fact that they have spent up to 12 years in a context in which this standard is taught, or at least used and modeled. One reason, of course, is the lack of adequate writing practice and instruction, a problem shared by almost all students in school (Applebee, 1981; Graves, 1978). In addition, however, there must be an explanation for the fact that nonmainstream students learn even less about writing than do mainstream students. It may be that in many schools these students, more often than mainstream students, remain in the "remedial track" and receive even less practice at actual writing (and reading) than do students in the regular and advanced tracks. Goodlad (1984) has suggested that students in lower ability tracks are repetitively given low-level skills exercises rather than work which challenges them to think, or to comprehend or write extended discourse.

A number of other reasons also have been posited to explain failure of nonmainstream students to develop writing skills. Some of these reasons are social and cultural and others are linguistic in nature. Most of these suggested explanations share a common assumption of a conflict between communicative systems, that is, between the ways the students use language at home and in their communities and the ways they are expected to do so in school.

Before discussing the potential conflicts between communicative systems, however, it is important to note other suggested explanations that underlie the conflict between communicative systems. Ogbu (1974, 1980) has linked the problems minority children face inside classrooms to broader problems of caste status and racism in the larger society of which schools are a part. Thus Ogbu calls for research that takes into account the world outside of classrooms, rather than solely focusing on micro-interactions within classrooms. Gilmore and Smith (1982), acknowledging Ogbu's concern, questioned why children, faced with unfamiliar ways of communicating, do not eventually adapt to the new situation and learn the new ways of using oral and written language. Children, after all, are known to be quick and facile learners of language and other aspects of the world around them. The fact that so many nonmainstream students do not learn standard English literacy leads Gilmore and Smith to conclude that there may be a systemic reason for this within the culture of the school, that perhaps the children's "survival needs are met by failing" (Gilmore & Smith, 1982, p. 7). From this perspective, such students may choose to fail because the personal costs of learning how to become members of the school culture are seen as too high.

In addition to locating the problem within cultural systems, either in the larger society or within the subculture of the classroom, negative teacher attitudes toward nonstandard dialects (and by extension toward those who use them) have been identified by many as a large part of the problem. Farr Whiteman (1980) and Chambers (1983) explore the controversial Ann Arbor court case. In this federal court case, a group of parents of Black English Vernacular (BEV)-speaking elementary school students brought suit against the Ann Arbor public schools. The parents claimed that the schools were denying their children their civil rights by failing to teach them to read and write standard English (SE), and Judge Harold Joiner, after extensive testimony by linguists and others on the extant research, ruled in the parents' favor in July 1979. Expert testimony pointed both to linguistic differences between BEV and SE and to negative attitudes toward nonstandard dialects as explanations for the school's failure. The remedy required by the court was teacher inservice education designed to inform them about the linguistic adequacy of nonstandard dialects and to turn negative attitudes into more positive ones.

These and other explorations of this educational problem undoubtedly provide at least partial explanations of the situation. Nevertheless, differences between communicative systems can be both extensive and deeply ingrained and, moreover, are the most evident features in the difficulties nonmainstream students face in learning to become literate. Explanations along these lines suggest both cultural conflict and linguistic conflict, and the following sections will explore each of these in turn.

Cultural Differences

Among the "cultural conflict" explanations offered is one suggested by Labov (1972a): peer group status among adolescents is associated with vernacular dialects, at least in the inner city. In a study of the relation of reading failure to peer-group status among adolescents in Harlem, Labov found that peer-group leaders who demonstrated (outside of school) all the scholastic and verbal ability needed to succeed in school still did not do so. He concluded that these teenagers had "turned their backs on school culture" because it conflicted with the street culture in which they were firmly grounded. Although Labov (1972a, 1983) also argues that there are structural (linguistic) differences between standard English and Black English Vernacular that do cause some problems in learning written standard English, he maintains that the primary conflict is a cultural one.

Because literacy is an essential goal of schooling, then students who reject schooling, reject literacy or, at least, what society perceives as the primary opportunity to become literate. Yet not all students, like Labov's peer group leaders, reject the school culture. Many try hard to do well in school, perhaps to live up to parental expectations (e.g., Heath, 1983) that doing well in school will lead to "success." Nonetheless, even these students, if they come from a nonmainstream culture, largely fail to acquire productive use of either oral or written standard English. Thus we are faced with an apparent enigma: given the complex linguistic capacities of all human beings, why should these students fail in this process, when they clearly have succeeded in learning to speak the language of their community? In other words, why is learning to become literate often so difficult, but learning to speak one's native language is not? This question is particularly perplexing if one does not accept a simple dichotomy between speaking and writing, that is, that speaking is contextualized and writing is decontextualized and, therefore, more difficult to generate.

Heath (1983) provides some answers to this question by describing in detail the ways in which children from two neighboring communities in the Piedmont area of North Carolina are socialized into the ways of using both the oral and written language that are characteristic of each group. In doing so, she illustrates why it is necessary to understand the beliefs and conceptual principles by which people live in order fully to understand their literacy practices. The ways people use both oral and written language are inextricably bound up with other patterns characteristic of their culture. For example, Heath contrasts the language socialization process in two nonmainstream communities, one she calls Trackton (a black, working-class, rural southern community), and one she calls Roadville (a white, working-class, rural southern community).

In Trackton, children learn to place high reliance on the context, and particularly on the nonverbal cues in that context, in negotiating language interactions with other members of their community. Consequently, they learn to be flexible and adaptable in their use of language, depending upon constantly changing situations and cues. They learn to switch roles with other members of the community, imitating the roles of others in verbal play. In this community, as in some other black communities (Kochman, 1972; Smitherman, 1977), creative verbal play, with frequent metaphors and similes, is highly valued, and there is a sustained focus, both in language use and in other aspects of the culture, on interpersonal relationships. Details in the context are assumed to be of prime importance, as was shown in the Heath study by the frequent questions that Trackton children asked to establish the context of any item newly introduced into a conversation (Heath, 1983, p. 107).

This pattern of seeing an object holistically in context, rather than as an accumulation of attributes, does not serve the Trackton children well in the early years of school, where the naming of attributes of objects (e.g., colors and shapes) is a common activity. Moreover, Trackton children have no preschool experience with answering questions about the attributes of objects, since Trackton parents believe children will learn by observing and participating, rather than by being taught explicitly. On the other hand, Trackton children have other ways of using language that should serve them well in school (e.g., creativity in the use of rhymes and metaphors). Nevertheless, they are often confused and discouraged by their early experiences in school, where written language is often taught as a series of subskills. As a result, they never progress to the point in school (usually at the end of third or the beginning of fourth grade) where the more innovative uses of language become more evident in the school curriculum. And, as noted earlier, some students remain for years in the remedial track, continuously repeating exercises on but never "mastering" what are presumed to be the subskills necessary to learn written language (Goodlad, 1984).

In Roadville, the other nonmainstream community that Heath (1983) describes, the language socialization process is quite different from Trackton's. In Roadville, adults believe that they "teach" their children how to talk and to learn before they begin formal schooling. Much emphasis is put upon babies learning to name objects around them, and, eventually, upon learning to name such attributes of various objects as their shapes and colors.

Practices such as these continue until the children in Roadville are about 4 years old. When the children enter school, parents seem to drop their "teaching" practices abruptly, expecting their children to continue their learning in school. Since much of the curriculum in the early school years is similar to the kinds of language practices preschoolers experience in Roadville homes, their initial transition to formal schooling is not a difficult one. This, of course, is not the case for the Trackton children, who experience a sharp discontinuity between the language practices at home and those at school.

Despite an initial familiarity with early elementary school routines on the part of the Roadville children, however, they too experience difficulty with formal schooling, usually in the upper elementary school years, when the curriculum places increasing emphasis on more interpretive and creative uses of language. Among the beliefs that people in the Roadville community live by are that behavior is either right or wrong, and that all knowledge about this can be found in literal form in the Bible. Verses from the Bible are learned verbatim by children at an early age, and they are continually referred to by community members in order to retrieve "morals" to live by. There is a corresponding emphasis upon factual and literally true accounts in community narratives.

This belief in what Heath terms "the finite nature of religious knowledge" stands in stark contrast to the emphasis on creative alternatives in Trackton. Although Trackton is also a religious community, its language and other cultural practices are quite different. In Trackton churches, for example, a written text (e.g., a prayer or a hymn) is presented orally with many interpretive variations. This is in contrast to Roadville where truth is literal, rather than metaphoric. When children socialized into these two communities confront the "new" culture of mainstream schooling, they are faced, in different ways, with learning vastly different ways of seeing the world and of using both oral and written language in that world.

Thus Heath (1983) provides a detailed ethnographic description of two communities whose children generally do not succeed in school. This work shows how the language practices of a particular community or culture are closely tied to the beliefs and conceptual principles by which the people in that community live, as well as how these practices may differ more or less starkly with the language practices of the school culture. Writing instruction, then, for those students who do not come from mainstream culture, is partially a matter of acculturation to mainstream culture. This acculturation includes learning to use specific language forms, or structures, in the more formal registers of language in the "new" culture. The next section discusses differences in language form across cultural groups, illustrating the kinds of conflicts between communicative systems that nonmainstream students face in the process of acculturation.

Linguistic Differences

Purely linguistic explanations (i.e., those due to differences in form between nonstandard dialects and written standard English) are another substantial explanation for the difficulties nonmainstream students experience in learning to write. Linguistic explanations may shed some light on why it seems so difficult, even for older, highly motivated composition students, to learn not to use vernacular features in their writing. Research has shown that this problem is generally limited to a few, frequently occurring nonstandard features (Farr & Janda, 1985; Farr Whiteman, 1981a; Sternglass, 1974). In addition, we know that, in the oral language of such nonstandard dialect speakers, these nonstandard features almost never occur categorically (i.e., 100% of the time), but usually alternate with the standard variant of the feature. Although the frequency of nonstandard features decreases with age, they persistently occur even in the writing of some adults (Farr Whiteman, 1976).

In addition to the deep-seated nature of linguistic rules, and to the high frequencies of occurrence of some nonstandard features, the inherent variability of particular features probably increases the difficulty of learning to produce standard English features. Much of the variation within a dialect is firmly conditioned according to a hierarchical set of constraints in the local, linguistic context, for example, the presence of a following vowel or consonant (Labov, 1972b). Such highly structured conditioning in a person's linguistic competence presumably is then reflected in both oral and written language performance. These unconscious but highly structured rules unfortunately may work against the kind of linguistic shift that is asked for in the more formal registers of language used in the classroom. That this may be the case points out, once again, how deep-seated and complexly structured all language use is, and, moreover, the difficulty of using conscious strategies to change largely unconscious processes.

Because linguistic differences among dialects can be complex as well as subtle, it is worth considering the specific ways in which communicative systems can conflict. Conflicts will be presented within a framework that includes five broad domains of language that can be said to comprise what speakers tacitly know about the dialect of their culture. Although linguists may disagree about how these domains are grouped and organized to represent a native speaker's linguistic knowledge, they generally would agree that these domains exist in some form. That is, all people who speak a language, or dialect of a language, have these five kinds of linguistic systems as part of their tacit knowledge about their language, and they presumably use this knowledge both when speaking and when writing. The five domains are

- Phonology (rules of pronunciation)
- Syntax (rules of grammar)
- Semantics (meanings associated with grammar, vocabulary, and patterns of discourse)

- Pragmatics (rules of use)
- Discourse (patterns of language beyond the sentence)

Phonology, of course, consists of the rules for pronouncing the words of a language. The differences among regional dialects in the United States are due largely to differences in phonology, or pronunciation. For example, southerners and New Englanders often omit -r sounds that occur after vowels (e.g., in *park, car, mother,* etc.). Occasionally, a student who pronounces words like these without the postvocalic -r will write the word without an r. In addition to regional dialect pronunciations, some students' writing occasionally will reflect features from an ethnic, or social dialect. For example, it is common for Black English Vernacular speakers to omit, in speech, the final member of a consonant cluster at the ends of certain words (e.g., *miss,* rather than *missed,* the last two sounds, not letters, of which are /st/). Sometimes, then, a BEV speaker will write such words without the final consonant. Although phonological dialect influence does not occur as frequently as other kinds of dialect influence (Farr Whiteman, 1981a), it does occur occasionally in the compositions of students who speak nonstandard dialects.

Syntax is that part of linguistic knowledge which, simply speaking, allows a speaker to generate sentences, and it includes rules of morphology and word order. In the United States, the differences between various social dialects and standard written English are often the result of differences in syntactic rules. For example, according to the rules of Black English Vernacular, the possessive -s suffix (a morpheme) may be used, but it does not have to be. Thus when a BEV-speaking student writes *My friend car,* without the -s morpheme, it sometimes is because he or she is drawing upon his or her tacit knowledge of BEV syntax, which does not require the inclusion of that morpheme.

Recent research has shown that, in addition to differences in the use of inflections such as -s and -ed, there are a number of other differences between standard English and BEV in the verb tense and aspect system (e.g., in the BEV use of *be, been, done,* and other features). Tense, of course, situates an event in time; aspect "communicates the *shape* of the event in time" (Labov, 1983, p. 35), that is, spread out in time (durative) or at many separate times (iterative or habitual). Although many of the special features that mark the BEV tense and aspect system usually occur only in "vernacular" contexts, they occasionally appear in writing (e.g., *He be smoking on the butt of the thing*) (Farr & Janda, 1985). Because all students draw on their tacit knowledge of English in writing sentences, it is important to understand exactly what comprises that tacit knowledge, or linguistic competence (Chomsky, 1965). The distinctive grammatical features of BEV are cogently and clearly described by Labov (1983).

Semantics, the third domain of language, deals with the meanings represented by words, sentences, and discourse patterns in a language. Although there has not been much research on differences in semantic systems between dialects, there are both clearly distinguished and more subtle differences between standard written English and various nonstandard dialects. Sometimes a word or a phrase is used to convey a meaning that is entirely different from the meaning conveyed in standard English; e.g., the use of *broom* meaning "fast getaway," as in *I don't have a car so I think I'll broom* (Kochman, 1972a). At other times, a word may be used similarly to standard English, but with an added negative or positive feature (e.g., the use of the word *attitude* in BEV to mean "a negative attitude," as in *That woman has an attitude*). According to Kochman's analysis, meanings in the semantic system of BEV are closely linked to the cultural norms of that community and a variety of usages often cohere around themes reflecting these norms. (Kochman, 1972a, explores the themes of movement, contest, and control.) Again, because students draw on such aspects of their linguistic competence in writing both sentences and longer discourses, it is important to understand how their linguistic competence differs from mainstream patterns of language and writing. (For an extensive description of culturally specific expressive uses of Black English, see all the essays in Kochman, 1972b.) Much less is known about other American English dialects than is known about BEV, but such information is equally important for all groups of nonmainstream students, and research is much needed in this area.

Pragmatics, the fourth domain of language in this framework, deals with the use of language in context. Some definitions of pragmatics focus on how the literal meaning of an utterance changes according to factors in the context of the utterance (e.g., the setting, the participants, their roles, what has occurred previously in the discourse, etc.). Other definitions include a focus on appropriateness: "Pragmatics is the study of the ability of language users to pair sentences with the contexts in which they would be appropriate" (Levinson, 1983, p. 24). For example, Levinson (1983, p. 43) uses the following two sentences to indicate differing levels of politeness, each of which would be appropriate in different contexts:

1. I want to see you for a moment.
2. I wondered if I could possibly see you for a moment.

Pragmatics also differentiates between the *form* of an utterance and its *function*. In a particular context, for example, an utterance that takes the form of a question can actually function as a directive: a teacher, noticing a student wandering around the room, might ask, "Have you finished your math?", meaning, "Sit down and finish your math." Thus an interrogative can actually be intended, and interpreted, as a directive, or an order to do something. It is not difficult to interpret the intended meaning of such an utterance, if both speaker and hearer share the same cultural background; however, differences across cultures can lend complexity to this process, and result in misunderstanding and even conflict.

Philips's (1972, 1983) account of the language use of Warm Springs Indian children at home and at school provides an example of the difficulty of cross-cultural communication, even when the same language is being used. In this study, Indian and Anglo children systematically responded differently to the teacher's imperatives and interrogatives, depending upon what Philips termed the "*participant structures*" in the classroom. Philips identified four participant structures: the whole class in interaction with the teacher, a small group in interaction with the teacher, one-to-one involvement between the teacher and a single student, and "desk work" (when a student's attention is focused on written materials on the student's desk). The first three structures influence the way verbal interaction is structured in the classroom; the latter, of course, does not involve such interaction.

Depending upon the participant structure being used, the Indian children often were silent in response to teacher questions and did not comply with teacher directives. Philips was able to determine that this occurred not because the children did not understand the linguistic structure of the interrogative or the imperative, but "because they [did] not share the non-Indian's assumption in such contexts that use of these syntactic forms by definition implies an automatic and immediate response from the person to whom they were addressed" (Philips, 1972, p. 392). These Indian children were perceived to be "non-comprehending" by many Anglo teachers because of such lack of response in certain classroom situations. Philips's ethnographic study, which contrasted patterns of language use at home and at school, illuminated the reasons for this characteristic lack of immediate response.

In communicative contexts which resembled those characteristic of language use at home, the Indian children were responsive. In the classroom, however, the "absence of the appropriate social conditions for communicative performance" accounted for the frequent lack of response by the Indian children. This and other such studies have shown us that the same linguistic form, for example, a question, actually is used differently in various contexts by different cultural groups, a fact that undoubtedly accounts for much miscommunication between people from different cultural backgrounds.

Although the above example deals with oral language use in the classroom and does not bear directly on writing, it is nevertheless an important example of how the communicative systems with which people unconsciously operate may conflict and thus interfere with all teaching and learning processes in the classroom. Further, it is not difficult to conceive of ways in which such conflicts might interfere with learning to write. For example, students who come from cultures in which it is inappropriate for individuals either to speak or to write as a solitary activity, without interaction with an audience (as was the case in Heath's study of the Trackton community), might find it strange and awkward to write in solitary contexts in school. For such students, the inter-active use of computers for writing might be a more appropriate and effective instructional strategy.

The final domain of language in the framework is discourse, a term that refers to patterns of language organization which extend over more than one sentence or utterance. Some studies of discourse have focused on the rules by which people unconsciously operate when engaging in conversation (e.g., the rules for turn-taking). Other studies of discourse have focused on the relations among sentences that cohere to comprise a text, either oral or written, rather than being simply a group of unrelated sentences (Halliday & Hasan, 1976). What is significant for writing research and instruction is that differences in the apparent coherence, or lack of it, in student compositions can sometimes be traced to cultural differences in communicative systems.

In several studies of Sharing Time (or Show and Tell) in various elementary-school classrooms (Cazden, Michaels, & Tabors, 1985; Michaels, 1981; Michaels & Collins, 1984) Michaels has identified two oral discourse patterns used to tell narratives. One of these patterns, which she termed "topic-centered," is typically used by standard English-speaking, mainstream children. The other pattern, which she termed "topic-associating," is typically used by BEV-speaking inner-city black children. Upon close analysis, she found that both patterns evidenced topic cohesion through the narrative, but that the topic-centered pattern showed the cohesion more explicitly by using lexical and syntactic devices (i.e., through explicit vocabulary and grammatical connectives). This type of pattern, though evidenced orally in this common classroom speech event, is close to what is expected in school literacy—it is, in fact, the kind of pattern students are taught to use when writing. Because of this match, students who already tacitly know and use this oral discourse pattern before coming to school probably have an easier transition to the formal teaching and learning of writing in school.

Those students who unconsciously know and use, as part of their native communication system, other discourse patterns that do not match the school's model of literacy presumably have a much more difficult transition to make. The topic-associating pattern identified by Michaels is one of these. In this discourse style, topics are implicitly connected through intonation contours rather than with explicit vocabulary and connectives (e.g., *then, so,* rather than *and*). Others have referred to a similar discourse style among other black Americans. Smitherman (1977) describes black adult narrative style as "concrete narrative . . . (whose) meandering away from the 'point' takes the listener on episodic journeys" (pp. 147–148).

In addition, Erickson (1984b), in a study of black adolescents informally discussing politics, found that shifts from one topic to another were not explicitly stated. Instead, meanings had to be inferred from a series of concrete anecdotes. Although this style of discourse can be difficult to follow for those who are not part of this cultural group, close analysis reveals "a most rigorous logic and a systematic coherence of the particular, whose internal system is organized not by literate style linear sequentiality but by audience/speaker interaction" (Erickson, 1984, p. 152). These descriptions by Michaels, Smitherman, and Erickson affirm the results of other studies of black American speech that describe it as culturally different from, but not deficient in regard to, mainstream uses of both oral language and literacy. The advantage that mainstream speakers have, of course, is that school literacy is modeled on their uses of language.

Clearly, conflicts between ways of using language in different cultural groups can cause both misunderstanding and problems in learning to write. Because of this, and also because there has been some debate, as well as confusion, about the role of dialects in learning to write (Farr Whiteman, 1976, 1980; Hartwell, 1980, 1985; Morrow, 1985), it is useful to consider here, briefly, what "dialects" actually are and how nonstandard dialects differ specifically from the written standard. The next section will describe what linguists mean by the term dialect, and what "being a (nonstandard) dialect speaker" means. It will also provide a concrete example of a set of linguistic rules that differentiate several nonstandard varieties of American English from the written standard. After these definitions and issues are clarified, the following section will reconsider the goal of "bidialectalism" in the light of recent research on linguistic variation and language change. Both of these sections hold significant implications for the teaching and learning of writing.

DIALECTS

All languages, even those with a small number of speakers, have dialects (Ferguson, 1977), which serve to identify speakers in either geographical or social space. Everyone who speaks a language speaks one dialect or another of that language. To be able to speak a dialect means, in general terms, that one has in one's linguistic repertoire those features that are characteristic of the dialect in question. Some speakers may use most of the features of a dialect, but at a lower frequency of occurrence than do others, who may be what Baugh (1983) has termed true "vernacular speakers," or those who live, work, and play among speakers of the same vernacular.

An ethnic dialect like BEV, then, is a model of what a particular group of language users know—that is, a linguistic description that has been abstracted from group language behavior. Many such linguistic descriptions, representing many dialects, together make up what has been called the sociolinguistic structure of English (Labov, 1972b). Therefore, the dialect described in linguistic studies as BEV is not used categorically by a finite group of speakers—e.g., all black Americans, or even all working class black Americans. Thus the term has a *linguistic* referent, not a social one.

Variation in the rules of a language, or, more often, slightly different versions of the same rules, distinguish speakers according to region, social status, sex, ethnicity, age, and other factors. The various dialects of American English share many linguistic rules, although there are also some that they do not share. It is important to understand differences in rules because students unconsciously call on such rules in writing sentences. The following set of linguistic rules, which allow for multiple negation in several nonstandard varieties of American English (Wolfram & Fasold, 1974, pp. 162–166), provide an example of how, specifically, dialects can differ from each other. The underlying strings (of meanings) upon which the following rules can operate are the following:

> NOT + ANY-BODY + DO-Z + KNOW + ANY-THING
> *(Nobody knows anything)* and
>
> NOT + HE + DO-Z + KNOW + ANY-THING
> *(He doesn't know anything)*

There are three primary rules that will generate negative sentences in various dialects. The first two rules are the same in all dialects, standard or nonstandard. The first rule places NOT, the negative marker, into the main verb phrase of the sentence:

1. In a negative sentence, place NOT in the main verb phrase. Applying this rule to the second underlying string results in *He doesn't know anything*.
2. In a negative sentence, if there is an indefinite element preceding the main verb, remove NOT from the main verb phrase and incorporate it into the indefinite element. Applying this rule (and others that are of no concern here) to the first underlying string results in *Nobody knows anything*.

The third rule has a standard version (3a) and two versions for different nonstandard dialects (3b, 3c).

3a. For emphasis, remove NOT from the main verb phrase and incorporate it in the first indefinite *after* the main verb phrase.
3b. For emphasis, incorporate a *copy* of the NOT, which is in the main verb phrase or preverbal indefinite, in *all* indefinites after the main verb phrase, but leave the original NOT intact.
3c. For emphasis, incorporate a *copy* of the NOT, which is in the main verb phrase or the preverbal indefinite, into the main verb phrase (if it is not there already) and in *all* indefinites after the main verb phrase, but leave the original NOT intact.

If rule 3a is applied after rule 1 (rule 2 does not apply in this case) after the second string above, instead of *He doesn't know anything*, we get *He knows nothing.* For many nonstandard dialects, rule 3b replaces rule 3a, which copies rather than moves NOT. This results in *He doesn't know nothing.* In fact, if there were more indefinites in such a sentence, all of them could have the negative copied onto them, resulting in a sentence with multiple negatives (*We ain't had no trouble about none of us pullin' out no knife or nothing*).

Rule 3c only exists in some nonstandard dialects. It allows a copy of the NOT from the preverbal indefinite to be copied onto the main verb phrase. If this rule is applied to the first string above, the result is *Nobody doesn't like it* (Which has the meaning of the SE *Nobody likes it*).

Obviously, the rules for negation are complex in any dialect. It is these differences in linguistic rules for negation that distinguish dialects in American English. Although multiple negation is not a feature that is found frequently, at least in older nonstandard dialect speakers' writing (e.g. Farr Whiteman, 1976), this example is useful as an illustration of how linguistic rules differ across dialects. Other features, which occur more persistently throughout schooling and beyond, e.g., *-s* and *-ed* suffix and copula (*is, are*) absence, (Farr Whiteman, 1981a), are also the result of such differences in linguistic rules.

Students who have rules in their linguistic competence that produce nonstandard features have difficulty editing their writing so that it reflects the written grammatical standard. Moreover, since such linguistic knowledge is unconscious, these students cannot use their linguistic intuition to understand the differences between standard and nonstandard versions of sentences. Particularly for adolescent and older students, some kind of instruction in the differences seems necessary to develop their awareness of different grammatical patterns for writing, as opposed to oral language. This is, of course, in addition to writing instruction that focuses on such higher level concerns as the elaboration and organization of content and audience awareness. The question of whether or not instruction in the standard grammar adds options to a student's linguistic repertoire or actually changes the student's dialect is addressed in the next section.

BIDIALECTALISM OR LINGUISTIC CHANGE?

For years, many scholars and educators have advocated "bidialectalism" as an educational goal for students whose native language is a nonstandard dialect. This position is based, first, on the assumption that nonstandard dialects are as valid as standard English as linguistic systems and that they are quite appropriate in certain situations. This assumption, of course, has been confirmed both by sociolinguistic studies of various nonstandard dialects and by ethnographic studies of language use in various situations. There is another assumption, however, which does not have such support from research, and it also often underlies the advocacy of bidialectalism. This is the assumption that, if one acquires a second dialect, one will have two linguistic systems to call upon in oral or written communication.

The concept of bidialectalism was modeled on that of bilingualism. This analogy is accurate insofar as it implies that a nonstandard dialect is as self-contained a linguistic system as a standard variety of a language. However, whether or not two dialects, or two languages for that matter, exist as separate systems in the minds of particular speakers is a question that can only be answered empirically. To date, the evidence from research is mixed and inconclusive, as has been pointed out by Ferguson (1977).

Recent research by Labov and his associates (Ash & Myhill, 1985; Graff, Labov, & Harris, 1983; Labov & Harris, 1983; Myhill & Harris, 1983) also provides evidence that indicates that actual bidialectalism with "code switching" may not be possible. In their research on linguistic change and variation, these researchers concluded that black and white dialects in Philadelphia, and quite possibly in the other major northern cities, are increasingly diverging. They speculate that this linguistic behavior reflects increasingly segregated societies. If this is true, the problems posed by such diversity for literacy instruction will become worse, not better. It may be, in fact, that better field-work in collecting natural language samples (in this project by Harris) is providing evidence for a dialect that was always divergent from standard English. Whether that is the case, or whether true Black English Vernacular is, in fact, moving in a different direction from white varieties of American English, we are faced with the same problem in educational terms.

By carefully documenting the social networks of the black and white speakers they studied, Labov and his associates were able to relate the occurrence of nonstandard features with patterns of social interaction, distinguishing two groups of people: those who have "meaningful contact" with the "opposite" ethnic group and those who do not (Ash & Myhill, 1985). They conclude that, although there is considerable "borrowing" of vocabulary and phonological (pronunciation) features across ethnic groups that have "meaningful contact" with each other, the case is quite different for grammatical features. In this case, "blacks who move in white circles show a major shift in their grammar in the direction of the white norm" (Ash & Myhill, 1985, p. 16), but the same is not true for whites who move in black circles. Although such whites can learn to "sound black" by using black pronunciation and vocabulary, they do not acquire BEV grammar. Such asymmetry is not surprising, of course, considering the social, political, and economic value of standard English, as opposed to BEV, in the mainstream society.

The educational implications of these findings, especially for writing, are substantial. Underlying grammatical patterns of standard English are apparently learned through "meaningful" and intensive interaction with those who already use standard English grammar, not "simply by exposure in the mass media or in schools" (Labov & Harris, 1983, p. 22). That is, only those nonstandard dialect speakers who "engage in structured interaction with (standard English speaking) whites, where they use language to negotiate their position or gain advantages, show a profound shift of their grammatical rules" (Labov & Harris, 1983, p. 23).

It seems clear from the work of Labov and his associates that learning written standard English probably does not entail acquiring a new dialect in addition to one's native dialect, and consequently maintaining two linguistic systems for use in "code-switching," as appropriate, in various contexts. What it may entail instead is a substantial shift, or change in one's underlying linguistic system, toward the features of standard English. Such a shift still would allow considerable variation within the speaker's own linguistic system, enabling shifts to more or less formal registers of use as appropriate in different situations. The linguistic change shown in Labov's research, significantly, only seems to occur when the learners interact meaningfully and frequently with standard English speakers.

Though Labov's results were obtained in a study of oral language use, it is reasonable to assume a parallel situation with writing and reading. When nonmainstream students learn to produce standard written English, they may be doing so by *changing* their linguistic systems, rather than by *adding* to their original linguistic repertoires. Since teaching writing is effectively, at least in part, teaching the linguistic patterns of standard English, it may result in a student's loss of his or her vernacular dialect, rather than the maintenance of that dialect alongside the standard written dialect. Such an educational change clearly can affect a student's relation to his or her original family and community (Rodriguez, 1983) and, as such, is a social and political issue. It is important, therefore, regardless of political stance, to acknowledge the potential linguistic and social ramifications of effective writing instruction.

LEARNING TO WRITE AMONG NONMAINSTREAM STUDENTS

Learning to write, of course, involves more than learning standard English grammar. It is reasonable to assume that when students "shift toward the standard" and learn to write, they are learning mainstream features of semantics, pragmatics, and discourse, as well as grammar. Written text provides many linguistic resources other than grammatical ones—for example, "literate" vocabulary and organizational structures of discourse. A number of studies have begun to show that children draw upon these resources from written text to learn how to write what is considered "good" (i.e., literate) prose (Scollon & Scollon, 1981, chap. 4; Sulzby, in press). Clearly, then, students need experience with written text (e.g., reading or being read to) to gather these resources. Sulzby (in press) shows that reading, or being read to, promotes understanding, particularly at the discourse level, of written language composition even before children are writing with the adult, conventional system.

Nagy, Herman, and Anderson (1985) show how reading, even for a brief period each day, builds vocabulary. Studies are needed to explore further how experience with written text facilitates nonmainstream students' learning to be literate, and also what effects such learning has on their own communicative competence. Finally, as discussed in a preceding section, the cultural orientations associated with Western literacy are often at odds with the orientations to language and literacy in the non-Western cultures and nonmainstream subcultures from which many students come. It is certainly possible, then, that experience with reading and writing mainstream academic prose induces cultural, as well as linguistic changes in students.

Why do so few nonmainstream students acquire mainstream literacy? In addition to the reasons discussed in the preceding sections, another explanation for the lack of such a shift for many such students may be that they do not experience enough "meaningful interaction," either with standard English speakers or with the standard written language to effect such a change. Most students, and particularly nonmainstream students, do not read or write extended prose (more than a few sentences) during the school day (Applebee, 1981; Goodlad, 1984). Instead the focus is on workbook exercises and short answer questions, neither of which generally challenges students to use higher level thinking processes. Moreover, these kinds of activities generally do not provide the discourse-level linguistic resources with which students need experience to learn to write.

Several studies have shown that when such experience is provided as a large part of time in school, students make substantial progress in learning to write. Some of these studies have been done in classrooms of mainstream children (Graves, 1982; King & Rentel, 1981, 1982, 1983), and others have been done in classrooms of nonmainstream children (Edelsky, 1986; Heath & Branscombe, 1985; Staton, 1982, in press). The Graves study (Calkins, 1983; Graves, 1982, 1983; Sowers, 1985) focused on teachers who turned from a "low-level skills" approach (of workbooks and similar exercises) to a "writing process" approach (in which children begin composing before they learn mechanics such as conventional spelling, are encouraged to write on their own topics, and read each other's writing). As a result of the change in approach, these elementary school students learned to read as well as those using a "skills" approach (as evidenced by standardized test scores), and they learned to write better than the other students (as evidenced by their compositions). Moreover, their learning of mechanical skills did not suffer; the study showed that these were best taught in context, usually in the frequent student-teacher conferences about particular pieces of student writing.

The King-Rentel study (1981, 1982, 1983), among other things, contrasted two classrooms, one that could be termed "skills-based" and one that could be called "literacy rich." In the skills-based class, primarily workbooks and worksheets were used to teach reading and writing (i.e., the skills of word recognition, decoding, handwriting, and spelling). In the literacy-rich class, instead of treating writing and reading as separate subject areas, a primary focus on stories and books (as wholes) was integrated into all content areas. For example, work on a science field trip included writing and reading extended text about the subject of the field trip. Predictably, the children with more experience with writing and reading extended text (those in the "literacy rich" classroom) surpassed the others on a number of measures of writing growth (e.g., higher proportions of cohesion in their compositions).

Both the Graves and the King and Rentel studies illustrate how all students can progress in learning to write as a result of specific instructional approaches. Thus, although the populations from these studies were primarily mainstream and middle class, the same approaches presumably would work with nonmainstream populations. Other studies have shown this to be the case. Staton (1982) analyzed the dialogue journals from one entire year in a sixth-grade classroom in a multicultural section of Los Angeles. The teacher in this classroom, consisting of children speaking 13 different languages, responded to daily entries in a journal by each of the students. By the end of the year an extended written conversation between each student and the teacher had developed. Analysis of the journals (Farr, 1982; Staton, 1982, in press) showed clear patterns of growth in writing, including elaboration of student-initiated topics, fluency, and control of English syntax (Kreeft & Shuy, 1985).

Because the writing in the journals was not evaluated for mechanics, but, instead, was responded to in terms of content, the students eagerly read each teacher response. Furthermore, the students wrote to communicate and therefore were fully "engaged" in their writing (and thus used their reasoning capacities). The Staton study, like the Graves and the King and Rentel studies, showed how students can learn to write when writing and reading are treated as functional activities (rather than as practice) and when students are allowed substantial experience with written text.

Heath and Branscombe (1985) also showed that involving students in meaningful interaction with written text leads them to adapt linguistic resources characteristic of mainstream expository prose. Heath and Branscombe worked as a researcher-teacher team with Branscombe's remedial-track ninth-grade English students (primarily nonmainstream blacks and a few nonmainstream whites in a southern city), using extensive letter writing and guiding the students in doing their own ethnographic research in their communities. The choice of letter writing was based on the assumption that "the development of written language depends on a rich, responsive context" (Heath & Branscombe, 1985, p. 30), and that the students needed to learn that expository writing required "linguistic devices and background information in explicated form if the addressee is to understand the [writer]" (Heath & Branscombe, 1985, p. 26).

Over the course of the year, these students wrote and read long letters to and from people they did not know (Heath, Heath's daughter, and Branscombe's 11th-grade students). As a result, they accumulated extensive experience with written text (including the depersonalized, decontextualized expository prose in Heath's letters). They used this experience as language input (as in oral language learning) "to *generate the needed internal rules or knowledge about how to make writing work* to communicate their feelings and knowledge" (Heath & Branscombe, 1985, p. 30). Consequently, they learned to use written language in ways similar to those of oral language acquisition, through "repeated trials and errors in attempting to communicate" (Heath & Branscombe, 1985, p. 31).

The results of all of these studies of the effective teaching of writing, with both mainstream and nonmainstream students, reinforces the conception of writing as language discussed in the first section of this chapter. Both speaking and writing draw on one's tacit knowledge about language, or one's communicative competence, and learning to write follows many of the same processes as learning to speak. Learning to write what society considers "good" expository prose, however, also entails learning how to use language in specific, culturally embedded ways, the ways of the more formal registers of mainstream standard English. Unless students have meaningful, and repeated, experience with this register, they will not have sufficient language input to learn how to use it.

CONCLUSION

This chapter has specified a framework within which the effect of cultural variation on writing and learning to write can be, but has only begun to be, studied. Within this framework writing is seen as one mode of language and as one way in which a language user can use his or her communicative competence. Furthermore, writing is seen not as a single entity (e.g., a single set of cognitive skills) that can be used in various contexts, but, rather, as a multifaceted way of using language, which, in fact, is defined variously in different contexts.

This chapter also reviewed what we know about standard language and writing among the mainstream middle class and how this model contrasts with characteristics of language and writing among various nonmainstream cultural groups. In exploring this contrast, the review investigated proposed reasons for the general failure among nonmainstream groups to learn to write according to mainstream expectations for academic prose. This investigation primarily focused first on cultural differences and then on linguistic differences.

Finally, the review briefly clarified the terms *dialect* and *bidialectalism,* especially as they relate to the teaching and learning of writing, and reviewed several studies of effective writing instruction to both mainstream and nonmainstream students. It seems clear from all the research reviewed that cultural and linguistic differences, because they are only unconsciously known by speakers and writers, are subtle and often difficult to specify. They are, nevertheless, of crucial importance for future research because of the role they play among nonmainstream populations in learning, or more significantly, in not learning to write.

REFERENCES

Amastae, J., & Elias-Olivares, L. (Eds.). (1982). *Spanish in the United States: Sociolinguistic aspects.* Cambridge, England: Cambridge University Press.

Applebee, A. (1981). *Writing in the secondary school: English and the content areas.* (Research Rep. No. 121). Urbana, IL: National Council of Teachers of English.

Applebee, A. (1984). *Contexts for learning to write: Studies of secondary school instruction.* Norwood, NJ: Ablex.

Ash, S., & Myhill, J. (1983). *Linguistic correlates of interethnic contact.* (Research Rep.) University of Pennsylvania, Linguistics Laboratory.

Baugh, J. (1983). *Black street speech: Its history, structure and survival.* Austin: University of Texas Press.

Bauman, R., & Sherzer, J. (Eds.). (1974). *Explorations in the ethnography of speaking.* Cambridge, England: Cambridge University Press.

Bloome, D., & Green, J. (1984). Directions in the sociolinguistic study of reading. In D. Pearson, R. Barr, M. Kamil, & P. Mosenthal (Eds.), *Handbook of reading research.* New York: Longman.

Calkins, L. (1983). *Lessons from a child: On the teaching and learning of writing.* Exeter, NH: Heinemann.

Cazden, C. (1982). Adult assistance to language development: Scaffolds, models, and direct instruction. In R. Parker & F. Davis (Eds.), *Developing literacy: Young children's use of language.* Newark, DE: International Reading Association.

Cazden, C., John, V., & Hymes, D. (1972). *Functions of language in the classroom.* New York: Teachers College Press.

Cazden, C., Michaels, S., & Tabors, P. (1985). Spontaneous repairs in sharing time narratives: The intersection of metalinguistic awareness, speech event, and narrative style. In S. Freedman (Ed.), *The acquisition of written language: Response and revision.* Norwood, NJ: Ablex.

Chafe, W.L. (1982). Integration and involvement in speaking, writing, and oral literature. In D. Tannen (Ed.), *Spoken and written language: Exploring orality and literacy.* (Vol. IX of *Advances in discourse processes*). Norwood, NJ: Ablex.

Chambers, J. (Ed.). (1983). *Black English: Educational equity and the law.* Ann Arbor, MI: Karama Press.

Cherry Wilkinson, L. (Ed.). (1982). *Communicating in the classroom.* New York: Academic Press.

Chomsky, N. (1965). *Aspects of the theory of syntax.* Cambridge, MA: MIT Press.

Dyson, A. (1985). Individual differences in emerging writing. In M. Farr (Ed.), *Advances in writing research: Children's early writing development.* Norwood, NJ: Ablex.

Edelsky, C. (1986). *Writing in a bilingual program: Habia una vez.* Norwood, NJ: Ablex.

Erickson, F. (1984a). Response to papers at session sponsored by Language Development/SIG at the annual meeting of the American Educational Research Association, Chicago.

Erickson, F. (1984b). Rhetoric, anecdote, and rhapsody: Coherence strategies in a conversation among black American adolescents. In D. Tannen (Ed.), *Coherence in spoken and written discourse*. Norwood, NJ: Ablex.

Farr, M. (1982). *Learning to write English: One dialogue journal writer's growth in writing*. Paper presented at the annual meeting of the American Educational Research Association, New York.

Farr, M. (1985a). *Some* new directions in *some areas* of composition research [Review of R. Beach and L. Bridwell (Eds.), *New directions in composition research*.] *Contemporary Psychology, 30*, 648–649.

Farr, M. (Ed.). (1985b). *Advances in writing research: Children's early writing development*. Norwood, NJ: Ablex.

Farr, M., & Janda, M. (1985). Basic writing students: Investigating oral and written language. *Research in the Teaching of English, 19*, (1), 62–83

Farr Whiteman, M. (1976). *Dialect influence in the writing of black and white working class Americans*. Doctoral dissertation, Georgetown University.

Farr Whiteman, M. (Ed.). (1980). *Reactions to Ann Arbor: Vernacular black English and education*. Washington, DC: Center for Applied Linguistics.

Farr Whiteman, M. (1981a). Dialect influence in writing. In M. Farr Whiteman (Ed.), *Variation in writing: Functional and linguistic-cultural differences*. Hillsdale, NJ: Erlbaum.

Farr Whiteman, M., (Ed.). (1981b). *Variation in writing: Functional and linguistic-cultural differences*. Hillsdale, NJ: Erlbaum.

Fasold, R. (1972). *Tense marking in black English*. Washington, DC: Center for Applied Linguistics.

Ferguson, C., & Heath, S.B. (Eds.). (1981). *Language in the U.S.A.* Cambridge, England: Cambridge University Press.

Ferguson, C. (1977). Linguistic theory. In *Bilingual education: Current perspectives*. Washington, DC: Center for Applied Linguistics.

Ferguson, C. (1985). Introduction. *Special language registers,* special invited issue, *Discourse Processes, 8* (4), 391–394.

Gilmore, P., & Glatthorn, A. (Eds.). (1982). *Children in and out of school: Ethnography and education*. Washington, DC: Center for Applied Linguistics.

Gilmore, P., & Smith, D.M. (1982). A retrospective discussion of the state of the art in ethnography and education. In P. Gilmore & A. Glatthorn (Eds.), *Children in and out of school: Ethnography and education*. Washington, DC: Center for Applied Linguistics.

Goelman, H., Oberg, A., & Smith, F. (Eds.). (1984). *Awakening to literacy*. Exeter, NH: Heinemann.

Goodlad, J.I. (1984). *A place called school*. New York: McGraw-Hill.

Goody, J., & Watt, I. (1963). The consequences of literacy. *Comparative Studies in Society and History, 5* (3), 304–345.

Graff, D., Labov, W., & Harris, W. (1983). *Testing listeners' reactions to phonological markers of ethnic identity: A new method for sociolinguistic research*. Paper presented at the annual conference on New Ways of Analyzing Variation in English, Montreal.

Graves, D. (1978). *Balance the basics: Let them write*. New York: Ford Foundation.

Graves, D.H. (1982). *A case study observing the development of primary children's composing, spelling and motor behavior during the writing process*. (Final rep. to the National Institute of Education NIE-G-78-0174). Durham, NH: University of New Hampshire.

Graves, D. (1983). *Writing: Teachers and children at work*. Exeter, NH: Heineman.

Green, J. (1983). Research on teaching as a linguistic process: A state of the art. In E.W. Gordon (Ed.), *Review of Research in Education, 10*. Washington, DC: American Educational Research Association.

Green, J. & Wallat, C. (Eds.). (1981). *Ethnography and language in educational settings*. Norwood, NJ: Ablex.

Greene, J. (1980). Which. In R.W. Shuy & A. Schnukal (Eds.), *Language use and the uses of language*. Washington, DC: Georgetown University Press.

Greene, J. (1985). Children's writing in an elementary school postal system. In M. Farr (Ed.), *Advances in writing research: Children's early writing development*. Norwood, NJ: Ablex.

Gumperz, J.J. (1982a). *Discourse strategies*. Cambridge, England: Cambridge University Press.

Gumperz, J.J. (Ed.). (1982b). *Language and social identity*. Cambridge, England: Cambridge University Press.

Gundlach, R., McLane, J.B., Stott, F.M., & McNamee, G.D. (1985). The social foundations of children's early writing development. In M. Farr (Ed.), *Advances in writing research: Children's early writing development*. Norwood, NJ: Ablex.

Halliday, M.A.K., & Hasan, R. (1976). *Cohesion in English*. New York: Longman.

Harste, J.C., Woodward, V., & Burke, C. (1984). *Language stories and literacy lessons*. Exeter, NH: Heinemann.

Hartwell, P. (1980). Dialect interference in writing: A critical view. *Research in the Teaching of English, 14* (2), 101–118.

Hartwell, P. (1985). Grammar, grammars, and the teaching of grammar. *College English, 47* (2), 105–127.

Heath, S.B. (1983). *Ways with words: Language, life and work in communities and classrooms*. Cambridge, England: Cambridge University Press.

Heath, S.B., & Branscombe, A. (1985). "Intelligent writing" in an audience community: Teacher, students, and researcher. In S. Freedman (Ed.), *The acquisition of written language: Response and revision*. Norwood, NJ: Ablex.

Hymes, D. (1962). The ethnography of speaking. In T. Gladwin & W.C. Sturtevant (Eds.), *Anthropology and human behavior*. Washington, DC: Anthropological Society of Washington.

Hymes, D. (1971). Competence and performance in linguistic theory. In R. Huxley & E. Ingram (Eds.), *Language in acquisition: Models and methods*. London: Academic Press.

King, M.L., & Rentel, V. (1981). *How children learn to write: A longitudinal study*. (Final rep. to the National Institute of Education, NIE-G-79-0137 and NIE-G-0039). Columbus: Ohio State University.

King, M.L., & Rentel, V.M. (1982). *Transition to writing*. (Final Rep. to the National Institute of Education, NIE-G-79-0137 & NIE-G-79-0031). Columbus: Ohio State University.

King, M.L., & Rentel, V.M. (1983). *A longitudinal study of coherence in children's written narratives*. (Final rep. to the National Institute of Education, NIE-G-81-0063). Columbus: Ohio State University.

Kinneavy, J.L. (1971). *A theory of discourse*. Englewood Cliffs, NJ: Prentice-Hall.

Kochman, T. (1972a). Toward an ethnography of black American speech behavior. In T. Kochman (Ed.), *Rappin' and stylin' out: Communication in urban black America*. Urbana: University of Illinois Press.

Kochman, T. (1981). *Black and white styles in conflict*. Chicago: University of Chicago Press.

Kreeft, J.P., & Shuy, R.W. (1985). *Dialogue writing: Analysis of student-teacher interactive writing in the learning of English as a second language.* (Final Rep. to the National Institute of Education, NIE-G-83-0030). Washington, DC: Center for Applied Linguistics.

Labov, W. (1972a). *Language in the inner city: Studies in the Black English Vernacular.* Philadelphia: University of Pennsylvania Press.

Labov, W. (1972b). *Sociolinguistic patterns.* Philadelphia: University of Pennsylvania Press.

Labov, W. (Ed.). (1980). *Locating language in time and space.* New York: Academic Press.

Labov, W. (Ed.). (1983). Recognizing black English in the classroom. In J. Chambers (Ed.), *Black English: Educational equity and the law.* Ann Arbor, MI: Karama Press.

Labov, W., & Harris, W. (1983). *De facto segregation of black and white vernaculars.* Paper presented at the annual conference on New Ways of Analyzing Variation in English, Montreal.

Langer, J. (1985). Musings. *Research in the Teaching of English, 19* (2), 117–119.

Langer, J. (1986). *Children reading and writing: Structures and strategies.* Norwood, NJ: Ablex.

Levinson, S.C. (1983). *Pragmatics.* Cambridge, England: Cambridge University Press.

Linell, P. (1982). *The written bias in linguistics.* Linkoping, Sweden: University of Linkoping, Department of Communication Studies.

McDermott, R.P., with Gospodinoff, K. (1976). *Criteria for an ethnographically adequate description of activities and their contexts.* Paper presented at the annual meeting of the American Anthropological Association, Washington, DC.

Michaels, S. (1981). Sharing time: Children's narrative style and differential access to literacy. *Language in Society, 10,* 423–442.

Michaels, S., & Collins, J. (1984). Oral discourse styles: Classroom interaction and the acquisition of literacy. In D. Tannen (Ed.), *Coherence in spoken and written discourse.* Norwood, NJ: Ablex.

Morrow, D.H. (1985). Dialect interference in writing: Another critical view. *Research in the Teaching of English, 19* (2), 154–180.

Myhill, J., & Harris, W. (1983). *The use of the verbal -s inflection in BEV.* Paper presented at the annual conference on New Ways of Analyzing Variation in English, Montreal.

Nagy, W., Herman, P., & Anderson, R.C. (1985). *Learning word meanings in context: How broadly generalizable?* (Tech. Rep. No. 347). Urbana, IL: Center for the Study of Reading.

National Assessment of Educational Progress. (1981). *Highlights and trends: Writing achievement, 1969–79.* Denver, CO: Education Commission of the States.

Odell, L., & Goswami, D. (1981). *Writing in non-academic settings.* (Final Rep. to the National Institute of Education, NIE-G-78-0224). Troy, NY: Rensselaer Polytechnic Institute.

Ogbu, J.U. (1974). *The next generation: An ethnography of education in an urban neighborhood.* New York: Academic Press.

Ogbu, J.U. (1980). *Literacy in subordinate cultures: The case of black Americans.* Manuscript prepared for Literacy Conference, Library of Congress, Washington, DC.

Olson, D. (1977). From utterance to text: The bias of language in speech and writing. *Harvard Educational Review, 47,* 257–281.

Philips, S.U. (1972). Participant structures and communicative competence: Warm

Springs children in community and classroom. In C. Cazden, V. John, & D. Hymes (Eds.), *Functions of language in the classroom*. New York: Teachers College Press.

Philips, S.U. (1983). *The invisible culture: Communication in classroom and community on the Warm Springs Indian Reservation*. New York: Longman.

Rodriguez, R. (1982). *Hunger of memory: The education of Richard Rodriguez*. New York: Bantam Books.

Rubin, D. (1979, spring). The myth of dialect interference in written composition. *Arizona English Bulletin*.

Schumacher, G.M. (1986). Reflections on the origins of writing: New perspectives on writing research. *Written Communication, 3* (1), 47–63.

Scollon, R., & Scollon, S.B. (1981). *Narrative, literacy and face in interethnic communication*. Norwood, NJ: Ablex.

Scribner, S., & Cole, M. (1981). *The psychology of literacy*. Cambridge, MA: Harvard University Press.

Smitherman, G. (1977). *Talkin' and testifyin': The language of black America*. Boston: Houghton Mifflin.

Sowers, S. (1985). Learning to write in a workshop: A study in grades one through four. In M. Farr (Ed.), *Advances in writing research: Children's early writing development*. Norwood, NJ: Ablex.

Staton, J. (1982). *Analysis of dialogue journal writing as a communicative event*. (Final Rep. to the National Institute of Education NIE-G-80-0122). Washington, DC: Center for Applied Linguistics.

Staton, J. (in press). *Dialogue journal writing: Linguistic, cognitive, and social views*. Norwood, NJ: Ablex.

Sternglass, M.S. (1974). Dialect features in the compositions of black and white college students: The same or different? *College Composition and Communication, 25*, 259-263.

Street, B. (1984). *Literacy in theory and practice*. Cambridge, England: Cambridge University Press.

Sulzby, E. (1985). Kindergarteners as writers and readers. In M. Farr (Ed.), *Advances in writing research: Children's early writing development*. Norwood, NJ: Ablex.

Sulzby, E. (in press). Young children's concepts for oral and written text. In K. Durkin (Ed.), *Language development during the school years*. London: Croom Helm.

Tannen, D. (Ed). (1982). *Spoken and written language: Exploring orality and literacy*. Norwood, NJ: Ablex.

Tannen, D. (Ed.). (1984). *Coherence in spoken and written discourse*. Norwood, NJ: Ablex.

Taylor, O. (1983). Black English: An agenda for the 1980's. In J. Chambers (Ed.), *Black English: Educational equity and the law*. Ann Arbor, MI: Karama Press.

Teale, W., & Sulzby, E. (Eds.). (1986). *Emergent literacy: Writing and reading*. Norwood, NJ: Ablex.

Wolfram, W., & Fasold, R. (1974). *The study of social dialects in American English*. Englewood Cliffs, NJ: Prentice-Hall.

Wolfram, W., & Christian, D. (1976). *Appalachian speech*. Washington, DC: Center for Applied Linguistics.

Wolfram, W. (1969). *A sociolinguistic description of Detroit negro speech*. Washington, DC: Center for Applied Linguistics.

Wolfram, W. (1974). *Sociolinguistic aspects of assimilation: Puerto Rican English in New York City*. Washington, DC: Center for Applied Linguistics.

Wolfram, W., Christian, D., Potter, L., & Leap, W. (1979). *Variability in the English of two Indian communities and its effects on reading and writing.* (Final Rep. to the National Institute of Education, NIE-G-77-0006). Washington, DC: Center for Applied Linguistics.

Zentella, A.C. (1981). Language variety among Puerto Ricans. In C. Ferguson & S.B. Heath (Eds.), *Language in the U.S.A.* Cambridge, England: Cambridge University Press.

Chapter 7

Knowledge and Process
in the Acquisition of Writing Skills

NANCY L. STEIN
University of Chicago

The major purpose of this article is to review and evaluate current knowl-edge-based and process approaches to the study of writing. Because of space limitations, only certain types of knowledge are considered. Although knowl-edge of spelling, grammar, and punctuation is essential to writing, the acqui-sition of lexical knowledge is not discussed. The focus is on a discussion of the importance of acquiring knowledge about the different goals and inten-tions that guide the writing process, the functions that different discourse forms serve, the comprehension processes of a reader, and specific topic do-mains.

Several general conclusions are reached as a result of the review. Although current models of writing emphasize the necessity of studying the interaction between process and knowledge, most research has not focused directly on this issue. The primary emphasis has been on a description of process with little attention given to an accurate description of the types of knowledge used during writing. As a result, many conclusions about the nature and develop-ment of writing skill need reevaluation. In particular, the assumption that poor writing results from a lack of metacognitive knowledge is seriously ques-tioned. Also, the belief that children lack metacognitive knowledge and knowledge about different forms of discourse, other than narrative, is shown to be in error. Children's knowledge and use of expository forms has been underestimated and their knowledge about stories has been overestimated.

Special thanks are due to John Bransford, Tom Trabasso, and Isabel Beck for their com-ments and thoughtful suggestions on an earlier draft of this paper. The writing of this paper was supported in part by a grant from the Benton Foundation. Facilities of the Department of Psychology at the University of California, Santa Barbara, were used in completing this man-uscript and are gratefully acknowledged.

The review also illustrates the problematic nature of writing instruction because of a primary emphasis on process. An analysis of current instructional methods in teaching effective writing shows a predisposition to adopt a social-interactive process approach to teaching. It is argued, however, that current studies using this approach confound the process or method of teaching with the content that is communicated. To the extent that instruction includes the elements necessary to learn new information, successful results will occur. A social-interactive approach does not necessarily guarantee that the prerequisites for learning will be met, nor does the occurrence of a traditional lecture signify poor instruction. A necessary component of instructional research is the inclusion and understanding of a theory of learning pertaining to writing skill.

Finally, the role that different types of knowledge play in the writing process is explored. It is concluded that an essential component of writing instruction must involve an assessment of the writer's goals for communicating and the reasons for using particular discourse forms to achieve these goals. At present, much instruction involves training children to use the appropriate structural dimensions of a discourse form without a discussion of how a writer's goals are met by the use of a specific form. Moreover, it is often assumed that the use of specific forms leads to the best possible writing and that the writer will gradually infer the correct goals that underlie the use of each form.

These assumptions are questioned on the basis of three considerations: (1) the different types of goals writers use to generate discourse, (2) the way in which these goals constrain the emergence of particular discourse forms, and (3) the importance of topic knowledge in organizing the structure of discourse. It is argued that good writing takes more diverse forms than those traditionally taught in writing classes, and that the emphasis on argument and analytic forms is inappropriate to many writing tasks. A variety of purposes underlie writing, and many of these are ignored in writing instruction. In addition, the structure and content of topic knowledge play a more important role in the emergence of good writing than originally thought. Thus, future research should focus on better descriptions of the knowledge needed to complete specific writing tasks, the types of discourse structures that best convey a writer's message, and the conditions under which knowledge pertaining to writing is acquired.

THE PROCESS OF CONSTRUCTING WRITTEN TEXTS

Writing is a complex act. The construction of a coherent text requires continual access to several different types of knowledge. The end product—the written text—does not necessarily reflect all of the knowledge accessed and used during composition. However, it is assumed that sophisticated writing reflects both unconscious and conscious access to such different types of knowledge as specific domain knowledge, principles of good communication, knowledge of a reader's beliefs and values, and so on that are used during each phase of writing.

Although all writers experience some difficulty during writing, especially when they are formulating new ideas, it is currently believed that the experienced writer expends much less conscious effort than a novice in interleaving different types of knowledge. The expert writer also has a more flexible organization of knowledge in both a specific content domain and in the principles underlying good communication and comprehension skill (Flower, in press; Flower & Hayes, 1981; Means & Voss, 1985; Resnick, 1985).

Children and/or novices, on the other hand, are thought to have much more difficulty with the writing process. They cannot coordinate different types of knowledge easily, they spend much more time on each segment of the text than the experts, and they perceive each part of the composition process as more effortful (Bereiter, 1980; Scardamalia, 1981; Bereiter & Scardamalia, 1985). To explain some of the difficulties encountered in writing, Bereiter (1980) has set forth a quasi-developmental framework that includes a description of how a person proceeds through a composition task. He argues for the necessity of automatizing different parts of the writing process so that a coherent text can be produced. He also implies that children and/or novices have not yet acquired the knowledge or strategies that allow automatic access to many essential components of the writing task.

Another model used to describe the nature of the writing process has been derived from Newell and Simon's (1972) general problem-solving model (hereafter referred to as the GPS model). The GPS model serves as a powerful metaphor because of the small number of finite processes that are assumed to comprise the act of writing. Thus, despite the complexity of writing, the GPS model labels and focuses on a limited number of transformations and processes critical to the production of any kind of text.

Another reason for the model's popularity is that it can be used to describe the representation and use of information in almost any topic domain. Researchers have used the GPS or a variant in describing mathematical and scientific problem-solving behavior (Bransford & Stein, 1984; Charles & Lester, 1984; Greeno, 1980; Mayer, 1982; Reed & Johnsen, 1977); story understanding (Graesser & Murachver, 1985; Lichtenstein & Brewer, 1980; Rumelhart, 1977; Stein, 1983b), and the development of social problem-solving behavior (Stein & Levine, 1986). In fact, in any domain where problem solving occurs, the GPS model can be used to describe the underlying cognitive processes relevant to task behavior.

Hayes and Flower (1980; Flower & Hayes, 1977, 1980, 1981) have used the heuristics of this model to describe the subprocesses specific to writing. An initial assumption made by these investigators is that the writer's store of knowledge and interpretation of task demands continually guide and control the three major subprocesses particular to writing: planning, translating, and reviewing.

Planning activities consist of setting specific goals for the writing process, generating information, and organizing it. The planning sequence usually requires that the writer first attempt an interpretation or representation of the task demand or problem at hand. Thus, the writer must encode information from an external source and integrate it with knowledge from long-term memory to set goals for how the writing process should proceed. Information relevant to those goals can then be retrieved from long-term memory and organized into a new knowledge representation to guide the construction of the text (Stein, 1983a, b).

Before text production begins, however, some sort of *translation* process must occur. The act of translation involves an attempt to match linguistic knowledge to the knowledge-based schema that results from the planning process. Thus, the writer attempts to bring linguistic processes to bear on a particular idea. Although Flower and Hayes never explicitly describe the nature and content of the writer's ideas or knowledge base, we can assume that writers have acquired and use rich repertoires of knowledge, much of which is *not* in verbal form. The arduous task that writers face in translation is to find ways of representing nonverbal concepts in verbal form.

Take as an example a skilled golfer who wants to write a book on how to play golf. Much of the knowledge about playing golf is organized and stored in visual representations and action sequences. In attempts to teach their skill to novices, golfers often use visual displays and motion pictures to illustrate the correct structure and organization of movements comprising various golf strokes. If a golfer decides to write a book that illustrates and describes the correct procedure for producing a particular golf stroke, pictures almost always accompany the text. The integration of the text with the information in the picture sequences serves as the ideal form, simply because some of the major dimensions inherent in the golf stroke cannot be described accurately in words alone.

However, when golfers are forced to translate some of their knowledge into a verbal form, they are able to focus on certain features of the visual action sequence that otherwise might prove difficult for a novice to encode. The instructor can elaborate on the component parts of the stroke and compare the correct way of executing a motor action sequence with an incorrect organization. Verbalization thus draws attention to various parts of the golf stroke that might go unnoticed in a visual representation. Verbalization also allows the instructor to emphasize certain behaviors as being more important and causally inducing other parts of the action sequence.

The third process, that of *reviewing,* consists of reading, editing, and revising the written text. Editing and revising consist of many different activities, many of which concern deleting, adding, or integrating information. The important feature of the review process is that writers can treat their written texts as a piece of discourse to be understood. Thus, writers can apply the same comprehension skills to their own texts as they would to texts written by other people. They can attempt to make sense of their own writing.

The process of reviewing is distinct from planning and translating because during the review the writer already has a piece of discourse at which to look. The major goal of the review is to ensure that the text makes sense and contains the critical information originally envisioned as important by the writer (Stein & Trabasso, 1985). During the initial writing process, the writer often generates a goal structure that is quite coherent and well organized. The difficulty of translating ideas into verbal concepts or of generating critical components of the written text often leaves writers unaware that inconsistencies exist in their text or that the text lacks a coherent structure. The review process allows the writer to process what is written without the burden of generating the entire structure.

In modeling the writing process, Hayes and Flower (1980) attempted to describe the interactions that occur between the various subprocesses by positing the existence of a "monitor." According to Hayes and Flower, disorganization would prevail without some type of overarching processing mechanism to monitor the interactions between all the subprocesses. A monitor was also necessary to account for the goal-directedness of the writing process, despite all of the interruptions that occur from incoming information. The subprocesses do not run off in a smooth fashion. Rather, some planning occurs, mixed with translation and review. Thus, the lack of linearity in the system necessitated reference to a mechanism that would impose some type of organization on the entire processing system.

The major impact of the Flower and Hayes work has been methodological and conceptual rather than theoretical. By introducing a process model to the field of writing, these investigators also advocated the use of the talk-aloud protocol as the optimal way to collect data on the processes underlying the act of writing. This methodology emerged directly from studies completed by Newell and Simon (1972) and has been defended as one of the better measurements of spontaneous thought during the problem-solving process (Ericsson & Simon, 1980). Many other researchers have used the technique (Bereiter & Bird, 1985; Lytle, 1985; Olson, Duffy, & Mack, 1985) and strongly support its usefulness in shedding light on the processing strategies used during both reading comprehension and writing. Collecting talk-aloud protocols allows access to many inferences and interpretations made during reading and writing. The content of these inferences is often predictive of errors made in the interpretation of text (Olson et al., 1985) and provides clues to the types of knowledge used to complete a composition task.

In many real world contexts, such as school classrooms, the use of talk-aloud procedures has had a direct impact on instruction in reading and writing. For the most part, the interpretation of text remains a covert activity that only emerges in final form on a required essay. By using the talk-aloud procedure to elicit a subject's interpretation of the task, the instructor can intervene to preclude serious misinterpretations of task demands. Also, the critical content required for comprehension can then be substituted. As we will see in the review of the instructional literature, a variant of the talk-aloud procedure has been used in several studies that provided the most effective instructional results in writing (Hillocks, 1984; Stein, 1984) as well as in reading (Palincsar & Brown, 1984).

The data generated by using talk-aloud procedures have also underscored the importance of representing writing as a nonlinear, recursive process. Although broad general stages may be used to describe the writing process (e.g., interpreting and representing the problem, planning and generating a solution, translating the plan into verbal form, reviewing and editing the text), the data on writing indicate the nonlinear interleaved nature of these subprocesses, even for the generation of one line of text. Almost all observational studies of the writing process, with or without the use of talk-aloud protocols, have included reference to a nonlinear phenomenon. This finding holds for experienced and less experienced writers (Hillocks, 1982; Stein & Hillocks, 1985). Emig (1971) and Pianko (1977, 1979) report that skilled student writers do not necessarily spend much time in advance planning before beginning to write. Writers tend to compose at fairly steady rates (Pianko, 1977, Stallard, 1974), which may indicate some access to automatic structures early in the writing process, depending upon the goals of the writer.

Writers have some conscious and verbal awareness of certain goals that underlie the oral and written composition process. Even young children can stop and identify some of the goals that motivate their composition behavior (Stein & Kilgore, 1985). Children can also identify many of the goals that motivate their social problem-solving behavior (Stein & Eulau, 1985; Stein & Jewett, 1986; Stein & Levine, 1985, 1986), *while* they are performing the behavior and *after* the behavior sequence is completed. This ability is apparent even in 3- and 4-year-old children who participate in problem-solving sequences (Stein & Levine, 1985) and composition activities (Stein & Salgo, 1986). Thus, at some level, there is conscious awareness of certain types of goals and knowledge that motivate and guide problem-solving and composition activities. The use of talk-aloud protocol and spontaneous generation procedures has allowed researchers and teachers access to much knowledge about thinking that is not readily accessible in many real world tasks.

Emphasis on process has also alerted researchers and teachers to the difficulty of producing written composition. Instead of focusing on the outcome of composition, the research community now tends to focus on the procedures used to generate written prose. According to Applebee (1982), viewing writing as a dynamic process is a radical departure from the norm. However, the results of this shift in attention to the process have been quite rewarding, especially in terms of understanding the *initial* thinking processes that precede or accompany the act of writing.

Many researchers (Bruner, 1985; Flower & Hayes, 1977; Graves, 1981) have found that in their initial attempt to draft a piece of prose, students first need to describe the context of events in which the focal information was originally encoded. For example, when telling a story about how she felt about a favorite aunt getting married, a young writer first had to tell about all the events at the wedding, what happened on the way to the church, and who was at the wedding. *Then* she could access and describe her feelings about her aunt getting married and the implications the marriage would have for the little girl's relationship to the aunt (Graves, 1981).

The necessity of accessing and describing the context in which focal information is embedded is an activity common to all writers. Almost anyone observing the writing, representational, or learning process has described similar strategies being used by adults and college students (Bruner, 1985; Flower & Hayes, 1977; Mandler, 1983, 1984; Stein & Colomb, 1985). Flower and Hayes (1977) have labeled this strategy as writer-based and the final composition strategy as reader-based. These labels indicate that the initial part of the writing process often involves the construction of a representation so that the *writer* better understands exactly what information is available about a topic. Stein (1983a, b) concurs with this evaluation and argues that writing for an audience cannot really proceed until writers have constructed some type of meaningful representation for themselves. Frequently, the initial act of writing serves as a retrieval mechanism for accessing highly organized information in a rapid automatic fashion and examining it for its meaning and appropriateness.

The necessity of constructing a writer-based text should also depend upon the amount of cognitive change and integration that has to precede the act of communication. If a writer is unsure that the goals of the writing task can be met or that enough information has been acquired about a topic, it may be necessary to write down what is currently known. The written text then can be used to assess whether more information needs to be acquired or whether writing for an audience can proceed solely with revision. If the writer is fairly sure of what is to be said, then the process of revision can begin with more planning and translation that is aimed at increasing the comprehensibility of the text for the reader. Consequently, it is clear that writing serves two main purposes: (1) to help the writer clarify and understand what is known about a topic, and (2) to inform, teach, or persuade others with reference to particular ideas.

EVALUATION OF A PROCESS APPROACH TO WRITING

Although the problem-solving approach is essential in focusing attention on the dynamics of the writing process, the theory, as it now stands, needs further elaboration and refinement. Two major aspects have not been addressed: the role of different types of knowledge used in the writing process and the nature of the interaction between knowledge and the use of specific writing strategies.

In all of their theoretical discussions, Flower and Hayes alert us to the importance of accessing knowledge at every point in the writing process. Furthermore, they use an implicit "novice-expert" metaphor (Flower & Hayes, 1980) to describe individual differences in the ability to construct coherent text (Flower, in press). However, these investigators have not provided explicit descriptions of *how* knowledge interacts with processing strategies or exactly *what* types of knowledge are necessary to construct a coherent text. This has led to several incorrect conclusions about the nature of instruction and the development of writing skill.

Consider first a writer's failure to carry out and complete different components of a writing task. Currently, poor writers are described as focusing more on the length of an assignment, the overt conventions of rhetoric, and the actual knowledge that is supposed to go into a text. Moreover, poor writers are reported not to modify their goals or perceptions of the task demands during the writing process (Flower & Hayes, 1980), nor are they able to maintain a coherent output without a continual review of the text already written (Atwell, 1981).

Two possible explanations exist for the lack of skill: (1) deficits in strategic knowledge (e.g., knowledge about *how* to carry out different parts of the writing task), or (2) deficits in declarative knowledge about different dimensions of the writing task (e.g., topic knowledge, knowledge about different forms of discourse, knowledge about the comprehension process, etc.). Advocating a strategic-process based hypothesis entails describing writing failure in terms of a lack of strategic knowledge about the three major subprocesses underlying the act of writing (planning, translating, and reviewing).

Some researchers have assumed that poor writers and/or children have difficulty because they lack the ability to formulate strategies critical to the *process* of writing. For example, children supposedly have more difficulty in planning ahead, detecting inconsistent information in their writing, isolating important information in text, and summarizing text material (Brown, 1980; Brown, Day, & Jones, in press; Flower, in press). These inabilities are generally referred to as a lack of "metacognitive" skill (Brown, 1980; Baker & Brown, 1985). The word megacognitive is used because it is believed that these skills are relatively content free and revolve around people's ability to reflect on and control their own thinking processes. Thus, metacognitive knowledge lies outside the realm of specific content knowledge about the comprehension and composition process.

The metacognitive viewpoint inadvertently leads to the conclusion that with development and/or experience basic changes occur in the ability to reflect and monitor one's thinking processes. The changes increase the amount and kind of processing skill children use to construct meaningful representations during comprehension and composition. Young children are thought to be incapable of engaging in many reflective activities (Baker & Brown, 1985; Scardamalia, 1981), and they are thought not to have an astute awareness of their own cognitive activities during the comprehension process (Brown, 1980; Markman, 1977, 1979).

Because of the belief in metacognitive deficits, several investigators have attempted to devise ways to train children, poor writers, and poor readers in the *processes* of comprehending and constructing written texts. An example of a process-oriented approach to teaching writing has been described by Hume (1983), who outlines various methods to improve each part of the writing process. For example, at the outset of a writing lesson, students are taught to deal with the problems of generating ideas. Word association and simile frame techniques, as well as answers to preset questions, are thought to increase generation capacity. Afterward, students are introduced to the process of grouping and rearranging their ideas. Clustering and shuffling techniques encourage the categorization of ideas. Spatial outlays and reference to temporal event sequences are also used to increase organizational skill. After children are coached in these strategies, they are asked to produce a piece of written prose. Strategies for revision follow.

Researchers or teachers who adopt a process approach to writing often believe that writers have acquired most of the necessary knowledge needed to complete the writing task. All that remains to be taught are the procedures that enable writers to use inert knowledge (knowledge that is not readily or easily retrieved during a problem-solving or composition task; see Bransford, Vye, Adams, & Perfetto, in press). Thus, the instructional strategies described by Hume (1983) assume that the most important types of knowledge needed for writing are organizational schemes for accessing and reorganizing already acquired information. Generating, grouping, and sequencing ideas fulfill these requirements.

Many writing difficulties, however, arise from a lack of specific content knowledge. An example of the obstacles created by content knowledge deficits will help underscore this point. In a training study, Day (1980) attempted to increase students' skill in summarizing expository texts. In order to devise effective procedures, she evolved a set of summarization rules derived from van Dijk and Kintsch's (1977) analysis of text comprehension. The rules consisted of deleting unimportant or redundant information, integrating information from several clauses into one, making general statements from several specific events, and inventing statements that would contain higher order "important" information not found in the text.

Day taught students how to use these rules and managed to elicit some improvement in summarization skill. However, many students still experienced great difficulty constructing good summaries. Day concluded that although training proved somewhat beneficial, most students still needed substantial instruction in summarization skill. The missing component, according to Day, was a method for teaching students how to identify important information in the text. Although the four summarization rules could be used, there were no rules to teach the definition of important information.

In a subsequent analysis of summarization skill, Stein and Garman (1986) argue that the identification of important information is essential to the construction of a summary. However, knowing the dimensions that define the concept of a good summary is also critical. Even when a writer knows how to identify important information, selection is still necessary. For example, in many narratives almost all of the events are included on the causal chain linking the beginning to the end (Stein & Garman, 1986; Trabasso & Sperry, 1985). Thus, almost all events can be said to be "important."

Since some events on the chain have more connections to other events, the level of importance is raised for those events having multiple connections. However, even for those events that have multiple connections (sometimes over 50% of the events), selection is still necessary. Certain types of events seem to carry more information in a summary than other events. For example, goals and outcomes are summarized more frequently than other types of events that have the same number of causal connections. Events that contain information about obstacles are also included frequently (Stein & Garman, 1986; van den Broek, 1985). Thus, the information in a summary appears to correspond to those dimensions that are used to define a good story (see Stein, 1982; Stein & Policastro, 1984), and these definitions can be specified and taught.

Therefore, the process of teaching students summarization skills is not simply a matter of applying a set of summarization rules for shortening, translating, and reorganizing knowledge. Writers must acquire and use specific types of conceptual knowledge in order to know what to delete, integrate, and generalize. In many writing contexts, the relevant conceptual knowledge has not yet been acquired and must be learned before students are asked to begin composing. (See Applebee, 1984, for an extended discussion of the relationship between learning and composing.)

Because the writing process has not been described with respect to the prerequisite conceptual knowledge needed to construct meaningful prose, the strategic skills of children and novices have been seriously underestimated and the skills of adults have been overestimated. If investigators focus on specific types of conceptual knowledge and ensure that their subjects have already acquired this information, even very young children are capable of using metacognitive or strategic skills.

As examples, preschool and elementary school children are able to engage in causal reasoning (Stein & Levine, 1985; Trabasso, Stein, & Johnson, 1981), in planning behavior (Goldman, 1982; Stein & Goldman, 1981; Stein & Levine, 1985; Wellman, in press), and in an assessment of the consequences of their own and other people's actions (Stein & Levine, 1985; Trabasso, Stein, & Johnson, 1981). Elementary school children can also pick out important information in text (Pichert, 1978; van den Broek, 1985) and make importance judgments in ways similar to adults (Worrall & Athey, 1985). The detection of inconsistent information is also a skill that most 5-year-old children manifest (Stein & Trabasso, 1985). Slobin (1978) has reported that even a 2-year-old child is sensitive to inconsistencies in discourse. Upon closer scrutiny, researchers are finding that very young children use the same strategic and organizing processes as adults in order to acquire, represent, and retrieve language concepts (Huttenlocher & Smiley, 1985; Huttenlocher, Smiley & Charney, 1983).

The major differences between studies that find young children capable of strategic processing and those that do not lie in the type and familiarity of materials and tasks used. The results of many different investigations (see Stein, 1983b, and Stein & Trabasso, 1982a & b, for reviews of the literature) show that when children are highly familiar with the content of a task, they perform similarly to adults. Furthermore, Chi (1978, in press) and Lindberg (1980) have shown that when children are more familiar with the task content and requirements than adults, children actually outperform adults.

Task familiarity also plays a critical role in predicting adults' comprehension and composition skill. Baker (1979) has shown that adults experience difficulty in detecting inconsistent logical reasoning when working with difficult text material. Furthermore, when a text contains omissions of information necessary to make causal inferences, adults' ability to remember the content dramatically decreases (Bransford et al., in press; Stein, 1983 a, b; Stein & Nezworski, 1978). Adults cannot successfully encode and remember texts containing randomly organized events sequences or texts containing information where certain functions or motives have been omitted (Bransford et al., in press; Thorndyke, 1977). Moreover, when adults have difficulty understanding the subject matter described in a text, they neither abstract important information nor write a cogent summary of the text contents (Stein, 1983a, b). In fact, skilled writers entering specialized areas of journalism often experience difficulty writing cogent texts for publication (C. Roberts, personal communication, July 6, 1986).

In assessing writing difficulty experienced in professions such as journalism or television, it is difficult to attribute the lack of expertise to the lack of strategic knowledge. Many novice reporters have been trained at the best undergraduate institutions in the country and have already shown "exceptional" talent in writing in specific content areas. Problems arise when new domains of knowledge are introduced. Acquiring expertise in political reporting necessitates an understanding of several different sources of information: topic knowledge, genre used in communication of political information, an understanding of the general level of audience knowledge in the political arena, the consequences of communication and persuasion, and so forth. A lack of information in any one of these areas might preclude the production of a coherent text.

The existence of *context-dependent* writing skill requires a reinvestigation and reformulation of our beliefs about the types of knowledge that lead to good writing and the generalizability of this skill across tasks. Many researchers believe that students can be classified as "good" and "poor" writers. Similar beliefs exist in the field of reading comprehension. In fact, current testing procedures for assessing reading or writing skill assume the existence of a general ability.

Although reading and writing do require substantial lexical knowledge that generalizes across domains, these activities also require the acquisition of domain-specific knowledge. Much of the available data on problem solving, thinking, and comprehension processes do not support a full-fledged generalist position (Anderson, 1977; Glaser, 1984; Resnick, 1985). Furthermore, professional writers rarely compose across topic domains. The food editor of *The New York Times* does not write political columns, nor does the political editor write articles for the science section. In fact, there is increasing specialization in news writing because of the difficulty of writing coherent text without the availability of critical knowledge specific to a domain.

Unless we begin to understand and specify the role of different types of knowledge during composing and comprehension, the chances of advancing theories of reading and writing remain limited. Similarly, understanding the role of different types of knowledge in the instructional process is equally important. At the moment, there are no coherent explanations for why teaching reading and writing succeeds. In fact, investigators who advocate different theoretical approaches to successful instruction often use similar training procedures.

As an example, Fitzgerald and Teasley (1985) selected fourth-grade children who demonstrated a lack of knowledge about story structure and trained these children to recognize and generate all the parts of a story episode. After intensive training, these researchers found that children's skill in generating well-formed, cohesive stories increased significantly. Moreover, children's ability to generate unique and creative content increased. The effectiveness of the training was atributed to providing knowledge about story structure that previously had been unavailable to children. Alternatively, Short and Ryan (1982) argue that children's skill at understanding stories suffers because they lack a critical metacognitive skill. In an attempt to improve comprehension, these investigators provided children with critical metacognitive training. The results of their study also showed significant increases in comprehension skill and accuracy. A comparison between the Short and Ryan study and the Fitzgerald and Teasley study ironically shows the use of similar procedures. Both sets of investigators taught children appropriate labels and definitions for the components of stories. Both taught children to generate the different parts of a story episode and to understand the ways in which knowledge about story structure could facilitate their comprehension and composition.

In evaluating the success of these training procedures, it is difficult to specify the exact reason for improvement in comprehension and composition. Clearly, both studies included direct instruction about the structure and content of story components. Thus, the significant increase in skilled behavior could be due to the acquisition of knowledge about story structure. However, both sets of investigators provided children with additional information about narratives. For example, children were told how learning about story structure could help them in writing future stories (Fitzgerald & Teasley, 1985). This type of information is equivalent to context information that ensures the appropriate use of schematic knowledge (Gick & Holyoak, 1983). Knowing the parts of a story does not necessarily guarantee the correct usage of such information. Knowing the conditions under which to use the information is also critical.

The difficulty with these two studies, besides supporting different explanations for similar results, is that we still do not know very much about the relative contribution of different types of knowledge to the composition and comprehension process. Fitzgerald and Teasley provided children with information about structural dimensions, purposes, functions, and thematic content in a given story. Short and Ryan provided children with specific knowledge about the structure and function of narratives, arguing that their training provided knowledge critical to metacognitive development.

Two aspects of these instructional studies are clear, however. First, there is little or no attempt to distinguish between metacognitive knowledge and knowledge about the content, functions, and purposes of different types of discourse. Second, both sets of investigators believe that any time knowledge about functions and purposes of discourse are given to children, this information should be labeled metacognitive knowledge. In addition, any time children are given information about the principles by which people comprehend text, the term metacognitive knowledge is used.

My interpretation of the situation is that children are being given specific content information about *theories* of comprehension, much like college and graduate students taking courses in theories of reading and writing. The knowledge being transmitted is specific to particular functions, content, and structures of discourse. Children's awareness of their own comprehension processes may increase as a direct function of providing critical content knowledge about the structure and function of particular discourse forms. However, the knowledge provided during instruction is not metacognitive. Because of the mislabeling of the knowledge being transmitted during instruction, few investigators have attempted to distinguish between (1) acquiring specific content knowledge about comprehension and discourse forms and (2) showing evidence of metacognitive skill.

Thus, to date, the major difficulty in understanding the role of knowledge in acquiring reading and writing skill is a lack of awareness and specificity about the types of knowledge transmitted during instruction. An attempt to define and differentiate metacognitive knowledge from specific types of factual knowledge has not been made. Instructing students in the comprehension process and illustrating different principles related to comprehension should not necessarily be classified as teaching metacognitive knowledge. Students are being taught factual, declarative information about the *principles* that facilitate the process of comprehension. They must take the knowledge they are given during instruction and incorporate it into already existing routines and procedural schemas.

Another obstacle in understanding the development of writing skill is the belief in the primacy of process over content. In most composition studies, the way in which information is transmitted (process) is thought to be more important than transmitted information. In his meta-analysis of effective composition training procedures, Hillocks (1984) concluded that the most powerful training techniques are *not* those currently used in most classrooms. The *naturalistic* mode of learning to write, in which the students initiate most of the interaction, proceed at their own pace, and seek feedback when necessary is not very successful. The *presentation* mode, embodying the more traditional method of lecturing to students, giving specific directions and requiring the development of a composition is not very effective either. The *environmental* mode of instruction *is* the most effective training procedure. This method entails using cooperative *interaction* among students to initiate discussion about the goals, content, and procedures associated with a composition task. The teacher, rather than lecturing, uses small groups and specific tasks to illustrate the dimensions under consideration. Students work on certain tasks in small groups before proceeding to independent composition tasks constructed in a similar fashion. Principles are "taught"—not simply announced as they are in the more traditional "presentational" mode of instruction.

Several other researchers (Anania, 1981; Bloom, 1984; Burke, 1983; Graybeal & Stodolsky, 1985; Johnson, Maruyama, Johnson, & Nelson, 1981; Palincsar & Brown, 1984; Slavin, 1980) also report success with various types of cooperative interactive procedures among teachers and students. Palinscar and Brown (1984), in particular, advocate a "reciprocal teaching" approach to comprehension, in which teachers and students alternate in guiding the processes relevant to comprehension.

The generalizations about the necessity of incorporating social interaction and cooperation to promote learning were made even though none of these studies advanced a theory of learning or an analysis of the *content* transmitted during the interaction. As a result, *process* has been confounded with *content* of the knowledge transmitted during instruction. Many different variables, besides those bearing on process, could account for effective reading and writing instruction.

If the types of knowledge transmitted during instruction were controlled in a systematic fashion, the effect of process could be examined more carefully. At this point, we cannot say that a particular mode or process of instruction is more powerful than another. The content of the information presented within a particular mode may be the critical factor in predicting successful acquisition of composition skill. In fact, it is our contention that the actual substance and organization of content is far more powerful in predicting successful instruction than is the mode of instruction (Nix, 1985; Stein, 1984). Thus, a traditional lecture could far outpace any "environmentally" based training procedure. The trick is to understand and manipulate the types of information that promote learning.

At the moment, tutorial, small group, and "environmentally" based instruction may be more effective in teaching composition skills because of the built-in sensitivity to the learning process (Stein, 1984). In a one-to-one tutorial session, teachers can assess and learn more about:

1. The types of knowledge students bring to the task.
2. The types of errors students make during the process of learning.
3. The types of additional knowledge students might need to understand the goals of the composition task.
4. The way in which students should make the transition from an initial knowledge state to a new one.

Thus, "environmentally" based procedures may allow the *teacher* to acquire new knowledge about the process of composition. Although we would like to believe that teachers have a good understanding of the learning and composition process, most do not. In fact, good teachers are constantly aware of the necessity to *expand* their knowledge of the composition process. Interactive cooperative procedures are useful as a method of tapping into the covert processes of their students. Teachers may use the interactive instructional mode, similar to the way in which researchers use the talk-aloud protocol: to understand the beginning knowledge states of their students.

However, successful instruction only *begins* when an astute assessment of a learner's initial state has been made. The next step is the development of methods or techniques that enable a student to make a transition from an initial state to a new state of knowledge. Since teachers and researchers lack critical information about the initial and transitional states of learning, they use cooperative interaction to generate what they hope will be the right types of instruction to promote learning. In the process of interacting with children, teachers may be able to use trial-and-error strategies to increase their own knowledge of learning.

Unless a fundamental understanding of the learning process is acquired, however, interactive techniques such as "environmental" interaction (Hillocks, 1984), "reciprocal" teaching (Palincsar & Brown, 1984), and "cooperative" learning (Slavin, 1980) will not necessarily lead to better instruction. Experimental studies using these techniques, such as those of Palincsar and Brown (1984), are highly constrained with respect to the type and complexity of the materials used. The importance of content or structure is not directly acknowledged in these studies. Many teachers do not operate with such highly constrained materials. More importantly, the conditions that truly promote the acquisition of composition and comprehension skills are occluded and may not be understood. A necessary step in advancing instruction in writing, as well as comprehension, is a framework for understanding how and what knowledge is used during composing, as well as understanding the mechanisms that promote learning.

THE ROLE OF KNOWLEDGE IN THE COMPOSING PROCESS

In order to understand how knowledge affects composing, the different types of prerequisite knowledge used during writing must be described. This is not as easy a task as it might appear to be. It is difficult, even for the most sophisticated teacher and researcher, to describe how and what knowledge writers use. The problematic nature of constructing detailed representations of the knowledge states necessary for composing can be seen when teachers instruct students in composition. Hillocks (1984, in press) reports that many teachers neither set detailed goals for composition tasks nor attempt to specify exactly what types of conceptual knowledge will facilitate composition. If goals are set, broad general aims such as "writing a story that is meaningful" or "learning how to write a good essay" are given as guidelines. Teachers rarely lay out a sequence of specific goals to be attained during composition instruction.

If a teacher *does* attempt to specify what students should be learning, the description often encompasses *only* the structural aspects of writing. In fact, both teachers and researchers tend to conceive of composition instruction as being the primary context for teaching students how to use such different types of discourse forms as a story, an argument, a description, a concept definition, an essay, and so on. Although the structural aspects of written composition are important, so are many other types of information. Failure to understand the nature of writing and the role of other types of knowledge are the reasons for some of the failures experienced in teaching composition (Stein & Colomb, 1985).

Most writing tasks are conceived and initiated in social contexts (Stein & Colomb, 1985), where writers have specific goals for communicating via the written word. The broad general goals of informing, explaining, and persuading underlie almost all acts of writing. The *reasons* for wanting to persuade, inform, and explain, the consequences of doing so (or not doing so), and knowledge about the social context guide the act of writing, both in terms of the content and structure of the discourse used.

Although researchers have emphasized the importance of the writer's knowledge in guiding the writing process (Flower & Hayes, 1977, 1980), few, if any, have explored the exact nature of the relationship between a writer's intentions and the outcome of the writing process. During composition instruction, the specificity of a writer's initial goal is not considered or manipulated in any systematic way. For example, when asking children to engage in storytelling, the most common form of instruction is to tell a story about a favorite activity, place, or event.

Although storytelling does serve the general purpose of communicating about and understanding personal-social experience, it is also important to provide specific reasons for telling stories, because each reason guides the storytelling process differently. For example, explaining why a character chose to interact in a certain way with people requires the use of different knowledge than when trying to teach someone *how* to adopt a particular strategy for interacting with other people. Convincing and persuading someone actually to undertake certain actions and adopt different values requires still additional knowledge.

Most stories generated by young children are not told for the purpose of explaining, convincing, teaching, or entertaining. Rather, most children's stories serve the function of *describing* characteristics of certain people and events or *resolving* specific types of personal problems (Stein, 1984, 1985; Stein & Salgo, 1986). Thus, if children can figure out successful solutions to a problem, or if they can understand why certain preconditions prevent successful goal attainment, then they believe they have told a good story (Stein, Kilgore, & Policastro 1986; Stein & Salgo, 1986).

It is difficult to conclude, however, that young children lack the potential skill to tell a greater variety of stories. Virtually no studies exist where (1) specific instruction is provided about the different purposes of storytelling, and (2) instruction is provided to children about the nature and process of *linking* particular functions to the act of storytelling.

It may be that when children are given no specific direction about the goals that can guide storytelling, they use the simplest strategy possible to satisfy their conception of a good story. Describing a stereotypical situation where familiar constraints apply or generating a routine way of solving a problem is cognitively easier and more economical than attempting to construct new solutions to a problem or attempting to figure out how someone can be persuaded to follow a certain course of action. Figuring out explanations for social actions also requires the acquisition of much new information.

If children were given information about those dimensions that characterize an explanatory or persuasive story and then were instructed in the *process* of constructing such a narrative, we might see even very young children using the story for social and moral purposes. In several analyses of social interaction (Berkowitz, 1985; Shantz & Shantz, 1985), children continually use narrative and argumentative discourse to persuade, explain, and convince others. A necessary step in advancing our understanding of composition is to understand why children succeed in using sophisticated strategies in some contexts but not in others.

Understanding how specific purposes guide the act of writing is important for another reason. The desire to inform, explain, persuade, compare and contrast, problem solve, and so on does *not* constrain the writer to a particular discourse form. Currently, several rhetorical analyses provide descriptions for how these goals influence the construction of expository texts (Meyer & Freedle, 1984). However, the same goals can guide the construction of virtually any form of discourse. Thus, it is misleading to identify rhetorical goals with expository text forms (e.g. definition, cause-effect, compare-contrast, problem-solution). The same goals and forms can be found in narratives, as well as in expository texts. The narrative is a form of discourse that primarily relates information about the resolution of personal and social problems. Embedded within its structure, however, are explanations for physical and personal actions, comparisons between the relative goodness of specific motives and/or interactions, and descriptions that define the characteristics of certain types of protagonists. Therefore, the narrative, as well as the expository text, contains all four of Meyer and Freedle's (1984) discourse forms.

Meyer and Freedle (1984) are really describing *goals* that regulate the generation of discourse. Each goal may result in a particular form or structure described in Meyer and Freedle's (1984) taxonomy. However, the resultant forms rarely occur independently of one another. As previously illustrated, one narrative can contain all four forms. Similarly, when a writer attempts to teach a reader a new concept, it is important to use a definition with several examples. However, a writer may also wish to show how a concept is similar to, or different from, another concept (compare and contrast), why a particular concept is essential in understanding other concepts (explanations), and how the concept can be useful in solving problems (problem-solutions). Thus, isolating four rhetorical goals and teaching the resultant forms in isolation may not be a productive strategy for composition.

If these goals are paired with higher order goals of wanting to teach a person a new concept or wanting to persuade a person to take a particular course of action, then talking about the different rhetorical subgoals becomes important. However, the writer must be taught that in most instances of real world writing, a good composition requires the sequencing and integration of such specific subgoals as defining, explaining, comparing, and contrasting. Stories, arguments, newspaper articles, letters, and the like are constructed by organizing and using a hierarchy of goals, depending upon the major social goal of the writer and the results expected after the text is completed.

Most important, however, functional knowledge allows writers to retrieve and use information about people (e.g., the audience) and specific social contexts at the *beginning* of the writing process. The rhetorical goal can then function as a pointer during composition, allowing the writer to assess whether the communicative goal is being accomplished. In many instructional studies, the focus is not on the goals of communication, per se. Rather, attention is focused on learning the dimensions unique to a specific discourse form (Fitzgerald & Teasley, 1985; Meyer & Freedle, 1984; Scardamalia & Paris, 1985; Short & Ryan, 1982). In these studies, children are not taught the *reasons* for using different discourse forms, nor are they given any information about the consequences of using one form versus another.

If a writer is taught to consider the intentions underlying communication and then is shown how certain types of intentions result in specific discourse forms, better decisions can be made about *how* the writing process is to proceed. As an illustration, consider the following problem: Jim, a 15-year-old student, has decided to write a composition specifically for his mother. The purpose: to persuade his mother to take him and his friend, Mark, to his favorite amusement park on Friday. The problem: the amusement park is closing for the season on Friday and Jim's friend, Mark, will be returning to his hometown for the school year. Jim needs a ride to the amusement park and the only person who can take him is his mother. The dilemma: Jim's mother works all week, except on Friday, which she uses to accomplish essential chores that consume the entire day. Thus, she is not available to take Jim and Mark to the amusement park, 50 miles away.

More than one type of composition can be created in an attempt to accomplish Jim's goal. A story could be told, an argument could be constructed, or a personal letter could be written. Each form, however, carries with it a different set of subgoals and different types of knowledge about the persuasion process. When 30 elementary school teachers were asked to resolve this dilemma, using one of three discourse forms, the content and solutions offered in the different discourse forms differed significantly (Stein & Colomb, 1985).

In the majority of generated stories, Jim accomplished his goal by making his mother understand his needs. However, his mother then put Jim's needs above her own and those of the rest of her family. In fact, Jim became a minor hero for advocating the importance of having a good time at the amusement park, so much so that his mother decided to accompany the boys to the amusement park instead of doing her chores. Thus, in the story composition, Jim achieves his goal, changes the goal of his mother, and shows the benefits of supporting his goals. The mother's goals, however, are ignored or dismissed as less important.

In the persuasive letter, over 70% of the teachers constructed a cooperative solution to the problem where both Jim's and his mother's goals were achieved. Because Jim wanted to go to the amusement park so badly, he and Mark offered to help his mother accomplish all of her chores by Friday. This would give Jim's mother the time to take them to the amusement park and pick them up. In addition, she would have free time to do whatever she wanted.

In the argument form, *all* of the teachers listed several reasons why Jim should get to go to the amusement park. Most of these reasons concerned the fulfillment of goals that Jim's mother had set for him during the summer (e.g., Jim deserved to go because he had completed all of his chores and did not break any rules the entire summer). Some concerned the fact that Jim had asked his mother several times and she had agreed that she would take him one Friday.

Over 75% of the teachers then acknowledged that if Jim's mother took him to the amusement park, she would not get her chores done. However, the solution to her problem was *her* responsibility, especially since she had made a promise to Jim. Thus, using an argument form resulted in an essay advocating the accomplishment of Jim's goals and *not* his mother's, similar to the narrative. However, in the argument, reference to moral obligations and responsibility were introduced. Moreover, evidence citing blame or fault was usually introduced (e.g., 52% of the teachers cited evidence suggesting that Jim's mother was *at fault* because her chores really did not consume an entire day). Thus, inferences were made about blame and intentional manipulation and evidence was introduced to discredit one party's claims.

The completion of the different essays constrained the writers in terms of how they used subgoals, as well as knowledge about specific social contexts in which the conflict arose. The argument form constrained the inferences made about goal solutions. An argument immediately implied that both Jim and his mother's goals could not be accomplished. Furthermore, most teachers supplied information explicitly suggesting that the mother had *violated* a promise or that the mother had been deceptive about the time spent in completing chores. In short, the concepts of blame, fault, and responsibility were introduced, as well as attempts to discredit the other person's assertions and viewpoints.

These concepts rarely occurred in the teacher's stories, although Jim achieved his goal and his mother did not achieve hers. In the stories, Jim's mother *voluntarily* changed her goals, substituting Jim's goals for her own. Therefore, the story, unlike the argument, did not have a structure in which two people's goals remained mutually exclusive. Even though goal substitution took place, some effort at cooperation and compromise were evident so that Jim's goals became his mother's.

Thus, using a particular discourse form conveyed different types of knowledge about the *conditions* and *consequences* for resolving conflict. Although teachers resolved the problem in each type of discourse, the use of one form versus another had different consequences. Ironically, when asked to judge which form of discourse would persuade them to respond to Jim's desires, almost all of the teachers chose the persuasive letter where both parties' goals were achieved (Stein & Colomb, 1985).

These preliminary data suggest that knowledge about a discourse form should be taught in close association with the unique goals that motivate the use of one discourse form versus another. Furthermore, the data suggest that a writer must consider the types of events and actions that would *persuade* a reader. Although an argument might contain all the features thought to be necessary for a coherent logical presentation of the evidence, constructing an argument may fail to *persuade* an individual to support a particular viewpoint. The beliefs and preferences individuals have about how problems should be solved (e.g., compromise, cooperation, win-lose strategy, etc.), as well as their beliefs about *how* people are *supposed* to act and feel, are critical in assessing whether a composition will be persuasive.

The importance of knowledge about audience has been recognized by almost everyone who studies the writing process. However, several dimensions of this type of knowledge have been ignored. It is assumed that the "good" writer always has access to important audience knowledge (Flower, in press). Although the sophisticated writer may indeed understand the importance of knowing exactly how a person will interpret and react to an essay, being able to acquire the prerequisite knowledge to accomplish the goals of persuasion is an ongoing process, even for the expert writer. For example, one of the greatest difficulties trial lawyers experience is being able to assess and predict accurately how a judge and jury will weight the evidence and interpret their arguments. Understanding the knowledge that jurors use to comprehend arguments and understanding how they make decisions is difficult even for the best lawyers (Pennington & Hastie, in press). Thus, constructing a good argument is not simply a matter of knowing that jurors must be convinced, nor is it simply a matter of knowing the correct way to present critical evidence. The content of the evidence (the specific justifications and consequences) and the interpretation of this content are just as important.

In many cases, even experienced writers cannot predict in advance how a particular audience will interpret or react to a written composition. Acquiring knowledge about an audience's belief systems and understanding the process of comprehension is an arduous task, dependent on access to cultural and social knowledge that is often outside the realm of even the best writer. Thus, understanding how different types of audiences might interpret a written composition should be an important instructional goal in most composition exercises.

The first step in such an instructional process would involve the acquisition of much knowledge about the way in which people's belief systems differ and how certain types of beliefs regulate the comprehension and interpretation of composition. Thus, before any writing took place, students would have to be exposed to an extensive amount of new information (Stein, 1983a). A great deal of learning would have to precede even the most rudimentary attempts at constructing a composition. Students also would quickly learn that the content of a composition might need to be altered dramatically, depending upon *who* was reading the composition (Perl, 1983; Stein, 1983a). At the moment, writing for specific types of audiences is not greatly encouraged. Student writers are usually instructed to construct an essay that would be comprehensible to the largest imaginable audience.

Understanding *general* principles of composition in terms of knowing how to create a coherent, comprehensible text is thought to be important (Trabasso & Sperry, 1985; Trabasso & van den Broek, 1985). In fact, the standard discourse forms (e.g., argument, story, description, concept definition, etc.) have survived because their use guarantees a certain level of general comprehensibility (Stein & Colomb, 1985). The structure of these forms corresponds to the way in which readers have organized much of their knowledge about the world. For these reasons, knowing and using general procedures to produce comprehensible texts is held to be important.

It is just as essential to understand how specific content in a particular discourse form affects the comprehension process. Many writers are capable of producing coherent text that is uninteresting and judged by many to be a piece of "poor" composition. Upon closer examination, many of these poor texts do not lack coherence (Stein et al., 1986). The problem is instead with the content of the composition rather than the form. Often, the reader does not agree with the assumptions made by the writer or, at times, the resolution to a problem offered by a writer violates the moral or ethical beliefs of the reader. Witness the recent purge by many school libraries of books long considered to be classics. These books were removed because of beliefs about their content and what children can learn from them. The form and coherence of the writing was incidental. In fact, part of the problem was that these classics were so well written that they left little doubt about the values and morals being supported.

In summary, then, there are several distinct types of knowledge important to the composing process:

1. *Knowledge about the goals of composing:* Understanding how these goals regulate and constrain the types of content knowledge retrieval during writing.

2. *Knowledge about different discourse forms:* Understanding the relationship between the use of a particular form and the way in which the writer's goals and content knowledge are constrained by the use of a particular form. Also knowledge about *why* the use of a particular discourse form results in coherent text.

3. *Knowledge about the belief systems of different types of audiences:* Understanding how specific beliefs influence the comprehension, interpretation, and persuasion process.

Finally, one type of knowledge that has not yet been discussed in any detail is knowledge of specific domains. This type of knowledge, which is sometimes referred to as discipline or topic knowledge (see Chi, 1978, 1985, in press; Glaser, 1984; Resnick, 1985, in press; Stein, 1983b; Voss, Greene, Post, & Penner, 1983), is probably the most essential knowledge for the production of discourse. Writing cannot proceed without access to information about specific events. Writers must have sufficient knowledge about a particular topic.

Currently, most topic knowledge is categorized according to traditional conceptions of school disciplines. For example, many recent studies have examined the development of knowledge in mathematics (Greeno, 1980; Mayer, 1982; Resnick, in press), biology (Carey, 1985), physics (Larkin, McDermott, Simon, & Simon, 1980), and the social sciences (Voss, Greene, Post, & Penner, 1983). Examinations of general social knowledge about people and conflict resolution also exist (Berkowitz, 1985; Shantz & Shantz, 1985; Stein & Jewett, 1986; Stein & Levine, 1985, 1986; Stein & Trabasso, 1982b, 1985). The development of knowledge in fields such as music, art, drama, and athletics also has been explored.

At present, the major problem in the field of writing research is the lack of any systematic effort to understand how discipline knowledge interacts with knowledge about the goals of communication, social contexts, and discourse forms. At the moment, the tendency of most writing researchers is to assume that the writer has acquired all of the prerequisite discipline or topic knowledge. Difficulties in writing are then attributed to the lack of strategies necessary to translate conceptual ideas into a verbal form (McCutcheon & Perfetti, 1982), the lack of knowledge about appropriate discourse forms (Scardamalia & Paris, 1985), or the lack of specific types of audience knowledge (Perl, 1983).

A knowledge deficit in any one of these areas could halt the writing process. Our contention is that the lack of knowledge specific to a topic or discipline and the lack of knowledge about how other people interpret and judge "good" writing lead to breakdowns in writing more frequently than has been assumed. The fact that different types of topic knowledge have not been examined or controlled at the outset of the writing process precludes an evaluation of this hypothesis. If we were to explore the role of discipline knowledge in the composing process, however, our understanding of learning and instruction might change significantly. The following example may help to illustrate the point.

In evaluating children's writing ability, most researchers have concluded that children have access to and know more about narratives than other forms of discourse. Children supposedly tell good stories but experience difficulty constructing good arguments and opinion essays (Bereiter & Scardamalia, 1982; Scardamalia & Paris, 1985), good concept definitions (Hillocks, in press), and good summaries (Brown et al., in press). Thus, young children's skill at constructing expository texts is supposedly deficient compared to their skill at constructing narratives.

Explanations for these deficiencies are rather murky and ambiguous, but two consistent hypotheses have emerged. First, children are thought to know more about narrative structure because of their continual exposure to stories in the kindergarten and elementary-school years (Stein & Glenn, 1979). Exposure to other discourse forms is less frequent. The predominant belief is that children lack the ability to understand and control expository discourse forms primarily because they lack exposure to and instruction in this type of writing.

Second, children are thought to be competent in narration because of their detailed knowledge of social interaction (Stein, 1982; Stein & Glenn, 1979) and because of the close correspondence between the organization of social-personal knowledge and the structure of narrative discourse. Topic domains such as mathematics, biology, and the social sciences are thought to be encountered less frequently in everyday interaction and more as a function of exposure to schooling. Thus, children are not thought to be exposed to and understand much of the content or the structure of expository discourse.

Although exposure to and instruction in discipline knowledge and discourse forms is essential in the development of writing skill, it is my contention that the prevailing beliefs about the structure and content of children's knowledge are not accurate. Their knowledge of narrative discourse forms has been overestimated and their knowledge of expository forms has been underestimated. Furthermore, children have acquired substantial knowledge about the properties of the physical and mathematical world (Resnick, 1985), just as they have acquired detailed knowledge about social interaction. An example of what children know about stories and argument forms will illustrate the nature of these misconceptions.

Most children over the age of 5 can produce stories that contain all of the structural elements of an ideal story form (Stein, 1985; Stein & Glenn, 1982; Stein & Salgo, 1986). However, up to the age of 11, children also produce other discourse forms that are not considered to be these ideal story forms. For example, when asked to tell "good" stories (Stein, 1985; Stein & Glenn, 1982), elementary-school children sometimes produce: *descriptions* of a character's personality traits, *scripts* of stereotypical action sequences, and *reactive sequences,* in which characters simply react emotionally and do not attempt to carry out any planned course of action designed to achieve a desired end-state.

The production of these descriptions and partial narratives cannot be attributed to conceptual difficulties experienced during the composition process, because at the end of that process, children were given opportunities to judge the goodness of their stories, and all the children who generated such partial narratives judged their texts to be examples of good stories (Stein, 1985). Subsequent research (Stein et al., 1986) has substantiated the finding that elementary-school children include more discourse forms in their concept of a story than adults do. Thus, children's conceptions of stories are broader and more varied than an adult's concept, changing later as a function of learning and instruction.

Rather than attribute successful instruction in story comprehension or composition to the provision of metacognitive information, as Short and Ryan (1982) have argued, the success of instruction could be due to the provision of information that allows children to narrow their concept of a good story. Teaching the components of a story allows children to initiate an explicit comparison between an ideal structure and their current conception of a story. Such comparisons enable children to update their conception of what makes a good story.

However, even when training in the structural aspects of discourse forms is successful (e.g., the training succeeds in having elementary-school children generate stories that conform to an ideal structure), Stein (1985) has shown that children's stories contain neither complex plots nor an analysis of different points of view, nor is there much effort to tell a story for the purposes of teaching, moralizing, entertaining, and persuading. Moreover, the solutions provided to problems are quite stereotypical and include direct aggression, obliteration of an opponent by magic or help of a third party, and direct appeals to authority. It is only with age that children begin to use complex planning strategies, strategies of compromise, and strategies dealing with internal goal conflicts. Thus, most children's "ideal" stories contain at least the first step in the process of generating a complex narrative: the construction of a coherent resolution to a particular problem.

The analysis of children's generated stories has several implications for learning and instruction in composition. First, the concept of a story is not well formed by the time of elementary school. Children gradually acquire the adult concept of a story, probably through a combination of direct and indirect instruction about the structure and definition of a story. Providing children with explicit information about the structural aspects of stories can prove helpful in allowing children to compare an ideal concept to their own. Children can then use the ideal form to guide generation of a story in much the same circumstances that are outlined in the Fitzgerald and Teasley (1985) study.

Providing information relevant only to the invariant properties of a good story, however, is limiting and probably not the most powerful instructional strategy. All stories do have a common structure, but certain dimensions vary as a function of the type of conflict or obstacle introduced into a story. Obstacles arise from three sources: from the environment, from other people, or from within a protagonist. Each of these obstacles carries with it particular methods of resolving a problem and particular outcomes associated with the resolution (Stein, 1983b, 1985). The knowledge associated with physical and environmental obstacles is different from that of interpersonal obstacles.

Instructing children in different types of conflict resolution provides a broader and more detailed understanding of the differences, as well as the similarities, that exist across stories. Training children to understand the different types of strategies that can be used to solve problems would force them to consider solutions not currently included in their narratives. For example, children rarely use a compromise solution in stories or rarely consider taking two different points of view in a narrative. When children are required to generate stories that result in different outcomes to the same problem, they can begin both to incorporate information relevant to the problem-solution structure of a story and to increase their content knowledge of social interaction. Conflict resolution training should also prove more powerful because the invariant structural properties of stories are used to talk about the different types of conflict resolutions. Thus, both structure and content are combined in an instructional procedure.

Another dimension to be considered during storytelling instruction is thematic knowledge, which refers to information about the different types of goals that motivate human behavior. Just as there are three categories of conflicts in stories (e.g. environmental, interpersonal, and intrapersonal, Stein, 1983b; Stein & Trabasso, 1982), so there are different types of tensions that comprise each one of these conflict categories.

As an example, at least five different types of tensions are included in the interpersonal conflict category:

1. A protagonist wants to achieve a particular relationship with another person and has not yet done so.
2. A protagonist has achieved a relationship with another person but perceives the relationship to be threatened in some way.

3. A protagonist wants to destroy or abandon a relationship with another person but has not yet done so.

4. A protagonist senses that another intends to harm him or her and seeks to protect him or herself.

5. A protagonist has suffered a loss of a relationship with another and seeks to replace it.

Each of these themes carries with it specific conditions that contribute to the tension (Stein & Jewett, 1986; Stein & Levine, 1985). Furthermore, each tension carries with it a set of obstacles or conditions that must be met in order to alleviate the tension. If children have not acquired the prerequisite knowledge about the conditions eliciting a particular tension, the obstacles that preclude goal attainment, and the methods that lead to success or failure, then their stories will suffer in terms of the coherence of the discourse or the appropriateness of the content included. Difficulties will ensue despite the fact that there has been training in the structural characteristics of stories. When children do not have the appropriate content information to fill in a particular category of a discourse structure, they either eliminate the category, fill it in with inappropriate information, or use routine stereotypical solutions to construct a coherent episode (Stein, 1985). Either of these strategies results in incoherent texts. Generating routine solutions to problems results in uninteresting texts and judgements of "mediocre" stories (Stein et al., 1986; Stein & Policastro, 1984).

Thus, training children to generate "good" stories involves providing them with information about functions, structure, conflicts, and themes (Stein, 1983b). To achieve this goal, a hierarchy of information about stories can be constructed. First, the functions and invariant properties of stories are introduced. Then, training in the different types of conflicts can be given, with attention focused on the nature of the differences that emerge when different types of obstacles are encountered by a protagonist. And, finally, children can begin to be instructed in the specific conditions, obstacles, and goal plans that prevail when a particular theme is introduced into a story.

Currently, children are rarely given an organized strategy for understanding the various themes that exist in stories, probably because of a strong belief that they have already acquired the prerequisite content knowledge necessary for story generation. Current studies of narrative and social knowledge do not support the latter conclusion (Berkowitz, 1985; Stein, 1983b, 1985; Stein et al., 1986). Thus, a series of instructional strategies needs to be developed to ensure that children receive explicit, detailed training in writing and understanding stories. Successful training procedures will have to incorporate knowledge about the function, structure, and content of stories, as well as information about how these knowledge types should be sequenced during instruction.

Similar comments can be made about the study of discourse forms such as an argument or concept definition. I believe it is incorrect to say that children lack knowledge of the argument form or the appropriate content since children have been observed to engage in argument construction from the preschool years onward (Berkowitz, 1985; Shantz & Shantz, 1985). Although the way in which they argue and the structure of their arguments may differ from the adult argument form described by Toulmin (1969), children do have enough knowledge to engage in forms of argumentation.

One of the problems in arriving at an accurate assessment of children's knowledge of such expository forms as the argument is that the form of argument varies as a function of the particular social context in which it occurs. Arguments occur in everyday social interaction, legal proceedings, political debates, scientific or artistic discussions, and so on. The belief that the structure of the argument form is invariant across contexts is erroneous (Toulmin, Rieke, & Janik, 1979). Although a detailed analysis of social contexts may provide certain properties of arguments that remain invariant across situations, differences will also exist. Thus, the argument, like the story, must be taught with respect to the similarities and differences that exist across situations.

Current instruction in writing arguments rarely corresponds to the way in which arguments actually evolve. When students are asked to write an opinion essay or an argument about an issue, they are responsible for generating both their point of view and their opponent's (see Scardamalia & Paris, 1985). In real world situations, such as a debate or legal proceeding, the social context provides the writer or orator with much of the content necessary to construct an argument. For example, lawyers do not need to generate the reasons for their adversaries' positions. They do need to counter their adversaries' reasons with their own, but the beliefs of the adversaries are made explicit.

In order better to assess children's skills at controlling and understanding expository discourse forms, a more systematic exploration will have to be made about the types of knowledge children have already acquired about these forms. Although structural information is relevant to learning how to argue, our contention, again, is that knowledge about the opposition's beliefs as well as knowing the specific reasons and conclusions that are convincing to others is just as essential. Sophisticated adults have difficulty with the argument form when they lack this information (Voss et al., 1983).

In the end, general advances in theories of composition and instruction will depend upon getting a better understanding and definition of knowledge and representation. Process is important in understanding composing behavior. However, process is not content free, and access to different content domains changes the type and quality of strategy used during both comprehension and composition. Understanding the exact nature of the knowledge used during composition will facilitate better descriptions of the interaction between processing strategies and knowledge retrieval.

Understanding the nature and structure in different disciplines will also be essential in advancing writing skill. To date, few research studies have examined how different types of discourse evolve out of different knowledge domains. The fact that arguments vary as a function of particular disciplines suggests that the knowledge acquired in a particular discipline may constrain the form of expression, rather than the form constraining the content. And, most important, understanding the development of writing entails a better understanding of social contexts. The goals underlying the act of writing emerge as a function of specific social conditions. It is essential to understand those conditions and to understand the nature and content of other people's beliefs. An advance in theories of writing requires the description and integration of these knowledge types into a process-oriented framework.

REFERENCES

Anania, J. (1981). The effects of quality instruction on the cognitive and affective learning of students. Doctoral dissertation, University of Chicago.

Anderson, R.C. (1977). The notion of schemata and the educational enterprise. In R.C. Anderson, R.J. Spiro, & W.E. Montague (Eds.), *Schooling and the acquisition of knowledge*. Hillsdale, NJ: Erlbaum.

Applebee, A.N. (1982). Writing and learning in school settings. In P.M. Nystrand (Ed.), *What writers know: The language, process, and structure of written discourse*. New York: Academic Press.

Applebee, A.N. (1984). Writing and reasoning. *Review of Educational Research, 54* (4), 577–596.

Atwell, M.A. (1981, November). The evolution of text: The interrelationship of reading and writing in the composition process. Paper presented at the annual meeting of the National Council of Teachers of English, Boston.

Baker, L. (1979). Comprehension monitoring. Identifying and coping with text confusions. *Journal of Reading Behavior, 11*, 363–374.

Baker, L., & Brown, A.L. (1985). Cognitive monitoring in reading. In J. Flood (Ed.), *Understanding reading comprehension*. Newark, DE: International Reading Association.

Bereiter, C. (1980). The development of writing. In L. Gregg & E. Steinberg (Eds.), *Cognitive processes in writing*. Hillsdale, NJ: Erlbaum.

Bereiter, C., & Bird, M. (1985). Use of thinking aloud in identification and teaching of reading comprehension strategies. *Cognition and Instruction, 2*, 131–156.

Bereiter, C., & Scardamalia, M. (1982). From conversation to composition. The role of instruction in a developmental process. In R. Glaser (Ed.), *Advances in instructional psychology* (Vol. 2). Hillsdale, NJ: Erlbaum.

Bereiter, C., & Scardamalia, M. (1985). Cognitive coping strategies and the problem of inert knowledge. In S. Chipman, J. Segal, & R. Glaser (Eds.), *Thinking and learning skills* (Vol. 2). Hillsdale, NJ: Erlbaum.

Berkowitz, M.W. (1985). *Peer conflict and psychological growth: New directions in child development*. San Francisco: Jossey-Bass.

Bloom, B. (1984). The search for methods of instruction as effective as one-to-one tutoring. *Educational Leadership, 41* (4), 4–18.

Bransford, J.D., & Stein, B.S. (1984). *The ideal problem solver.* New York: Freeman.

Bransford, J.D., Vye, N.J., Adams, L.T., & Perfetto, G.A. (in press). Learning skills and the acquisition of knowledge. In R. Glaser (Ed.), *Advances in instructional psychology* (Vol. 3). Hillsdale, NJ: Erlbaum.

Brown, A.L. (1980). Metacognitive development and reading. In R. Spiro, B. Bruce, and W.F. Brewer (Eds.), *Theoretical issues in reading comprehension.* Hillsdale, NJ: Erlbaum.

Brown, A.L., Day, J. & Jones, R. (in press). The development of plans for summarizing text. *Child Development.*

Bruner, J. (1985). Narrative and paradigmatic modes of thought. In E. Eisner (Ed.), *Learning and teaching: Ways of knowing. Eighty-fourth yearbook of the National Society for the Study of Education, Part II.* Chicago: University of Chicago Press.

Burke, A.J. (1983). Students' potential for learning contrasted under tutorial and group approaches to instruction. Doctoral dissertation, University of Chicago.

Carey, S. (1985). *Conceptual change in childhood.* Cambridge, MA: MIT Press.

Charles, R.I., & Lester, F.K. (1984). An evaluation of a process oriented instructional program in mathematical problem solving in grades 5 and 7. *Journal for Research in Mathematics Education, 15* (1), 15–34.

Chi, M.T.H. (1978). Knowledge structures and memory development. In R.S. Siegler (Ed.), *Children's thinking: What develops.* Hillsdale, NJ: Erlbaum.

Chi, M.T.H. (1985). Interactive roles of knowledge and strategies in development. In S. Segal, S. Chipman, & R. Glaser (Eds.), *Thinking and Learning: Current research and open questions* (Vol. 2). Hillsdale, NJ: Erlbaum.

Chi, M.T.H. (in press). Representing knowledge and meta-knowledge: Implications for interpreting meta-memory research. In R.H. Kluwe & F.E. Weinart (Eds.), *Metacognition, motivation, and learning.* Hillsdale, NJ: Erlbaum.

Day, J.D. (1980). Training summarization skills: A comparison of teaching methods. Unpublished doctoral dissertation, University of Illinois, Champaign-Urbana.

Ericsson, K.A., & Simon, H.A. (1980). Verbal reports as data. *Psychological Review, 87* (3), 215–251.

Emig, J. (1971). *The composition process of twelfth graders.* Urbana, IL.: National Council of Teachers of English.

Fitzgerald, J., & Teasley, A. (1985). Effects of instruction in narrative structure on children's writing. Unpublished manuscript, University of North Carolina.

Flower, L. (in press). Taking thought: The role of conscious processing in the making of meaning. In E. Maimon, B. Nodine, & F. O'Connor (Eds.), *Thinking, Reasoning, and Writing.* New York: Longmans Press.

Flower, L., & Hayes, J.R. (1977). Problem solving strategies and the writing process. *College English, 39,* 449–461.

Flower, L., & Hayes, J.R. (1980). The cognition of discovery: Defining rhetorical problems. *College Composition and Communication, 30,* 21–32.

Flower, L., & Hayes, J.R. (1981). Plans that guide the composing process. In C.H. Frederiksen & J.F. Dominic (Eds.), *Writing: The nature, development, and teaching of written composition.* Hillsdale, NJ: Erlbaum.

Gick, M.L., & Holyoak, K.J. (1983). Schema induction and analogical transfer. *Cognitive Psychology, 15,* 1–38.

Glaser, R. (1984). Education and thinking: The role of knowledge. *American Psychologist, 39,* 93–104.

Goldman, S.R. (1982). Knowledge systems for realistic goals. *Discourse Processes, 5,* 279–303.

Graybeal, S.S., & Stodolsky, S.S. (1985). Peer work groups in elementary schools. *American Journal of Education, 93* (3), 409–428.

Graesser, A.C., & Murachver, T. (1985). Symbolic procedures of question answering. In A.C. Graesser & J.B. Black (Eds.), *The psychology of questions.* Hillsdale, NJ: Erlbaum.

Graves, D.H. (1981). *Writing: Teachers and children at work.* Durham, NH: Heinemann Educational Books.

Greeno, J.G. (1980). Trends in theory of knowledge for problem solving. In D.T. Tuma & F. Reif (Eds.), *Problem solving and education: Issues in teaching and research.* Hillsdale, NJ: Erlbaum.

Hayes, J.R., & Flower, L. (1980). Identifying the organization of the writing process. In L. Gregg & E.R. Steinberg (Eds.), *Cognitive processes in writing.* Hillsdale, NJ: Erlbaum.

Hillocks, G., Jr. (1982, June). Some issues in composition instruction. Paper presented at the Learning to Read and Write Conference, University of Chicago.

Hillocks, G., Jr. (1984). What works in teaching composition: A meta-analysis of experimental treatment studies. *American Journal of Education, 93* (1), 133–170.

Hillocks, G., Jr. (in press). *Research in written composition: New directions for teaching.* Urbana, IL.: National Council of Teachers of English.

Hume, A. (1983). Putting writing research into practice. *Elementary School Journal, 84* (1), 3–18.

Huttenlocher, J., & Smiley, P. (1985). Early word meanings: The case of object names. Unpublished manuscript, University of Chicago.

Huttenlocher, J., Smiley, P. & Charney, R. (1983). The emergence of action categories in the child: Evidence from verb meanings. *Psychological Review, 90* (1), 72–93.

Johnson, D.W., Maruyama, G., Johnson, R., & Nelson, D. (1981). Effects of cooperative, competitive, and individualistic goal structures on achievement: A meta-analysis. *Psychological Bulletin, 89,* 47–62.

Larkin, J., McDermott, J., Simon, D.P., & Simon, H.A. (1980). Expert and novice performance in solving physics problems, *Science, 208,* 1335–1342.

Lichtenstein, E.H., & Brewer, W.F. (1980). Memory for goal directed events. *Cognitive Psychology, 12,* 412–445.

Lindberg, M. (1980). The role of knowledge structures in the ontogeny of learning. *Journal of Experimental Child Psychology, 30,* 401–410.

Lytle, S.L. (1985). Comprehension styles of twelfth grade readers: What verbal protocols can and can't tell us. Paper presented at the American Educational Research Association, Chicago.

Mandler, J.M. (1983). Representation. In J.H. Flavell & E.M. Markman (Eds.), *Cognitive Development.* Vol. III of P. Mussen (Ed.), *Handbook of child psychology.* New York: Wiley.

Mandler, J.M. (1984). *Stories, scripts, and scenes: Aspects of schema theory.* Hillsdale, NJ: Erlbaum.

Markman, E. (1977). Realizing you don't understand: A preliminary investigation. *Child Development, 46,* 986–992.

Markman, E. (1979). Realizing you don't understand: Elementary school children's awareness of inconsistencies. *Child Development, 50,* 643–655.

Mayer, R.E. (1982). Memory for algebra story problems. *Journal of Experimental Psychology, 74,* 199–216.

McCutcheon, D., & Perfetti, C. (1982). Coherence and connectedness in the development of discourse production. In *New directions in cognitive models of discourse processing*, special issue of *Text, 2* (1–3).

Means, M.L., & Voss, J.F. (1985). Star wars: A developmental study of expert and novice knowledge structures. *Journal of Memory and Language, 24* (6), 746–757.

Meyer, B.F., & Freedle, R. (1984). Effects of discourse type on recall. *American Education Research Association Journal, 21* (1), 121–143.

Newell, A., & Simon, H.A, (1972). *Problem solving.* Englewood Cliffs, NJ: Prentice-Hall.

Nix, D. (1985). Notes on the efficacy of questions. In A.C. Graesser & J.B. Black (Eds.), *The psychology of questions.* Hillsdale, NJ: Erlbaum.

Olson, G.M., Duffy, S.A., & Mack, R.L. (1985). Thinking out loud as a method of studying real time comprehension processes. In D. Kieras & M. Just (Eds.), *New methods in the study of comprehension processes.* Hillsdale, NJ: Erlbaum.

Palincsar, A.M., & Brown, A.L. (1984). Reciprocal teaching of comprehension and comprehension fostering activities. *Cognition and Instruction, 1* (2), 117–175.

Perl, S. (1983). How teachers teach the writing process. *Elementary School Journal, 84* (1), 19–26.

Pennington, N., & Hastie, R. (in press). Evidence evaluation in complex decision making. *Journal of Personality and Social Psychology.*

Pianko, S. (1977). Reflection: A critical component of the composition process. *College Composition and Communication, 30* (3), 275–278.

Pianko, S. (1979). A description of the composing process of college freshman writers. *Research in the Teaching of English, 13,* 317–336.

Pichert, J. (1978). Sensitivity to what is important in prose. Unpublished doctoral dissertation, University of Illinois, Champaign-Urbana.

Reed, S., & Johnsen, J.A. (1977). Memory for problem solutions. In G.H. Bower (Ed.), *The psychology of learning and motivation* (Vol. 11, pp. 161–201). New York: Academic Press.

Resnick, L.B. (1985). Education and learning to think. Special report to the Commission on Behavioral and Social Sciences and Education, National Research Council.

Resnick, L.B. (in press). Constructing knowledge in school. In L.S. Lieben & D.H. Feldman (Eds.), *Development and learning: Conflict or congruence.* Hillsdale, NJ: Erlbaum.

Rumelhart, D.E. (1977). Understanding and summarizing brief stories. In D. LaBerge & J. Samuels (Eds.), *Basic processes in reading: Perception and comprehension.* Hillsdale, NJ: Erlbaum.

Scardamalia, M. (1981). How children cope with the cognitive demands of writing. In C.H. Frederiksen & J.F. Dominic (Eds.), *Writing: The nature, development, and teaching of written communication* (Vol. 2). Hillsdale, NJ: Erlbaum.

Scardamalia, M., & Paris, P. (1985). The function of explicit discourse knowledge in the development of text representations and composing strategies. *Cognition and Instruction, 2*(1), 1–39.

Schnotz, W. (1984). Comparative instructional text organization. In H. Mandl, N.L. Stein, & T. Trabasso (Eds.), *Learning and comprehension of text.* Hillsdale, NJ: Erlbaum.

Shantz, C., & Shantz, D. (1985). Conflict between children: Social cognitive and sociometric correlates. In M.W. Berkowitz (Ed.), *Peer conflict and psychological growth: New directions in child development.* San Francisco: Jossey-Bass.

Short, E.J., & Ryan, E.B. (1982). Meta-cognitive differences between skilled and less skilled readers: Remediating defects through story grammar. Unpublished manuscript, Frank Porter Graham Child Development Center, University of North Carolina.

Slavin, R.E. (1980). Cooperative learning. *Review of Educational Research, 50,* 315–342.

Slobin, D. (1978). A case study of early language awareness. In A. Sinclair, D.J. Jarvella, & W.J.M. Levelt (Eds.), *The child's concept of language.* New York: Springer-Verlag.

Stallard, C. (1974). An analysis of the writing behavior of good student writers. *Research in the Teaching of English, 8,* 206–218.

Stein, N.L. (1982). The definition of a story. *Pragmatics, 6,* 487–507.

Stein, N.L. (1983a). Methodological and conceptual issues in writing research. *The Elementary School Journal, 83* (1), 100–108.

Stein, N.L. (1983b) On the goals, functions, and knowledge of reading and writing. *Contemporary Educational Psychology, 8,* 261–292.

Stein, N.L. (1984, November). Critical issues in the development of literacy: Toward a theory of learning and instruction. *American Journal of Education, 93* (1), 171–199.

Stein, N.L. (1985). The development of storytelling skills. Unpublished manuscript, University of Chicago.

Stein, N.L., & Colomb, G. (1985). Learning and development: Institutional Proposal for the Center for the Study of Writing, submitted to the National Institute of Education.

Stein, N.L., & Eulau, S. (1985). Children's understanding of emotional episodes: A study of shifting emotions. Unpublished manuscript, University of Chicago.

Stein, N.L., & Garman, D. (1986). The role of episodic structure and causal relations on the composition of summaries. Unpublished manuscript, University of Chicago.

Stein, N.L., & Glenn, C.G. (1979). An analysis of story comprehension in elementary school children. In R.O. Freedle (Ed.), *Advances in discourse processes: Vol. 2. New directions in discourse processing.* Norwood, NJ: Ablex.

Stein, N.L., & Glenn, C.G. (1982). Children's concept of time: The development of a story schema. In W.J. Friedman (Ed.), *The developmental psychology of time.* New York: Academic Press.

Stein, N.L., & Goldman, S. (1981). Children's knowledge about social situations: From causes to consequences. In S. Asher & J. Gottman (Eds.), *The development of friendship.* New York: Cambridge University Press.

Stein, N.L., & Hillocks, G., Jr. (1985, January). Learning and development: Planning proposal for the Center for the Study of Writing, submitted to the National Institute of Education.

Stein, N.L., & Jewett, J. (1986). A conceptual analysis of the meaning of basic negative emotions: Implications for a theory of development. In C.E. Izard & P. Read (Eds.), *Measurement of emotion in infants and children* (Vol. 2). New York: Cambridge University Press.

Stein, N.L., & Kilgore, K. (1985). The story concept: A test of alternative definitions. Unpublished manuscript, University of Chicago.

Stein, N.L., Kilgore, K., & Policastro, M. (1986). The development of the story concept: From social to narrative scheme. Unpublished manuscript, University of Chicago.

Stein, N.L., & Levine, L. (1986). Thinking about feelings: The development and use of emotional knowledge. In R.E. Snow & M. Farr (Eds.), *Aptitude, learning, and instruction: Vol. 3. Cognition, conation, and affect.* Hillsdale, NJ: Erlbaum.

Stein, N.L., & Levine, L. (1985). The development of knowledge structures underlying the meaning of happiness, anger, and sadness. Unpublished manuscript, University of Chicago.

Stein, N.L., & Nezworski, M.T. (1978). The effect of organization and instructional set on story memory. *Discourse Processes, 1*, 177–193.

Stein, N.L., & Policastro, M. (1984). The concept of a story: A comparison between children's and teachers' perspectives. In H. Mandl, N.L. Stein, & T. Trabasso (Eds.), *Learning and comprehension of text*. Hillsdale, NJ: Erlbaum.

Stein, N.L., & Salgo, D. (1984). The relationship between explicit discourse knowledge and storytelling skills. Paper presented at the annual meeting of the Psychonomics Society, San Antonio, TX.

Stein, N.L., & Salgo, D. (1986). The development of structure, goal-plans, and themes in children's generated stories.

Stein, N.L., & Trabasso, T. (1982a). What's in a story: An approach to comprehension and instruction. In R. Glaser (Ed.), *Advances in instructional psychology* (Vol. 2). Hillsdale, NJ: Erlbaum.

Stein, N.L., & Trabasso, T. (1982b). Children's understanding of stories: A basis for moral judgment and resolution. In C.J. Brainerd & M. Pressley (Eds.), *Verbal processes in children*. New York: Springer-Verlag.

Stein, N.L., & Trabasso, T. (1985). The search after meanings: Comprehension and comprehension monitoring. In F. Morrison, C. Lord, & D. Keating (Eds.), *Advances in applied developmental psychology* (Vol. 2). New York: Academic Press.

Thorndyke, P. (1977). Cognitive structures in comprehension memory and discourse. *Cognitive Psychology, 9*, 97–110.

Toulmin, S. (1969). *The uses of argument*. Cambridge, MA: MIT Press.

Toulmin, S., Rieke, R, & Janik, A. (1979). *Reasoning*. New York: Macmillan.

Trabasso, T., Stein, N.L., & Johnson, L.R. (1981). Children's knowledge of events: A causal analysis of story structure. In G. Bower (Ed.), *Learning and motivation*, Vol. 15. New York: Academic Press.

Trabasso, T., Secco, T., & van den Broek, P. (1984). Causal cohesion and story coherence. In H. Mandl, N.L. Stein, & T. Trabasso (Eds.), *Learning and comprehension of text*. Hillsdale, NJ: Erlbaum.

Trabasso, T., & Sperry, L.L. (1985). Causal relatedness and importance of story events. *Journal of Memory and Language, 24*, 595–611.

Trabasso, T., & van den Broek, P. (1985). Causal thinking and the representation of narrative events. *Journal of Memory and Language, 24*, 612–630.

van den Broek, P. (1985). Judging the importance of events in stories: The influence of structural variation and grade level. Unpublished doctoral dissertation, University of Chicago.

van Dijk, T.A., & Kintech, W. (1977). Cognitive psychology and discourse: Recalling and summarizing stories. In W.U. Dressler (Ed.), *Trends in text linguistics*. New York: De Gruyter.

Voss, J.F., Greene, T.R., Post, T.A., & Penner, B.C. (1983). Problem solving in the social sciences. In G.H. Bower (Ed.), *The psychology of learning and motivation: Vol. 17. Advances in research theory*. New York: Academic Press.

Wellman, H. (in press). The growth of meta-cognitive skill. *Child Development*.

Worrall, N., & Athey, L. (1985). Developmental changes in evaluating the importance of story elements. Unpublished manuscript, University of London, Institute of Education.

Chapter 8

Levels of Inquiry into the Nature of Expertise in Writing

CARL BEREITER and MARLENE SCARDAMALIA
Centre for Applied Cognitive Science
Ontario Institute for Studies in Education

Research on writing is notable for its extreme diversity and for the lack of interconnections. Scardamalia and Bereiter (1985b) describe nine separate strands of research that are currently prominent: research on the early development of written symbolism, discourse analysis, story grammar, basic writers, the "new" rhetoric, writing "apprehension," classroom practices, teacher and peer response to writing, and the nature of the composing process. To say that these strands are separate is to say that there is little cross-referencing of research across strands and that findings from one strand seldom impinge on findings from another. Undoubtedly this is partly a reflection of the newness of many of these lines of research, but it is also a reflection of the pre-paradigmatic state of writing research (Emig, 1978)—the lack of agreed-upon constraints on theoretical questions and answers.

The Levels of Inquiry schema (Bereiter & Scardamalia, 1983b) provides a framework within which research on various questions, using diverse methods, can be brought into conjunction. A major reason for developing this schema was the belief that the current diversity in kinds of inquiry into writing has led to artificial and unnecessary polarities. As in most other fields, research into writing ranges from kinds of inquiry that stay close to everyday concerns and to the lived experience of writing to inquiry that addresses writing at quite an abstract or formal level. It is pointless, however, to debate the relative merits of these approaches or to accept the inevitability of a trade-off between phenomenological richness and generality, between wholism and rigor. Rather, it should be possible for research of a variety of kinds to feed into a common effort at understanding. That is what the Levels of Inquiry schema is intended to support. The schema is prescriptive as well as descriptive. It is proposed that research on writing should go on at different levels of inquiry and that there should be a systematic relationship between studies at different levels.

Table 1 provides a sketch of the Levels of Inquiry schema as applied to research on the composing process. The six levels are ordered on a dimension that runs from subjective reflection on the actual experience of writing through successively more abstract levels of analysis. Two central premises of the schema are (a) that findings at one level often give rise to questions that must be answered by moving to a more abstract or formal level and (b) that this process is cyclical: research needs to keep returning to Level 1 in order to renew contact with phenomenal reality and to integrate what has been found out with common sense or tacit knowledge. The schema emphatically does *not* reflect an ordering on the basis of levels of sophistication or rigor. Such virtues can be found in varying degrees at all levels. Neither should the levels be confused with a continuum of basic to applied research. Both basic and applied research (however these might be conceived) can go on at any level, and as we shall see some of the most practical findings, in the form of instructional innovations, can arise from Level 6 (simulation), which is the farthest removed from ordinary experience.

In this chapter, the Levels of Inquiry schema is applied to inquiry into the nature of expertise in writing. We use the term "expertise" here in the non-evaluative sense that is typical in contemporary studies of expert-novice differences. That is, experts are identified by external criteria: prize-winners, people who earn their livings by the skill, people who earn higher grades in writing courses, or simply people who are at a more advanced stage of education than those designated as novices. *How* they differ from those designated as novices, whether in fact experts have anything intrinsically in common at all, is not presupposed but is rather the object of investigation.

Even a superficial analysis indicates that the nature of expertise in writing can be approached in a variety of ways. There are the well-charted routes of rhetoric and literary criticism, which examine expertise from the standpoint of literary products and the qualities and strategies they reveal. There is the route of individual differences research, which looks for traits that distinguish the expert from the inexpert writer. And then one can look at processes—at what expert writers *do* that may be different from what others do. Processes may be overt—for instance, the kinds and extent of revision a writer carries out—or they may be covert, perhaps not even accessible to the writer's own awareness, but possibly inferable by crafty experimental means. Our task here is not to itemize these and other ways of approaching the topic, but rather to show how such diverse lines of inquiry might lead to a coherent understanding of the nature of expertise in writing.

LEVEL 1: REFLECTIVE INQUIRY

The database for reflective inquiry is one's accumulated experience. Hence those who are in a favored position for reflective inquiry about writing are those who have extensive experience as writers or as teachers of writing. We

Table 1
Levels of Inquiry in Research on the Composing Process

Level	Characteristic Questions	Typical Methods
Level 1: Reflective inquiry	What is the nature of this phenomenon? What are the problems? What do the data mean?	Informal observation Introspection Literature review Discussion, argument, private reflection
Level 2: Empirical variable testing	Is this assumption correct? What is the relation between x and y?	Factorial analysis of variance Correlation analysis Surveys Coding of compositions
Level 3: Text analysis	What makes this text seem the way it does? What rules could the writer be following?	Error analysis Story grammar analysis Thematic analysis
Level 4: Process description	What is the writer thinking? What pattern or system is revealed in the writer's thoughts while composing?	Thinking aloud protocols Clinical-experimental interviews Retrospective reports Videotape recordings
Level 5: Theory-embedded experimentation	What is the nature of the cognitive system responsible for these observations? Which process model is right?	Experimental procedures tailored to questions Chronometry Interference
Level 6: Simulation	How does the cognitive mechanism work? What range of natural variations can the model account for? What remains to be accounted for?	Computer simulation Simulation by intervention

have before us a book titled *How to Write: By Those Who Can* (Watson, undated). It consists entirely of comments by published writers about writing. These comments, though often fascinating, reveal striking limitations in what "Those Who Can" are able to convey about the nature of their expertise. On the matter of style, for instance, we are told by Julius Caesar that "Choice of words is the origin of eloquence" and by Arnold Bennett that "Good style is not a bird that can be brought down with a shot-gun." Only one, William Cobbett, comes forth with a usable principle: "The first word that occurs is always the best." But Cobbett, a political writer of the Romantic era, was better known for the violence of his opinions than for the excellence of his style.

Educators have developed their own notions about the nature of competence in writing, presumably through reflecting on their experience as writers and teachers. Rose (1981) has critically examined the implicit theories of writing that have found their way into composition textbooks. Typical of the genre, before a new wave of research and thinking about writing began to have an effect, is the 1963 edition of Warriner's *English Grammar and Composition: Grade 11*. Writing a composition is divided into seven steps: choosing and limiting the subject, assembling materials, organizing materials, outlining, writing the first draft, revising, and writing the final draft. Expertise, the text seems to say, consists of skill and care in executing each of these steps.

Rose (1981) credits cognitive research—in particular the process description research that we will discuss as Level 4—with having revealed the falsity of such conceptions of the writing process. The point we wish to make here, however, is that Level 1 inquiry is fully sufficient to have replaced the old step-by-step conception of writing with a more valid one. A good case in point is an essay by Donald Murray (1978), reflecting on his own experience as a writer.

Murray begins by declaring, in accord with many other writers, that "Writing is rewriting" (p. 85). Thus, what figures as but one out of seven steps in the Warriner (1963) scheme is elevated to the central position. "Rewriting is the difference between the dilettante and the artist, the amateur and the professional, the unpublished and the published," Murray goes on to say, thus claiming that rewriting is the essence of expertise.

Although Murray recognizes stages in writing not unlike those of Warriner, he also perceives that "The writing process is too experimental and exploratory to be contained in a rigid definition; writers move back and forth through all stages of the writing process as they search for meaning and then attempt to clarify it" (p. 86). This idea has been formalized by Hayes and Flower (1980) as the recursive property of the composing process. The most original contribution of Murray's essay is a distinction between "internal" and "external" revision. External revision is the familiar marking up and recasting of text to ready it for presentation to an audience. Internal revision, however, is carried out for the writer's own benefit and is mainly concerned with understanding more fully what one has said and developing it further. This idea has been formalized by Scardamalia and Bereiter (in press) as a property of a "knowledge-transforming" as opposed to a "knowledge-telling" model of writing.

The distinction between external and internal revision is of interest in light of general considerations of the nature of expertise. In a variety of expert-novice comparisons from different domains, a recurrent finding is that novices attend to the external or surface features of phenomena, whereas experts attend to underlying structures (Glaser, 1984). External revision, which is the only kind of revision that shows, is naturally therefore the province of the novice, whereas internal revision, as Murray asserts, occupies the larger part of the expert's attention.

We have dwelt on Murray's essay to indicate the important contributions that Level 1 inquiry can make to understanding writing and writing competence. Similar demonstrations could be made by examining the reflections of writers like Galbraith (1981) and Smith (1982) or, in a more educational vein, those of Moffett (1968) and Elbow (1973). It appears that the database available to writers, derived from their own experience, is very substantial. We doubt that reflection on personal experience could ever produce comparable insights about reading, for instance, because much of the reading process is too rapid and automatic to leave much of a trace in memory.

The experiential database available to writers does have limits, however, and these are the limits of Level 1 inquiry as a means of understanding the nature of expertise in writing. Murray (1978) generalizes with caution to other professional writers, recognizing that he has only anecdotal evidence to support such generalizations. More systematic inventorying of writer's self-reports would take one at least to a Level 2 inquiry. It is also true, of course, that one does not have unobstructed access even to the data of one's own experience. As it happens, Donald Murray, whose Level 1 inquiry we have been examining, also served as the subject of a Level 4 process description study (Berkenkotter, 1983). Our discussion of Level 4 inquiry will compare what that study revealed with what Murray's independent reflections had educed. The great dark spot left by Level 1 inquiry into writing, however, is what goes on in the minds of inexpert writers. Do they in fact only carry on external revision (if that), or do they also engage in internal revision but with less awareness or effect? As we shall see, such questions are extremely difficult to answer, and require integration of findings from all levels of inquiry.

LEVEL 2: EMPIRICAL VARIABLE TESTING

One way to approach the question, "What is the nature of expertise in writing?" is by translating it into the question, "What variables distinguish relatively more expert from relatively less expert writers?" In so doing, one has reformulated the question in a manner appropriate to Level 2 inquiry. Level 2 inquiry may be defined as the investigation of how one or more variables (e.g., reading ability, syntactic complexity) are related to one or more other variables (e.g., writing ability, content complexity). A great deal of writing research has been of this kind. Indeed, an influential monograph intended to raise the quality of writing research (Braddock, Lloyd-Jones, & Schoer, 1963) dealt with it exclusively, leaving the impression that Level 2 inquiry and scientific inquiry are coextensive.

Level 2 research is beset by a number of inherent difficulties, to such an extent that its popularity among behavioral scientists has declined drastically since the days of the Braddock et al. (1963) monograph. One of these inherent difficulties is the proliferation of variables. Almost any aspect of the human condition that one can imagine might be hypothesized to have some relationship to writing ability. Thus, if the aspect can be measured in some way, one has the makings of a Level 2 investigation.

To restrain the proliferation of variables, it is customary to insist that Level 2 researchers have some coherent rationale for the selection of variables and not simply play hunches. As Mosenthal (1983) shows, however, there are initial decisions about the selection of variables that arbitrarily limit the kinds of rationales that can subsequently be constructed. Mosenthal proposes a tetrahedral model in which writing competence is represented by five classes of variables (or "contexts," in Mosenthal's terminology): task, writer, setting, materials, and situation organizers (audience and/or assigner of the writing task). But no investigator can deal with all five contexts, Mosenthal argues. Instead, what happens is that the researcher selects one favorite context out of the five and uses it as the source of causal variables and selects another favorite context and uses it as the source of effect variables.

Mosenthal (1983) optimistically suggests that, out of an accumulation of such limited studies, an understanding of writing competence as a whole will emerge. As Cronbach (1975) noted, however, as soon as one begins considering the interactions among variables, higher and higher order interactions are generated. The result is a combinatorial explosion of relationships that quickly exceeds any possibility of human comprehension. It is not clear how Level 2 research can avoid this explosion except by arbitrarily limiting the scope of inquiry.

Writing research has seen a host of such limited studies, in which one of the variables is a measure of writing performance and the other variable is some characteristic of the writer, such as age or score on an ability test, or some characteristic of the text, such as clause length or number of revisions. As far as understanding the nature of expertise in writing is concerned, the results of these investigations are unilluminating. Good writers tend to be better at everything than poor writers. This result reflects another of the inherent weaknesses of Level 2 research when it is applied to questions of competence—the problem of positive manifold. Positive manifold is the tendency, so named by Spearman (1927), for all human abilities to be positively correlated. It is a good bet that, if enough cases were tested, good writers would be found to be significantly better than poor writers at tying their shoelaces.[1]

These observations seem to suggest that Level 2 research has nothing to contribute to studying the nature of expertise in writing. Indeed, we believe it has much less to contribute than the Braddock et al. (1963) monograph, for instance, implies; but there is a role for Level 2 research that cannot be supplanted by research at any other level. Level 1 reflection, except when it is entirely introspective, relies on empirical generalizations about the world that are often questionable. The job of Level 2 research is to provide dependable empirical generalizations.

The "writing crisis" that provided the impetus for the current wave of research on writing was fired by an apparently widespread conviction that competence in writing was declining (*Newsweek,* 1975). But was it really? Human beings are notoriously poor at deriving and using base rates. Instead, they tend to generalize from memorable instances (Tversky & Kahneman, 1974). Fortunately, the National Assessment of Educational Progress (1975, 1980a, 1980b, 1980c) was able to provide data on trends in writing performance based on nationwide sampling and carefully controlled scoring procedures. These data did, in fact, show evidence of declines across the 1969–1979 period, especially in higher-order variables of organization and effectiveness.

The National Assessment findings are subject to the typical objections that can be brought against Level 2 studies. One can object to the particular variables used and to the manner of data collection (would results be different if students wrote under more motivating conditions?). One can also question what the numerical magnitudes mean. With large samples, even very small trends can be statistically significant. But are they of any consequence? Such a question is typically unanswerable. The point we wish to make, however, is that in spite of these weaknesses Level 2 studies provide an important supplement to generalizations based on informal recollection of personal experience.

Another valuable role for Level 2 research is in testing assumed causal relationships. On the basis of the great importance attached by expert writers to revision (as discussed in the preceding section), one might infer that revising is a key to writing improvement and that encouraging students to revise more would be a sure way to improve their writing. As it happens, however, these causal inferences have not received resounding support from empirical research. Several investigators of high school and university-level writers found that students who revised more did not produce better compositions

(Bridwell, 1980; Faigley & Witte, 1981; Hansen, 1978). Bracewell, Scardamalia, and Bereiter (1978) found that at grade 8, students' revisions actually tended to lower the rated quality of their compositions. Beach (1979) also found that instructional treatments designed to increase revision activity did not improve writing quality.

One's response to these findings might be, "Well, of course, revision in and of itself isn't necessarily a good thing. It depends on having a purpose and on having the necessary skills and knowledge." If Level 2 research did nothing more than induce people to temper their pronouncements in this way it would serve a useful purpose. However, significant Level 2 inquiry usually has the effect of raising questions that call for further research. The cited findings concerning revision raise, for instance, the question of under what conditions (if any) revisions by students tend to be successful, and the question of what characteristics distinguish successful from unsuccessful revisers. These are questions that lead to further Level 2 inquiry. But one might also ask whether there is some pattern or apparent method to revisions that are judged to be detrimental. This is a question calling for Level 3 text analysis. Alternatively, one might ask whether unsuccessful revisers follow different cognitive strategies from successful revisers—a question that could be pursued through Level 4 process description. Finally, one may ask whether revision is a theoretically useful notion at all for understanding writing competence. Is there any essential difference between rethinking content and language *after* text has been written and rethinking them *before* words are put on paper (Scardamalia & Bereiter, 1985b)? Such a question cannot even be satisfactorily answered by describing the mental activities of writers. There needs to be a principled basis for deciding what counts as one process and what counts as another, and this requires formulating and testing theories at Level 5. Level 2 research, it seems, can seldom provide satisfactory answers to questions about writing competence, but it can be of value both in raising questions and in ruling out overly simple answers.

LEVEL 3: TEXT ANALYSIS

We have mentioned the fallacy of equating study of the composing process with thinking-aloud protocol analysis. It is equally fallacious to equate text analysis with study of the product as opposed to study of the process. Matsuhashi and Quinn (1984) review contributions that discourse analysis can make to a cognitive understanding of writing. It is true that a finished text reveals little about the process of its creation—and the better the text the less it reveals (cf. Flower, 1979). Nevertheless, analysis of texts can reveal a great deal about the knowledge that must have been used by the writer, and understanding the nature of the expert's knowledge is a large part of understanding the nature of expertise (Glaser, 1984).

Level 3 inquiry may be defined as a search for implicit principles in texts.

In studying the texts of novice college-level writers, Flower (1979) identified an implicit principle underlying what she called "writer-based" prose. The principle is that of presenting ideas by recapitulating their development in the mind of the writer. It is not suggested that this principle is consciously entertained by writers. How the principle gets implemented in the composing processes of novice writers will be taken up in the discussion of inquiry at Level 5. But even without an understanding of the process, it is still significant to know that such a principle does characterize novice writing and serves to distinguish it from expert writing.

The study of rhetoric, on the other hand, may be thought of as Level 3 inquiry aimed at identifying the implicit principles that characterize expert writing. This is most evident in modern rhetorical research that has attempted to place its findings within a cognitive psychological framework. Beaugrande and Colby (1979) and Brewer (1980, 1985) have approached the much-researched issue of story structure with the question of what makes stories interesting, involving, worth telling and listening to. The result has been analyses of how effects are achieved by manipulations of sequence and of what information is given or withheld. Although the resulting principles are used to characterize stories, they must surely have some counterpart in the knowledge of the skilled story writer. Otherwise it is unlikely that writers could with any consistency produce mystery stories that arouse puzzlement and curiosity or adventure stories that arouse suspense. Again, it cannot be assumed that the knowledge in the mind of the writer has precisely the form of principles given by text analysis, but it must be functionally equivalent. There is, in fact, evidence that conscious knowledge of how suspense is created in stories develops with age and is related to ability to produce suspensefulness (Bereiter & Scardamalia, 1984).

Not all research involving texts is Level 3 inquiry, of course. Counting the number of misspelled words, or the lengths of clauses, or the number of cohesive ties is a matter of measuring certain variables that happen to be extracted from texts and that will normally be used in Level 2 research (for instance, studying age trends in the length of syntactic units). Historically most of the educational and developmental research using texts has been Level 2 research (see, for instance, the review by Blount, 1973). The potential for Level 3 inquiry to identify underlying principles has only recently begun to be pursued by educational researchers.

An example of a systematic study that exploits the possibilities of Level 3 text analysis is provided by Bracewell and Frederiksen (1985). Oral stories produced by children in grades 2 and 4 were analyzed. One kind of analysis concerned story structure and included the demarkation of episodes and of events within episodes. Another kind of analysis concerned topicalization, which is a matter of what information is presented first in a sentence (e.g., "We went to the party afterwards," versus "Afterwards we went to the party").

Conventional statistical treatment of variables drawn from these analyses might have led to a Level 2 study testing for grade-level differences in the variables. However, Bracewell and Frederiksen's particular interest was in whether children used topicalization to signal shifts between episodes. In brief, the finding was that children at grade 4 did but children at grade 2 did not.

This finding is intriguing with respect to the development of expertise in writing. There was already substantial evidence that by grade 2 children's writing exhibits both structural knowledge of stories and knowledge of lexical and syntactic patterns relevant to textual cohesion (King & Rentel, 1981). What is not clear is whether any of this knowledge is used strategically, that is, for effect. Bock (1982) has argued that in ordinary discourse syntactic variations (which make options available in topicalization) serve to facilitate production. They make it possible to begin uttering a sentence without having planned how it will end. On this view, strategic use of topicalization would represent a significant step beyond ordinary expediency-based choices of what to say in what order. The Frederiksen and Bracewell results suggest that somewhere between grade 2 and 4 syntactic choices begin to be influenced by considerations of text structure, which seems to be a remarkable step in the direction of strategic control of an otherwise automatic process.

Whether fourth graders are actually using text structure knowledge in making syntactic choices or whether some less sophisticated process accounts for their performance is a question not likely to be answerable by Level 3 inquiry. It is not likely to be answerable by Level 4 process description either, but will require Level 5 theory-testing. Nevertheless, it should be clear that Level 3 research concerned with identifying the competence implicit in written texts can play a very important role in understanding the nature of expertise in writing.

LEVEL 4: PROCESS DESCRIPTION

Description of the composing process, especially through the use of thinking-aloud protocols, has probably been the most popular innovation in writing research in recent years. From an educational standpoint, process descriptions offer the promise of describing expertise in terms of actions rather than states or achievements—actions that students might be taught to carry out. The actions, of course, are mainly mental actions, and that is what has led to the practice of having people think aloud while they compose. Thinking aloud is not the only source of data on processes, however. Ordinary observation can provide information on such things as extent and timing of rereading and revision (Stallard, 1974). Fine-grained analysis of pauses in writing, when combined with text analysis and retrospective reports by writers, can be used for quite penetrating inquiry into local processes of composition (Matsuhashi & Quinn, 1984). With children, thinking-aloud protocols are often scanty, more interactive procedures being required to bring thoughts to light. Scardamalia and Bereiter (1983) describe a variety of interactive methods, such as involving the child in concrete activities that provide more specific events to comment on and introducing procedural changes that allow the child to compare current experience with past experience.

There has been a great deal of concern about the trustworthiness of various self-reporting procedures for getting at mental processes during composition (Boice, 1985; Clifford, 1984; Hayes & Flower, 1983; Tomlinson, 1984). That self-reports give a limited picture of what goes on in the mind seems to be granted by everyone. Whether self-reporting alters the processes it is meant to expose is less certain, although there is some evidence to this effect (Black, Galambos, & Reiser, 1984). It is not clear, however, why these are taken as such serious drawbacks. As far as explaining the composing process is concerned, no data can be taken at face value; it is theories, not data, that do the explaining, and data do not need to have perfect validity in order to be useful in suggesting and testing theories. (See the subsequent discussion of Level 5 inquiry.)

With respect to educational applications, it may well be that the limitations of Level 4 inquiry and the limitations of instruction coincide advantageously. Process-tracing research gets at those mental activities that are most accessible to the writer during the actual process of writing. If students are deliberately to incorporate expert strategies into their composing processes, they also must be able to have access to them during the ongoing process of writing. Therefore, although Level 4 research may identify only certain components of expertise, these may be the only components that are directly teachable, the rest having to be acquired by less direct means. (For a related discussion with supporting data pertaining to reading comprehension strategies, see Bereiter & Bird, 1985.)

An interesting test case on the value of process description research is provided by Donald Murray, whose essay on internal and external revision was examined as an example of Level 1 inquiry. Subsequently Murray served as the subject in a thinking-aloud study of composing (Berkenkotter, 1983). In a face-off between the two studies there is no contest: Murray's essay is vastly more insightful and instructive than the protocol analysis, which tells us in some detail what Murray did but very little about why or how. Within the Levels of Inquiry schema, however, one should not be asking whether one level of inquiry is better than another; one should ask whether one level adds anything to the other. And, on this account, a positive answer seems justified.

The thinking-aloud protocol showed that much of what Murray called internal revision occurred before a first draft was completed. This finding is in accord with other protocol analyses of expert writers (e.g., Flower & Hayes, 1980a) and contrary to Murray's own earlier report (1978). It would appear, as Murray himself suggests (1983), that his earlier formulation of internal revision was unduly influenced by a conception of writing as taking place in distinct phases. The other finding of special interest was that Murray did much less searching for the meaning of what he was saying than his essay would imply. Murray (1983) reported surprise and concern over this finding, which suggested that he had become so facile at writing about certain things that the writing was no longer an occasion for reflection and discovery. The issue of how experts manage to resist slickness, rigidity, staleness, and other negative effects of long practice is an important one for further research.

A study that shows how Level 4 inquiry can extend our understanding of expertise in writing is a protocol analysis study by Flower and Hayes (1980a) that compared the planning activities of expert and novice writers. The main finding of this study was that novice writers tended to take the writing assignment as given whereas expert writers constructed an elaborate representation of the writing problem, which contained a number of constraints in addition to those given by the assignment. The assignment was to write about one's job for an article for *Seventeen* magazine. Whereas the novices approached this as a relatively straightforward expository task, the experts elaborated on what would be required to make the article interesting or meaningful to such a magazine's audience and discovered that they were facing quite a formidable problem. One might say that the problem was implicit in the assignment and that the experts were simply better at recognizing it, but that is not how the process looks as revealed by the protocols. The protocols show a more active kind of work going on, which is better represented by saying that the experts *constructed* the elaborated problem representation, using the assignment as a basis.

The Flower and Hayes (1980a) article is aptly titled "The Cognition of Discovery." Murray (1978) and many other writers have testified to the phenomenon of discovering meaning through the composing process, but how the phenomenon is brought about has not been described in sufficiently procedural terms to suggest what one might try teaching to a novice. The Flower and Hayes analysis does not, of course, yield a step-by-step procedure, but it does identify a more definite goal to put before the student than had previously been available—the goal of elaborating on the writing problem to be solved.

This study illustrates another more general point about Level 4 inquiry. The findings concerning problem representation did not arise from a simple recording and cataloguing of observations but depended instead on interpreting those observations within a conceptual framework provided by cognitive research on problem solving. Other conceptual frameworks might prove equally useful, but some such framework appears to be essential. Many of the complaints against thinking-aloud studies seem to be based on the premise that the composing process, if properly revealed, should be immediately accessible to common sense. Level 4 researchers may have encouraged such a fallacy by speaking of thinking aloud as providing a window on the composing process. More cautiously, Matsuhashi and Quinn (1984, p. 332) refer to text analysis as providing "clues for understanding the writing process." That would seem to be the strongest claim that should be made for process-tracing methods as well.

LEVEL 5: THEORY-EMBEDDED EXPERIMENTATION

Inquiry at any level may be guided by theory. A large part of the research done at Level 4 has been carried out within the framework of Flower and Hayes's (1981) theory of the composing process. The Level 3 text analyses of Bracewell and Fredericksen were guided by linguistic theory and by their own theory of the nature of text production. Level 2 studies often mine all kinds of theories as sources of variables to investigate. And by Murray's own report (1983), his 1978 Level 1 inquiry was influenced by a sequential stage theory of the composing process. What distinguishes Level 5 inquiry, therefore, is not that it is guided by or otherwise *makes use of* theory. Rather, what distinguishes Level 5 inquiry is that the research is actually derived from a theory and serves to extend or test the theory.

Generally speaking, in order for a theory to have generative power, it must constitute a proposed solution to a theoretical problem. The literature on writing as a whole is remarkable for its lack of mention of theoretical problems— for its lack of *how* or *why* questions. However, one fruitful question has been raised. This is the question of how writers manage to deal with the multitude of constraints that require more-or-less simultaneous attention in writing— syntactic constraints, text-structure constraints, audience-related constraints, constraints related to meaning and purpose, and so on (Flower & Hayes, 1980b; Scardamalia, 1981). Level 4 analyses of competent writers suggested that planning is the major means they use to keep from being overwhelmed by constraints during the process of generating text, since planning allows them to deal with a few constraints at a time in a coherent fashion (Flower & Hayes, 1980b). Revising and rewriting also permit constraints to be dealt with serially rather than all at once. But these answers further raise the question of how novice writers function who do little planning or revision and for whom the overall processing load of writing would be expected to be high, because component processes would not have been compiled or automatized (Scardamalia, 1981).

The "knowledge-telling" model (Bereiter & Scardamalia, 1983a, 1985, in press; Scardamalia & Bereiter, 1985b) has been developed as a proposed solution to the question of how it is possible for novice writers to produce coherent, well-structured prose, given no more high-level planning than is revealed in their thinking-aloud protocols and planning notes (Burtis, Bereiter, Scardamalia, & Tetroe, 1983). The very framing of the problem immediately raises the question of whether it is true that young writers do little planning or whether their planning simply does not show under ordinary procedures of Level 4 inquiry. But this question itself requires theoretical formulation before it can be pursued. If one looks for more indirect indicators of planning activity, one needs a theoretical basis for deciding what should count or not count as an indicator. Thus it is a model or theory as a whole that needs to be constructed and tested, not isolated theoretical questions. That is the role of Level 5 inquiry.

Level 5 inquiry may be illustrated by one study designed to test implications of the knowledge-telling model. Briefly, the knowledge-telling model presents a process for generating text content that uses only two kinds of cues for retrieving content from memory—topical cues based on knowledge of what the text is supposed to be about and structural cues based on implicit knowledge of discourse types (narrative, argument, comparison, etc.). The model therefore implies that higher-level kinds of knowledge, such as knowledge of goals or of main ideas, even though these might be available to the writer, cannot be called upon by the composing process. How does one test the fit of such a model to real-life novices, assuming that one is unwilling to take at face value the absence of high-level planning statements from their protocols?

One test is presented by Scardamalia and Paris (1985, Study 2). The reasoning behind this study was that if higher-level representations play a role in composing, then they should also play a role in recall of things about the text. This expectation follows from reconstructive views of memory, which assign an important role to top-down processes in the recall of meaningful material. Accordingly, mature and immature writers were asked to think aloud as they tried to recall various things about texts they had previously written—actual language, intentions, main ideas, and structure, as well as particular facts such as how many times they used a certain key word and how much of the text was devoted to certain functions. The interest of the study was not in accuracy of recall but in the kinds of knowledge appealed to in the process of trying to recall. According to the knowledge-telling model, novice writers should rely mainly on recall of specific language and content, with some use of structural knowledge, but only the more expert writers should advert to intentions and main ideas, since only they would have made explicit use of such information in creating the text in the first place. The findings of the study precisely bore out these predictions.

Several observations may be made about this study that apply generally to Level 5 inquiry. First, the study only makes sense within a theoretical context. This is the most marked distinction between Level 2 and Level 5 research. On the surface Level 2 and Level 5 studies may be similar; both kinds typically involve empirical tests of relationships among quantified variables. But in Level 2 research, the variables must be significant and meaningful in their own right. In Level 5 research the variables draw their meaning by inference from theoretical propositions. Although on the surface the Scardamalia and Paris (1985) study is about memory for text, it is not in fact motivated by an interest in how well people are able to remember what they write, and it would no doubt have been designed differently had it been so motivated. As it is, the study must stand or fall on its relevance to the theoretical issues it was designed to test.

A second observation is that, notwithstanding their origins in a particular theory, individual Level 5 studies are usually open to alternative explanations. The results just described might be explained, for instance, on grounds that immature writers give less complete recall protocols or have less sophisticated recall strategies, and that therefore the results cannot be taken as convincing support for the knowledge-telling model. This is just another way of saying there are no crucial experiments. A theory gains strength over series of experiments if it is able to make good predictions whereas different and ad hoc counterexplanations are required to explain away the results of each individual experiment (Lakatos, 1970). In the case of the knowledge-telling model, there has accumulated quite a variety of supporting evidence that would have to be accounted for coherently by a rival explanation (Bereiter & Scardamalia, in press).

It could perhaps be argued that Level 5 research on writing is premature—on the premise that any explanatory theory that could be constructed in the present state of knowledge is bound to be limited, simplistic, and wrong. The premise is undoubtedly correct, but the conclusion that Level 5 research is premature does not follow from it. In healthy domains of scientific inquiry, theories are not usually rejected because they are limited, simplistic, or wrong, but because they have been overtaken by a better theory. As we have suggested, all levels of inquiry into writing rely to some extent on theory. If those theories are to become better or more relevant, research must also be done that focuses on theory development and testing itself.

LEVEL 6: SIMULATION

Simulation means representing a theory in the form of something that runs and that accordingly may or may not do what was expected of it. Thus simulation has potentialities both for verification and for discovery. Simulation via computer has emerged as a particularly powerful tool for developing and testing cognitive theories (Anderson, 1983; Boden, 1977). Because of the complexity of writing, both in the processes it involves and in the knowledge it draws on, computer simulation is likely for some time to have only limited application in writing research, but these applications can nevertheless be valuable. In this section we shall describe a type of human experimentation that can also be considered simulation, and which opens possibilities that are currently not accessible to computer simulation.

Probably the most ambitious use of computer simulation of writing has been Meehan's work (1976) on computer-generated stories. In this kind of work, the interest is not so much in simulating the process by which people compose text but in investigating the kinds of knowledge and capabilities that must be built into a simulation in order for it to produce the kinds of stories that human beings are able to generate. As Black, Wilkes-Gibbs, and Gibbs (1982) show in a review of this work, it reveals that extremely detailed and complex knowledge of the world is required in order to generate even a simple story that makes sense. As examples, they offer:

One detail is that if a character drops something then he no longer physically possesses it because it is at a different location than he is, so the kind of plan that will regain it involves a change in location. The second detail is that if the story character who owns an object is yourself, then you do not have to bargain for the object because you already own it (p. 329).

The need for such unlikely knowledge is brought to light by the absurd stories generated when the program does not have that knowledge.

At present such simulation research is not in a position to shed light on expert-novice differences, it being enough of a challenge to simulate minimally adequate story generation. But it is easy to see how the approach can eventually be extended to identifying the kinds of knowledge required to produce a story or other composition that has recognizably expert-like characteristics.

A computer simulation that does deal with differences in writing ability is reported by McCutchen and Perfetti (1982). In this case, the production of text was not simulated but only the selection of text content. McCutchen and Perfetti were trying to simulate the kinds of text content generated by students at grades 2, 4, and 6. The knowledge base was held constant, and what varied was the number of constraints that were honored. The assignment imposed three constraints: to write about (a) a single activity that is (b) fun and that is also (c) dangerous. Text content similar to that of the second graders could be generated by applying only one constraint—for instance, by listing things that are fun. Fourth-grade content could be generated by applying two constraints, and sixth-grade content by applying all three.

Simulation research on content generation has great promise for exploring expert-novice differences. It bypasses the immense problems of language production and yet deals with an aspect of expertise which, as the preceding discussion has indicated, appears to be of major importance according to other kinds of inquiry. It should be possible, for instance, to simulate both the knowledge-telling model and models of more expert or knowledge-transforming (Scardamalia & Bereiter, in press) processes of content generation.

Several investigators have noted that instructional experiments can be used as a form of simulation for testing theories of competence (Brown & Campione, 1981; Butterfield, Siladi, & Belmont, 1980). As applied to writing, the idea is that a conjecture about the nature of expert versus novice competence could be investigated by teaching novices the particular competence in question and observing whether it has the expected effect on writing processes or performance. This kind of research, which we shall refer to as *simulation by intervention,* need not be limited to instructional interventions. Equally appropriate are procedural facilitations (Scardamalia & Bereiter, 1985a), in which students are provided with supports for the exercise of new cognitive procedures.

Simulation by intervention is to be distinguished from research aimed simply at instructional improvement. An intervention that produced an all-around improvement in performance would be counted a success from the standpoint of instructional improvement research but would usually not be counted a success from the standpoint of simulation by intervention. It would not be sufficiently informative. In the long run, however, simulation by intervention may contribute to instructional improvement by providing knowledge about how particular kinds of cognitive changes may be brought about.

These points may be illustrated by a series of studies related to revision, reported by Bereiter and Scardamalia (in press). These studies were based on a model of expert performance in writing that posits a COMPARE process that repeatedly compares actual text with intentions, a DIAGNOSE process that is invoked when a mismatch is detected, followed by a choice of whether to change the text or change the plan. If the choice is to change the text, this is accomplished through an OPERATE process that includes choosing a general tactic and then generating a text change. It was conjectured that immature writers might possess competence in some of these processes, but that such competence was not evident because the procedure as a whole was not executed.

Accordingly, an intervention was devised to provide elementary-school students with procedural support in executing the COMPARE-DIAGNOSE-OPERATE procedure. Children were prompted to carry out the procedure after each sentence. The COMPARE process was facilitated by providing a set of evaluative statements to choose from. The DIAGNOSE process was not facilitated, but was prompted by asking children to explain the basis for their choices of evaluative statements. The OPERATE phase was facilitated by providing a fixed set of general tactics to choose from (leave it as is, delete a part, say more, change the wording, etc.), but no facilitation was provided for the actual generation of text changes. Children in grades 4 through 8 all proved capable of executing the procedure and typically declared it was the sort of thing they knew they were supposed to do but never did in writing. At all grade levels the children showed considerable competence at the COMPARE process. The evaluative choices of children at grades 6 and 8 closely corresponded to those made by a semiprofessional writer. Their diagnoses and choices of tactic, however, corresponded much less closely to those of the expert. As for actual changes to their texts, changes for the better outnumbered changes for the worse by a statistically significant though small margin, but global ratings of their texts showed no improvement.

These results were taken as supporting the notion that experts are distinguished by having an effective executive procedure for bringing evaluative, diagnostic, and remedial capabilities to bear on text production and that the evaluative capabilities of novice writers are disabled by lack of an executive procedure for putting them to use. Might the same be true of diagnostic capabilities? The study was uninformative on this point, because no procedural facilitation was provided for diagnosis. A subsequent study by Brett (also reported in Bereiter & Scardamalia, in press) examined the effects of facilitating diagnosis. Evaluation was facilitated for both an experimental and a control group, but the experimental group additionally received facilitation of diagnosis, again by providing a limited set of diagnostic statements to choose from each time a problem was noted. There was a significant treatment effect on quality of diagnoses for students at both grades 6 and 12, although only the 12th graders in the experimental group came close to matching the diagnoses made by a professional editor. However, the procedural facilitation raised the quality of diagnoses made by 6th graders to the level of unfacilitated 12th graders. Thus, again the results indicated the important role of an executive procedure for bringing available competence to bear on text production.

In a final study (Cohen & Scardamalia, 1983, also reported in Bereiter & Scardamalia, in press), all phases of the COMPARE-DIAGNOSE-OPERATE procedure were facilitated and, in addition, students were taught a variety of basic revision moves. This intervention resulted in a significant global improvement in the rated quality of compositions and also a very large increase in the frequency of revisions at the level of ideas (as opposed to revisions at the level of mechanics and single words). By itself, this final study would stand as an instructional improvement study and would not be informative about the nature of expertise. Taken in conjunction with the more focused results of the earlier studies, however, it suggests that the components of the COMPARE-DIAGNOSE-OPERATE procedure and the executive structure for controlling it constitute an important and teachable part of expertise in writing. Finally, it should be noted that the instructional procedure that ultimately proved to yield overall improvement in performance included components that would probably never have been arrived at through a frontal attack on the teaching of revision skills but that emerged from efforts to investigate competence through simulation.

CONCLUSION

In this chapter the issue of the nature of expertise in writing was used mainly as a vehicle for explaining the Levels of Inquiry schema. Certain claims about levels of inquiry remain to be addressed, however. One is a claim about the whole being greater than the sum of parts—a claim that something should arise from a bringing together of research at different levels that is more than just an agglomeration of topically related findings. The present discussion of research on writing expertise need not necessarily live up to that claim, since the cited research was not carried out within an integrative levels schema. Nevertheless, we suggest that something worthwhile does emerge from the conjunction of studies cited in this chapter.

What emerges is a picture that is quite different from the conventional image of experts as the ones who know, who have all the necessary knowledge and skills at their fingertips. From the Level 1 and Level 4 studies cited, we get the impression that, if anything, experts struggle rather more with writing than novices do. Thinking-aloud protocols indicate that this is because they create more complex problems for themselves to solve in writing. Although protocol analyses tell us quite a bit about what experts do, they leave us more in the dark about novices, whose protocols are mainly distinguished by what is not there. Level 5 research was cited, however, which supports a theoretical model of novice competence indicating how novices can produce generally acceptable prose while avoiding most of the higher-level goal-setting and problem-solving in which experts engage. These results raise the educationally important question of what stands between novice and expert competence. Level 6 simulations by intervention suggest that an important barrier to the development of novice writers' competence is lack of an executive structure for applying evaluative, diagnostic, and remedial abilities. There are indications from related instructional research that development of such an executive structure can be supported effectively. Thus, a progression through the levels of inquiry, as traced in the preceding discussion, takes us from an intuitive description of the kind of thought an expert puts into writing, through a formulation of this kind of thought in terms that make it relatable to other things we know about human problem solving, to a formulation of how this thought differs from that of the novice, and finally to some insight into what kinds of cognitive acquisitions might allow the novice to think more like an expert.

Another claim made at the outset of this chapter was that movement through the levels of inquiry should be cyclical, with continual return to Level 1, reflective inquiry. Very likely that was the case which much of the research cited. Although what gets reported may be straightforward Level 3, Level 4, or Level 5 research, it is likely that its actual history involved inquiry at Level 1 and other levels. Speaking for ourselves, it is clear that the knowledge-telling model did not spring directly from experimental findings or protocol analyses but rather from reflection on a variety of formal and informal observations. The first discussion of knowledge-telling as a strategy appeared, in fact, in a reflective essay rather than in a research-based report (Bereiter & Scardamalia, 1983a). This point is probably annoyingly obvious to other researchers, but there is a growing movement bearing such names as "critical social science" and "interpretive science" that seems to be based on the premise that only nonempirical researchers ever think very much about what things mean. If this were true, it is doubtful that there could be any progress in science at all.

In a progressive program of inquiry, Level 1 reflection should be continually advancing on the basis of facts, insights, and formalisms developed at other levels of inquiry. Where this is not the case, one tends to get stagnation because generations of thinkers keep mulling over the same data—the data of ordinary experience (Bereiter, 1984). The possibilities of progressive development of Level 1 inquiry are illustrated by the work touched upon in this chapter. Murray's (1978) reflective essay ostensibly focused on the virtues of thoughtful revision. Level 2 studies introduced the sobering fact that revision in and of itself is not necessarily beneficial. Level 4 protocol analyses, including the protocol analysis of Murray himself, indicated that what Murray was calling "internal revision" appears indistinguishable from planning (Berkenkotter, 1983). Studies at Levels 5 and 6 support processing models in which revision as such does not figure. Rather, the tendency of novices to revise little and only superficially and the tendency of experts to revise more deeply is seen as a natural consequence of differently structured systems for generating text content (Scardamalia & Bereiter, in press). With these findings in mind, one can go back and reread Murray's essay, not as a discourse on revision but as a reflection on the theoretically as well as educationally significant issue of how rhetorical and ideational considerations interact during composition so as to transform the writer's understanding.

This chapter has dealt mainly with cognitively based research, because that is the kind of research that has given most attention to the nature of expertise. A different topic—such as problems of basic writers or how children first learn to express themselves in writing—might draw on an altogether different body of research from a different tradition; but we believe the same basic schema would apply. (Whether all six levels would currently exist is another matter; our only claim would be that all six levels could—and ultimately should—exist to make up a vigorous research program.) The intent of the Levels of Inquiry framework, we must emphasize, is not to rule out certain kinds of research, but neither is it to endorse an amorphous eclecticism. Rather, it is to show how research of a variety of kinds can be combined into a systematic effort to get to the bottom of deep questions about writing.

NOTE

[1] We say nothing here about the multivariate methods that have been developed to extract meaning from intercorrelated variables (see, e.g., Marascuilo & Levin, 1983). Such methods have hardly been used at all in writing research; but in the absence of clear ideas about what is being looked for, it is doubtful that they could be used to much purpose.

REFERENCES

Anderson, J.R. (1983). *The architecture of cognition.* Cambridge, MA: Harvard University Press.

Beach, R. (1979). The effects of between-draft teacher evaluation versus student self-evaluation on high school students' revising of rough drafts. *Research in the Teaching of English, 13,* 111–119.

Beaugrande, R. de., & Colby, B.N. (1979). Narrative models of action and interaction. *Cognitive Science, 3,* 43–66.

Bereiter, C. (1984). The limitations of interpretation [Review of writing and the writer]. *Curriculum Inquiry, 14,* 211–216.

Bereiter, C., & Bird, M. (1985). Use of thinking aloud in identification and teaching of reading comprehension strategies. *Cognition and Instruction, 2,* 131–156.

Bereiter, C., & Scardamalia, M. (1983a). Does learning to write have to be so difficult? In A. Freedman, I. Pringle, & J. Yalden (Eds.), *Learning to write: First language, second language* (pp. 20–33). New York: Longman.

Bereiter, C., & Scardamalia, M. (1983b). Levels of inquiry in writing research. In P. Mosenthal, S.A. Walmsley, & L. Tamor (Eds.), *Research on writing: Principles and methods* (pp. 3–25). New York: Longman.

Bereiter, C., & Scardamalia, M. (1984). Learning about writing from reading. *Written Communication, 1,* 163–188.

Bereiter, C., & Scardamalia, M. (1985). Cognitive coping strategies and the problem of "inert knowledge." In S.F. Chipman, J.W. Segal, & R. Glaser (Eds.), *Thinking and learning skills: Research and open questions* (Vol. 2, pp. 65–80). Hillsdale, NJ: Erlbaum.

Bereiter, C., & Scardamalia, M. (in press). *The psychology of written composition.* Hillsdale, NJ: Erlbaum.

Berkenkotter, C. (1983). Decisions and revisions: The strategies of a publishing writer. *College Composition and Communication, 34,* 156–168.

Black, J.B., Galambos, J.A., & Reiser, B.J. (1984). Coordinating discovery and verification research. In D.E. Kieras & M.A. Just (Eds.), *New methods in reading comprehension research.* Hillsdale, NJ: Erlbaum.

Black, J.B., Wilkes-Gibbs, D., & Gibbs, R.W., Jr. (1982). What writers need to know that they don't know they need to know. In M. Nystrand (Ed.), *What writers know: The language, process, and structure of written discourse* (pp. 325–343). New York: Academic Press.

Blount, N.S. (1973). Research on teaching literature, language and composition. In R.M.W. Travers (Ed.), *Second handbook of research on teaching* (pp. 1072–1097). Chicago, IL: Rand McNally.

Bock, J.K. (1982). Toward a cognitive psychology of syntax: Information processing contributions to sentence formulation. *Psychological Review, 89,* 1–47.

Boden, M.A. (1977). *Artificial intelligence and natural man.* New York: Basic Books.

Boice, R. (1985). Cognitive components of blocking. *Written Communication, 2,* 91–104.

Bracewell, R.J., & Frederiksen, C.H. (1985). *Children's story production: Signalling frame structures with text structure.* Paper presented at the meeting of the American Educational Research Association, Chicago.

Bracewell, R.J., Scardamalia, M. & Bereiter, C. (October, 1978). The development of audience awareness in writing. *Resources in Education* (ERIC Document Reproduction Service No. ED 154433).

Braddock, R., Lloyd-Jones, R., & Schoer, L. (1963). *Research in written composi-

tion. Champaign, IL: National Council of Teachers of English.

Brewer, W.F. (1980). Literary theory, rhetoric, and stylistics: Implications for psychology. In R.J. Spiro, B.C. Bruce, & W.F. Brewer (Eds.), *Theoretical issues in reading comprehension* (pp. 221–239). Hillsdale, NJ: Erlbaum.

Brewer, W.F. (1985). The story schema: Universal and culture-specific properties. In D.R. Olson, N. Torrance, & A. Hildyard (Eds.), *Literacy, language and learning: The nature and consequences of reading and writing* (pp. 167–194). Cambridge: Cambridge University Press.

Bridwell, L.S. (1980). Revising strategies in twelfth grade students' transactional writing. *Research in the Teaching of English, 14,* 107–122.

Brown, A.L., & Campione, J.C. (1981). Inducing flexible thinking: A problem of access. In M. Friedman, J.P. Das, & N. O'Connor (Eds.), *Intelligence and learning* (pp. 515–529). New York: Plenum.

Burtis, P.J., Bereiter, C., Scardamalia, M., & Tetroe, J. (1983). The development of planning in writing. In G. Wells & B.M. Kroll (Eds.), *Explorations in the development of writing* (pp. 153–174). Chichester, England: Wiley.

Butterfield, E.C., Siladi, D., & Belmont, J.M. (1980). Validating theories of intelligence. In H.W. Reese & L.P. Lipsitt (Eds.), *Advances in child development and behavior* (Vol. 15, pp. 95–162). New York: Academic Press.

Clifford, J. (1984). Cognitive psychology and writing: A critique. *Freshman English News, 13,* 16–18.

Cronbach, L.J. (1975). Beyond the two disciplines of scientific psychology. *American Psychologist, 30,* 116–127.

Elbow, P. (1973). *Writing without teachers*. London: Oxford University Press.

Emig, J. (1978). Hand, eye, brain: Some "basics" in the writing process. In C.R. Cooper & L. Odell (Eds.), *Research on composing: Points of departure* (pp. 59–71). Urbana, IL: National Council of Teachers of English.

Faigley, L., & Witte, S. (1981). Analyzing revision. *College Composition and Communication, 32,* 400–414.

Flower, L.S. (1979). Writer-based prose: A cognitive basis for problems in writing. *College English, 41,* 19–37.

Flower, L.S., & Hayes, J.R. (1980a). The cognition of discovery: Defining a rhetorical problem. *College Composition and Communication, 31,* 21–32.

Flower, L.S., & Hayes, J.R. (1980b). The dynamics of composing: Making plans and juggling constraints. In L.W. Gregg & E.R. Steinberg (Eds.), *Cognitive processes in writing* (pp. 31–50). Hillsdale, NJ: Erlbaum.

Flower, L.S., & Hayes, J.R. (1981). A cognitive process theory of writing. *College Composition and Communication, 32,* 365–387.

Galbraith, J.K. (1981). *A life in our times*. Boston, MA: Houghton Mifflin.

Glaser, R. (1984). Education and thinking: The role of knowledge. *American Psychologist, 39,* 93–104.

Hansen, B. (1978). Rewriting is a waste of time. *College English, 39,* 956–960.

Hayes, J.R., & Flower, L.S. (1980). Identifying the organization of writing processes. In L.W. Gregg & E.R. Steinberg (Eds.), *Cognitive processes in writing* (pp. 3–30). Hillsdale, NJ: Erlbaum.

Hayes, J.R., & Flower, L.S. (1983). Uncovering cognitive processes in writing: An introduction to protocol analysis. In P. Mosenthal, L. Tamor, & S. Walmsley (Eds.), *Research on writing: Principles and methods* (pp. 207–220). New York: Longman.

King, M.L., & Rentel, V.M. (1981). Research update: Conveying meaning in written texts. *Language Arts, 58,* 721–728.

Lakatos, I. (1970). The methodology of scientific research programmes. In I. Lakatos & A. Musgrave (Eds.), *Criticism and the growth of knowledge* (pp. 91–195). Cambridge: Cambridge University Press.

Marascuilo, L.A., & Levin, J.R. (1983). *Multivariate statistics in the social sciences: A researcher's guide*. Monterrey, CA: Brooks/Cole.

Matsuhashi, A., & Quinn, K. (1984). Cognitive questions from discourse analysis: A review and a study. *Written Communication, 1*. 307–339.

McCutchen, D., & Perfetti, C.A. (1982). Coherence and connectedness in the development of discourse production. *Text, 2,* 113–139.

Meehan, J.R. (1976). *The metanovel: Writing stories by computer* (Research Rep. No. 74). New Haven, CT: Yale University, Department of Computer Science.

Moffett, J. (1968). *Teaching the universe of discourse*. Boston: Houghton Mifflin.

Mosenthal, P. (1983). Defining classroom writing competence: A paradigmatic perspective. *Review of Educational Research, 53,* 217–251.

Murray, D.M. (1978). Internal revision: A process of discovery. In C.R. Cooper & L. Odell (Eds.), *Research on composing* (pp. 85–103). Urbana, IL: National Council of Teachers of English.

Murray, D.M. (1983). Response of a laboratory rat—or, being protocoled. *College Composition and Communication, 34,* 169–172.

National Assessment of Educational Progress (1975). *Writing mechanics, 1969–1974: A capsule description of changes in writing mechanics* (Rep. No. 05-W-01). Denver, CO: National Assessment of Educational Progress.

National Assessment of Educational Progress (1980a). *Writing achievement, 1969–79: Results from the third national writing assessment (Vol. 1: 17-year-olds)* (Tech. Rep.). Denver, CO: National Assessment of Educational Progress. (ERIC Document Reproduction Service No. ED 196 042)

National Assessment of Educational Progress (1980b). *Writing achievement, 1969–79: Results from the third national writing assessment (Vol. II: 13-year-olds)* (Tech. Rep.). Denver, CO: National Assessment of Educational Progress. (ERIC Document Reproduction Service No. ED 196 043)

National Assessment of Educational Progress (1980b). *Writing achievement, 1969–79: Results from the third national writing assessment (Vol. II: 13-year-olds)* (Tech. Rep.). Denver, CO: National Assessment of Educational Progress. (ERIC Document Reproduction Service No. ED 196 043)

Rose, M. (1981). Sophisticated, ineffective books—The dismantling of process in composition texts. *College Composition and Communication, 32,* 65–74.

Scardamalia, M. (1981). How children cope with the cognitive demands of writing. In C.H. Frederiksen & J.F. Dominic (Eds.), *Writing: The nature, development and teaching of written communication* (pp. 81–103). Hillsdale, NJ: Erlbaum.

Scardamalia, M., & Bereiter, C. (1983). Child as co-investigator: Helping children gain insight into their own mental processes. In S. Paris, G. Olson, & H. Stevenson (Eds.), *Learning and motivation in the classroom* (pp. 61–82). Hillsdale, NJ: Erlbaum.

Scardamalia, M., & Bereiter, C. (1985a). Fostering the development of self-regulation in children's knowledge processing. In S.F. Chipman, J.W. Segal, & R. Glaser (Eds.), *Thinking and learning skills: Research and open questions* (Vol. 2, pp. 563–577). Hillsdale, NJ: Erlbaum.

Scardamalia, M., & Bereiter, C. (1985b). Research on written composition. In M. Wittrock (Ed.), *Handbook of research on teaching* (3rd ed. Also note, pp. 778–803). New York: Macmillan Education.

Scardamalia, M., & Bereiter, C. (in press). Knowledge telling and knowledge transforming in written composition. In S. Rosenberg (Ed.), *Advances in applied psycholinguistics* (Vol. 1). New York: Cambridge University Press.

Scardamalia, M., & Paris, P. (1985). The function of explicit discourse knowledge in the development of text representations and composing strategies. *Cognition and Instruction, 2,* 1–39.

Smith, F. (1982). *Writing and the writer.* New York: Holt, Rinehart & Winston.

Spearman, C. (1927). *The abilities of man.* New York: Macmillan.

Stallard, C.K. (1974). An analysis of the writing behavior of good student writers. *Research in the Teaching of English, 8,* 206–218.

Tomlinson, B. (1984). Talking about the composing process: The limitations of retrospective accounts. *Written Communication, 1,* 429–445.

Tversky, A., & Kahneman, D. (1974). Judgment under uncertainty: Heuristics and biases. *Science, 125,* 1124–1131.

Warriner, J.E., Mersand, J., & Griffith, F. (1963). *English grammar and composition, 11.* New York: Harcourt, Brace, & World.

Watson, R. (undated). *How to write: By those who can.* Ottawa, Canada: Graphic Publishers.

Why Johnny can't write. (1975, Dec. 8). *Newsweek,* pp. 59–62.

III.

COMPOSITION OF THE TEACHING FORCE

Chapter 9

Compensation for Teachers

DAVID STERN
School of Education
University of California, Berkeley

INTRODUCTION

Two main questions arise about compensation for teachers. First, can monetary incentives attract and retain a sufficient number of qualified teachers? Second, does the compensation structure affect teachers' performance? The research on these questions, as they pertain to public elementary and secondary school teachers in the United States, is reviewed in this chapter.

Questions about the power of money to attract and retain teachers have arisen because most practicing teachers say they are in the profession for other reasons, mainly having to do with their intrinsic desire to teach (see Bacharach, Lipsky, & Shedd, 1985). Social norms also prescribe some altruistic dedication on the part of teachers. However, the evidence reviewed in the next section consistently indicates that both prospective and practicing teachers are influenced by salary levels. Whether material incentives complement or conflict with teachers' intrinsic motivation is considered in the final section of this chapter.

Questions also are raised about the structure of teachers' compensation. In the period from 1917 to 1950 almost all public school districts in this country adopted some version of the uniform or single salary schedule (Miller, 1985). This is a two-dimensional grid on which a teacher is positioned according to years of service and formal educational attainment. Salary increments are automatically awarded for each year or two of additional service, but usually no increments are given beyond the 15th or 20th year. In addition, teachers receive higher pay when they accumulate credits for education beyond the bachelor's degree. The accumulation of seniority and educational credits results in higher salaries for older teachers than for younger ones. However, as will be shown, the age-earnings profile for teachers is relatively flat compared to college graduates in other occupations.

Several models of efficient compensation will be presented. According to one model, it is efficient for employees with more seniority to receive larger salaries even if they are no more productive than employees with less seniority—provided that meeting minimum standards of performance is a necessary condition for an individual to keep accumulating seniority. This has direct implications for teachers, as will be explained. Other models reviewed are extra pay for superior performance, and skill-based pay. The application of these models to teaching is also discussed. The general conclusion is that certain changes in the structure of teachers' compensation would probably help to make schools more effective, but only if combined with other organizational changes.

EFFECT OF SALARY LEVELS ON RECRUITMENT AND RETENTION

Trends in the level of teachers' salaries follow trends in student enrollment. The number of students in the United States enrolled in kindergarten through 12th grade grew continuously from 1946 through 1969, then declined. The average salary of public school teachers, in constant dollars, also rose continuously through this period, and did not reach its peak until 1972 (Everett, 1985). There is a lag between growth in enrollment and the rise in teachers' salaries because it takes time for school authorities to respond. The continued rise in teachers' inflation-adjusted salaries for three years after enrollment had reached its peak represents the lagged response to shortages a few years earlier. After 1972, however, the level of teachers' salaries declined, not only relative to inflation, but also relative to salaries in other occupations requiring a bachelor's degree. According to Feistritzer (1983, Table 41), starting salaries of public school teachers in current dollars (*not* adjusted for inflation) increased by 65% between 1973 and 1981—compared to a 99% increase in starting salaries for engineers, 84% in business administration, and 75% for liberal arts graduates. In Feistritzer's list of 10 fields other than teaching, only accounting had smaller growth (60%) in starting salaries. Additional evidence of the relative decline in teachers' salaries following the drop in student enrollment is provided in the next section.

The fact that trends in teachers' salaries follow trends in student enrollment does not necessarily imply that higher salaries bring about an increase in the number of people available for teaching jobs. Conceivably, local school districts could raise salaries in an attempt to bid teachers away from each other without having any effect on the total supply available.

However, the evidence consistently indicates that the total supply of teachers does in fact respond to salary levels. Zarkin's (1985b) analysis of trends in total supply and demand in the United States found that the number of people available to teach is positively related to the level of teachers' salaries, and negatively related to the level of salaries in alternative occupations. Zarkin's (1985a) analysis of aggregate trends also indicates that more people enter teaching when they expect salaries to rise due to growing enrollments.

The data on individuals are consistent with these findings from aggregated data. Manski (1985) analyzed information on individuals from the National Longitudinal Study of the High School Class of 1972. Among college graduates who were employed in 1979, Manski found a positive association between salary and SAT score for nonteachers, but not for teachers. He also found that individuals with higher SAT scores were less likely to be teaching. These findings are consistent with the theory that salaries influence occupational choice in general, and, in particular, that individuals with high SAT scores are relatively unlikely to choose teaching because they can obtain bigger salaries in other fields. Manski's analysis implies that raising teachers' salaries would make it feasible to establish a minimum SAT score for teachers and still attract the same number of young people into teaching. For instance, he estimated that setting the minimum SAT score (verbal plus math) at 1,000 would require raising teachers' salaries approximately $90 per week (in 1979 dollars), if the fraction of high school graduates who eventually enter teaching were to be held constant.

The likelihood that an individual will leave teaching for another occupation has been found to be positively related to the amount by which the individual is underpaid as a teacher, compared to potential earnings in other fields (Baugh & Stone, 1982). Additional corroboration comes from analysis of data from the United Kingdom by Zabalza, Turnbull, and Williams (1979). They found that the level of teachers' salaries relative to other fields was positively related to the number of new entrants into teaching, and negatively related to the number of teachers who left the profession.

All these results are consistent with economic theory and common sense. They clearly indicate that both prospective and practicing teachers respond to monetary considerations. Raising salaries will attract and retain more teachers. Manski's (1985) results also suggest higher salaries can be used to recruit new teachers with higher SAT scores. Whether monetary inducements will also attract more teachers of "virtue" (Jackson, 1985) is not known, but some discussion of intrinsic and extrinsic motivations for teachers is in the concluding section of this chapter.

RELATIVE EARNINGS OF TEACHERS, BY AGE

A young person considering a career in teaching could find out how much money teachers make, relative to other occupations, by looking at U.S. Census reports. Bits and pieces of this information can also be obtained, with varying degrees of accuracy, from newspapers and magazines, placement offices, families, and acquaintances. One way or another, the basic facts about teachers' pay are easily discovered. They are presented in Figure 1.

The age-earnings profiles shown for different groups in Figure 1 vary in height, steepness, and curvature. With regard to height, the most striking difference is between males and females. In both 1969 and 1979, the average man, whether in teaching or not, earned more than the average woman. This was true for earners with 4 years of college (solid lines) or with 5 or more years (broken lines).

The large male-female difference in annual earnings in Figure 1 is due in part to the fact that the proportion of earners who work for pay less than 50 weeks a year is larger among women than among men. But the comparisons in Figure 1 could not be restricted to full-time, year-round earners because most teachers, both male and female, work for pay less than 50 weeks a year.

Earnings profiles for male teachers were much lower than for all male earners in both 1969 and 1979. However, among females there was very little difference between teachers and the college-educated labor force as a whole. The similarity of earnings profiles for female teachers and the whole group is due in part to the fact that female teachers comprised a large fraction of the whole female college-educated labor force: 50% in 1969 and 33% in 1979. If teachers' earnings profiles were compared with nonteachers' separately, the differences would be more pronounced than in Figure 1, but still less pronounced for women than for men.

It has been said that increasing participation of college-educated women in occupations other than teaching is making it more difficult to recruit women into teaching. Indeed, the sharp decline in the proportion of college-educated female earners who are teachers—from one half in 1969 to one third in 1979—was part of a general decline in occupational segregation by sex (Holden & Hansen, forthcoming). If the occupations women are entering in larger proportions pay more than teaching, the earnings of female teachers relative to all female earners should decline, especially in the younger age groups where desegregation is occurring more quickly, and the decline in relative pay should be greater for female teachers than for male teachers. However, the numbers charted in Figure 1 do *not* show a greater decline for female teachers than for male teachers. Among 25–34 year olds, female teachers' relative mean earnings fell between 1969 and 1979, from 97.6 to 89.4% of mean earnings of all women with 4 years of college; for those with 5 or more years of college, teachers' earnings fell from 102.7 to 97.3% of the overall mean. But the decline in relative pay for teachers between 1969 and 1979 was just as large among 25–34 year old males: from 72.5 to 69.8% among earners with 4 years of college, and from 81.2 to 75.9% for those with 5 or more years. Whether they were female or male, young teachers did relatively less well in 1979 than in 1969.

It remains to be seen whether the entry of more women into previously

FIGURE 1. Mean earnings by age for male and female K-12 teachers, and experienced civilian labor force, by years of education, 1969 and 1979.

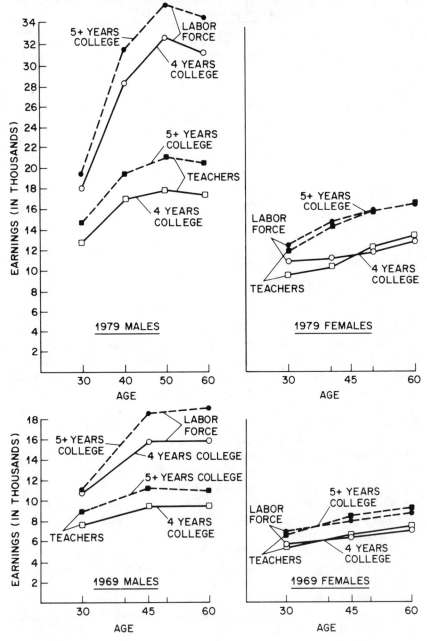

TABLE 1
Ratio of mean earnings in highest-paid age group to mean earnings of 25–34 year-olds, for male and female K–12 teachers and experienced civilian labor force, by years of education, 1969 and 1979.

Category	Age group with highest mean earnings		Ratio to mean earnings of 25–34 year-olds	
	Male	Female	Male	Female
1969				
Labor force				
4 yrs. college	55–64	55–64	1.49	1.23
5+ yrs. college	55–64	55–64	1.75	1.37
Teachers				
4 yrs. college	35–54	55–64	1.21	1.32
5+ yrs. college	35–54	55–64	1.27	1.27
1979				
Labor force				
4 yrs. college	45–54	55–64	1.79	1.17
5+ yrs. college	45–54	55–64	1.84	1.32
Teachers				
4 yrs. college	45–54	55–64	1.43	1.36
5+ yrs. college	45–54	55–64	1.43	1.36

Source: U.S. Census, 1970 and 1980.

male-dominated occupations (e.g., law, medicine) will cause the earnings profile for teachers to fall below that of other earners in the older age groups. This is clearly the pattern for males in Figure 1: the earnings gap between teachers and other college-educated earners grows wider with age. In other words, age-earnings profiles are much steeper for men who do not teach than for men who teach. However, among college-educated women there has been no such difference in steepness of the earnings profile among teachers and nonteachers. This may change in the future, as more college-educated women work in previously male-dominated occupations.

Table 1 presents a simple measure of steepness for each of the profiles in Figure 1. It is the mean earnings in the age group where mean earnings are highest, divided by mean earnings of 25–34 year olds. According to this measure, female teachers' age-earnings profiles became slightly steeper between 1969 and 1979, while the profiles for all college-educated female earners actually became *less* steep. The age-earnings profile for females who do not teach therefore became *less* similar to the male profile during the 1970s. The steepness or flatness of earnings profiles may have important behavioral implications, which are discussed in the next section.

At this point, what conclusion would a young person draw from this information about teachers' pay? For a young man it is clear: teachers' pay starts bad and gets worse. No improvement is evident from recent data. For a college-educated woman, prospective earnings in teaching still look very similar to earnings in other fields. In the next 20 to 30 years, women who have recently entered nonteaching occupations that were predominantly male may raise average earnings in the older age groups more than in the past. But implementation of "career ladder" plans for teachers (see the final section) may have the same effect for those who choose teaching.

MODELS OF EFFICIENT COMPENSATION

Does the relative flatness of teachers' age-earnings profiles affect their behavior? What difference does it make if teachers' salaries are tied to seniority, knowledge, or performance? While some research pertaining to these questions has been done on teachers specifically, a great deal more research has been conducted on compensation in settings other than schools. This section presents five distinct models or principles of efficient compensation drawn from the literature in economics, organizational psychology, and personnel management. The aim here is to extract ideas that are relevant to compensation for teachers. Readers interested in more comprehensive reviews are referred to the sources cited, especially International Labour Office (ILO, 1984), Lawler (1971, 1981), Yellen (1984), Henderson (1979), and Heneman (1984).

Predetermined Pay, with Minimum Standard of Performance

The most common kind of employment contract in capitalist economies commits the employer to pay an agreed upon amount of compensation periodically, in exchange for which the employee promises to do a certain job. If the employee fails to perform at or above some minimum standard, the employer may terminate the contract by firing the employee.

Unless employees have some intrinsic motivation to do the job (an important proviso in thinking about teachers; see the concluding section), it is not rational for them to perform above the minimum standard since higher performance requires effort that is presumably unpleasant. With this kind of employment contract, therefore, performance at the minimum standard, or only a little above it, would be expected.

Prevailing practices in the labor market determine a range of acceptable "effort bargains" for each kind of work. If an employer sets a high standard of minimum performance but does not pay a high enough wage or salary, the employer will be unable to recruit or retain the desired number of qualified workers. In determining levels of pay and performance for a particular job, the employer therefore has some range of choice, within which both pay and minimum performance standards can be set either relatively high or relatively low.

Economists have analyzed this choice problem for a profit-seeking employer. In theory, the firm's profit-maximizing solution is to set pay and performance levels at the point where an additional 1% increase in pay would permit an increase in required performance of exactly 1% (see Solow, 1979; Stiglitz, 1976). If different firms offer an array of effort bargains, workers can sort themselves into jobs where each obtains the most preferred combination of earnings and effort, given the available technology of production.

In practice, the most explicit application of this kind of contract—predetermined pay with minimum standards of performance—has been to production workers in manufacturing, mining, or trade. Here an employee may perform the same operation, day after day. "Measured daywork" is a term sometimes used in this context to describe contracts with explicit minimum standards (Henderson, 1979, p. 364; ILO, 1984). Where contracts are written down in collective bargaining, provisions for enforcement of minimum standards are sometimes spelled out. For example, one contract specified:

When an employee is charged only with inefficiency, such employee and the union shall have 10 work days written notice thereof. If the inefficiency shall not have been corrected within 10 work days from the period of said notice, such employee (if hourly paid) may be subject to discharge (U.S. Bureau of Labor Statistics, 1979; p. 8).

Another stipulated:

The right of the company to establish and enforce production standards is recognized. Such production standards shall be fair and equitable and the time allowed for performing an operation shall be the time necessary for a normal experienced operator, familiar with the operation, tools, equipment, and material provided, and the quality of the finished part shall be up to the standard required with the operator working at a pace he can maintain day after day without mental sickness or physical injury to himself or his fellow employees (U.S. Bureau of Labor Statistics, 1979, p. 23).

For managerial and professional employees, or for production workers in service industries, minimum performance standards are usually more difficult to define in precise, objective terms. However, large employers almost always conduct periodic, formal appraisals of performance by managerial, professional, and service workers. These appraisals are most often written by supervisors. They inevitably include subjective judgment, but employers have incentives to make the appraisals as valid and reliable as possible, both for more efficient management and to avoid lawsuits or grievances (see Henderson, 1979, chap. 14). An employee who receives bad ratings is more vulnerable to discharge, especially at times when business is slack and the company is eliminating jobs. Though far from perfect, performance appraisals do permit employers to enforce minimum standards.

Extra Pay for Superior Performance

In addition to (or instead of) enforcing minimum performance standards by discharging employees who do not meet them, employers may also provide extra pay for employees who perform at a high level. There are two main forms of positive incentive pay: the one-time bonus and the recurrent salary increase.

In the first version, extra pay is awarded as a one-time bonus at the end of the period when the employee's performance was high. This kind of bonus pay based strictly on current performance has been applied mainly to production and sales employees in profit-seeking firms, but there have also been attempts to apply it to public employees (Greiner, Dahl, Hatry, & Millar, 1977; National Commission on Productivity and Work Quality, 1975), and to managerial and professional workers in the private sector (Heneman, 1984). Usually, the bonus is paid immediately but then is given again only when the individual's performance again rises to the meritorious level.

Bonus pay for production workers in the United States and other industrialized countries became more widespread from the 1920s to the 1950s (ILO 1984, chap. 8). This was a period when base wages were becoming more "sticky" due to changing social norms and direct governmental restraints on employers (Mitchell, 1985). By making more use of bonus pay for high performance, employers could maintain some flexibility in payroll costs so that payroll obligations would not exceed revenues, but without resorting to cuts in base wages. The spread of bonus pay incentives also reflected growing acceptance of "scientific management" principles.

Since the 1950s there has been some decline in the use of bonus pay to reward current performance, especially for individual employees (ILO 1984, chap. 8). The period from approximately 1955 to 1970 was a time of relatively steady growth for the western industrial economies. Miles (1976) has suggested that prevailing practice, especially in large corporations, accordingly came to emphasize planning and attainment of minimum production targets, rather than cost-effectiveness. Tying pay to performance might motivate employees to increase productivity, but would also add an undesired element of unpredictability. Instead, the concern was to achieve mass production targets and to prevent failure by enforcing minimum standards.

Now the economic climate has become less stable again. There is evidence that employers in the 1970s and 1980s have again made more use of bonus pay for production workers—but increasingly now for groups rather than individuals (ILO 1984, chap. 8; Lawler, 1981). Group incentives will be described further below.

The second major form of individual incentive pay is a raise in salary for the high-performing employee. This is the more relevant form of reward for managerial and professional workers. At the beginning of each pay period the level of compensation for that period is predetermined. But superior performance may lead to higher compensation in the future, and once the level of compensation rises, it ordinarily will not fall back to the previous level.

It is surprisingly difficult to verify in practice whether salary increases for managers and professional workers are really tied to their performance. Unlike one-time bonus payments, which are triggered automatically by an explicit formula, salary raises are not tied to performance in such a mechanical way. Lawler (1971, p. 158) reported several studies that failed to confirm a link between salary and performance even in companies where pay based on merit was the stated policy. More recently, studies by Medoff and Abraham (1980, 1981) and a review by Abraham and Medoff (1983) have found that corporate managers and professional workers within a given job classification obtain higher salaries if they have been there longer—but those who have been there longer do *not* obtain higher performance ratings on average. Medoff and Abraham conclude that most salary increases are in fact attributable to seniority itself, not to performance. A limitation of their studies, and those reported by Lawler, is that they compare employees only within the same job classifications because performance appraisals cannot be compared across different job categories. Therefore, these studies do not rule out the possibility that promotion from one job category to another is determined by merit. Even so, these studies cast serious doubt on the proposition that salaries are strongly tied to performance among managers or professional workers within the same job classification in large private firms.

Is a compensation system that awards higher pay for superior performance more efficient for the organization than one that does not? Psychological theory and common sense imply that tying pay to performance is efficient *if:* workers' performance can be clearly linked to the organization's objectives; financial incentives are sufficiently large; workers have sufficient control over their own performance; the measurement of performance is seen as legitimate by employees but is not too costly or time-consuming; and workers trust management not to raise standards when performance improves (ILO 1984, chap. 3 & 4: Lawler, 1971). Unfortunately, clear empirical tests of these propositions have not been conducted (see Heneman, 1984), since compensation practices in actual organizations are not amenable to rigorous experimentation. However, if a certain practice has been widely used by firms in a competitive environment, this is at least prima facie evidence that the practice is efficient. On these grounds, one-time bonus payments tied to current performance appear to be efficient for some production and sales workers.

As for the second form of performance-based pay—building performance awards into recurrent salary—it is not even clear that it has been widely practiced. If this kind of incentive does operate in practice, it is mainly by promotion from one job grade to the next. Competing for promotion may motivate individuals who are still contenders, but those who feel their chances for promotion have come and gone may give up and stop working hard if there is no other incentive (Rosenbaum, 1984). This may be one reason why salary differences within large organizations have been found, in fact, to depend more on seniority than on performance.

Pay for Seniority

When an employee is expected to continue working for the same employer for a number of years, it may be efficient for the employment contract to promise steady increases in pay from year to year, as long as performance meets minimum standards. Failure to meet minimum standards is grounds for dismissal. Other than that, pay does not depend on performance.

To see why this kind of contract may be efficient, consider an extreme counterexample. Suppose the employment relationship is expected to last for a number of years, but the employer foolishly offers to pay the whole present value of the expected future salary in one lump sum on the first day. This would create a strong temptation for the employee to pocket the money and flee. Even if the employer succeeded in recovering the money, this kind of contract obviously is not going to result in getting a maximum amount of work done.

More generally, Lazear (1981) has constructed an ingenious theoretical demonstration that rational employees and employers would agree to long-term contracts that pay employees *less* than the value of what they produce during the early part of their career, but then pay *more* than what they produce toward the end of the contract, as long as they meet minimum performance standards. This is rational because by not paying employees much money up front, the contract avoids tempting them to take the cash and run. The contract also gives senior employees a strong incentive to keep working, at least up to minimum standard, because they can collect the full amount of extra pay that comes with seniority only by remaining with the same employer. This kind of contract therefore results in more work getting done, and thus more total income for employees.

A good deal of evidence about labor markets is consistent with this theory of seniority pay. Many studies have demonstrated that additional years of work experience are associated with larger earnings, but that an employee who has remained with the same employer tends to earn more than one who has changed employers (see Chapman & Tan, 1980; Duncan & Hoffman, 1979). Within organizations, Lawler (1971) and Medoff and Abraham (1980, 1981) found, as mentioned earlier, that seniority increments were *not* related to performance ratings.

Abraham and Medoff (1983) also conducted a survey of large corporations, which indicated a widespread commitment to giving senior workers more protection in the event of layoffs. This protection was strongest for unionized, hourly employers. But even for nonunion or managerial employees, seniority provided some protection against layoff, as long as they were not significantly less valuable to the company. Existence of this protection is necessary if the kind of long-term contract described by Lazear is really going to work, as employees would have no reason to accept low pay early in their careers if employers did not honor the bargain by keeping senior workers on the payroll to collect their reward. However, if senior employees are paid more than the value of what they produce, the employer will not agree to a contract that allows employees to stay on the payroll as long as they like—and this, Lazear points out, can logically explain why there is mandatory retirement.

Pay for Know-How

In most large organizations, the amount of pay a person receives is determined by the job classification to which he or she is currently assigned. Formally, pay depends on the job, not on characteristics of the person, although personal qualifications influence eligibility for various jobs. In the conventional personnel system, an employee's pay can change relative to others in the organization only if the employee's job classification changes.

Pay for know-how changes all that. This innovative concept, often called "skill-based pay" (Gupta, Jenkins, & Curington, forthcoming; Jenkins & Gupta, 1985; Lawler & Ledford, 1985), makes a person's current rate of pay depend on demonstrated mastery of certain skills and knowledge—*not* on the job being performed during the current pay period. Employees advance up the pay scale by progressing through a sequential "curriculum" of skills and knowledge used in the particular workplace.

The first organization to install a full-fledged system of pay for know-how seems to have been General Foods, at the pet food factory built in Topeka, Kansas in 1971 (Lawler, 1981, pp. 66–68; O'Toole, 1973; Walton, 1980). The concept has spread rapidly since then. A 1985 survey by Gupta et al. (forthcoming) found more than 7% of companies listed on the New York or American Stock Exchange were operating at least one workplace with pay for Exchange were operating at least one workplace with pay for know-how.

To date, the concept of pay for know-how has been applied mainly in new manufacturing plants where production workers are given a large amount of responsibility for running the operation. It seems especially applicable in highly automated, continuous-process industries such as chemicals, food, and paper where the work consists largely of monitoring controls and solving problems. Unlike a conventional assembly plant, where operators handle materials and the speed of the line depends on how fast employees move, in a continuous-process facility the pace of production depends on how fast employees think.

The "curriculum" in a system of pay for know-how can include some diffuse behavioral objectives in addition to highly specific skills and concepts. For example, a Procter & Gamble factory in Modesto, California, offers technicians two alternative career paths in advanced assembly line skills. One path is called "mechanical," the other "operational." To reach advanced level one in the operational sequence, a technician must first acquire prerequisite skills in 4 functional areas, then demonstrate mastery of 21 specific additional parts of the line operation, as well as satisfying 16 behavioral expectations. The 21 specific proficiencies include some that are tested by actual performance, and others tested by answering questions. For instance, one of the 21 parts of the line is a rotary folding machine. Here the candidate must perform 11 distinct tasks, for example "adjust the clearance between tucker and gripper roll." The candidate also must answer 6 questions on the rotary folder, including "If you are getting a 'bull nosed' pad from the rotary folder, what malfunction might you expect from the opening cam?" In addition to the hundreds of detailed proficiencies in line operation, the technician seeking advancement also has to satisfy behavioral expectations such as "proactively works to eliminate downtime problems," "trains new technicians on safety in the area," and "encourages others to join in problem solving discussions of line problems."

Usually pay for know-how is only one in a set of several organizational features that support employee participation in problem-solving. A list of these features provided by Hirschhorn (1984, pp. 115–117) shows how pay for know-how fits in. The list is worth summarizing here because it represents an increasingly common paradigm for employee participation in high-tech production:

- "Workers are paid salaries, not wages." A salary is determined not by the tasks a worker is currently performing, "but by how much he or she has learned. The pay-for-learning system is organized on the basis of skill clusters . . . for example, there will be separate clusters for line, maintenance, warehouse, and laboratory work."
- "The workers are organized into teams based on natural segments of the production process, such as packaging, processing, and laboratory work." Teams have considerable autonomy, sometimes their own budgets.
- "Workers train one another and rotate through the teams to learn the full complement of skills. Since particular teams are limited to particular parts of the plant, a team member must temporarily transfer to other teams to develop new skills. This means that workers and their teams negotiate temporary transfer arrangements with others . . . [M]ost often there is one worker on the team who orients new members and sits on a general committee supervised by the training coordinator for the whole plant."
- "Workers evaluate one another for pay raises." Based on written tests and on-line performance, teams decide whether individuals have mastered the skills. In some plants a negative evaluation can be appealed.
- "The role of first-line supervision is changing. In some plants the supervisor acts as a facilitator or coordinator assigned to a particular team, while in others he is responsible for a functional area, such as training or health and safety."

- "An elaborate system of committees and task forces manages the plant. Some of these focus on particular projects and problems, such as training and plant expansion, while others review the entire design."
- "Few of the plants are unionized. Many were built from scratch in regions where unions are weak."

In the context of these "high commitment work systems," as Walton (1980) calls them, pay for know-how has several advantages. From the employee's point of view, it helps keep the work interesting by rewarding accomplishment of new tasks. From the employer's standpoint, maintaining employees' motivation is itself a good thing. In addition, pay for know-how improves the organization's capacity for problem-solving since each individual comes to understand more of the whole production process (Lawler & Ledford, 1985). A final advantage for employers is that turnover of experienced employees becomes less disruptive and costly because no employee develops a monopoly on knowledge about a particular part of the operation. To the extent that these advantages can also be realized in other manufacturing and service industries, pay for know-how will continue to spread.

Group Incentives

The four preceding models of efficient compensation all pertain to employees as individuals, but the first two can also be applied directly to groups. Minimum performance standards can be defined for a group just as for an individual, although in practice this seems to have been done only in a few organizations as part of work restructuring experiments (ILO 1984, p. 111). The application to groups of extra pay for superior performance is more common in practice. In U.S. collective bargaining contracts, such incentives are in fact mentioned four times more often for groups than for individuals (U.S. Bureau of Labor Statistics, 1979, p. 4).

The other two concepts described above—pay for seniority and pay for know-how—are inherently applicable only to individuals. However, organizations can and do combine these principles of individual compensation with incentives for groups.

Group incentives have obvious advantages when jobs are interdependent. One advantage is the lower cost of monitoring output for a group of related jobs than for each job in the group. In some work settings, the time and effort required to measure performance by individuals can exceed the benefit of improved performance. According to Silverman (1983), this is what happened when individual merit pay was instituted for federal government employees. A second advantage of creating incentives for groups instead of individuals is that, if jobs are interdependent, overall performance is likely to be better if individuals are motivated to help each other, instead of each one trying to look good at the others' expense.

Even if jobs are not highly interdependent, it may be more effective to reward groups rather than individuals for superior performance. A well-known drawback of individual incentive plans is the tendency to create peer pressure against "rate busters"—individuals whose superior performance threatens to cause the employer to raise the standards (Whyte, 1955). These counterproductive sentiments should not arise among members of a group whose performance is rewarded collectively, although such feelings might well exist between groups that compete against each other. Another general advantage of group incentives is the greater inducement for more able and experienced employees to train or coach the others.

In theory, rewarding performance by groups rather than individuals also has the disadvantage of diluting the incentive. Especially in large groups, individuals may feel no inducement to improve their own performance, being content instead to let others bring home the bacon. On the other hand, if the group is small enough so that individual members can perceive each others' performance, instituting rewards for the group might instead create a new kind of peer pressure *against* such "free riding." In the absence of a material incentive for the group, high-performing members can appeal to their less motivated coworkers only on moral grounds. Given a material incentive, the appeal can be made on the basis of shared self-interest. Unfortunately, there is no available evidence on how group incentives affect these group dynamics in practice.

Since approximately 1960, use of group incentives has become more widespread among private firms in the United States and Western Europe (ILO 1984, chap. 8). One form of group reward is profit-sharing. In the United States, employers since 1974 have been able to receive tax credits for sharing profits with all employees (not just top managers), through the mechanism of Employee Stock Ownership Plans (ESOPs). The National Center for Employee Ownership (NCEO) estimates that approximately 8,000 companies had taken steps to establish ESOPs as of 1984. These companies employ approximately 8% of the work force nationwide. The 1984 Deficit Reduction act contained several provisions that are expected to spur the growth of ESOPs even further.

However, the size of a company's profits depend not only on employees' performance but also on exogenous factors such as fluctuations in demand for the company's product. For this reason, some authors do not consider profit-sharing or stock ownership schemes to be true incentive plans at all.

There is another type of group incentive plan that has also become more widespread in recent years. Often called gain-sharing, this kind of plan is sometimes applied to the firm as a whole, like profit-sharing. Alternatively, gain-sharing can also apply to single establishments in a multiplant firm, or to individual divisions, departments, or work groups. The idea of gain-sharing is to promote improvement in a group's work procedures by awarding bonus pay to employees in the group when they improve their productivity. The amount paid out in bonuses is a predetermined share of the total monetary benefit to the company due to the group's higher productivity (Bullock, 1984).

The best-known version of gain-sharing is the Scanlon plan, which originated in the 1930s. Joseph Scanlon, then a union officer in a Pennsylvania steel mill, devised an agreement between the union and management that brought the company through financial crisis by enlisting workers to improve efficiency. Increased wages ensued. Scanlon moved to union headquarters, and then went to work at MIT with Douglas McGregor. Here the plan was formulated and refined through experience in a number of companies (Katzell & Yankelovich 1975, pp. 355–356).

Scanlon plans have different features in different companies, but there are said to be three defining characteristics: (1) a set of committees to communicate problems and develop ideas for improving efficiency; (2) a formula for distributing money to a group of employees in proportion to measured improvements in productivity, which promotes productive collaboration in a group of employees, and an equitable distribution of gains from higher productivity; (3) the philosophy and practice of cooperation (Moore & Ross, 1978). This includes sharing knowledge and information between employees and management. Ultimately, it may amount to "the merging of personal goals with those of the organization," so that employees "desire to make higher levels of contributions to the attainment of organizational goals" (Moore & Ross, 1978, p. 4). In sum, the Scanlon plan uses group incentive pay along with other organizational practices to create a high-commitment work system.

The durability of the Scanlon concept, the number of companies that have adopted at least some form of it, and the documentation of success stories in individual companies—for example, Donnelly Mirrors (see Iman, 1975; Rush, 1973)—all testify to the effectiveness of this particular group incentive plan. Furthermore, according to Lawler (1981, p. 148), interest in the Scanlon plan has "increased tremendously since 1970."

EFFICIENT COMPENSATION FOR TEACHERS

The preceding general principles of efficient compensation have four definite implications for changing teachers' salary structures: (1) minimum performance standards should be better enforced; (2) the additional education for which teachers receive salary increments should be more closely related to what teachers actually do; (3) it is possible to award higher pay to teachers whose performance is superior, but (4) this should be done in the context of a more general organizational strategy for maintaining teachers' commitment to their work. This section explains these four propositions.

Enforce Minimum Performance Standards

Some teachers, usually said to be a small minority, fail to perform up to reasonable minimum standards. Unlike their more able or more dedicated colleagues, they lack the necessary talent or intrinsic motivation to give students the kind of instruction and care that is expected. Yet it is hard to dismiss a teacher for incompetence or nonfeasance. After teachers pass through their initial probationary period, laws in most states protect them against dismissal except for cause, and with due process. This statutory right is protected by the Fourteenth Amendment of the U.S. Constitution. In districts with collective bargaining, contractual grievance procedures provide another layer of legal protection. Finally, dismissing a teacher usually requires action by the school board itself (Bridges, 1984, p. 5), and can therefore become entangled in board politics.

In contrast, most employees in the private sector enjoy far less job security. Some large companies do seek to maintain the loyalty and commitment of skilled employees by promising to use layoffs only as a last resort in the event of a business downturn (Stern, 1982). Furthermore, recent court rulings in several states have protected employees against firing that stems from an employer's demonstrable "bad faith" (*Business Week,* July 8, 1985, pp. 74–75). But, in spite of these limitations, millions of private-sector employees lose their jobs every year because they did not meet minimum performance standards or their employers cut payrolls.

Since it is relatively difficult to discharge a teacher once he or she has obtained tenure, the main opportunity for enforcing minimum performance standards is during the probationary period after a teacher is newly hired. There is evidence that principals do succeed in weeding out some unsuccessful teachers during this initial period (Murnane, 1984). However, some unsuccessful teachers survive probation, especially in times and places where teachers are scarce. Furthermore, if it is practically impossible to dismiss a tenured teacher, then teachers with tenure have practically no material incentive to exert themselves. Those who do continue to work hard do so *despite* the lack of material incentive.

Logically, not enforcing minimum performance standards for tenured teachers destroys the rationale for basing pay on seniority. As explained in the previous section, pay for seniority is efficient only if employees can be dismissed for "shirking." In a long-term employment relationship, awarding higher pay for seniority—over and above any pay differences associated with higher productivity—is likely to deter shirking by senior employees because they will forfeit their seniority bonus if dismissed. While most salary schedules for teachers do include increments for seniority, no efficiency gain can be expected if minimum performance standards are not enforced. This could be the most important reason for better enforcement.

There are other, more obvious reasons. Students benefit directly if substandard teaching is improved, whether by helping unsuccessful teachers upgrade their performance or by replacing them with other, more effective teachers. Enforcing standards also benefits successful teachers, because seeing other teachers perform poorly and get away with it can make successful teachers wonder about the rationality of their own efforts, and because all teachers are tarred by the brush of public contempt for the ineffective ones.

Enforcing minimum standards for teaching is not easy. It means adopting measurable criteria and determining whether teachers satisfy them; ensuring that supervisors have the time, incentive, and capability to assess teachers' performance; providing help to teachers who need it; and following due process at each step, up to and including a formal hearing, if necessary (Bridges, 1984). All of this, in turn, requires resources, and determination on the part of top management.

Unlike firms that sell products or services in competitive markets, public schools *as organizations* have no incentive to take on the difficult task of enforcing minimum performance standards for employees. Public schools are not like firms that lose revenues and eventually go out of business if they fail in market competition. If there is any link between what teachers do and how much money the schools have, the connection is too indirect to matter. Schools therefore lack any survival imperative to enforce minimum standards.

For economists and others who see competitive markets as the best mechanism for allocating resources, absence of competition is the public schools' main problem (Friedman & Friedman, 1979, chap. 6). An article in *Fortune* magazine declared,

. . . the problems of education are immediately seen as the problems typical of any socialized monopoly. The public school system is the American version of Soviet agriculture, beyond help as currently organized because its incentive structure is all wrong (Brimelow, 1983, p. 64).

In this view, an obvious—though drastic—cure for the problems of schools is a voucher system, which would allocate public money only to schools where parents choose to send their children. The resulting competition, it is said, not only would eliminate substandard teaching and reward superior performance, but also would produce more *kinds* of good education (Coons & Sugarman, 1978). On the other hand, critics of the voucher idea have pointed to possible negative consequences for social cohesion (Wise & Darling-Hammond, 1983). It is possibly for this reason that voucher proposals in this country have so far been defeated at the polls.

A less sweeping proposal for enforcing minimum standards at the organizational level, without the radical changes entailed by a voucher system, was suggested in a report issued by the Committee for Economic Development (CED, 1985), a group composed mainly of business executives. "When a school district grossly fails to meet its obligations to its students," it should be declared educationally bankrupt and placed in "receivership." The state or local educational authority invoking receivership would take over the schools and bring them "up to standard" (p. 29). The feasibility and effectiveness of this procedure have not been tested. The point is that no such mechanism now exists.

Award Salary Increments Only for Relevant Knowledge

Conventional salary schedules for teachers currently have two main dimensions. One is seniority. The other is educational attainment, measured by graduate degrees and "units." As explained earlier, the potential benefit to students of basing teachers' pay on seniority may be lost if there is no enforcement of minimum performance standards. Similarly, the potential advantage of basing teachers' pay on education may be lost if that education is not relevant to what teachers actually do, or try to do.

Numerous studies have looked for statistical relationships between characteristics of teachers and student performance, usually measured by test scores. Hanushek (1981) compiled results from almost 100 such studies. Of 89 studies that tested the relationship between students' outcomes and the amount of education their teacher had, only 5 found a significant positive association, while 4 found a significant negative one. Twenty-five studies reported a negative association that was not statistically significant, and 17 reported a nonsignificant positive relationship. In contrast, the association between student outcomes and teachers' experience was positive in 53 of 92 studies, and statistically significant in 28 of the 53. Evidently, student performance is more strongly related to teachers' seniority than to their educational attainment.

Furthermore, there is a theoretical rationale for paying higher salaries to more senior teachers, even if effectiveness does not increase with seniority (see the previous section)—but the justification for paying more to teachers with more education depends entirely on the presumption that education improves performance. In contrast to the skill-based pay plans described in the preceding section, teachers in fact can progress along the salary schedule by accumulating "units" of education that are only tangentially related to their actual work.

Education for teachers can conceivably improve performance by broadening or deepening their knowledge. *Broadening* means acquiring additional know-how, expanding their repertory of teaching techniques. *Deepening* means more "know-why," a better understanding of basic principles related to students' learning and the nature of schools. Districts could map out educational sequences for teachers in different subjects and grade levels, providing choices for individual teachers to reflect differences in professional interests and prior preparation. Unless more districts make the effort to align teachers' ongoing education with their actual classroom practice, it seems unlikely that salary increments for education will buy any benefits for students.

Extra Pay for Superior Performance

The idea of tying teachers' pay to performance arouses strong feelings. For example, Genck has proclaimed "Any school board member who is spending the public's money on teacher salaries without pay-for-performance plans should be thrown out of office" (Cramer, 1983, p. 35). In contrast, Rosenholtz (1985) assails the "fatuous assumptions that schools can be motivated to improve through pecuniary incentives, that schools now withhold services to students that they would supply if the rewards were greater, and, finally, that schools *can* improve if only they are properly motivated to do so" (p. 11).

Many school districts at one time or another have implemented pay-for-performance plans. Proponents of the idea cite this as evidence that it can work. However, detractors point out that most plans have been discontinued. Furthermore, evidence about effects on students' learning is virtually nonexistent. Therefore, like the literature on merit pay in other kinds of organizations (Heneman, 1984), the literature on paying teachers for performance contains much advice that is only tenuously related to findings from actual experience with performance-based pay. Most of the recent advice literature is cautionary, skeptical, or plainly antagonistic to the idea of paying teachers for performance (Bacharach et al., 1985; Johnson, 1984a; McLaughlin, Pfeiffer, Swanson-Owens, & Yee, 1985; Mitchell, Ortiz, & Mitchell, 1983; Thompson, 1979).

Before wading into the controversy, it is useful to attempt some dispassionate description. Fortunately, a picture of recent practice can be pieced together from surveys by the Educational Research Service (Calhoun & Protheroe, 1983; Porwoll, 1979), along with informative case studies and analysis by Hatry and Greiner (1985), Cohen and Murnane (1985), Murnane and Cohen (forthcoming), and Johnson (1984b).

Four major types of pay-for-performance plans can be distinguished. First, and most common in practice, are one-time bonus payments for individual teachers whose performance is judged to be meritorious. These are usually awarded on an annual basis. A teacher who receives a bonus for one year can receive another in a subsequent year only if he or she is once again judged to have earned it. Current or recent examples of such plans are in Bryan, Texas; Lebanon, Connecticut; Penn Manor, Pennsylvania; and Seiling, Oklahoma (Hatry & Greiner, 1985). This kind of plan is what seems to be usually meant by "merit pay."

A second kind of plan also awards one-time bonuses, but to groups rather than individuals. Usually the group consists of all teachers in a school. Group-bonus plans appear in Dallas (Webster & Olson, 1984) and Florida (Abalos, Jolly, & Johnson, 1985). The bonus-pay plan in Houston, Texas, also includes a group-based component (Miller & Say, 1982), and an experimental group-bonus plan has been tried in Norwalk-La Mirada, California (Bruno & Nottingham, 1974).

The third and fourth kinds of pay-for-performance plans are both versions of the career ladder idea. In both varieties, teachers' salaries increase as they move up the ladder. In one kind of plan, promotion depends mainly or entirely on meritorious performance of regular teaching responsibilities. Primary among these is actual instruction of students, but teachers' regular responsibilities also include interaction with parents and the community, helping with extracurricular activities, serving on committees, and sponsoring student teachers. Ladue, Missouri, and Evanston, Illinois, are well-known examples of such merit-based promotion plans (Cohen & Murnane, 1985; Hatry & Greiner, 1985). The other kind of career ladder gives teachers distinct new kinds of responsibility as they move up (Burden, 1985; Murphy & Hart, 1985). New responsibilities may include conducting in-service programs for other teachers, developing new curricula, supervising apprentice teachers, and collaborating in research. Examples of this second type of ladder are the Charlotte-Mecklenburg, North Carolina, career development program (Schlechty, Joslin, Leak, & Hanes, 1985) and the California mentor teacher program.

In theory, the difference between the two career ladder plans is that one keeps all teachers doing essentially the same things but recognizes some individuals for doing a better job, while the other version creates a new structure of roles and responsibilities within a school. The former is more like merit pay, the latter more like the differentiated staffing plans of the 1960s (Bornfriend, 1985; English, 1985; Freiberg, 1985). In practice, the merit-pay version currently predominates, with many of the career-ladder plans in use requiring periodic reevaluation of upper-track teachers as a condition for continuing to receive higher salaries.

All discussions of paying teachers for performance agree that evaluating performance is the central problem. The two most commonly used plans—one-time bonuses for individuals and merit-based career ladders—both require judgments that some individual teachers are performing better than others. These judgments usually are not based mainly on student test scores, because existing tests are assumed not to measure the subtle, multidimensional effects of good teaching, or because attaching pay to test scores would explicitly raise hard questions about the relative value of different kinds of achievement for different students (Murnane, 1985).

In practice, therefore, selection of better teachers depends on observation of the teaching process, and sometimes on dossiers compiled by teachers to document their own accomplishments. Classroom observations are often done not only by the principal, but by others as well, and on more than one day. Selection committees are created to review all the evidence and pick the winners. The evaluation process must be very time-consuming so that judgments of relative merit will be accepted as accurate and fair. If enough attention is not given to this, the pay-for-performance plan is likely to be destroyed by dissension. Even spending a great deal of time and effort on evaluation does not guarantee that the outcome will be accepted as legitimate, since there still may be implicit conflict over which parts of the curriculum are more important, and which students should receive more attention. Most districts that have tried but later discontinued a pay-for-performance plan cited failure of the evaluation process as the reason for stopping it (National Education Association, cited in Newcombe, 1983, p. 41; Porwoll, 1979).

The difficulty of making fair and accurate evaluations of performance is not unique to teaching. A handbook on compensation, though subtitled "Rewarding Performance," states frankly,

If there is an ambiguous area in the entire compensation process, it is the assessment of worker performance. . . . Performance appraisal has become a 'damned if you do, damned if you don't' process. Appraising performance is one of management's most important responsibilities. (Henderson, 1979, p. 317)

Given the inherent difficulty of evaluating individual performance, and given the importance of using teachers' evaluations as a guide for professional self-development (Wise & Darling-Hammond, 1985), tying individual evaluations to merit pay may overburden the evaluation process. In fact, districts that have maintained merit-pay systems for relatively long periods of time usually find ways to avoid betting too much on the process of evaluation. They may keep the monetary stakes small, or pass out bonuses to nearly everyone (Cohen & Murnane, 1985). Districts also learn to avoid publicizing the winners, not only to spare embarrassment for the losers, but also to avoid causing all parents to request placement of their own children with the winning teachers (Benson, 1978, p. 242).

These tactics help ensure survival of merit pay, but they also subvert its purpose (Cohen & Murnane, 1985). Whatever effect cash prizes might have on teachers' motivation is lost if they are given to almost everyone, are of negligible size, or are so private that no one knows who the winners are.

The conclusion from practice, therefore, seems to be that existing procedures for evaluating teachers cannot adequately justify large, conspicuous, cash awards to individuals for meritorious teaching. Individual merit-pay plans tend to crash either because judgments of relative merit are not seen as legitimate, or because the effort required to maintain legitimacy is not felt to be worth whatever gains are achieved. Merit pay seems to survive only in small, affluent school districts where the public shares a strong desire for high-quality education (Cohen & Murnane, 1985).

Paying bonuses to groups rather than individuals simplifies the evaluation problem because it necessarily focuses more on what students learn than on what teachers do. Instead of using classroom observations and teachers' individual dossiers, group incentive plans rely on students' test scores, which may be adjusted statistically to control for differences in students' home background and prior achievement (Abalos et al., 1985; Webster & Olson, 1984). If achievement tests do not measure what teachers are trying to teach, then group incentives do not solve the problem of legitimacy, especially when statistical adjustment procedures are not used or understood. However, if tests do measure what teachers think they are teaching, then using test scores makes identification of superior performance more straightforward and far less time-consuming than when teachers are judged on classroom behavior and dossiers.

Some of the theoretical advantages and disadvantages of group incentives compared to individual incentives were mentioned in the previous section above. Generally, the relative advantages of group incentives are greater if jobs are interdependent. With regard to schools, it is often said that teachers now are too isolated from each other (Lortie, 1975). For example, Glickman (1985) observes, "It is remarkable that teachers can work in the same building on the same common task (instruction) with the same clientele (students) with virtually no knowledge of what other teachers are doing" (p. 39). Glickman gives a vivid example of how teachers actually impede each other: when one teacher leaves, other teachers often remove any useful materials, equipment, or furniture from the classroom, sometimes replacing them with their own discards, so that the next teacher to use the room finds it full of leftovers. One can easily think of other examples of teachers undermining each other: for instance, seeking to have troublesome students assigned to someone else, or making negative remarks about other teachers to administrators, students, or parents. Incentive pay for individuals can aggravate these divisive tendencies (Rosenholtz, 1985).

Conversely, incentives for groups might promote more collaboration on curriculum, instructional technique, discipline, keeping track of individual students from one year to the next or one subject to the next, relations with parents, extracurricular activities, and other matters that affect students' performance. If a whole school is rewarded for good performance, then teachers who are already inclined to accept schoolwide responsibility might have more incentive to do so, and they also have an additional argument for their colleagues to do the same. (As noted earlier, however, there is always the possibility of some "free riding.") The demonstration of school vouchers in the Alum Rock school district in California in the early 1970s provided evidence that group incentives can stimulate creative collaboration among teachers (Stern, deLone, & Murnane, 1975). There is evidence that some teachers are more receptive to group incentives than to individual merit pay. The president of Florida's teacher association, who is also chief negotiator for teachers in Dade County, reported that teachers like Florida's "merit school" program because "it creates a team effort. . . . It doesn't pit teacher against teacher" (Currence, 1985, p. 16). If combined with a bigger role for teachers in decision-making, group incentives in schools could produce benefits similar to the Scanlon plan in private firms.

Despite these theoretical advantages of group incentives—and their increasing prevalence outside education—they are still a rarity in schools. Some of the reasons for this are technical. Available achievement tests often are not closely aligned with school curricula. The importance of testing what is to be taught became evident in a set of field experiments with group performance contracting, conducted by the federal Office of Economic Opportunity in 1970–71: subjects in which test scores were not explicitly included in performance contracts were underemphasized by teachers (Gramlich & Koshel, 1975). Another technical problem is that statistical procedures to adjust test scores for the background and prior achievement of students in different schools are still the subject of theoretical dispute (Rogosa, Brandt, & Zimowski, 1982). Also, movement of students and teachers in and out of schools complicates the task of giving credit to a particular group of teachers for the achievements of a particular group of students. Whether group incentives become more popular in the future will depend in part on whether current experiments can solve these problems.

The most talked-about pay-for-performance idea in the early 1980s has been the career ladder for individual teachers. While serving as Secretary of Education, Terrell Bell proclaimed it necessary to "provide an opportunity for the most outstanding teachers to earn a new distinction beyond the level of the regular teaching ranks." He called the absence of such opportunity part of "the fundamental problem with the current condition of the teaching profession" (Bell, 1983, pp. 3–4). The Secretary's Discretionary Fund in 1984 distributed 51 planning grants to states and localities for the development of teacher incentive structures. Several "education governors," notably Alexander of Tennessee and Graham of Florida, also attracted attention by initiating proposals to recognize and reward master teachers. As of early 1985, 6 states had career ladders under way, 14 were conducting pilot tests, 15 had plans under consideration, and 8 were developing ideas (Murphy & Hart, 1985).

Career ladders have three stated purposes: (1) to attract talented people into teaching; (2) to provide more inducement for the best teachers to keep at it; and (3) to motivate all teachers to improve. The first purpose is to be achieved by increasing a prospective teacher's expected lifetime earnings, especially if he or she expects to reach the top of the ladder. This effect depends on how much additional salary is paid, and what the chances of getting it are. In Tennessee, to take a well-publicized example, a top-ranked teacher will be paid up to $7,000 more (for a 12-month contract) than regular teachers with the same education and seniority, but only about 10% of the teachers are expected to reach the top rank (Parish, 1983). An optimistic young person might therefore expect the career-ladder plan to increase his or her peak earnings by about $1,000, in today's dollars. Referring back to the age-earnings profiles above, and assuming that profiles in Tennessee have a shape similar to the national average, the result of the career-ladder plan there would be to increase the average ratio of peak to starting salary from roughly 1.4 to 1.5. This seems unlikely to make much difference in a young person's perception of the monetary rewards from a teaching career. Furthermore, for a person who is averse to risk, an uncertain payoff with an expected value of $1,000 is worth less than a risk-free payoff of the same amount. For this reason, and also because a given amount of money is worth more if paid now than if paid later, Zabalza et al. (1979) found that it is more cost-effective to recruit new teachers by raising starting salaries than by making the age-earnings profile steeper.

The effectiveness of performance-based career ladders in motivating teachers, and also in retaining those who perform best, will depend in part on whether the process of selecting teachers for advancement is seen as legitimate. This is difficult, as we have observed. In addition, the effectiveness of these plans also will depend on how well they enhance teachers' intrinsic motivation, the issue to which we now turn.

Support the Art of Teaching

A number of writers have questioned the basic assumption that money can motivate teachers to achieve or maintain a high level of performance (Bacharach et al., 1985; Mitchell et al., 1983; Rosenholtz, 1985). At some risk of oversimplification, we can distinguish two kinds of evidence on which this skepticism is based: psychological experiments and statements by teachers.

Psychologists have conducted numerous experiments demonstrating that extrinsic incentives can inhibit intrinsic motivation (Deci, 1972, 1975; Lepper & Greene, 1978). These experiments involve tasks that at least some people will do without any extrinsic reward or punishment—for example, adults spending a few minutes working on puzzles, or children doing an art project. The experiments have found that individuals who receive extrinsic rewards or punishments as an anticipated consequence of performing the activity will subsequently, when the extrinsic incentives are removed, spend less time on the activity than other individuals who were never given extrinsic inducements. This has been interpreted to signify that people become less interested in doing the task for its own sake after they have learned to see it as a means to receive extrinsic rewards or avoid punishment. Related experiments have also shown that extrinsic incentives can reduce risk-taking and incidental learning.

The danger suggested by these studies is that teachers in a pay-for-performance system will come to care less about students and more about money. This kind of goal displacement leads to what Murnane (1985), following Williamson (1975), calls "opportunism." However, it is important to bear in mind that the psychological studies have usually found performance of the experi-

TABLE 2
Opinions of California Public School Teachers (percentages)*

Statement	Strongly disagree 1	2	3	4	Strongly agree 5
Teachers' salaries should be related in part to teachers' effectiveness.	25	12	20	21	23
Teachers should participate in the evaluation of their colleagues.	30	14	23	18	15
Teachers should have a career ladder, which allows them to earn more as they take on diversified professional responsibilities.	4	2	13	24	57
I feel I am making a significant difference in my students' lives.	0	2	13	34	51

*Percentages may not add to 100 due to rounding errors.
Source: Koppich et al. (1985).

mental task increases during the time when extrinsic incentives are applied. It is only after they are removed that performance declines. This suggests that paying teachers for performance might be productive as long as it continues. The worst thing to do would be to start paying for performance, and then stop, which is exactly what has often happened in the past.

An obvious reason to be cautious about applying the results of experimental studies to teachers (or other employees) is that the experimental tasks usually take only a few minutes, but teaching is a day-in, day-out affair. After years in a classroom, intrinsic motivation can lose its intensity. A teacher carrying home a stack of students' papers to correct might find consolation in knowing there is the possibility of a monetary reward—especially if students have been neither enthusiastic nor cooperative.

Opponents of performance-based pay for teachers also point to statements by teachers about why they enter, remain in, or leave the profession. Usually these statements emphasize intrinsic satisfaction from the teaching process itself—or, in the case of leavers, the lack of such satisfaction. Teachers can derive deep fulfillment from knowing they have helped students grow and learn.

However, when asked directly about performance-based pay, many teachers approve of the idea. A nationwide poll of teachers in 1983 by the *American School Board Journal* found 62.7% of respondents agreed that "Teachers who are more effective in the classroom should receive larger salary increases than teachers who are less effective" (Rist, 1983). A similar result was obtained from a representative sample of public school teachers in California (Koppich, Gerritz, & Guthrie, 1985). Table 2 shows answers to some of the questions in that survey. A substantial fraction favor salary differences related to effectiveness, and there is even stronger support for a career ladder based on differentiated responsibilities. At the same time, the great majority of these respondents feel they are having the kind of effect on students that makes teaching rewarding in itself. It is possible that their intrinsic interest in teaching would diminish if performance-based pay were actually instituted. However, most of these teachers appear to see no conflict between their intrinsic motivation and the principle of paying more for better performance.

Possibly, basing part of teachers' pay on performance could help teachers justify to themselves (and their families) the hours of effort for which no thanks are given. Unfortunately, the research to date provides no clear guidance for combining extrinsic and intrinsic rewards most effectively. The trick is to keep results in mind, to encourage teachers to keep doing the tedious chores that are necessary to achieve those results, but at the same time to allow as much opportunity as possible for teachers to enjoy the work. Dewey described this ideal in a famous passage about work and play.

It is important not to confuse the psychological distinction between play and work with the economic distinction. Psychologically, the defining characteristic of play is not amusement nor aimlessness. It is the fact that the aim is thought of as more activity in the same line, without defining continuity of action in reference to results produced. Activities as they grow more complicated gain added meaning by greater attention to specific results achieved. Thus they pass gradually into work. *Both are equally free and intrinsically motivated* [italics added], apart from false economic conditions which tend to make play into idle excitement for the well to do, and work into uncongenial labor for the poor. Work is psychologically simply an activity which consciously includes regard for consequences as a part of itself; it becomes constrained labor when the consequences are outside of the activity as an end to which activity is merely a means. Work which remains permeated with the play attitude is art—in quality if not in conventional designation (Dewey, 1923, pp. 241–242).

More recent literature provides some evidence and much advice on how to sustain intrinsic motivation of employees in general (Katzell & Yankelovich, 1975) and teachers in particular (Bacharach et al., n.d.; Mitchell et al., 1983). For teachers, creating greater diversity in responsibilities from day to day or year to year could help. More opportunity for constructive interaction with colleagues also could be beneficial. A fuller discussion of ideas for restructuring the work of teachers is beyond the scope of this chapter. However, this review has pointed to the possibilities, and the difficulties, of using the compensation system more effectively to support the work of teaching.

REFERENCES

Abalos, J., Jolly, S.J., & Johnson, R. (1985). Statistical methods for selecting merit schools. Paper presented at the annual meeting of the American Educational Research Association, Chicago.

Abraham, K.G., & Medoff, J.L. (1983). *Length of service and the operation of internal labor markets* (Working paper #1394–83). Cambridge, MA: Sloan School of Management, Massachusetts Institute of Technology.

Bacharach, S.B., Lipsky, D.B., & Shedd, J.B. (1985). *Teacher compensation systems and the quality of education*. Ithaca, NY: Organizational Analysis and Practice.

Baugh, W.H., & Stone, J.A. (1982). Mobility and wage equilibration in the educator labor market. *Economics of Education Review, 2* (3), 253–274.

Bell, T.H. (1983). Building a better teaching profession. *American Education, 19* (2), 2–4.

Benson, C.S. (1978). *The economics of public education* (3rd ed.). Boston: Houghton Mifflin.

Bornfriend, A.J. (1985). Career ladders and the debureaucratization of education. In H.C. Johnson, Jr. (Ed.), *Merit, money, and teachers' careers.* Lanham, MD: University Press of America.

Bridges, E.M. (1984). *Managing the incompetent teacher.* Eugene, OR: ERIC Clearinghouse on Educational Management.

Brimelow, P. (1983, September 19). What to do about America's schools. *Fortune,* pp. 60–64.

Bruno, J.E., & Nottingham, M.A. (1974). Linking financial incentives to teacher accountability in school districts. *Educational Administration Quarterly, 10* (3), 46–62.

Bullock, R.J. (1984). Gainsharing—a successful track record. *World of Work Report, 9* (8), 3–4.

Burden, P.R. (1985). Career ladders: Retaining academically talented teachers. In H.C. Johnson, Jr. (Ed.), *Merit, money, and teachers' careers.* Lanham, MD: University Press of America.

Calhoun, F.S., & Protheroe, N.J. (1983). *Merit pay for teachers: Status and descriptions.* Arlington, VA: Educational Research Service.

Chapman, B.J., & Tan, H.W. (1980). Specific training and inter-industry wage differentials in U.S. manufacturing. *Review of Economics and Statistics, 62* (3), 371–378.

Cohen, D.K., & Murnane, R.J. (1985). The merits of merit pay. *The Public Interest,* No. 80, 3–30.

Committee for Economic Development (1985). *Investing in our children.* New York: author.

Coons, J.E., & Sugarman, S.D. (1978). *Education by choice, the case for family control.* Berkeley: University of California Press.

Cramer, J. (1983). Yes—merit pay can be a horror, but a few school systems have done it right. *American School Board Journal, 170* (9), 28–34.

Currence, C. (1985). Teachers' unions bringing reform issues to the bargaining table. *Education Week, 4* (34), 1, 16.

Deci, E.L. (1972). The effects of contingent and noncontingent rewards and controls on intrinsic motivation. *Organizational Behavior and Human Performance, 8* (2), 217–229.

Deci, E.L. (1975). *Intrinsic motivation.* New York: Plenum Press.

Dewey, J. (1923). *Democracy and education: An introduction to the philosophy of education.* New York: Macmillan.

Duncan, G.J., & Hoffman, S. (1979). On-the-job training and earnings differences by race and sex. *Review of Economics and Statistics, 61* (4), 594–603.

English, F.W. (1985). We need the Ghostbusters! A response to Jerome Freiberg. *Educational Leadership, 42* (4), 22–25.

Everett, G. (1985). Supply and demand for teachers: a look at national trends. Berkeley: University of California, School of Education.

Feistritzer, C.E. (1983). *The condition of teaching.* Princeton, NJ: The Carnegie Foundation for the Advancement of Teaching.

Foster, C.A., & Marquart, D.J. (1984). *Performance-based funding in public schools.* Sacramento, CA: Sequoia Institute.

Freiberg, H.J. (1985). Master teacher programs: Lessons from the past. *Educational Leadership, 42* (4), 16–21.

French, R.L. (1985). Dispelling the myths about Tennessee's career ladder program. *Educational Leadership, 42* (4), 9–13.

Friedman, M., & Friedman, R. (1979). *Free to choose.* New York: Avon.

Glickman, C.D. (1985). The supervisor's challenge: Changing the teacher's work environment. *Educational Leadership, 42* (4), 38–40.

Gramlich, E.M., & Koshel, P.P. (1975). *Educational performance contracting.* Washington, DC: Brookings Institution.

Greiner, J.M., Dahl, R.E., Hatry, H.P., & Millar, A.P. (1977). *Monetary incentives and work standards in five cities: Impacts and implications for management and labor.* Washington, DC: Urban Institute.

Gutpa, N., Jenkins, G.D., Jr., & Curington, W.P. (forthcoming). Paying for knowledge: Myths and realities. *National Productivity Review.*

Hanushek, E.A. (1981). Throwing money at schools. *Journal of Policy Analysis and Management, 1,* 19–42.

Hatry, H.P., & Greiner, J.M. (1985). *Issues and case studies in teacher incentive plans.* Washington, DC: The Urban Institute.

Henderson, R.I. (1979). *Compensation management.* Reston, VA: Reston Publishing.

Heneman, R.L. (1984). Pay for performance: exploring the merit system. Elmsford, NY: Work in America Institute.

Hirschhorn, L. (1984). *Beyond mechanization: Work and technology in a postindustrial age.* Cambridge, MA: MIT Press.

Holden, K.C., & Hansen, W.L. (forthcoming). Part-time work, full-time work, and occupational segregation. In C. Brown & J. Pechman (Eds.), *Gender in the workplace.* Washington, DC: Brookings Institution.

Iman, S.C. (1975). The development of participation by semiautonomous work teams: The case of Donnelly Mirrors. In L.E. Davis and A.B. Cherns (Eds.), *The quality of working life* (Vol. 2). New York: Free Press.

International Labour Office (1984). *Payment by results.* Geneva, Switzerland: Author.

Jackson, P.W. (1985). Does virtue merit pay? Reflections on the better-teachers-deserve-more-money argument. In H.C. Johnson, Jr. (Ed.), *Merit, money, and teachers' careers.* Lanham, MD: University Press of America.

Jenkins, D.G., Jr., & Gutpa, N. (1985). The payoffs of paying for knowledge. *National Productivity Review, 3,* 121–130.

Johnson, S.M. (1984a). Merit pay for teachers: A poor prescription for reform. *Harvard Educational Review 54* (2), 175–185.

Johnson, S.M. (1984b). *Pros and cons of merit pay.* Bloomington, IN: Phi Delta Kappa Educational Foundation.

Katzell, R.A., & Yankelovich, D. (1975). *Work, productivity, and job satisfaction.* New York: Harcourt Brace Jovanovich.

Koppich, J., Gerritz, W., & Guthrie, J.W. (1985). *California teachers' opinions on working conditions and school reform proposals.* Berkeley: University of California, School of Education.

Lawler, E.E., III. (1971). *Pay and organizational effectiveness: A psychological view.* New York: McGraw-Hill.

Lawler, E.E., III. (1981). *Pay and organization development.* Reading, MA: Addison-Wesley.

Lawler, E.E., & Ledford, G.E. (1985). Skill-based pay: A concept that's catching on. *Personnel, 62* (9), 30–37.

Lazear, E.P. (1981). Agency, earnings profiles, productivity, and hours restrictions. *American Economic Review, 71* (4), 606–620.

Lepper, M.R., & Greene, D. (1978). *The hidden costs of reward.* Hillsdale, NJ: Erlbaum.

Lortie, D.C. (1975). *Schoolteacher: A sociological study.* Chicago: University of Chicago Press.

Manski, C.F. (1985). *Academic ability, earnings, and the decision to become a teacher: Evidence from the National Longitudinal Study of the High School Class of 1972* (Working Paper No. 1539). Cambridge, MA: National Bureau of Economic Research.

McLaughlin, M.W., Pfeiffer, S., Swanson-Owens, D., & Yee, S. (1985). State policy and teaching excellence (Project Report No. 85–A5). Stanford, CA: Stanford University, Institute for Research on Educational Finance and Governance.

Medoff, J.L., & Abraham, K.G. (1980). Experience, performance, and earnings. *Quarterly Journal of Economics, 95* (4), 703–736.

Medoff, J.L., & Abraham, K.G. (1981). Are those paid more really more productive? The case of experience. *Journal of Human Resources, 16* (2), 186–216.

Miles, R.E. (1976). Compensation, organizational structure, and control: Toward a balance. *Proceedings of the Twenty-Eighth Annual Winter Meeting of the Industrial Relations Research Association,* 137–144.

Miller, L., & Say, E. (1982). This bold incentive pay plan pits capitalism against teacher shortages. *American School Board Journal, 169* (9), 24–25.

Miller, P. (1985). *The complexity of the single salary schedule versus merit pay issue.* Berkeley: University of California, School of Education.

Mitchell, D.E., Ortiz, F.I., & Mitchell, T.K. (1983). *Work orientation and job performance: The cultural basis of teaching rewards and incentives.* Riverside: University of California.

Mitchell, D.J.B. (1985). Wage flexibility in the United States: Lessons from the past. *American Economic Review, 75* (2), 36–40.

Moore, B.E., & Ross, T.L. (1978) *The Scanlon way to improved productivity: A practical guide.* New York: Wiley.

Murnane, R.J. (1984). Selection and survival in the teacher labor market. *Review of Economics and Statistics, 66,* 513–518.

Murnane, R.J. (1985). The rhetoric and reality of merit pay: Why are they different? In H.C. Johnson, Jr. (Ed.), *Merit, money, and teachers' careers.* Lanham, MD: University Press of America.

Murnane, R.J., & Cohen, D.K. (forthcoming). Merit pay and the evaluation problem: Why most merit pay plans fail and a few survive. *Harvard Educational Review.*

Murphy, M.J., & Hart, A.W. (1985). *Career ladder reforms.* Salt Lake City: University of Utah.

National Center for Employee Ownership. *Employee ownership,* monthly newsletter. Washington, DC.

National Commission on Productivity and Work Quality (1975). *Employee incentives to improve state and local government productivity.* Washington, DC: Author.

Newcombe, E. (1983). *Rewarding teachers: Issues and incentives.* Philadelphia, PA: Research for Better Schools.

O'Toole, J. (1973). *Work in America.* Cambridge, MA: MIT Press.

Parish, J. (1983). Excellence in education: Tennessee's 'master' plan. *Phi Delta Kappan, 64* (10), 722–726.

Porwoll, P.J. (1979). *Merit pay for teachers.* Arlington, VA: Educational Research Service.

Rist, M.C. (1983). Our nationwide poll: most teachers endorse the merit pay concept. *American School Board Journal, 170* (9), 23–27.

Rogosa, D., Brandt, D., & Zimowski, M. (1982). A growth curve approach to the measurement of change. *Psychological Bulletin, 92* (3), 726–748.

Rosenbaum, J.E. (1984). *Career mobility in a corporate hierarchy.* Orlando, FL: Academic Press.

Rosenholtz, S.J. (1985). Career ladders and merit pay: Capricious fad or fundamental reform? Urbana-Champaign: University of Illinois.

Rush, H. (1973). *Organization development: A reconnaissance.* New York: The Conference Board.

Schlechty, P.C., Joslin, A.W., Leak, S.E., & Hanes, R.C. (1985). The Charlotte-Mecklenburg teacher career development program. *Educational Leadership, 42* (4), 5–8.

Silverman, B.R.S. (1983). Why the merit pay system failed in the federal government. *Personnel Journal, 62* (4), 294–302.

Solow, R. (1979). Another possible source of wage stickiness. *Journal of Macroeconomics, 1,* 79–82.

Stern, D. (1982). *Managing human resources.* Dover, MA: Auburn House.

Stern, D., deLone, R.H., & Murnane, R.J. (1975). Evolution at Alum Rock. *The Review of Education, 1* (3), 309–324.

Stiglitz, J. (1976). The efficiency wage hypothesis, surplus labour, and the distribution of income in L.D.C.s. *Oxford Economic Papers, 28,* 194–227.

Thompson, S. (1979). Motivation of teachers. Burlingame, CA: Association of California School Administrators.

United States Bureau of the Census. *1980 census of population, earnings by occupation and education* (PC80-2-8B). Washington, DC: U.S. Department of Commerce.

United States Bureau of the Census. *1970 census of population, earnings by occupation and education* (PC(2)-8B). Washington, DC: U.S. Department of Commerce.

United States Bureau of Labor Statistics (1979). *Major collective bargaining agreements: Wage-incentive, production standard and time-study provisions* (Bulletin 1425-18). Washington, DC: U.S. Department of Labor.

Walton, R.E. (1980). Establishing and maintaining high commitment work systems. In J.R. Kimberly & R.H. Miles (Eds.), *The organizational life cycle.* San Francisco: Jossey-Bass.

Webster, W.J., & Olson, G.H. (1984). An empirical approach to identifying effective schools. Paper presented at the annual meeting of the American Educational Research Association, New Orleans.

Whyte, W.F. (1955). *Money and motivation.* New York: Harper & Bros.

Williamson, O.E. (1975). *Markets and hierarchies: Analysis and antitrust implications.* New York: The Free Press.

Wise, A.E., & Darling-Hammond, L. (1983). Educational vouchers: Regulating their efficiency and effectiveness. *Educational Researcher, 12,* 9–12, 17–18.

Wise, A.E., & Darling-Hammond, L. (1985). Teacher evaluation and teacher professionalism. *Educational Leadership, 42* (4), 28–33.

Yellen, J.L. (1984). Efficiency wage models of unemployment. *American Economic Review, 74* (2), 200–205.

Zabalza, A., Turnbull, P., & Williams, G. (1979). The economics of teachers supply. Cambridge, England: Cambridge University Press.

Zarkin, G.A. (1985a). Occupational choice: an application to the market for public school teachers. *Quarterly Journal of Economics, 100,* 409–446.

Zarkin, G.A. (1985b). *The importance of economic incentives in the recruitment of teachers.* Final report to National Institute of Education (NIE-G-83-0068). Durham, NC: Duke University.

Chapter 10

Union-Made Teaching:
The Effects of Labor Relations on Teaching Work

CHARLES TAYLOR KERCHNER
Claremont Graduate School

The union label on a product or service is, in effect, an assertion. It proclaims that the union has changed the conditions of production, the social and economic status of the worker, or the nature of what is produced. Thus, the garment workers' emblem sewn in a collar indicates that the shirt was produced under decent conditions. The framed membership certificate from the bar association (a powerful union if there ever was one) establishes the social position of the lawyer. The guild hallmark on fine silver proclaims that the product was produced to high craft standards. Teachers, however, seldom have such overt labels. Teachers do not affix "union-made" stamps to report cards, nor are "union shop" placards found behind teachers' desks. Insignia are seldom worn except by union officers and staff members. However, it is argued here that in less visible ways, the unionization of the vast majority of America's 1.9 million public school teachers has altered teaching.

Finding a union effect on teaching is more than a matter of casual interest. If unions have, in fact, changed teaching, they have carried off a powerful intervention, one that runs counter to the persistent belief that nothing changes teaching very much very fast (Cuban, 1984; Kirst, 1983). A substantial union effect on teaching would suggest that unions have become potent agents of change in education and that they have the capacity to be deliberate engines of educational reform. Such a realization would cast unions in a substantially different role than has been the case historically, and it would focus the attention of policy and research on the relationship between unionization and teaching rather than the relationship between unionization and school governance.

This chapter considers the extent of union effects on three aspects of teaching:

1. *Teaching work itself.* Jobs exist within a set of rules that help define the occupation. They shape the activities that constitute the work, and they influence the working conditions. But, more fundamentally, the set of rules, norms, and understandings that surround an occupation help to define what kind of work is undertaken. We readily understand, for instance, the differences between work where the activities are highly defined and those where workers are expected to define their own tasks. Unionism, the evidence suggests, has aided the formalization and rationalization of these rules and thus serves as a bureaucratizing influence.

2. *Teaching as an occupation.* An occupation is partly characterized by status—the financial rewards and social respect accorded its members—and partly characterized by the extent to which the occupation protects its members and determines their competence. Here, the influence of unions has been mixed. Unions do influence teacher salaries, but not enormously, but the relative social status of teaching appears unchanged. And, the role of unions in teacher protection and competence varies widely from place to place.

3. *Teaching in organizational context.* Public school teaching is strongly shaped by the organizations in which it takes place, and teachers shape those organizations. Unionism has powerfully altered the role of teachers as they interact with school districts: it has changed what teachers do when they are dissatisfied, changed the definition of teacher loyalty, and changed teacher interaction with social and education reforms.

After a brief introduction to labor relations research, the chapter will consider the research evidence in each of the three areas of impact on teaching.

INTRODUCTION: THE LABOR RELATIONS LITERATURE

Collective bargaining research has concentrated on governance impacts precisely because that is where the effects were thought to be. Unionization was variously perceived as a social revolution or an occupational turf fight, and the emergence of unionized teachers raised two central problems: conflict management and school governance protection. Conflict management became a central concern because collective bargaining opened the door for the legitimate and open disagreement between teachers and school managers (Perry & Wildman, 1970). The possibility of strikes and the means of industrial peacemaking became a central subject of research (Bruno & Nelken, 1975; Burton & Krider, 1970; Cole, 1969a; Delaney, 1983; Richardson, 1977). Governance was a central issue because it was assumed that the collectivization of public-sector workers posed a real threat to the orderly and democratic operation of government. Probably more than any other single

work, Wellington and Winter's essay (1969; expanded in 1971) set the tone
for the decade of research that followed. Allowing employee strikes would

be so effective a pressure as to skew the results of the "normal American political process." One
should straightaway make plain that the strike issue is not *simply* the essentiality of public
service as contrasted with services or products produced in the private sector. . . . The problem
is that because market restraints are attenuated and because public employee strikes cause in-
convenience to voters, such strikes too often succeed. Since other interest groups with conflicting claims on municipal government do not, as a general proposition, have anything approaching the effectiveness of this union technique . . . they are put at a significant disadvantage in the
political process. (Wellington & Winter, 1969, p. 1120)

Collective bargaining was thus envisaged almost exclusively as a monopoliz-
ing force among workers. Attention was drawn to teachers' unions as economic monopolies, which have a tendency to raise wages above competitive
levels, and as political monopolies, which possess an unjustified influence
over the political process (Grimshaw, 1979; Lieberman, 1980).

However, there is a "second face" to unionism. As Freeman and Medhoff
(1979, 1984) put it, unionism can also be viewed from an institutional perspective, which they call "the collective voice/institutional response face"
(1984, p. 7). Examination of this second face of unionism requires that we
consider how the beliefs and activities of unionization are integrated into
school operations as a whole: how administrators respond to what teachers
do, how values change, how status differences are recognized. This approach
to labor relations requires that one understands how statutes, contracts, and
union structures are socialized into organizational behavior and teachers' perception of themselves as workers.

While there are enough data to reveal the collective voice/institutional response face of unionism, it is necessary to add a sense of tentativeness to its
interpretation. First, teacher unionization did not occur in social isolation.
Thus, when one finds that teaching has changed, one cannot automatically
conclude that unionization caused the change. Second, unlike the situation in
the private sector, there are relatively few nonunion comparison groups available and most of those are in states that prohibit collective bargaining. For
instance, there is practically no recorded research on school districts whose
managements and teachers deliberately adopted a union-free environment
stance (Kerchner & Mitchell, 1981). Third, there is a general shortage of
published research on labor impacts. Although more than 400 doctoral dissertations in this field are recorded, only a handful have been published as
books or excerpted in academic journals. The level of sponsored research on
educational labor relations has been very low, probably less than $1 million
from all sources over the past 20 years. As a consequence, most studies are
quite limited in scale, relying on field data from a single district or secondary
analysis of data bases gathered for purposes other than research on unions.

Since this review is limited to that portion of the larger research on labor relations that helps to illuminate the effects of labor relations on teaching, there are many areas of the more general labor relations research literature that are not covered here but for which separate collections, reviews, or bibliographies are referenced (Cresswell & Murphy, 1976). These include the rather substantial literature on organization (Moskow, Lowenberg & Koziara, 1970; Urban, 1982); negotiations (Cooper & Bussey, 1980; Cresswell & Murphy, 1976, 1980); strikes and strike alternatives (Cole 1969a; Colton, 1977; Cooper, 1982; Tomkiewicz, 1979; Weintraub & Thornton, 1976); public-sector bargaining and state governance (Cresswell & Spargo, 1980; Cresswell & Wachter, 1983; Kerchner, 1978, 1979; Ross 1980); principals and administrator unions (Bridges & Cooper, 1976; Cooper, 1979; Lutz & Caldwell, 1979; Murphy & Ellman, 1974); and studies of union organizations themselves (Braun, 1972; Cole, 1969b; Donley, 1976; Eaton, 1975; Jessup, 1978; Sanzare, 1977; Selden, 1985; Stinnett, 1968; Stinnett, Kleinmann & Ware, 1966; Tooredman, 1978).

EVIDENCE ABOUT TEACHING WORK ACTIVITIES

All occupations are shaped by what Dunlop (1958) called a "web of rules." First of all, rules emerge from organizations and the particular work process itself. Thus, one can look for effects of unionization in new rules that change working conditions and activities. A new schedule, team teaching, subject matter specialization, a homework policy, or working with an aide changes teaching work, just as introducing a new mining or factory process changes work in those settings. Second, teaching is a socially constructed reality, and changes in work rules take on added significance when they affect the central beliefs of the occupational or organizational culture (Dunlop, 1958, p. 17; see also Deal & Kennedy, 1982; Ouchi, 1980). Consequently, we can ask whether teaching is more or less of a profession than it used to be, more or less an individual undertaking, more or less formalized or ritualized.

The Labor Contract

In labor relations, the most visible part of the web of rules is the collective contract. Collective bargaining is what the vast majority of unions do. The contract is an explicit output—a legally binding document enforceable through the grievance mechanism and through the courts. Symbolically, the contract is the "artifact of the relationship" (Cresswell & Murphy, 1976), the signal that a relationship has been formed or reshaped, and the boxscore that determines how well or poorly each party did.

Scholars who have engaged in the exacting and frequently tedious work of examining and classifying thousands of pages of contracts have produced a nearly universal conclusion: contracts have extended well beyond traditional bread-and-butter issues into areas of organizational policy. Over time, contracts tend to cover more subjects and to be more detailed and specific about the subjects that they include.

An examination of five large contract studies shows that the hours, conditions, and duties of work are increasingly a matter of contractual agreement (Eberts & Stone, 1984; Goldschmidt, Bowers, Riley & Stuart, 1984; Johnson, Nelson & Potter, 1985; McDonnell & Pascal, 1979b; Simpkins, Mc-Cutcheon & Alec, 1979). As Table 1 shows, provisions for adjudicating grievances, often referred to as the heart of the contract because they make the other parts more easily enforceable, have become nearly universal. Provisions for school hours have increased in frequency and have become nearly universal in larger school districts. Class-size requirements are present in almost half of the districts, although there is some evidence that the prevalence of these provisions is declining. (It should be noted that none of the studies uses exactly the same classification scheme, and none reports a classification of all contractual items. Also, the Simpkins et al. (1979) report relies on questionnaires from school districts rather than on contracts themselves.)

McDonnell and Pascal's (1979b) comparison of 150 school district contracts demonstrates the extent to which labor contracts have become the vehicle for dealing with a school district's current problems. For example, notice the rapid increase in reduction-in-force procedures from 11% in 1970 to 37% in 1975, which occurred during a time of real and projected enrollment declines that presented schools (and unions as teachers' representatives) with the need for an orderly way to dismiss teachers. Transfer criteria also became more common. By the time of Johnson's 1984 study, voluntary transfer criteria were present in 57% of agreements and involuntary transfer criteria were present in 60%. Notice also the increasing attention given to dismissals and teacher evaluation.

Clearly, the scope of teacher labor contracts has expanded over the years, and in this way teacher labor relations mirror those of other workers (Weitzman, 1974). However, the expansion of bargaining has been interpreted quite differently. Most frequently, expansion of the scope of bargaining is seen in terms of intrusion into managerial prerogatives or policy areas reserved for public determination. Much of the critique of bargaining from the citizen's action perspective takes this tack (Cheng, 1976; Englert, 1979; Institute for Responsive Education, 1975; Pierce, 1975). The vision is of labor pushing to expand and management resisting. There are suggestions, however, that this is not always the case. The scope of labor contracts also expands through the common desires of the parties to solve problems and through pressure from management to formalize or specify its rights (Kerchner, 1978; Mitchell, Kerchner, Erck, & Pryor, 1981). Sometimes these management-inspired changes take the form of rollbacks or takebacks of past concessions (Eberts & Stone, 1984, pp. 25, 28; Perry, 1979, p. 16), but they can also serve as evidence that management has become the aggressive party in labor relations

TABLE 1
Percentage of Contracts Providing Particular Provisions

Provision	McDonnell & Pascal 1970 N-151	McDonnell & Pascal 1975 N-151	Goldschmidt et al. 1981–1982 N-80	Simpkins, et al.[a] 1978 Small N-258	Simpkins, et al.[a] 1978 Large N-5	Johnson et al. 1985 N-155	Eberts & Stone Michigan 1972 N-454	Eberts & Stone Michigan 1976 N-454	Eberts & Stone New York 1972 N-455	Eberts & Stone New York 1976 N-45
Grievances	70	83	93	97	100				96	99
Teacher evaluation	42	65		64	100		40	79	67	87
Probationary						50				
Nonprobationary						75				
School hours	39	58	61	89	100					
Pupil exclusion	28	46	31	31	100					
Assignment refusal	21	27								
Class size	20	34	49	35	80	15	84	67	62	56
Promotion rules	20	32				15				
Transfer criteria	19	29		46	60					
Voluntary						57				
Involuntary						60				
Instructional committee	16	31	68				62	42	37	39
RIF procedure	11	37		65	80				12	40
By seniority							70	83		
Dismissal procedures						27				
Aides	11	29					35	24		
Early retirement						32				
Curriculum			46	25	40					
Student placement			64							
Teacher selection and assignment			96							
Management rights						92				
Budget priorities				3	20	66				

[a]Undertaken by survey of superintendents rather than reading contracts themselves. Small school districts are those having fewer than 2,500 students. Large districts have more than 100,000 students.

Sources: Eberts & Stone (1984); Goldschmidt et al. (1984); Johnson et al. (1985); McDonald & Pascal (1979b); Simpkins et al. (1979)

seeking to "manage through the contract rather than around it" (Mitchell et al., 1981, p. 183). Eberts & Stone (1984, p. 25), for instance, show that the number of districts in which class size appears in contracts and where class size is a grievable item *declined* markedly in Michigan school districts between 1972 and 1976. These changes appeared unrelated to the financial condition of the district or changes in enrollment (Eberts & Stone, 1984, p. 35). Johnson, Nelson, and Potter (1985, pp. 117–124) show the managerial influence quite clearly. A management rights clause was found in 66% of the contracts, and while teacher assignment was considered in 92% of the contracts, 27% of those contracts had clauses saying that assignment was the province of administrative discretion, and an additional 19% had teacher preference clauses, such as: "To the extent that [teachers'] wishes do not conflict with the instructional requirements and best interests of the school system and the pupils, [they will be granted]" (Johnson, Nelson, & Potter, 1985, p. 118). There were also strong managerial influences apparent in transfer clauses.

Some researchers trace a greater union effect on teacher work activities and conditions to sources outside the contract than to the contract itself (Jessup, 1985; Mitchell et al., 1981; Perry, 1979). Perry and Wildman (1970) pointed to the significant potential for union influence through consultation at central and school levels. In a restudy of some of the same districts, Perry (1979) found increases in the number of joint committees, particularly in large cities, "assigned tasks ranging from reviewing the schedule of increments for extracurricular activities to evaluating a teacher-aide program and developing a teacher evaluation program" (p. 16). Perry's finding about increased regular contact between union and management is also evident in studies of New York City (Klaus, 1969), Chicago (Grimshaw, 1979), and, to a limited extent, Los Angeles (Thomas, 1982). However, it is not universal. Eberts and Stone's (1984, p. 28) analysis of New York and Michigan contracts and Kerchner and Mitchell's (1981, pp. A22-A40) ethnographic studies suggest that in some cases unions abandon interactionist roles and confine themselves to teacher protection issues. This is particularly the case during periods of prolonged high conflict. And, interestingly, somewhat fewer teachers reported that they were as involved in committee work as they had been a decade earlier (Gardner, 1982, p. 63).

Characterization of Teaching Work

Have changes in the contract changed the character of teaching work? The answer is a qualified yes. Teaching has become more preplanned and structured, more bureaucratized in the sense that "bureaucratization is the rationalization of collective activities," and in the sense that it "evokes slowness and ponderousness" to adapt (Crozier, 1964, pp. 62–65). One hastens to add that there is nothing in the data to suggest that teachers' unions *intended* to encourage bureaucratization. On the contrary: Union leaders talk of their jobs in terms of freeing teachers to teach. But the primary union instrument is the creation of new, written rules of behavior, and as Wise (1979, p. 200) notes, "Unions will seek new rules and procedural safeguards, and management will counter with rules of their own." This sets the stage for using the instruments of unionism—contract negotiation and adjudication—for the standardization of instruction. The presence of unions, and the explicit division of the work force into workers and managers, supports the belief that instruction should be organizationally planned and overseen.

Based on ethnographic evidence, Mitchell and Kerchner (1983) reasoned that the fundamental character of teaching work could be determined according to how tasks were assigned and how the work was inspected. Under this typology, one can discriminate between tasks that are highly preplanned and rationalized and those that are highly flexible and situationally adaptive. One can also discriminate between work whose processes or products are directly overseen by supervision or quality assurance mechanisms and work settings that require their occupants to be tested and certified before they are allowed to begin to practice an occupation. The intersection of these characteristics produces four ideal-type work conceptions: *labor, craft, profession, and art.* Mitchell and Kerchner's case studies led them to the conclusion that unionization was making teaching more rationalized and more highly inspected, meaning that the laboring work roles were being emphasized. Other studies generally support the contention that teaching has tended to become more rationalized and preplanned (Belasco & Alluto, 1969; Bickel & Bickel, 1979; Wollett, 1969). Teaching also is being more heavily inspected, but the dominant drive for inspection appears to be coming from the school reform movement rather than from labor relations.

The bureaucratizing effects of unions are seen strongly in the specification of duties and the requirements for due process when duties are changed. Restriction and specification of teachers duties have added to the division of labor, making teaching somewhat like an à la carte menu. School managers specify those duties that they want performed and those for which they are prepared to pay. Teachers frequently remove items from the menu by refusing to provide services that are contractually optional. In negotiations, the issue of specifying duties most commonly arises in terms of relief from nonteaching assignments, such as a guarantee of a duty-free lunch period (Perry, 1979, p. 13).

Since then, this thrust has carried into nonteaching activities such as faculty meetings, parent conferences, preparation of report cards, supervision of sporting events, and leadership of student activities. The goal of teachers in this area has been to make such activities voluntary or compensable. Teachers across nine systems have been quite successful in this quest as a direct result of collective bargaining. Most systems now provide for faculty meetings, parent conferences, and report-card preparation on school time and require little or no teacher participation in after-school activities. Most systems now also provide for larger and far more pervasive pay premiums for teacher participation in student extracurricular activities, and some systems are beginning to face demands that teachers can be assigned to such activities only with their consent. (Perry, 1979, p. 13)

While the extra-pay-for-extra-work concept was certainly not introduced by collective bargaining, it was powerfully extended by bargaining (Johnson, 1984, p. 91). Furthermore,

teachers' attitudes were said to have changed. In those districts where participation was not required by contract or board policy, principals had to rely on friendly persuasion or veiled threats to ensure sufficient coverage. It was not so much that teachers sought pay for their work. Rather, the widespread introduction of stipends reinforced the notion that teachers' professional obligations were defined rather than diffuse and that they, rather than their principals, had the right to determine whether they would participate outside their classrooms. (Johnson, 1984, p. 95. See also Mitchell et al., 1981, p. 156.)

In addition to the division of teaching work into mandatory and optional duties, school duties increasingly are being divided between teachers and such other employees as aides, playground and lunchroom supervisors, and other paraprofessionals. This change of duties results from an economic substitution of lower priced paraprofessional services for higher priced teacher services. That is, when school districts found they would have to pay someone for supervising lunchrooms, they chose to pay someone who made less than a teacher. This effect is frequently noted in labor relations and can be seen in studies of police unionism where sworn officers have been increasingly relieved of paperwork duties (Juris & Feuille, 1973). It may also represent an assertion on the part of teachers that "they were not to be regarded as full-time caretakers, but as professionals with instructional expertise" (Johnson, 1984, p. 107). In an organizational sense, however, it means that someone must decide in advance what kinds of work teachers are to do and when they are to do it.

The number of support personnel such as psychologists, aides, and coordinators grew between 1961 and 1971 at a rate 3 to 5 times as fast as the teacher work force (Kirst, 1983, p. 436). California, with more than 30 categorical programs in addition to the federal ones, reported particularly large increases in pupil services personnel (California Legislative Analyst, 1980).

A further dimension of bureaucratization is seen in the extent to which work rules are used to standardize teaching, making all teachers the same. This allows work to be easily transferred from one employee to another or for workers to be transferred to different assignments or work places. This tendency has been found in manufacturing (Slichter, Healy, & Livernash, 1960), as well as in education (Kerchner & Mitchell, 1981). For teachers, the argument has been made that specialists find it difficult to garner special treatment at the expense of so-called regular classroom teachers who constitute the vast majority of a bargaining unit. In observing bargaining and tracing issues through the process, it was found that counselors, subject-matter specialists, psychologists, and support personnel in the teacher bargaining unit frequently made contract proposals that were seldom accepted (Mitchell et al., 1981). Kulleseid (1982) observed tensions between teachers and librarians. Special education appears to be an exception. Studies reveal clauses dealing with special education policy in 44% of the contracts and clauses dealing with special education teacher compensation, training, and other matters in 60% of the contracts (Goldschmidt, Bowers, Riley, & Stuart, 1984; Sosnowsky & Coleman, 1971). Clearly, special education teachers have been recognized as having a *bona fide* specialty. However, their legitimation came through legislation rather than labor negotiation, and much of what appears in their contracts is simply memorialization of statutory requirements. Groups of teachers who do not have their specialties recognized in statute appear to be less successful in gaining special work rules.

When differences among teachers are contractually recognized, as in the case of special education teachers, additional rules are created to specify how they shall interact with other teachers. The special education contracts analyzed by Goldschmidt and colleagues (1984, p. 61) provide rules designed to determine in advance which classifications of students will be placed in special education classrooms and which in regular classrooms. They call for notice to be given to regular classroom teachers before students are placed in their classrooms, and for rights of appeal.

Clearly, unionization has had a major impact on the rule-making machinery and on the specification of the web of rules. It is somewhat surprising, therefore, to observe that many of the most basic structural dimensions of teaching work appear to be largely unchanged. In the National Education Association's 5-year surveys (the best longitudinal data available), teachers appear to work about the same amount of time as they did in 1961. The required school hours are still 36 hours a week, and the reported work week has declined by only 1.2 hours to 45.9 hours a week. The school year remains about the same: 180 days with 6 nonteaching days (see Table 2). Lunch periods have been shortened by 7 minutes to 33 minutes.

Longitudinal studies using individual district data, however, do suggest that changes have taken place in teacher work loads, "particularly in the areas of contact time and extracurricular responsibilities" (Perry, 1979, p. 14). Other case studies indicate a minimization of teacher work effort during prolonged negotiations and labor-management tension (Mitchell et al., 1981, pp. 158–159).

One major change in teaching work, which accompanied unionization, was the decrease in class size from 29 to 25 in elementary schools and from 27 to 23 in secondary and departmentalized elementary schools (Table 2). The number of pupils that each teacher saw per day in secondary and departmentalized elementary schools dropped from 156 to 118. The National Center for Educational Statistics broader measures report similar declines in class size (Pilsko & Stern, 1985).

Certainly, unionization was not the only cause of class-size declines. Declining enrollments and increases in special education services also pushed

TABLE 2
Longitudinal Comparison of Teacher Work Activities

Category	1961	1966	1971	1976	1981
Hours per week					
Required school hours	36.80	36.50	36.50	36.30	36.30
Compensated extra hours	na	na	6.20	9.60	7.00
Noncompensated hours	na	10.20	8.20	8.50	8.70
Total workweek	47.10	47.40	46.90	46.10	45.90
Teaching days per year[a]		181	181	180	180
Nonteaching days		5	4	5	6
Minutes in lunch period	40.00	38.00	37.00	35.00	33.00
Class size					
Nondepartmentalized elementary	29	28	27	25	25
Secondary and dept. elementary	27	27	26	25	23
Pupils per day in secondary and dept. elementary schools	156	132	134	127	118
Assignment within college prep area, secondary	62.30	66.40	76.20	76.50	80.30
No team teaching in school			63.40	60.40	65.40
Have or share an aide			29.30	33.30	28.00
Participate in					
Curriculum committee			40.80	44.70	34.20
Other committee			35.20	38.60	32.60

[a]Teacher's total workweek estimates taken from a different answer than previous questions; does not add.
Source: Gardner, 1982.

down average class sizes. However, those who have undertaken field studies of unionization generally subcribe to the view "that changes in class size would not have been made without collective bargaining" (Johnson, 1984, p. 98. See also Grimshaw, 1979, p. 70.).

Eberts (1984) reports the most ambitious attempt to use the economic concept of a production function to explain union effects. While not a direct test of student achievement, Eberts' research associates unionism with variables that the school effectiveness literature links to achievement. Unionism appears to have mixed effects or, as the author puts it, "The net effect of collective bargaining on teacher productivity is not clear" (Eberts, 1984, p. 346).

Unionization appears to decrease the amount of time teachers spend in direct instruction, which arguably would lower student achievement, and raise the amount of time teachers spend in preparation of instruction, a variable associated with increased achievement. The 2,071 union-represented teachers in Eberts' data base (see Hemenway, 1978, for a description of the data base) spent about 3% less time in direct instruction than did their 1,180 nonunion counterparts: about 9 minutes a day or 5 days a school year. However, the unionized teachers spent about 4% more time on preparation, about 13% more time on administrative or clerical duties, and about 8% more time meeting with parents. Though statistically significant, the union effect on direct instructional time is much weaker than the effect of the overall length of the school day (Eberts, 1984, p. 356) and the length of the school day is not significantly affected by unionization (Eberts, 1984, p. 355).

THE EVIDENCE ON TEACHING AS AN OCCUPATION

In addition to the characterization of work based on differences in work activities, occupations are described in terms of how they compare to other lines of work. For teachers, the research provides us some evidence about the relative position and union influence on: (1) wages and salaries, (2) social status, and (3) protection of teachers and competence of the teacher work force.

Wages and Salaries

While there is substantial disagreement about the exact impact of unionization, it is clear that collective bargaining has not brought about a massive shift in the economic fortunes of teachers. As has been the case for the past half-century, teachers find themselves marching in the middle ranks of the nation's wage earners, following much of the professional, technical, and managerial work force. Since 1929, teacher salaries have remained in a relatively narrow band around the mean wage paid to all salaried workers nationwide (see Table 3). In comparison with all other workers, teachers fared best—their pay was about 1.2 times the average wage nationally—in the early 1970s when enrollments were at their peak and when teacher unionization was spreading rapidly. They fared worst during World War II when factory wages were high, male teachers were scarce, and female teachers were frequently paid less than males.

Teachers, like many other workers, suffered declining real incomes during the 1970–1980 decade for a loss of about 13.4% (Lipsky, 1982, p. 15). Teachers suffered larger declines than steel workers or auto workers and, by the end of the decade, teaching, when considered on a weekly salary basis, paid about the same as jobs in those elite blue-collar industries (Lipsky, 1982, p. 19). Thus, teaching retains its historic place at the bottom of the college-educated work force, although just how far below other white-collar jobs depends on what calculations are being used. The average yearly starting salary for teachers in 1981–1982 was $12,769 compared to $15,444 for college graduates with a liberal arts degree, $16,980 for accounting graduates, and $22,368 for engineers (National Education Association, 1983, p. 22). Even making generous assumptions about moonlighting and summer earnings,

TABLE 3
Average Annual Salary of Instructional Staff in Public Elementary and Secondary Schools and Average Annual Earnings of Full-Time Employees in All U.S. Industries

| Year | Wages Adjusted for Changes in Living Costs[a] | | Ratio of Teacher to Worker Wages | Educational Expenses As % of GNP |
	Teachers	All Workers		
1929–30	$ 7,185	$ 7,013	1.0245	3.1
1931–32	8,513	7,198	1.1827	3.9
1933–34	8,024	7,315	1.0969	4.1
1935–36	8,091	7,315	1.1061	3.7
1937–38	8,316	7,529	1.1045	3.3
1939–40	8,930	7,944	1.1241	3.5
1941–42	8,378	8,762	0.9562	2.6
1943–44	8,597	10,099	0.8513	1.8
1945–46	9,478	10,794	0.8781	2.0
1947–48	9,805	10,002	0.9803	2.8
1949–50	11,008	10,715	1.0273	3.4
1951–52	11,365	10,943	1.0386	3.4
1953–54	12,315	11,679	1.0545	3.8
1955–56	13,389	12,642	1.0591	4.2
1957–58	14,247	12,956	1.0996	4.8
1959–60	15,251	13,653	1.1170	5.1
1961–62	16,418	14,194	1.1567	5.6
1963–64	17,513	15,079	1.1614	6.1
1965–66	18,089	15,834	1.1424	6.6
1967–68	19,424	16,405	1.1840	7.2
1960–70	20,271	16,818	1.2053	7.5
1971–72	21,257	17,541	1.2118	7.8
1973–74	20,769	17,914	1.1594	7.5
1975–76	20,484	17,515	1.1695	8.0
1977–78	20,340	17,755	1.1456	7.4
1979–80	18,720	16,589	1.1285	7.0
1980–81	18,409	16,050	1.1470	6.8
1982–83	18,678	18,200	1.0263	na

[a]Wages in 1980 dollars
Sources: Grant & Eiden (1980), Grant & Snyder (1983)

teachers still rank last. (About 27% of all teachers reported income from jobs other than teaching. The mean income of those who reported outside earnings was $2,464. If these added earnings were applied to all beginning teachers, the annual income for new teachers would be $15,223, still below that of liberal arts graduates [Gardner, 1982, p. 82]). While these data do not speak directly to the union-wage effect question, they clearly rule out the conclusion that public sector unionism has been a very strong economic force.

Saying that unionization has not made teachers rich does not preclude the possibility that it has made them less poor. At the most crude level of comparison, Table 3 illustrates that the relative position of teachers to the mean U.S. salary was 1.06 in the years prior to unionization, 1929 to 1965. Particularly during the latter part of that period, there were continuing shortages of public school teachers. During the period 1965 to 1981, however the wage ratio climbed to 1.15—even though there was a glut of teachers and declining enrollments in many school districts during part of that period.

The 40 or so studies of wage impact (reviewed in Lipsky, 1982) suggest that there is a union-wage effect in the range of 5% to 10%. While this is not the stuff out of which Porsches are purchased, it does represent an annual salary increment of $750 to $2,500 for most teachers, a very handsome return on union dues. Wage effects of this magnitude are consistent with the lower end of the union-effect results found in private-sector unions where effects on the order of 10% to 25% are commonly found (Ashenfelter, 1972; Lewis, 1963; Ryscavage, 1974).

The fundamental technique used in union-effect studies has been econometrics, or regressions in which a number of predictor variables are associated with a wage or salary. Within this fundamental technique, however, there have been substantial differences in which variables are included as predictors, what sample of salaries is used, and how the presence, absence, or degree of unionism is considered. As a consequence, the range of reported union effects has been quite large, from 0 to 30%. (All the studies were carried out between the late 1960s and mid-1970s; the latest study was based on 1977 data. The studies also differ somewhat on what they measure as salary. Some consider only entry-level salaries, some use several points on the salary scale, and others the average of salaries in the district.)

The studies that found the smallest union effect tended to be those that took state averages of salaries and regressed a number of other variables upon them. Wage effects that approximated zero were found by Mitchell (1979), Balfour (1974), and Smith (1972). (Smith's study did not use multiple regression.) Kasper (1970) also found wage effects that approximated zero. Studies that used school-district level data within a state tended to find effects in the 3% to 6% range (Gallagher, 1978; Hall & Carroll, 1973; Lipsky & Drotning, 1973; Treacy, Harris & Blake, 1974; Zuelke & Frohreich, 1977). Frey (1973) found smaller effects. These studies had the advantage of controlling for differences that are caused by state-level variations, including the wealth of the state itself. Studies comparing school districts across state boundaries largely tended to fall in the same range (Baird & Landon, 1972; Gustman & Segal, 1976; Thornton, 1971). A major exception was Schmenner (1973) who found effects ranging from 7% to 16%.

There is reason to believe that these studies generally understate the union effect because of their inattention to the extent to which wage settlements in unionized organizations set the tone or standard for settlements in nonunionized organizations. Chambers (1977, 1980) attempted to account for this union spillover effect by including the extent of teacher unionization in the *region*, as well as the presence of a union contract in an individual school district. The regional effect proved substantially stronger than the school-district effect, and Chambers concluded that there was an overall union-wage effect of between 6% and 12%. Since Chambers's initial studies, however, the almost universal spread of teacher unionism in many states has made calculation of spillovers based on regional teacher union membership more difficult. No studies were found that attempted to relate teachers' wage levels to the extent of unionization in all sectors of the economy. (Regarding spillover effects, it should be noted that Goldschmidt et al. [1984, p. 14] found teacher contracts more likely to contain topics of explicit organizational policy where more than 27% of the state's work force was unionized.)

A few studies have compared individual teacher salaries rather than school district salary schedules (Baugh & Stone, 1982; Eberts, 1982; Holmes, 1976). Baugh and Stone's union effects are among the largest reported: 7% in one year and 21% in another. Baugh and Stone use an hedonic approach to wage analysis, which assumes that employers and employees may have different preferences about the characteristics of the workers they hire or the characteristics of the work to be undertaken (Antos & Rosen, 1975). Thus, a person considering a position would weigh not only the salary but also satisfaction obtained from the work itself and working conditions, as it has long been argued that teachers do. Similarly, employers may value some employee attributes more than others, and different employers may value different attributes.

Using New York state data, Eberts and Stone (1984, pp. 63–81) regress variables associated with bargaining strength, teacher attributes such as experience and education, and job attributes against teacher salary. In the resultant coefficients, bargaining strength variables relating to class-size provisions and gaining a reduction-in-force agreement enter the regression significantly. This, the authors suggest, supports the contention that unions with sufficient bargaining strength are able to move beyond the employer's demand curve for labor achieving higher levels of employment and higher levels of compensation than would have been predicted by a demand-constraint depiction of the teacher labor market.

Using Current Population Survey data, Eberts and Stone calculated the apparent union-wage effect in regression equations that, in addition to union/nonunion status, also consider the sex of the teacher, number of years of teaching, number of years of education, and big city location. Although all these factors were significant predictors of teacher salary, union membership remained a significant effect, increasing salaries by 7% in 1974 and 21% in 1977.

Using individual teacher data allows the regression equation to capture differences in sex, age, and experience, but it makes it very difficult to capture important school district characteristics, including the fiscal capacity of the district. It has been suggested that this omission leads to an overestimation of the union-wage effect (Finch & Nagel, 1984, p. 1597; Lipsky, 1982, p. 35). Eberts and Stone acknowledge attributes of their study that would tend to bias their findings on the high side, but they also note that their data include only base salary, not fringe benefits, which tend to be higher in unionized environments.

A second example of the hedonic approach is found in Chambers's (1985) comparison of public and private school teachers' salaries. Although it is not a direct study of a union effect, it is illuminating because it suggests that the wage difference between the heavily unionized public sector and the very lightly unionized private sector may not be as great as commonly believed. Chambers compared salaries of San Francisco area public and private (church-related and independent) school teachers. He included in his regression equations such teacher characteristics as years taught and education, and such employment characteristics as class size.

As expected, public school teachers were better paid than their counterparts in independent or church-related schools. However, they were paid for different attributes, particularly a state teaching credential. Chambers went on to estimate what the sample of public school teachers would have earned had they taught in the private sector and what the private school teachers would have earned had they taught in the public sector. Again, as expected, the simulations revealed that private school teachers would earn more if they sold their talents to a public school employer, but the regression analysis showed that they would make substantially less than the existing pool of public school teachers because they lacked the education, experience, or credentials valued by public employees. And public school teachers would make more than the existing private school teachers if they went to work in private schools. As Chambers put it, "On average, within our sample, public school teachers possess greater levels of those characteristics which are compensated in the market for school teachers than teachers in other sectors" (1985, p. 38).

Status of Teachers

One obtains quite different readings of the union effect on teacher occupational status from ethnographic or case-study evidence than one gains from looking at broad-gauge public opinion surveys. Interview respondents frequently reflect a unions-have-wrecked-teaching opinion, of which the following from a school superintendent is typical:

Teachers have lost their image as being public servants and are relegating themselves to being comparable to the dinner bucket, hard-hat union members. The community opinion is that the teacher really isn't interested in my youngster. (Kerchner & Mitchell, 1981, p. IV:12)

Unions have been depicted as fostering disengenuousness when facing educational reforms (Finn, 1983, 1985), particularly the ways in which teachers are paid and evaluated (Murnane & Cohen, in press). In fact, some of the most colorful language in academe is found in the critique of unionism, as

Long's foreword to Grimshaw's (1979) book on the Chicago Teachers Union illustrates:

> What Grimshaw shows is the frightening degree to which a profession with strong pretensions to serving its clients—the city's children—could, through the union device, legitimize a degree of callous selfishness that surpassed that of the managerial elite of [urban] reform and even the rapacity of the [Chicago political] machine. (p. xxiii)

However, it is very difficult to infer any union effect on the status of teaching or reputation of education from surveys of public opinion. Confidence in education as an institution has fallen over the past decade, but not greatly, and education retains higher approval ratings than most social institutions. In the National Opinion Research Center survey (NORC, 1982), 67% of respondents reported only "some" or "not much" confidence in education, as compared with 63% in 1972. Organized labor, in which 88% of the NORC respondents said they had little confidence, edged out the Congress (87%), television (86%), the press (82%), and the federal executive branch (81%) in the race for low approval ratings. Survey data show teachers in approximately the same social position that they have occupied for decades—near the bottom of the professions but ahead of skilled workers, athletes, businessmen, and journalists (*Public Opinion,* 1981). No studies were found that directly compared the status of union and nonunion teachers or comparative public perceptions of the two.

Protection and Teacher Competence

Protecting teachers from arbitrary and capricious managerial decisions was one of the primary attractions of unionism. Within the unionized labor-management environment, these employee protections are found in a standardized salary schedule, uniform work rules, seniority and transfer provisions, and an elaborate grievance system. These structural aspects, which often predated unionism, are reinforced in most teacher unions by active representation of teachers by local union officers and executives, representation that in some respects is the first stage of grievance processing, but which often extends into aspects of employee treatment that may not in themselves be grievable. While the idea of employee protection is seldom attacked, the system frequently is seen as a costly, formalizing, and cumbersome mechanism that protects incompetence behind a veil of due process (Lieberman, 1980). Thus, in the public mind, the question of teacher protection and teacher competence are joined.

The evidence on this subject suggests three findings. First, due process protection works. Unions are vigorous in their protection of teachers, and they frequently act without the formality of a written grievance. In fact, one of the hallmarks of contract implementation is that the grievance system is relatively infrequently used, particularly in smaller school districts (Simpkins, McCutcheon, & Alec, 1979). Rather, principals are socialized to solve problems at the school site before they require attention of the central administration (Kerchner, 1985). Teachers frequently are able to use these informal interactions to renegotiate the substantive meaning of work rules. Grievance protection is substantially expanded in those districts in which school policies and practices *outside the contract* are also subject to grievance adjudication (Grimshaw, 1979, p. 69).

Second, there is evidence that discharges are more difficult under unionization than they otherwise would be. As a result, schools employ some marginal teachers who would probably have been dismissed had it not been for the union representation. Grimshaw (1979, p. 67) compared the dramatic drop in teacher terminations in Chicago in the political-machine rule era (1933–1946) when there were an average of 22.6 dismissals a year with the administrative-reform rule era (1947–1966), 6.6 dismissals per year, and the more recent union-rule era (1967–1971) when there were an average of .6 dismissals per year in the Chicago public schools. One of the primary reasons for the decline is that administrators and school boards are reluctant to initiate dismissal proceedings that will expose evaluation procedures and necessarily subjective judgements about teacher quality to courtroom scrutiny (Johnson, 1980, p. 230).

Relatively recently, however, some union locals have successfully negotiated peer review agreements in which specially designated senior teachers evaluate probationary teachers and, in effect, determine whether their contracts will be renewed, and other union locals are studying the possibility. The results from Toledo, Ohio, where such an arrangement has been in force since 1981, suggest that first-year supervision becomes more rigorous and that the number of teachers dismissed increases (Waters & Wyatt, 1985). Peer review, once an anathema, is gaining a serious hearing in union circles (Currence, 1985; Shanker, 1985).

Third, while union protection against arbitrary treatment has not translated into employment security for the vast majority of teachers (Harris, 1979; National Education Association, 1980), unions may have protected their memberships somewhat from the winds of declining enrollment. More than anything else, unions have channeled and rationalized enrollment-driven layoffs (Murnane, 1980). The majority of districts now have seniority-based layoff procedures, but these can be of quite different types, and frequently involve consideration of specialty area and performance in the calculation of who is to be vulnerable to layoff. For teachers, seniority in job protection is frequently thought of as fair treatment or an equity issue rather than as an issue that should be decided on performance alone (Johnson, 1980, p. 74).

EVIDENCE ON THE RELATIONSHIP BETWEEN TEACHERS AND ORGANIZATIONS

In addition to affecting teacher work and teaching as an occupation, unionization has changed the relationship between teachers and the organizations in which they work. Principally, unionization changed the teachers/school district relationship by altering the rules for how one behaves when dissatisfied, unhappy, affronted, or angry. Before unionism, teachers most often had the option of accepting their employment setting as it was or of leaving to find another job. After unionism, teachers' options for voicing their complaints were dramatically increased. Organizational life changes profoundly when dissatisfied workers give voice to their complaints instead of quietly leaving.

Two consequences of unionized teacher organizational voice have a direct implication for shaping teaching work roles and the occupational ethos. The first consequence is a changed definition of teacher loyalty: Good teachers, loyal ones, act differently now than they did before unionization. Before unionization, the administrator spoke for "good" teachers who either supported the administration or at least worked circumspectly to subvert that which they did not like. After unionization, teachers spoke for themselves and saw no conflict between organizational loyalty and teacher voice. Teacher leadership came to mean strength and independence, not support and obsequiousness. The second consequence is the struggle over the teacher union's proper role in schools as organizations. This tension is particularly evident as one looks at educational reform and efforts to change schools.

The New Definition of Loyalty

Legitimizing voice on the part of teachers changes the definition of what teachers consider as organizational loyalty. Teachers come to believe that their alternative social system (Mitchell & Kerchner, 1982) is not inconsistent with their being good teachers and loyal employees. Because the existence of the union is ultimately socially legitimated within the school district (in addition to being legalized within the state), teachers come to believe that being pro-union is not necessarily being antischool. Vocal teachers, "willing to take a stand," are not necessarily viewed by principals as disloyal or their actions inappropriate (Johnson, 1984, p. 37). Similarly, unionized teachers come to view their principals without animosity, and even use such union mechanisms as grievances to gain central office actions that the principal cannot individually command (Kerchner, 1985; Murphy & Ellman, 1974). A new social relationship emerges between principals and teachers that is based on reciprocity of influence more than on obedience to authority. Principals seek teacher support and fear teachers' ability to organize against them. At the same time, principals act as gatekeepers for what the unions want (Johnson, 1984, pp. 41, 46–47).

The new definition of loyalty, in which good teachers give voice to their complaints, produces two anomalous situations: (1) employees who complain but who do not quit, and (2) union leaders who are militant but happy in their work.

Complaining vs. Quitting

Legitimation of unionism, acceptance of a bargained contract offering better wages and benefits, a grievance system, and organizational voice in determining employment conditions *do not* appear to be associated with voiced employee satisfaction, either in teaching or in the private sector (Freeman & Medhoff, 1984, pp. 137–140). Eberts and Stone (1984, pp. 82–83) found teachers in unionized schools less satisfied with their schools than those in nonunion settings. Unionized teachers also felt their schools were less effective in instruction. Others report similar findings (Bilsky, 1982). Feistritzer (1986) reports teachers in largely nonunion private schools more satisfied with their work than in the largely unionized public schools. (One should note, however, that this does not mean that most teachers say they are dissatisfied with their jobs. In a 1984 Metropolitan Life Insurance survey, 81% of all teachers said that they were satisfied or very satisfied with their jobs. This was somewhat lower than the national cross-section of workers, 87% of whom said they were satisfied or very satisfied [*American Teacher,* 1984]). Although Feistritzer (1986) found 70% of public school teachers quite satisfied with their jobs, more than 80% were dissatisfied or very dissatisfied with their salaries.

One would expect dissatisfied employees to quit their jobs more frequently than satisfied ones. This is generally the case, but as the University of Michigan Quality of Employment Survey and numerous other studies suggest, unionized employees exhibit *both* lower satisfaction and lower intended and actual quit rates (see Freeman & Medhoff, 1984, pp. 139–139). Studies of teachers reveal similar tendencies. In the only direct measure found, union membership decreased the probability that a teacher would move by 5% in 1974–1975 and 16% in 1977–1978 (Eberts & Stone, 1984, p. 93). Union membership, however, was distinctly less powerful in predicting job mobility than differences in salary.

Another way of seeking evidence on this question is to examine the rates at which teachers quit their jobs over the span of years involved in teacher unionization. As one examines the rates reported from different years, there is a slight upward trend from about 7% to 8% in 1957 to 11% to 12.5% in 1974, but the studies involved are not strictly comparable and involve different populations (Carroll, 1963; Lindenfield, 1963; Murnane, 1980; National Education Association 1957, 1972).

To explain the paradox of simultaneously lowered satisfaction and lowered mobility, Freeman and Medhoff (1984, p. 139) differentiate between *actual* dissatisfaction, which causes employees to leave their jobs, and *voiced* dissatisfaction, "which results from critical attitudes towards the workplace and a willingness to complain about problems." Voiced dissatisfaction is the legitimated mechanism by which the union communicates its and the workers' interests to employers. And it is *expected* that voiced dissatisfaction will increase under unionism just as one expects more vocal citizens in a democracy than in a dictatorship.

Happy Warriors

One would normally expect militants, those who organize unions and lead them during the "to-the-barricades" period, to be very dissatisfied with their jobs but, frequently, they are not. Corwin (1970, p. 186) reports that a teacher's career satisfaction increases with the number of conflicts in which the individual has been involved. Militancy and conflict add purpose and a sense of mission to employment (Kerchner & Mitchell, 1981), and unions create offices and titles that accord militants recognition and the status of "teacher leaders" (Cheng, 1976; Cresswell & Murphy, 1980). In the three school districts studied by Jessup (1985), union leaders were not quiet or satisfied, but they reported an "improvement in an overall sense of well being" (p. 205).

The legitimation of voice for the dissatisfied gives rise to a new type of teacher leadership that is both militant and independent. Union leaders are seldom the teachers with whom school managers would have chosen to deal. As one superintendent reported:

The radical leadership of the union are the kind that never had an opportunity to be heard. They are always suspect [by the principal], always wondering whether they'd get rehired or not, or whether . . .[the principal is] going to step into their classrooms at any moment and jump on them about something or the other. . . . They're the ones that [now] spend many, many hours in the superintendent's conference room discussing everything they want about working conditions, etc. (Kerchner & Mitchell, 1981, p. III:5)

There is substantial variation from district to district in how union leaders are different from the administratively chosen teachers, as well as in how independent and vocal they are. Virtually every investigator also has reported substantial differences among union organizations (Jessup, 1985; Johnson, 1984; Perry, 1979). Generally, however, union leaders stood out as distinctly as they did in Corwin's (1970) study, which took place very early in the unionization process.

Organizational Functioning

The problem of voiced teacher dissatisfaction is also evidenced in the continuing tension over the proper relationship of the teachers' union to school operations. This tension is often perceived as a turf fight over organizational influence. In a more fundamental sense, the tension represents a search for an

ideology, or shared belief to which school districts and unions jointly subscribe and around which they operate when working out their disagreements.
Lacking a shared belief system, their relationship is unstable (Dunlop, 1958,
p. 17), and we know that periodically labor relations do become unstable
(Erck, 1983; Jessup, 1985; Kerchner & Mitchell, 1981, p. I:8).

Certainly, the embrace of collective bargaining itself represented a major
ideological struggle for the National Education Association (Bushman, 1982;
Donley, 1976). But, more pointedly, the acceptance of a new central idea is
worked out in each local union through what Jessup (1985, p. 187) calls "patterns of change" and Kerchner and Mitchell (1981, p. I:5–6) identify as "generations of labor relations." The struggle for a central ideology is not simply
tension *between* labor and management, it is also tension *within* both the managerial hierarchy and the union leadership. Acceptance of bargaining came
with great difficulty in some districts, and although the tension over *de jure*
recognition has been resolved in most jurisdictions by state statute, there remain substantial numbers of school districts in which the teachers' union is
still not *de facto* the legitimate voice of teachers in that district.

While the struggle to legitimate collective bargaining is widely recognized,
it is no less of a struggle than that which accompanies efforts to work out the
union's role in other, often externally created, issues such as fiscal change,
desegregation, or school reform (Cresswell, Juris, Nathanson & Tooredman,
1978). Particularly in recent years, management has become the aggressive
party, bringing its agenda to the bargaining table rather than responding to the
union's demands: managing through the contract rather than around it (Mitchell et al., 1981). Labor relations and policy are explicitly joined in two ways:
(1) as the implementation of externally mandated changes, and (2) as the
results of political action in which the quality of school operations has become
an issue.

The union effect on the implementation of externally mandated changes can
be seen in the union reaction to reform initiatives in the 1980s. In California,
for instance, the legislature (through the Hughes-Hart Educational Reform
Act of 1983) established a program of Mentor Teachers, each of whom would
receive a state-financed stipend of $4,000. Implementation of the act quickly
became joined with labor relations (Johnson, Nelson, & Potter, 1985, p. 38),
although the law specified that school district entrance into the Mentor
Teacher program was not a bargainable subject. The unions insisted, however,
that undertaking the program meant a change in the working conditions for
other teachers, and hence was inherently a subject for negotiations. Some
districts did not enter the program because of union opposition, and their
opposition became the subject of a gubernatorial threat to excise further
school reform funds. Moreover, the statute required that Mentor Teachers be
selected by a mechanism whose representation included a majority of teachers. The unions held that they were the proper body to do the choosing and,
in some cases (Johnson et al., 1984, p. 38), unions negotiated selection pro-

cedures and mentor's responsibilities. In effect, the union served as a policy broker defining, through implementation, what the reform act actually meant. And, in at least one setting, the union changed its position from one of opposition because Mentor Teacher looked too much like merit pay to one of cautious acceptance on the basis that if "we good teachers don't get involved in this, someone else will" (Johnson et al., 1985, p. 42).

Desegregation is another issue in which unions sometimes hesitantly enter into policy determination. Desegregation was a difficult issue for United Teachers of Los Angeles (Thomas, 1982). Teachers opposed involuntary transfers and did not legitimate the union leadership's involvement in social issues. However, in one southern school district, the union and administration reached agreements that, in effect, subordinated seniority considerations to staff racial balancing, even though the district had not explicitly been ordered to balance staff by the courts (Johnson et al., 1985, p. 48). In this district, the union executive director cultivated a personal political base with "legislators, senators, representatives, and the commissioner—the whole works" and thus was somewhat insulated from cross-pressures of the membership (Johnson et al., 1985, p. 49).

In the case of school reform and desegregation, the external reform was joined to labor relations during implementation. There are other cases of organizational change in which labor relations become the *object* of political efforts at reform. For instance, in the case called Industrial City (Kerchner & Mitchell, 1981), a new superintendent was recruited and handed what he called "the mandate of heaven" to rewrite the labor contract eliminating clauses that impinged on managerial flexibility. Similarly, in East Port (Johnson et al., 1985, p. 61), a new superintendent took office "intent on regaining management prerogatives," especially of the teacher-transfer system and of the teacher-evaluation mechanism that was perceived as protecting incompetents. In Midland Heights (Johnson et al., 1985, p. 89), the union resisted the superintendent's reforms and supported sympathetic school board candidates. Their success at the polls fueled "rumors that the school board would no longer defer to the superintendent and that he would eventually leave" (Johnson et al., 1985, p. 92).

The research on unions and reforms indicates both a substantial capacity for reform and real limitations on the unions' ability to respond to reform measures that are not popular with their members. Jessup (1985, pp. 9–10) forms the question in terms of two different traditional goals of teacher unionism: (1) welfare, "raising workers' consciousness and energies to press collectively for improvement in their own work situations," and (2) professional responsibility, "an ideology stressing the importance of service to clients . . . and responsibility of the occupational group for the quality of this service." In looking at the case histories of three districts, Jessup found that in one case the union leadership's professional interests were eroded by economic pressures, internal organizational conflict, and community strife that transformed "what started out as an idealistic and professionally oriented union into a fairly traditional, protective labor organization by the late 1970s" (Jessup, 1985, p. 16). In another community, the union was able to balance professional and welfare agendas. In a third, the union was formed in a climate of perceived school board hostility, and its agenda was always one of teacher protection. In this case, the welfare agenda remained publicly paramount, but the union leadership and the administration were able to develop patterns of accommodation.

In sum, the union reaction to reform is "not reflexive," but depends on the context of the reform proposal (Johnson et al., 1985, p. 9), the qualities of union leadership, the strength of professional norms, and the mechanisms for reinforcing professional commitment (Jessup, 1985, p. 13).

PROSPECTS FOR THE UNION LABEL

We can safely conclude that there is a union effect on teaching, an effect that follows the dimensions enumerated at the outset of this chapter: teaching as work, teaching as an occupation, and teaching in organizational context. We can say with some certainty that teachers are better paid, better protected by the shield of due process, and much more given to institutional voice than they would have been without unions. We can say that teaching work is more rationalized and rule-directed than it would have been without unions. We can say that teaching as an occupation is organized differently, and that the institutional response face of unionism is plainly visible. The consequence of these findings is to raise three substantive problems for research and for labor relations practice: (1) understanding that the important problems in labor relations change periodically, (2) matching research to the problems, (3) expressing the relationship of unionism to teaching as an ideal.

The first substantive problem is to align labor relations with today's educational issues. American unions have prospered by being pragmatic, by solving real, felt problems of the society and their members. This focus on the here and now has been the hallmark of unionism since the 19th century when Gompers' American Federation of Labor grew in response to worker wage and working condition concerns while the more revolutionary Knights of Labor faded. For teachers' unions, the "problem of today" is no longer to settle fights and to divide the spoils of interest group conflict. The problem is to make the institution of public education conspicuously successful. For the union label to become a badge of occupational distinction, it must assist schools toward a public recognition that they do superb work. Failure to do so invites public disinvestment, "exit" in Hirschman's (1970) word.

Focusing on a new problem is a much more complex undertaking than we have heretofore admitted: A unionism that is about protecting the institution, enforcing quality standards, socializing new teachers, and training them. The range of activities that are central to understanding an occupation is far different than the range of activities that are involved in pursuing conventional narrow-range collective bargaining and contract enforcement (Kerchner & Mitchell, in press; Kochan, McKersie, & Capelli, 1984; Kornbluh, 1984; Wirth, 1982, 1983). Thinking about the problem of today thus requires consideration of new forms of interaction between labor and management, new structures, and new ways of considering success or failure.

Far too much of the research on unionization—particularly dissertation research—essentially deals with yesterday's problems, psychological perceptions of changed roles (particularly those of school principals), or measures of teacher militancy. In terms of informing policy or practice, the answers are largely meaningless, and they add little to the storehouse of social knowledge about union effects that was known when Slichter, Healy, and Livernash (1960) wrote a generation ago. The problem of unionism and teaching is more fruitfully addressed by looking to the series of natural experiments being carried out by teachers' unions themselves. In school districts throughout the country, unions have had to solve the problem of integrating reforms and their activities. Relatively little attention has been paid to the ways in which unions have worked with the reform agenda of school districts and school building. Little attention has been paid to studying the internal operation of unions, aside from the few organizational histories that have appeared as dissertations. And very little has been done that captures the richness of the natural experiment between union leaders and school managers whose relationship transcends the collective contract.

The second substantive problem is to create a research tradition that matches the dynamics of unions themselves. Unfortunately, most of the research on labor relations is not suitably constructed to serve this purpose. Whereas unionization is widely thought to be a dynamic process of social change, a substantial amount of the research undertaken has been cross-sectional—either econometric research at a single time point, or survey research on teachers and school districts. If one believes that labor relations are fundamentally developmental (and it is hard to believe otherwise), then static, cross-sectional designs are not likely to yield much. However, the incentives of academe are stacked against taking the long view.

There are some practical countermeasures. New, badly needed, longitudinal data bases are being constructed to track students, teachers, and school environments. As a part of these data bases, or attendant to them, we need data on teachers and their careers. With slight additions, these data bases could be used to track teaching policies as they are modulated by labor relations. Furthermore, standardization or compatibility among surveys and reports by employers, unions, and state public employment relations boards would allow aggregation of these data into meaningful, multiyear forms. The existence of such data bases would make it possible for graduate students and others with single-year schedules to take a longitudinal perspective in their work.

The final and most difficult problem is to give concrete expression to a new idea of labor relations. Affirming the existence of a union effect means that those interested in labor relations practice and research also need to be concerned with the fundamentals of the sociology and economics of teaching. Neither academic nor practitioner can plead that procedures for teacher-rights' protections do not interact with organizational functioning or with student learning. When the relationship between teaching work rules and policy is recognized, the distinction between what is inherently managerial and what is inherently labor becomes blurred, and the roles of each party require redefinition.

Linking unionism with educational policy and achievement requires, first of all, that unions and managements rethink the scope of their interactions. Just as industrial organizations have found it necessary to focus labor relations on productivity and product quality, schools will need ways to consider new divisions of labor implicit in career-ladder schemes, job redesign, and new means of teacher motivation, and of teacher evaluation. Second, labor and management will need new means of interaction. Agreements other than conventional contracts will probably be necessary and, in innovative settings, such agreements already occur. Frequent union-management interaction for problem solving will also be needed. Third, consideration needs to be given to how groups of teachers can aggregate to form a portion of their own work rules, curriculums, assignments, and schedules (Little, 1985). Such flexibility enhances the quality of work life and adds importantly to the ability of schools to develop the authentic cultures so important to organizational excellence.

REFERENCES

The American Teacher. (1984). New York: Metropolitan Life Insurance.

Antos, J., & Rosen, S. (1975). Discrimination in the market for public school teachers. *Journal of Econometrics, 3*,(2), 123–150.

Ashenfelter, O. (1972). Racial discrimination and trade unionism. *Journal of Political Economy, 80*, 435–464.

Baird, R., & Landon, J. (1972). The effect of collective bargaining on public school teachers' salaries: Comment. *Industrial and Labor Relations Review, 25*, 410–416.

Balfour, G.A. (1974). More evidence that unions do not achieve higher salaries for teachers. *Journal of Collective Negotiations, 3*, 289–303.

Barbash, J. (1969). Rationalization in the American union. In G. Somers (Ed.), *Essays in Industrial Relations Theory* (pp. 147–162). Ames: Iowa State University Press.

Baugh, W., & Stone, J.A. (1982). Teachers, unions, and wages in the 1970s: Unionism now pays. *Industrial and Labor Relations Review, 35*, 368–376.

Belasco, J., & Alluto, J. (1969). Organizational impacts of teacher negotiations. *Industrial Relations, 9*, 67–79.

Bickel, W., & Bickel, D. (1979). *A study of a district teacher organization's impact on educational policy.* Paper presented at the annual meeting of the American Educational Research Association, San Francisco.

Bilsky, D. (1982). *An analysis of the relationship between teachers' job satisfaction and teachers' union attitudes in a large midsouthern city.* Unpublished doctoral dissertation, Memphis State University.

Bird, T., & Little, J.W. (in press). How schools organize the teaching occupation. *Elementary School Journal.*

Braun, R.J. (1972). *Teachers and power: The story of the American Federation of Teachers.* New York: Simon & Schuster.

Bridges, E., & Cooper, B. (1976). Collective bargaining for school administrators. *Theory Into Practice, 15,* 306–315.

Bruno, J., & Nelken, I. (1975). An empirical analysis on the propensity for teachers to strike. *Educational Administration Quarterly, 2,* 66–85.

Burton, J.F., Jr. (1979). The extent of collective bargaining in the public sector. In B. Aaron, J. Grodin, & J. Stern (Eds.), *Public-sector bargaining* (pp. 1–43). Washington, DC: Bureau of National Affairs.

Burton, J.F., Jr., & Krider, C. (1970). The role and consequences of strikes by public employees. *The Yale Law Journal, 79,* 418–433.

Bushman, P. (1982). *Collective bargaining in California public education: A historical perspective.* Unpublished doctoral dissertation, Claremont Graduate School.

California Legislative Analyst. (1980). *Administrative and pupil service personnel.* Sacramento: Author.

Carroll, S. (1963). *Analysis of the educational personnel system: III* (R-1308-HEW). Santa Monica, CA: Rand.

Chambers, J. (1977). The impact of collective bargaining for teachers on resource allocation in public school districts. *Journal of Urban Economics, 4,* 324–339

Chambers, J. (1980). *The impact of bargaining and bargaining statutes on the earnings of public school teachers: A comparison in California and Missouri* (Report 80–86). Stanford, CA: Institute for Educational Finance and Governance.

Chambers, J. (1985). *Patterns of compensation of public and private school teachers.* Stanford, CA: Institute for Educational Finance and Governance.

Cheng, C. (1976). Community representation in teacher collective bargaining. *Harvard Educational Review, 46,* 153–174.

Cohen, E. (1984) *Sociology in the classroom: 1972–1984.* Paper presented at the annual meeting of the American Educational Research Association, New Orleans.

Cole, S. (1969a). Teachers' strike: A study of the conversion of predisposition into action. *American Journal of Sociology, 74,* 506–520.

Cole, S. (1969b). *The unionization of teachers: A case study of the UFT.* New York: Praeger.

Colton, D. (1977). The influence of an antistrike injunction. *Educational Administration Quarterly, 13,* 47–70.

Cooper, B. (1979). The future of middle management in education. In D. Erickson & T. Reller (Eds.), *The principal in metropolitan schools* (pp. 272–299). Berkeley, CA: McCutchan.

Cooper, B. (1982). *Collective bargaining, strikes, and financial costs in public education: A comparative review.* Eugene, OR: ERIC Clearinghouse on Educational Management.

Cooper, B., & Bussey, J. (1980). *Collective bargaining in public education—and other sectors: A comparative review of research.* Dartmouth, NH: Dartmouth College, Dept. of Education.

Corwin, R. (1970). *Militant professionalism: A study of organizational conflict in high schools.* New York: Appleton-Century-Crofts.

Cresswell, A., & Murphy, M. (1976). *Education and collective bargaining.* Berkeley, CA: McCutchan.

Cresswell, A., & Murphy, M., with Kerchner, C. (1980). *Teachers, unions, and collective bargaining in public education*. Berkeley, CA: McCutchan.

Cresswell, A., & Spargo, F. (1980). *Impacts of collective bargaining policy in elementary, and secondary education: A review of research and methodology; Recommendations for new research*. Denver, CO: Education Commission of the States.

Cresswell, A., & Wachter, G.F. (1983). Control of collective bargaining in education. Paper presented at the annual meeting of the American Educational Research Association, New Orleans.

Cresswell, A., Juris, H., Nathanson, L., & Tooredman, K. (1978). The impact of state labor relations and school finance policies on educational resource allocation. Paper presented at the annual meeting of the American Educational Research Association, Toronto,

Crozier, M. (1964). *The bureaucratic phenomenon*. Chicago: University of Chicago Press.

Cuban, L. (1984). *How teachers taught: Constancy and change in American classrooms, 1890–1980*. New York: Longman.

Currence, C. (1985, May 15). Teachers' unions bringing reform issues to bargaining table. *Education Week, 4*,(1), 16.

Deal, T., & Kennedy, A. (1982). *Corporate cultures*. Reading, MA: Addison-Wesley.

Delaney, J.T. (1983). Strikes, arbitration and teacher salaries: A behavioral analysis. *Industrial and Labor Relations Review, 36*, 432–446.

Donley, M.O. (1976). *Power to the teacher: How America's educators became militant*. Bloomington: Indiana University Press.

Dunlop, J. (1958). *Industrial relations systems*. New York: Holt.

Eaton, W. (1975). *The American Federation of Teachers, 1916–1961: A history of the movement*. Carbondale: Southern Illinois University Press.

Eberts, R. (1982). *Unionism and nonwage effects: A simultaneous equations model*. Eugene: Center for Educational Policy and Management, University of Oregon.

Eberts, R. (1984). Union effects on teachers' productivity. *Industrial and Labor Relations Review, 37*, 346–368.

Eberts, R., & Pierce, L. (1982). *Time in classroom: The effect of collective bargaining on the use of teacher time*. Eugene: Center for Educational Policy and Management, University of Oregon.

Eberts, R.W., & Stone, J.A. (1984). *The effect of collective bargaining on American education*. Lexington, MA: Heath.

Elam, S. (1981). The National Education Association: Political powerhouse or paper tiger? *Phi Delta Kappan, 63*, 169–174.

Englert, R. (1979, April). *Third-party participation in the 1978 teacher negotiations in Philadelphia: The politics of bargaining*. Paper presented at the annual meeting of the American Educational Research Association, San Francisco.

Erck, W. (1983). *An analysis of the relationship between teacher collective bargaining and altered managerial behavior in selected Illinois school districts*. Unpublished doctoral dissertation, University of Illinois.

Feistritzer, E. (1982). *The condition of teaching: A state-by-state analysis*. Princeton, NJ: Carnegie Foundation for the Advancement of Teaching.

Feistritzer, E. (1986). *Profiles of teachers in the U.S.* Washington, DC: National Center for Education Information.

Finch, M., & Nagel, T. (1984). Collective bargaining in the public schools: Reassessing labor policy in an era of reform. *Wisconsin Law Review, 1984*, 1573–1670.

Finn, C. (1983). Teacher politics, *Commentary, 75*, 29–41.

Finn, C. (1985). Teacher unions and school quality: Potential allies or inevitable foes? *Phi Delta Kappan, 66,* 331–338.

Fox, W., & Wince, M. (1976). The structure and determinants of occupational militancy among public school teachers. *Industrial and Labor Relations Review, 30,* 47–58.

Freeman, R., & Medhoff, J. (1979). The two faces of unionism. *The Public Interest, 57,* 69–93.

Freeman, R., & Medoff, J. (1984). *What do unions do?* New York: Basic Books.

Frey, D. (1973). *Wage determination in the public schools and the effects of unionization* (Working paper 42E). Princeton, NJ: Princeton University, Industrial Relations Section.

Gallagher, D. (1978). De facto bargaining and teacher salary levels: The Illinois experience. *Journal of Collective Negotiations in the Public Sector, 7,* 243–254.

Gallagher, D.G. (1979). Teacher negotiations, school district expenditures, and taxation levels. *Educational Administration Quarterly, 15,* 67–82.

Gardner, S. (1982). *Status of the American public school teacher, 1980–1981.* Washington, DC: National Education Association.

Goldschmidt, S., Bowers, B., Riley, M., & Stuart, L. (1984). *The extent and nature of educational policy bargaining.* Eugene: Center for Educational Policy and Management, University of Oregon.

Grant, W., & Eiden, L. (1980). *Digest of educational statistics.* Washington, DC: National Center for Educational Statistics.

Grant, W., and Snyder, T. (1983). *Digest of educational statistics.* Washington, D.C.: National Center for Educational Statistics.

Grimshaw, W.J. (1979). *Union rule in the schools.* Lexington, MA: Heath.

Gustman, A., & Segal, M. (1976). *The impact of teachers' unions.* Final report to National Institute of Education, U.S. Department of Health, Education, and Welfare.

Hall, W., & Carroll, N. (1973). The effects of teachers' organizations on salaries and class size. *Industrial and Labor Relations Review, 26,* 834–841.

Harris, L. (1979, February). Most recommended profession for a young person starting out. *ABC News-Harris Survey,* Feb. 15, 1979.

Hemenway, J. (1978). *The measures and variables in the sustaining effects study.* Rep. #9. Santa Monica CA: Systems Development Corporation.

Herrick, M. (1971). *The Chicago schools: A social and political history.* Beverly Hills, CA: Sage.

Hirschman, A. (1970). *Exit, voice, and loyalty: Responses to decline in firms, organizations and states.* Cambridge, MA: Harvard University Press.

Holmes, A. (1976). Effects of union activities on teachers' earnings. *Industrial Relations, 15,* 328–332.

Institute for Responsive Education. (1975). *The community at the bargaining table.* Boston: Author.

Jessup, D. (1978). Teacher unionization: A reassessment of rank and file motivation. *Sociology of Education Journal, 51,* 44–55.

Jessup, D. (1985). *Teachers, unions and change.* New York: Praeger.

Johnson, S.M. (1980). Performance-based staff layoffs in the public schools: Implementation and outcomes. *Harvard Educational Review, 50,* 214–233.

Johnson, S.M. (1984). *Teachers unions in schools.* Philadelphia: Temple University Press.

Johnson, S.M., Nelson, N., & Potter, S. (1985). *Teacher unions, school staffing, and reform.* Cambridge, MA: Harvard Graduate School of Education.

Juris, H., & Feuille, P. (1973) *Police unionism.* Lexington, MA: Heath.

Kasper, H. (1970). The effects of collective bargaining on public school teachers' salaries. *Industrial and Labor Relations Review, 24,* 57–72.

Kerchner, C. (1978). From scopes to scope: The genetic mutation of the school control issue. *Educational Administration Quarterly, 14,* 64–79.

Kerchner, C. (1979). The impacts of collective bargaining on school governance. *Education and Urban Society, 11*(2), 181–207.

Kerchner, C. (1984). *The impact of labor relations on teaching.* Eugene: Center for Educational Policy and Management, University of Oregon.

Kerchner, C., & Mitchell, D. (1981). *The dynamics of public school collective bargaining and its impacts on governance, administration and teaching* (Rep. G-79-0038). Washington, DC: National Institute of Education. (ERIC Document Reproduction Service No. ED 221 925).

Kerchner, C., & Mitchell, D. (in press). Teacher reform and union reform. *Elementary School Journal, 86.*

Kirst, M. (1983) Teaching policy and federal categorical programs. In L. Shulman & G. Sykes (Eds.), *Handbook of Teaching and Policy.* New York: Longman.

Klaus, I. (1969). The evolution of a collective bargaining relationship in public education: New York City's changing seven-year history. *Michigan Law Review, 67,* 1033–1066.

Kochan, T., McKersie, R., & Capelli, P. (1984). Strategic choice and industrial relations theory. *Industrial Relations, 23,* 16–39.

Kornbluh, H. (1984). Work place democracy and the quality of work life: Problems and prospects. *American Association of Political Science Annals, 473,* 88–95.

Kuhn, J. (1961). *Bargaining in grievance settlement.* New York: Columbia University Press.

Kulleseid, E. (1982). *A study of survival: Three New York City elementary school library media centers and their support components.* Unpublished doctoral dissertation, Columbia University.

Lewis, G. (1963). *Unionism and relative wages in the United States.* Chicago: University of Chicago Press.

Lieberman, M. (1956). *Education as a profession.* Englewood Cliffs, NJ: Prentice-Hall.

Lieberman, M. (1980). *Public-sector bargaining: A policy reappraisal.* Lexington, MA: Heath.

Lieberman, M., & Moskow, M. (1966). *Collective negotiations for teachers.* Chicago: Rand McNally.

Lindenfield, F. (1963). *Teacher turnover in public elementary and secondary schools, 1959–1960.* Washington, DC: Office of Education, Circular 675.

Lipsky, D. (1982). The effect of collective bargaining on teacher pay: A review of the evidence. *Education Administration Quarterly, 18,*(1), 14–42.

Lipsky D., & Drotning J. (1973). The influence of collective bargaining on teachers' salaries in New York State. *Industrial and Labor Relations Review, 27*(1), 18–35.

Little, J. (1985). Teachers as colleagues. In V. Koehler (Ed.), *Educator's handbook: Research into practice.* New York: Longman.

Lortie, D. (1975). *Schoolteacher: A sociological study.* Chicago: University of Chicago Press.

Lutz, F., & Caldwell, W. (1979). Collective bargaining and the principal. In D. Erickson & T. Reller (Eds.), *The principal in metropolitan schools.* Berkeley, CA: McCutchan.

McDonnell, L., & Pascal, A. (1979a). National trends in collective bargaining. *Education and Urban Society, 11*(2), 129–151.

McDonnell, L., & Pascal, A. (1979b). *Organized teachers in American schools.* Santa Monica, CA: Rand.

Meyer, J.W. (1981). *Organizational factors affecting legalization in education* (Program Rep. 81–B10). Stanford, CA: Institute for Educational Finance and Governance.

Meyer, J., & Rowan, B. (1978). The structure of educational organizations. In M. Meyer and associates (Eds.), *Environments and organizations.* San Francisco: Jossey-Bass.

Mitchell, D., & Kerchner C. (1982). *Teacher organizations as alternative social systems.* Paper presented at the annual meeting of the American Educational Research Association, New York.

Mitchell, D., & Kerchner, C. (1983). Labor relations and teacher policy. In L. Shulman & G. Sykes, *Handbook of teaching and policy* (pp. 214–238). New York: Longmans.

Mitchell, D., Kerchner, C., Erck, W., & Pryor, G. (1981). The impact of collective bargaining on school management and policy. *American Journal of Education, 89,* 147–188.

Mitchell, D.J.B. (1979) The impact of collective bargaining on compensation in the public sector. In B. Aaron, J. Grodin, & J. Stern (Eds.), *Public sector bargaining.* Washington, DC: Bureau of National Affairs.

Moskow, M., Loewenberg, J., & Koziara, E. (1970). *Collective bargaining in public employment.* New York: Random House.

Murnane, R. (1980). *Seniority rules and educational productivity: Understanding the consequences of a mandate for equity* (Project rep. 80-A17). Stanford, CA: Stanford University, Institute for Educational Finance and Governance.

Murnane, R., & Cohen, D. (in press). Merit pay and the evaluation problem: Understanding why most merit pay plans fail and a few survive. *Harvard Educational Review.*

Murphy, M., & Ellman, N. (1974). The building principal and the union: A study in mutual accommodation. *IAR Research Bulletin, 14,* 3–5.

National Education Association. (1957). *Status of American public school teachers.* Washington, DC: Author.

National Education Association. (1972). *Status of the American public school teacher, 1970–1971.* Washington DC: Author.

National Education Association (1980). *Nationwide teacher opinion poll, 1980.* Washington, DC: Author.

National Education Association. (1983). *Prices, budgets, salary and income.* Washington, DC: Author.

National Opinion Research Center. (1982). *General social surveys, 1972–1982: Cumulative codebook.* Chicago: University of Chicago Press.

Ouchi, W. (1980). Markets, bureaucracies, and clans. *Administrative Science Quarterly, 25,* 129–141.

Perry, C. (1979). Teacher bargaining: The experience in nine systems. *Industrial and Labor Relations Review, 33*(1), 3–17.

Perry, C., & Wildman, W. (1970). *The impact of negotiations in public education: The evidence from the schools.* Worthington, OH: Jones Publishing.

Pierce, L. (1975). Teachers' organizations and bargaining: Power imbalance in the public sphere. In S. Weinstein & D. Mitchell (Eds.), *Public testimony on public schools.* Berkeley, CA: McCutchan.

Pilsko, V., & Stern, J. (Eds.). (1985). *The condition of education, 1985 edition.* Washington, DC: U.S. Department of Education.

Public Opinion, (1981, August–September), *33*.

Ream, M.A. (1977). *Status of the American public school teacher, 1975–76*. Washington, DC: National Education Association.

Rhemus, C., & Wilner E. (1965). *The economic results of teacher bargaining: Michigan's first two years*. Ann Arbor: University of Michigan, Institute of Labor and Industrial Relations.

Richardson, R. (1977). *Collective bargaining by objectives: A positive approach*. Englewood Cliffs, NJ: Prentice-Hall.

Ross, D. (1980). *State involvement in educational labor relations: A report on four states*. Denver, CO: Education Commission of the States.

Ryscavage, P.M. (1974). Measuring union-nonunion earnings differences. *Monthly Labor Review, 97*(12), 3–9.

Sanzare, J. (1977). *A history of the Philadelphia Federation of Teachers, 1941–1973*. Philadelphia: Philadelphia Federation of Teachers.

Schmenner, R. (1973). The determination of municipal employee wages. *Review of Economics and Statistics, 55*, 83.

Selden, D. (1985) *The teacher rebellion*. Washington, DC: Howard University Press.

Shanker, A. (1985). *The making of a profession*. Expansion of a speech delivered to the representative assembly of the New York State United Teachers, April 27, 1985. Washington, DC: American Federation of Teachers.

Simpkins, E., McCutcheon, A., & Alec, R. (1979). Arbitration and policy issues in school contracts. *Education and Urban Society, 11*, 241–254.

Slichter, S., Healy, J., & Livernash, E.R. (1960). *The impact of collective bargaining on management*. Washington, DC: Brookings Institution.

Smith, A. (1972). Have collective negotiations increased teachers' salaries? *Phi Delta Kappan, 52*, 268.

Smith, S. (1983). *Improving the attractiveness of the K–12 teaching profession in California*. Sacramento: California Round Table on Educational Opportunity.

Sosnowsky, W., & Coleman, T. (1971). Special education in the collective bargaining process. *Phi Delta Kappan, 52*, 610–613.

Stinnett, T.M. (1968). *Turmoil in teaching: A history of the organizational struggle for America's teachers*. New York: Macmillan.

Stinnett, T.M., Kleinmann, J.H., & Ware, M.L. (1966). *Professional negotiation in public education*. New York: Macmillan.

Thomas, S.A. (1982). *The organizational behavior of a teachers' union attempting to influence school district policy: The response of the United Teachers of Los Angeles to school desegregation*. Unpublished doctoral dissertation, University of California at Los Angeles.

Thornton, R. (1971). The effects of collective negotiations on teachers' salaries. *Quarterly Review of Economics and Business, 2*, 37–46.

Tomkiewicz, J. (1979). Determinants of teacher militancy: Factors affecting the decision to strike. *Journal of Collective Negotiations, 8*, 91–96.

Tooredman, K. (1978). *Local teacher union leadership: Participation and democracy in majority-female labor organizations*. Unpublished manuscript. Evanston, IL: Northwestern University, Graduate School of Education.

Treacy, J., Harris, R., & Blake, C. (1974). *Salaries, strikes, shutdown, split shifts and collective bargaining in Ohio public schools* (Final rep.). Washington, DC: National Institute of Education.

Urban, W. (1982). *Why teachers organized*. Detroit: Wayne State University Press.

Walters, C., & Wyatt, T. (1985). Toledo's internship: The teachers' role in excellence. *Phi Delta Kappan, 66*, 365–368.

Weintraub, A., & Thornton, R. (1976). Why teachers strike: The economic and legal determinants. *Journal of Collective Negotiations, 5,* 193–206.

Weitzman, J. (1974). *The scope of bargaining in public employment.* New York: Praeger.

Wellington, H., & Winter, R.K., Jr. (1969). The limits of collective bargaining in public employment. *Yale Law Journal, 78,* 1107–1127.

Wellington, H., & Winter, R., Jr. (1971). *The unions and the cities.* Washington, DC: Brookings.

Wirth, A. (1982, June). Alternative philosophies of work: Some questions for educators. *Phi Delta Kappan, 63* (10), 677–679.

Wirth, A. (1983). *Productive work in school and industry.* Lanham, MD: University Press of America.

Wise, A. (1979). *Legislated learning: The bureaucratization of the American classroom.* Berkeley: University of California Press.

Wollett, D. (1969). The coming revolution in public school management. *Michigan Law Review, 67,* 1017–1032.

Zuelke, D., & Frohreich, L. (1977). The impact of comprehensive collective negotiations on teachers' salaries: Some evidence from Wisconsin. *Journal of Collective Negotiation, 6,* 81–88.

IV.
META-ANALYSIS

Chapter 11

Issues in Meta-Analysis

LARRY V. HEDGES
University of Chicago

A decade ago Gene Glass coined the term meta-analysis in his presidential address to the annual meeting of the American Education Research Association. He defined meta-analysis as "the statistical analysis of a large collection of analysis results from individual studies for the purpose of integrating the findings" (1976a, p. 3). Since 1976 literally hundreds of reviews have been conducted using meta-analytic methodology and dozens of other papers have presented refinements of that methodology.

In this chapter, I use the term "meta-analysis" in a broad sense to connote any literature review that makes explicit use of quantitative methods to express the results of studies or to combine those results across studies. This usage seems consistent with Glass's original intent and with the current usage of the term in many areas of social, biological, and medical sciences. It is, however, somewhat less restrictive than the more detailed prescriptions offered by Glass and his associates (Glass, McGaw, & Smith, 1981) or, for example, by Hunter, Schmidt, and Jackson (1982). The broad definition has the advantage of including all relevant activity while obviating unprofitable debates (e.g., over orthodoxy, that is, about the infinitesimal details of what is and what is not a real meta-analysis). This broad conception of meta-analysis also serves clearly to identify meta-analysis as a variety of research review, specifically a research review that involves the use of quantitative methods. This is particularly appropriate since much of the discussion about meta-analyses applies equally well to any research review.

There are now seven books about procedures for conducting meta-analyses. One of these (Fricke & Treines, 1985) is in German, but the others

This chapter was written while the author was at Michigan State University. The author wishes to thank Betsy Jane Becker, Harris M. Cooper, and Richard J. Light for their helpful comments on an earlier draft of this manuscript.

(Cooper, 1984; Glass, McGaw & Smith, 1981; Hedges & Olkin, 1985; Hunter, Schmidt, & Jackson, 1982; Light & Pillemer, 1984; Rosenthal, 1984) are in English and should be both accessible and valuable to those interested in meta-analysis. Three edited volumes of collected papers (Light, 1983; Rosenthal, 1980; Yeaton & Wortman, 1984) are also valuable. The purpose of this chapter is not to summarize all of the material in these works or even the most important material. Similarly, this chapter is *not* a comprehensive review of the several hundred meta-analytic research reviews that are the substantive products of meta-analysis. Instead, the purpose of this chapter is to review important issues in meta-analysis that have emerged in the last decade.

THE IMPORTANCE OF META-ANALYSIS

Perhaps because of Glass's original definition, some have seized upon the quantitative aspect of meta-analysis and argue that meta-analysis is an advance because it is a quantification of the previously qualitative endeavor of research reviewing. This has led to what is essentially a replication of the debate about qualitative versus quantitative research methods (see Reichardt & Cook, 1979) in the context of literature review. This debate obscures what may be the real importance of meta-analysis. The most significant contribution is not that meta-analysis has led to more applications of quantitative methods in research reviews, but rather that it has helped to focus attention on the issue of methodological *rigor* in research reviewing. The signal contribution of meta-analysis is that it has led to serious examination of methodological standards in research reviewing.

Methodological Rigor

Methodological standards in original research help ensure the validity of the research. These standards exist because it is known that some procedures are subject to biases that render research results invalid or at least uninterpretable. For example, some methods of problem formulation (e.g., post hoc hypothesis formulation), data collection (e.g., purposefully biased or nonrandom sampling), data evaluation (e.g., eliminating subjects whose behavior contradicts the research hypothesis), data analysis (e.g., failure to use statistical methods to evaluate stochastic evidence), and reporting (e.g., failure to describe procedures clearly) may lead to difficulties in interpretation or to invalid research results. The methodological standards that are familiar to most researchers are an attempt to control biases and improve the validity of original research studies.

Research reviews involve many of the same procedures as original research, including problem formulation, sampling, data evaluation, data analysis, and reporting. It seems obvious that some variations of these procedures can lead to biases that may reduce the validity of the conclusions of a research review (Cooper, 1982, 1984). That is, methodological standards serve the same function (of helping to ensure validity) in research reviews as they do in original research. Given the importance of methodological standards in ensuring the validity of the results of research reviews and given the importance of literature reviews in the generation of scientific knowledge, it is astonishing that there was an almost complete lack of attention to methodological standards for literature reviews in the social sciences prior to 1976.

Reviews Prior to 1976

An illuminating study by Jackson (1978, 1980) reveals a great deal about the methodological quality of research reviews a decade ago. One aspect of Jackson's study was a search for explicit descriptions of systematic procedures (standards) for research reviews in the social sciences. He reported that none in his sample of 39 books on general research methodology in social sciences devoted more than two pages to literature reviews. Jackson also searched extensively for journal articles on methodological aspects of research reviewing in education, psychology, and sociology. Only three relevant articles were found during the 4-year period investigated (1973 to 1976). Finally Jackson surveyed journal editors and "officials of 10 organizations thought to have major responsibilities for integrative reviews" (1980, p. 458) in an attempt to discover systematic methodological standards that were used to evaluate literature reviews. Neither group of respondents provided very specific guidelines and both groups indicated that they relied almost exclusively on the judgments of authors or reviewers.

The lack of formally articulated standards for reviews would not be a problem if the standards for original research methodology were applied to research reviews. Jackson found, however, that they were not. He conducted a survey of the quality of reviews sampled from prestigious periodicals in education, psychology, and sociology. He found little evidence of the use of systematic procedures in these reviews and very serious deficiences in the sampling of studies to be reviewed, the representation of study results, and the reporting of the reviews. Jackson concluded:

It appears that relatively little thought has been given to methods for doing integrative reviews. Such reviews are crucial to science and social policy making yet most are done far less rigorously than is currently possible (1980, p. 459).

Inadequacy of Methods for Summarizing Research

Jackson's research did not detail the methods used to arrive at general conclusions from individual research results, but other investigators discovered a lack of rigorous procedures in this aspect of reviews as well. Examinations of the procedures used to arrive at general conclusions suggest that reviewers tended to rely heavily on the statistical significance of the individual results. Light and Smith (1971) argued that many reviewers used the proportion of statistically significant treatment effects to decide if the treatment has an overall effect. They labeled this procedure "vote counting" because each study in effect casts a vote (via its result) for or against the efficacy of the treatment. Analytical analysis of vote-counting methodology (Hedges & Olkin, 1980) demonstrated that it can be a highly misleading inference procedure. Vote counting not only has very low power to detect effects under the conditions in which it is usually used, but the power may actually decrease (tending to zero) as the number of available studies increases!

A related, misleading analytical procedure found in reviews is the use of statistical significance to determine if studies give consistent results (Humphreys, 1980). It is most simply illustrated by considering the case of two studies. Reviewers typically regard two similar studies whose significance tests yield the same result (both significant or both nonsignificant) as indicating replication of the research result. A situation in which one study yields a significant result and the other does not is regarded as a "failure to replicate." Neither conclusion is justified, nor is the generalization that several studies that find significant results provide evidence of consistent treatment effects.

Both of these erroneous procedures were used in many reviews, although their use was often implicit rather than explicit, and hence the actual procedure that was used had to be deduced from the reviewer's argument. The widespread use of these erroneous procedures for data summary is evidence of another failure of reviews to use rigorous procedures; in this case, analytical procedures.

Specific Contributions of Meta-Analysis

Although quantitative methods are not inherently more rigorous or scientific than qualitative methods, the discussion centering around meta-analysis has been accompanied by improvements in the rigor of all kinds of research reviews, including qualitative ones. This general increase in concern for the use of rigorous systematic procedures in research reviews is viewed as progress even by the critics of meta-analysis (e.g., Slavin, 1984).

Meta-analysis has led to a greater concern about data collection in research reviews. The identification of studies to be reviewed is now properly recognized as a sampling activity that can have a profound effect on the results of the review. Similarly, making complex judgments about such characteristics of studies as quality of research designs is now properly seen as a measurement process that must be treated as such with the tools of modern psychological measurement.

Meta-analysis has also contributed to the conceptualization that the magnitude of treatment effects may be more important than statistical significance (see Rosenthal, 1984). Meta-analysis has often involved representing the results of each study by an estimate of effect size and then combining these estimates across studies. Although there have been many advocates of the use of effect magnitude (Bakan, 1966; Cohen, 1965; Greenwald, 1975; Hays, 1963; Lykken, 1968), statistical significance has traditionally played a dominant role in the interpretation of statistical analyses in reviews, as well as in primary research. Meta-analysis based on effect sizes has represented something of a fortunate departure from that tradition.

Finally, meta-analysis has led to better analytic methods for research reviews. This includes research that led to a better understanding of the failings of procedures previously used in research reviews (Hedges & Olkin, 1980, 1985). More significant perhaps is the development of analytic methodology for expressing results (Glass, McGaw & Smith, 1981; Rosenthal & Rubin, 1982a), and for studying the variability of research results (Hedges, 1982a,b,c, 1983a,b; Hedges & Olkin 1983a,b; Kraemer, 1983; Raudenbush & Bryk, 1985; Rosenthal & Rubin, 1982b).

Although it might be comforting to dwell upon the many positive aspects of meta-analysis, it is also important to examine the areas in which meta-analysis is deficient or has room for improvement. In the rest of this chapter, I examine issues that arise when considering meta-analysis as scientific explanation. Some of the issues arise purely from the logical analysis of methodology. Other issues are suggested by recurrent criticisms that imply that meta-analysis has not been completely successful as explanation.

ISSUES IN PROBLEM FORMULATION

Problem formulation is often conceptualized as the first step in any research or research review (Cooper, 1984; Light & Pillemer, 1984). It involves formulating the precise questions to be answered by the review. One aspect of formulating questions is deciding whether the purpose of the review is confirmatory (hypothesis testing) or exploratory (hypothesis generating). Problem formulation also involves deciding on the constructs that underlie independent variables, study characteristics, and outcomes that are appropriate for those questions, and deciding on the operations that will be regarded as corresponding to the constructs. That is, the reviewer must develop both construct definitions and a set of rules for deciding which concrete instances (of treatments, controls, or measures) correspond to those constructs.

Selecting Constructs and Operations

The criticism that meta-analysis combines incommensurable evidence (apples and oranges) is essentially a criticism of the breadth of constructs and operations chosen. In one sense, breadth of constructs and operations chosen must reflect the breadth of the question addressed by the review. The issue is complicated by the fact that reviewers often report that they distinguish constructs and operations more narrowly than is reflected in the final presentation of results. Thus the issue of constructs and operations actually is first an issue of what constructs and operations are to be *included* in the review and then what constructs and operations are to be *distinguished* in the data analysis of the review, and finally which constructs and operations are *presented* in the results of the review. Meta-analyses have tended to use rather broad constructs and operations in their presentation of results (Cook & Leviton, 1980). This may have resulted from the arguments of Glass and his associates (Glass, McGaw, & Smith, 1981) who urged meta-analysts to seek general conclusions. The use of broad constructs and operations may also be a consequence of the ease with which quantitative methods can analyze data from large numbers of studies (Cooper & Arkin, 1981). It is important to recognize, however, that while broad questions necessitate the *inclusion* of studies with a broad range of constructs and operations, they need not inhibit the meta-analyst from distinguishing variations of these constructs in the data analysis and in presentation of results.

Broad versus Narrow Constructs

The advantage of broad constructs and operations is that they may support the broad generalizations sought by Glass and his associates. Because they are very inclusive, broad constructs and operations obviate most arguments about studies that should have been included, but were not.

However, the uncritical use of very broad constructs in meta-analysis is problematic. Analyses based on operationalization of broad constructs are vulnerable to the criticism that overly broad choices of construct obscure important differences among the narrower constructs subsumed therein. For example, Presby (1978) argued that the broad categories of therapies used by Smith and Glass (1977) obscured important differences between therapies and their effectiveness. A similar argument may be made about the breadth of outcome constructs.

Moreover, empirical data sometimes confirm the truth of these arguments. Substantial differences among effect sizes are often functions of variations in treatment (Becker, 1986; Giaconia & Hedges, 1982; Raudenbush, 1984). Variations in outcome *construct* can also result in variations in treatment effect size. For example Giaconia and Hedges (1982) found that the effects of open education depended strongly on the type of outcome construct (e.g., mathematics achievement versus self-concept). Similar results have been obtained by Thomas and French (1985). Other meta-analyses have shown how even slight variations in outcome construct sometimes lead to different patterns of results. An extraordinarily careful meta-analysis of sex differences in spatial ability conducted by Linn and Peterson (1985) demonstrated that the results were highly sensitive to the definition of the spatial ability construct. By dividing what is usually called spatial ability into three constructs (spatial visualization, spatial perception, and mental rotation), each with a psychological and psychometric rationale, Linn and Peterson obtained different patterns of results for the three constructs.

Using Broad Constructs

Perhaps the most successful applications of broad or multiple constructs in meta-analysis are those that may *include* broad constructs in the review but *distinguish* narrower constructs in the data analysis and presentation of results. This permits the reviewer to examine variations in the pattern of results as a function of construct definition. It also permits separate analyses to be carried out for each narrow construct (see, e.g., Cooper, 1979; Linn & Peterson, 1985; Eagly & Carli, 1981; Thomas & French, 1985). A combined analysis across constructs may be carried out where appropriate, or distinct analyses for the separate constructs may be presented. Note that merely estimating a main-effect difference between constructs is usually not enough to assure that different constructs produce the same pattern of results. The absence of both main effects and interactions of construct with other between-study variables is necessary to assure that the pattern of results is the same across constructs.

Broad versus Narrow Operations for Constructs

Another issue of breadth arises at the level of operationalization of constructs. The reviewer will almost always have to admit several different operations for any given construct. Treatments will not be implemented identically in all studies, and different studies will measure the outcome construct in different ways. Thus, the reviewer must judge whether each operation is a legitimate representation of the corresponding construct. This involves obtaining as much information as possible about the treatment actually implemented and the outcome actually used in each study. This may involve the use of secondary sources such as technical reports, general descriptions of treatment implementations, test reviews, or published tests.

In spite of the difficulty they may present to the reviewer, multiple operations can enhance the confidence in relationships between constructs, if the analogous relationships between operations hold under a variety of different (and each imperfect) operations (Campbell, 1969). However, increased confidence comes from multiple operations only when the different operations are in fact more closely related to the desired construct than to some other construct. (For a discussion of multiple operationism, see Webb, Campbell, Schwartz, Sechrest, & Grove, 1981). Thus, although multiple operations can lead to increased confidence through "triangulation" of evidence, the indiscriminate use of broad operations can also contribute to invalidity of results via confounding of one construct with another (see Cooper, 1984).

Exploratory versus Confirmatory Reviews

A crucial aspect of problem formulation is distinguishing whether the purpose of the review is to *test* a small number of reasonably well-defined hypotheses, or to *generate* new hypotheses. Obviously, new hypotheses (even new variables) arise in the course of meta-analyses, just as in any scientific activity. The critical issue is to distinguish the clearly a priori hypotheses from those that are suggested by the data. This distinction has implications for the choice of statistical analysis procedures used in the meta-analysis and for interpretation of results. Most statistical tests calculate levels of statistical significance assuming that the hypothesis is a priori and is tested in isolation. When statistical tests are suggested by the data, the usual procedures for assessing statistical significance are misleading (Miller, 1981). Similarly, when many statistical analyses are conducted on the same data, the usual significance levels will *not* reflect the chance of making *at least* one Type I error in the collection of tests (the simultaneous significance level). In each case, the usual methods for testing statistical significance will make the results appear more significant than they should be. Thus, when conducting many tests in an exploratory mode, there is a tendency to "capitalize on chance" (Hunter, Schmidt, & Jackson, 1982).

Particularly flagrant examples of this problem are meta-analyses that calculate 50 tests of significance of the effects of study characteristics on effect size, often from barely that number of effect sizes. Interpretation of those tests of significance is problematic. The situation is even worse when many tests are conducted but only those that attain significance are reported by the reviewer.

One method of dealing with the problem of exploratory analysis in research reviews is to use statistical methods that are specifically designed for exploratory analysis—such as clustering methods (Hedges & Olkin, 1983, 1985). Another alternative is to adjust the significance level to reflect the fact that many tests are conducted on the same data (Hedges & Olkin, 1985). The problem with this and all other simultaneous procedures is that they reduce the power of statistical tests, and the effect is dramatic when many tests are conducted simultaneously.

Another alternative is the use of procedures that do not involve statistical significance. The simplest procedures are simply descriptive statistics. Graphical procedures such as Light and Pillemer's (1984) funnel diagrams, Hedges and Olkin's (1985) confidence interval plots, or many of the graphical ideas presented by Tukey (1977) may also be helpful.

A third alternative is to divide the data into two subsets randomly. The first subset is used to generate hypotheses whose statistical significance is then evaluated (cross-validated) on the second subset (Light & Pillemer, 1984.)

ISSUES IN DATA COLLECTION

Data collection in meta-analysis consists of assembling a collection of research studies and extracting quantitative indices of study characteristics and of effect magnitude (or relationship between variables). The former is largely a sampling process in selecting studies that may contain information relevant to the specific questions addressed in the review. The latter is a problem of obtaining quantitative representations of the measures of effect magnitude and the other characteristics of studies that are relevant to the specific questions addressed by the review. This is essentially a measurement process similar to other complex tasks or judgments that researchers are sometimes required to make in other research contexts. The standard psychological measurement procedures for ensuring the reliability and validity of such ratings or judgements are as appropriate in meta-analysis as in original research (Rosenthal, 1984; Stock, Okun, Haring, Miller, Kinney, & Ceurvorst, 1982).

Sampling in Meta-Analysis

The problem of assembling a collection of studies is often viewed as a sampling problem; that is, of obtaining a representative sample of all studies that have actually been conducted. Because the adequacy of samples necessarily determines the range of valid generalizations that are possible, the procedure used to locate studies in meta-analysis has been regarded as crucially important. Much of the discussion on sampling in meta-analysis (e.g., Cooper, 1984; Glass, McGaw, & Smith, 1981; Hunter, Schmidt, & Jackson, 1982; Rosenthal, 1984) concentrates on the problem of obtaining a representative or exhaustive sample of relevant studies. Another equally important sampling question is whether the samples of subjects and treatments in the individual studies are representative of the subject populations and treatment populations of interest.

The importance of representative sampling of experimental populations is obvious. For example, studies of the effects of psychotherapy on college students who do not have psychological problems may not be relevant to the determination of the effects of psychotherapy on patients who have real psychological problems. The importance of representative sampling of treatments is perhaps more subtle. The question is whether the treatments that occur in studies are representative of the situations about which the reviewer seeks knowledge (Bracht & Glass, 1968). For example, one criticism (Slavin, 1984) of Glass and Smith's (1979) meta-analysis of the effects of class size is that many of the class sizes represented in the studies (e.g., of the effects of tutoring) were too small to be representative of school settings. A representative sample of studies, each of which involves a nonrepresentative sample of subjects or treatments, brings us no closer to useful conclusions about the subjects or treatments that are of interest to us.

Consequently, there are two levels of sampling to be concerned about in meta-analysis. One level concerns the representativeness of the sample of studies that are actually conducted. The other concerns the representativeness of the individual studies as studies of the phenomenon of interest to the reviewer. The situation is much like that of two-stage samples in sample surveys. The reviewer samples clusters or secondary sampling units first, then the individual subjects or primary sampling units are sampled from the clusters.

Strategies for obtaining representative or exhaustive samples of studies have been discussed by Glass, McGaw, and Smith (1981) and Cooper (1984). The problem of obtaining representative samples of subjects and treatments is constrained by the nature of the studies that have been done and, therefore, is not under the complete control of the reviewer. The reviewer can, however, present descriptions of the samples of subjects and treatments and examine the relationship between characteristics of these samples and study outcomes. Such assessments of the representativeness of treatments and subjects are obviously crucial in evaluation of the external validity of studies.

Missing Data in Meta-Analysis

Missing data create a problem that plagues many forms of applied research. Survey researchers are well aware that the best sampling design is ineffective if the information sought cannot be extracted from the units that are sampled (Cochran, 1963; Madow, Nisselson, & Olkin, 1983). Of course, missing data are not a substantial problem if they are "missing at random," that is, if the missing information is essentially a random sample of all the information available (Rubin, 1976). Unfortunately, there is usually very little reason to believe that missing data in meta-analysis are missing at random. On the contrary, it is often easier to argue that the causes of the missing data are systematically related to effect size or to important characteristics of studies. When this is true, missing data pose a serious threat to the validity of conclusions in meta-analysis. The specific cases of missing data on effect size and missing data on study characteristics are considered separately.

Missing Data on Effect Size

Studies (such as single case studies) that do not use statistical analyses are one source of missing data on effect size. Other studies use statistics but do not provide enough statistical information to allow the calculation of an effect size estimate. This is sometimes a consequence of failure to report relevant statistics. More often, it is a consequence of the researcher's use of a complex design that makes it difficult or impossible to construct an effect size estimate using the proper metric (McGaw & Glass, 1980) or standard deviation. Unfortunately, both the sparse reporting of statistics and the use of complex designs are plausibly related to study outcomes. Both result, at least in part, because the most selective journals in psychology and education often discourage reporting of all but the most essential statistics. Perhaps the most pernicious sources of missing data are studies that *selectively* report statistical information. Such studies typically report only information on effects that are statistically significant, exhibiting what has been called reporting bias (Hedges, 1984b). Missing effect size data from studies that report complete data on only significant effects can lead to very serious biases, identical to those caused by selective publication that are discussed in the section on publication bias.

One strategy for dealing with incomplete effect size data is to ignore the problem. This is almost certainly a bad strategy. If nothing else, such a strategy reduces the credibility of the meta-analysis because the fact that at least some data are missing is obvious to knowledgeable readers. Another problematic strategy for handling missing effect size data is to replace all of the missing values by the same imputed value (usually zero). Although this strategy usually leads to a conservative (often extremely conservative) estimate of the overall average effect size, it creates serious problems in any attempt to study the variability of effect sizes and the relationship of study characteristics to effect size. A better strategy is to extract from the study any available information about effect size. The direction of the effect (the sign of the effect size) can often be deduced even when an effect size cannot be calculated. A tabulation of these directions of effects can therefore be used to supplement the effect size analysis (e.g., Crain & Mahard, 1983; Giaconia & Hedges 1982). Such a tabulation can even be used to derive an estimate of effect size (Hedges & Olkin, 1980, 1985).

Although a tabulation of directions of effects is a contingency table, it should be noted that the use of *standard* statistical methods (e.g., chi-square tests, log-linear models, or logistic regression) to analyze such a table cannot be justified. The reason is that the counts are not identically distributed within cells of the table, even if the underlying effect size is the same for all studies. The probability that a study gives a positive result when it has a given (population) effect size is a function of its within-study sample size. Because these sample sizes vary across studies, so does the probability of a positive result and, consequently, the individual observations (counts) are not identically distributed.

Perhaps the best way to deal with missing effect size data is the use of the many analytic strategies that have been developed for handling missing data in sample surveys (Madow, Nisselson, & Olkin, 1983; Madow & Olkin, 1983; Madow, Olkin, & Rubin, 1983). These strategies generally involve using the available information (including study characteristics) to estimate the structure of the effect size data and the relationships among study characteristics and effect sizes. They can also be used to study the sensitivity of conclusions to the possible effects of missing data. Although these strategies have much to recommend them they have not been used in meta-analysis.

Missing Data on Study Characteristics

Another less obvious form of missing data is missing data on study characteristics that results from incompletely detailed descriptions of the treatment, controls, experimental procedure, or the outcome measures. In fact, the generally sketchy descriptions of studies in the published literature often constrain the degree of specificity possible in schemes used to code between-study differences.

The problem of missing data about study characteristics is related to the problem of breadth of constructs and operations for study characteristics. Coding schemes that use a high degree of detail (and have higher fidelity) generally result in a greater degree of missing data. As a result, relatively vague study characteristics are often coded on all studies or more specific characteristics are coded on a relatively few studies (see Orwin & Cordray, 1985). Neither procedure alone seems to inspire confidence among some readers of the meta-analysis.

One method for dealing with missing information about study characteristics is to have two levels of specificity: a broad level that can be coded for nearly all studies and a narrower level that can be coded for only a subset of the studies. This strategy may be useful if suitable care is exercised in describing the differences between the entire collection of studies and the smaller number of studies permitting the more specific analysis. A more elegant solution is the use of the more refined methods for handling missing data in sample surveys as discussed previously.

Two other strategies for dealing with missing data on study characteristics are little used but deserve more attention. One is the collection of additional information from other sources such as technical reports, other more general descriptive reports on a program, test reviews, or articles that describe a program, treatment, or measurement method. The appropriate references are often published in research reports. Direct examination of published tests is a good way to get information on those instruments. A second, and often neglected, source of information is the direct collection of new data. For example in a meta-analysis of sex differences in helping behaviors, Eagly and Crowley (1986) surveyed a new sample of subjects to determine the degree of perceived danger in the helping situations examined in the studies. This rating of degree of perceived danger to the helper was a valuable factor in explaining the variability of results across studies.

Publication Bias

An important axiom of survey sample design is that an excellent sample design cannot guarantee a representative sample if it is drawn from an incomplete enumeration of the population. The analog in meta-analysis is that an apparently good sampling plan may be thwarted by applying the plan to an incomplete and unrepresentative subset of the studies that were actually conducted.

The published literature is particularly susceptible to the claim that it is unrepresentative of all studies that may have been conducted (the so-called publication bias problem). There is considerable empirical evidence that the published literature contains fewer statistically insignificant results than would be expected from the complete collection of all studies actually conducted (Bozarth & Roberts, 1972; Hedges, 1984b; Sterling, 1959). There is also direct evidence that journal editors and reviewers intentionally include statistical significance among their criteria for selecting manuscripts for publication (Bakan, 1966; Greenwald, 1975; Melton, 1962). The tendency of the published literature to overrepresent statistically significant findings leads to biased overestimates of effect magnitudes from published literature (Hedges, 1984b; Lane & Dunlap, 1978); a phenomenon that was confirmed empirically by Smith's (1980a) study of 10 meta-analyses, each of which presented average effect size estimates for both published and unpublished sources.

Reporting bias is related to publication bias based on statistical significance. Reporting bias also creates missing data when researchers fail to report the details of results of some statistical analyses, such as those that do not yield statistically significant results. The effect of reporting bias is identical to that of publication bias: Some effect size estimates are unavailable (e.g., those that correspond to statistically insignificant results).

Publication or reporting bias may not always be severe enough to invalidate meta-analyses based solely on published articles (see Hedges, 1984b; Light & Pillemer, 1984). Theoretical analysis of the potential effects of publication bias showed that even when nonsignificant results are never published (the most severe form of publication bias), the effect on estimation of effect size may not be large unless both the within-study sample sizes and the underlying effect size are small. However, if either the sample sizes in the studies or the underlying effect sizes are small, the effect on estimation can be substantial.

The possibility that publication or reporting bias may inflate effect size estimates suggests that reviewers may want to consider investigating its possible impact. One method is to compare the effect size estimates derived from published (e.g., books, journal articles) and unpublished sources (e.g., conference presentations, contract reports, ERIC documents, or doctoral dissertations). Such comparisons, however, are often problematic because the source of the study is often confounded with many other study characteristics. An alternative procedure is to use Hedges's (1984b) corrections for estimation of effect size under publication bias. If these corrections produce a negligible effect, this suggests that publication and reporting bias are negligible. Another less specific alternative is the use of Rosenthal's (1979) file-drawer number, but the reader may want to examine the discussion of the limitations of this technique in Hedges & Olkin (1985).

There have been relatively few detailed statistical analyses of the existence and magnitude of publication and reporting bias. Such studies are badly needed as are refinements of statistical analysis tools to handle less extreme and more realistic censoring models than those considered thus far.

Conceptualization of Effect Size

Meta-analysis always involves summarizing the results of a research study by an index of effect magnitude or a relationship between variables. When studies of a treatment do not all use identical outcome measures, the index of effect magnitude that is most often used is the standardized mean difference or effect size. The sample effect size is usually defined as

$$g = (\bar{Y}^E - \bar{Y}^C)/S$$

where $\bar{Y}^E$ is the sample mean of the subjects in the experimental or treatment group, $\bar{Y}^C$ is the sample mean of the subjects in the control group, and S is a within-group sample standard deviation.

There are three fundamentally different means of conceptualizing effect sizes, which have not always been clearly distinguished. Two of these conceptualizations give the effect size different meanings within the context of a two-group experiment. The third relates the effect size to summary indices of outcome in different experimental situations. These three conceptualizations give rise to different interpretations of effect size analyses, and hence the conceptualization of effect size may influence both methodology and generality of conclusions in meta-analysis.

Effect Size as an Index of Overlap Between Distributions

One of the earliest conceptions of effect size is as an index that is related to the degree of overlap between distributions. For example, Cohen (1977) justified his choices of numerical values corresponding to small, medium, and large effect sizes by referring to the visible degree of overlap between distributions. He also explicitly used a transformation of effect size to an index U of overlap between distributions. Some of the early interpretations given by Glass (1976a,b, 1978) and by Glass, McGaw, and Smith (1981) stress the notion of overlapping distributions or the equivalent notion that a given effect size implies that the average person in the treatment group would be at a specific percentile in the control group. For example "an 'effect size' of + 1 indicates that a person at the mean of the control group would be expected to rise to the 84th percentile of the control group after treatment" (Glass, 1976b, p. 13).

The use of effect size as an indicator of *overlap between distributions* is actually a special (univariate) case of the more general idea of Mahalanobis's (1936) distance, which is used as an index of the overlap between multivariate distributions (see, e.g., Morrison, 1967). This conceptualization of effect size is important because overlap between distributions is a concept that has the same interpretation regardless of whether the distributions are distributions of measures of the same (or similar) constructs. Hence, in this conceptualization, effect sizes are comparable even when they are calculated based on observations of such different variables as self-concept, IQ, mathematics achievement, or freedom from neuroses. This conceptualization is appropriate even when combining effect sizes based on a very broad array of outcome constructs. However, this conceptualization is only indirectly linked to the notion of a treatment effect on a (psychometrically) well-defined outcome variable. Thus, it may be appropriate to conclude that an average effect size of 1 implies that the treatment moves the average person to the 84th percentile, but there may be no single, well-defined variable to which this percentile relates.

Effect Size as Scale-Free Treatment Effect

The effect size has also been characterized as a scale-free index of treatment effect whose value does not change (is invariant) under linear transformations of the original observations (Hedges, 1981, 1982a). The importance of this conceptualization comes from the fact that in classical measurement theory, different measures of the same construct are linearly equatable (perfectly correlated). Different studies are liable to use different measures (different instruments) to assess study outcomes. However, if all studies actually measure the same outcome *construct,* then the outcome measures should be roughly linearly equatable. Because the effect size is scale invariant, it provides an index of treatment effect that does not depend on the particular outcome measure used. The effect sizes therefore are a way of putting treatment effects (on a particular outcome construct) from different studies on the same "scale." This scale corresponds to an equivalent (linearly equatable) version of the outcome that is chosen to yield unit variance within groups. Thus, the effect size is the treatment effect (mean difference) that would have been observed if a study had used an equatable outcome measure with unit variance.

Note that this interpretation of effect size depends on the idea that the outcomes of different studies are measures of the same underlying construct. It is only appropriate when the reviewer uses a relatively narrow definition (set of operationalizations) of the outcome variable. One advantage of this conceptualization of effect size is that a precise interpretation of the effect size is sensible within the context of classical test theory. A second advantage of this conceptualization is that effect size analyses can be justified as the natural analogue to pooling raw data (from all k studies) into a single two treatments by k studies analysis (see Hedges, 1984a; Hedges & Olkin, 1985).

Effect Sizes as Equivalent to Other Summaries

Yet another conceptualization of effect size is as one of many equivalent ways to express the magnitude of a relationship between variables. For example, Cohen (1977) demonstrated a method to transform effect sizes into correlation coefficients. Similarly, Hyde (1981) used both effect sizes and Hays's index ω^2 to express the magnitude of gender differences in cognitive abilities. Rosenthal and Rubin (1982a) showed how to construct a 2 × 2 contingency table (a binomial effect size display) in which the magnitude of the relationship corresponded to a given effect size. Although some have sought to exploit such transformations to simplify statistical analyses (Hedges & Olkin, 1985; Hunter, Schmidt, & Jackson, 1982; Kraemer, 1983; Rosenthal, 1984), the most important use of this conceptualization has been to aid in interpreting the magnitude of effects. Rosenthal and Rubin (1982a) demonstrated convincingly that treatment effects which looked small when expressed as effect sizes, correlation coefficients, or squared correlations (proportions of variance accounted for), often appeared to be much larger when expressed in the binomial effect size display.

Effect Sizes from Complex Designs

Most meta-analyses involve combining effect sizes, each of which is an estimate of a treatment effect derived from a contrast between a treatment group and a control group. However, the research designs employed in studies may be considerably more complicated than just a treatment group and a control group. Frequently, independent variables other than the treatment are employed, often as design (blocking) factors or covariates to increase the power of statistical tests by reducing error variability. Alternatively, pretest-posttest designs sometimes utilize gain scores to reduce bias due to preexisting differences and to increase precision. Increased precision is, of course, desirable but the reduction of error terms has the effect of making it more difficult for the meta-analyst to obtain effect size estimates that are comparable from study to study.

To make effect sizes comparable across studies, the reviewer must express the effect sizes in terms of the same type of standard deviation in each study, usually that of raw outcome scores (see McGaw & Glass, 1980; Glass, McGaw, & Smith, 1981). This is not a problem when raw data or complete descriptive statistics are available, but these fundamental data are usually not available in research reports. Thus, the reviewer must usually recover effect size estimates from t or F test statistics using formulas provided, for example, by Glass, McGaw, and Smith (1981).

Problems arise when the test statistics from complex designs are based on a different and smaller "operative standard deviation" than that of the posttest scores. Cohen (1977) has described the situation by saying that statistical tests in complex designs have a larger "operative effect size" than that of the simple experimental-control group design. While this creates no problem for statistical testing in primary research, it can create a problem for meta-analysis because the magnitude of the "operative effect sizes" is a function of experimental design, as well as the actual treatment effect (McGaw & Glass, 1980). If all studies used the same design, then operative effect sizes would be comparable from study to study and meta-analysis based on operative effect sizes might be reasonable—if it were properly interpreted. Unfortunately, experimental designs vary across studies and so effect size estimates must be transformed to provide estimates in a uniform metric (that is, with reference to the same type of standard deviation).

Glass, McGaw, and Smith (1981) provide formulas that relate the operative standard deviations in various designs to the desired (pooled within-groups) posttest standard deviation. These transformations are all of the form

$$\sigma_Y = c\,\sigma_{Y'},$$

where σ_Y is the posttest standard deviation, $\sigma_{Y'}$ is the operative standard deviation for the test statistic in the design, and c is a constant depending on the design. These transformations are used in meta-analysis to convert an estimate of operative effect size g' obtained from test statistics (and based on an operative sample standard deviation S') into an estimate of the desired effect size g (based on the posttest standard deviation) via

$$g = g'/c.$$

For example in the experimental-control group design with one covariate, Y' is a covariate adjusted score, Y is the raw (unadjusted) posttest score, and

$$c = 1/[1 - \rho^2_{XY}]^{\frac{1}{2}}$$

where ρ_{XY} is the within-group correlation between the covariate and the posttest. Hence the desired effect size g (based on raw posttest scores) is

$$g = g'\,[1 - \rho^2_{XY}]^{\frac{1}{2}}$$

where g' is the operative effect size derived from ANCOVA test statistics.

Implications of Transformations for Statistical Analyses.

Most technical treatments of modern statistical methods for meta-analysis describe the setting for their methods in terms of two-group experiments in which the assumptions of the t test are met (Hedges 1981, 1982a,b,c, 1983a, 1984; Hedges & Olkin, 1983, 1985; Kraemer, 1983; Rosenthal, 1984; Rosenthal & Rubin, 1982b). This has apparently led to confusion about how to proceed when effect size estimates must be derived from test statistics or from transformations from operative effect sizes in complex designs. The calculation of effect size estimates from t or F test statistics in a simple two-group design has no implications for statistical analysis since the estimate so obtained is algebraically equivalent to that obtained directly from means and standard deviations. However, the calculation of effect size estimates via transformations from operative effect sizes does necessitate slight changes in statistical analyses.

Modern statistical methods for effect size analyses all involve sampling theory for effect size estimates that applies to the *operative* effect sizes. However, the transformations from operative effect sizes (g' values) to the effect sizes of interest (g values) always involve division by a constant,

$$g = g'/c.$$

The effect of this transformation is to change the variance of g' by a factor of $1/c^2$. In other words, the variance of the effect size estimate of interest (g) is $1/c^2$ times the variance of g'. All that is required to carry out any of the modern statistical analyses for effect sizes (e.g., from Hedges & Olkin, 1985) is to replace the usual variance v of g by v/c^2 in the statistical computations.

For example, if g was calculated from the operative effect size g' in a two-group design with one covariate, then the $c = 1/[1 - \rho^2_{XY}]^{\frac{1}{2}}$ and the sampling variance of g would be

$$v[1 - \rho^2_{XY}]$$

where ρ_{XY} is the within-group correlation between posttest and covariate and

$$v = \frac{n^E + n^C}{n^E n^C} + \frac{(g')^2}{2(n^E + n^C)},$$

the usual sampling variance of g' (see, e.g., Hedges & Olkin, 1985). Note that because ρ_{XY} will almost always be substantial, the effect size estimate obtained from g' will be more precise (have smaller variance) than that obtained from a simple experimental-control group design with the same sample size and no covariates. It will generally be true that more complex designs that reduce error variance by covariates, matching, or gain scores yield effect size estimates that are more precise than simple designs using the same sample size.

Transformations of Nonparametric Statistics to Effect Sizes

Researchers sometimes use nonparametric statistics or proportions of subjects reaching a criterion to analyze the results of comparative experiments. Glass, McGaw, and Smith (1981) proposed several strategies for estimating effect sizes in such situations. For example, when nonparametric statistics are reported, they propose a transformation from the significance level to an effect size estimate. When proportions of subjects reaching a criterion are reported, they propose the use of probit analysis (Finney, 1971) to obtain an estimate of effect size. These procedures are often employed in meta-analysis, yet little is known about their conceptual and statistical properties. It seems likely that both transformations from significance levels and probit analysis are sensitive to violations of assumptions on which they are based. It also seems likely that both of these procedures result in effect size estimates with larger standard errors than those obtained directly from means and standard deviations. The one available study of estimation of effect size based on transformations of p-values from nonparametric statistics suggests that these estimates can have substantial bias in small samples (Reynolds & Day, 1984). More investigation of the properties of these estimates is needed, including both coherent large sample theory and at least simulations of small sample behavior.

ISSUES IN DATA EVALUATION

Data evaluation in meta-analysis is the process of critical examination of the corpus of information collected to determine which study results are expected to yield reliable information. Judgments of study quality are the principal method of data evaluation. Such judgments are useful both for identifying a subsample of high-quality studies on which to base the data analysis and for use in studying the relationship between study quality and study results. A second aspect of data evaluation is the use of empirical methods to detect outliers or influential data points. When properly applied, empirical methods have uses in both meta-analysis (Hedges & Olkin, 1985) and primary research (Barnett & Lewis, 1978; Hawkins, 1980).

Assessing Study Quality

Meta-analysts and other reviewers of research have sometimes used a single binary (high/low) judgment of the quality of research studies. Although such aggregate judgments may be useful for some purposes, such as deciding which studies to exclude from the review, it is seldom advisable to make such judgments directly. Instead, most meta-analysts, at least initially, characterize study quality by using multiple criteria. One approach to criteria for study quality is the threats-to-validity approach, in which each study is rated according to the presence or absence of some general threats to validity such as those presented by Campbell and Stanley (1963) or Cook and Campbell (1979). A second approach is the methods-description approach (Cooper, 1984) in which the reviewer exhaustively codes the stated characteristics of each study's methods. A third approach to assessing study quality is a combination of the first two approaches, involving coding of the characteristics of study methodology and assessing threats to validity that may not be reflected in the characteristics of study methods (Cooper, 1984).

Defining Study Quality Empirically

Glass (1978) and Glass, McGaw, and Smith (1981) argued that the effects of study quality could be examined by determining whether high-quality studies gave different results on the average than did low-quality studies. They argued that study quality could, in effect, be defined empirically. If high-and low-quality studies gave the same results, they argued that low-quality studies should be included in the evidence used to draw conclusions. Based on an analysis of several meta-analyses, Glass, McGaw, and Smith (1981) concluded that "as a general rule there is seldom more than .1 standard deviation difference between average effects for high-validity and low-validity experiments" (p. 226).

Glass and his associates implied that high- and low-quality studies gave the same results essentially because the flaws in different studies resulted in conflicting biases that cancelled across studies. This argument may be sensible if the primary methodological flaws lead to biases that act in opposite directions. However, several investigators have noted that the biases in some research areas tend to share the same direction (Campbell & Erlebacher, 1970; Cook & Leviton, 1980; Slavin, 1984; Yeaton & Wortman, 1984). The general rule that study results are unrelated to study quality now seems somewhat dubious since a substantial number of meta-analyses have found that indices of study quality are related to effect size (Carlberg, 1979; Chalmers, 1982; Crain & Mahard, 1983; DerSimonian & Laird, 1983; Gilbert, McPeek, & Mosteller, 1977; Glass & Smith, 1979; Hartley, 1977; Smith 1980b; Smith & Glass, 1980; Wortman, 1981).

Even if study quality were found to be empirically unrelated to study results, there are several reasons to evaluate carefully the general decision to base conclusions on both high- and low-quality studies. First, the determination that there is no main effect of study quality does not imply that high- and low-quality studies give the same *pattern* of results. There may be interactions of study quality with other study characteristics. To demonstrate adequately that high-quality studies give the same answers as low-quality studies requires examining *all* of the interactions of study quality with other study characteristics.

Second, even if high-quality studies and low-quality studies give the same answer on the average, the variability of their results may not be the same. In fact, if low-quality studies are subject to biased results (perhaps in different directions), the major effect of poor experimental control should be increased variability in study results. Because both sampling error and variability of underlying effect sizes contribute to variability in observed effect sizes, the raw standard deviations of effect size estimates are not a reliable index of the variability of study results (Hedges, 1983a). An analog to variance components estimation is needed to estimate the variability in underlying population effect sizes. The use of such procedures often reveals that the underlying effect sizes from studies with poor experimental control yield effect size variance components that are substantially more variable than those from highly controlled studies. For example, Cohn (1984) found that poorly controlled studies of the effects of creativity training had effect size variance components that were two to four times as large as those of well-controlled studies.

Third, even if low-quality studies do give essentially the same answers as high-quality studies, their inclusion may decrease the credibility of the results. Some readers may tend to dismiss the review as based on faulty evidence, if they cannot easily isolate the evidence based on high-quality studies. For these readers, the extra evidence provided by the low-quality studies does not increase their confidence in the results, but in fact tends to decrease it.

Specificity of Indicators of Study Quality

Regardless of what method is used to develop indicators of study quality, these indicators can be treated either as completely general or with reference to the specific research area. For example, a threat to validity might be viewed generally as the danger that treatment and control groups are not equivalent. In a specific research context, such as the evaluation of a compensatory education program, that threat might be more specifically interpreted as the danger that the treatment group had lower initial ability than the control group, or that the control group suffered from selective attrition as more concerned parents attempted to obtain the treatment for their children. Sophisticated researchers have specific knowledge of the threats to validity (or alternatively of the study methods) appropriate in their areas. Not all threats to validity are equally important in every specific research area, and sophisticated researchers pay more attention to the more salient methodological difficulties. Generalized descriptions and indicators of study quality may not inspire confidence in a sophisticated reader for two reasons. First, they may fail to demonstrate that the reviewer has grasped the *specific* methodological issues of the particular field. Second, general classifications may confound several specific issues that are not viewed as (and may not be) equivalent in their effect on research results. Meta-analysts can avoid the difficulties produced by overly broad indicators of methodological quality by reading previous reviews and other literature in the area so that they can confront the specific issues (and use the specific language) of the research areas that they review.

Model Diagnostics and Outliers

Another source of information in data evaluation comes from data analyses themselves. It often happens that one or more observations (estimates of effect magnitude) fail to fit the pattern of the other observations. That is, one or more of the data points fail to conform to the same model as do the other observations. These deviant observations or outliers may be the result of studies or situations in which the treatment is exceptionally powerful or exceptionally weak. In some cases, a careful examination of details of study design or procedures suggests plausible reasons for the exceptional treatment effect. For example, in Hall's (1986) analysis of sex differences in nonverbal communication, a study identified statistically as an outlier was one in which the individuals communicating were 10 feet apart. All other studies involved face-to-face communication at distances more typical of dyadic interaction.

Sometimes the examination of studies that yield outlying effect size estimates reveals that the effect size estimate is calculated incorrectly, that it is based on suspicious data, or that it is not comparable to other effect sizes because it is based on a different standard deviation (a different metric). Calculation of effect size estimates often involves a substantial amount of computation such as repooling sums of squares from complex designs (see Glass, McGaw, & Smith, 1981). Computational errors can and do occur. In other cases, the data reported in a study are suspicious because they are contradictory. For example, it may be possible to calculate an estimate of effect size in two different ways (e.g., from means and also from a test statistic). If these two estimates differ substantially, then one of them must be incorrect but it may be difficult to tell which one. Hence, neither estimate of effect size is highly credible. Finally, effect size estimates in a study may be calculated using a different type of standard deviation than that of other studies, rendering them incomparable to the estimates from other studies. For example, Becker and Hedges (1984) found that the study identified as an outlier used group means as a unit of statistical analysis and therefore produced spuriously large effect sizes (since they were based on the standard deviation of the *means* of randomly selected groups).

Although statistical methods may be used to detect outliers in meta-analysis (Hedges & Olkin, 1985), the question of what to do about them cannot always be resolved so easily. Outliers that result from detectable (and remediable) errors in computation should, of course, be replaced by estimates based on the correct calculations. Outliers resulting from effect sizes that are not "on the same metric" should probably not be included in the same statistical analysis. Aggregates of such dissimilar objects are bound to be misleading. When outliers are based on suspicious data, then a cautious data analyst might want to delete, or at least consider separately, such suspicious observations.

The most difficult problem arises when examination of the outlying studies reveals no obvious reason why their effect sizes should differ from the rest. The analysis of data containing some observations that are outliers (in the sense of not conforming to the same model as the other studies) is a complicated task. It invariably requires the use of good judgment and the making of decisions that are, in some sense, compromises. There are cases (Rocke, Downs, & Rocke, 1982; Stigler, 1977; Tukey, 1977) where setting aside a small proportion of the data (less than 15-20%) has certain advantages. If nearly all the data can be modeled in a simple, straightforward way, it is certainly preferable to do so, even at the cost of requiring elaborate descriptions of the studies that are set aside.

Studies that are set aside should not be ignored since they often reveal patterns that are interesting in and of themselves. Occasionally, these deviant studies share a common characteristic that should be added to the model as a predictor. One of the reasons it is preferable to use a model that includes most of the data is that the results of studies that are identified statistically as outliers often do not deviate enough to disagree with the substantive result of the model. That is, an effect size estimate may exhibit a statistically significant difference from those of other studies, yet fail to differ from the rest to an extent that would make a practical or substantive difference. However, it is crucial that all data be reported and that any deleted data be clearly noted.

ISSUES IN DATA ANALYSIS AND INTERPRETATION

Data analysis and interpretation in meta-analysis is the process of utilizing statistical methods to draw general conclusions based on the data extracted from individual studies. Of the seven books on meta-analysis, all of one (Hedges & Olkin, 1985) and at least half of three others (Fricke & Treines, 1985; Hunter, Schmidt, & Jackson, 1982; Rosenthal, 1984) are devoted to statistical methods. In addition, there have been dozens of papers on the subject. This section is not an exhaustive review of previous work on data analysis and interpretation but an examination of critical issues in the area.

What Can Be Achieved by Statistical Methods in Meta-Analysis

Statistical methods in meta-analysis are easier to understand by considering an idealized case that preserves the essential features of meta-analysis, but has no unnecessary complexities. This idealized case is one in which conventional data analysis procedures are appropriate and thus the statistical methods are familiar (Hedges, 1984a).

Perhaps the simplest research synthesis is one in which the raw data from several experiments are available and can be pooled directly. For example, suppose that we have a series of k two-group experiments, each of which investigates the effect of a treatment using an experimental/control group design. Assume that each study measures a normally distributed outcome variable using the same instrument and the same sampling plan so that the within-group population variances of the outcome scores are identical.

While this situation is idealized because all studies use the same instrument to measure the outcome variable, it preserves the other essential features of meta-analysis. The studies need not be exact replications, but may have different sample sizes, use different types of subjects, use different experimental procedures, use different variations of the treatment, and be conducted by different investigators. The only unrealistic requirement is that the studies use the same outcome measure. There are meta-analyses, in fact, which come very close to this idealization in that all studies use the same measure of the outcome variable (DerSimonian & Laird, 1983; Underwood, 1957).

The situation defined in this idealization is one in which the raw data from the individuals in all the studies are directly comparable. Consequently, the outcome scores of the individuals can be combined and analyzed in one global statistical analysis. This is a format familiar to most social scientists, who would probably use the data from all individuals in a $2 \times k$ (two treatments by k studies) analysis of variance. In our idealized case, the assumptions of the analysis of variance will be met.

What does one learn from the analysis of variance? There are three omnibus F tests in the textbook analysis of such a situation. The F test for the main effect of studies tests whether the average value of the outcome variable (averaged over both experimental and control groups) differs across studies. This test is not particularly interesting in this context. The other two F tests are more interesting. The F test for the treatment factor tests whether the treatment group performs better than the control group on the average across all k experiments. The F test for the treatment-by-studies interaction tests whether the treatment effect is consistent across studies. The interpretation of the statistical analysis rests largely on these latter two tests. A large treatment effect with a negligible interaction is interpreted to mean that the treatment produces a large consistent effect across studies. If the interaction is not negligible, then interpretations become more complicated. An interaction suggests that the treatment effect is larger in some studies than in others. Statements about the main effects must be qualified by the fact that treatment effects vary significantly across studies.

A significant interaction signifies that one should begin to look for reasons why the treatment effect varies across studies. Variations across studies in treatment, experimental procedure, conditions of measurement, or sample composition might enter into an explanation of variations in treatment effect. If a suitable explanatory variable were found, it should be included in the statistical analysis as another independent variable or as a (blocking) factor. The new statistical analysis would reveal (by an appropriate F test) whether the new variable accounted for a significant amount of variation in the treatment effects and whether variations in the treatment effect across studies within levels of the new factor remained substantial. That is, we can test whether a proposed explanatory factor succeeds in removing or "explaining" the variations in treatment effects across studies. This test is conceptually analogous to the original test for the treatment-by-studies interaction.

Note that if the reviewer has a priori hypotheses about how treatment effects vary across studies, such hypotheses could be treated via contrasts (planned comparisons). Contrasts are probably the best (most powerful) way to detect a few specific effects. It is important, however, to recognize that finding a few specific contrasts show no differences does *not* guarantee that there is no variation among study results. Substantial variation might exist that could be detected by other contrasts. The omnibus test for study by treatment interaction is valuable precisely because it tests the hypothesis that *all possible* contrasts among treatment effects are zero. Hence the omnibus test simultaneously examines all possible contrasts among treatment effects (including those not conceived by the reviewer).

Note also that it is possible to conduct a purely exploratory analysis of differences among treatment effects. There are many procedures for testing a posteriori hypotheses constructed after examination of the data in analysis of variance (Miller, 1981). Some of these procedures, such as multiple range tests, are designed essentially to identify clusters of studies whose treatment effects do not differ. Other procedures are designed to test the significance of differences between specific pairs of studies while controlling for the effects of post hoc selection of the differences that are examined. In both situations, special procedures are used to protect against capitalizing on chance due to the exploratory (post hoc) nature of the analysis.

In our idealized meta-analysis, where the raw data can be combined directly, the statistical analysis addresses four kinds of questions:

1. What is the average treatment effect and is it different than zero?
2. Are the treatment effects from different studies consistent?
3. Are explanatory variables involving differences between study characteristics consistently related to treatment effects?
4. Are the treatment effects from different studies consistent except for the effects of the explanatory variable? That is, do the explanatory variables account for the variation in treatment effects?

This examination of the idealized case of research synthesis demonstrates what is possible if the raw data from each study are available and can be combined into one analysis. It also illustrates the fact that most educational researchers would probably know both what statistical analysis was appropriate and how to interpret the analysis. In real meta-analyses, unfortunately, different studies rarely use identical outcome measures and thus raw data will never be directly comparable from study to study, even if they are available.

Modern statistical methods for meta-analysis, however, permit the reviewer to answer essentially the same questions as can be answered in the idealized case. In contrast, conventional statistical procedures in meta-analysis fail to answer one or more of the questions of interest. Moreover, the use of some conventional analyses for effect size data frequently involves serious violations of the assumptions of these techniques. Thus conventional statistical procedures in meta-analysis are problematic for both conceptual and statistical reasons. Specific problems of conventional statistical procedures in meta-analysis will be discussed below.

Applications of Conventional Statistical Methods in Meta-Analysis

Early statistical analyses in research synthesis were greatly influenced by the pioneering work of Glass. He suggested combining the results of studies by first calculating an estimate of effect size *g* to put the results of each study on the same scale. He then suggested that the research synthesizer should combine these estimates across studies, or treat the effect sizes as raw data for statistical analyses (analysis of variance or multiple linear regression) that relate characteristics of studies to treatment effects (Glass, 1976; Glass, 1978; Glass, McGaw, & Smith, 1981).

Conceptual Problems with Conventional Statistical Methods in Meta-Analysis

Comparing effect size analyses with the idealized analysis reveals conceptual difficulties with the application of conventional statistical methods in meta-analysis. In the idealized case, the treatment effect (mean difference) corresponds to the effect size for the study. In conventional analysis, the effect sizes can be averaged to obtain an estimate of the average treatment effect and a *t* or *F* test can be used to test whether the average effect size is zero. Similarly, the effect of any particular explanatory variable can be tested by using that variable as a blocking factor in an analysis of variance (or as a predictor in a regression analysis) that uses the effect size as the dependent variable. Thus the conventional effect size analysis can answer two of the questions addressed by the statistical analysis in the idealized case.

However, the conventional analysis fails to answer two of the crucial questions addressed by the idealized analysis. First, it is impossible to directly test the consistency of effect sizes across studies in the conventional analysis. That is, there is no analogue to the test for treatment-by-study interactions. The conventional analysis for testing systematic variation among *k* effect sizes has $k - 1$ degrees of freedom for systematic variation among effect sizes and one degree of freedom for the grand mean, so that there are no degrees of freedom left over for estimation of the error or nonsystematic variation. Consequently, it is impossible in the conventional framework to construct a test to determine whether the systematic variation in *k* effect sizes is larger than the nonsystematic variation exhibited by those effect sizes.

In the conventional analysis, it is possible to construct a test for differences among the average effect sizes of two or more groups of studies, as long as at least one group contains two or more effect sizes. The multiple effect sizes within the group(s) serve as replicates from which an estimate of nonsystematic variance is obtained. Then the test is constructed by comparing "systematic" variance among group mean effect sizes to the "nonsystematic" variance of effect sizes within groups. However, such a test is conceptually and statistically perilous. How does the investigator know that the effect sizes exhibit only nonsystematic variability within the groups? If the investigator chooses the wrong groups, considerable systematic variance may be pooled into the estimate of the error variance. Moreover, conventional wisdom would suggest that there are many reasons to *expect* systematic variation between study results due to differences in study design, treatment implementation, and samples of subjects (see, e.g., Presby, 1978). The inclusion of systematic variation in the estimates of error terms decreases the sensitivity of the statistical test for systematic variation (Madow, 1948).

The conceptual problem in the conventional analysis is that the amount of systematic variation among observed effect sizes is unknown. Further, even if the tests for specific contrasts among effect sizes were not conceptually problematic, such tests could not substitute for a direct test for treatment by study interaction. As was noted earlier, omnibus tests for treatment-by-study interaction examine the hypothesis that *all* possible contrasts are zero, including contrasts not anticipated by the investigator.

In the conventional framework, precisely the same conceptual problem plagues an attempt to construct a test for the variation in effect sizes that remains after employing an explanatory variable. If the investigator tries to "explain" variation in effect sizes by grouping studies with similar characteristics (or using a linear predictor), there is no way to assess whether there is still variation (in addition to sampling error) among the effect sizes.

Statistical Problems with Application of Conventional Statistical Methods in Meta-Analyses

The analysis of effect sizes or correlation coefficients by using conventional statistical methods is also problematic for purely statistical reasons. Conventional statistical procedures (*t* tests, the analysis of variance, multiple regression analysis) rely on parametric assumptions about the data. All of these procedures require that the nonsystematic variance associated with every observation be the same (the so-called homoscedasticity assumption). That is, if we think of each observation as composed of a systematic part and an error part, then the errors for all observations must be equally variable. In the analysis of variance, we check that within-cell variances are similar in value for all cells in the design. In regression analysis, we check this assumption by determining whether the residual variance about the regression line is reasonably constant for all values of the predictor variable.

In estimating the effect magnitude (either correlation coefficients or effect sizes), the nonsystematic variance of an observation can be calculated analytically. The nonsystematic variance of estimates of effect size is inversely proportional to the sample size of the study on which the estimate is based. Therefore, if studies have different sample sizes, which is usually the case, effect size estimates will have different error variances. If the sample sizes of the studies vary over a wide range, so will the error variances. In many meta-analyses, it is not unusual for the range of sample sizes to be on the order of 50 to 1. In such cases, the error variances are substantially heterogeneous.

The effects of heterogeneity of variance on analysis of variance *F* tests have been studied extensively (see, for example, Glass, Peckham, & Sanders,

1972). Furthermore, heterogeneous variances have only small effects on the validity of the F tests in a conventional analysis of variance. However, the situation in research synthesis is usually quite different from that in which robustness of F tests is usually studied. Studies of the effects of heterogeneity of variance in ANOVA usually give a different variance to one or more *groups* in the design. Thus, every observation in the same group has the same variance and there are at most two to three different variances in the entire experiment.

In the case of research synthesis, the heterogeneity is usually more pronounced. Every observation (study) may have a different variance. Moreover, the range of variances studied in connection with the robustness of F tests is usually rather limited, often less than 5 to 1. The studies that examine the effects of very wide ranges of variances and groups of unequal size find that the F test is not necessarily robust to substantial heterogeneity of variance. For example, Glass, Peckham, and Sanders (1972) note that when the ratio of variances is 5 to 1 and the sample sizes are unequal, then the actual significance level of the F test can be 6 times as large as the nominal significance level, say, 0.30 instead of 0.05.

Thus, the violation of the homogeneity of variance assumption in the analysis of variance and in regression analysis is severe in research synthesis. Moreover, this type of violation of the assumptions has not been extensively studied. It is, however, mathematically equivalent to the type of violation of assumptions that occurs when error terms are correlated (that is, when observations are not independent), a violation of assumptions against which the F test is demonstrably *not* robust (see Box, 1954; Scheffé, 1959, pp. 359–360). Thus, there is little reason to believe that the usual robustness of the F test will somehow prevail. The statistical problem of violation of the assumptions of conventional statistical procedures, and the potential problem of bias due to pooling of systematic variation into estimates of error variance, raise severe questions about the validity of conventional statistical procedures in meta-analysis. There is no rigorously defensible argument for the use of conventional t tests, analysis of variance, or regression analysis to analyze effect sizes or correlations in most meta-analyses. These procedures can be misleading and should no longer be used now that there is an extensive set of valid statistical methods for meta-analysis.

Modern Statistical Methods for Fixed Effects Meta-Analysis

Modern statistical methods for effect sizes overcome both the conceptual and the statistical problems that plague conventional statistical analyses. These methods exploit the properties of effect sizes and provide statistical analyses that are analogous to those provided by conventional statistical methods such as t tests, the analysis of variance, and multiple regression analysis. Only analyses based on effect sizes (standardized mean differences) are discussed below, but analogous procedures based on other indices of effect size (such as correlation coefficients) are available (see Hedges & Olkin, 1985). This section outlines the procedures available for fixed effects meta-analysis, which are described in detail elsewhere (Hedges & Olkin, 1985).

Effect Sizes

For meta-analysis in education, the effect size or standardized mean difference is the fundamental quantity in between-group studies. Let us begin by focusing on the effect size for a single study. Glass (1976) defined the effect size (estimate) as the difference between the experimental group mean and the control group mean, divided by the standard deviation of the control group:

$$g = (\bar{Y}^E - \bar{Y}^C)/S. \tag{1}$$

If there is no concrete reason to believe that the within-group variances differ, the standard deviation of the control group can be replaced by a pooled within-group standard deviation which has better statistical properties (Hedges, 1981).

The effect size estimate g can be decomposed into a systematic part, which reflects a true or population treatment effect, and an unsystematic part, which reflects sampling error of the individual scores used to calculate the effect size. The systematic part is called the population effect size:

$$\delta = (\mu^E - \mu^C)/\sigma, \tag{2}$$

where μ^E and μ^C are the population means of scores in the experimental and the control groups respectively, and σ is the population standard deviation within the groups of the study. The Greek letters δ, μ^E, μ^C, and σ are used to indicate that the population effect size δ is a population parameter defined by population parameters μ^E, μ^C, and σ of the observations in the study.

The unsystematic part of the effect size estimate g is the within-study sampling error $\varepsilon = g - \delta$. Thus, the decomposition of g follows directly as

$$g = \delta + \varepsilon. \tag{3}$$

Note that the within-study sampling error of g is a consequence of the sampling error in the estimates $\bar{Y}^E$, $\bar{Y}^C$, and S of μ^E, μ^C, and σ. Therefore, this sampling error is totally determined by the sampling of subjects that occurs within a study.

The decomposition of effect size estimates into population effect size and within-study sampling error is important because it highlights a crucial feature of meta-analysis. That is, all systematic relationships in meta-analysis are relationships involving δ, the population effect size. The sampling error ε is nonsystematic by definition and, therefore, it has no systematic relationship to anything. The estimate of effect size g is useful only because it provides information about δ. Thus, if the meta-analyst uses regression or analysis of variance to study the relationship between study characteristics and effect size, the systematic relationship is between the study characteristics and population effect size.

Investigation of the sampling properties of g shows that g has a slight bias when it is based on a small sample of subjects. Unless within study sample sizes are very small ($n < 10$ per group), this bias is negligible but it can be corrected by multiplication by a simple correction factor to give an unbiased estimator d via

$$d = g\left[1 - \frac{3}{4n^E + 4n^C - 9}\right], \tag{4}$$

where n^E and n^C are the experimental and control group sample sizes, respectively (Hedges, 1981). Under fairly general assumptions, it can be shown that the effect size estimate d has a sampling distribution that is approximately normal with mean δ and variance

$$v = \frac{n^E + n^C}{n^E n^C} + \frac{d^2}{2(n^E + n^C)}. \tag{5}$$

Alternatively, we could say that the within-study sampling error is normally distributed with the mean zero and variance given in (5). The variance of d is completely determined by the sample sizes and the value of d. Consequently, the sampling variance of d can be computed from a single observation. The ability to determine the nonsystematic variance of d from a single observation of d is the key to modern statistical methods for meta-analysis. This relationship allows the meta-analyst to use all the degrees of freedom among different d values for estimating systematic effects, while still providing a way of estimating the unsystematic variance needed to construct statistical tests.

Combined Estimates of Effect Size

One of the first statistical questions that arises is how to combine estimates of effect size. Suppose that a series of k studies with sample sizes $n_1^E, n_1^C, \ldots, n_k^E, n_k^C$ provides k independent effect size estimates (that is, effect size estimates based on independent samples) $d_1, \ldots, d_k$. One way of combining the estimates is simply to take the average d. The most precise combination, however, is a weighted average that takes the variances $v_1, \ldots, v_k$ of $d_1, \ldots, d_k$ into account. This weighted average, denoted $d.$, is defined as follows:

$$d. = \sum_{i=1}^{k} w_i d_i / \sum_{i=1}^{k} w_i \qquad (6)$$

where

$$w_i = 1/v_i = \frac{2(n_i^E + n_i^C)n_i^E n_i^C}{2(n_i^E + n_i^C)^2 + n_i^E n_i^C d_i^2}. \qquad (7)$$

If all k studies share a common population effect size δ, the weighted mean $d.$ is approximately normally distributed with a mean of δ and a variance of

$$v. = 1/\sum_{i=1}^{k} w_i, \qquad (8)$$

which can be used to construct confidence intervals or statistical tests for δ. For example, a chi-square test that is analogous to the F test for the main effect of treatment in the idealized analysis uses the test statistic $(d^2/v.)$, which is compared with the critical value of a chi-square distribution with one degree of freedom.

Testing Homogeneity of Effect Size

Combining estimates of effect size across studies is reasonable if the studies have a common population effect size δ. In this case, the estimates of effect size differ only by unsystematic sampling error. However, if the studies do not share a common underlying effect size, it can be misleading to combine estimates of effect size across studies. For example, if half of the studies have a large positive population effect size and half of the studies have a negative population effect size of equal magnitude, then the average—zero—is not representative of the effect size in any of the studies. The obvious question is: How is it possible to determine whether population effect sizes are relatively constant across studies? That is, how do we test for treatment-by-study interactions?

A test for homogeneity of effect size has been given by Hedges (1982a) and independently by Rosenthal and Rubin (1982b). The test involves computing

$$H_T = \sum_{i=1}^{k} w_i (d_i - d.)^2, \qquad (9)$$

where $w_i = 1/v_i$ is the weight given in (7) and $d.$ is the weighted mean given by (6). The H_T statistic is simply the weighted sum of squares of the effect size estimates $d_1, \ldots, d_k$ about the weighted mean $d.$. If all studies share a common effect size, δ, the statistic H_T has approximately a chi-square distribution with $(k - 1)$ degrees of freedom. Thus, the test for treatment-by-study interaction rejects homogeneity of effect size for large values of H_T.

An Analog to Analysis of Variance for Effect Sizes

When effect sizes are not homogeneous across studies—that is, when treatment-by-study interactions are present—the meta-analyst may want to relate variations in effect sizes to variations in coded characteristics of studies. One way of proceeding is to group studies that share characteristics that are expected to influence effect size. Thus, the meta-analyst would seek to create groupings in which the variability of effect sizes was small, and use the statistical methods to test the hetereogeneity of effects both within and between groups of studies.

A statistical procedure that permits this kind of analysis for effect sizes was introduced by Hedges (1982b). This analog to analysis of variance for effect sizes permits the meta-analyst to test the significance of variations in effect sizes between groups of effect sizes. It also allows the investigator to test whether the remaining variation within groups of effect sizes is significant. Thus, it enables the meta-analyst to determine whether the explanatory grouping variable adequately explains the treatment-by-study interaction.

The analysis of variance for effect sizes involves a partitioning of the overall homogeneity statistic H_T given in (9) into two independent homogeneity statistics: H_B, reflecting between-group homogeneity, and H_W, reflecting within-group homogeneity. These homogeneity statistics are related by the algebraic identity $H_T = H_B + H_W$, which is analogous to the partitioning of sums of squares in analysis of variance.

The between-group homogeneity statistic H_B is a weighted sum of squares of weighted group mean effect size estimates about the overall weighted mean effect size. It is analogous to the F statistic used for testing between-group differences in the conventional analysis of variance. When there are p groups and there is no variation between group mean effect sizes, the statistic H_B has approximately a chi-square distribution with $(p - 1)$ degrees of freedom. Thus, the test for variation in effect sizes between groups rejects the null hypothesis of no variation between groups of studies when H_B is large.

The within-group homogeneity statistic is the sum of the homogeneity statistics (9) calculated for each of the p groups separately. That is,

$$H_W = H_{W1} + \ldots + H_{Wp}, \tag{10}$$

where $H_{W1}, \ldots, H_{Wp}$ are the homogeneity statistics (9) calculated as if each group were an entire collection of studies. Whenever a group contains more than one study, its within-group homogeneity statistic can be used to test the homogeneity of effect sizes within that group. The total H_W provides an overall test of homogeneity of effect size within the groups of studies.

If a total of k studies is divided into $p < k$ groups, then H_W has a chi-square distribution with $(k - p)$ degrees of freedom when the effect sizes are homogeneous within groups. The test for homogeneity of effect size within groups rejects the null hypothesis of no within-group variability when H_W is large.

Suppose that the meta-analyst "explains" the variations in effect sizes by finding that effect sizes are reasonably homogeneous within groups but that they differ between groups. If there are only two groups of studies, then a significant H_B statistic indicates that there is a significant difference between their population effect sizes. If there are more than two groups, then the meta-analyst may want to use comparisons or contrasts analogous to those in analysis of variance to explore the differences among effect sizes for the different groups. Procedures for testing comparisons among the effect sizes of different groups have been discussed by Hedges (1982b) and Hedges and Olkin (1985).

An Analog to Multiple Regression Analysis for Effect Sizes

Another alternative analysis when effect sizes exhibit heterogeneity is the use of a general linear model to investigate the relationships between one or more quantitative explanatory variables and the effect sizes. An analog to multiple regression analysis for effect sizes was developed by Hedges (1982c). It uses a weighted regression procedure with weights given by (7) to estimate and test the relationship between several predictor variables and effect size. It also provides a way of testing whether the regression model is adequately specified, that is, whether significant systematic variation in effect sizes remains unexplained by the data analysis model.

Suppose that we have k independent effect size estimates $d_1, \ldots, d_k$ and p predictor variables $X_1, \ldots, X_p$ that we believe to be related to effect sizes. Under the data-analysis model described here, the systematic part of the effect sizes (the population effect sizes) $\delta_1, \ldots, \delta_k$ is determined as a linear function of the values of the predictor variables $X_1, \ldots, X_p$. That is,

$$\delta_i = \beta_0 + \beta_1 x_{i1} + \ldots + \beta_p x_{ip},$$

where $\beta_0, \beta_1, \ldots, \beta_p$ are unknown regression coefficients, and x_{ij} is the value of the jth predictor variable for the ith study. One object of the statistical analysis is to use the observed estimates of effect size $d_1, \ldots, d_k$ and the values of the predictor variables to estimate the relationship between $X_1, \ldots, X_p$ and the effect sizes—that is, to estimate the unknown regression coefficients. Another object of this analysis is to test whether the regression model is correctly specified, that is, whether significant systematic variation remains unexplained by the regression model.

Packaged computer programs can be used to perform the weighted regression analysis, which yields estimates $\beta_0, \ldots, \beta_p$ of the regression coefficients and tests of their statistical significance (Hedges 1982c; Hedges &

Olkin, 1985). If the number k of studies exceeds $(p + 1)$, the number of predictors plus the intercept, then a test for model specification is possible. The test uses the weighted sum of squares H_E about the regression line. This statistic is sometimes called the residual or error sum of squares. When the population effect sizes are completely determined by the predictor variables—that is, when the regression model is correctly specified—then the statistic H_E has a chi-square distribution with $(k - p - 1)$ degrees of freedom. Model specification is rejected if H_E exceeds the critical value. Thus, the test for model specification is a test for greater than expected residual variation.

Fixed, Random, and Mixed Effects Models for Data Analysis

Researchers familiar with the analysis of variance will recall that there are three related conceptualizations of the analysis: fixed, random, and mixed effects models. The procedures for data analyses in these models involve the same main effects and interactions, but the details and interpretations of statistical tests are somewhat different.

The description of the idealized data analysis procedure and the analog to the analysis of variance and regression correspond to fixed effects analyses. In this conceptualization, the true or population values of the treatment effects in the study are an (unknown) function of study characteristics. By studying the relationship between study characteristics and treatment effects, the data analyst tries to deduce stable relationships that explain essentially all of the variability in study results, except for that attributable to within-study sampling variability. The evaluation of particular explanatory models is part of this process. However, fixed effects models are not the only way to conceptualize data analysis in meta-analysis.

The random effects conception arises from a model in which the treatment effects are *not* functions of known study characteristics. In this model, the true or population values of treatment effects vary randomly from study to study, as if they were sampled from a universe of possible treatment effects (see Hedges, 1983a). The random effects conceptualization is consistent with Cronbach's (1980) proposal that evaluation studies should consider a model in which each treatment site (or study) is a sample realization from a universe of related treatments. The primary difference between the interpretation of fixed and random effects models is that between-study variation in treatment effects is conceived to be unsystematic in random effects models and consequently explanation of this variance is not possible. Instead, the data analyst usually seeks to quantify this variation by estimating a (treatment by studies interaction) "variance component": an index of the variability of population treatment effects across studies.

Estimation of variance components to characterize the variability of effect sizes in meta-analysis is necessary for the same reason that the estimation of variance components is necessary in the analysis of variance. Just as sampling error and the variability in treatment effects contribute to mean squares in the analysis of variance, both within-study sampling errors and variability in the underlying (population) effect sizes contribute to variability in the observed effect size estimates. Because the object of the random effects analysis is to obtain an estimate of the variability of the underlying effect sizes, special procedures are needed (Hedges, 1983a; Hedges & Olkin, 1985; Hunter, Schmidt, & Jackson, 1982).

Mixed models involve a combination of the ideas involved in fixed and in random effects models. In these models, some of the variation between treatment effects is fixed (i.e., explainable) and some is random. Consequently, the data analyst seeks to explain some of the variation between study results and quantify the remainder by estimating a variance component (Raudenbush & Bryk, 1985). Such models have considerable promise as data analytic tools for situations in which it is useful to treat some of the variability between study results as random.

Problems of Dependence

One of the most persistent statistical issues raised in discussions of meta-analysis is the potential lack of statistical independence among effect size estimates. Such statistical dependence can arise in at least four ways. First, several different effect size estimates may be calculated from different measurements on the same subjects. This situation typically arises in meta-analysis when several effect size estimates are calculated in a study using measures of several different outcome constructs or several different measures of the same construct. The second sort of dependence arises from calculation of several effect sizes in a study, each of which uses the same control group or the same treatment group. For example, in a study with one control group and two treatment groups, the two effect sizes computed with reference to the same control group are correlated. A third sort of dependence arises because several different samples in the same study are used to calculate effect size estimates. The fourth type of dependence arises because a series of studies conducted by the same investigator or research team may not give results that are completely independent.

The first type of dependence (which arises from multiple effect sizes calculated on different measures from the same subjects) has received the most explicit attention. One of the reasons that such dependence arises is that many meta-analysts (e.g., Glass, McGaw & Smith, 1981) choose to code every possible effect size estimate to avoid "loss of information." The rationale is that if each different measurement provides additional information, then effect size estimates based on those measurements provide additional information about the underlying effect size. However Hedges and Olkin (1985) studied the situation analytically and found that the actual amount of additional information (measured by increased precision of the estimate making optimal use of all information) was quite modest. They showed, for example, that using two or three correlated effect sizes based on measures of the same construct was unlikely to increase statistical precision by more than 10–20%.

Consequently, Hedges and Olkin argued that the use of several effect sizes on the same individuals was seldom justified solely to increase statistical precision. Instead, they suggested using a simple effect size estimate for each study obtained either by choosing one estimate at random or by taking the median of the effect sizes that are based on the same outcome construct.

Dependence arising when several effect size estimates make use of the same control group (or, conceivably, the same treatment group) poses different problems. In this situation, the additional effect sizes may add substantially to the precision of estimation. Because the correlation between the estimates can be calculated exactly in this situation (if the sample sizes of all the groups are the same it will be about .5), the multivariate procedures derived by Hedges and Olkin (1985) can be used to provide a statistical analysis that takes into account the dependence of the estimates. Obviously, if there are very few such correlated estimates, another, but suboptimal, solution is to cautiously ignore the dependence or to delete all but one of each set of dependent estimates.

The other two forms of dependence, arising from multiple samples within studies and from a series conducted by the same investigators, are more difficult to accommodate. The implication of these sorts of dependence is that the underlying (population) effect sizes within studies or from a series of studies by the same investigator are less variable than are the other effect sizes. Such dependence can attenuate relationships in fixed effects models and should lead to difficulties in obtaining adequate model specification. Fortunately, the strong tests for model misspecification can help to detect such problems in fixed effects models. The effects of this sort of dependence in random and mixed effects models may be more serious for two reasons. First, the dependence results in a serious misspecification of the error structure of the model. Second, there is no obvious way to detect problems of dependence *that have not been anticipated*. Because misspecification may lead to biases in parameter estimates, undetected dependence in random and mixed effects models may lead to serious biases in inference. Specific dependencies that are anticipated can be incorporated and even tested as hypotheses in both fixed effects models (by appropriate coding strategies) and in random or mixed effects models by proper parameterization of error covariance matrices. Serious consideration should always be given to possible sources of dependence, and the data analyst should investigate the possibility of dependence whenever there is reason to believe that it may be serious.

Limitations of Statistical Methods

One of the advantages of meta-analysis is that many issues of judgment about the potential effects of study characteristics on research outcomes can be empirically tested (Glass, McGaw, & Smith, 1981). For example, questions of the effects of study quality can be assessed by testing empirically whether study quality is related to study effect sizes. Similarly, questions about the effects of study design, study procedure, and measurement methods can all be subjected to empirical test. However, the mechanism of empirical test is sometimes abused in meta-analysis. Most of the abuses stem from failures to recognize the limitations of empirical methods based on a given set of data.

Not All Propositions Can Be Tested in a Given Set of Data

One way that empirical tests are abused in meta-analysis is by their ubiquity. A very large number of study characteristics may be examined, leading to a very large number of statistical tests. In some cases, the number of statistical tests may equal or exceed the number of independent effect size estimates. Such large numbers of statistical tests are difficult to interpret because the meta-analyst runs a great risk of capitalizing on chance (see Hunter, Schmidt, & Jackson, 1982). Unless special methods are used, the chance that at least one of the statistical tests leads to erroneous rejections of the null hypothesis increases with the number of hypothesis tests (see the section on exploratory versus confirmatory reviews). Simultaneous test procedures that control adequately for this source of error reduce the power of the tests, and the reduction in power is proportional to the number of tests. Thus, there is a definite limit to the number of tests that can be supported (in the sense of having acceptably small error rates) by a given collection of studies. This is a limitation of the data and places a limitation on the number of propositions that can be adequately tested in a single analysis. This limit is usually far less than the number of possible main effect and interaction hypotheses that could arise from even a modest list of study characteristics.

The responsible meta-analyst must therefore recognize the limitations of the data available and test only a subset of all *possible* propositions. Presumably, the hypotheses chosen for testing should be those that are most central to the purpose of the meta-analysis or those most crucial for its interpretation. Note that these hypotheses must be selected on conceptual (a priori), rather than empirical (a posteriori), grounds.

Propositions Are not Independent of One Another

A second abuse of statistical testing stems from the fact that study characteristics are not, in general, independent of one another. Consequently, it is difficult or impossible to disentangle the effect of one study characteristic from those of all the others. Tests that purport to show that one study characteristic has no relation to effect size may in fact be confounded by the action of other study characteristics. Conversely, what appears to be the effect of one study characteristic on effect size can often be equally well described as the effect of another (correlated) study characteristic. Thus, the problem of interpreting the relationships between study characteristics and effect size is essentially like that of interpreting a correlational (nonexperimental or observational) study. Essentially all relationships are confounded and many rival hypotheses are possible. In this situation purely technical (statistical) methods are unlikely to lead to credible conclusions because, as in any instance of multicolinearity, the data alone are insufficient to distinguish all of the relationships of interest.

The only alternative is to proceed in a manner similar to that used in other highly confounded situations such as the interpretation of quasi-experiments. Patterns of results from the data analysis and other evidence in addition to the data can be used to build an argument for the credibility of a proposition (see Cook & Campbell, 1979). Rival hypotheses can be posed and perhaps eliminated by various means. Sometimes, of course, rival hypotheses cannot be eliminated and therefore weaken the conclusion to the extent that they are plausible as explanations.

META-ANALYSIS AS EXPLANATION

The function of research reviews in the sciences is to do more than collect and tabulate research results. It is no accident that the most prestigious journals that publish research reviews seek reviews that are "critical," "integrative," or "synthetic," or that the words "research synthesis" are sometimes used as a synonym for "research reviewing." These descriptions of research reviews imply something beyond tabulation. They suggest that reviews will not only present results and generalizations, but will offer *explanations* in support of those generalizations. The important issue is that the explanation consists of more than the generalization and a sketchy summary of the data on which it is based. All explanations relate the phenomenon to be explained to other ideas that are presumably understood and perceived to be relevant by the recipient of the explanation. The explanation usually involves demonstrating the ways in which the new phenomenon fits into patterns that are familiar and are perceived to be relevant in some way. We understand by discovering the many linkages between a new phenomenon and existing beliefs, relationships, and empirical data. The function of the explanation is to make the linkages clear, to make obvious the ways in which the new phenomenon fits into the matrix of background beliefs, theories, empirical data, and relationships. Note that a perfectly correct generalization alone is not necessarily a good explanation if the links to appropriate context are not made obvious. The purpose of this section is to raise the questions of how good meta-analysis is as explanation and how it can be improved.

Meta-analysis has prompted a considerable amount of debate during its 10-year history. Perhaps the controversy is understandable as a natural consequence of the introduction of a new research paradigm. Some of the controversy seems to be based on a misunderstanding of meta-analysis. Part of it may be an inevitable consequence of the rough edges of the first few studies produced by any new research paradigm. But some of the criticisms seem to suggest that meta-analyses have sometimes failed as explanations. This is disturbing because research reviews using meta-analysis must succeed as explanations if they are to be useful. Moreover, if they are to have any lasting impact they must be convincing explanations to the researchers and policy makers who are most knowledgeable about the subject matter under review. Meta-analyses that convince only other experts in meta-analysis are not useful. The question is, why do meta-analyses sometimes fail as explanation and how can they be improved?

Why Meta-Analyses Face Difficulty as Explanation

Meta-analyses, and indeed any research reviews that offer precise conclusions, are likely to face some difficulties as credible explanation. The reason is that to make generalizations across studies, the reviewer must ignore a great many differences among those studies. Glass, McGaw, and Smith (1981) have argued that generalizing across studies is not logically different from generalizing across individual subjects within an experiment. While this may be true at some level, the analogy ignores an important perceptual difference between generalizations within and across studies. The experimental paradigm predisposes researchers to view the generalization across subjects as natural because, by definition, the differences between subjects are "experimental errors" (see Cronbach, 1957). The few systematic individual difference variables recognized in the experimental paradigm are incorporated into the design and all other differences are by definition nonsystematic.

Differences between studies, on the other hand, are viewed as systematic because the same experimental paradigm stresses the importance of the design of research studies. A great deal of the training and professional effort of researchers is devoted to learning about, planning, and implementing systematic aspects of research studies that make one study different from another. I emphasize that the differences between studies are viewed by knowledgeable researchers as *systematic*, because researchers strive to make their studies systematically different from those of other researchers to obtain new information. They do so because they believe these differences could have an effect on the results of the study. Moreover the differences between studies are not usually unidimensional. The design and execution of research studies is so complex that even "similar" studies often differ in many ways. For this reason, it would be expected that researchers would have difficulty with any method of generalizing across studies because such methods implicitly relegate the many complex and important differences between studies to the status of "error" or unsystematic variation. Even more problematic to researchers are statistical methods for generalizing across studies that explicitly define all of the unmodeled variation between study results to be sampling error.

Conventional statistical methods (such as *t* tests, analysis of variance, and multiple regression analysis) applied to effect sizes are examples of this type. Statistical methods developed specifically for meta-analysis separate variation between studies that is due to sampling error within studies from that which is due to systematic variation between studies. Conventional statistics define as error all between-study variation *except* what is explicitly modeled. Modern statistical methods for meta-analysis do the opposite. They define as *systematic* all between-study variation except that explicitly due to within-study sampling error. Thus the use of modern statistical methods for meta-analysis is consistent with the researcher's intuitive notion that between-study variation in study results is likely to be systematic except for the inevitable within-study sampling error.

The most persistent criticisms of meta-analysis stem, in part, from the perspective of researchers who feel that differences among studies and among their results are systematic and that meta-analysis fails in some way to recognize those differences. The most common criticisms of meta-analysis (which could be criticisms of any review) are the "apples and oranges" criticism and the "garbage-in, garbage-out" criticism.

The apples and oranges criticism is that meta-analysis combines evidence from studies that do not have the "same" procedures, independent variables, or dependent variables. Thus, meta-analysis is combining the incommensurable because studies exhibit systematic differences. Another statement of essentially the same criticism (Presby, 1978) is that combining research studies into overly broad categories obscures important differences between those studies and their results. In each case the fundamental issue is the breadth of constructs that are the "same," and the critic's position is that only aggregation across a rather narrow range of treatment, control, and outcome constructs is sensible.

The "garbage-in, garbage-out" criticism (Eysenck, 1978) is that by abandoning "critical judgement" about the quality of research studies reviewed, meta-analysis places too much emphasis on studies of low quality. Because studies of low quality are presumably subject to many biases, they cannot be the foundation of reliable knowledge. Meta-analysis, therefore, becomes another case of garbage-in, garbage-out. Although the criticism concerns the question of methodological quality, it is firmly rooted in the conception that there are systematic differences (in methodology) between studies that influence study results.

Improving Meta-Analysis as Explanation

The improvement of meta-analysis as explanation depends on greater attention to both methodological detail and to persistent criticisms of meta-analysis. Critics tell us why they do not find meta-analyses to be convincing as explanation. Attempts to respond to those criticisms (where they do not conflict with other requirements of methodology) are likely to yield more persuasive meta-analyses. Many of these criticisms are among the issues discussed in earlier sections of this chapter, but two general issues emerge. One is the issue of specificity versus generality of constructs. The other is the appropriate use of quantitative methods.

The issues of specificity arise because researchers tend to think of studes in terms of specific and rather narrow constructs. This tendency toward specificity is reflected in the usually narrow choice of constructs in conentional reviews (Cook & Leviton, 1980). Meta-analyses are likely to be more credible as explanation if they use (or at least distinguish) constructs of treatment, control, and outcome that are relatively narrow and relatively specific to the research domain at hand. Meta-analyses are also likely to be more credible if they use conceptions of study quality that recognize the specific difficulties associated with the domain under study. By treating between-study differences in rather specific ways, meta-analyses will offer a richer variety of connections with researchers' conceptualizations of the research domain.

The issues of appropriate use of quantitative methods might be interpreted to include all issues of the formal (mathematical) appropriateness of statistical methods in a given situation. More important is the question of when statistical methods should be used, given that they are formally correct. Researchers are not always comfortable with the use of quantitative methods to empirically "define" the differences among studies that deserve consideration. For example, the argument that study quality can be defined empirically by determining which groups of studies give different answers has not always been persuasive. Critics seem to be saying that quantitative analyses cannot carry the whole load. Meta-analyses are likely to be more persuasive if they use qualitative conceptual analyses as a supplement to quantitative methods to determine interesting differences among studies. Researchers know both that quantitative methods cannot resolve all questions and that these methods must be guided and set in context by qualitative analysis. Qualitative information that is not explicitly coded as between-study differences has an important role in interpretation and should not be neglected, even if it requires rather lengthy descriptions of important aspects of individual studies (Light & Pillemer, 1984).

The net effect of these suggestions would be to make meta-analyses look more like conventional narrative reviews, involving perhaps fewer studies distinguishing narrower constructs, and providing more detailed qualitative and conceptual arguments. In fact, earlier conventional reviews of an area may be a model for conceptualization and level of operational detail that are appropriate. The most persuasive meta-analysis is likely to be one that combines the strengths of qualitative reviews and those of serious quantitative methodology.

REFERENCES

Bakan, D. (1966). The test of significance in psychological research. *Psychological Bulletin, 66,* 423–437.

Barnett, V., & Lewis, T. (1978). *Outliers in statistical data.* New York: Wiley.

Becker, B.J. (1986). Influence again: An examination of reviews and studies of gender differences in social influence. In J.S. Hyde & M.C. Linn (Eds.), *The psychology of gender: Advances through meta-analysis.* Baltimore, MD: Johns Hopkins University Press.

Becker, B.J., & Hedges, L.V. (1984). Meta-analysis of cognitive gender differences: A comment on an analysis by Rosenthal and Rubin. *Journal of Educational Psychology, 76,* 583–587.

Box, G.E.P. (1954). Some theorems on quadratic forms applied in the study of analysis of variance problems: II. Effect of inequality of variance and of correlation of errors in the two-way classification. *Annals of Mathematical Statistics, 25,* 484–498.

Bozarth, H.D., & Roberts, R.R., Jr. (1972). Signifying significant significance. *American Psychologist, 27,* 774–775.

Bracht, G., & Glass, G.V. (1968). The external validity of experiments. *American Educational Research Journal, 5,* 437–474.

Campbell, D.T. (1969). Definitional versus multiple operationism. *et al., 2,* 14–17.

Campbell, D.T., & Erlebacher, A. (1970). How regression artifacts in quasi-experimental evaluations can mistakenly make compensatory education look harmful. In S. Hellmuth (Ed.), *Compensatory education: A national debate.* New York: Brunner/Mazel.

Campbell, D.T., & Stanley, J.C. (1963). *Experimental and quasi-experimental designs for research.* Chicago: Rand McNally.

Carlberg, C. (1979). *Meta-analysis of special education treatment techniques.* Unpublished doctoral dissertation, University of Colorado.

Chalmers, T.C. (1982). The randomized controlled trial as a basis for therapeutic decisions. In J.M. Lachin, N. Tygstrup, & E. Juhl (Eds.), *The randomized clinical trial and therapeutic decisions.* New York: Dekker.

Cochran, W.G. (1963). *Sampling techniques.* New York: Wiley.

Cohen, J. (1965). Some statistical issues in psychological research. In B.B. Wolman (Ed.), *Handbook of clinical psychology.* New York: McGraw-Hill.

Cohen, J. (1977). *Statistical power analysis for the behavioral sciences* (2nd Ed.). New York: Academic Press.

Cohn, C.M.G. (1984). *Creativity training effectiveness: A research synthesis.* Unpublished doctoral dissertation, Arizona State University.

Cook, T.D., & Campbell, D.T. (1979). *Quasi-experimentation.* Chicago: Rand McNally.

Cook, T.D., & Leviton, L.C. (1980). Reviewing the literature: A comparison of traditional methods with meta-analysis. *Journal of Personality, 48,* 449–472.

Cooper, H.M. (1979). Statistically combining independent studies: A meta-analysis of sex differences in conformity research. *Journal of Personality and Social Psychology, 37,* 131–146.

Cooper, H.M. (1982). Scientific guidelines for conducting integrative research reviews. *Review of Educational Research, 52,* 291–302.

Cooper, H.M. (1984). *The integrative research review: A systematic approach.* Beverly Hills, CA: Sage.

Cooper, H.M., & Arkin, R.M. (1981). On quantitative reviewing. *Journal of Personality, 49,* 225–230.

Crain, R.L., & Mahard, R.E. (1983). The effect of research methodology on deseg-regation-achievement studies: A meta-analysis. *American Journal of Sociology,* *88,* 839–854.

Cronbach, L.J. (1957). The two disciplines of scientific psychology. *American Psychologist, 12,* 671–684.

Cronbach, L.J. (1980). *Toward reform of program evaluation.* San Francisco: Jossey-Bass.

DerSimonian, R., & Laird, N. (1983). Evaluating the effectiveness of coaching for SAT exams: A meta-analysis. *Harvard Educational Review, 53,* 1–15.

Eagly, A.H., & Carli, L.L. (1981). Sex of researchers and sex-typed communications as determinants of sex differences in influenceability: A meta-analysis of social influence studies. *Psychological Bulletin, 90,* 1–20.

Eagly, A.A., & Crowley, M. (1986). Gender and helping behavior: A meta-analytic review of the social psychological literature. *Psychological Bulletin, 99,* .

Eysenck, H.J. (1978). An exercise in mega-silliness. *American Psychologist, 33,* 517.

Finney, D.J. (1971). *Probit analysis.* Cambridge, England: Cambridge University Press.

Fricke, R. & Treines, G. (1985). *Einführung in die metaanalyse.* Bern: Hans Huber.

Giaconia, R.M., & Hedges, L.V. (1982). Identifying features of effective open education. *Review of Educational Research, 52,* 579–602.

Gilbert, J.P., McPeek, B., & Mosteller, F. (1977). Progress in surgery and anesthesia: Benefits and risks of innovation therapy. In J. Bunker, B. Barnes, & F. Mosteller (Eds.), *Costs, risks, and benefits of surgery.* New York: Oxford University Press.

Glass, G.V. (1976a). Primary, secondary, and meta-analysis of research. *Educational Researcher, 5,* 3–8.

Glass, G.V. (1976b). Presidential address, annual meeting of the American Educational Research Association, San Francisco.

Glass, G.V. (1978). Integrating findings: The meta-analysis of research. In L.S. Schulman (Ed.), *Review of research in education,* Vol. 5. Itasca, IL: Peacock.

Glass, G.V., & Smith, M.L. (1979). Meta-analysis of the relationship between class size and achievement. *Educational Evaluation and Policy Analysis, 1,* 2–16.

Glass, G.V., McGaw, B., & Smith, M.L. (1981). *Meta-analysis in social research.* Beverly Hills, CA: Sage.

Glass, G.V., Peckham, P.D., & Sanders, J.R. (1972). Consequences of failure to meet assumptions underlying fixed effects analysis of variance and covariance. *Review of Educational Research, 42,* 237–288.

Greenwald, A.G. (1975). Consequences of prejudice against the null hypothesis. *Psychological Bulletin, 82,* 1–20.

Hall, J. (1986). Smiling and gazing. In J.S. Hyde & M.C. Linn (Eds.), *The psychology of gender: Progress through meta-analysis.* Baltimore, MD: Johns Hopkins University Press.

Hartley, S.S. (1977). *Meta-analysis of the effects of individually paced instruction in mathematics.* Unpublished doctoral dissertation, University of Colorado.

Hays, W.L. (1963). *Statistics.* New York: Holt, Rinehart & Winston.

Hawkins, D.M. (1980). *Identification of outliers.* London: Chapman & Hall.

Hedges, L.V. (1981). Distribution theory for Glass's estimator of effect size and related estimators. *Journal of Educational Statistics, 6,* 107–128.

Hedges, L.V. (1982a). Estimation of effect size from a series of independent experiments. *Psychological Bulletin, 92,* 490–499.

Hedges, L.V. (1982b). Fitting categorical models to effect sizes from a series of experiments. *Journal of Educational Statistics, 7,* 119–137.

Hedges, L.V. (1982c). Fitting continuous models to effect size data. *Journal of Educational Statistics, 7,* 245–270.

Hedges, L.V. (1983a). A random effects model for effect sizes. *Psychological Bulletin, 93,* 388–395.

Hedges, L.V. (1983b). Combining independent estimators in research synthesis. *The British Journal of Mathematical and Statistical Psychology, 36,* 123–131.

Hedges, L.V. (1984a). Advances in statistical methods for meta-analysis. In W.H. Yeaton & P.M. Wortman (Eds.), *New directions for program evaluation: Issues in data synthesis* (No. 24). San Francisco: Jossey-Bass.

Hedges, L.V. (1984b). Estimation of effect size under nonrandom sampling: The effects of censoring studies yielding statistically insignificant mean differences. *Journal of Educational Statistics, 9,* 61–85.

Hedges, L.V., & Olkin, I. (1980). Vote counting methods in research synthesis. *Psychological Bulletin, 88,* 359–369.

Hedges, L.V., & Olkin, I. (1983a). Clustering estimates of effect magnitude from independent studies. *Psychological Bulletin, 93,* 563–573.

Hedges, L.V., & Olkin, I. (1983b). Regression models in research synthesis. *American Statistician, 37,* 137–140.

Hedges, L.V., & Olkin, I. (1984). Nonparametric estimators of effect size in meta-analysis. *Psychological Bulletin, 96,* 573–580.

Hedges, L.V., & Olkin, I. (1985). *Statistical methods for meta-analysis.* New York: Academic Press.

Humphreys, L.G. (1980). The statistics of failure to replicate: A comment on Buriel's (1978) conclusions. *Journal of Educational Psychology, 72,* 71–75.

Hunter, J.E., Schmidt, F.L., & Jackson, G.B. (1982). *Meta-analysis: Cumulating findings across research.* Beverly Hills, CA: Sage.

Hyde, J.S. (1981). How large are cognitive gender differences? *American Psychologist, 36,* 892–901.

Jackson, G.B. (1978). *Methods for reviewing and integrating research in the social sciences.* Final report to the National Science Foundation. (NTIS No. PB28374–7/AS).

Jackson, G.B. (1980). Methods for integrative reviews. *Review of Educational Research, 50,* 438–460.

Kraemer, H.C. (1983). Theory of estimation and testing of effect sizes: Use in meta-analysis. *Journal of Educational Statistics, 8,* 93–101.

Lane, D.M., & Dunlap, W.P. (1978). Estimating effect sizes: Bias resulting from the significance criterion in editorial decisions. *British Journal of Mathematical and Statistical Psychology, 31,* 107–112.

Light, R.J. (Ed.). (1983). *Evaluation studies review annual, vol. 8.* Beverly Hills, CA: Sage.

Light, R.J., & Pillemer, D.B. (1984). *Summing up: The science of reviewing research.* Cambridge, MA: Harvard University Press.

Light, R.J., & Smith, P.V. (1971). Accumulating evidence: Procedures for resolving contradictions among different research studies. *Harvard Educational Review, 41,* 429–471.

Linn, M.C., & Peterson, A.C. (1985). Emergence and characterization of sex differences in spatial ability. *Child Development, 56,* 1479–1498.

Lykken, D.T. (1968). Statistical significance in psychological research. *Psychological Bulletin, 70,* 151–159.

Madow, W.G. (1948). On a source of downward bias in the analysis of variance and covariance. *Annals of Mathematical Statistics, 19,* 351–359.

Madow, W.G., Nisselson, H., & Olkin, I. (1983). *Incomplete data in sample surveys: Vol. 1. Report and case studies.* New York: Academic Press.

Madow, W.G., & Olkin, I. (1983). *Incomplete data in sample surveys: Vol. 3. Proceedings and the symposium.* New York: Academic Press.

Madow, W.G. & Olkin, I., & Rubin, D.B. (1983). *Incomplete data in sample surveys: Vol 2. Theory and bibliographies.* New York: Academic Press.

Mahalanobis, P.C. (1936). On the generalized distance in statistics. *Proceedings of the National Institute of Science of India, 12,* 49–55.

McGaw, B., & Glass, G.V. (1980). Choice of metric for effect size in meta-analysis. *American Educational Research Journal, 17,* 325–337.

Melton, A.W. (1962). Editorial. *Journal of Experimental Psychology, 64,* 553–557.

Miller, R.G. (1981). *Simultaneous statistical inference* (2nd ed.). New York: Springer.

Morrison, D.F. (1967). *Multivariate statistical methods.* New York: McGraw-Hill.

Orwin, R.G., & Cordray, D.S. (1985). Effects of deficient reporting on meta-analysis: A conceptual framework and reanalysis. *Psychological Bulletin, 97,* 134–147.

Presby, S. (1978). Overly broad categories obscure important differences. *American Psychologist, 33,* 514–515.

Raudenbush, S.W. (1984). Magnitude of teacher expectancy effects on pupil IQ as a function of the credibility of expectancy induction: A synthesis of findings from 18 experiments. *Journal of Educational Psychology, 76,* 85–97.

Raudenbush, S.W., & Bryk, A.S. (1985). Empirical Bayes meta-analysis. *Journal of Educational Statistics, 10,* 75–98.

Reichardt, C.S., & Cook, T.D. (1979). Beyond qualitative versus quantitative methods. In T.D. Cook & C.S. Reichardt (Eds.), *Qualitative and quantitative methods in evaluation research.* Beverly Hills, CA: Sage.

Reynolds, S., & Day, J. (1984). *Monte Carlo studies of effect size estimates and their approximations in meta-analysis.* Paper presented at the annual meeting of the American Psychological Association, Toronto.

Rocke, D.M., Downs, G.W., & Rocke, A.J. (1982). Are robust estimators really necessary? *Technometrics, 24,* 95–101.

Rosenthal, R. (1979). The "file drawer problem" and tolerance for null results. *Psychological Bulletin, 86,* 638–641.

Rosenthal, R. (Ed.). (1980). *New directions for methodology of social and behavioral science: Quantitative assessment of research domains* (No. 5). San Francisco: Jossey-Bass.

Rosenthal, R. (1984). *Meta-analytic procedures for social research.* Beverly Hills, CA: Sage.

Rosenthal, R., & Rubin, D.B. (1982a). A simple, general purpose display of magnitude of experimental effect. *Journal of Educational Psychology, 74,* 166–169.

Rosenthal, R., & Rubin, D.B. (1982b). Comparing effect sizes of independent studies. *Psychological Bulletin, 92,* 500–504.

Rubin, D.B. (1976). Inference and missing data. *Biometrika, 63,* 581–592.

Scheffé, H. (1959). *The analysis of variance.* New York: Wiley.

Slavin, R.E. (1984). Meta-analysis in education: How has it been used? *Educational Researcher, 13,* 6–15.

Smith, M.L. (1980a). Publication bias in meta-analysis. *Evaluation in Education: An International Review Series, 4,* 22–24.

Smith, M.L. (1980b). Sex bias in counseling and psychotherapy. *Psychological Bulletin, 87,* 392–407.

Smith, M.L., & Glass, G.V. (1977). Meta-analysis of psychotherapy outcome studies. *American Psychologist, 32,* 752–760.

Smith, M.L., & Glass, G.V. (1980). Meta-analysis of class size and its relationship to attitudes and instruction. *American Educational Research Journal, 17,* 419–433.

Sterling, T.D. (1959). Publication decisions and their possible effects on inferences drawn from tests of significance—or vice versa. *Journal of the American Statistical Association, 54,* 30–34.

Stigler, S.M. (1977). Do robust estimators work with real data? *Annals of Statistics, 5,* 1055–1098.

Stock, W.A., Okun, M.A., Haring, M.J., Miller, W., Kinney, C., & Ceurvorst, R.W. (1982). Rigor in data synthesis: A case study of reliability in meta-analysis. *Educational Researcher, 11,* 10–14, 20.

Thomas, J.R., & French, K.E. (1985). Gender differences across age in motor performance: A meta-analysis. *Psychological Bulletin, 98,* 260–282.

Tukey, J. (1977). *Exploratory data analysis.* Reading, MA: Addison-Wesley.

Underwood, B.J. (1957). Interference and forgetting. *Psychological Review, 64,* 49–60.

Webb, E., Campbell, D., Schwartz, R., Sechrest, L., & Grove, J. (1981). *Unobtrusive measures: Nonreactive research in the social sciences.* Boston: Houghton Mifflin.

Wortman, P.M. (1981). Randomized clinical trials. In P.M. Wortman (Ed.), *Methods for evaluating health services.* Beverly Hills, CA: Sage.

Yeaton, W.H., & Wortman, P.M. (Eds.). (1984). *New directions in program evaluation: Issues in data synthesis* (No. 24). San Francisco: Jossey-Bass.

Index

ability grouping, 116–120

achievement tests, role in evaluating teachers, 306–308

age-earnings profiles: male/female, teacher/nonteacher comparisons, 288–290

age-graded schools, 143

American English dialects: American Indian English, 198; Appalachian English, 198; Black English Vernacular, 198–214 passim; Puerto Rican English, 198; Standard Black English, 199

analog to analysis of variance, 384–385

analog to multiple regression analysis, 385–386

basal reading materials: described, 92; danger of overreliance on, 113; need for improvement of, 113–114

bidialectalism, 212–214

British Infant School Model, 24

bureaucratization of teaching, 323–328

career ladders, 305–308; teacher approval of, 310–311

Cherokee syllabary, 130

class size: contract provisions about, 321; decrease in, over time, 326

cognitive activities to promote reading comprehension, 101–104; advance organizers, 101–102; prompts for comprehension, 102; generative learning, 102–103

collective bargaining, see labor contracts, teacher unionization

compensation for teachers: affected by unionization, 328–332; age-earnings profiles, 288–290; effect on teacher supply, 285; efficient models of, 291–300; historic trends, 328–329; increasing efficiency of, 300–311; in public vs. private schools, 332; single salary schedule, 285; trends since 1946, 285

computer-generated stories, 274

conceptualization of effect size, 366–367

Confederacy, textbooks published in, 132

constructs: chosen as part of research problem formulation, 357; broad vs. narrow, 357–359; specific vs. general, 393

content-area reading, 145–146

content of schoolbooks: affected by marketing considerations, 141–142; affected by social views, 137; early American, 135, 136; influence of, 137; in 19th century, 134–137; modern constraints on, 144

context-dependent writing skill, 236

context in writing, 231–232

cultural attitudes: in textbooks, 5; toward literacy, 5–6; See also social contexts

cultural conflict: in literacy learning, 200, 208; role in school success of nonmainstream students, 202

cultural identity: effect on language use, 198, 203–204; effect on learning of writing, 195

curriculum history, 159–160

dependence: problem in meta-analysis, 387–388

depth of word knowledge: developmentalist perspectives, 54–55; educators' perspectives, 55; fast mapping, 55; missing feature plus haphazard example theory, 54; needed research, 58; semantic feature hypothesis, 54

Dewey, John and Evelyn, 3

dialects: defined, 210; examples of varying rules in, 211–212; loss of, when standard English is learned, 213–214; negative teacher attitudes towards, 201

direct instruction, 97–98

disadvantaged students, vocabulary size of, 52–53

discourse: differences among dialects, 209–210; nature and possibilities of, 242; uses of various forms of, 243, 245

district schools, 157

early writing development: concurrent with reading development, 18; need for research, 21; various strategies in, 19 educational reform movement (19th century), 143

educational research: factor in switch from oral to silent reading, 151; impact on curriculum, 137; modern trends in, 152

effect size: basis for meta-analysis, 356–357; conceptualization of, 366–367; derived from complex designs, 368–371; function of treatment and of outcome construct, 358; missing data on, 362; overestimation of, caused by publication bias, 365; related to study quality indices, 372; scale-free treatment effect, 367; use of modern statistical methods, 381–388

elocution, 143, 146, 147

emergent literacy: defined, 3; implications of research on, 32–37; research influenced by cognitive psychology, 16

extra pay for extra work, 325

fixed effects models, 380–387

functions of language, children's, 122

gain-sharing, 299–300

generative vocabulary instruction: using context clues, 68–73; using morphological elements, 73–77

homogeneity of effect size, 383–384

incentive pay, 292–294, 298–300

informed strategy instruction, 105–106

isolation of teachers, 307

juvenile literature: concepts in, 134; contents of, 135, 143–144

Kamehameha Early Education Project, 36, 118

kindergarten movement, 143

knowledge in writing: about audience, 245–247; about forms of discourse, 245; about goals, 243–245; about specific domains, 247–248; interaction with process, 228–229, 232; relationship to revision, 263; role in composing process, 240; role in composition, 232–235; several kinds needed, 236–237; testing use of, 271–272; type important in instruction, 238

"knowledge-telling" model, 271–273

labelling skills, in very young child, 175–176

labor contracts, 291–292, 320–323

language experience approaches to reading, 100

language functioning, 8

language interactions, 32, 33

language learning: includes reading and writing, 173; result of adult-child interactions, 174; promoted by specific teaching activities, 184

language use in school: reflects mainstream culture, 200–210; and cultural conflict in nonmainstream students, 198, 200, 208

language variation, 195

Levels of Inquiry schema: empirical variable testing, 264–266; process description, 268–271; reflective inquiry, 260–263; simulation, 274–276; text analysis, 266–268; theory-embedded experimentation, 271–273

limitations of statistical methods, 388–390

linguistic development, 8

linguistic differences among dialects, 205–210; discourse, 209–210; phonology, 206; pragmatics, 207–209; semantics, 207; syntax, 206

literacy events: in families, 8–9; in classrooms, 33–34

literacy instruction: effective, components of, 185–188; related to literacy learning, 171–172; as social process, 171

literacy learning: constrained by social context, 171–172; implications of children's oral language abilities for, 14–16; as individual process, 171; related to instruction, 171; two processes involved in, 16

literature, role in reading instruction, 143–144

McGuffey's *Reader,* 129–147 passim

management, use of labor contract by, 321, 323, 334

Mann, Horace: influence on reading instruction, 133

mathemagenic activities, 102

merit pay, 304–306

meta-analysis: data analysis and interpretation in, 375–390; data collection in, 360–371; data evaluation in, 371–375; conventional statistical methods in, 377–387; defined, 353; as explanation, 390–393; importance of, 354; problem formulation in, 357–360; specific contributions of, 356–357

metacognition: applied to reading curriculum, 108; cultivated by effective teachers, 105–106; defined, 104; developed through adult-child interactions, 179; importance to skilled reading, 104; use in reading instruction, 111–112

metacognitive skills: children trained to use, 237; problems in identifying, 237–238; shown by very young children, 235; use in writing process, 232–233

metalinguistic knowledge, 7–8, 9–10

methodological rigor, 354

metric for effect size, 369, 374

middle-class students, vocabulary size of, 52–53

minimum performance standards: for groups, 298; need to enforce in teaching, 300–302; role in usual employee compensation, 291–292

minority students: experience greater problems with learning to write, 195–196; school problems linked with societal problems, 201

missing data: caused by publication bias, 365; crucial to validity of meta-analytic conclusions, 362; strategies for dealing with, 362–364

mixed effects models, 386–387

morphology, use in vocabulary instruction, 73–77

motivation: of students, 116–117; of teachers, 309–310

multiple negation, 200, 211–212

multiple operations, 359

National Society for the Study of Education *Yearbooks,* 93–95, 145–146

New England Primer, 129–147 passim

one-room schoolhouse, 157

operations: broad vs. narrow, 357–359; chosen as part of research problem formulation, 357

operative effect size, 368–369

oral language, use to comprehend written text, 100

oral reading: importance until late 19th century, 143; switch to silent reading, 149–150

outliers, 371, 373–375

parents: importance of story reading by, 26–29; importance to children's understanding of language function, 12; influence on children's literacy, 6–7, 29; language instruction by, 7, 8; metalinguistic terms taught by, 7; use of scaffolding conversations, 25

pay-for-performance plans: described, 304; drawbacks of, 305–306; for groups of teachers, 306–308; performance evaluations in, 305; teacher approval of, 310–311

peer review of teachers, 334

performance appraisals: need for, in merit pay plans, 305; as tool to enforce minimum work standards, 292

Pestalozzi, 140

Pestalozzian principles, 142

phonemic awareness, 21–25

phonology: kinds of linguistic differences among dialects, 206

positive manifold, 265

pragmatics: kinds of linguistic differences among dialects, 207–209

preschool children: common family literacy events, 9; early reading development, 17–18; emergent reading attempts, 27; emergent writing, 18–21; labelling skills, 175; phonemic awareness, 23; reading awareness, 4; use of language, 197

problem formulation in research, 357–359

procedural facilitation, 183–184

process description research, 268–271

process in writing: by experts and by novices, 227, 264–266; general problem-solving model of, 227; interaction of knowledge with, 228–229, 252–253; major subprocesses in, 227–229; often confused with content in instruction, 239; research in description of, 268–271; training in, 233

process-oriented research, 188

profit-sharing, 299

programmed instruction, 96–97

Progressive Movement in education, 134

proplectic teaching, 181

Protestant ethic, effect on schoolbook content, 139

publication bias, 364–365

random effects models, 386–387

reading achievement, correlated with linguistic awareness, 21–22

reading comprehension instruction: assessment in, 114–115; cognitive prompts in,

101–103; historical facets of, 147–148; metacognition in, 104; motivational techniques in, 116–117; social context in, 117–120; strategies in, 104–112; use of basal materials for, 113–114

reading instruction: direct instruction in, 97–98; language experience approach to, 100; programmed instruction in, 96–97; promoting comprehension in, 99–115; related-activity approaches to, 93–94; skills approaches to, 92–99; teaching to read for meaning, 182; Wisconsin Design for Reading Skill Development, 96–97

reading instruction, historical: changes over time, 158; comprehension instruction in, 147–148; content-area reading in, 145; linkage of reading achievement to, 159; methods in, 148–149; modern evaluation of, 158; outcomes hard to assess, 152–156; research perspectives on, 132; source materials in, 130; stages in, 134

reading instruction methods: alphabetic or ABC method, 132–133, 149; look-say method, 133, 149, 153; phonics approach, 132–133, 152; whole-word approach, 132–133, 149

reading remediation programs, 34–37, 182–183

reciprocal teaching, 110, 181–182, 184, 238–240

recruitment and retention of teachers, 286

religious content of schoolbooks, 134–138

remedial track, 201, 203

research methodology, 354

research reviews: expected to offer explanations, 390; exploratory or confirmatory purpose of, 359–360; improved by meta-analysis, 356–357; methodological standards in, 354–355

rote memorization, 135

sampling, 356, 360, 361–362

SAT scores, correlated with salaries, 287

scaffolding, 25, 109–111; demonstrated in instructional studies, 188–191; described, 173; gradually internalized by child, 179, 187–188; as part of tutorial interactions, 177–178; to support early language learning, 175; use in instructional interactions, 181, 185–188; use in language acquisition, 197; use in textbooks, 185

Scanlon plan, 300

self-control training, 106–108

semantics: kinds of linguistic differences among dialects, 207

seniority, pay for, 295

silent reading, 143, 147

single salary schedule, 285

skill-based pay, 296–298

social context: affects community language practices, 203–204; affects language use, 197; and curriculum history, 160–161; essential for language learning, 174; and language awareness, 9; for learning to talk, 7; for literacy, 5–7; of 19th century literacy, 156; of oral and written language, 197–198; of reading comprehension instruction, 117–120; shapes individual development, 171; underlies most writing tasks, 241; use of, in curriculum development, 36

social interaction, 174, 178–179

social views, and schoolbook content, 136–142

socioeconomic status: effect on literacy, 6–7; and family literacy events, 9; and story reading at home, 28

special education: recognition of, in contracts, 326

standard English: oral, described, 199; written, described, 200; best learned through meaningful exposure, 213–215

standardized tests, 115, 152

story reading, 26–32

story structure, 249–251, 267

storytelling, 241–242, 248, 249–251

student enrollment trends, 286

syntax: kinds of linguistic differences among dialects, 206

talk-aloud procedures, 229–230, 268–270, 277

teacher protection through unionization, 333–334

teacher status, 332–333

teacher unionization: directions for future, 340; effects on policy determination, 337–340; effects on relationships between teachers and school systems, 335–337; effects on teacher compensation, 328–332; effects on teacher protection, 301, 333–334; effects on teacher status, 332–333; effects on teaching activities, 320–328; history of research on, 318–320; need for further research, 341–342

text analysis, 266–268

text revision, 262, 265–266

thinking-aloud protocols, 229–230, 268–270, 277

time-on-task, 154

vocabulary instruction: attributes of effective methods, 62–63; in basal readers, 77–78; in classrooms, 77–78; comprehensive plan for, 80; effect on reading comprehension, 60–62; effect on writing, 62–63; in McGuffey's *Readers,* 140; needed research, 68

vocabulary instruction methods: concept teaching, 66; context method, 63; keyword method, 65–66; looking up and defining words, 65; semantic feature analysis, 63; semantic mapping, 67

vocabulary size: among various populations, 52–53; contemporary studies on, 51–53; early studies on, 50; gained from normal reading, 70; importance of determining, 50; needed research, 58

vocabulary testing, 56–57

vocabulary of written texts, 58–60

vote-counting methodology, 356

voucher system, 302, 307

Webster's (blue-back) speller, 134–147 passim

weighted mean effect size, 384

Wisconsin Design for Reading Skill Development, 96–97

word-learning tasks, 65–68

writing: computer simulation of, 274; dealing with constraints, 271; goals, 230, 242–244; kinds of research on, 259; major subprocesses, 227–229; nature of expertise, 260; as a nonlinear process, 230; planning, 270; purposes, 231; requires many types of knowledge, 226–227; in social contexts, 241; task familiarity, 235; variables affecting ability in, 264

"writing crisis," 265

writing instruction: difficulties of teaching composition in, 240–241; effective practices for mainstream and nonmainstream students, 214–217; to improve children's storytelling, 249–251; ineffective and effective techniques, 238; reflects mainstream culture, 204; use of cooperative interaction, 238–239; in various discourse forms, 252–253

written language: best learned through meaningful interaction with written text, 214–215; changes societies and individuals, 196; culturally specific, 199; differs from oral language, 9–14, 196–197; important to cognitive growth, 173; as language, 196; as a social practice, 199; transition from oral language, 14–16

zone of proximal development, 25, 37, 109, 186